The Routledge Handbook of Criminal Justice Ethics

The enormous financial cost of criminal justice has motivated increased scrutiny and recognition of the need for constructive change, but what of the ethical costs of current practices and policies? Moreover, if we seriously value the principles of liberal democracy then there is no question that the ethics of criminal justice are everybody's business, concerns for the entire society. *The Routledge Handbook of Criminal Justice Ethics* brings together international scholars to explore the most significant ethical issues throughout their many areas of expertise, anchoring their discussions in the empirical realities of the issues faced rather than applying moral theory at a distance. Contributions from philosophers, legal scholars, criminologists and psychologists bring a fresh and interdisciplinary approach to the field.

The *Handbook* is divided into three parts:

- Part I addresses the core issues concerning criminal sanction, the moral and political aspects of the justification of punishment, and the relationship between law and morality.
- Part II examines criminalization and criminal liability, and the assumptions and attitudes shaping those aspects of contemporary criminal justice.
- Part III evaluates current policies and practices of criminal procedure, exploring the roles of police, prosecutors, judges, and juries and suggesting directions for revising how criminal justice is achieved.

Throughout, scholars seek pathways for change and suggest new solutions to address the central concerns of criminal justice ethics.

This book is an ideal resource for upper-undergraduate and postgraduate students taking courses in criminal justice ethics, criminology, and criminal justice theory, and also for students of philosophy interested in punishment, law and society, and law and ethics.

Jonathan Jacobs is Professor, Presidential Scholar, Chair of Philosophy, and Director of the Institute for Criminal Justice Ethics at the John Jay College of Criminal Justice, CUNY, and editor of the journal, *Criminal Justice Ethics*.

Jonathan Jackson is Professor of Research Methodology at the London School of Economics and Political Science, and an editor of the *British Journal of Criminology*.

"The timing could not be more appropriate for a wide-ranging and sophisticated discussion of ethics in criminal justice. With its stellar line-up of contributors addressing the most pressing normative debates in the field, *The Routledge Handbook of Criminal Justice Ethics* is easily the decade's most important new handbook among an increasingly crowded field in criminal justice research."

Shadd Maruna, Dean and Professor, Rutgers School of Criminal Justice, Rutgers University-Newark, USA

The Routledge Handbook of Criminal Justice Ethics

Edited by Jonathan Jacobs and Jonathan Jackson

Routledge
Taylor & Francis Group
LONDON AND NEW YORK

First published 2017
by Routledge
2 Park Square, Milton Park, Abingdon, Oxon OX14 4RN

and by Routledge
52 Vanderbilt Avenue, New York, NY 10017

First issued in paperback 2020

Routledge is an imprint of the Taylor & Francis Group, an informa business

British Library Cataloguing-in-Publication Data

A catalogue record for this book is available from the British Library

Library of Congress Cataloging-in-Publication Data
Names: Jacobs, Jonathan A., editor. | Jackson, Jonathan, 1974– editor.
Title: The Routledge handbook of criminal justice ethics / edited by Jonathan Jacobs and Jonathan Jackson.
Description: Abingdon, Oxon; New York, NY: Routledge, 2016. | Series: Routledge international handbooks | Includes bibliographical references and index.
Identifiers: LCCN 2015046950 | ISBN 9780415708654 (hardback) | ISBN 9781315885933 (ebook)
Subjects: LCSH: Criminal justice, Administration of—Moral and ethical aspects.
Classification: LCC HV7419 .R68 2016 | DDC 174/.9364—dc23
LC record available at http://lccn.loc.gov/2015046950

ISBN 13: 978-0-367-58158-9 (pbk)
ISBN 13: 978-0-415-70865-4 (hbk)

Typeset in Bembo
by codeMantra

Contents

Figures

Contributors

Ben Bradford is Departmental Lecturer at the Centre for Criminology, University of Oxford. His research mainly focuses on procedural justice and issues of trust, legitimacy, cooperation and compliance as these pertain particularly in the relationship between the police and the policed.

Leonidas K. Cheliotis is Assistant Professor of Criminology in the Department of Social Policy, London School of Economics and Political Science. He is also Book Review Editor of the *British Journal of Criminology*.

Alexandra Cox is Assistant Professor of Sociology at the State University of New York at New Paltz. She is a former Gates Cambridge Scholar and Soros Justice Fellow.

Richard Dagger is E. Claiborne Robins Distinguished Chair in the Liberal Arts at the University of Richmond. His publications in political and legal philosophy include *Political Ideologies and the Democratic Ideal* (with Terence Ball), *Civic Virtues: Rights, Citizenship, and Republican Liberalism,* and the forthcoming *Playing Fair: Political Obligation and the Problems of Punishment.*

Mark R. Fondacaro is a Professor and Director of the Psychology & Law Doctoral Training Area at the CUNY Graduate Center and John Jay College of Criminal Justice. He received his PhD in clinical psychology from Indiana University–Bloomington, his JD from Columbia Law School, and completed postdoctoral studies in social ecology at Stanford Medical School. With Steven Penrod, Cathy Widom, Margaret Kovera and Diana Falkenbach, he serves as a faculty liaison to the Beijing Normal University China-US Center for Forensic Psychology.

Phillip Atiba Goff is Assistant Professor of Social Psychology at the University of California, Los Angeles. He is the co-founder and president for research of the Center for Policing Equity. He is an expert in contemporary forms of racial bias and discrimination as well as the intersections of race and gender.

Thomas Douglas is Senior Research Fellow at the Oxford Uehiro Centre for Practical Ethics, Faculty of Philosophy, University of Oxford, and Editor of the Journal of Medical Ethics. He is dual-trained in medicine (MBChB) and philosophy (DPhil) and works chiefly in normative and medical ethics.

Rachel D. Godsil is Eleanor Bontecou Professor of Law at Seton Hall University School of Law. She is the co-founder and director of research for the Perception Institute. She focuses her current scholarship on the application of research on race, gender, and other lines of difference from social psychology to law, policy, institutions, and individual behavior.

Hannah Graham is Lecturer in Criminology in the Scottish Centre for Crime and Justice Research (SCCJR) at the University of Stirling, Scotland. She is the author of three books published internationally by Routledge: *Rehabilitation Work: Supporting Desistance and Recovery* (2016) and two books co-authored with Rob White, *Innovative Justice* (2015) and *Working with Offenders: A Guide to Concepts and Practices* (2010). Prior to moving to Scotland, Hannah lectured in Criminology and Sociology at the University of Tasmania, Australia.

Peter A. Hanink is a lawyer and PhD student in Criminology, Law & Society at the University of California, Irvine. His research focuses on race and policing.

Maria Hartwig is Associate Professor of Psychology at John Jay College of Criminal Justice. In 2008, she received an Early Career Award by the European Association for Psychology and Law, and in 2012, she received the Saleem Shah Award for Early Career Excellence in Psychology and Law, awarded by the American Psychology-Law Society and the American Academy of Forensic Psychology.

Aziz Z. Huq is the Frank and Bernice J. Greenberg Professor of Law at the University of Chicago. His scholarship on criminal procedure, terrorism and the law and constitutional design has been published in dozens of leading law reviews and peer-reviewed journals, and his book *Assessing Constitutional Performance* (co-edited with Tom Ginsburg) is forthcoming in 2016.

Douglas Husak is Distinguished Professor of Philosophy at Rutgers University. He holds both a JD and PhD and is the author of several books, including *Drugs and Rights* (Cambridge, 1992); *Overcriminalization* (Oxford, 2008); *The Philosophy of Criminal Law* (Oxford, 2010); and *Ignorance of Law* (Oxford, forthcoming). He is the Editor-in-Chief of *Criminal Law and Philosophy* and a former Editor-in-Chief of *Law and Philosophy*.

Jonathan Jacobs is Professor and Chair of Philosophy, as well as Director of the Institute for Criminal Justice Ethics at John Jay College and member of the Doctoral Faculty of Philosophy at the Graduate Center of CUNY. He is author of nine books and over 80 articles and Editor of the journal, *Criminal Justice Ethics*. He works in ethics, history of philosophy, moral psychology, and philosophical theology as well as criminal justice.

Jonathan Jackson is Professor of Research Methodology at the London School of Economics. He is an editor of the *British Journal of Criminology*. His research focuses primarily on public attitudes toward crime, policing, punishment and the law.

John Kleinig is Emeritus Professor of Philosophy and Criminal Justice, John Jay College of Criminal Justice and the PhD Program in Philosophy, Graduate Center, CUNY, and Adjunct Research Professor, Centre for Applied Philosophy and Public Ethics, CSU. He has authored or edited over 20 books and 150 articles and book chapters.

Stephen Koppel is a student in John Jay College's Doctoral Program in Criminal Justice, and a pre-doctoral fellow at National Development and Research Institutes. He is a graduate of Brooklyn Law School, and a member of the New York State Bar.

Richard L. Lippke is Professor in the Department of Criminal Justice at Indiana University. He is the author of *Rethinking Imprisonment* (OUP, 2007), *The Ethics of Plea Bargaining* (OUP, 2011), and *Taming the Presumption of Innocence* (OUP, 2016).

Timothy J. Luke is Postdoctoral Researcher and Adjunct Assistant Professor of Psychology at John Jay College of the City University of New York. He has co-authored several papers on issues concerning techniques in the use of evidence.

Matt Matravers is Professor of Law and Director of the Morrell Centre for Toleration at the University of York. His publications include *Justice and Punishment* (OUP, 2000), *Responsibility and Justice* (Polity, 2007), and papers in legal and political theory.

Seumas Miller is Professorial Research Fellow at the Centre of Applied Philosophy and Public Ethics at Charles Sturt University (Canberra) and the 3TU Centre for Ethics and Technology at Delft University of Technology (The Hague). He is the author (with Ian Gordon) of *Investigative Ethics: Ethics for Police Detectives and Criminal Investigators* (Blackwell, 2014) and *Terrorism and Counter-terrorism: Ethics and Liberal Democracy* (Blackwell, 2009).

Jeffrie G. Murphy is Regents' Professor of Law, Philosophy, and Religious Studies at Arizona State University. He is a past president of the American Philosophical Association.

Gabe Mythen is Professor of Criminology at the University of Liverpool. He is also Regional Director of the ESRC North West Doctoral Training Centre and President of the International Sociological Association Sociology of Risk and Uncertainty Group.

Jill Peay is Professor of Law at the London School of Economics and Political Science. She is also a member there of the Mannheim Centre for Criminology. She is the author of *Decisions and Dilemmas: Working with Mental Health Law* (2003) and *Mental Health and Crime* (2011).

Adam Perry is an Associate Professor in the Faculty of Law at the University of Oxford and the Garrick Fellow and Tutor at Brasenose College. His interests are in administrative law, constitutional law, and legal philosophy.

Elaine Player is Professor of Criminology and Criminal Justice at the Dickson Poon School of Law, King's College, London. Her published research focuses on the treatment of women in the criminal justice system, sentencing, and prisons. She is vice-chair of the Centre for Crime and Justice Studies, a charity which aims to inform and educate about all aspects of crime and the criminal justice system.

Jonathan Pugh is Postdoctoral Research Fellow in Applied Moral Philosophy at the University of Oxford. He has written on a variety of topics including penal theory, informed consent in medical ethics, and reproductive ethics.

Jon Shute is a criminologist at the University of Manchester. His research interests are youth crime, family stress, and mass violence. He is a Co-investigator on the ERC programme Corpses of Mass Violence and Genocide.

Michael Skerker is an Associate Professor in the Leadership, Ethics, and Law Department of the United States Naval Academy. He is the author of *An Ethics of Interrogation* (University of Chicago Press, 2010) and several articles on military and intelligence ethics.

Justin Tosi is Postdoctoral Research Fellow in the philosophy department at the University of Michigan. He holds a PhD in political philosophy from the University of Arizona.

Sandra Walklate is Professor and Eleanor Rathbone Chair of Sociology at the University of Liverpool and Adjunct Professor in the School of Justice, QUT, Brisbane. Her recent publications include: *The Contradictions of Terrorism* (2015) with Gabe Mythen, published by Routledge.

Geoff Ward is Associate Professor of Criminology, Law, and Society at the University of California, Irvine. He is the author of *The Black Child-Savers: Racial Democracy and Juvenile Justice*, an award-winning study of the rise, fall, and lasting remnants of Jim Crow juvenile justice in the US.

Brandon Warmke is Postdoctoral Research Associate at the University of Notre Dame. He works in moral philosophy and moral psychology, primarily on issues related to blame, forgiveness, and punishment.

Rob White is Professor of Criminology at the University of Tasmania, Australia. Among his recent books are *Environmental Crime and Collaborative State Intervention* (edited with Grant Pink), *Environmental Crime and Social Conflict* (edited with Avi Brisman and Nigel South), and *Innovative Justice* (with Hannah Graham).

Sappho Xenakis is Senior Lecturer in Criminology at the School of Law, Birkbeck, University of London. She is also a Book Review Editor of *Critical Criminology*.

Acknowledgements

It has been a pleasure working with Thomas Sutton, Senior Editor, Criminology at Routledge. He made the initial approach regarding this project, and he has been helpful and encouraging throughout its development and execution. We are especially grateful for the latitude we have been given in formulating the overall aim and character of the *Handbook* while also being given valuable guidance. Tom was clear that the *Handbook* should aim to be more than a compilation and that it should comprise new works. We were urged to think of the *Handbook* as aiming to develop criminal justice ethics as an area of study, and we appreciate the free hand we have been permitted in that effort.

Others at Routledge, in particular Heidi Lee and Hannah Catterall, have been patient, supportive, responsive … and more patient. We are grateful to them for the numerous ways they have helped at each step of the project.

We are very grateful to the contributors to the volume, especially for their willingness to offer new work. The extra effort required by the commitment to the distinctive character of this project is much appreciated.

Jonathan Jacobs would like to thank the Earhart Foundation for a Fellowship Research Grant, which supported his work on this project, both in regard to my contribution and in regard to work on the project overall. The grant supported research and consultation visits to the UK and supported my editorial collaboration with Jon Jackson. Time spent with scholars at the Institute of Criminology at Cambridge and with Jonathan Jackson has been important to the development of my work on issues at the intersection of Ethics, Politics, and Criminal Justice.

Jonathan Jackson would like to thank Yale School Law, Harvard Kennedy School and John Jay College of Criminal Justice (Department of Psychology) for hosting him while he worked on this project. He is also grateful to the UK's Economic and Social Research Council for funding that research leave (grant number ES/L011611/1).

Editor's preface to *The Routledge Handbook of Criminal Justice Ethics*

Jonathan Jacobs

Issues that beset criminal justice, especially in the United States but in other countries as well, are not only receiving considerable scholarly attention across a broad range of disciplines and methodologies, but are also increasingly acknowledged as serious, even urgent issues, by the wider society. One consideration that has motivated the increased interest, at least in the United States, is the enormous cost of criminal justice. From policing to incarceration, to the damage done to neighborhoods and communities as a result of mass incarceration, to the troubling rates of recidivism the cost of criminal justice runs into the hundreds of billions of dollars per year. It would be encouraging if moral concerns were motivating the enlarged public interest, and indeed concerns for justice are being voiced—more and more audibly. But even if cost is what is triggering the drive to make constructive changes, the fact that interest is enlarged is especially important because it provides an opening for bringing a multitude of issues more fully to the public's attention and making more people aware of how numerous and how serious the issues are.

At least in the United States, no one aware of the facts could think that the current state of things is satisfactory or that current policies and practices just need some adjustment and refinement. The issues are at a complex intersection of political, social, ethical, and economic factors, and they have implications through all of those dimensions. In criminal justic e in the US issues of race and poverty are especially acute. In the US and the UK there is an enormous literature on criminal justice including government reports, scholarly research and analysis, and increasing discussion in the media. The issues are increasingly recognized as everybody's business. Given their significance and scale they are not issues only for researchers and persons directly involved in criminal justice. They merit consideration across and throughout society and, directly or indirectly, they have an impact on everybody.

Issues concerning criminal justice are not just the business of victims of crime and those who have been charged with crimes or punished for committing them. Nor is criminal justice concerned only or even primarily with punishment. As John Kleinig points out in the Introduction difficult questions concerning what should be criminalized and what should be the powers and procedures of those with official roles in the administration of justice—all throughout the institutions of justice, and not just concerning police—are vitally important and shape many aspects of the social world.

We should not need crisis to persuade people of that fact. The papers in this *Handbook* address enduring, fundamental issues of criminal justice ethics and also address contemporary circumstances and the concrete forms of those issues. They speak to some of the most pressing current issues but do so within a larger setting of perennially important questions and issues. The US and the UK are the main focus of most of the papers but they include some discussion of the issues in other nations, such as Australia, and they address the issues in ways that are relevant to many liberal democracies whether or not they are part of the English-speaking world.

The issues of criminal justice ethics have global relevance, even though it is in liberal democracies that they tend to be most openly and thoroughly studied and discussed. In addition, while this may be a time when the United States begins to take substantial steps in the direction of significant reform, some of the issues are becoming more pronounced and garnering more attention in other parts of the world. As this is being written many European countries are contending with large influxes of people from war-torn and poor countries in North Africa and the Middle East. There could be a rapid increase in the ethnic, religious, and cultural diversity of the populations in many countries, and as the national populations of many European countries become increasingly ethnically and religiously heterogeneous the current liberal and humane practices and attitudes concerning criminal justice could be challenged quite powerfully.

Countries such as Germany, Norway, Sweden, and others, among those often pointed to as not having the very troubling issues so notable in US criminal justice, are starting to face issues concerning law enforcement, relations between police and culturally diverse communities, the need for new approaches to risk-assessment, and so forth on a new scale. This is not to say that the problems in US criminal justice will be replicated, but there is little doubt that the stresses consequent upon current trends of immigration and the movement (and the needs) of impoverished refugees are largely unaccustomed (at least in the era after European post-war reconstruction) and that the difficulties of addressing them will be substantial.

Some of the chapters in this volume reflect the value and importance of comparative study and approaches that involve collaboration of new types and on a larger scale. There are, after all, a number of issues that are shared by liberal democracies despite the many differences among them. Moreover, given the very nature of liberal democracy all sorts of issues concerning criminal justice merit and should receive attention concerning their empirical, conceptual, and normative aspects. If one takes seriously the values and principles of liberal democracy and has any concern with the character of civil society there is no question that the issues of criminal justice ethics require attention from many angles of approach.

What is the character of the present collection of papers, and what makes this a *handbook* of criminal justice ethics in more than just its title? The aspiration of this volume extends beyond offering new work by excellent scholars on a diversity of issues. We conceived the project not only as a compilation of new work done in criminal justice ethics but primarily with a view to giving shape and direction to criminal justice ethics as an area of study. That is different from a collection of ethical perspectives on criminal justice issues. We were hoping that those who accepted the invitation to write for the *Handbook* would show how their expertise and methodological approaches can give shape and orientation to central problems of criminal justice ethics in ways that will help develop it as an area addressing empirical and normative considerations in an integrated manner.

At the same time, the editors (and the publisher) have had no specific commitments in mind, as to the views to be elaborated and defended. This is not a volume of papers aimed at jointly making a case for some specific perspective on the issues. Contributors were invited to explore what they take to be the most significant ethical aspects of the specific topics they examine, and the volume is editorially wide open in regard to the views presented by contributors. In our letter of invitation to potential contributors we wrote:

> We are inviting contributors to help develop criminal justice ethics as a field, to help shape the direction and the aims of criminal justice ethics, and to bridge empirical and philosophical inquiry. This does not mean that we expect all the contributors to somehow manage to acquire expertise in methods and technical vocabularies other than their own. However, we are encouraging invitees to be willing to include reflections on the normative presuppositions of methods of inquiry, on ethical questions regarding policies and practices and their ethically relevant implications, and, in general, to develop their contributions so that ethical considerations receive explicit attention. One need not be an ethicist to say important things about ethical issues and such issues can arise throughout the contexts of criminal justice.

This approach was motivated by the thought that such an approach can be much more illuminating than having ethical theory over here, empirical issues and social scientific explanations over there, and connecting them by some notion of how to 'apply' the former to the latter. The reality of ethical issues is not like that, and the notion of 'applied' philosophy is somewhat suspect or at least misleading. One does not apply moral theory the way one might apply a recipe or the instructions for assembling a piece of furniture purchased as a set of parts. There just isn't a clean break between "here are the facts" and "here are the relevant ethical considerations." Thus, it is probably more accurate to speak of *practical* philosophy or practical ethics. Practical ethics is the study of the ethical features of specific issues and practices, explicating the ethical considerations to which those issues and practices give rise. It concerns what we should *do*, what practices are normatively most sound, what terms of evaluation are most relevant and significant. Criminal justice ethics could not be a more practical project.

Moreover, from the perspective of many contemporary philosophers the putative 'fact/value' distinction, at least in the most familiar forms it took during much of the twentieth century, has been subject to so much destructive critique that it can almost seem surprising that at one time the distinction was very much in ascendance. This is not the place for a detailed examination of its ascendance and the various strands of destructive critique of it. Moreover, the critique has not led to any sort of consensual view of the relations between values and non-valuative facts and properties. There are persistent, important issues of the metaphysics and epistemology of value, and the semantics of value-discourse provides plenty of work for philosophers. However, insisting on the mutual exclusivity of facts and values, of objectivity and subjectivity, or of cognition on the one hand and expressing attitudes on the other often does little to illuminate the issues. More is to be gained by ethical thought and judgment engaging and being informed by the complex realities of contexts of action and decision and by the willingness to try to articulate the ethical significance of those realities.

To be sure, philosophical theorizing about moral value has distinctive theoretical concerns and issues, and the method of philosophical reasoning and analysis is different from that of empirical inquiry. There are problems of moral philosophy that are distinctively philosophical problems, and they will not be resolved by empirical inquiry. At the same time, while there surely is a role for philosophical theorizing at a highly general level regarding metaethics, i.e., the metaphysics, epistemology, and semantics of moral value, it is not at all clear how such theorizing might bear directly on issues concerning criminal justice ethics. The Introduction highlights the fact that the chapters in this volume do not seek to formulate a "grand theory" of criminal justice and that many of them engage extensively with empirical considerations and suggests that is a merit of the volume. In addition, at least in the US—and this may be true of numerous other countries, too—there is not really a criminal justice *system* in the sense of a deliberately designed, integrated, overall approach, each main element of which having been planned in conjunction with the others.

Of course, whether or not criminal justice reflects an overall system, progress formulating and addressing issues of criminal justice ethics will be made most effectively by examining those issues in their empirical specificity and complexity. Ethical thought can be coherent and illuminating without aspiring to be as explicitly systematic as possible. In addressing concrete, specific issues of practice, action, moral evaluation, and decision ethical reasoning and judgment need to be thickly informed by empirical understanding. In important respects ethical thought needs to be elaborated and articulated through reflective attention to the normative significance of criminal justice realities. That reflective attention might issue in more clearly systematic understanding and more systematic approaches to the issues—which would be a welcome development. But getting to that point may be helped along most by seeing how general and systematic points and principles are supported by engagement with the empirical realities of the issues.

The normative significance of those is unavoidable because criminal justice concerns institutions, practices, and policies connected with the employment of coercive power, the rule of law, and concrete, and often urgent, matters of social and economic life. That, of course, is one of the main reasons that reflection on the fundamental values and principles of the political/legal order is so important. Still, while taking that into account, many problems of criminal justice ethics need to be addressed by ethical thought that develops through negotiating the conceptual, empirical, and normative aspects of the issues as a joint, complex undertaking rather than bringing ethical thought to the issues from an external source. We encouraged contributors to look at their topics in that way and to be willing to see themselves as helping to shape the discourse of criminal justice ethics, explicating issues, addressing problems, offering suggestions through the perspectives of their expertise, seeing that expertise as a resource for helping to make ethical considerations more fully intelligible. That way the discussions are firmly anchored in the several types of relevant facts but do not limit themselves to some attempt at 'value free' description and explanation disconnected from ethical reasoning and analysis.

While description and explanation disconnected in that way might be an attempt to maintain the putative value-neutrality of the facts, free of the distortion of a valuative lens, it can be a way of failing to register and articulate the ethical significance of what we find to be the case. The role of values is not inevitably distorting. Moral commitments and theories are not items in an ideological salad bar from which one chooses what is most congenial or what is least disruptive of one's antecedent views. The rationales for them need to be more fully connected with what we understand about the relevant contexts, institutions, and agents. The ethical reasoning needs to work its way into and through the facts, articulating the values those realities reflect and also making the case for values and principles that should inform the realities and orient policy and practice. The facts can be crucially important considerations in support of ethical judgments, reasoning, and recommendations. And, anyway, what is valuatively significant is perhaps what is most important about understanding the facts.

The papers in this volume approach criminal justice ethics in the spirit of examining the complex texture of the issues in ways meant to explicate the ethical significance of the various elements of them. Ethical theories are conceptual resources for thinking through the issues, but it is in the thinking-through that the real work is done. (Little is gained by showing how, 'if one is a Kantian, one would maintain X' or 'if one is a utilitarian, one would maintain Y,' and so forth. A very similar point, illustrated similarly, is made by John Kleinig in the Introduction, though it had occurred to us independently of each other.) Moral thought and judgment require (i) forms of discerning attention (to notice morally relevant considerations), (ii) the weighing of diverse considerations with a view to ascertaining what is morally most significant, and (iii) fashioning a reasoned approach to the issues, one responsive to the potentially diverse moral considerations and how they figure in a coherent conception of what is morally at stake.

Accordingly, we asked contributors to consider how their expertise could help explicate ethically significant features of criminal justice; how their understanding might be part of an ethically illuminating appreciation of the issues they study and the methods they employ. The wide range of disciplines and methods supplies a multitude of sources of 'data' for ethical thought and rich intellectual resources for formulating and addressing the issues. We hope that this way of proceeding will help give shape and orientation to further work in criminal justice ethics, developing it as a study to which scholars in a great many disciplines and also practitioners can contribute.

There are multiple connections to a large number of disciplines, and it is clear that the humanities, the social sciences, and the natural sciences all have important roles in formulating and addressing the issues. Whatever one's disciplinary 'home,' whatever one's methodological approach, it can have a voice needing to be heard in the discussion of criminal justice. The issues are not only significant, they are also as multidimensional as any issues could be. There can be little doubt of that with regard to both theory and practice, and that is another reason it is helpful to have several different methodologies represented. We hope that the discussions will be seen as relevant to each other and as contributing jointly to the understanding of the issues.

Among the most difficult and disputed aspects of issues of criminal justice ethics, both theoretically and practically, is the question of how one goes from data to policy. There are complex debates about how to explanatorily interpret data, i.e., about what the data tell us about the social world and human behavior in explanatory terms; and there are complex debates about the prescriptive significance of the data. What changes in law and policy are rationalized and justified by the data? How should the intersection of law and morality be understood? How should considerations of the efficacy of policies be weighed in relation to valuative commitments and ideals? What sorts of different attitudes and habits would be needed for criminal justice to be both more just and more civil? The step—basically, from data to policy—is critically important, and it is sometimes taken too swiftly, without sufficiently careful consideration of assumptions and implications. The papers in this volume help explicate some of the conceptual and normative complexity of the landscape that needs to be negotiated in taking the step from data to policy.

We hope that the contents of this volume, both individually and as elements of an overall project, help readers make the step from data to policy with more sure footing, if a bit more slowly than is sometimes the case. While there are many issues of criminal justice the *Handbook* does not address directly—the number and variety of important issues are enormous—we hope that reading these papers will motivate reconsideration of approaches to the issues discussed and others, as well. Success will be measured by the extent to which these papers motivate further analysis, argumentation, objections, responses, and elaboration in ways that deepen and enlarge understanding of the ethical issues. We hope that you will find this volume's multiple angles of approach a valuable guide, highlighting key features of the terrain of criminal justice ethics and indicating directions for developing it as an area of inquiry, theorizing, and practice. The issues discussed extend all the way from fundamental considerations concerning the nature of the rule of law and the basic principles of political order, to highly specific matters of practice and policy.

Though this volume is aimed primarily at scholars and students of criminal justice, the topics addressed have plenty of connections with what we read in the news and in the opinion sections of major newspapers, what we see on television news, and what is on the minds of many politicians and citizens. This collection is well suited to a great many topics and issues analyzed and discussed in many classrooms in many disciplines. We hope that the arguments and the perspectives herein will reach many students focusing their studies in criminal justice and also reach many who are interested in it but may be focusing elsewhere.

Many of the contributors to this volume are scholars whose work has had a considerable impact on the study of the issues, and other contributors are younger scholars whose work is garnering attention and having a growing role in their areas of study. We are very grateful to all of the contributors for writing new works for this volume and, in many cases, writing with a focus a bit different from that to which they may be most accustomed. Developing criminal justice ethics as a field will need that kind of intellectual generosity. While the contents of the volume represent numerous fields and methods, we think that they can help develop criminal justice ethics as a coherent, integrated set of concerns of undoubted theoretical complexity and undoubted practical significance.

The main sections of the volume are as follows:

I: Morality, law, and criminal justice
The first part of the volume addresses fundamental issues concerning criminal sanction, moral and political aspects of the justification of punishment, and some important contemporary issues requiring important deliberations concerning policy. The papers take up some of the most enduring core issues concerning criminal sanction, having to do with the legal and political order, with what kinds of considerations should figure in fashioning sanctions, and with the role of various attitudes and sentiments in regard to punishment and offenders.

II: Criminalization, decriminalization, and punishment
The second part pursues some of those major issues with explorations of specific issues concerning criminalization and criminal liability and with analysis of widely shared assumptions and attitudes and how they shape some of the troubling realities of contemporary criminal justice. The discussions include suggestions regarding possible remedies regarding policies and attitudes. The contributions include works by philosophers, legal scholars, criminologists, and psychologists.

III: Institutions, policies, and practices
The third part deepens the empirical exploration of issues and it, too, includes contributions from scholars in several different disciplines. They evaluate in detail a number of prevalent policies and practices of criminal procedure, and they indicate important directions in which ethical reconsideration of them is required.

Introduction

John Kleinig

Philosophical interest in criminal justice is as long-standing as philosophical interest in civil society, and the more restricted interest in criminal justice ethics—albeit not under that rubric—is of similar antiquity. Humans are first and foremost social beings, but beings whose societal existence has always been fractured by conflicts having moral and ethical (and often religious) significance. Responses to those conflicts are likewise suffused with such significance. Punishment, seen as an ethically appropriate response to wrongdoing, has figured in the reflections of almost every ethically oriented philosopher and thinker from the Hebrews and Greeks to the present.[1] Punishment for crime—societally prohibited wrongdoing—has engaged almost every moral, legal, and political philosopher. There have been skeptics, to be sure, but they have not been able to ignore such concerns. Interest in criminal justice and the ethical questions it generates are unavoidable dimensions of human and philosophical inquiry.

Criminal justice ethics, as a discrete domain of ethical inquiry, and as envisaged in this series of handbooks, is a much more recent phenomenon, part of a profuse division of intellectual labor that (for the most part) began in the nineteenth century and increased in its specificity after World War II. University courses in criminal justice were first instituted in the 1930s. With the development in the late 1960s of a systems approach to criminal justice, which sought to promote coordination among the largely uncoordinated institutions of criminal justice—policing, prosecution, adjudication, sentencing, and criminal sanctions—a relatively distinct focus for intellectual and more specifically ethical inquiry was "created."

The earliest investigations into criminal justice ethics so conceived also reflected the return of a practical focus for philosophical ethics that began to gather momentum during the 1960s, leading, most notably, to the formation of new journals such as *Philosophy & Public Affairs*, *Philosophy and Public Policy*, and the *Journal of Applied Philosophy*; the re-orientation of older journals such as *Ethics*; and then, in the early 1980s, the commencement of *Criminal Justice Ethics*. It is within this latter movement that the current volume stands—a maturing expression of the diversification and deepening of practical philosophical inquiry, sufficiently self-conscious and confident of its integrity to open itself to the broader frameworks within which it is situated.

There are three ways in which the present volume distinguishes itself from some earlier work in criminal justice ethics. First, it does not seek to "derive" ethical conclusions from what might be termed "grand theory"—the general ethical theories beloved of moral philosophers and constructed to provide a unified account of right and wrong, good and bad, virtue and vice. Without casting aspersions on such projects (though their unifying pretensions may legitimately be interrogated), the concerns of the present volume see the project of grand theory construction and critique as being several steps removed from those of more direct interest in criminal justice ethics. The central questions are not: What would a Kantian approach to punishment or a consequentialist understanding of sentencing or a contractualist approach to policing look like—though such questions may have a legitimate place—but: What kinds of ethical considerations bear most appropriately on the state's authority to punish or on the determination of penalties, or what grounds and limits police authority? The quest is for reasons that will sustainably bear on these issues, without some immediate resort to highly contestable grand theory or theories. For the most part we do better to develop theory from the ground up than from the top down—or, if we do not wish to lose sight of the larger picture, we may content ourselves with some version of what John Rawls termed "reflective equilibrium," a general methodological strategy in which broader theory and practical intuitions moderate each other.

Second, the present volume recognizes that "criminal justice"—and hence criminal justice ethics—is not exclusively concerned with policing, adjudication, and punishment, but first with them as arms of the state (Dagger; Bradford and Jackson; Mythen and Walklate, in this volume) and embedded in larger social institutions such as political traditions and legislatures, which determine the kinds of conduct that are appropriately criminalized or socially responded to in other kinds of ways (Husak; Peay and Player; Cheliotis and Xenakis; Matravers, in this volume); police organizations that enforce the law as understood and maintain social order (Goff and Godsil; Miller; Hartwig, Luke, and Skerker, in this volume); a judicial process that interprets and applies the legislative will (Koppel and Fondacaro; Perry; Lippke, in this volume); and prisons and other penal or corrective practices that impose the determinations of adjudication and sentencing (Jacobs; Murphy; Graham and White, in this volume). Beyond this core there may extend a range of interconnected issues, such as private policing and imprisonment, terrorism and illegal immigration, police unions and strikes, and mandated drug treatment. Centrally, though, the current volume sees the domain of criminal justice ethics as encompassing questions about the criminalization of wrongdoing (Dagger; Peay and Player, in this volume), the distinction between crime and tort, the concerns and limits of criminal law, law enforcement discretion, grounds for the state's punitive activity (Murphy; Husak, in this volume), and the legitimacy of imprisonment. True, these questions are themselves connected to larger questions about the nature and legitimacy of political authority, the nature and justification of human rights, the "criminal mind," and the attribution of moral responsibility, mercy, and forgiveness, and it is important to recognize that such questions sometimes hover in the near background. For the purposes of the present inquiry, though, they are approached via their proximity to a criminal justice context (Jacobs; Tosi and Warmke, in this volume).

The present volume also recognizes that the political process of criminalization and rectification makes presumptions about the nature and sources of criminality and thus about the appropriateness of punitive and other responses to criminalized conduct (Koppel and Fondacaro; Matravers, in this volume). And so it sees the questions traditionally explored by criminologists as raising legitimate issues for criminal justice ethics, thus broadening its scope from merely institutional concerns to those of moral psychology and character (Jacobs; Cox, in this volume).[2]

Finally, the present volume recognizes—in a way that was not always apparent in earlier philosophical inquiries—that "applied" or "practical" philosophy does not operate in an empirical vacuum. Philosophical inquiry that directly engages with real world issues cannot presume to resolve them independently of an engagement with the contours of their appearance. It is not enough to resolve questions about imprisonment with an inquiry into the normative and conceptual connections between wrongdoing and hard treatment. We must also engage with empirical data about the conditions and individual and social effects of punishment. Attempts to carve out a domain for philosophical and ethical inquiry that is impervious to (or dismissive of) what we otherwise know about our world are not only alien to the history of philosophical inquiry, but also hubristic in their pretensions. One need not deny the distinctiveness of philosophical inquiry to acknowledge the contributions that many other forms of human inquiry may make. That goes for criminal justice ethics no less than the philosophy of science or law. There is an increasingly large body of comparative and non-comparative legal, sociological, psychological, and scientific research that bears on questions that are central to criminal justice ethics—the implications of neuroscientific research (Pugh and Douglas, in this volume); whether, for example, criminal offenders can be held responsible for their conduct (Koppel and Fondacaro, in this volume); whether particular punishments deter; whether imprisonment rehabilitates or damages moral capacity (Jacobs, in this volume)—as well as more specific concerns: whether police should be permitted to stop, question, and frisk and, if so, under what circumstances; whether tasers are life-threatening, and if so, under what circumstances; whether exclusionary rules adequately deter police misconduct; the effects of interrogation on vulnerable populations; whether supermax prisons have psychologically and therefore ethically deleterious side-effects; or whether taping jury deliberations would distort them. The possibilities are almost endless.

Ethical inquiry and empirical research may engage with each other in various ways. Philosophers whose research is motivated primarily by ethical questions will draw upon the research of sociologists and psychologists whose work bears on the empirical presumptions required by their questioning. Social scientists will find their empirical inquiries triggered by social and ethical concerns, or find that their data prompts such concerns. Both approaches are represented in the present volume. More recently a hybrid approach has developed, largely as a reaction to the sharp division of labor that has occurred in academic research—what is known as "experimental philosophy." One of the frustrations often encountered by those who engage in criminal justice ethics has been the difficulty of finding empirical data that would help inform certain ethical questions or, if available, data in a form that is of unambiguous relevance to philosophical and ethical concerns. Although much classical philosophy developed in the context of an undifferentiated inquiry into human activity, including ethical judgments, its fragmentation into many disciplinary strands has led to an unfortunate isolation of one form of inquiry from others. Experimental philosophy represents a—sometimes faltering[3]—attempt to link interdisciplinary projects more productively, allowing philosophical questions to shape empirical inquiries that will assist in their resolution. In any event, it heralds a philosophical re-engagement with empirical data that had become muted with the rise of analytic philosophy in the early part of the twentieth century.

There is also, along with the confidence that goes with a maturing understanding, a certain humility that should accompany the recognition of historical embeddedness. Contributors to the present volume are mostly comfortable with the liberal democratic political framework within which much criminal justice ethical thinking and practice take place; they recognize, however, that that framework not only has a particular historical configuration but may also be contested in various ways. Are there, for example, ways in which current understandings or at least embodiments of liberal democracy undercut some of the ethical expectations relating to the legitimacy of state punishment? Are, there, moreover, implications from neuroscientific inquiry that call into question presumptions about human agency and moral responsibility (Pugh and Douglas, in this volume)? Although we do not possess the benefits of a god's-eye-view of our world, we cannot ignore what—*sub specie humanitatis*—we discern from our broader inquiries into the world and our place within it.

The idea of a criminal justice system is largely a product of the 1960s, crystallized in a flowchart published in the 1967 Report of the (US) President's Commission on Law Enforcement and Administration of Justice, *The Challenge of Crime in a Free Society*, and updated in 1997(Figure I.1)

Characterizing it as a "system" is somewhat misleading, as its various elements, though connected and dominated by the phenomenon of crime and a series of causally related social responses to it, have often developed fairly independently and without a central coordinating mechanism. This has led to many tensions—particularly between the police and courts, and the courts and corrections. Notably, however, rather than the standard oversimplified division of police, courts, and corrections, the flowchart reveals more of the system's inner complexity by expanding it into a five-part division—entry into the system, prosecution and pretrial services, adjudication, sentencing and sanctions, and corrections. In addition, each part of that division comprises a range of possibilities, along with its ethical challenges. We are reminded, for example of the (contested) division between adult and juvenile offenders and the different processes through which they generally pass (Cox, in this volume). In each case there are critical ethical problems that attend both the division and the institutional procedures that are followed. And as for the corrections phase, rather than seeing it uniformly in terms of imprisonment (which garners most of the discussion), along with the multitude of ethical questions raised by confinement, we are reminded that there are further distinctions between probation and parole, jails and prisons, and incarceration and community sanctions, even though they receive a small fraction of the ethical attention given to imprisonment. No doubt the radical loss of liberty that incarceration involves makes it a critical site for ethical inquiry; but each of these (and other) options raises distinctive ethical questions of its own. And these questions become more diverse the closer we get to actual correctional practices—say, the use of diversionary and community sanctions, the criteria for granting parole or treating probation violations, and the racial disparities involved (Ward and Hanink; Goff, in this volume).

Despite its welcome gesture toward the complexity (moral and otherwise) of the criminal justice system, the flowchart possesses some significant inadequacies. For one thing, it takes crime for granted, rather than seeing the criminalization process as an integral part of the "system" (Peay and Player; Dagger; White; Husak, in this volume). Some years ago, when I was invited to write an introductory textbook on criminal justice ethics, I had to argue strenuously for the inclusion of a section on criminalization. Yet determining what act-kinds will be denominated crimes is a critical and controversial component of criminal justice, with important implications for criminal justice ethics as well as having ramifications for the rest of the system. So, if one is going to consider crime and the response to it systemically, it is important to include references to the legislative actions that precede the social phenomenon of crime. The processes of criminalization bring with them a complexity of as much significance as that found at other points in the system. The so-called majesty of the law is deeply embedded in a political system that determines what kinds of actions and sanction fall within the criminal justice system's purview, and along with that politicization have come some of the most acute ethical problems in criminal justice (such as "the war on drugs"). Some of the ethical questions arising from the process of criminalization are addressed in Parts I and II of the present volume (to which I'll return).

At the other end of the flowchart, there is little to indicate the ethical problems of re-entry that confront those who have passed through the system and have been sanctioned in some way. The notion that those who have been imprisoned and released have now "paid their dues" or that they can return to the society from which they were taken "with a clean slate" is completely at variance with social reality. The tentacles of the system often reach deeply into prison afterlife via a range of disqualifications that make employment and various social eligibilities (such as voting, jury service, educational grants, and loans) difficult if not impossible. In the United States,

What is the sequence of events in the criminal justice system?

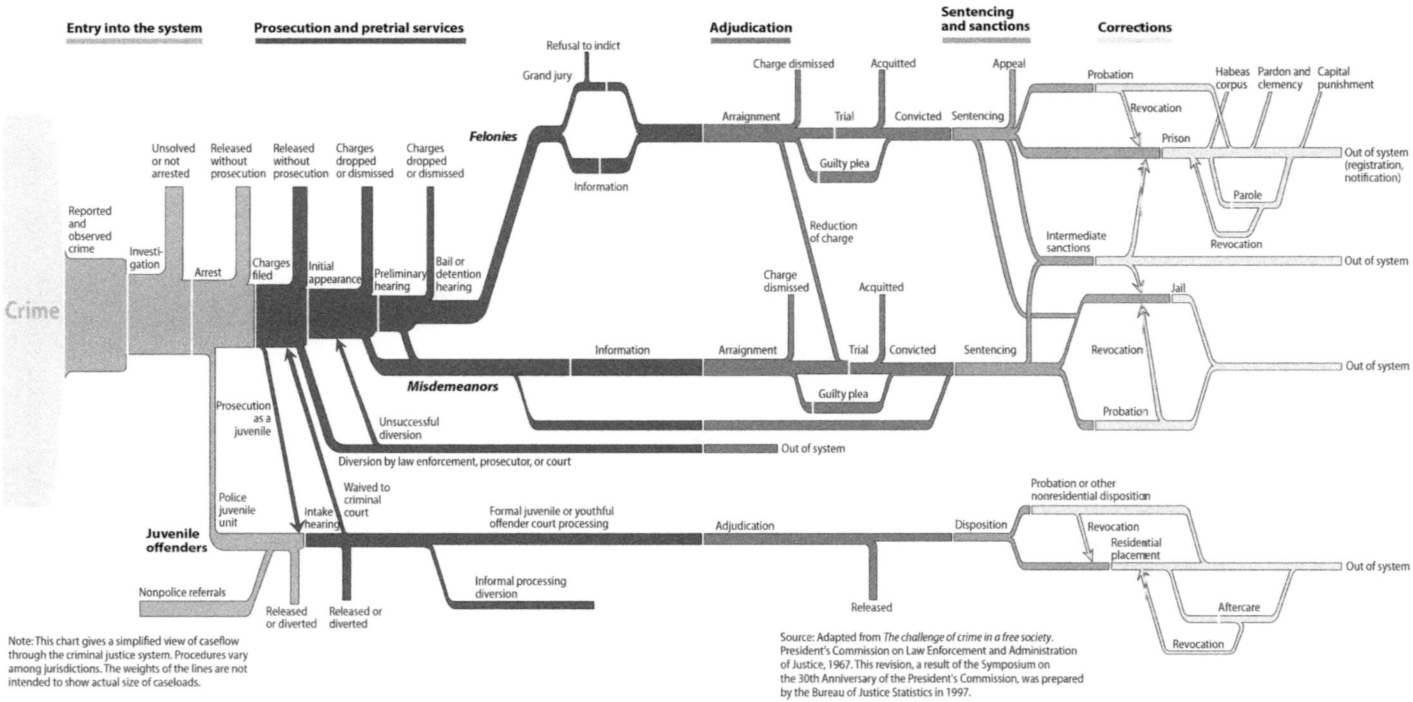

Figure I.1 United States criminal justice system flowchart.

© Bureau of Justice Statistics[4]

more than half a million individuals annually re-enter the wider society after a period of incarceration, and most of them face formidable obstacles to resuming a normal social life. Many of them will be sufficiently daunted (or corrupted) by their prison experience, and subsequent opportunities to lapse again into criminalized activity and their recidivism pose additional ethical challenges for the system (Lippke, in this volume).

The flowchart also leaves out of account the role that a range of ancillary services—such as police dispatchers, forensic laboratories, expert witnesses, medical providers, prison social workers, and mental health professionals—may play in the system and the ethical problems that arise therefrom. The cozy relationship often existing between forensic specialists and prosecuting agencies has frequently been a source of ethical concern, as has the use of "tame" expert witnesses.[5] The tension between prison and social welfare and mental health priorities is an ongoing source of ethical dilemmas. Although prisoners are the only citizens with a constitutional right to medical treatment, its delivery is frequently flawed. Also, the long sentences imposed in the 1980s and 1990s for drug-related crimes have precipitated a raft of ethical problems for an aging prison population.

Yet another omission is constituted by larger social and structural questions concerning the system. Until fairly recently in the United States, "tough on crime" measures have been politically and socially popular, with the consequence that between about 1972 and 2008, when it peaked, the incarceration rate increased from approximately 160 per 100,000 to over 750 per 100,000, with the numbers of incarcerated persons increasing from roughly 200,000 to 2.3 million (Figures I.2-I.4). The United States accounts for approximately 5 percent of the world's population, but 25 percent of the world's imprisoned population. Add to these the several million under court supervision. It is the most punitive country in the world. Disproportionately, young black males are affected, with drug offenses implicated in many cases (even though whites and blacks do not differ significantly in their drug use[6]).

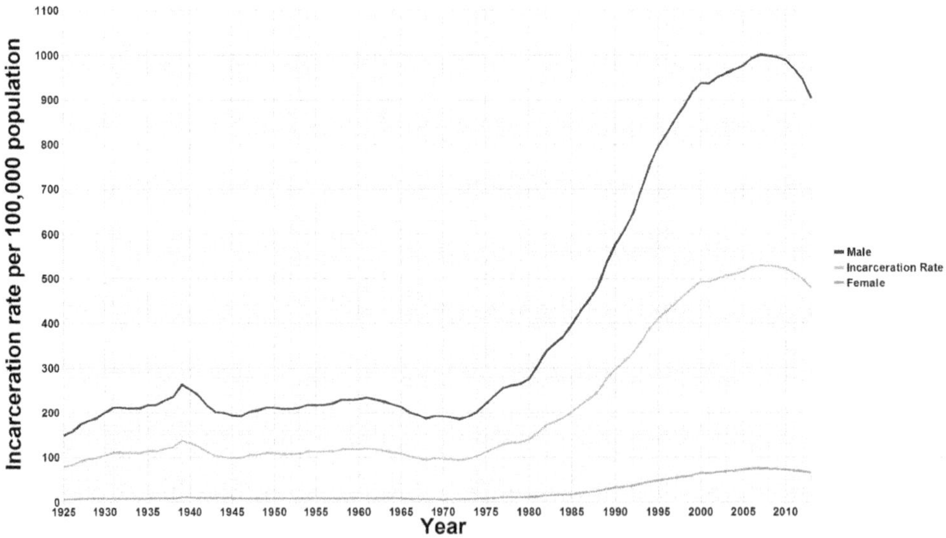

Figure I.2 Incarceration rate of inmates incarcerated under state and federal jurisdiction per 100,000 population, 1925–2013.

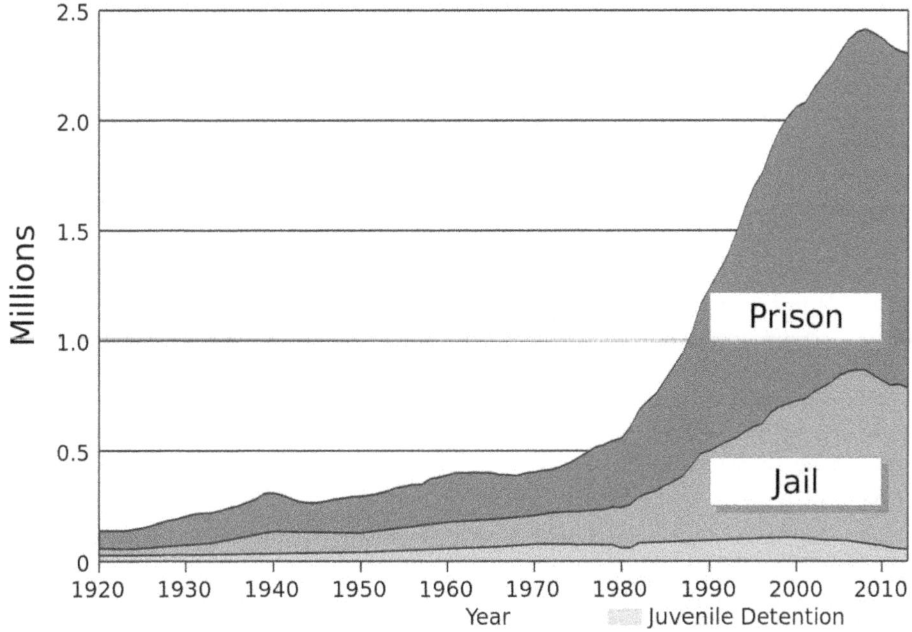

Figure I.3 Incarcerated Americans, 1920–2014.

©Wikimedia Commons[8]

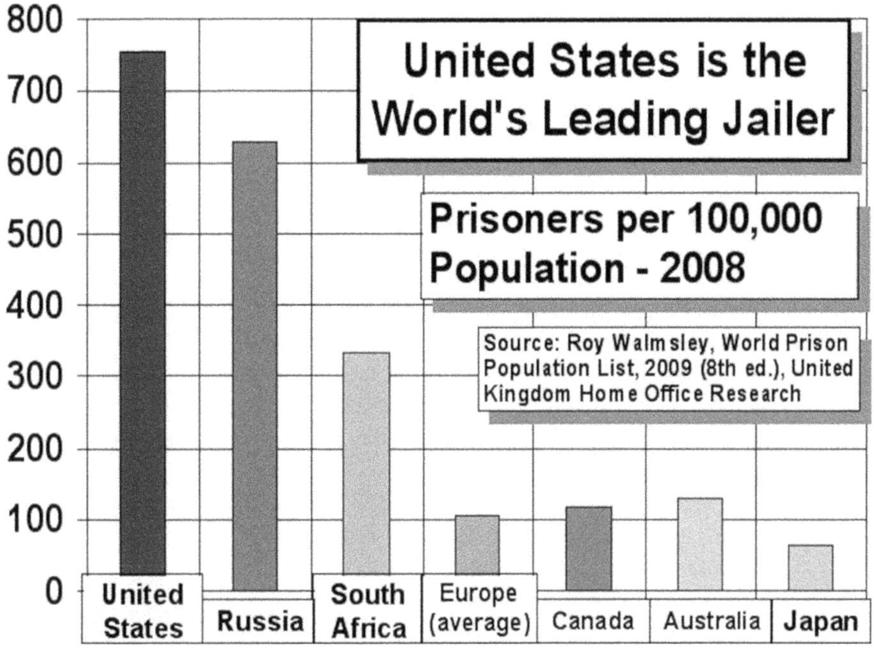

Figure I.4 Incarceration rates worldwide.

©November Coalition, Wikimedia Commons[9]

For a variety of reasons, a retreat has now begun. For some it has been motivated primarily by economics—the huge expenditures involved in incarcerating and supervising so many people (aggravated by the financial crisis of 2008); for others, the enormous social cost and dislocation has been a prime factor (blighted neighborhoods as the result of mass incarceration); yet others have revisited the foundations of criminalization and asked whether behaviors now criminalized or punished by imprisonment (especially drug-related offenses) might be better addressed in some other way (as public health rather than public safety issues). Even standard and longstanding punitive practices have been called into question by advocates for some form of restorative justice, in which reconciliation and recompense are at the forefront. Although the flowchart (Figure I.1) makes one or two gestures toward alternatives to the status quo, it is framed in a fairly conservative manner.

That said, one of the virtues of a flowchart such as the one above (recognizing, however, that different jurisdictions are likely to have somewhat different flowcharts) is that it helps to identify junctures at which ethical issues are likely to arise—for example, in the decision to arrest or (multiply or) reduce charges, or in negotiating a guilty plea (plea bargaining), reviewing prosecutorial, judicial, and jury conduct, or in sentencing determinations. Each of these phases generates its own series of ethical questions or challenges.

As the graphs above indicate (Figures I.2-I.3), there has been a shift since 2008, a shift that is likely to increase in the coming years as a bipartisan concern about incarceration intensifies, supported by a shift in public sentiment, *even as* the 2016 US Federal, state, and local elections loom. The shift is memorialized in a publication of New York University's Brennan Center, *Solutions: American Leaders Speak Out on Criminal Justice,*[10] in which prominent personalities, including presidential candidates, stake out their case for significant decarceration. In some states, such as California, Supreme Court decisions have prodded change, in recognition that many of the incarcerated also suffer from significant mental and other health problems.[11] But a good deal of this shift is also associated with a recognition that, however devastating some drug addictions may be, the prosecution and incarceration of drug users (often for lengthy periods) has constituted poor public policy.

At the legislative level, a critical question will be the determination whether to levy criminal sanctions on some form of socially disapproved behavior (Peay and Player; Matravers; White; Husak, in this volume). Is it necessary or even sufficient that the behavior is considered immoral, and by whom? If something other or more is required, such as harm or offense, how is it to be understood and to whom must it be caused? Must the relevant harms have individual victims, or may they be diffused and cumulative or remote? Are the sanctions intended to express social condemnation, secure deterrence of some kind, enable rehabilitation, vindicate the law, or more than one of these, and if so, how are we to prioritize them? Should failed attempts receive less punishment than completed crimes? And if certain distinctions are to be made here—such as the one commonly drawn between crimes and misdemeanors—can this be ethically sustained? If criminality requires culpability as well as harm, what counts as such? Must it involve deliberate intent, and if so, intent to what? What about reckless disregard? Why and how, for example, should we distinguish criminal from merely tortious negligence? Of course, most of these questions have legal counterparts—indeed, are cast in terms that are enshrined in legal practice—but legal distinctions, because of their practical effects, are susceptible to moral scrutiny, and even if they stand up to scrutiny there may be a hiatus between their legal and moral manifestations. There has been a long-standing and difficult negotiation between legal and moral responsibility. Reforming the law may require not only attention to the details of that negotiation but also a broader attention to the complex and contentious intersections of law and morality.

The various ethical questions generated by the process of criminalization have some significance for our understanding of "the criminal mind." Perhaps in some cases criminals do not have criminal minds—they simply fall foul of some criminalizing legislative fiat. And what should we say about corporate crimes? Nevertheless, given that some form of criminal intent is usually seen as critical, our responses to it may be linked to a range of ethically suffused issues—the so-called "rotten background" syndrome, brain plasticity in young people, effective rehabilitative strategies, links (or distinctions) between intent and motivation, the relevance of character, and so forth.

When a crime is committed or reported, it may trigger an investigation, most commonly by police. The investigative process itself generates a host of ethical questions—some relating to organizational prioritization, others stemming from strategies and techniques used. There are general questions about the limits of discretion; the targeting of suspects; the use of force and deceptive or manipulative techniques; invasions of privacy; and more specific ones concerning the deployment and management of informants, tasers, and chokeholds and the construction and use of profiles, stings, wiretaps, and other forms of surveillance. Custodial interrogation raises its own questions about coerciveness, whether police should see their role as one of fact finding or gaining inculpatory evidence, whether to videotape proceedings, badger, falsify evidence, conduct a strip search, or use polygraphs.

Ethical questions that confront law enforcement are by no means exhausted by police-suspect relations. In the dealings that police have with prosecutors (assuming, as in the United States, that police do not also have prosecutorial functions), in the giving of police testimony in courtroom settings, and in the relations that police officers have with their own departments there are ample occasions for further ethical challenges—concerning prosecutorial collusion, determinations about which cases to pursue, testimonial deception, and the observance of regulatory or supervisory constraints, just to take a few examples. The fact that prosecutors in the US are most often elected raises its own set of questions (as also do alternative means of prosecutorial appointment).

Indeed, it may be stated generally, not only of police but also of all participants in the criminal justice system, that insofar as what they do bears on the interests of others (whether individually, collectively, or at an institutional level), substantial ethical questions may arise. Although some of these questions may arise at a basic human level—what we owe to each other—others are likely to be shaped by the criminal justice context in which they arise. As role occupants, their actions will have a distinctive ethical character. It is particularly the latter that will be of interest to scholars of criminal justice ethics. The acceptance of gratuities will have a different ethical significance within policing from the significance that it has in a restaurant setting; if a police officer draws his weapon or attaches handcuffs, the ethical questions it raises will have a different import from those raised when a civilian draws a weapon or dominatrix handcuffs a client. Although criminal justice ethics might ultimately touch upon the most general questions about how people should regard and respond to each other, as a specific form of ethical inquiry it is shaped by the context, institutions, and occupational roles of criminal justice.

It is not only the ethical dimensions of the primary interactions that may be shaped by the institutional context in which they occur, but also the ways in which we set about responding to them. If, for example, police are developing use-of-force policies, who should be involved in determining them? Should they develop such policies internally, guided only by legal and judicial constraints? Should they consult with and involve a broader citizenry? Should prison policies regarding access to health care be developed exclusively by corrections officials, or should those who need and provide the care also have significant input into their formulation? How we resolve ethical questions is of ethical importance along with their actual resolution.

It is common to assume that the flow of a criminal case will involve a police investigation, the arrest of a suspect, a trial, and adjudication by a judge or jury, followed by sentencing and sanctions (should the suspect be found guilty). But this is not how the "system" generally works. In almost 95 percent of criminal cases in the US (albeit significantly less in other countries), there is no "trial." Some form of guilty plea is entered after a presumed-to-be voluntary negotiation among the prosecutor, defendant, and the defendant's lawyer, in which, usually in exchange for some mitigation, the defendant assents to plead guilty to an agreed-upon offense. The process in question—plea bargaining—is usually deemed central and essential to the viability of the US criminal justice system. Yet it is fraught with ethical problems that are given inadequate attention within the domain of criminal justice ethics.[12]

It is understandable that, because the impact of some role occupants on individual human lives can be so visceral, particular attention is given—at one end—to police-citizen encounters and—at the other end—to the sanctions that are imposed on those found guilty of criminal transgressions. But what happens between arrest/arraignment and the implementation of criminal sanctions also raises ethical questions of the greatest import. There is often an assumption that the prosecutorial process through to judicial determination is less vulnerable to ethical usurpation than other phases of the system. But that is an illusion. First of all, there are large assumptions about the structure that an adjudicatory system should have. Is it true, as is sometimes suggested, that the adversarial system favored by the United States and some other Western countries is more "rational" in its processes than the "inquisitorial" system that predominates in many European countries? Once we move beyond the theoretical attractions of one or the other, it becomes clear that each system has its strengths and weaknesses, and each generates its own ethical challenges and is subject to its own ethical pitfalls. Although, in the end, it may be difficult to say that *tout court* one system is manifestly preferable to the other, it is clear that, as with all human institutions, each is vulnerable to serious ethical failure and each must work—maybe in some Popperian incrementalist fashion[13]—to eliminate or mitigate the significant ethical problems to which it gives rise. Along with the larger structural questions there are many smaller but no less important ones concerning jurisprudential principles and standards, such as the presumption of innocence and the burden of proof, which have important ethical as well as epistemic dimensions.

Within jurisprudential—though not so much mainstream ethical—inquiry there is a substantial literature about prosecutorial, defense, judicial, and jury misconduct. The ethical issues, however, concern not only ethical failure but also the ethical contours and limits to the role played by these actors within the adjudicatory phase of the criminal justice system. Should the defense lawyer answer primarily to the court, to the law, or to the interests of his or her client, or are they integrated in certain ways? Are judges answerable to those who appoint them or to a particular professional conception of the judicial role and, if the latter, what does that involve? Even the well-worn responses to the latter—such as impartiality, independence, integrity, and competence[14]—are open to various articulations and interpretations, and whether and how particular configurations of circumstances constitute, say, derogations of duty or conflicts of interest, remain live and controversial issues.

Juries (both grand and petit), time-honored and revered within the US judicial system, are not so highly regarded (or at least used) in many other liberal democratic systems, but their employment, even if ethically defensible, is also a source of ethical concern, as we review the ways in which they are chosen and utilized. Yet their rationale and workings, by and large, have been often been ignored by philosophers who take an interest in criminal justice.[15] Perhaps one reason for this (despite the plethora of television dramas) is the dominance of plea bargaining, though, as already noted, even plea bargaining has attracted limited philosophical interest.

The United States is one of the few liberal democracies that retain capital punishment among their sentencing options. It may not be the "capital" of capital punishment (that is China, followed by some Islamic states). But the fact that the US continues (albeit with decreasing enthusiasm) to support the death penalty is an issue of considerable ethical interest. Is there some morally compelling reason (a matter of desert or deterrence?) for keeping capital punishment as a viable sentencing option? Or should redemptive possibilities remain even for those who commit the most heinous of crimes? And even if compelling reasons are theoretically available, are the processes of justice so flawed (or politicized) that it is inadvisable to impose a penalty that cannot be reversed?

Once a judicial determination has been reached, then, if one is found guilty, there must be a decision about an appropriate sanction. Here again the reach of a legislature may be deep, though there are important ethical debates about whether judges should have a discretionary role and if so, how they should exercise it. And there is an equally important though often assumed debate about whether the sanction should take the form of imprisonment. Too often questions of punishment are presumed to be questions about imprisonment. It is easy to forget that routine imprisonment is a relatively modern phenomenon, and that although it may originally have been seen as a humane alternative to other sanctions that preceded it, it has subsequently accumulated a large number of ethical problems. These include general questions about the appropriateness of using the deprivation of liberty as a "standard" sanction (after fines), very specific questions about prison conditions, and the so-called rights of prisoners. When a convicted person is delivered into the hands of those who have been delegated responsibility for carrying out a court's determinations—jail or prison, probation, or diversionary or community sanction, new sets of ethical issues arise. Those relating to prisons are the most familiar. They frequently house many more inmates than they were constructed for and in conditions that exacerbate the mental health problems of many who are incarcerated and do little to improve prospects for productive citizenship after release. Only rarely are the courts willing to intervene, encouraging a situation of institutional impunity that is usually shielded from other forms of public scrutiny. Even efforts to divert people from incarceration, including what has become known as therapeutic jurisprudence, raise problems of their own, especially given the discretion permitted to those who administer alternative systems.

But They All Come Back. Not Quite. But the ambiguous (to where?) title of Jeremy Travis's book on prisoner re-entry reminds us, on the one hand, that for most imprisonment is not "forever" and, on the other, that some two-thirds of those released will be re-arrested within a few years. Unless one has an implausible theory of criminality, there have to be serious ethical problems with a system that does not work hard to ensure that its occupants, as well as society, are better off after the incarcerative process has ended. Here, as in a number of other places, we have a good deal of sociological data but relatively little detailed ethical discussion. How do we justify spending on prisoner education programs when many in society cannot afford access to the education they need? How do we balance expenditures on security against expenditures on rehabilitation? Should ex-prisoners be barred from certain occupational roles by virtue of their criminal records or be required to state on employment applications that they have a criminal record (or even been arrested)?

As this brief overview indicates, at every point of the criminal justice process ethical issues come into play. They come into play because the process is one in which actors within the system affect the interests of others in ways that bear on their dignitarian status. Many of these are situations in which the authority conferred by roles is used to subject others to some form of constraint or imposition. But the ethical questions are generated not only at the interface of authoritative action, but also more generally as actions are given collective and institutional expression. What is done and calls for ethical judgment in the individual case often has broader ramifications for groups and institutions.

The present *Handbook*, insofar as it moves between particularities and generalities within the orbit of criminal justice, reflects but by no means exhausts the diversity of ethical questions that emerge from its processes. It provides an empirically informed insight into the actual ethical questions that emerge from the criminal justice system as we have it. Moreover, it offers a paradigm of the depths of ethical reasoning to which the processes of criminal justice may be pursued and, insofar as its contributors were asked to focus on questions of current and critical relevance, it offers cutting-edge access to many of the issues that confront the criminal justice system. May it inspire the in-depth ethical reflection and debate that the field demands.

Notes

1 This is not to deny the relevance or contribution of other traditions, but to keep the volume manageable and reasonably unified, it pretty much limits itself to what is called the Western tradition.
2 In the United States, an institutional divide occurred in which some who were previously associated with the American Society of Criminology (ASC) formed the Academy of Criminal Justice Sciences (ACJS). See Frank Morn, *Academic Politics and the History of Criminal Justice Education,* Westport, CT: Greenwood Press, 1995. Although the two societies continue to operate separately, there is now a considerable overlap of membership and focus.
3 That is not always easy. It can be difficult to operationalize a research question so that it is testable.
4 Available at Bureau for Justice Statistics, http://www.bjs.gov/content/largechart.cfm.
5 Even with important Supreme Court decisions such as *Daubert v. Merrell Dow Pharmaceuticals*, 509 US 579 (1993), the adversarial nature of the court system has encouraged an industry in which specialized partisan "experts" with widely varying expertise regularly testify for prosecution or defense (usually the latter).
6 See, e.g., R.A. Miech, L.D. Johnston, P.M. O'Malley, J.G. Bachman, & J.E. Schulenberg, *Monitoring the Future: National Survey Results on Drug Use, 1975–2014: Volume I, Secondary School Students* (Ann Arbor, MI: Institute for Social Research, The University of Michigan, 2015); L.D. Johnston, P.M. O'Malley, J.G. Bachman, J.E. Schulenberg, & R.A. Miech, *Monitoring the Future: National Survey Results on Drug Use, 1975–2013: Volume 2, College Students and Adults Ages 19–55* (Ann Arbor, MI: Institute for Social Research, The University of Michigan, 2014), available at http://monitoringthefuture.org/pubs.html#monographs.
7 Available at Wikipedia Commons, https://en.wikipedia.org/wiki/File:U.S._incarceration_rates_1925_onwards.png.
8 Available at Wikipedia Commons, https://en.wikipedia.org/wiki/File:US_incarceration_timeline-clean.svg.
9 Available at Wikipedia Commons, https://en.wikipedia.org/wiki/File:Incarceration_rates_worldwide.gif.
10 See Inimai Chettiar and Michael Waldman (eds.), *Solutions: American Leaders Speak out on Criminal Justice*, Brennan Center for Justice, NYU School of Law, 2015, available at: https://www.brennancenter.org/sites/default/files/analysis/Solutions_American_Leaders_Speak_Out_On_Criminal_Justice.pdf.
11 *Brown v. Plata*, No. 09–1233. Decided May 23, 2011.
12 Though see, for a recent philosophical discussion, Richard L. Lippke, *The Ethics of Plea Bargaining,* Oxford: Oxford University Press, 2011.
13 In his two influential books, *The Poverty of Historicism,* London: Routledge, 1957 and *The Open Society and Its Enemies,* 5th ed., Princeton, NJ: Princeton University Press, 1966, Popper distinguished "holistic social engineering" from "piecemeal social engineering," strongly favoring the latter. Without adopting every

detail of Popper's distinction, the history of holistic movements represents a strong cautionary tale—and a good pragmatic reason for a more piecemeal and incremental approach to resolving social problems.

14 See, for example, the Bangalore Principles of Judicial Conduct (2002), available at: http://www.unodc.org/pdf/crime/corruption/judicial_group/Bangalore_principles.pdf.

15 Although proportionately neglected, there are exceptions. See, e.g., Jeffrey Abramson, *We, the Jury: The Jury System and the Ideal of Democracy*, rev. ed., Cambridge, MA: Harvard University Press, 2000; John Kleinig and James Levine (eds.), *Jury Ethics: Juror Conduct and Jury Dynamics,* Boulder, CO: Paradigm Publishers, 2006.

Bibliography

Abramson, J. (2000) *We, the Jury: The Jury System and the Ideal of Democracy*, rev. ed., Cambridge, MA: Harvard University Press.

Bangalore Principles of Judicial Conduct (Judicial Group on Strengthening Judicial Integrity), (2002) available at: http://www.unodc.org/pdf/crime/corruption/judicial_group/Bangalore_principles.pdf.

Bradford, B. and Jackson, J. (2016) 'Enabling and constraining police power: on the moral regulation of policing', in this volume.

Cheliotis, L.K. and Xenakis, S. (2016) 'The moral psychology of penal populism', in this volume.

Chettiar, I. and Waldman, M. (eds.) (2015) *Solutions: American Leaders Speak out on Criminal Justice*, Brennan Center for Justice, NYU School of Law, available at: https://www.brennancenter.org/sites/default/files/analysis/Solutions_American_Leaders_Speak_Out_On_Criminal_Justice.pdf.

Cox, A. (2016) 'Fetishizing the will in juvenile justice policy and practice', in this volume.

Dagger, R. (2016) 'Crime, morality, and republicanism', in this volume.

Goff, P. and Godsil, R. (2016) 'The moral ecology of policing: a mind science approach to race and policing in the United States', in this volume.

Graham, H. and White, R. (2016) 'The ethics of innovation in criminal justice', in this volume.

Hartwig, M., Luke, T. and Skerker, M. (2016) 'Ethical perspectives on interrogation: an analysis of contemporary techniques', in this volume.

Husak, D. (2016) 'Retributive desert and deterrence: how both cohere in a single justification of punishment', in this volume.

Jacobs, J. (2016) 'Resentment, punitiveness, and forgiveness: an exploration of the moral psychology of punishment', in this volume.

Johnston, L.D., O'Malley, P.M., Bachman, J.G., Schulenberg, J.E. and Miech, R.A. (2014) *Monitoring the Future: National Survey Results on Drug Use, 1975–2013: Volume 2, College Students and Adults Ages 19–55,* Ann Arbor, MI: Institute for Social Research, The University of Michigan, available at http://monitoringthefuture.org/pubs.html#monographs.

Kleinig, J. and Levine, J. (eds.) (2006) *Jury Ethics: Juror Conduct and Jury Dynamics,* Boulder, CO: Paradigm Publishers.

Koppel, S. and Fondacaro, M. (2016) 'The retribution heuristic', in this volume.

Lippke, R.L. (2011) *The Ethics of Plea Bargaining,* Oxford: Oxford University Press.

Lippke, R.L (2016) 'The ethics of recidivist premiums', in this volume.

Matravers, M. (2016) 'De-moralising retributivism: agency, blame, and humanity in criminal law theory and practice', in this volume.

Miech, R.A., Johnston, L.D., O'Malley, P.M., Bachman, J.G. and Schulenberg, J.E. (2015) *Monitoring the Future: National Survey Results on Drug Use, 1975–2014: Volume I, Secondary School Students,* Ann Arbor: Institute for Social Research, The University of Michigan, available at http://monitoringthefuture.org/pubs.html#monographs.

Miller, S. (2016) 'The moral justification for the police use of lethal force', in this volume.

Morn, F. (1995) *Academic Politics and the History of Criminal Justice Education,* Westport, CT: Greenwood Press.

Murphy, J. (2016) 'Last words on retribution', in this volume.

Mythen, G. and Walklate, S. (2016) 'Justice, but not as 'we' know it: anticipatory risk, pre-emption, and ethics', in this volume.

Peay, J. and Player, E. (2016) 'The ethics of criminalisation: intentions and consequences', in this volume.

Perry, A. (2016) 'Mercy and the roles of judges', in this volume.

Popper, K.R. (1957) *The Poverty of Historicism,* London: Routledge.

Popper, K.R. (1966) *The Open Society and Its Enemies,* 5th edn, Princeton, NJ: Princeton University Press.

President's Commission on Law Enforcement and Administration of Justice. (1967) *The Challenge of Crime in a Free Society: Report,* Washington, DC: Government Printing Office, available at www.ncjrs.gov/pdffiles1/nij/42.pdf.
Pugh, J. and Douglas, T. (2016) 'Neurointerventions as criminal rehabilitation: an ethical review', in this volume.
Tosi, J. and Warmke, B. (2016) 'Punishment and forgiveness', in this volume.
Travis, J. (2005) *But They All Come Back: Facing the Challenges of Prisoner Reentry,* Washington, DC: Urban Institute Press.
Ward, G. and Hanink, P. (2016) 'Deliberating racial justice: toward racially democratic crime control', in this volume.
White, R. (2016) 'Eco-justice and the moral fissures of green criminology', in this volume.

Cases

Brown v. Plata, No. 09–1233. Decided May 23, 2011.
Daubert v. Merrell Dow Pharmaceuticals, 509 US 579 (1993).

Part I

Morality, law, and criminal justice

1

The ethics of recidivist premiums

Richard L. Lippke

Recidivist premiums are sentence enhancements given to individuals for their most recent criminal offenses because they have continued to commit crimes after having previously been punished for other offenses. Though considerable variation in such enhancements exists, they can be found, in some form or other, in most legal jurisdictions throughout the world (Bagaric 2010: 10; Roberts 2008a: 468). However, the ubiquity of this sentencing practice is hard to square with its insecure theoretical foundations. Though numerous defenses of recidivist premiums have been advanced, most have been found wanting (Frase 2012; Bagaric 2010; Roberts 2008a). Some sentencing theorists react to the unimpressive arguments for recidivist premiums by advocating their elimination (Bagaric 2010). Other theorists doubt that the public's appetite for such premiums can be so blithely ignored (Roberts 2008b). It seems fair to say that the public's support of recidivist premiums, though apparently strong, is somewhat undifferentiated in the sense that it does not translate into highly specific recidivist sentencing policies. This, in turn, suggests that public demands for such policies might be tutored in order to produce recidivist sentencing practices that are more constructive and fair than is often the norm.

The discussion that follows is divided into three sections. In the first, I briefly survey the kinds of recidivist premiums that can be found in existing legal jurisdictions and discuss the theoretical defenses that have been proffered for at least some of them. Like others, I find the arguments given on behalf of recidivist premiums unconvincing, though I agree with those theorists who are reluctant to simply urge their elimination. In the second section, I advance a hypothesis concerning the public's support of recidivist premiums. When sentencing practices are commonplace, the theoretical bases of which are suspect, it makes sense to ask whether something else, besides theory, explains them. I suggest that certain basic facts about human social cooperation might explain the tendency to enhance the sentences given to repeat offenders. Individuals might be rather crudely evaluated by their fellow citizens as either being on board with the rules of the group or prepared to disobey them. When individuals are perceived as being unwilling to abide by the rules of the group, the punishments meted out to them steadily escalate with an eye toward limiting their access to the group for longer and longer periods of time. By contrast, offenders who appear remorseful signal their allegiance to group norms. In response, such offenders are typically granted some sentence mitigation, though they have flouted the rules of the community. Importantly, the theoretical basis for such mitigation has likewise been challenged. Yet, even if we must honor the largely instinctive reactions of the public to what the conduct and attitudes of offenders signal about rule-compliance, little else follows about sensible sentencing practices. This is where the lessons that have emerged from the scholarship of recidivist premiums might be drawn upon in crafting better sentencing policies.

In the third section, I apply these lessons, arguing that the public sentiments that engender recidivist premiums should be steered away from disproportionate and costly versions of them. Not only might the public be convinced to give young, first-time offenders some mitigation of their sentences, the public might be led to see how progressively enhanced recidivist premiums make little sense in light of the fact that most offenders naturally desist from further offending as they age. Also, if evidence of rule-compliance is crucial, the public should support early release of offenders who show signs of being rehabilitated. Furthermore, the retention of lengthy sentence enhancements for a narrowly defined group of particularly violent recidivists might serve to reassure the public that a more general easing off of recidivist premiums will not come back to haunt it.

One recurring theme throughout the discussion involves what I term the "social deprivation narrative." Many if not most criminal offenders come from socially deprived backgrounds (Clear 2007: 61). Their lives are already difficult, which makes following the rules society enforces more challenging for them than for other citizens. Further, their encounters with the criminal justice system harm them in a variety of well-documented ways (Haney 2006; Western 2006). Our responses to evidence of rule non-compliance are often insensitive to these complications. But the interesting question is whether our punitive responses might be tempered by a better understanding of social deprivation and the corrosive effects of legal punishment. I contend that there is reason to believe that they might be, though our patience with the rule-defiant will inevitably have its limits.

Part one: The theory of recidivist premiums

Sentencing policies for repeat offenders can be conceived of in terms of two extremes: At one extreme, we might adopt what are termed "flat-rate" sentences for such offenders, by which each crime that they commit is punished according to an estimation of its seriousness with no enhancement for previous offenses (Ashworth 1995: 152). In effect, a flat-rate approach elides an offender's criminal history in sentencing her for her most recent offense. At the other extreme, we might adopt "escalating" sentences, wherein repeat offenders receive sentences for their current crimes that reflect the seriousness of those crimes plus an enhancement based on the length of their criminal histories. The longer their criminal histories, the greater the enhancement could, in theory, become. Indeed, the criminal history enhancement could exceed if not dwarf the sentence for the current offense. Again, few, if any, legal jurisdictions have flat-rate sentencing for recidivists. Few also have the more extreme forms of escalating sentencing, though some jurisdictions in the United States come close and their "habitual offender" or "three strikes" sentencing provisions produce sentences in which the premiums for recidivism exceed, by a considerable margin, the sentences assigned offenders for their most recent convictions (Greenberg 2002: 238). Most legal jurisdictions fall somewhere in-between flat-rate and the more draconian forms of escalating sentencing.

To simplify things, I will focus on retributive and crime reduction rationales for recidivist premiums. Other theories of sentencing exist, but retribution and crime reduction are invariably the predominant concerns of the legislators, sentencing commissions, or judges who determine sentencing policies. Retributive, or desert-based, rationales for recidivist premiums seem especially unpersuasive. The reason for this is succinctly captured by Mirko Bagaric (2010: 13; see also Fletcher 1978). Recidivist premiums seem to punish offenders repeatedly for crimes for which they have already been punished. Suppose that offender S commits a crime at time T1 and at T2 receives the deserved punishment for that offense. Suppose also that S then commits another crime at T3 and at T4 receives not only punishment for his second crime but also an enhancement based on his previous offense. How can we avoid the conclusion that S is being punished twice for his crime at T1? The answer might be that his offending at T3 is somehow made worse (that is, more culpable) by his offending at T1, and therefore he is deserving of harsher punishment at T4 than his second offense, all by itself, would warrant. It could be argued, for instance, that his continued offending reveals S's bad character, which renders him more blameworthy for his subsequent offenses; his punishment at T4 reflects that. Alternatively, it could be argued that in spite of his having been put on notice that his conduct at T1 was unacceptable, his continued offending shows that he is defiant. S has not absorbed the lesson conveyed by the punishment for his first offense about the importance of following the legal rules. His enhanced sentence at T4 is deserved because his defiance makes S more blameworthy.

Neither of these rationales for recidivist premiums seems convincing. Retributivists should balk at punishing people for their bad character. You can have a thoroughly bad character, but as long as you do not break the law, you do not deserve to be legally punished (Bagaric 2010: 15). When you do break the law, you deserve punishment for that infraction, based on its seriousness. Crime seriousness is typically held by retributivists to be a function of the harm inflicted or risked by an offense and the culpability of the offending agent—in particular, whether she inflicted or risked harm deliberately, recklessly, or negligently (von Hirsch 1993: 29). Bad character sentence enhancements punish people for who they are, not for what they have done and how blameworthy they were in doing it. Also, would each subsequent offense demonstrate that an individual had even worse character and therefore is eligible for increasing enhancements? It would seem so, but then the problem is that, at some point, recidivist sentencing enhancements will exceed the sentences for individuals' most recent offenses. Such an outcome should be worrisome to retributivists for two reasons: First, sentences for repeat offenders might exceed cardinal proportionality limits, that is, become so harsh that they are non-comparatively unjust (von Hirsch 1993: 18). For instance, a 25-year sentence for a petty theft is unjust no matter how lengthy an individual's criminal history. Second, sentences for repeat offenders might exceed ordinal proportionality limits. This will occur if the sentences assigned to repeat offenders for their most recent crimes wind up being significantly harsher than the sentences they ought to be assigned for considerably more serious offenses (Roberts 2008b: 475; Frase 2012: 183). A petty thief with a long criminal history should not be punished as if he were guilty of having committed homicide.

Similarly, people can have defiant attitudes toward the criminal law, regarding it as little more than an oppressive regime aimed at protecting the rich and powerful at the expense of the poor and weak, yet as long as they otherwise remain within its strictures, they do not merit punishment. It is not apparent why the attitudes individuals have toward the criminal law suddenly become relevant to determining their sentences once they have committed one or more crimes. Also, the defiance rationale seems incapable of explaining why recidivist premiums should continue to increase with each subsequent offense. Even if it makes sense to punish second-time offenders more than first-time ones, due to the former's defiance of the rules, once such an enhancement has been added to an offender's sentence, why keep increasing it for each subsequent offense he commits? Defiance seems all-or-nothing, and so unlike character, which can range from bad to worse. This suggests that defiance-based sentence enhancements should not increase with each subsequent offense. If in spite of this they do increase, then the likelihood that such enhancements will run afoul of cardinal and ordinal proportionality limits comes into play.

A different approach to recidivist premiums has been urged by Andrew von Hirsch and several of his co-authors over the years. Von Hirsch claims that first- and perhaps some second-time offenders are less culpable for their criminal acts than third- or fourth-time offenders; hence first- or second-time offenders might be reasonably punished less than their crimes would otherwise merit (Wasik and von Hirsch 1994: 410; von Hirsch and Ashworth 2005: 148; von Hirsch 2010). First-time (and some second-time) offenders might have simply "lapsed" from otherwise law-abiding lives, a common enough form of human frailty that should be acknowledged with reduced punishment. However, if individuals persist in offending, it is no longer plausible to view their offending as a lapse and so they deserve full (but not enhanced) punishment. The "progressive loss of mitigation" (or PLM) approach is not designed to support harsh recidivist premiums of the kinds found in many jurisdictions. For many theorists, this is a strong point in its favor. Against the PLM approach, it has been argued that not all first-time offenses appear to be "lapses." They are deliberately planned crimes by adults (Frase 2012: 182); as such it is not clear why the punishment of such offenders should be reduced. Another problem is that we should hesitate to give people too much credit for their past law-abidingness. Maybe they have just been lucky, never encountering sufficiently compelling temptations to offend.

It could be argued that we punish more harshly those whose bad characters or defiance have been revealed not because they are more blameworthy but because we reasonably fear that they will go on to commit other crimes and wish to deter or incapacitate them from doing so. At first glance, a crime reduction approach to defending recidivist premiums appears to be on firmer ground. Individuals who continue to offend after having been punished for earlier offenses would seem to be in need of stronger incentives, in the form of enhanced sentences, to desist from future offending. The longer their offending persists, the stronger those incentives might have to become. Or if enhanced sentences do not work to reduce crime via deterrence, at least incapacitating repeat offenders for progressively longer periods of time might seem to be in order. After all, one of the best predictors of future offending is past offending (Frase 2012: 178). At the extreme, individuals with lengthy criminal records might be justifiably incapacitated under habitual offender or "three strikes" provisions designed to imprison them for many years, if not for the rest of their lives.

Critics of crime reduction rationales for recidivist premiums point out that the evidence linking longer sentences with desistance from crime is singularly unimpressive (Frase 2012: 189; Doob and Webster 2003). Even as the "price" of crime goes up, there seems little detectable decrease in the demand for it. As for recidivist premiums and incapacitation, there is no gainsaying the fact that when individuals are locked up in prisons, their abilities to reoffend are limited. However, the evidence strongly suggests that by their mid-thirties, most individuals discontinue their criminal careers all on their own (Nagin 1998: 364). This "aging out" phenomenon means that substantial recidivist premiums assigned once offenders have reached their late twenties will produce few incapacitation effects but will be enormously costly. Habitual offender or "three strikes" provisions might uselessly and expensively keep offenders imprisoned into old age. Also, at least for certain kinds of offenses, removing individuals from society by imprisoning them does little to reduce offending in communities, since "replacements" quickly emerge to take up their roles in drug or property theft rings (Nagin 1998: 365).

Overlaying all of these difficulties with the standard rationales for recidivist premiums is what might be termed a "social deprivation narrative." The fact is that many criminal offenders come from socially deprived backgrounds and will return to them once they have served whatever sentences are assigned to them for their crimes. The diminished opportunities such individuals faced before they were convicted are constricted further once they acquire criminal records (Western 2006). Moreover, imprisonment often warps their personalities in predictable and worrisome ways, especially in societies (like the United States) in which efforts to rehabilitate offenders are half-hearted or non-existent (Haney 2006). It is thus hardly surprising that many of the individuals who have acquired criminal records continue offending; their past records leave them with relatively few viable alternatives for earning income or gaining social status. Add to this the well-known fact that it is generally easier to police the crimes of the poor than those of the rich or middle class (Stuntz 1998). This means that the profile of offenses that the criminal justice system processes is skewed in ways that make the poor look like worse rule-breakers than they probably are, at least compared with their fellow citizens who are better off.

This social deprivation narrative bears on the theoretical debate about recidivist premiums in a number of ways. For one thing, it casts doubt on the notion that recidivist premiums are justified because repeat offenders have worse characters for which they should be punished more harshly or are more defiant in the face of the reasonable rules of civil society. Such offenders might instead be more desperate than other citizens and so arguably less culpable for their crimes. Also, the already bleak options such individuals have will be further reduced by their criminal records and the corrosive impact of imprisonment upon them. The picture of repeat offenders as individuals who have had decent chances in life and who have freely chosen instead to keep defying the rules is, to put it mildly, a bit simplistic. Others in society may be just as defiant with regard to the rules, but less likely to get caught or better able to ward off convictions if they are caught. In addition, the narrative helps to explain why enhanced sentences may have few discernible deterrent effects. Even if individuals are aware of the toll recidivist premiums will exact from them, many will be tempted to risk them in the face of their otherwise limited options, at least until they reach early middle age and the many burdens of continued offending shift enough to outweigh its attractions. In fact, if our aim is to reduce offending, then recidivist premiums visited on young offenders—if they involve imprisonment under conditions that are mostly harsh and degrading—might frustrate more than promote it.

Part two: Understanding the public demand for recidivist premiums

In spite of their shaky theoretical bases, it is clear that the public supports recidivist premiums. Public opinion polls consistently show that citizens believe that repeat offenders should be punished more harshly than first-time offenders and more so the lengthier their criminal records (Spiranovic et al. 2012; Roberts 2008b). As Julian Roberts has suggested, the lengthier an individual's record, the more the public seems to attribute responsibility for crimes to the individual, rather than to social or other factors, whether rightly or wrongly (2008b: 193). Hence, whatever we might conclude about recidivist premiums as a theoretical matter, practically speaking, they seem unlikely to disappear. We can roundly condemn them, as some scholars have, or we can work with the public attitudes that underlie them and try to limit their impact on sentencing schemes.

How might we understand the public attitudes that underlie recidivist premiums? As mentioned at the outset, my hunch is that these attitudes are connected with the importance to human social groups of having rules (including legal rules) with which most of the members of the group comply. Noncompliance is perceived as a threat to the welfare of the group, and when the rules in question prohibit such things as violence, force, and theft, or are instrumental in coordinating social activities or allocating scarce resources, such a perception has considerable merit. Repeat offending by individuals is naturally taken as a signal that individuals are unwilling to abide by the rules. The longer such offending persists, the more individuals seem a threat to the welfare of the group. The public's response to persistent offending might be somewhat crude—increasingly harsh sentences meted out with little regard for their proportionality or cost. But the public's frustration with those who defy basic social rules seems undeniable, and harsh habitual offender provisions make some sense in light of it. At some point, complete exclusion of persistent offenders from the social order might seem the only recourse.

To develop this further, consider the common practice of granting reduced sentences to convicted offenders who demonstrate remorse for their crimes. Remorse-based sentence mitigation has equally been subjected to criticism by punishment theorists (Bagaric and Amarasekara 2001; Lippke 2008). From a retributive perspective, it is not apparent why it matters how offenders feel after they have committed their crimes. If crime seriousness is a function of the harm done (or risked) and the culpability with which the offender acted, remorse comes too late to affect either of those factors. It also is not clear that feelings of remorse, even sincere ones, are reliably related to reduced risk of future offending, as a crime reduction defense of remorse-based sentence mitigation would have to demonstrate. Whether or how often remorse can be or is put to effective use in modifying the desires or dispositions that led individuals to offend in the first place is, one suspects, an empirical question concerning which we do not have reliable data. Then there is the practical problem of distinguishing real from feigned remorse, one that we might doubt sentencing judges will be well-equipped to take on. In spite of all of this, there is something about the expression of remorse by offenders that consistently elicits reduced punitive responses in the US and other criminal justice systems (Bagaric and Amarasekara 2001; Tudor 2008).

As Julian Roberts has suggested, perhaps what expressions of remorse are taken to signal is an understanding by the offender of the importance of the legal rules, along with some resolve to abide by them in the future (2008b: 77). Such a signal reassures us that the offender is still "with us," at least in the sense that he acknowledges the importance of the rules and sees his failure to abide by them as regrettable. And notice this: It might not matter too much to us whether such signals are reliable (as conveying genuine remorse). If individuals reoffend, their subsequent displays of remorse will be viewed more skeptically by sentencing judges, and offenders will begin to accrue recidivist premiums. In short, recidivist premiums, understood as somewhat undifferentiated punitive responses by the public to what it perceives as rule-defiance, serve as natural correctives to previous, insincere expressions of remorse.

To be clear, I am not suggesting that the preceding account justifies either recidivist premiums or remorse-based sentence reductions in any of their current forms, only that it might help to explain their ubiquity. It matters enormously and predictably to humans whether and to what extent their fellow humans accept and abide by certain basic rules that make social life possible, and beyond this, minimally worthwhile. But these facts about humans tell us relatively little about how sentencing policies must be crafted to acknowledge and accommodate them. In a way, that is a good thing, for it means that though we ignore the public's responses to such signals about rule-compliance, or the lack thereof, at our peril, there might be considerable room to educate and thus shape public responses to them with a view toward limiting their damage and making them more constructive. In the next section, I explore this possibility with respect to recidivist premiums.

Part three: Shaping recidivist premiums

Again, even if there is an almost instinctive response to repeat offending according to which we take it as an increasingly strong signal about the unwillingness of individuals to comply with important social rules, little else follows about the magnitude of the sentence enhancements meted out to recidivists. Repeat serious offending, especially when it is violent, might generate intense public pressure on those who devise and administer sentencing schemes to keep the individuals in question out of circulation for some time. Fortunately, most repeat offenders are unlikely to fall into this category and so the public might be generally satisfied with modest sentence enhancements for the vast majority of recidivists. Strict retributivists might bridle at the weight given an incapacitation aim in the public's sentencing calculus, but the public's eclecticism about the aims of legal punishment is unlikely to disappear anytime soon (Roberts 2008b: 183). We need not abandon retributive limits on legal punishment in order to accommodate public concerns about and reactions to recidivists. There is, in fact, some evidence that the public is prepared to accept proportionality limits on recidivist premiums, a point I will come back to shortly (Roberts 2008b: 167).

To begin, the hypothesis that repeat criminal offending is interpreted by the public as a signal about the willingness of individuals to comply with vital social rules might help us to make some sense of von Hirsch's progressive loss of mitigation approach to recidivist premiums. A first offense conveys some information about an individual's commitment to rule-compliance, but what it conveys might depend on the age of the offender and the seriousness of the offense. Most individuals start their criminal careers when they are young (Nagin 1998: 364). Youths are widely understood to be "works in progress" when it comes to rule-compliance, so the public might be convinced to be somewhat forgiving of youthful indiscretions as long as they are not too serious (Roberts 2008b: 170). Also, the public might have some sense that entanglement with the criminal justice system can be life-changing in negative ways, especially for the young and impressionable. Thus, it might support efforts to minimize the impact of criminal sanctions so long as the value of rule-compliance is affirmed. Of course, if offending continues, there will come a point at which the public is unwilling to support further sentence mitigation, even for youthful offenders. Once the importance of rule-compliance has been affirmed once or twice to individuals, the public might draw the not unreasonable conclusion that continued offending shows indifference to the value of rule-compliance.

Next, though support for recidivist premiums is widespread, we should be able to make some headway in curbing them if the public can be made to understand and accept the validity of the "aging out" phenomenon. To the extent that recidivist premiums are based on the desire to incapacitate repeat offenders for increasingly lengthy periods of time, the fact the most offenders will desist from crime in their thirties makes lengthy sentence enhancements patently useless and socially costly policies beyond a certain point. As numerous critics of "habitual offender" and "three strikes" provisions have pointed out, it makes no sense to imprison people into their fifties, sixties, and seventies in order to limit their criminal activities (Greenberg 2002: 240). Convincing a cost-conscious public of this ought to be possible, at least if it can be assured that the few crimes that will thereby be prevented, at considerable cost, are not all that serious to begin with. Moreover, such an approach to limiting recidivist premiums need not conflict with retributive support for longer sentences for more serious offenses. It is one thing to support lengthy prison sentences for murderers or rapists because they deserve them. It is quite another to support them (in the form of recidivist premiums) for repeat drug or property offenders because it is thought that we might thereby prevent such offenders from committing further offenses of the same or similar kinds. The aging out phenomenon should discourage sentence enhancements aimed at reducing crimes, though it tells us little about deserved sentences for more serious offenders.

Another way in which we might be able to convince the public to limit recidivist premiums draws upon the public's apparent unease with disproportionate criminal sanctions. Again, though opinion polls show widespread support for recidivist premiums, they likewise show support for proportionality limits on punishment (Roberts 2008b: 167). Even if there is an almost instinctive demand to punish repeat offenders more than first-time offenders, it is not clear how much more we need to punish recidivists in order to satisfy this demand. One possibility, embodied in numerous sentencing schemes, is to have sentence ranges for offense types set at the high and low ends either by desert or crime reduction considerations, or perhaps some combination of the two (Morris 1982; Frase 2012). The sentence for a specific offense, or offense token, would then be set initially by taking into account specific features of the token or of the offender, excluding considerations of criminal history. Assuming that this did not yield a sentence at the top of the sentence range for the type of offense in question, repeat offenders could be given somewhat higher sentences within the range than their crimes would otherwise merit. This enhancement would be a recidivist premium, albeit a modest one, and one that would usually be limited by the severity of the highest sentence within the relevant sentencing range. Those with longer criminal histories could be given correspondingly greater enhancements, though still within the relevant sentencing range. Those whose punishment for the current offense already put them at the top of the range might be given enhancements that took them slightly above it—in effect sentencing them as if they had committed a crime of the next most serious type in the sentencing scheme. True, departures of this kind would breach ordinal proportionality limits, but we could view such limits as presumptive rather than absolute. As presumptive limits, they could be exceeded only if a criminal history justification for doing so was provided by sentencing judges. We might hope that they would rarely have to do so. Notice also that such an approach to sentencing would permit less-than-deserved or optimally crime reductive sentences for first-time offenders, in recognition of their youthfulness and the negative impact of criminal sanctions.

Two challenges that such a top and bottom bounded sentencing scheme must confront are, first, finding some articulable means of setting the tops and bottoms of the various offense sentencing ranges, and, second, determining the extension of the relevant ranges. For instance, considerations of ordinal proportionality, that is, of the comparative seriousness of offense types, can help us with ranking offenses from more to less serious and ensure that the more serious offenses are punished by sentence ranges that encompass harsher sanctions than less serious offenses. But ordinal proportionality gets us only so far. To fix sentence ranges, we need some solution to what von Hirsch has termed the "anchoring" problem (von Hirsch 1993: 36). This is the problem of finding one or more offense types whose sentence ranges can be determined non-comparatively. Once we have some anchoring points, that is, offense types whose sentence ranges are intuitively just, considerations of ordinal proportionality can be brought in to determine sentence ranges for comparatively more and less serious offense types. The anchoring problem is a vexed one in sentencing theory, one for which various solutions have been advanced (von Hirsch 1993; Frase 2012; Lippke 2012). Fortunately, it need not detain us since any solution that yields sentence ranges is consistent with the approach to recidivist premiums herein being proposed. As long as there is room within offense type sentencing ranges for movement upwards (and downwards) from presumptive sentences for offense tokens, sentence enhancements for repeat offenders will be possible.

Solving the second problem—that of determining by how far the tops and bottoms of the sentence ranges for offense types should be separated—is more important for our purposes. For if the ranges wind up being narrow, then sentence enhancements for repeat offenders will likewise be modest. This might not comport well with public support for such enhancements. If the ranges wind up being quite large, then such sentence enhancements might exceed or even dwarf the deserved sentence for the most recent offense. If our aim is to honor instinctive support for criminal history enhancements while keeping them in check, then permitting them to exceed the deserved sentence for the most recent offense is undesirable. Standard retributive logic would seem to support sentence ranges that are not too large, especially if the harm inflicted or risked by offense types is the primary determining factor in sentencing. Granted, within offenses types, there will be some variation in the harm done or risked by agents. Some armed robberies risk more harm than others, just as some sexual assaults do more harm than others. But the range of standard harms risked or inflicted by any given offense type is not apt to be enormous, unless offenders have committed and therefore should be charged with more than one type of offense. Richard Frase has suggested that the sentence at the top of an offense range should be no more than twice as long as the sentence at the bottom of an offense range (2012: 192). Though this stipulation is, as he recognizes, somewhat arbitrary, it corresponds, at least roughly, with the recognition that harms inflicted or risked by individuals who commit the same type of offense are likely to vary within a relatively narrow range. Frase's proposal would permit significant recidivist premiums, ones that we might hope will satisfy the public's demand for them, while keeping sentences within proportionality limits.

Further, we might attempt to mollify public concerns about particular kinds of recidivists by adopting narrowly tailored habitual violent offender provisions. There is, it could be argued, some discernible wisdom in the public's impatience with repeat violent offenders, individuals who on numerous occasions have demonstrated their unwillingness to abide by the most basic rules of social life. Even punishment theorists who are otherwise harshly critical of habitual offender or "three strikes" provisions concede that carefully crafted and narrowly applied provisions of these kinds might be defensible (Morse 1996: 149; Duff 2001: 170). We would have to specify clearly the number and kinds of violent offenses that would make individuals eligible for such highly enhanced recidivist premiums and develop fair procedures for determining which offenders met the eligibility requirements. Such enhancements could be understood as occasionally justified significant upward departures from the sentences individuals deserve given their most recent offenses. To make such a provision less draconian, we could allow the possibility of early release from such harsh sentences if the individuals subject to them could somehow demonstrate a renewed and thoroughgoing commitment to abide by the rules of civil society (see Duff 2001: 172).

Should we likewise adopt some provision for releasing other offenders from their sentences, including any sentence enhancements they received for prior offending, if they can convince us that they have changed and are now ready to honor the rules of civil society? Such provisions used to be common in the form of parole for prisoners who could persuade duly constituted parole boards that they were rehabilitated. Yet sentencing policies of the last 40 years in the United States have systematically sought to limit early release options, often by eliminating discretionary parole decisions (Tonry 2013). I believe that conceiving of offending and repeat offending as conveying signals to the public about the willingness of individuals to abide by the basic rules of social life provides some support for policies of parole or early release. It ought to matter to the public, at least somewhat, whether individuals who have served some part of their sentences appear to be rehabilitated in the sense that their commitment and willingness to abide by the rules is rejuvenated. As we have seen, displays of remorse are routinely taken as signals that offenders understand the importance of the rules they have violated, such that mitigating their punishment is in order. By the same token, sincere efforts by prison inmates to turn their lives around ought to attract some sympathy from a public focused on rule-compliance. Hence, even if the public's concerns about rule-compliance require us to retain recidivist premiums, their impact could be limited further by reinstating discretionary parole.

Finally, there is the social deprivation narrative sketched earlier and the question of whether it can be made to have any traction with a public that insists on recidivist premiums in some form or other. The narrative, as we have seen, undermines the intuitive plausibility of the logic of recidivist premiums. Social deprivation limits the viable income-earning options of individuals, and for young males focused on gaining status and respect from others, the temptation to offend will be hard to resist (Lippke 2011). Socially deprived youths who succumb to the temptation and are convicted of crimes will encounter yet more limited options and might be targeted by the authorities in ways that make future arrests more or less inevitable. Until they age out, a criminal career path will be one to which many socially deprived youths are drawn. The way to the public's heart, it seems to me, is to lay bare just how difficult such individuals' lives are from the start. These are not individuals who have the kinds of opportunities that affluent or even middle class youths have and who have squandered them by offending. Neither are they individuals who, having been arrested, charged, and convicted, simply refuse to heed the norm-reinforcing message conveyed by legal punishment and, once again, waste abundant opportunities to earn income and status within the confines of the legal rules. Moreover, many of their crimes are not violent. Fully 80 percent of the offenses processed by the legal system are misdemeanors and therefore mostly not-too-serious property, drug, or other offenses (Roberts 2011: 281). The image of recidivists as violent predators, rather than immature or feckless human beings with limited and dwindling options, might fuel the demand for harsh recidivist premiums, but it is a misleading image in many cases and should be exposed as such.

Also, the public should be reminded that its current penal regime is hardly focused on helping offenders to avoid recidivism. It is one thing to support lengthy recidivist premiums if our penal practices are structured to get at and remedy some of the root causes of offending, and thereby give young offenders the tools they need to re-enter society and function as responsible citizens. If we were making concerted efforts to help socially deprived offenders gain a toehold in society, it would make sense for us to react in a strongly negative fashion when they chose, instead, to return to offending. It is another thing if we leave social deprivation intact (or permit it to grow worse) and then harshly sanction offenders, with little apparent thought given to the social, psychological, and economic impact of such measures. Public enthusiasm for recidivist premiums seems too often founded in a combination of denial and delusion about repeat offenders. To temper that enthusiasm, efforts to inform and educate the public about offenders, especially the limited life options many of them have, ought to be made. The public foots the bill for many of its (or its elected political leaders') counter-productive choices about the treatment of repeat offenders; too often, the indiscriminate use of lengthy recidivist premiums raises the costs of the criminal justice system while providing little additional protection to the public from the violent repeat offenders who are likely its intended targets.

Bibliography

Ashworth, A. (1995) *Sentencing and Criminal Justice*, London: Butterworths.

Bagaric, M. (2010) 'Double punishment and punishing character: the unfairness of prior convictions', *Criminal Justice Ethics*, 19: 10–28.

Bagaric, M. and Amarasekara, K. (2001) 'Feeling sorry?—Tell someone who cares: the irrelevance of remorse in sentencing', *The Howard Journal*, 40: 364–76.

Clear, T.R. (2007) *Imprisoning Communities: How Mass Incarceration Makes Disadvantaged Neighborhoods Worse*, New York, NY: Oxford University Press.

Doob, A.N. and Webster, C.M. (2003) 'Sentence severity and crime: accepting the null hypothesis', *Crime and Justice: A Review of Research*, 30: 143–89.

Duff, R.A. (2001) *Punishment, Communication, and Community*, Oxford: Oxford University Press.

Fletcher, G. (1978) *Rethinking Criminal Law*, Boston, MA: Little, Brown.

Frase, R.S. (2012) *Just Sentencing: Principles and Procedures for a Workable System*, New York, NY: Oxford University Press.

Greenberg, D. F. (2002) 'Striking out in democracy', *Punishment & Society*, 4: 237–52.

Haney, C. (2006) *Reforming Punishment: Psychological Limits to the Pains of Imprisonment*, Washington, DC: American Psychological Association.

Lippke, R.L. (2008) 'Response to Tudor: remorse-based sentence reductions in theory and practice', *Criminal Law and Philosophy*, 2: 259–68.
Lippke, R.L. (2011) 'Social deprivation as tempting fate', *Criminal Law and Philosophy*, 5: 277–91.
Lippke, R.L. (2012) 'Anchoring the sentencing scale: a modest proposal', *Theoretical Criminology*, 16: 463–80.
Morris, N. (1982) *Madness and the Criminal Law*, Chicago, IL: University of Chicago Press.
Morse, S.J. (1996) 'Blame and danger: an essay on preventive detention', *Boston University Law Review*, 76: 112–55.
Nagin, D.S. (1998) 'Deterrence and incapacitation', in M. Tonry (ed.), *The Handbook of Crime and Punishment*, New York, NY: Oxford University Press, pp. 345–68.
Roberts, J. (2011) 'Why misdemeanors matter: defining effective advocacy in the lower criminal courts', *University of California-Davis Law Review*, 45: 277–372.
Roberts, J.V. (1996) 'Public opinion, criminal record, and the sentencing process', *American Behavioral Scientist*, 39: 488–99.
Roberts, J.V. (1997) 'The role of criminal record in the sentencing process', *Crime and Justice: A Review of Research*, 22: 303–62.
Roberts, J.V. (2008a) 'Punishing persistence: explaining the enduring appeal of the recidivist sentencing premium', *British Journal of Criminology*, 48: 468–81.
Roberts, J.V. (2008b) *Punishing Persistent Offenders: Exploring Community and Offender Perspectives*, Oxford: Oxford University Press.
Roberts, J.V. and von Hirsch, A. (2010) *Previous Convictions at Sentencing: Theoretical and Applied Perspectives*, Oxford: Hart Publishing.
Spiranovic, C.A., Roberts, L.D., Indermaur, D., Warner, K., Gelb, K., Mackenzie, G. (2012) 'Public preferences for sentencing purposes: what difference does offender age, criminal history, and offence type make?' *Criminology and Criminal Justice*, 12: 289–306.
Stuntz, W.J. (1998) 'Race, class, and drugs', *Columbia Law Review*, 98: 1795–1842.
Tonry, M. (2013) 'Sentencing in America, 1975–2025', *Crime and Justice: A Review of Research*, 42: 141–98.
Tudor, S.K. (2008) 'Why should remorse be a mitigating factor in sentencing?' *Criminal Law and Philosophy*, 2: 241–57.
von Hirsch, A. (1993) *Censure and Sanctions*, Oxford: Clarendon Press.
von Hirsch, A. (2010) 'Proportionality and the progressive loss of mitigation: some further reflections', in Roberts and von Hirsch 2010.
von Hirsch, A. and Ashworth, A. (2005) *Proportionate Sentencing: Exploring the Principles*, Oxford: Oxford University Press.
Wasik, M. and von Hirsch, A. (1994) 'Section 29 revisited: previous convictions in sentencing', *Criminal Law Review*, 1994: 409–18.
Western, B. (2006) *Punishment and Inequality in America*, New York, NY: Russell Sage.

2

Last words on retribution

Jeffrie G. Murphy

Mourn no more, children. Those to whom
the night of earth gives benediction
should not be mourned. Retribution comes.
Sophocles, *Oedipus at Colonus*

Introduction

For the past 45 years or so I have drawn upon, with varying degrees of enthusiasm, a retributive account of punishment—an account that makes the concept of *desert* central in the justification of punishment. I have been drawn to this account because of my belief that, at its best, it is based on the Kantian idea of *human dignity.* One of the ways that we respect the dignity of persons is through holding them responsible and sometimes resenting or even punishing them for what they do instead of insulting them by regarding them as sick or helpless victims of their fixed natures or social circumstances. (Of course, if conclusive evidence establishes that they are indeed such victims—delusional psychotics, for example—then we should not hold them responsible, but that should never be our default position.) I must admit, however, that I have not always been as clear or consistent on what I mean by the concept of retributive desert as I perhaps should have been. I have, for example, changed my mind about the nature of retributive desert several times—sometimes, influenced by Herbert Morris, meaning a debt owed in fairness by the criminal to the law abiding, at other times meaning deep evil of character, what Kant called "inner wickedness" (*inneren Bösartigkeit*).[1] I have highly qualified my commitment to both of those meanings and have recently identified and articulated six different conceptions of retributive desert—all with some merit in my view (2012: Chapter 6). I tend to write what I believe at the time of writing a particular essay and have not paid very much attention to checking if what I say at that time is consistent with what I have said earlier. I may thereby have contributed, alas, to the belief of many that the very idea of retributive desert is inherently vague—too much so to play a significant role in deciding which people, if any, may legitimately be punished. Ultimately we simply are the people that we are, however, and I have never had either the talent or (because of limitations of talent) the inclination to develop a grand overarching career defining philosophical theory of the kind that we can find in the great geniuses of twentieth-century moral, political, and legal philosophy—John Rawls and Ronald Dworkin, for example.

In the present essay I will not worry much about what I have said before, but I will seek to be as clear as I can be about the current view that I will here put forward—put forward with the clear understanding that my commitments to aspects of it are tentative and that I may at some future point be persuaded to change my mind about these aspects. When I speak of retributive desert in this essay I will mean by this the use in justifying punishment of the idea of *moral evil*–of act, mental state, motive, or character.

Problems of clarity, of course, are not the only problems facing retributivism. In recent years I have become alarmed at the degree to which the language of retributive desert has been coopted by the forces of darkness in order to claim that absurdly long prison sentences and unspeakably horrendous treatment of prisoners is simply to give criminals exactly what they deserve. And I have also come to realize that the high-sounding rhetoric of just deserts often functions, as Nietzsche claimed, as a cover (perhaps unconscious) for the base passion that he called *ressentiment*—an unwholesome brew of malice, spite, envy, and cruelty (Murphy 2012: Chapters 2 and 4). Surely these problems with at least the language of retribution or just deserts must give us pause before we continue to use that language—might even make us skeptical about the underlying values themselves.

In spite of these worries, however, I am not yet prepared to give up all of my retributive commitments and still wish to think in terms of what in an earlier publication I called "the two faces of retribution"—one the face that respects the dignity of responsible individuals and one the face that tempts us to cruelty (2012: Chapter 4). I want to retain the good face and will even argue that retributive values are themselves, when properly understood, sometimes the best way to weaken the temptations posed by the bad face.

In the remainder of this essay I will, in the next two sections, identify and dismiss two confusions that often tempt people to reject retributivism. In the final section I will state and defend what I regard as the strengths of retributivism and also identify what I regard as the limitations of this value in the justification of punishment. I should note, by the way, that when I use the phrase "Last words" in the title of this essay I do not mean to suggest that there will be nothing more worth saying about retribution once my essay has been published. I mean something much more personal—namely, that these will almost surely be *my* last words on the topic. I am getting pretty old and—to quote Stravinsky when he was asked why he had stopped composing—it is possible that "my muse has gone out on a wildcat strike" —at least with respect to the issues of the present essay. Some, of course, may think that even this one is one too many and that I should have stopped some time ago. I leave that for others to judge.

Retribution and punishment

I have used as an epigraph for this essay a passage from Sophocles' final play, *Oedipus at Colonus*—a passage that seems to use the word "retribution" in a way that is increasingly uncommon but should not be ignored. As one knows from the play *Oedipus the King*, Oedipus was declared a polluted sinner and driven into exile because he had killed his father and had sexual relations with his mother. It made no difference that he had not known or indeed had no way of knowing that the man he killed in self-defense on the road to Thebes was his father or that the woman whom he married after his arrival in Thebes and with whom he fathered children was his mother. The system of liability was what we would now call a strict or absolute liability system in which mental states such as knowledge or intention or foresight of consequences played no role in determining the way in which he deserved to be regarded and treated. Oedipus so internalized the values of this grotesquely unjust system that he regarded himself as evil, accepted exile willingly, and even blinded himself so that he would not have to see his vile reflection in a pool of water.

In *Oedipus at Colonus,* Oedipus is now an old man who has spent many years as an exile—traveling in disgrace throughout the land, accompanied and cared for by his daughters Antigone and Ismene. He has given much thought to the punishment that he has endured and has reached the conclusion that it was totally unjust—should not have been imposed by Creon (his successor as ruler of Thebes) and should not have been internalized by him since what he did was in no sense his fault. He says "the law acquits me as innocent of any wrongdoing in what I have done" and, instead of being repentant and apologetic when visited by his son, Eteocles, and Creon (who now want him to return to Thebes since he has, unbeknownst to him, become a venerated individual who could bring blessings to Thebes) he angrily rebukes them and sends them away. He is then, as the play closes, swept up by the gods in a kind of miraculous divine intervention that confirms his status as a blessed individual to be venerated and not shunned—presumably because, by seeing the injustice of the system under which he was condemned but enduring it with patience when he still believed it was just, he has attained a state of wisdom—has "suffered unto truth." And how is all this described? In the Fitzgerald translation it is described as "retribution" (*nemesis* in the Greek). Since what is happening to him is surely not punishment (but more like a reward) the world "retribution" here must mean, not "punishment," but simply "being treated as he *deserves* to be treated" or "getting his due as a matter of justice." So let us keep that meaning of "retribution" in mind during what follows in this essay.[2]

Why is it important to keep this in mind? Because it is often mistakenly thought that those who embrace a retributive justification of punishment must always be in enthusiastic favor of punishment—and probably very harsh punishment at that. But this is a mistake. Retributivists believe in punishment only when it is deserved and will always oppose it when it is not deserved. Many people who condemn retributivism seem to remember only the application of the theory to support punishment and forget the equally important application of the theory to condemn punishment when it is unjust—condemning any punishment at all for those who do not deserve it and condemning punishment in excess of what is deserved for those who deserve punishment to some lesser degree. As I have argued elsewhere, the out of control nature of excessive punishments and horrendous prison conditions in the United States cry out for rejection on retributive grounds, for these horrors are affronts to human dignity and far beyond what any person could reasonably be said to deserve—whatever their possible deterrence value, which may be considerable.[3]

As I understand the retributive theory of punishment at its best, it is not a foundational primitive (the claim that we can see as self-evident that the deserving should be punished) but a view about punishment that must be located within broader concerns about justice, fairness, and desert (both punitive and non-punitive).[4]

I think that the above point is often missed because many critics of retributivism (and some of its defenders) think that desert of punishment always requires punishment. Carlos Nino and T. M. Scanlon, for example, regard it as a serious objection to retributivism that it will never allow consequential considerations to override considerations of retributive desert in cases in which not to do this seems just plain wrong (Nino 1996 and Scanlon 1999). Consider Chile, for example, after Pinochet left office. Although no longer in office he retained considerable control of the military and might have used that to topple the new and fragile democratic regime if he and his officers were put on trial and punished for the atrocities that were common under his rule. It seems correct that such punishment should be avoided if necessary to preserve democratic institutions, and if a retributivist cannot see this necessity because of a belief that those who commit atrocities deserve to be punished, this surely—according to Nino and Scanlon—reveals a great and perhaps fatal flaw in a retributive theory of punishment.

But must a retributivist reject the necessity? I think not. Even Kant, often put forward as a paradigm retributivist, argued that there can be some circumstances in which punishment, although deserved, should be avoided (1996: 475).[5] So, in my view, it would simply be a mistake to regard the following as two defining claims of retributivism: (1) Desert is a *necessary condition* for justified punishment and (2) Desert is a *sufficient condition* for justified punishment.

I am inclined to accept (1) as it stands. However, although some retributivists might assert (2), I would not. I would instead replace (2) above with this: Desert is always a *very strong reason* that favors punishment and, other things being equal, the punishment that is deserved should be inflicted. But other things are not always equal since not all evils are part of the legitimate concern of the liberal state (a point I will discuss in a bit more detail later) and since consequences of sufficient gravity sometimes require that certain principles—including desert principles—be overridden. As I have noted above, for example, I believe that much of the treatment given prisoners in the United States is so inhumane that it is wildly beyond what any human being deserves. Does this mean that I believe that the doors of all the prisons in America should immediately be opened and everyone in them, including the most violent and dangerous, be allowed to run free and prey on the innocent? No. (I might, however, favor letting out many non-violent offenders for these reasons.) Also, I would support *not* punishing those who deserve to be punished if so doing would, as it probably would have in Chile and South Africa, cause serious threat of the collapse of democratic government and a return to tyranny or something of a similarly horrendous nature. Absent such threats, however, I would favor punishing at least the worst of them (the torturers, rapists, and murderers and those in power who instructed them to act in this way) and might even favor punishing them with *ex post facto* legislation if necessary simply because these morally evil thugs deserve it. This might cause tension with the rule of law and respect for law, however, and that concern might regrettably trump the retributive value of retroactive punishment. On the other hand, when citizens see evil get what is deserved through very narrow and constrained retroactive law, this might strengthen (particularly among those who have been victims of atrocity) citizens' respect for law. This is, of course, a matter for empirical investigation and cannot be resolved merely by philosophical reflection.

In saying the above, however, I would insist that we should stay vividly aware that—when desert values are being trumped by consequential considerations—we are not simply doing what is right (end of story) but are rather, out of a regrettable necessity, *violating an important principle* if we continue to punish in excess of desert or do not punish those who are deserving. This is a choice between evils, and in such a choice the evil that is left in place (because one chose to avoid an even greater evil) *remains an evil.* A retributive outlook preserves this sense of something wrong having regrettably been necessary in a way that a consequential theory would not.

Of course, as I have noted earlier and have argued at length elsewhere, the language of retribution and desert has an unfortunate tendency to engage—as Nietzsche argued—some very base passions—in particular the one he called *ressentiment.* And this language remains susceptible to similar corruption in our own day, as when a couple of years ago one of my criminal law students said in class that those young people who are raped in prison are just getting what they deserve for breaking the law. And more recently, in a CNN interview, some of my fellow citizens expressed the view that a recent execution in Arizona that took over two hours and seemed to cause the victim non-trivial pain was deserved—one even saying that the convicted man deserved to take longer to die in pain. But this is not a fair charge against retribution properly understood—just as it is not a fair charge against utilitarianism that it must, in all its forms, approve of punishing the innocent.

The best argument against utilitarianism and the punishment of the innocent, by the way, is not that the theory cannot oppose such punishment but rather that it opposes it for the *wrong reason.* The standard way in which utilitarians tend to oppose punishment of the innocent is to argue that the principle of utility (promote the greatest good for the greatest number) is to be applied, not to every act to be evaluated, but rather to *social rules* to be evaluated—rules that tell us which acts are permissible and which are impermissible. It is then argued that a rule that allowed the intentional punishment of the innocent would not promote utility because it would leave everyone nervous that he might be selected for sacrifice to the general welfare. It is not difficult, however, to imagine how one might have a rule allowing intentional punishment of the innocent that would not have such adverse consequences on the general welfare—for example, a rule that would limit such punishment to an easily identified minority of which the majority would not have to fear membership. And such a rule could have, just as a similarly restricted rule allowing slavery could have, considerable general utility. But surely intentionally punishing even one innocent person would still be wrong—as would enslaving even one person. Why? Because that person would not *deserve* it—not because punishing him would make other people twitchy. To act otherwise is simply not to accord the individual the equal concern and respect that is owed to his dignity as a person. So the best way to oppose the utilitarian "solution" to the problem of punishing the innocent is one based on the concept of desert—a concept that is itself based on the idea of the dignity of each individual person and the respect that is owed to this dignity.

Punishment and pain

The philosopher T. M. Scanlon (whom I have already discussed above) and others have condemned a retributive account of punishment because of a belief that those who favor punishment on such grounds must favor causing pain or hard treatment—something that these critics believe can never be justified by the claim that it is deserved. In his essay "Giving Desert Its Due" (Scanlon 2013) Scanlon makes the following claims:

> I regard as morally repugnant [the idea] that it is good that people who have done wrong should suffer. (102)[6]
>
> The infliction of pain is part of the purpose of acts of punishment. (103)
>
> It is never a good thing, morally speaking, for anyone to suffer, no matter what they have done. (104)
>
> Fines, imprisonment and other forms of hard treatment are not justifiable unless they are necessary and effective means to protect citizens against serious wrongs. (103)

There are two serious problems with this critique of retribution: (1) It is simply *not true* that all retributivists must believe that the criminal wrongdoer deserves either pain or hard treatment. (2) In considering those retributivists who might consider inflicting some degree of pain as appropriate because deserved, it is not clear (at least to me) that it is always wrong to favor some degree of pain or unpleasantness for wrongdoers. Scanlon simply assumes this, gives no argument for it, and thus seems to beg some very important questions on the issue under discussion. I also find it odd that he does not discuss at all the well-known and sophisticated arguments given by those who defend retributive views—Herbert Morris (1976), Herbert Fingarette (1977), Michael Moore (1987, 1997), and Jean Hampton (1991–1992), for example.[7]

I do not wish to be unfairly critical here, however, so let me say this in at least partial defense of Scanlon's omissions: Scanlon is a very important philosopher who has made contributions of lasting value to moral, legal, and political philosophy. His work on freedom of expression, for example, forced me to modify my own views on this important topic. He has written very little on punishment, however, and many philosophers might well like to know his views on this topic *just because they are Scanlon's* and will not care if he does not immerse himself in the vast body of literature that specialists on the philosophy of punishment tend to study. Also, Scanlon and those who are close students of his work might—if they are so inclined—be able to develop a defense for some of his views on punishment by drawing on his general theory of contractualism. Perhaps the most charitable way to interpret Scanlon's work on punishment is to see it as an attempt to answer this question: To what degree can those who reject retributivism accommodate the intuitions that tend to draw people to retributivism and show that many of these intuitions can be provided with a foundation that is not retributivist?

But now let me return to the two problems I previously noted with respect to Scanlon's claims that (1) retributivists favor causing pain on grounds of desert and (2) it is always wrong to inflict pain on someone because of a belief that the person deserves it.

With respect to (1), why do Scanlon and other critics believe that retributivists must favor pain? I think that this is very likely due to a semantic confusion. The retributivist does believe that criminals deserve to *suffer*, and in common language suffering is often identified with pain. (Scanlon and others sometimes seem to use the terms "pain" and "suffering" interchangeably.[8]) The concept of suffering I regard as central in retributivism, however, is to be found in the original and primary meaning of the word: "to *endure* something that is not within the control of one's own will." (Think here of "To suffer woes which hope thinks infinite" from Shelly's *Prometheus* or the common phrase "He does not suffer fools gladly.")

So the operative concept of "to suffer" that I regard as central to retribution has no intrinsic connection to pain but is rather to be understood as "to endure." Herbert Fingarette, for example, has made a powerful retributive case that the criminal wrongdoer, having presumed to exercise a level of will that is incompatible with the rule of law, must endure having his will "humbled"—deserving to have his ability to control his own life by his own will limited or restricted to some degree (Fingarette 1977). There is no reason to think, however, that what will be endured by the wrongdoer must be painful—unwelcome, of course, but not necessarily painful in any ordinary sense of the word "pain."

And while on the subject of linguistic distinctions let me simply say that I regard it as very strange to call fines and imprisonment examples of "hard treatment" and thus presumably on the same list of supposed immoralities as intentionally causing pain. Some instances of fines and imprisonment could be open to moral objections, of course—if the fines are excessive or unfairly burdensome, for example. But fines *per se* as hard treatment? Surely not. If I am fined 50 dollars for illegally parking in a space marked as reserved for handicapped people (no personal experience involved here I assure you) I would never for a moment be even tempted to say that I had experienced hard treatment. And why the fine anyway? It is surely in part, of course, to deter the non-handicapped from using one of these spaces. This cannot be the only reason, however, since the fine might well be appropriately waived for someone who parked in the space to deal with a serious emergency. So, in addition to deterrence, an additional reason for imposing the fine is probably based on an idea of retributive desert: People who are so morally insensitive that they think that their mere convenience is sufficient to outweigh accommodating those who are handicapped are simply getting what they deserve.

What about imprisonment? If we are thinking about the unspeakable conditions often found in contemporary United States jails and prisons, then I would agree that the phrase "hard treatment" is appropriate to apply—the only objection to the phrase being that it is likely too weak to adequately condemn these pest holes. (In the United States it has apparently been forgotten that we should send people to prison *as* punishment, not *for* punishment.) But imprisonment *per se* as hard treatment? As with fines, I think this depends on the nature of the imprisonment. If (dream on) our system were changed so radically that inmates would be confined for a reasonable amount of time in safe, healthy, and civilized quarters—and provided with therapy if needed and an opportunity to study and learn skills that might make their lives outside the prison more likely to be those of good citizens—I see no reason to think of this as hard treatment unless one thinks that anything at all that is not the product of one's own will is hard treatment. But, at least to my ear, this usage sounds wrong. When I try to think of examples of what I would call hard treatment I call forth images of someone breaking rocks on a chain gang, not someone reading law books in a prison library.

Let me now move to (2) above and ask if it is really true that it is *always* morally wrong to believe it appropriate that someone experience pain (even painful punishment) simply because they deserve it? If so, why? Is it not all a matter of the *degree and nature* of the pain involved? Suppose, for example, I allow myself to wish that Bernard Madoff from now on has a very unhappy life—most of his remaining hopes and dreams unfulfilled—and do not have this wish because I believe his unhappiness will have deterrence value or will bring comfort to his victims (since I would retain the wish even if his misery was not generally known). I want him to be unhappy simply because, given the harm he brought others through his greed and selfishness, I think he *deserves* to be unhappy. Does having this wish make me a bad person or an irrational person? If so, I fail to see why and would like to hear an argument. And if it is morally acceptable to see value in this kind of pain, why would it be unacceptable to generate if possible this kind of pain (or something like it) as punishment? Of course, if I wished him to get cancer and die in screaming agony or wanted him to be tortured or wanted prison guards to turn him over to some prison gang so that he would be repeatedly raped, I would reveal myself as a bad person because I would be wanting for him things that would compromise his dignity as a human being—things that no decent person would want for another person and certainly would not approve of as punishment. I think that the infliction of any *physical* pain runs this risk since it addresses the offender's animal nature and not his human rational nature.[9]

Having attempted to meet what I regard as two ill-founded objections to retribution, let me now attempt to say something positive on behalf of the concept and its legitimate use in the justification of punishment. I will not attempt a detailed analysis of the concept of desert itself but will instead operate by noting examples, paradigm cases one might say, in which the idea of desert (understood as some combination of an evil act and an evil will—intention, motive, or character—that produced the act) will do a better job of putting us in reflective equilibrium than any consequential analysis.

What is retributive desert, and what role should it play in punishment?

There is no doubt that one of the main obstacles to taking the idea of retributive desert seriously is the large number of different meanings that have been given to the concept in the literature and the many different roles that have been envisioned for it in punishment. At one extreme it has been used to mean simply legal guilt and at the other extreme to mean evil of character all the way down—what Kant called "inner wickedness" (*inneren Bösartikeit*). As noted earlier, I can—depending on the role it is to play—see some virtues in both of these and in several other understandings of the concept as well.

With respect to its legitimate role in punishment, retributive desert has been conceptualized as a limit (a side constraint) on a practice whose main purpose is the consequential one of crime control through such mechanisms as deterrence and incapacitation. Following the distinction introduced by H. L. A. Hart, this view regards crime control as the "general justifying aim" of the practice of punishment and desert as an answer to the "distributive question" of "whom should we punish under this consequentially justified practice?"[10] This has often been called "negative retributivism," and one common version, found in Rawls for example, is that we should use punishment to control crime only on those who deserve it in the weak sense of being actually guilty of the crime in question—i.e., never intentionally punishing the legally innocent (Rawls 1955).

Given this very weak version of negative retributivism, it is easy (though in my view mistaken) to believe that there is no trouble of reconciling a utilitarian (or other consequential) view of punishment with a retributive view since it would probably be highly disutilitarian to attempt to control crime with a system that intentionally punished those innocent of any criminal wrongdoing. Under such a system all citizens would be very insecure (having no guarantee that they could avoid punishment by choosing to avoid crime) and could not use the criminal law as a way to plan their lives—a vital feature in a system that would seek to control conduct in a way that would maximize utility. As Rawls claimed, this would be like trying to control economic behavior with a price system that told people the price of an item only after they had already purchased it. This is a good reason to avoid intentionally punishing the innocent but not, as I argued earlier, the only or even the best reason.

At the other extreme, the retributive view—now sometimes called "positive retributivism"—might be interpreted as the claim that the sole purpose of punishing people is to give evil people who do evil things what they deserve and that consequential considerations should play no role at all in the matter. Both Michael Moore and Kant have been—perhaps mistakenly—interpreted in this way.

The view of retributive desert that I now wish to defend (who knows for how long?) might be called "enriched negative retributivism" or perhaps "negative utilitarianism" or "negative consequentialism." The former label will call attention to the claim that the legitimate retributive constraints on punishment are far more complex and robust than merely "do not intentionally punish the innocent" and that these constraints cannot be defended solely with consequentialist arguments. The latter two labels will call attention to the claim that at least one important reason for having a system of punishment is to give morally evil people the suffering that they deserve, but that only a subset of such people, for consequential reasons, will actually be identified as legitimate targets for punishment—namely, bad people whose badness has a tendency to undermine the social order of rights that it is the business of the liberal state to maintain.[11] I am not sure at present which label I prefer, but the practical outcome of each may be the same.

First, let me say why I think that the strongest form of retributivism must be rejected—the form that claims that the sole purpose of punishment is to give evil people the suffering that they deserve. As I have argued elsewhere, it is important to see that justifying punishment is not just a moral matter but also a political matter—the mere fact that something is morally good not being a sufficient reason by itself to use state power to bring it about (Murphy 1985). All reasonable people will surely agree, for example, that the moral education of children is very important, but not all such people (some fearing state indoctrination perhaps) will agree that developing and imposing such a program is a legitimate use of state power. Turning to punishment, it is hard to imagine—thinking in liberal social contract terms—that rational people designing institutions under which they will live would, given how expensive and intrusive the practice of punishment will be, adopt it for the sole purpose of making sure that bad people will get whatever suffering is believed properly proportional for their badness. Surely, at the very least—and this invites the labels "negative utilitarianism" or "negative consequentialism"—they would want to limit state punishment to instances of moral evil that pose a danger to the ability of the law-abiding to live in peace and reap the benefits of social cooperation—the objective here being to curtail dangerous anti-social conduct. In other words, Hobbes was on to something important in his justification for the rule of law.

Consider, for example, what are generally called "victimless crimes"—crimes in which people engage in conduct that, though believed to be evil, really causes no threat to peace, stability, and personal security. Even those who believe (quite wrongly in my view) that private homosexual conduct is evil and should perhaps even be punished by God as these evil people deserve should, if rational, oppose using the criminal law to deal with such private activities since any small benefits (benefits in their view) of such punishment will be greatly outweighed by staggering costs in treasure and privacy invasions. And consider also the betrayal of friendship and intimacy. I regard such betrayal as very, very evil and can easily welcome suffering for people who are given to such vices—hoping, for example, that whatever they wished to gain by such betrayal will produce loss and misery instead. But it would be quite irrational for me to think that this kind of evil should be part of the *state's* legitimate business and that the machinery of criminal law should be brought to bear on these people.

So, in short, I believe with Hart that *a* (if not *the*) general justifying aim of having the practice or institution of criminal law is the consequential one of crime control. I also believe, however, that this aim must be joined by retributive desert as another general justifying aim or, at the very least, have the aim of crime control constrained by a variety of related retributive desert considerations—considerations that include, of course, legal guilt but also involve far more than legal guilt. This is why I have considered the label "enriched negative retributivism." Rawls's version of negative retributivism—intentionally punish only the legally guilty—was his way of answering Hart's distributive question. We might label Rawls's approach as "minimalist negative retributivism."

Hart's own answer, however, was much more complex and gave me the idea for the label "enriched negative retributivism."[12] His list of required side constraints on a system of crime control includes, in addition to no intentional punishment of the innocent, requirements of *mens rea* for statutory definitions of crimes, proportionality in grading offenses to be based on "a commonsense scale of gravity," rich doctrines of justification, excuse, and mitigation, and consideration of such states of character as remorse as relevant in sentencing and clemency. He often tries to defend these side constraints as demands of procedural fairness—an argument that, as I have argued elsewhere, does not work for many of them (1995). At other times, however, he sometimes refers to them simply as "*retribution* in the distribution of punishment" (italics mine)—clearly recognizing that they have a value independent from and not reducible to the value of crime control as his general justifying aim of punishment. He also sometimes defends these side constraints consequentially in terms of maximizing the role of choice in law but for some of them maintains that they cannot plausibly be defended by utilitarian or other consequential considerations and will often defend them simply by arguing that "commonsense morality" would not tolerate a system that did not incorporate them. I do not think that Hart had in mind here the taking of an opinion poll of the general public but was probably (but without current philosophical jargon) suggesting that a system without the noted constraints would fail to put informed and thoughtful people in a state of reflective equilibrium.

Let me now—expanding on Hart's rich analysis—list some additional ways in which, in my view, the concept of retributive desert should play a role (and sometimes already does play a role) in the design of a morally acceptable system of criminal law—even if a primary goal of such a system is to control crime. It is my hope that most of my readers will find themselves in reflective equilibrium with the role that I will suggest in each case for the value of retributive desert:

1. *There should be radical limitations on the current practice of avoiding trials through plea bargaining.* Plea bargaining as it stands sometimes involves frightening a defendant (who may be of limited intelligence and provided with poor legal representation) into pleading

guilty to something he did not do by persuading him that if he goes to trial he will almost certainly be convicted of something even worse (that he also did not do) with a longer sentence. More common is the problem that because prosecutors are able to stack multiple (and often overlapping) charges against a defendant, he is effectively terrorized into pleading guilty to avoid the risk of trial. This substantially conserves resources and sometimes functions to get genuinely guilty people out of circulation for a period that is socially useful. Too frequently, however, it leads to inappropriate punishment—that is, punishment that is sometimes more than (and sometimes less than) the punishment that is deserved. If this strikes the reader, as it strikes me, as a kind of assembly line "justice" that ignores the kind of individuation that is required by respect for the dignity of persons, then one is being drawn to retributive values even if one does not like the word "retribution." Surely in these cases the defendant *deserves* better.

2. *The crime itself will be defined with considerations of retributive desert playing a significant role, e.g., mens rea will be required for all offenses (no strict liability) even if this might undermine utility.* This will require, among other things, that the United States will join all other civilized democratic countries and eliminate the doctrine of felony murder—a doctrine that in the United States allows the punishment for murder (normally requiring intention to kill) of a person who, without any intention to kill, commits a felony that is a significant causal contributor to a wrongful death—even if the person did not intend the death, had good reason to believe that no death would result, and would not have committed the felony if he thought that a death would result. Think, for example, of a large and imposing man who agrees to go along, for intimidation value, with a man who persuades him to join in robbing a convenience store (a felony). The man with the plan claims, however, that the gun he will use is a toy and that he simply wishes to frighten the clerk. The gun is real, however, and the lying robber shoots and kills the store's clerk. It may promote utility to have a doctrine of felony murder—making people more careful when they commit felonies or perhaps even giving them incentives to avoid the underlying felony altogether—but does anyone *deserve* to be branded as a murderer and convicted of murder when he was just negligent perhaps with respect to the resulting death? He certainly deserves some non-trivial punishment as the robbing thug that he is, but does he deserve the same punishment as the killer? Surely not. And is there a better way to make this point than one employing the concept of retributive desert? Being constrained by a reasonable conception of retributive desert would also make us doubt the value of making some instances of conduct looked on with disfavor by most people crimes at all. Consider all the people swept up and jailed as a part of our so-called "war on drugs." Some of them certainly deserve to suffer punishment (major distributors, for example) but I find it hard to accept that individual users are bad enough to deserve significant punishment—perhaps not bad at all but just stupid or addicted or otherwise ill. Consider also those who visit computer sites that offer child pornography but who never even consider abusing children much less actually abusing them. I find such people rather disgusting and perhaps a bit sick, but I would not brand them as evil such that they deserve to be punished for their viewing habits. And if the argument is given, as it often is, that these consumers must be punished in order to dry up a market that depends on the actual exploiting of children, is this not (in Kantian terms) merely to use these people as means rather than as ends in themselves—a wrong to them that the concept of desert would help to block?
3. *The grading of criminal offenses will be a function of retributive desert. The higher the grade the heavier the punishment.* Consider the current grading of criminal homicides in the

United States. A common grading (from most serious to least serious, most severe punishment to least severe punishment) is this: *First Degree Murder*: intentional, premeditated, and deliberate killing. *Second Degree Murder*: intentional killing. *Voluntary Manslaughter*: intentional killing under provocation or extreme emotional disturbance for which there is a rational explanation. *Involuntary Manslaughter*: negligent or reckless killing.

Since dead is dead, the ranking here cannot be a function of harm caused since it is the same in all grades. Is the ranking then based on dangerousness? Surely not since I and all of my readers stand in much greater danger of being killed by a negligent or reckless driver than by someone who deliberates and premeditates before intentionally killing us. Why then the current ranking? I think it is probably based on the concept of retributive desert—the thought being that deliberate premeditating killers are simply morally worse (more evil) than those lower on the grading list and thus deserve the most punishment.

It is interesting to note, in this regard, that the primary challenges to this ranking are themselves based on the concept of retributive desert.[13] Consider, for example, the mercy killer. He deliberates and premeditates prior to intentionally killing, but is he—given his motives—the worst of the worst and deserving of a first degree murder conviction and the punishment attached to that? Many people will answer no to this question and might even suggest that it is certain wantonly reckless killers who are really the worst of the worst and should be guilty of first-degree murder. Some states have a category of homicide labeled as "depraved heart murder"—a killing produced by conduct so wantonly reckless that it reveals a "hardened, abandoned, and malignant heart totally indifferent to the value of human life." In states that have this grade of murder it is murder in the second degree, but perhaps it should be first degree murder and mercy killing moved to murder of a lesser degree.

My main point here is this: The debate about degrees of homicide is carried out mainly in terms of the value of retributive desert, and I do not see how it could plausibly be carried out in terms of any other value.

4. *A variety of justifications and excuses will be provided as criminal defenses—some mitigating and others completely freeing from criminal responsibility and punishment.* A person deserves to be treated as an individual, and this requires an individuated response to his culpability—one that explores in some depth specific and often unique things about the defendant that either mitigate (make him seem better) or aggravate (make him seem worse) than we might have thought on a superficial analysis. We already do this to a considerable degree in the justifications and excuses we currently allow in United States criminal law, and we expand radically the range of factors to be considered when the sentence of death is a possibility. In an ideal world, we would—out of a respect for the dignity of the individual—extend such inquiries beyond the realm of capital punishment and into the realm of all serious crimes. But our world is not ideal, and doing this to a much greater degree than at present might well be more costly in time and resources than we could afford, since there are many other important and expensive things the state must do besides operate a system of criminal punishment. If these consequential factors carry the day, then we should at least admit to ourselves that we are regretfully departing from the demands of justice, giving defendants less or more than they actually deserve, and thus failing fully to respect their dignity as persons. And even if we cannot do a great deal more in the realm of individuation, we should always be open to considering some expansions given what we might learn

about diminished responsibility from such new areas of research as neuroscience and considering some contractions if we come to think that some current defenses are empirically ill-founded and often result in less punishment than is deserved. Whether rightly or wrongly, for example, the criminal law seems to be moving away in skepticism from allowing the so-called "battered woman syndrome" to function as a trigger for the justification of self-defense and admitting it only as an evidential matter to overcome a likely jury presumption that, since the woman did not leave, then the abuse she claims could not have been all that bad.

5. *After conviction, considerations of desert will play a significant role in clemency or parole—at which time such character states as remorse or its absence may be regarded as relevant.* Many state governors (including the current governor of my own state) are very stingy in the granting of clemency—often overriding even unanimous recommendations from their own clemency boards. This often means that truly repentant and reformed individuals who have turned their lives around are treated the same as individuals who remain hardened, hateful, and unrepentant. This seems deeply wrong to me, and I cannot think of a better way to mark this wrongness than by saying that their differences are morally relevant and should be legally relevant.[14] To put it in my preferred language, the former have a good case that they deserve early release (unless their crime was truly horrendous) and the latter a good case that they should stay put and serve their full sentence. Here is a case, however, where the quarrel is not mainly between the values of retributive desert and the values of social utility but rather between moral values of any kind and the narrow desire of politicians to curry favor with a vengeful populace by demonstrating a tough stance on crime. Here the perception of political expediency generally wins.
6. *Prison conditions will be considered as a part of punishment and 8th Amendment constraints against cruel and unusual punishments will meaningfully and significantly apply to them.* As I have noted in a previous essay (2014: Note 11) the United States Supreme Court has, except in one kind of situation, been unwilling to extend the 8th Amendment ban on cruel and unusual punishments to such things as a failure to prevent prison rape, failure to control abuse from prison gangs, or putting a stop to those long periods of solitary confinement that are destructive of an inmate's very personality. The general court doctrine has been that these are not punishments but are rather prison conditions—a piece of pure formalism if ever there was one. In the noted essay I expressed my outrage over this in the following way:

> A Kantian retributivist would be first in line to condemn much of what goes on in the [United States prison system]—condemn it because its harshness and cruelty are not deserved by any human being, any being having that precious value that Kant called dignity.[15]

Conclusion

I have attempted in this essay to say what I think is correct about the application of the concept of retributive desert in the justification of punishment. I have also attempted to expose what I think are limitations of the legitimate use of that concept—to regard giving wrongdoers what they deserve as the sole justification for a system of punishment, for example. Much of what I have said is tentative, and I remain conflicted in my own mind about many aspects of punishment and its justification. Perhaps this is a good thing. At the very least, those who are tentative, hesitant, and conflicted about punishment are much less likely to be cruel or support cruelty. At another time in history combating excessive leniency, rather than combating cruelty, might be an important goal, but in our present time—with the discussion of crime dominated by what Judge Richard Posner has called "a vengeful populace and resource-starved penal sysem"[16]—excessive leniency seems to be the least of our worries.

Notes

1 I have discussed in detail Kant's views on punishment in Murphy (1987). Kant's use of the concept of inner wickedness can be found in Kant (1996: 474).

2 I am in no sense an expert in the literature of ancient Greece and have no reading knowledge of the language. I do know, however, that in some other translations of the play *nemesis* is interpreted as a warning that the gods will be angry if their acts are taken as a cause of mourning. I first saw *nemesis* rendered simply as "retribution" when I was exposed to the Robert Fitzgerald translation in the wonderful play/film adaptation of *Oedipus at Colonus* with the title *The Gospel at Colonus*—where the context is the overcoming of grief and mourning through the realization that a wonderful thing has happened to Oedipus (Sophocles 1977: 172). So I consulted some people I know who do have expertise in the ancient Greek language and learned that, in spite of the fact that we now tend to use both *nemesis* and "retribution" to mean punishment or even vengeance, the literal and original meaning of *nemesis* is simply "the dispensing of what is due."

3 There is considerable anecdotal evidence that the thing that many people fear the most about going to prison is the likelihood that they will be raped or otherwise brutalized by the gangs that currently control many aspects of the lives of inmates (Murphy 2014).

4 One might defend one's theory of punishment with a model of rational choice (in social contract terms perhaps), by deriving it from a more general moral principle (fairness perhaps), or by arguing that it does a better job than any alternative theory of putting us in what John Rawls called "reflective equilibrium" with respect to the largest set of our pre-theoretical moral convictions. My own preference is the route of seeking reflective equilibrium, and I think that the idea of retributive desert—moral desert as a function of the moral evil of the act and the moral wickedness of the person performing the act—provides, at least for most (but certainly not all) reflective people, the best concept around which to discuss and defend most (but not all) important issues raised by the practice of criminal punishment.

5 Kant argues that if the accomplices in wrongdoing are so great that to punish them all would destroy the state and throw the community back into the state of nature, then not punishing with deserved severity all the wrongdoers would be both rational and moral—although regrettable.

6 In this essay Scanlon shows more sympathy with the concept of desert than he had shown in his earlier writings on punishment, but he still has no sympathy for the use to which retributivists (in his view) put the concept.

7 Some readers will perhaps note that I do not include my own name on this list and may suspect that this is because I do not want it to appear that my critique of Scanlon is in part motivated by some personal pique that he does not engage with my work on punishment. This is not my reason. I have left my name off this list because it does not belong on the list. I have often drawn on retributive ideas when I have written on punishment, and I hope that I have sometimes said some illuminating things when doing so. Unlike these four writers, however, I have never made an attempt to develop a detailed systematic explanation of and justification for a retributive theory of punishment. I have in this regard mainly pledged allegiance to the work of others.

8 Just a few weeks ago I was sent for to review an essay by a very talented young philosopher who, drawing on Scanlon's work, sometimes spoke of "pain" and other times of "suffering" in a way that seemed to recognize no possible difference in meaning between the two words.

9 Kant is quite explicit in his claim that punishment must never involve cruelty or any other kind of mistreatment that would fail to respect the dignity of the person being punished (Kant 1996: 474).

10 "Consequential" does not necessarily mean "utilitarian" since the relevant consequence might be the protection of important rights, not the maximization of general happiness. Hart's famous distinction between these two basic questions occurs in Hart (2008: Chapter 1).

11 My colleague Mary Sigler, who has provided me with many useful comments on an earlier draft of this essay, has reminded me that a similar view has been defended by Michael Moore (Moore 1997: 78–80).

12 In my summary and interpretation of Hart's views on consequential and retributive values in punishment, I am drawing on Hart (2008: Chapters 1, 2, and 3). For his views on repentance as a possible ground for sentence reduction, I draw on Hart (1963) and Murphy (2013).
13 My argument in this section has been greatly influenced by Pillsbury (1998).
14 Antony Duff and others have argued that claims for mercy based on such factors as offender remorse may sometimes be justified if grounded on values extrinsic to the retributive factors required for just punishment but that they are not intrinsic to the retributive factors and indeed must always be in tension with those retributive factors. I have argued against this view in Murphy (2012: Chapter 6). In Murphy (2012: Chapter 7) I have argued that, because of the danger of faking, claimed remorse should probably not be given much weight in sentencing but can legitimately play a role in clemency.
15 In *Farmer v. Brennan* (511 U. S. 824 (1994)) the United States Supreme Court allowed 8th Amendment appeals of possibly cruel and unusual prison conditions. The Court set a standard for successful appeals, however, that will provide very little protection to inmates. The standard requires a showing that the prison officials were themselves consciously aware of the conditions and yet took no steps to correct them (a recklessness standard). Such recklessness is very difficult to prove.
16 *Johnson v. Phelan*, 69 F.3d 144, 152 (7th Cir. 1993) (Posner, C. J. Dissenting).

Bibliography

Fingarette, H. (1977) 'Punishment and suffering', *Proceedings and Addresses of the American Philosophical Association*, 50(6): 499–525.
Hampton, J. (1991–1992) 'Correcting harms versus righting wrongs: the goal of retribution', *UCLA Law Review*, 39: 1659–1702.
Hart, H.L.A. (1963) *Law, Liberty, and Morality*, Stanford, CA: Stanford University Press.
Hart, H.L.A. (2008) *Punishment and Responsibility*, 2nd edn, Oxford: Oxford University Press.
Kant, I. (1996) *Practical Philosophy*, ed. and trans. M.J. Gregor, Cambridge: Cambridge University Press.
Moore, M. (1987) 'The moral worth of retribution', in F. Schoeman (ed.) *Responsibility, Character, and the Emotions,* Cambridge: Cambridge University Press, pp. 179–219.
Moore, M. (1997) *Placing Blame: A General Theory of the Criminal Law*, Oxford: Clarendon Press.
Morris, H. (1976) 'Persons and punishment' in his *On Guilt and Innocence*, Berkeley, CA: University of California Press, pp. 31–58.
Murphy, J.G. (1985) 'Retributivism, moral education, and the liberal state', *Criminal Justice Ethics*, 4(1) Winter/Spring: 3–11.
Murphy, J.G. (1987) 'Does Kant have a theory of punishment?', *Columbia Law Review*, 87(3) April: 509–32.
Murphy, J.G. (1995) 'Legal moralism and liberalism', *Arizona Law Review*, Spring: 73–93.
Murphy, J.G. (2012) *Punishment and the Moral Emotions–Essays in Law, Morality, and Religion*, Oxford and New York, NY: Oxford University Press.
Murphy. J.G. (2013) 'A failed refutation and an insufficiently developed insight in Hart's *Law, Liberty, and Morality', Criminal Law and Philosophy*, 7(3) October: 419–34.
Murphy, J.G. (2014) '*In the Penal Colony* and why I am now reluctant to teach Criminal Law', *Criminal Justice Ethics*, 33(2) July: 72–82.
Nino, C. (1996) *Radical Evil on Trial*, New Haven, CT: Yale University Press.
Pillsbury, S. (1998) *Judging Evil: Rethinking the Law of Murder and Manslaughter*, New York, NY: New York University Press.
Rawls, J. (1955) 'Two concepts of rules', *The Philosophical Review*, 64(1) January: 3–32.
Scanlon, T.M. (1999) 'Punishment and the rule of law', in H. Hongju and R.C. Slye (eds.) *Deliberative Democracy and Human Rights*, New Haven, CT: Yale University Press, pp. 257–71.
Scanlon, T.M. (2013) 'Giving desert its due', *Philosophical Explorations*, 16(2): 101–16.
Sophocles (1977) *The Oedipus Cycle*, trans. D. Fitts and R. Fitzgerald (Fitzgerald the sole translator of *Oedipus at Colonus*), New York, NY: Harcourt, Inc.

3

Crime, morality, and republicanism

Richard Dagger

One of the abiding concerns of the philosophy of law has been to establish the relationship between law and morality.[1] Within the criminal law, this concern often takes the form of debates over *legal moralism*—that is, "the position that immorality is sufficient for criminalization" (Alexander 2003: 131). This paper approaches these debates from the perspective of the recently revived republican tradition in politics and law. Contrary to what is usually taken to be liberalism's hostility to legal moralism, and especially to attempts to promote virtue through the criminal law, the republican approach takes the promotion of virtue to be one of the necessary aims of a polity. The virtue in question, however, is a specifically *civic* virtue, and calling for its promotion does not entail that the criminal law should be a straightforward reflection of the conventional morality of a society. What republicanism offers, instead, is a form of legal moralism resting on a distinctively *civic* morality that lays particular stress on such virtues as fair play and tolerance.

According to the republican conception of the criminal law, the questions of what should count as a crime and how a polity should respond to criminal offenses are to be answered by the members of a polity. In answering, though, they should not think themselves free to respond to these questions however they please, or however the majority at the time pleases. Moral and other practical considerations must play a part in determining what counts as a crime and how to respond to those who commit crimes. Such considerations, however, are not resolved by straightforward appeal to what is morally right and wrong, or to what criminals do and do not deserve. Some conception of the polity, and of how its members stand in relation to one another, is also necessary.

In this way the republican version of legal moralism occupies the ground between "pure" legal moralism, which holds that "acts that are immoral and degrading may be criminally punished, even if they are harmful in no other way" (Alexander 2003: 132), and the "liberal" position, according to which harmfulness rather than moral wrongness should determine whether an action or activity is criminal. To establish the soundness of this position, however, I shall need to say something about the varieties of both legal moralism and republicanism. These are the tasks I take up in the first two parts of this essay, respectively. In Part Three, I elaborate the republican conception of legal moralism—a conception resting on the civic morality of fair play—and conclude by demonstrating how it underpins the criminal law.

Part one: Legal moralism and its varieties

Legal moralism emerged in the course of two controversies over the proper extent of the criminal law. The earlier of these involved John Stuart Mill and his British compatriot, the jurist James Fitzjames Stephen. In 1873, the year of Mill's death, Stephen published a rebuttal to the "one very simple principle" that Mill had advanced 14 years earlier in *On Liberty*. According to Mill's principle, "the only purpose for which power can be rightfully exercised over any member of a civilized community, against his will, is to prevent harm to others. His own good, either physical or moral, is not a sufficient warrant" (Mill 1991: 14). In response, Stephen maintained that the criminal law quite properly affirms "a principle which is absolutely inconsistent with and contradictory to Mr. Mill's—the principle, namely, that there are acts of wickedness so gross and outrageous that, self-protection apart, they must be prevented as far as possible at any cost to the offender, and punished, if they occur, with exemplary severity. ..."[2]

Although this nineteenth-century controversy looms in the background, the term "legal moralism" itself seems to be a product of the second controversy, which has come to be known as "the Hart-Devlin debate." What sparked this debate was the official Wolfenden Committee Report of 1957, which recommended that neither homosexual activity nor prostitution should be outlawed in Britain when conducted in private between consenting adults. This report provoked a British judge, Lord Patrick Devlin, to argue that "society is justified in taking the same steps to preserve its moral code as it does to preserve its government and other essential institutions. The suppression of vice is as much the law's business as the suppression of subversive activities. ..."[3] Devlin, in turn, provoked a retort from the legal philosopher H. L. A. Hart, who defended both the committee's recommendation and Millian liberalism more generally. Indeed, Hart seems to be the one who gave legal moralism its name: "In England in the last few years the question whether the criminal law should be used to punish immorality 'as such' has acquired a new practical importance; for there has, I think, been a revival there of what might be termed *legal moralism*" (Hart 1963: 6; emphasis in original).

This revival was not only something that Hart deplored but something he did much to discourage. Among legal philosophers, at least, "legal moralism" became associated in the 1960s and '70s with a smothering imposition of social norms that would deprive individuals of the essential freedom of self-expression. More recently, however, such prominent legal theorists as Michael Moore and Antony Duff have proclaimed their adherence to legal moralism, while others have tendered it a grudging respect.[4] Two considerations seem to lie behind this shift. The first is the growing appreciation of the *expressive* or *communicative* function of criminal punishment, and the second is the recognition that morality may be entwined with the criminal law in a more complicated fashion than Devlin's arguments had suggested.

In 1965, in the midst of the Hart-Devlin debate, Joel Feinberg published an article that raised the first of these considerations. In that article Feinberg drew attention to a characteristic of punishment that distinguishes it from other penalties. That characteristic, he argued, "is a certain expressive function: punishment is a conventional device for the expression of attitudes of resentment and indignation, and of judgments of disapproval and reprobation, on the part either of the punishing authority himself or of those 'in whose name' the punishment is inflicted" (Feinberg 1970: 98). Following Feinberg's lead, other legal philosophers have taken this expressive, reprobative, or condemnatory function to be a key feature of legal punishment, including some who have argued that the function is better described as "communicative," because "communication involves, as expression need not, a *reciprocal* and *rational* engagement" on the part of those who are punished (Duff 2001: 79; see also Hampton 1992; Morris 1981: 274; and Pettit 2015: 135). Rather than simply expressing or venting society's anger, in other words, the aim of punishment is to communicate both social disapproval and the reasons for holding the wrongdoer's actions to be deserving of punishment. Moreover, this communication should proceed in ways that will help to restore him to good standing in society.

Whether we call it the expressive or the communicative function, the point is that punishment and criminalization are tied to the moral censure—to "resentment and indignation" and "judgments of disapproval and reprobation," in Feinberg's terms—that the offender's unjust actions provoke. Punishment certainly has its "conventional" aspect as a matter of "[p]ublic condemnation," according to Feinberg (98, 114), for it is an expression of a social reaction to a public offense, not a disinterested reaction to an abstract moral wrong. One cannot take this view of punishment, however, without also taking the view that the criminal law is somehow bound up with morality. To be sure, it is possible to hold that murder, robbery, rape, and other central examples of criminal wrongdoing are wrong not because they are immoral but because they are harmful, with "harm" defined in a way that excludes moral considerations.[5] But even those who are tempted by such a view must concede that the expression or communication of social resentment and indignation through punishment involves at least an implicit appeal to justice and morality. If we are to regard punishment as a form of moral censure, in other words, we must also regard the criminal law as upholding in some sense the moral standards of the polity. In that respect, the expressive or communicative aspect of punishment lends support to legal moralism.[6]

That is not to say, though, that anyone who conceives of punishment in this way must also conclude that the criminal law either is or should be a straightforward reflection of the conventional morality of a society. The relationship between law and morality—indeed, morality itself—is more complicated than that. Hart himself pointed in this direction by distinguishing "the morality actually accepted and shared by a given social group," or "positive morality," from "critical morality"—that is, "the general moral principles used in the criticism of actual social institutions, including positive morality" (Hart 1963: 20). Positive morality might well endorse, for example, "morals legislation" proscribing "vice crimes" that are not obviously harmful to anyone, including those who engage in those "vices." Devlin and the early advocates of legal moralism seemed content with this conclusion, but theirs is not the kind of legal moralism its current advocates are propounding.[7] As Moore takes pains to point out, a circumscribed conception of morality and a presumption in favor of liberty, among other considerations, has led him to a highly qualified form of legal moralism that is no less hesitant than Mill and Hart to reject much of "morals legislation." Immoral actions should indeed count as crimes, Moore insists, but his "spare view" of morality leaves no room for "duties to others with respect to many of the items about which customary morality so fusses and fumes, such as sex" (Moore 2008: 32).

Duff reaches a similar conclusion in part for similar reasons, but also by way of the traditional distinction between civil and criminal law (Duff 2014: 222–24). Both branches of law are concerned with wrongs, but one has to do with private and the other with public wrongs. Someone who breaches a contract, for example, is ordinarily guilty of wrongdoing, but the law, regarding it as a private wrong, leaves the aggrieved party to decide whether to bring suit in civil court or not. Someone arrested for burglary or some other crime, on the other hand, is liable to prosecution by the state or commonwealth regardless of whether the victim wants to press charges. In the case of a crime, in other words, the wrong is not only to the immediate victim or victims but in some sense to the public as a whole. Hence, the concern of criminal law with public rather than private wrongs.

Of course, whether a wrong is private or public is not always a clear-cut matter. Some legal systems regard defamation of character as a public wrong and thus a crime, for example, while others take it to be a private wrong (Dagger 2009: 162–65). Some might even hold that breach of contract is properly a criminal offense because, by weakening trust in the security of contracts, it constitutes a public wrong. Whatever one thinks of these particular cases, the point is that some guidance is necessary if we are to find a principled way of distinguishing private from public wrongs. Duff suggests that such guidance is to be found in political rather than moral theory and particularly in the political theory of republicanism. His remarks in this connection are brief, though, and require the kind of elaboration I try to provide in the following sections of this paper (Duff 2007: 50, 53; 2014: 222–24). For the present, the important point is that Duff takes the distinction between private and public wrongs to lead to a "modest" form of legal moralism that eschews the "kind of moral witch hunt" in which "we must collectively seek out wrongdoing (of the appropriate kind) in order to make sure that it is criminalized and punished" (Duff 2014: 222).

In this respect, as I have noted, Duff's conclusion is much the same as Moore's. There are differences between them, however, as Duff observes while developing a useful taxonomy of the varieties of legal moralism. First he distinguishes between negative and positive versions of legal moralism; and then, within the latter category, he distinguishes modest from ambitious forms. According to negative legal moralism, only immoral actions or activities should be outlawed; according to the positive version, the immorality of an action or activity is always a reason—but not always a *conclusive* reason—to outlaw it (Duff 2014: 218; also Duff 2012: 179–204, esp. 186). The distinction, however, is not a dichotomy, for one may accept both negative and positive legal moralism, as Duff says both he and Moore do. The difference between them is that Moore takes the *ambitious* view that "criminal law must punish all and only those who are morally culpable in the doing of some morally wrongful action" (1997: 35), while Duff holds the *modest* view that "only certain kinds of moral wrongdoing are even in principle worthy of criminalization …" (2014: 222).[8] In particular, as we have seen, he argues that the proper concern of the criminal law is with public wrongs, for "the criminal law is not simply the moral law given institutional form," as it would have to be were it to reflect the ambitious version of positive legal moralism (Duff 2014: 223).

Duff's case for a modest version of positive legal moralism is both powerful and persuasive. Nevertheless, three difficult questions remain to be answered: (1) How firm is the distinction between public and private wrongs? (2) Are such paradigmatic crimes as murder, rape, and robbery really *public* wrongs? And (3) are *mala prohibita* offenses, such as speeding or driving without a license, really *moral* wrongs? Duff and his sometime co-author, Sandra Marshall, have provided answers to these questions, but fully adequate answers are only available through a full-fledged embrace of the civic morality of republicanism. To appreciate why that is so requires a brief consideration of the answers they have ventured.

The first question is important because failure to establish a firm distinction between private and public wrongs could lead to the kind of ambitious legal moralism that Moore embraces but Duff eschews; it could even lead, in the absence of Moore's circumscribed conception of morality, to a pure and decidedly immodest form of legal moralism.[9] Marshall and Duff open themselves to the latter possibility by resting their argument on the idea of *shared* wrongs, with crime taken to be "socially proscribed wrongdoing" (Marshall and Duff 1998:13). This understanding leads to a position uncomfortably close to Devlin's claim that society has as much reason to defend itself against immorality as against treason: "We must ask [write Marshall and Duff] … what kinds of wrong should be seen as wrongs against 'us'; and this is to ask which values are (which should be) so central to a community's identity and self-understanding … that actions which attack or flout those values are not merely individual matters which the individual victim should pursue for herself, but attacks on the community" (Marshall and Duff 1998: 21–22). So stated, one could conclude that acts that apparently "attack or flout" a community's dominant values concerning sex, religion, or ethnic homogeneity are "attacks on the community" to be counted as "socially proscribed wrongdoing." If the aim is to advance a modestly positive form of legal moralism, then Duff (and Marshall) will need to find some less communitarian way to distinguish public from private wrongs. The civic morality of republicanism, as I shall argue below, is both available and appropriate.

The second and third questions both trade on the familiar distinction between actions wrong in themselves (*mala in se*) and those that are wrong only because they are prohibited (*mala prohibita*). In the case of paradigmatic crimes such as rape, robbery, and murder, it is easy to see how, as *mala in* se, they are morally wrong. The problem is to show how they constitute *public* wrongs. In contrast to perjury, tax evasion, and treason, which are by definition wrongs to the public, the paradigmatic crimes are wrongs to individuals. Again, Marshall and Duff have a response, which is to argue that such crimes are *not only* wrongs done to their individual victims: "an attack on a member of the group is thus an attack on the group—on their shared values and their common good. … '[H]er' wrong is also 'our' wrong insofar as we identify ourselves with her" (Marshall and Duff 1998: 20). But this prompts the further question of *how* the wrongs are shared or common. Is it a matter of choice or identification—of what "we" choose as our values and mutual concerns, or of how "we" define our values and ourselves as a group? Here again, I shall argue, republican theory provides the adequate answer.

The third question—how to account for *mala prohibita* as moral wrongs—arises because the proscribed acts or activities may be obviously public but not obviously immoral. Speeding, driving without a license, and drinking alcohol in a city park provide clear examples. If relevant statutes or ordinances proscribe them, all three are *legally* wrong even though none of them seems to be intrinsically immoral. But if *mala prohibita* need not be moral wrongs, then immorality cannot be the necessary condition of criminality that negative legal moralists—and negative *plus* positive legal moralists, such as Duff and Moore—take it to be. In response to this challenge to legal moralism, Duff has drawn a distinction between *pre-criminal* and *pre-legal* wrong. To use his example, failure to comply with tax laws can only be morally wrong if there are such things as tax laws; there is thus no pre-legal wrong of failing to pay taxes. Once tax laws do exist, however, failure to comply with them, *ceteris paribus*, counts as a morally wrongful failure to do one's civic duty. When other laws make a crime of failing to pay one's taxes, they make a crime of an action that was pre-criminally, but not pre-legally, a moral wrong (Duff 2014: 219; see also Duff 2012: 198–204, and Duff 2007: 91–2). The idea, then, is that actions that do not seem to be morally wrong in themselves, such as speeding or driving on the left-hand side of the street, can become wrongful when relevant laws are promulgated, such as traffic laws. Something that was not wrong pre-legally thus becomes a wrong pre-criminally—that is, even before it is designated as a crime or infraction—which is consistent with the legal moralist's claim that only immoral actions should be made crimes.

This distinction between pre-legal and pre-criminal is, I believe, both sound and to the point. It fails, however, to account for the *moral* element of the pre-legal wrongfulness that Duff has identified. Paying taxes may be a legal duty, and failure to pay them a legal (but pre-criminal) wrong, but what makes it a *moral* duty, the violation of which counts as a moral wrong? Duff appeals in passing to republicanism to forge the link between legal and moral wrongfulness, referring to civic duties and using the language of fair shares (Duff 2014: 219, 222, 227; also Duff 2012: 203), but these are references and appeals that must be supported by an account of republicanism as a matter of fair play. That account I shall now try to provide, beginning with a brief synopsis of republican political and legal theory.

Part two: Republicanism as fair play

Perhaps the simplest way to distill the leading themes of its long and complicated history is to say that republicanism is largely a matter of *publicity* and *self-government*. That republicanism involves publicity is evident from the term's derivation from the Latin *res publica*, the business of the public. To the republican, government and law are not the purview of a single ruler or a small set of rulers, who may dispose of people and territory as if they were the ruler's personal property. On the republican view, government and law are the people's business, to be conducted on the people's terms (Pettit 2012). For that reason, republicanism also involves publicity in the sense of openness. That is, the public's business is to be conducted *in public*, open to the scrutiny and criticism of members of the public.

Quentin Skinner's and Philip Pettit's influential writings have brought the second feature of republicanism, self-government, to the center of attention in recent years (esp. Skinner 1998 and Pettit 1997). Pettit's contributions are especially important here, for he has explicitly connected republican freedom to the concerns of criminal law (esp. Braithwaite and Pettit 1990 and Pettit 2015). His conception of freedom as non-domination stops short of where I think republican freedom takes us, which is to freedom understood as autonomy (Dagger 2005), but the essential point is that republicans believe freedom is more than a matter of being left alone. Whether regarded as freedom from domination or as autonomy, republican freedom requires self-government under, by, and through the law. Hence the proclamation, from Roman antiquity to modern times, that a republic is an empire of laws, not of men. That is, the republic is the rule of free citizens who govern themselves through laws that they enact or ratify, if not directly, then through their elected representatives.

How, though, do these republican concerns, publicity and self-government, bear on criminal law or legal moralism? Part of the answer is that together they underpin the republican commitment to the rule of law; another is that they represent a civic morality grounded in the principle of fair play.

With regard to the rule of law, the republican element is evident in all three themes that Brian Tamanaha has discerned in the rule of law (2004: ch. 9). First, the rule of law entails a commitment to limited government. No one is to hold absolute or unchecked power, and the aims of those in positions of authority must be limited to the service of the public good. Second, the rule of law is, in the old republican formula, the rule of *law*, not of men—not, that is, rule by the arbitrary will or whims of those in power. Finally, in order to satisfy the two previous conditions, the rule of law also requires *legality*. For a rule or ordinance to be a law, in other words, it must meet certain formal requirements regardless of what its substance is. Thus, among other things, a law must be general in its application, must be made known to the public, and must not contradict itself or other laws.[10] All of these themes, in short, bear traces of the republican concern for publicity and self-government. In the case of legality, moreover, there is a clear connection to the idea of fair play. For it is simply not fair to hold people accountable to "laws," or expect them to "play by the rules," when these people have no way of knowing what the rules are; nor is it fair to subject them to "laws" that apply to some but not to others, or that simultaneously require and prohibit an action.

The rule of law, then, is linked not only to republicanism but also to the sense of fair play. Nor is this simply a coincidence. Implicitly if not explicitly, republicans are committed to the moral principle of fair play, which forms the basis of republicanism's civic morality. This connection to fair play admittedly is not a feature of standard accounts of republicanism, but I shall try to demonstrate why it should be in three steps. The first is to define the principle of fair play and to identify its key features; the second is to show how this principle connects to the main concerns of republicanism; and the third is to explain how following the principle of fair play leads to a civic morality that underpins a modest form of positive legal moralism.

Step one: The principle of fair play

Fairness and fair play are ancient concepts, grounded in widely and firmly held intuitions about right and wrong conduct. Straightforward formulations of the principle of fair play, however, are little more than half a century old. The first appeared in 1955, before the Hart-Devlin debate, in H. L. A. Hart's "*Are There Any Natural Rights*?" As Hart there wrote, "when a number of persons conduct any joint enterprise according to rules and thus restrict their liberty, those who have submitted to these restrictions when required have a right to a similar submission from those who have benefited by their submission" (Hart 1970 [1955]: 70). Hart did not refer explicitly to "fairness" or "fair play" in this passage, but John Rawls did in his 1964 essay, "*Legal Obligations and the Duty of Fair Play*." There Rawls explained "the principle of fair play" in this way.

> Suppose there is a mutually beneficial and just scheme of social cooperation, and that the advantages it yields can only be obtained if everyone, or nearly everyone, cooperates. Suppose further that cooperation requires a certain sacrifice from each person, or at least involves a certain restriction of his liberty. Suppose finally that the benefits produced by cooperation are, up to a certain point, free: that is, the scheme of cooperation is unstable in the sense that if any one person knows that all (or nearly all) of the others will continue to do their part, he will still be able to share a gain from the scheme even if he does not do his part. Under these conditions a person who has accepted the benefits of the scheme is bound by a duty of fair play to do his part and not to take advantage of the free benefit by not cooperating.
>
> (Rawls 1964: 9–10; see also Rawls 1999: 96)

Taking Hart's and Rawls's formulations together, we can identify four key elements in the principle of fair play. First, the principle applies to *cooperative practices*; second, these practices are governed by *rules* or *laws*; third, these rule-governed practices are subject to *collective-action problems*; and fourth, coercion is necessary to *assure* the people engaged in such a practice that their compliance will not be exploited or wasted. None of these points is novel, but they do require brief explanation.

Regarding the first point, the principle of fair play applies only to those activities involving a *cooperative practice*. Those who find themselves in a street fight or anything that counts as a "free for all," such as a Hobbesian state of nature, are not engaged in a cooperative practice in which the participants have a duty of fair play to one another. Cooperative practices must be mutually beneficial, as Rawls said, for otherwise there would be no point to the cooperation. But they also must be in some way burdensome. A group of musicians must cooperate if they are to play together, but their playing will not constitute a cooperative enterprise if it is all benefit to them and no burden. There must be some hardship—at least some restriction of their liberty, in Hart's terms—that is necessary to the achievement of the good or benefit the participants aim to achieve. In the case of the musicians, there must be occasions on which one or more of them would rather not play a certain piece or would prefer not to rehearse so often or so long. Something similar is true of all cooperative practices.

Cooperative practices are also ongoing. They may begin with spontaneous, unrehearsed activity, but they will need *rules* or *laws* to continue. That is the second key element of cooperative practices that raise considerations of fair play. In some cases these rules are nothing more than informal and perhaps unspoken norms. In a small group, when the point of the activity and the need for cooperation are obvious, the rule may be nothing more than "You do your part, I'll do mine, and no shirking." In larger groups, and especially in those in which the cooperation is supposed to extend well into the future, formal rules that specify the nature of the required cooperation will be necessary.

The third feature of a cooperative practice is that it is susceptible to *collective-action* problems. As Hart's and Rawls's formulations indicate, the principle of fair play applies to cooperative enterprises that produce *public* or *collective goods*—that is, goods that are indivisible, non-excludable, and non-rival, so that one person's enjoyment of a good does not deprive another of an equal opportunity to enjoy it. Such goods, of course, are not likely to require universal cooperation to produce, as the standard examples of national defense and clean air attest. They are, instead, goods that non-cooperators may enjoy as fully as those whose cooperative efforts produce the goods in question. Cooperative practices are thus open to free riders who hope to benefit from others' cooperative labors and sacrifices without themselves bearing those burdens. Cooperative practices typically can tolerate some free riders, but at some point free riding will lead to the collapse of the enterprise. That is why coercive measures are usually necessary if the practice is to survive.

Coercion or some other means of preventing or punishing free riders thus speaks to the fourth fair-play element of cooperative practices, the need for *assurance*. Even people who are willing to make cooperative sacrifices will be unwise to do so when their sacrifices will be in vain. It makes no sense, for example, to pay membership dues to a club or organization when few of the other supposed members are doing so. Cooperative practices must find some way to assure those who would willingly cooperate that their cooperation will not be wasted. Such people will quite happily acknowledge that they have a duty of fairness to contribute to the support and maintenance of the cooperative practice, but they must be given security against those who would take unfair advantage of their cooperative good nature and endanger the practice with their attempts at free riding.

This analysis of fair play and cooperative practices bears on political and legal philosophy because Hart and Rawls, among others, believe that we should regard political societies and legal systems as cooperative enterprises. For Rawls, in fact, the idea "of society as a fair system of cooperation over time, from one generation to the next," is "the fundamental organizing idea" of his theory of justice as fairness (Rawls 2005: 15). To be sure, some political regimes have been so despotic, tyrannical, oppressive, and exploitative that they could not be properly described as cooperative enterprises. All political regimes rely on some degree of cooperation, however, and many of them have been cooperative enough to qualify as the mutually beneficial and reasonably just schemes of social cooperation that Rawls took to warrant duties of fair play. That is why the principle of fair play has found its chief employment in discussions of political obligation and the justification of punishment. In both cases the arguments are controversial, but the underlying idea is that the citizens of a polity that may be reasonably regarded as a cooperative venture have a general duty to obey its laws. Those who do not comply with this duty make themselves liable to punishment by the legal authorities. Other things being equal, in short, fair play requires obedience to the law and justifies punishing those whose disobedience violates the duty of fair play.[11]

Two further points remain before turning to the connection of fair play to republicanism. The first is that the duty of fair play is something that every member of a cooperative practice owes to the other members, or at least to those whose cooperative efforts help to support and sustain the practice. We often speak of duties or obligations that are owed to "the state" or "the law," but that is simply a short-hand way, according to the fair-play view, to refer to obligations owed to one another as cooperating members of the practice—to the law-abiding members of the polity, for instance. The second is that the principle of fair play has a critical and aspirational aspect. Because the principle applies only to cooperative practices, it requires us to subject political regimes to scrutiny in order to determine whether they truly qualify. If they fall well short of the ideal of a cooperative practice—if they are thoroughly oppressive and exploitative—then there will be no duty of fair play to comply in general with their ordinances. In other cases the question will be whether a regime is cooperative *enough* to qualify as a cooperative practice. For that matter, even the best regimes will not completely realize the ideal of a fully cooperative practice. There will always be something further to aspire to if a body politic is to be a mutually beneficial and just scheme of social cooperation. And that is why the principle of fair play has a critical and aspirational aspect.

Step two: Fair play and the republic

The most direct way to mark the connection between fair play and republicanism is to attend to a word often used to render *res publica* into English. That word is *commonwealth*. The republic is the public's business, as we have seen, and the *weal*, *wealth*, or *well-being* of the public is a matter of common concern. It is not the business of one or a few, nor of a faction or sect, but of the people in their common capacity as citizens. If the republic truly is to succeed, the people must cooperate, as citizens, to ensure that it provides the public goods of order and security under law. They must bear the burdens involved in establishing and maintaining the rule of law, in other words, in order to enjoy its benefits.

Like other cooperative practices, then, the republic is a rule-governed enterprise. Cicero made that point two millennia ago when he defined the republic as "an assemblage of some size associated with one another through agreement on law and community of interest" (1999: 18). In order to provide the rule of law, however, the citizens of the republic must cooperate by paying taxes and bearing other burdens; but because the rule of law is a public good, some citizens will be tempted to become free riders. In the face of this temptation, the republic must find ways to assure those who are willing to bear their shares of the cooperative enterprise that their efforts will not be futile.

This is to say that republics rely on the spirit of fair play. Of course, they must employ coercion against those who would take unfair advantage of other citizens; but coercion cannot by itself generate the *spirit* of fair play. The threat of coercion may lead to a grudging acceptance of the need to do one's fair share by paying taxes and obeying other laws that one would rather disobey. But republics need more than grudging acceptance. They need citizens who are willing to put the public good ahead of their personal desires not because they fear coercion but because they want to do their duty. To put the point in time-honored republican terms, republics need to foster *civic virtue*. And civic virtue, I am suggesting, is largely a matter of fair play.

To reinforce this point, we should consider what the classical republicans took to be the antithesis and enemy of civic virtue—namely, *corruption*. Corruption takes various forms, but at bottom it is a matter of acting selfishly rather than civically—of putting one's interests and desires ahead of the public good that one shares with one's fellow citizens. If civic virtue is largely a matter of fair play, then corruption, or civic vice, is largely a matter of refusing to play fair. Two terms frequently linked in republican discourse, *ambition* and *avarice*, are instructive in this regard. Ambition, to republicans, is the overweening desire for personal power that threatens the stability of the republic and the freedom of its citizens. Avarice is the desire for personal wealth that blinds some people to the duty to contribute to the public enterprise and may even lead them to steal from it. Both are failures to act with proper regard to the rights and interests of one's fellow citizens and therefore violations of the duty of fair play.[12]

By saying this, I do not mean to suggest that public corruption is no worse than the failure to play fair in a game. The ambitious man who tries to seize power by overthrowing a republic is far worse than someone who cheats while playing tennis, as is the avaricious woman who betrays the public trust by embezzling public funds. But that simply means that some violations of fair play are worse than others, just as some corrupt actions are worse than others. The point here is that surrendering to avarice or ambition counts as corruption because it is a failure of fair play. It is also a violation of the republican commitment to publicity.

The same point holds with regard to republicanism's second leading feature, self-government. For republicans, I have noted, to be free is to be self-governing under, by, and through the law. To be free in this way, however, requires more than forbearance or lack of coercion or interference from others. It requires others to do their part in maintaining the rule of law that makes self-government possible; and this is a matter of fair play.[13] Freedom under law thus requires the citizens to bear the burdens of legal cooperation so that all of them may enjoy the benefits of self-government. This is in large part a matter of obeying the law. Laws do not write themselves, though, and republican citizens bear some responsibility for determining what the laws are to be. They may also have some duty to enforce the law, as they do in countries that require citizens to serve on juries. If citizens are to be self-governing, in short, they owe it to one another to pay some attention to public affairs and cast at least an occasional vote for a representative. This is a matter of civic virtue, but it is also a matter of freedom as self-government. With regard to both elements of republicanism, in sum, self-government as well as publicity, fair play is a crucial ingredient.

To clarify this point, it may be helpful to draw a contrast with another conception of self-government. According to this other conception, freedom or self-government is mainly a matter of being left alone to do as one wants without restraint. With regard to law, this means that self-government amounts to *freedom from* law or, as Hobbes put the point, the liberties of subjects depend largely on "the silence of the Law" (1985 [1651]: 271). The republican view of self-government stands in contrast to this conception because, as I have said, it takes freedom to be something achieved under, or through, or by the law. In terms that Pettit frequently invokes, the difference is between "the freedom of the heath"—that is, the liberty of life in a lawless wilderness—and "the freedom of the city"—that is, the liberty of life in a civilized society under the rule of law (e.g., Pettit 1989). Self-government in the latter, republican sense is to be understood not as freedom from restraint, but as the liberty possible under *shared* government; for the freedom one can enjoy as a member of a republic is as much a matter of *interdependence* as it is of *independence*. Self-government under and through the rule law, or of restraints that people impose upon themselves, is in this way intimately connected with cooperative fair play.

Step three: Implications of fair play for republicanism

What follows for criminal law theory from this fair-play conception of republicanism? The answer is a modest form of legal moralism, as I shall explain in Part Three. It is necessary to begin, though, by considering briefly two broad implications of the fair-play conception of republicanism. The first is that republics must cultivate the spirit of fair play among their citizens; the second is that republics must play fair with their members.

Implications of the first kind begin with the reminder that we cannot simply assume that citizens will be imbued with the spirit of cooperative fair play. That assumption might be warranted in a small, tightly knit community, but not in anything as large as a republican polity. Indeed, one of the principal challenges for modern republics is to help their members to appreciate the cooperative foundations of their political and legal systems. That is a difficult task when political and legal authority are likely to seem remote from people's lives and more coercive than cooperative in their bearing. There are ways to meet this challenge, however, with civic education probably the most widely accepted among republicans. Especially important in this regard is education in the rights and responsibilities of citizens under the rule of law.

The second broad implication of conceiving of republicanism as fair play is that the republic itself must be worthy of cooperative, fair-playing citizens. If people are to think of themselves as participants in a cooperative venture, and therefore subject to a duty of fair play, then the practice must treat its members fairly. Taxation again provides an example. Government and the rule of law are public goods, and taxes are part of the burden we bear to provide them. But what if the tax collectors are filling their pockets with our tax payments? Or what if relatively few people are paying their full and fair shares of the tax burden? In these circumstances, there seems to be no duty—and certainly none based on fair play—to pay one's taxes. For that duty to be in force, the tax system itself must operate fairly. The same point holds for other legal institutions. We simply cannot expect people to play fair when they are not themselves treated fairly.

Pressing this point farther, republics must see to it that their members have good reason to think of themselves as parts of a *common*wealth. Among other things, that means that economic inequality will be a subject of concern. There is no single republican formula that determines how much inequality of wealth and property is tolerable, but Rousseau grasped the essential point when he declared, in the footnote that ends Book I of his *Social Contract*, that everyone must have something and no one too much. Everyone must have enough, that is, to live as a self-governing citizen free from dependence upon those whose superabundant resources put them in position to dominate others.[14]

Beyond economic considerations, treating people fairly within a republic involves treating them as *citizens*. Their individual characteristics—sex, religion, ethnicity, sexual orientation, and so on—are irrelevant. The important consideration is whether a person is subject to, and will contribute to, the republic understood as a cooperative practice. If so, then that person deserves the same concern and respect under law as every other citizen; but she owes that same concern and respect, as a matter of fair play, to her fellow citizens. This is in some respects a social matter, for it relates to the attitudes of citizens and their spirit of cooperation. But it is also a legal issue insofar as the law must be concerned with fostering the spirit of fair play if the rule of law is to survive.

Part three: Republican legal moralism

Criminals, though, do not play fair. Thieves, for example, want others to respect their property, but they do not respect the property of their victims. To be sure, we must make allowances for situations in which the criminal law itself is unjust, either in what it proscribes or in how it is enforced. The burdens of fair play fall upon polities and legal systems too; that is part of republicanism's critical and aspirational aspect. When a polity is reasonably regarded as a cooperative enterprise, however, we can say that criminals violate the civic morality of republicanism by taking unfair advantage of their fellow citizens, whose cooperation makes the rule of law possible. In that sense, all crimes are crimes of unfairness. This claim strikes some not only as counterintuitive but false, despite the defenses of it I have offered elsewhere (1993 and 2008; but cf. Duff 2008). Here I shall try to extend and strengthen that defense by way of legal moralism.

From the standpoint of legal moralism, the question of whether to declare an act or activity to be criminal means that we must begin, at least conceptually, with the suspicion that the act or activity is likely to be immoral. From the standpoint of republican and modest legal moralism, we must also have reason to believe that the act or activity constitutes not only a moral but a public wrong. To make the case for criminalization, we must therefore be able to provide satisfactory responses to the three questions raised earlier concerning Duff's (and Marshall's) modest legal moralism.

The first question—how firm is the distinction between private and public wrongs?—poses a difficulty for Duff (and Marshall), I have argued, because the attempt to draw the distinction by defining public wrongs as *shared* wrongs implies a communitarian position that seems uncomfortably close to Devlin's version of legal moralism. For an answer more congenial to modest legal moralism, we should ask instead whether the putative wrong inhibits or endangers the rule of law as a cooperative practice. Lying and promise breaking, for example, will not in general have this effect. Indeed, were we to try to bring the law to bear on every lie or broken promise, we would almost surely bring about the collapse of the rule of law. Some lies, though, such as perjury and false accusations, are clearly threats to the rule of law. The same holds for some kinds of promise breaking, such as breach of contract, that are typically counted as civil rather than criminal wrongs. Whether such forms of lying and promise breaking should be subject to the criminal law will then depend largely on the question of whether civil law provides suitable remedies. If it seems to, as in the case of breach of contract, then the wrong should be regarded as a private matter to be left to individuals to pursue through the civil law. If the offense is on the order of fraud, though, then the offender is guilty of an intentional violation of fair play and thus guilty of a public wrong deserving of the communicative or condemnatory force of the criminal law.

The second question—are such paradigmatic crimes as murder, rape, and robbery really *public* wrongs?—poses another difficulty for the conception of crimes as shared wrongs. In this case, the problem is to explain how the wrong is *shared*. How is it, that is, that the murder of Jones or the robbery of Smith constitutes a wrong the rest of us share? To say, as Marshall and Duff do, that the sharing is the result of our identification with the victims—of seeing the attacks on them as somehow attacks on us—is to invoke notions of sympathy and community that may prove embarrassing. For suppose that Jones and Smith are not—for reasons of race, religion, language, or numerous other factors—persons with whom "we" fully identify as members of "our" community. In that case, is the murder of Jones or the robbery of Smith really a shared wrong? If it *ought to be* so regarded, as Marshall and Duff no doubt believe, then we will have to have some reason other than identification or fellow-feeling to account for these offenses as public wrongs.

In these cases, again, the civic morality of fair play provides the reason. Anything that makes it difficult or impossible to play one's part as a self-governing participant in the cooperative practice of the polity counts as a public wrong—and hence is a candidate for criminalization. Murder, rape, robbery, arson, and the other paradigmatic crimes fall into this category. When the victims of such crimes survive, they are often crippled, physically or otherwise, in ways that inhibit their participation in the polity. Nor are the immediate or direct victims the only ones who suffer from these crimes, which bring in their wake not only the attitudinal costs associated with fear and the sense of injustice but also insurance and avoidance costs for the secondary or indirect victims of crime. These are the reasons even the paradigmatic crimes are as much public as private wrongs.

Finally, the third question—how to account for *mala prohibita* as *moral* wrongs—is important because any theory of criminalization that claims to be grounded in legal *moralism* must be able to show that *mala prohibita* are not merely *legal* offenses. Duff's distinction between pre-legal and pre-criminal wrongs goes some way toward meeting this challenge, as we have seen, but it does not itself account for the *moral* wrongfulness of *mala prohibita*. To do this, as his gestures toward republicanism indicate, the distinction must be grounded in a political theory that provides a credible basis for invoking civic *qua* moral duty. What Duff misses, though, is the critical importance of the principle of fair play to republicanism.

That this principle is linked to the justification of *mala prohibita* is not surprising. Indeed, it is difficult to see what is wrong with many of the prohibited activities other than the unfairness of those who engage in them. To return to the example of tax evasion, it is hardly obvious that any *harm* will result from the average citizen's failure to pay his taxes. Other things being equal, though, his failure to pay is morally wrong because he is taking unfair advantage of those whose cooperation enables him to enjoy, as a free rider, the rule of law and other public goods. That is why even those who doubt the validity of the fair-play account of *mala in se* offenses, including Duff, often acknowledge the account's plausibility when applied to *mala prohibita* (Duff 1986: 211).[15] What must be recognized, however, is the vital role that this principle plays in republican legal and political theory.

Conclusion: Legal moralism and republican virtue

Recognizing this role, and elaborating it, will further advance two aims of fundamental importance to criminal law and justice. One of these is to strengthen the case for legal moralism. As I have argued above, republican civic morality provides the underpinning for a version of legal moralism that is both modest and attractive—and attractive largely because of its modesty. Legal moralism of this kind allows us to capture the intuition that criminal acts are morally wrong without turning criminal law into the legal instrument of a polity's conventional morality or licensing "the kind of moral witch hunt" that Duff and others have rightly deplored (Duff 2014: 222). According to a modest and republican form of legal moralism, criminal acts are *public* wrongs, deserving of public condemnation, because they are immoral *at least* in the sense of violating the spirit of fair play and endangering the cooperative practice of the polity, including the rule of law.

Recognizing and elaborating the role of fair play within republicanism should also advance republican legal moralism, and republican theory more broadly, by deflecting concerns about the republican emphasis on virtue. Because of its association with civic virtue, republicanism is sometimes taken to be a threat to individual rights and liberties—and especially to rights and liberties that protect activities at odds with conventional conceptions of virtuous conduct (Gey 1993; Goodin 2003). Adding republicanism to legal moralism, according to this view, is simply to encourage moral witch hunts and other attempts to stamp out vice. When republican virtue is understood in terms of the civic morality of fair play, however, these worries should disappear. So understood, republican virtue is fundamentally a matter of playing one's part as a citizen engaged in the cooperative practice of the polity, and playing this part includes respecting the rights and liberties and tolerating the personal preferences, orientations, and activities of everyone who is also doing her civic duty. Republican legal moralism will indeed endorse attempts to suppress vice by means of criminal law, but those attempts will aim at violations of *civic* morality rather than the standard "vice crimes."

This is not to say that republican legal moralism will neatly or swiftly dispose of every controversy concerning what should or should not be deemed a crime. It does, however, provide essential guidance. If an activity or action poses no threat to the republic as a cooperative practice, then it cannot be considered civically vicious, and it should not be proscribed. Those who would make a crime of some form of sexual activity between consenting adults would thus have to show that the activity in question poses a serious threat to the polity as a cooperative practice. That case, I take it, would be difficult to make. In other cases, though, the judgment will not be as easy to reach. One could argue, for instance, that the production and/or consumption of any drug that renders people incapable of fair play or of carrying out their duties of civility should be a crime. Couched in those terms, the proposal is perfectly acceptable under the republican version of legal moralism.

But those who are charged with determining what is to count as a crime would then have to make an informed judgment as to which drugs, if any, do in fact have these propensities. Once they have identified such drugs, if any, they would then have to make the further determination of whether the criminal sanction is the appropriate way to deal with the problem and, if it is, whether a blanket prohibition or a more limited response is better. In the case of alcohol, there is little doubt that its consumption at some point inhibits civility and the spirit of fair play. Laws against public drunkenness and enhanced punishment for those who harm or endanger others while drunk, though, seem likely to address the problem more effectively than outright prohibition of the production, sale, and/or consumption of alcohol. Nor would such criminal laws place an unfair burden on anyone, neither those who fail to play fair because of their drunkenness nor those who consume alcohol without endangering others or otherwise threatening fair play within the polity. Extending this republican reasoning to drugs that are widely proscribed at present would almost certainly result in a dramatic reduction in drug laws, with corresponding reductions in drug crimes and in prison populations, especially in the United States.

The point, again, is not that republican legal moralism offers straightforward resolutions to controversial aspects of the criminal law. But it does offer essential guidance, as the examples above should show, and it does so while preserving the connection between criminal law and morality. This modest form of legal moralism, however, connects the criminal law not with the positive or conventional morality of any society, but with the civic morality of fair play within a republican polity. If it happens that the conventional morality of a society is in large part consistent with the civic morality of republicanism, then it will be a fortunate society indeed.

Notes

1 I am grateful to Antony Duff and Jonathan Jacobs for valuable comments on an earlier draft of this essay, including comments I have not been able to address here.

2 Stephen, *Liberty, Equality, Fraternity*, quoting from the selection reprinted in Stephen 1994: 35.

3 From Devlin's 1959 lecture, 'The enforcement of morality', reprinted as 'Morals and the criminal law' in Devlin 1971: 36–37.

4 For Moore's legal moralism, see Moore 1997: chs. 1, 16, and 18; and 2008. For Duff's views, see Duff 2007, esp. ch. 4, and 2014: 217–35. For the grudging respect legal moralism now elicits, see Husak 2008: 196–206; and Murphy 2012: 69–76.

5 Indeed, one familiar response to earlier arguments for legal moralism has been to draw a distinction between actions that are harmful and those that are immoral, with only actions in the first category to be deemed criminal. Such a view is often attributed to Mill in *On Liberty*. I think it more plausible to read Mill as holding that the law ought to concentrate on proscribing actions that are harmful to others who have not consented to take part in them, because those actions—and not those "vices" that are merely contrary to conventional morality—are the truly immoral actions. In this respect I follow Louch (1968), both in his reading of Mill and in his general position with regard to the "libertarian" opponents of Devlin's legal moralism.

6 Note, e.g., Duff's claim (2014: 219) that "Negative Legal Moralism … seems plausible" because criminal law "inflicts not just penalties, but punishments—impositions that convey a message of censure or condemnation; the convictions that precede punishment are not mere neutral findings of fact, that this defendant breached this legal rule, but normative judgments that this defendant committed a culpable wrong."

7 One of the current advocates, Antony Duff, has suggested in personal correspondence that Devlin was not a legal moralist, properly speaking, but "a proponent of the harm principle, with some curious views about how various kinds of conduct could cause social harm." Thus Devlin believed that failure to uphold and enforce the conventional morality of a society—including proscriptions of homosexuality, prostitution, and other sexual practices—could lead to the harmful outcome of social dissolution.

8 Moore does constrain his ambitious legal moralism, however, by allowing that some immoral activities and actions should not be deemed criminal because treating them as crimes would prove too limiting or inhibiting of autonomy (e.g., Moore 1997: 75–80). The difference between Moore's ambitious

and Duff's modest versions of legal moralism thus proves to be a difference in principle rather than a substantial one in what each would count as criminal.

9 Failure to establish a firm distinction between private and public wrongs also raises the possibility that so-called crimes are really private wrongs, and thus to the absorption of criminal into tort law. See, e.g., Barnett 1977.

10 The *locus classicus* of discussions of legality is Fuller 1969: ch. 2.

11 I defend these contentions at length in a forthcoming book, *Playing Fair: Political Obligation and the Problems of Punishment.*

12 For apposite remarks about Aristotle's criticism of "grasping" persons who want "more than their fair share of benefits and less than their fair share of burdens," see Yankah 2013: 72. Here and elsewhere in his essay Yankah uses the language of fair-play theory without explicitly connecting it to republicanism.

13 Note in this regard John Finnis's statement about the "desiderata" of the rule of law: "The fundamental point of the desiderata is to secure to the subjects of authority the dignity of self-direction and freedom from certain forms of manipulation. The Rule of Law is thus among the requirements of justice or fairness" (Finnis 1980: 273).

14 Indeed, in Pettit's view, "the most crucial idea for a theory of criminalization is that of equal freedom as non-domination" (2015: 136).

15 But cf. Morison 2005, n. 160, which holds that fair play can account for both *mala prohibita* and *mala in se*; and Husak 2008: 118–19, for the argument that fair play is limited even as an account of *mala prohibita*.

Bibliography

Alexander, L. (2003) 'The legal enforcement of morality', in R.G. Frey and C.H. Wellman (eds.) *A Companion to Applied Ethics*, Oxford: Blackwell.

Barnett, R. (1977) 'Restitution: a new paradigm of criminal justice', *Ethics*, 87: 279–301.

Braithwaite, J. and Pettit, P. (1990) *Not Just Deserts: A Republican Theory of Criminal Justice*, Oxford: Oxford University Press.

Cicero. (1999) *On the Commonwealth and On the Laws*, ed. and trans. J.E.G. Zetzel, Cambridge: Cambridge University Press.

Dagger, R. (1993) 'Playing fair with punishment', *Ethics*, 103: 473–88.

Dagger, R. (2005) 'Autonomy, domination, and the republican challenge to liberalism', in J. Christman and J. Anderson (eds.) *Autonomy and the Challenges to Liberalism*, Cambridge: Cambridge University Press.

Dagger, R. (2008) 'Punishment as fair play', *Res Publica*, 14: 259–75.

Dagger, R. (2009) 'Republicanism and crime', in S. Besson and J.-L. Martì (eds.) *Legal Republicanism: National and International Perspectives*, Oxford: Oxford University Press.

Dagger, R. (forthcoming) *Playing Fair: Political Obligation and the Problems of Punishment.*

Devlin, P. (1971) 'Morals and the criminal law', in R.A. Wasserstrom (ed.) *Morality and the Law*, Belmont, CA: Wadsworth.

Duff, R.A. (1986) *Trials and Punishment*, Cambridge: Cambridge University Press.

Duff, R.A. (2001) *Punishment, Communication, and Community*, Oxford: Oxford University Press.

Duff, R.A. (2007) *Answering for Crime: Responsibility and Liability in the Criminal Law*, Oxford: Hart.

Duff, R.A. (2008) 'The incompleteness of "punishment as fair play": a response to Dagger', *Res Publica*, 14: 277–81.

Duff, R.A. (2012) 'Political retributivism and legal moralism', *Virginia Journal of Criminal Law*, 1: 179–204.

Duff, R.A. (2014) 'Towards a modest legal moralism', *Criminal Law and Philosophy*, 8: 217–35.

Feinberg, J. (1970) 'The expressive function of punishment', in J. Feinberg, *Doing and Deserving: Essays in the Theory of Responsibility*, Princeton, NJ: Princeton University Press.

Finnis, J. (1980) *Natural Law and Natural Rights*, Oxford: Oxford University Press.

Fuller, L. (1969) *The Morality of Law*, rev. edn, New Haven, CT: Yale University Press.

Gey, S. (1993) 'The unfortunate revival of civic republicanism', *University of Pennsylvania Law Review*, 141: 801–98.

Goodin, R. (2003) 'Folie Républicaine', *Annual Review of Political Science*, 6: 55–76.

Hampton, J. (1992) 'An expressive theory of retribution', in W. Cragg (ed.) *Retributivism and Its Critics*, Stuttgart: F. Steiner, Verlag.

Hart, H.L.A. (1963) *Law, Liberty, and Morality*, Stanford, CA: Stanford University Press.

Hart, H.L.A. (1970 [1955]) 'Are there any natural rights?', in A.I. Melden (ed.) *Human Rights*, Belmont, CA: Wadsworth.
Hobbes, Thomas (1985 [1651]) *Leviathan*, C.B. Macpherson (ed.), London: Penguin Books.
Husak, D, (2008) *Overcriminalization: The Limits of the Criminal Law*, New York, NY: Oxford University Press.
Louch, A.R. (1968) 'Sins and crimes', *Philosophy*, 43: 38–50.
Marshall, S.E. and Duff, R.A. (1998) 'Criminalization and sharing wrongs', *Canadian Journal of Law and Jurisprudence*, 11: 7–22.
Mill, J.S. (1991) 'On liberty', in J. Gray (ed.) *On Liberty and Other Essays*, Oxford: Oxford University Press.
Moore, M. (1997) *Placing Blame: A Theory of Criminal Law*, Oxford: Oxford University Press.
Moore, M. (2008) 'A tale of two theories', *Criminal Justice Ethics*, 28: 27–48.
Morison, S. (2005) 'The politics of grace: on the moral justification of executive clemency', *Buffalo Criminal Law Review*, 9: 1–138.
Morris, H. (1981) 'A paternalistic theory of punishment', *American Philosophical Quarterly*, 18: 263–71.
Murphy, J.G. (2012) 'Legal moralism and retribution revisited', in Murphy, *Punishment and the Moral Emotions*, Oxford: Oxford University Press.
Pettit, P. (1989) 'The freedom of the city: a republican ideal', in A. Hamlin and P. Pettit (eds.) *The Good Polity*, Oxford: Blackwell.
Pettit, P. (1997) *Republicanism: A Theory of Freedom and Government*, Oxford: Oxford University Press.
Pettit, P. (2012) *On the People's Terms: A Republican Theory and Model of Democracy*, Cambridge: Cambridge University Press.
Pettit, P. (2015) 'Criminalization in republican theory', in R.A. Duff, L. Farmer, S.E. Marshall, M. Renzo and V. Tadros (eds.) *Criminalization: The Political Morality of the Criminal Law*, Oxford: Oxford University Press.
Rawls, J. (1964) 'Legal obligation and the duty of fair play', in S. Hook (ed.) *Law and Philosophy*, New York, NY: New York University Press.
Rawls, J. (1999) *A Theory of Justice*, rev. edn, Cambridge, MA: Harvard University Press.
Rawls, J. (2005) *Political Liberalism*, expanded edn, New York, NY: Columbia University Press.
Skinner, Q. (1998) *Liberty before Liberalism*, Cambridge: Cambridge University Press.
Stephen, J.F. (1994 [1873]) 'The doctrine of liberty in its application to morals', in G. Dworkin (ed.) *Morality, Harm, and the Law*, Boulder, CO: Westview Press.
Tamanaha, B. (2004) *On the Rule of Law: History, Politics, Theory*, Cambridge: Cambridge University Press.
Yankah, E. (2013) 'Legal vices and civic virtue: vice crimes, republicanism, and the corruption of lawfulness', *Criminal Law and Philosophy*, 7: 61–82.

4

Resentment, punitiveness, and forgiveness

An exploration of the moral psychology of punishment

Jonathan Jacobs

This essay examines some moral-psychological issues relevant to criminal sanction. It is meant to sketch out some of the main contours of attitudes and sentiments almost unavoidably connected with punishment, either as motives for it, as reasons for it, as responses to wrongdoing and wrongdoers, or otherwise impacting how individuals and a society regard offenders and punishment. I cannot hope to provide an adequate account of even just the essentials in an essay on the present scale. The issues are complex, involving causal considerations, normative considerations, and important aspects of how members of a society regard and treat each other. Still, I hope that the discussion attains a measure of helpful clarity at least in regard to formulation of some of the main issues.

Of course, one reason for exploring these issues is that, at least in the United States, it is plausible to think that criminal justice is excessive in its punitiveness and that attitudes toward offenders and ex-offenders are often hostile and unforgiving. Moreover, the conditions of incarceration for large numbers of prisoners are truly awful, and it is widely felt that prisoners deserve no better. Topics such as resentment, punitiveness, and forgiveness are important aspects of moral life in any case, with especially pronounced importance in regard to criminal justice. Given the problems besetting criminal justice in the United States (and elsewhere) the issues have undeniable contemporary relevance, even urgency.

The discussion is shaped in large part by some of Adam Smith's insights and arguments in *The Theory of Moral Sentiments*. I neither offer nor presuppose a defense of Smith's moral theory overall, but his treatment of some of the most fundamental sentiments involved in moral experience and moral judgment offers valuable resources for addressing the present topic. Those resources include a great deal that is strongly relevant to criminal justice and civic culture and to the causal and normative relations between them in the United States, the United Kingdom, and other countries, as well.

My aim is not to make a case for Smith's moral theory as an approach to criminal justice but to explicate how elements of his view illuminate some of the morally most important aspects of how a society regards criminal sanction.

The consideration of resentment is especially important. It is the basis for the discussions of punitiveness, forgiveness, and the character of civil society. The first section of this essay focuses on the moral psychology of resentment. The second considers punitiveness as an attitude and motive, and both sections consider the relations between those sentiments and criminal justice. The third section discusses forgiveness in relation to criminal justice. It does not address the very significant role of forgiveness as a moral matter between individuals in their private relations, whether as family members, friends, neighbors, strangers, or otherwise. Its concern is with forgiveness in regard to a society's institutions and practices of criminal justice. The fourth, final section of the essay discusses the implications of the foregoing for the civility of civil society generally. It considers the impact of sentiments and attitudes concerning criminal justice on civic culture, especially in the contemporary United States. Thus, the discussion starts with a look at an early modern view of moral sentiments and works its way toward a brief explication of how it can illuminate some of the most troubling challenges in contemporary America, and elsewhere.

A role for resentment

Resentment gets a good deal of bad press, much of it deserved. It is widely regarded as toxic, mean-spirited, something to be minimized, having no proper place in moral life. It is a painful sentiment, and it can corrupt motives and attitudes in ways that result in moral damage to both the person resented and the resentful person. Nietzsche famously explicated the way that *ressentiment* could be not only an attitude and a motive that poisons relations between people but also the source of a system of values, one that he took to be profoundly unhealthy and damaging.[1] There is little doubt that resentment can undermine trust, fuel suspicion and malice, and overall, reflect some of the least admirable and most destructive attitudes and types of conduct possible for human beings. However, a blanket condemnation of resentment is too quick, too summary and fails to discern ways that resentment can be apt.

To understand why, it is very helpful to consider why Smith regarded resentment as a *basic* moral sentiment and also why he regarded gratitude as similarly basic. In Smith's view, those two sentiments have fundamental roles in moral life and experience. They figure in some of the most regular and important ways people regard and treat each other. Gratitude is a core element of appreciative regard for others, and resentment is a core element of recognizing and responding appropriately to the ill-desert of others.

In explicating desert, Smith says:

> … he, therefore, appears to deserve reward, who, to some person or persons, is the natural object of a gratitude which every human heart is disposed to beat time to, and thereby applaud: and he, on the other hand, appears to deserve punishment, who in the same manner is to some person or persons the natural object of a resentment which the breast of every reasonable man is ready to adopt and sympathize with.
>
> (Smith 1982: 69–70)

And he wrote:

> Our whole sense, in short, of the merit and good desert of such actions, of the propriety and fitness of recompensing them, and making the person who performed them rejoice in his turn, arises from the sympathetic emotions of gratitude and love, with which, when we bring home to our own breast the situation of those principally concerned, we feel ourselves naturally transported towards the man who could act with such proper and noble beneficence.
>
> (Smith 1982: 75)

Gratitude and resentment have roles in many types of situations and relations between people. It is no accident that they are fundamental attitudes. Only voluntary, rational agents can be proper objects of gratitude and resentment because only such agents can merit responses on the basis of *desert*. Such agents not only bring about this or that; their conduct has more than causal efficacy. It can be appreciated, and it can be censured on the basis of what sorts of intentions and motives are reflected in their conduct. Through *gratitude* we show our appreciation of the benefactor, even if the person benefited is not one's self (as in the quoted passage above). Through *resentment,* we express the sense of ill-desert of a wrongdoer; it is a sentiment we feel even when it is someone else who has been wronged. (Smith uses "resentment" in contexts where we might use "indignation.") As sentiments, motives, and attitudes, gratitude and resentment pervade moral life. There are myriad contexts and ways in which they have a proper place. Also, they can influence the character of the social world overall in ways we will discuss.

For Smith, a moral sentiment is more complex than just being something *felt*. For example, the elements of gratitude include our sympathetic grasp of how another feels when enjoying the beneficence of others, a notion of the sort of motive that led to being the benefactor, the enjoyment accompanying beneficent action, and the propriety and merit of so acting. This is a nexus of feeling, normative judgment, and sympathetic representation or reconstruction of others' states of mind as though we were in the agent's situation.

If we try to imagine what sorts of bonds, attitudes, and relations there would be between human beings without gratitude and resentment shaping and giving energy to motives, judgments, and decisions we can very quickly become disoriented. Gratitude and resentment are not mere accessories to the kinds of lives human beings live. They are integral to the normative contours of human relations.

> Gratitude and resentment, therefore, are the sentiments which most immediately and directly prompt us to reward and to punish. To us, therefore, he must appear to deserve reward, who appears to be the proper and approved object of gratitude; and he to deserve punishment, who appears to be that of resentment.
>
> (Smith 1982: 69)

> To punish, too, is to recompense, to remunerate, though in a different manner; it is to return evil for evil that has been done.
>
> (Smith 1982: 69)

Moreover, "The want of proper indignation is a most essential defect in the manly character, and, upon many occasions, renders a man incapable of protecting either himself or his friends from insult and injustice" (Smith 1982: 243). To be lacking in that sentiment is to exhibit a deficiency of proper respectful regard for the persons harmed or mistreated. And though envy is a vice, "The man, however, who, in matters of consequence tamely suffers other people, who are entitled to no such superiority, to rise above him or get before him, is justly condemned as mean-spirited" (Smith 1982:16). This is the case even if it is "a sort of ill-judged magnanimity" (Smith 1982: 16).

Smith was alert to the ways in which resentment can harm relations among people, corrupt judgment, and poison motivation. But his view was not just an attempt to somehow domesticate resentment, to find a way to accommodate it, given that we would feel it inevitably. Rather, it has a positive role, which we can bring into view by considering the question, "How would you regard the state of affairs in which no one ever felt resentment on your behalf despite the fact that you had been wrongfully harmed?" That, I think, can help us see that resentment can indeed be appropriate and that there are ways in which its absence can reflect a moral *defect*. Nor is the defect discernible only in thinking about one's own case. Consider the situation in which no one felt resentment on behalf of others who are unjustly, deliberately harmed. Even if one were fortunate in never being a victim, the fact that there would be no resentment on behalf of others who *are* victims of injustice would be morally troubling.

It is not that we want others to be vengeful on behalf of victims. It is that we want that people should have sufficient regard for each other's standing as members of the moral community so that wrongful actions should be recognized as objects of ill-desert. It should *matter* that persons have been wrongly injured, and resentment reflects the judgment that it does indeed matter. An absence of resentment on behalf of victims would suggest a "want of proper indignation," "a most essential defect." The case is similar with regard to gratitude. Its absence, too, would constitute a normatively significant alteration in human relations and their normative significance.

To not ever feel resentment, and for resentment to never have any motivational role, would not be an unmixed blessing, a washing away of a moral taint. Instead, we would be ill-equipped to set right the normative order of human relations after it has been violated by wrongful conduct. At the same time, "we ought always to punish with reluctance, and more from a sense of the propriety of punishing, than from any savage disposition to revenge" (Smith 1982: 172). Guarding against that by resolute commitment to propriety is crucial. But that is not because resentment, as such, is something better unfelt. Discussing anger, John Casey writes:

> To be angry with someone is to be disposed to rebuke him, to remonstrate with him, demand that he apologize, have him punished. One could not satisfy one's anger simply by causing another person to be harmed. One cares about his attitudes as well as his acts. If one's anger cannot be appeased by apology or restitution, and if it concentrates not upon someone's attitudes and emotions, but purely on what he has done, or even on what he is, then it has ceased to be anger and has become hatred.
>
> (Casey 1991: 12)

And:

> So it is part of the nature of anger that one make certain demands, that one seek a certain response. The angry man claims that his feelings and attitudes be taken seriously. He makes certain claims, and considers himself justified. Anger and apology are concerned with claims, justification, Recompense.
>
> (Casey 1991: 13)

"Anger entails reacting to someone personally, setting a value on his attitudes and intentions. It implies treating him as an agent capable of accepting or rejecting reasons for action. And that means treating him as free" (Casey 1991: 15). The resentment Smith refers to is a form of anger that is motivated by an agent acting unjustly. It is anger motivated by the agent's ill-desert, and we can resent wrongs done to others.

Casey's discussion includes additional elements similar to what we find in Smith (though he does not mention Smith in regard to his discussion of moral emotions). Anger requires sympathetic imagination. To be angry on behalf of another person involves sympathetic appreciation of the wronged person's injury and sympathetic appreciation of the motives and aims of the person who has committed the wrong. When someone (with reason) is angry with us, we experience that anger

> as a claim that we treat the other as a person, take his attitudes seriously, enter into a world of reciprocal relations where rebuke, apology, forgiveness, are intelligible. And that must be

> the world of beings who can make claims, can incur and acknowledge obligations, can be wronged, can be the objects of and can reciprocate love, respect, hatred and contempt.
>
> (Casey 1991: 21)

Casey goes on to note that if "all I feel is dumb, subterraneous resentment" that is not proper anger, and "I may be failing to regard myself as on terms of equality with the person at whom my feeling is directed" (Casey 1991: 21). There certainly is such resentment, and that is one of the "toxic" varieties. There is also healthy resentment, and it is connected with a constellation of beliefs about oneself and others and with a judgment of the fitness of certain affective states and acts motivated by those beliefs and that affect. The resentment Smith focused on is not "dumb, subterraneous" anger; it has to do with proper acknowledgment of the status of the parties involved—wrongdoer, victim, and the person feeling resentment. It concerns a complex notion of what is due to each, that notion achievable through a training of the capacity for sympathy and imagination.

Moreover, resentment is not a proper response to just *any* conduct that we find objectionable. The person who fails to recompense a benefactor is guilty of impropriety but not in a manner that elicits our resentment. This is because "he does no positive hurt to any body" (Smith 1982: 79). However:

> Resentment would prompt us to desire, not only that he should be punished, but that he should be punished by our means, and on account of that particular injury which he had done to us. Resentment cannot be fully gratified, unless the offender is not only made to grieve in his turn, but to grieve for that particular wrong which we have suffered from him. … The natural gratification of this passion tends, of its own accord, to produce all the political ends of punishment; the correction of the criminal, and the example to the public.
>
> (Smith 1982: 69)

Resentment, justice, and punitiveness

There is an especially significant relation between resentment and *justice* because of resentment's relation to desert. In regard to justice, resentment performs a vital function.

> Nature has implanted in the human breast that consciousness of ill-desert, those terrors of merited punishment which attend upon its violation, as the great safe-guards of the association of mankind, to protect the weak, to curb the violent, and to chastise the guilty.
>
> (Smith 1982: 86)

Granted, resentment is painful, disagreeable, just as consciousness of our own ill-desert often is painful and disagreeable. However, that a sentiment is painful or disagreeable or that it can motivate impropriety or unjust conduct is not, as such, a reason for thinking it cannot have a valuable, even positive role. Resentment does, indeed, have such a role, and there is a basis for it in the capacities and susceptibilities constitutive of human nature.

Resentment involves a punitive aspect. But the punitiveness is based upon an appreciation of what is due to each person in the situation, a situation in which someone has been unjustly wronged. Again, consider the state of affairs in which punitiveness is altogether absent. Is it a state of affairs in which something morally commendable or desirable is *lacking*? I suggest that it is. To never experience punitive sentiments, or to never seek to impose punishment—regardless of the conduct of the putative wrongdoer—those are ways of failing to properly acknowledge the reality of the wrongful harm done. Granted, punitiveness is susceptible to excess, and it can include taking malicious pleasure in the suffering of the punished wrongdoer. But punitiveness rooted in properly proportional resentment is not just a passion fueling a desire to cause pain and suffering. It is the practical dimension of commitment to principles of justice and to what is required to properly respect the rights, interests, and standing of persons who have been wronged.

Nor need punitiveness be experienced as wholly alienating one from the object of punitiveness. It can be a mode of addressing the person punished as a rational, accountable agent capable of recognizing his moral wrong and perhaps also righting himself. It can be understood as an essential element in a "dialogue" between persons in that it is both expressive and communicative. Punitiveness expressed by censure and imposed by punishment in a way that is responsive to morally relevant features of agency and accountability is not only morally permissible but, when appropriately calibrated by self-command and propriety, can be morally commendable, serving an important function in the ordering of moral life.

It is a mistake to think of punitiveness as *only* malicious, as either malicious desire to harm or malicious pleasure in imposing suffering on a wrongdoer. Retributive theories of punishment are often pejoratively described by critics as poorly disguised vengeance, dressed up perhaps in a rhetoric of "balancing the scales" of justice or "annulling a false assertion of superiority" or some other metaphor. (Of course, those employing the metaphors do not regard them as misleading or meaningless rhetorical ornaments.) Often, the charge is that retributivism claims to express a fundamental moral truth—perhaps even what is claimed to be an *evident* moral truth—when, in fact, underneath is something quite unlovely. But retributivism need not be claimed to express a rationally evident moral principle, and it is not true that it must hold that desert is a *sufficient* ground for punishment.

In fact, while there is a retributivist element in Smith's view of punishment it included considerations having to do with motivating reform—an educative function for punishment—and considerations of deterrence as well as punishment communicating censure and reflecting desert. He wrote of the person punished:

> He must be made to repent and be sorry for this very action, that others, through fear of the like punishment, may be terrified from being guilty of the like offence. The natural gratification of this passion tends, of its own accord, to produce all the political ends of punishment; the correction of the criminal, and the example to the public.
>
> (Smith 1982: 69)

And, as Jeffrie Murphy writes in "Last Words on Retribution" in this volume:

> As I understand the retributive theory of punishment at its best, it is not a foundational primitive (the claim that we can see as self-evident that the deserving should be punished) but a view about punishment that must be located within broader concerns about justice, fairness, and desert (both punitive and non-punitive).
>
> (Murphy 2016: this volume)

Thus, it is not even the case that desert always requires punishment. Instead, "[d]esert is always a *very strong reason* that favors punishment and, other things being equal, the punishment that is deserved should be inflicted" (Murphy 2016: this volume). Nor does retributivism imply severity. There just is no logical or conceptual connection between desert and harshness, though there is a connection between desert and proportionality, and desert is "a concept based on the idea of the dignity of each individual person and the respect that is owed to this dignity" (Murphy 2016: this volume).

It is important to recognize that neither punitiveness nor retribution is committed to the notion that criminals should suffer in the sense of experiencing considerable pain and being made miserable by inhumane conditions. Rather, a criminal is to suffer punishment in the original and primary meaning of the word: "to *endure* something that is not within the control of one's own will" (Murphy 2016: this volume). The proportionality requirement of retributivism, in conjunction with the recognition of the dignity of offenders as participants in the moral/legal community are inherent impediments to resentment-based retributivism involving vengeance as a motive and the offender's pain and suffering as an aim, one to be enjoyed by others.

Though it is plain that retributive resentment *can easily become excessive* it is not intrinsically malicious or inevitably morally objectionable. Nietzsche was almost certainly correct that, when sublimated or repressed, resentment builds, intensifies, and often is misdirected, woundingly expressed in unfair and hurtful ways, directed at inappropriate persons. In many cases this is because the resentful person lacks the courage to direct this anger at the person who has caused it. In any event, undischarged resentment does not evaporate; it can deepen its roots, is easily aggravated, and can become a troubling, troublesome preoccupation.

An abundant risk of real harm can come from misguided or disproportionate resentment and from corrupted forms of retributivism. Smith was alert to this. He held that, "[t]he insolence and brutality of anger, in the same manner, when we indulge its fury without check or restraint, is, of all objects, the most detestable" (Smith 1982: 24). The impartial spectator could never approve of punitive resentment unregulated and uncontained by the employment of sympathy and imagination in a critically reflective process. Smith wrote:

> But we admire that noble and generous resentment which governs its pursuit of the greatest injuries, not by the rage which they are apt to excite in the breast of the sufferer, but by the indignation which they naturally call forth in that of the impartial spectator; which allows no word, no gesture, to escape it beyond what this more equitable sentiment would dictate; which never, even in thought, attempts any greater vengeance, nor desires to inflict any greater punishment, than what every indifferent person would rejoice to see executed.
>
> (Smith 1982: 24)

Even punitiveness, in proper measure, can be a mode of addressing the person punished as a rational, accountable agent. It can be part of the "conversation" among participants in the moral community.[2] The wrongdoer should be able to recognize that others cannot endorse the motives and attitude that resulted in his unjust act. Punitiveness can be expressed by censure and imposed by punishment but in neither case is it also unavoidably intended to *injure* and certainly not to *worsen*.

However, when resentment and punitiveness are aimed at persons whose agency or voluntariness is constrained it may be that they are then not directed at their proper objects and are liable to cause needless harm. If the scope of one's agency and voluntariness is diminished by (i) mental illness, (ii) a genuine paucity of alternatives to crime, or (iii) conditions that plausibly motivate alienation, anger, and resentment of injustice then punitive resentment toward such persons, even when they commit crimes, may be, at least to some degree, undeserved.

Consider that in the contemporary United States, a striking disproportion of minority and poor persons are incarcerated, especially those who have less than a high school education. By 2008 the incarceration rate for young African-American men who had dropped out of high school was above 35 percent. At the end of 2013 the overall state and federal imprisonment rate for African Americans was nearly six times that of white Americans though for the latter group, the incarceration rate for young high school dropouts was also very high. Individuals with few marketable skills, little education, and living in poverty—often multi-generational poverty—are arrested and incarcerated at alarmingly high rates. For many such people property crime, drug crime, and violent crime are nearly ubiquitous features of their lives rather than uncommon disruptions.

The question of whether such conditions of life constitute excusing or justifying conditions is complex, and it is probably a mistake to assert unqualified generalizations about poverty excusing or justifying what would otherwise be blameworthy conduct. At the same time, it is almost certainly true that many such persons are regarded as criminals—and not anything other than that—by many who are better off, and to whatever degree a given individual's wretched predicament and poor prospects are his or her own fault, there is often a serious deficit of a civil disposition toward such a person. On one side there is anger, frustration, despondency, and even rage, while on the other there is a too-ready punitiveness or disdain, as though such person is not a full member of society, anyway. The complicated issues regarding the appropriateness of the resentment and punitiveness directed at many poor and poorly educated persons who commit criminal acts extend beyond the scope of the present discussion. However, one significant—and morally intelligible—form of resentment is that felt by the disadvantaged in regard to what they take to be the injustice of their predicament. The interaction of excessive punitiveness on the one side and resentment on the other does real damage to the civility of civil society, each group blaming the other for being the chief source of the contraction of civility. That resentment is distinct from the present focus, but they are jointly elements of the overall social and moral culture of society.

Even acknowledging the relevance of serious social issues, their complex interaction with criminal justice, and the ways that disordered or corrupt sentiments aggravate threats to civility and mutual respect, we should not lose sight of the fact that there are ways of feeling anger and resentment that are morally sound, even commendable. Resentment and punitiveness can be proper responses, and the attempt to exclude them altogether, or the claim that one strives to be above them, with no need to feel such disagreeable sentiments is morally dubious. When one is slighted or clearly and deliberately disrespected, that is a reasonable basis for resentment. There are ways of *failing* to feel it and exhibit it that are failures to uphold one's own dignity and standing or a failure to resent injustice done to others.[3]

That does not make anger, *as a standing disposition* or as a stand-alone disposition, a virtue; far from it.[4] This is even more clear in regard to punitiveness. If anger or punitiveness becomes a persisting disposition in its own right, the agent may fail to be alert to how easily those dispositions can be morally corrupt and damaging. Both in regard to the individual's character and sensibility and in regard to the overall character of the social world, the task is to direct resentment and punitiveness at their proper objects.

Consider some of the general features of a healthy civic culture. Among its ingredients are the following: (i) That people generally exhibit stable dispositions to regard and treat each other as participants in a common moral world with each having equal status as members on the basis of their inherent dignity. (This does not foreclose on some people being morally more worthy, admirable, and excellent than others.) (ii) That people are regularly able to interact, even with strangers, on a basis of trust and reciprocal good will; (iii) That criminal sanction reflects widely endorsed measures of proportionality, ordered in accord with the gravity of offenses; (iv) That incarceration does not involve conditions that damage or worsen offenders in terms of their agential capacities and ability to reintegrate into civil society; (v) That sanction is not imposed out of malice or contempt, and that it is only imposed when the offender had a genuine option of compliance with the law; (vi) That punishment does not go on unofficially via impediments and disqualifications after completion of sentence. (Certain kinds of official disqualification may be appropriate for certain types of offenders. That is a distinct matter.)

In general, ex-offenders should not have to endure continuing obstacles and forms of exclusion once sentence has been served. As Murphy has remarked of the contemporary situation in America, "In the United States it has apparently been forgotten that we should send people to prison *as* punishment not *for* punishment" (Murphy 2016: this volume). The appalling conditions in many prisons, the official and unofficial impediments to ex-prisoner reentry into civil society and the ways in which many ex-offenders are stigmatized are all grounds for significant moral objections to current practices.[5] Such features of the current carceral regime are manifest violations of retributive principles; they are not examples of retributivism at work.

How could we plausibly answer the question, "what is the proper place of anger in moral life and experience?" if we ask about it in a way that is independent of its objects, causes, and so forth? The same holds for resentment and punitiveness. One of the strengths of the moral psychology Smith elaborates is its alertness to the different kinds of considerations that figure in the relevant phenomena and his textured appreciation of how they figure. He does not focus narrowly on how a particular sentiment feels or only on one or another paradigmatic type of experience of it. He sees that sentiments have complex relations with beliefs, other sentiments, moral imagination, and the representation of other's motives and perspectives.

The complexity of forgiveness

We have not commented on forgiveness, the capability for which is widely regarded as among the morally best capabilities of human beings. Examples of forgiveness can be powerful examples of moral excellence, and no doubt, most of us have had the experience of wishing to be forgiven and perhaps even to be more forgiving.

The complexity—logical, moral, and psychological—of forgiveness is considerable, and I will not try to sketch even the outlines of a theory of it.[6] However, we can identify some of the main questions concerning it and consider its relations to the issues discussed so far. They include (1) Is forgiving always virtuous? Is it ever a moral mistake to forgive? (2) Can we forgive on behalf of others? (3) How should we understand the relation between forgiving and punishing? (4) Is forgiving ever a moral requirement? (5) Is it a condition of forgiveness that the wrongdoer has apologized, experienced remorse, and repented? What if, as sometimes appears to be the case, it is forgiveness that *motivates* remorse and repentance? (6) What is the relation between forgiving others and self-forgiveness?

As a tentative, informal characterization of forgiveness we can say it is a forswearing of resentment (and punitiveness) toward someone, in such a way that the original cause of anger no longer has a place in the forgiving person's attitude toward, and treatment of, the person forgiven.

It is widely, and plausibly held that only the person wronged has the standing to forgive. Others who may feel resentment and punitiveness toward Y over the fact that X has been wronged by Y, may follow X's lead in the sense that, because X has forgiven Y they, too, cease to feel punitive anger toward Y. But it is plausible to maintain that it is not for anyone apart from the victim to forgive Y. If Y *killed* X then X's family members and other intimates might consider forgiving Y for the grievous harm done to *them* in taking X's life. They cannot, however, forgive Y *for* X, even if we have reason to believe X *would have* forgiven Y. If X survived Y's attack family and friends may manage to persuade X to forgive Y. They may cease to feel anger toward Y. But they are not in a position to forgive Y for what Y did to X. At least, this seems a plausible claim about forgiveness;

that it is a change in attitude, sentiment, and regard *on the part of the person who has been wronged.* That person alone has the standing, so to speak, to offer forgiveness.

Also, for the offer to be genuine forgiveness (rather than something else) it is to be motivated by moral reasons and not just a felt need to overcome rage or painful memories or feelings of vulnerability or some other psychological need on the part of the victim. Those may indeed be important; I am not dismissing their significance. But forgiving is a *gift*. Those other reasons to forswear resentment and moral hatred may do considerable good for the victim and the wrongdoer, but they change the relations between them by a means other than *giving* (something that is not owed).

Is forgiveness ever *owed*? It might be thought that we should regard punitiveness and resentment as morally acceptable only if they are stages on the way to forgiveness, and that there is a moral requirement to strive to be forgiving. Suppose that after wronging X, Y is genuinely repentant. Y apologizes and tries to "make X whole" for whatever loss or suffering was caused; Y acknowledges the wrong done and the harm caused; Y expresses sincere resolve to ethically reorient herself; and Y engages in the appropriate types of conduct to realize that aspiration. Would it be *overly* punitive, hardhearted or unfair of X to not forgive Y? Does X owe it to Y to forgive Y?

It would be unfair and wrong for X to continue hating Y if by "hating" we mean that X regards Y as morally abandoned or wholly unworthy of trust, as incapable of moral decency having forfeited the dignity one has as a moral agent, or as someone incapable of understanding and being responsive to moral reasons. If X insisted that there are no grounds on which Y can be self-forgiving or that *nothing* Y *could do could count* as repentance or genuine moral self-correction that would be unreasonable and callous on X's part.

Yet, one could acknowledge that the wrongdoer has recognized the wrong done and perhaps even apologized, but this person may still have reasonable reservations about forgiving. This is not necessarily a matter of X being unable to "get over" the wrong, remaining unhealthily preoccupied with it. Also, it would be morally dubious if the unwillingness or inability to forgive is a prideful version of "I don't *do* forgiveness," perhaps underwritten by the "certainty" that one could never do anything as awful as what Y has done. What might be going on is that though the victim is not preoccupied with the past wrong the reality of the history is a lasting impediment to a clean slate in one's relation to the wrongdoer. In such a case, not forgiving need not be evidence of being *unforgiving* in a morally objectionable way. It is not a mean-spirited withholding of something, but it may reflect honest self-knowledge that one does not have that gift to give because of the reality of the wrong that was done in the past. It is a mistake to assume that the only explanations for not forgiving are unreasonable bitterness or punitiveness or a self-wounding preoccupation with resentment. While acknowledging that there could be moral gains from restored relations with the wrongdoer or at least from forgiving even without seeking new relations with the wrongdoer, the victim may (reasonably) insist that not forgiving is not itself a moral error.

It is not clear that forgiveness can be strictly *merited.* That is one way it differs from, say, gratitude. Gratitude can indeed be merited and in some cases, failure to be grateful is blameworthy. On the other hand, while someone might have done things that merit admiration that is not meriting in as strict a sense as gratitude is merited. If A fails to admire B that might be on account of a moral failing on A's part (envy, perhaps or jealousy or misplaced resentment) but it is not an injustice on A's part not to admire B. It might be "small" or inappropriate but not a failure to acknowledge what justice requires. "Gratitude is something which is justly owed, and which can be claimed. Someone entirely without a sense of justice (if he could be imagined) could neither feel grateful nor claim gratitude from others" (Casey 1991: 174). And:

> Gratitude is not simply the faithful fulfillment of a contract. Someone with no sense of justice could still understand his contractual obligations, and could have good reasons—for

> instance, of a utilitarian sort—for honouring the contract. Gratitude, like anger, is essentially directed at the attitudes of others, and not simply at their deeds.
>
> (Casey 1991: 174)

A connection between justice and forgiveness is even less clear and direct than in the case of admiration. We might say that X was just in forgiving Y, but that would make the most sense if, for instance, X needed to overcome bitterness or deep anger in order to forgive and realized that his bitterness was excessive. Having finally come to see that, and having overcome it, X was able to go further and forgive. But the justice is in overcoming *the excess of bitterness* and in not doing things that the bitterness might have motivated, not actually in the forgiving. There are situations in which we think, "It would be unfair, ungenerous, not to forgive him. He has taken numerous steps to make things right and there is every reason to believe those steps are genuine." But is the withholding of forgiveness an injustice? Not forgiving a wrongdoer does not imply that the non-forgiving person is unjustly adding to or continuing the punishment of the wrongdoer.

Imagine a person who claims that she forgives anyone who has wronged her and regards doing so not only as a moral good, but also as a liberating aspect of moral good health. She feels that carrying a burden of resentment and anger is a danger to oneself and that forgiveness is critically important to mutual respect as equal participants in a common moral world. The view might be that we are all flawed; we have all been unkind or unjust; and forgiveness is not only a gift that can benefit the recipient, it benefits the giver, as well. However, it is important to be reminded that forgiving requires effort. It is work, not just a decisional episode. The kind of change in regard and attitude that forgiveness involves does not come easily and cannot be made a routinized matter of personal *policy* in the way that writing thank-you notes (even heartfelt, meaningful ones) might be a personal policy. A different kind of effort is required.

Just as there are apologies that are less than genuine and there is less than genuine remorse, there are dubious and counterfeit forms of forgiveness. Some are spoiled by a kind of narcissism of virtue, the forgiver overly concerned with the moral figure she presents to herself and others. In addition, the person who claims to always forgive, to *of course* forgive, may be avoiding looking closely at the morally disturbing features of the ways she has been wronged and failing to come to terms with them. One way to avoid becoming angry and resentful because of the ways one has been wronged is to deceive oneself about the nature and seriousness of the wrong, persuading oneself that it wasn't "really" a wrong, or failing to acknowledge one's vulnerability and susceptibility to being abused, mistreated or otherwise unjustly ill-served. Weakness—of a type we are loath to acknowledge—can become a motive for (less than genuine) forgiveness.

As Michael Moore put it, "By repressing anger at wrongful violation, we may be attempting to deny that we live in a society in which there really are fearful and awful people" (Moore 2010: 143). Focusing on forgiving can be a way of averting one's eyes from ugly moral realities, which we should have the courage to look at honestly. (How much moral good is done by a hollow apology meeting with scripted or merely rhetorical forgiveness? It makes the situation worse.)

Smith himself commented on a related phenomenon of moral sensibility. Once the wrongdoer is under the control of the criminal justice system we may feel inclined to forgive or at least to advocate mercy. We may begin to see the offender as a victim of a sort. Commenting on this dynamic, Smith writes:

> When the guilty is about to suffer that just retaliation, which the natural indignation of mankind tells them is due to his crimes; when the insolence of his injustice is broken and humbled by the terror of his approaching punishment; when he ceases to be an object of fear, with the generous and humane he begins to be an object of pity. The thought of what

> he is about to suffer extinguishes their resentment for the sufferings of others to which he has given occasion. They are disposed to pardon and forgive him, and to save him from that punishment, which in all their cool hours they had considered as the retribution due to such crimes. Here, therefore, they have occasion to call to their assistance the consideration of the general interest of society. They counterbalance the impulse of this weak and partial humanity by the dictates of a humanity that is more generous and comprehensive. They reflect that mercy to the guilty is cruelty to the innocent, and oppose to the emotions of compassion which they feel for a particular person, a more enlarged compassion which they feel for mankind.
>
> (Smith 1982: 88–89)

Smith was not advocating hardheartedness or encouraging us to take pleasure in the suffering of the offender. Nor was he morally repudiating forgiveness. He urged a focus on the morally most central features of the situation, warning against becoming distracted from the merits of the case by our own sympathetic affect. To become distracted would be a failure of impartiality, slighting the rights and the interests of the victim and failing to uphold the normative principles applicable to the situation. Distraction of this type indicates failure of compassion rather than a virtuous enlargement of it.

None of what has been pointed out thus far is material for a case *against* forgiveness. Still, it is significant that forgiving is not an unqualified moral good. It can be morally mistaken in ways that offend against justice. Moreover, it is certainly possible to both punish *and* forgive. Even if one is disposed to forgive prior to punishment being carried out, that disposition does not supply a strong reason to *not* punish. Punishment can be merited in a strict sense while forgiveness can be morally intelligible though it is not something merited. Punishment is a response to desert, and forgiving and punishing are not antithetical. They respond to different considerations.

Moreover, at the social level the issue is even more complicated, and it is doubtful if forgiveness can be a *policy* though groups and institutions can behave *as if* forgiving. For example, debt can be forgiven, i.e., written off. But that is generally different from moral forgiveness. In many cases, debt is forgiven when (and *because*) there is no reasonable expectation of the debt being paid and there are prudential or pragmatic reasons to not require repayment. By moral forgiveness we do not mean an acknowledgment that the wrongdoer cannot be expected to morally right himself. Typically, forgiveness between creditor and debtor is a very different matter from moral forgiveness.

Also, there may be ways in which reconciliation is possible even when there is not forgiveness. Reconciliation can be a *policy* undertaken at the social level. There can be institutionalized practices that aim at reconciliation in ways that are not available with regard to forgiveness. Perhaps effective reconciliation can motivate forgiveness, at least some of the time. But reconciliation—even when it involves a real willingness to trust—can occur without forgiveness. Forgiveness involves a more complete change of heart toward the wrongdoer, a durable willingness to cease feeling resentment and a willingness to erase the previous wrong as a component of any shared history. Those may figure in reconciliation, but some forms of reconciliation do not also involve those types of depth. Moreover, when reconciliation involves institutions or associations there may not be the sorts of directly personal relations between individuals that make for the intimacy that forgiveness typically involves. This is not to say that reconciliation is dilute or superficial; this is just an observation about the different pragmatics often involved. It may be that reconciliation between groups or involving institutions creates an environment in which forgiveness is made more possible. And forgiving certainly should involve reconciliation, but it involves more, as well.

Inability to forgive others may be connected with inability to forgive oneself.[7] Recognizing the need for self-forgiveness and the gains from it can have a powerful impact, motivating a change in how one sees the possibility and point of forgiving others. An unwillingness or inability to forgive oneself can be burdensome and very costly in regard to one's prospect for happiness and even self-respect. If one starts to see that, and sees how damaging punitiveness directed at oneself can be, that can make a substantial change in how one judges whether others are to be forgiven and what that means for moral life. It can be very difficult to attain an honest, accurate perspective on oneself and one's vices and wrongdoing. It can be as damaging and pathological to regard oneself as unforgivable as it is to too casually forgive oneself. Perhaps, in this context, too, it is possible to strive to be virtuous even if one struggles to forgive (oneself).

Also, it can be difficult to know how to do that. Religious traditions have rich and textured disciplines of repentance and seeking forgiveness. Those with no religious sensibility or no appreciation for the insights of religious traditions might see all of that as little more than (morally questionable) theater. Yet, there is wisdom in recognizing that repentance and forgiveness (and here they are not being understood in a distinctively Christian sense) need guidance, and that certain practices can support and orient the revision in sensibility and attitude. Additionally, the respects in which repentance and forgiveness can integrally involve public aspects, and are not entirely and exclusively interior and undertaken alone, can be important supports and guidance. The revisions in attitude and perspective, and the matter of how to *effect* those revisions, can often involve ways of seeing ourselves that require more than an ego-situated view.

Alexander Broadie remarks of Smith's view, "In a Smithian way we are all engaged in a regulatory role, in which, however, we spectate as a condition of regulating the behavior not only of others but also of ourselves" (2010: 81). Smith's impartial spectator has a key role in moral self-understanding, making it quite evident how important it is to be able to look and see in ways that are not confined to the sphere of one's own spontaneous sensibility. Would the impartial spectator automatically endorse forgiveness? Much depends on what one takes to be possible reasons for not forgiving, on the wrong that was done, and how other relevant moral considerations figure in the judgment of what is the morally sound approach to one's situation.

Forgiveness, when genuine, overcomes resentment and punitiveness, at least with regard to the individual(s) forgiven. That is not to say that if one is capable of forgiving, one overcomes resentment and punitiveness altogether. Those can still be morally appropriate responses even if, in certain instances, the agent also forgives. Justice requires that punitive resentment come to an end and that the punishment of the offender not go on past completion of sentence. Justice itself (mainly through proportionality of desert) requires a limit. It does not require forgiveness. Not forgiving does not, as such, imply an excess of punitive resentment.

Above, we made note of an important deficit of civil disposition in the US. It involves attitudes and sentiments that are often unfair and certainly could not be endorsed by the persons who are the objects of them. There are several regards in which that uncivil disposition is morally objectionable. Being unforgiving is among them but is probably not the chief cause of the ways in which it is damaging to civil society.[8] There are important forms of reconciliation that could help restore civility even if they do not also include forgiveness, though there is little doubt that punitive unwillingness to forgive aggravates incivility. It is damaging because of the dependence of civil society on stable dispositions of trust and trustworthiness and an expectation of good faith, honesty, and mutual respect.

The civility that it is crucial to civil society cannot accommodate regarding offenders as effectively expelled from civil society, never to return to it, even upon release after serving sentence. If conviction and punishment are seen as marks of a fundamental and irreversible diminution of standing, as though the offender can no longer have a place in free society then, that is both uncivil and unjust. To be sure, many offenders are very bad people, and it can be—rightly—very difficult to sympathetically represent their outlooks, motives, attitudes, and intentions. Sympathizing, in the neutral sense of mentally representing without endorsement, can be obstructed by the wrongdoer's vices. A morally decent person may find it impossible to grasp the offender's perspective and motives except by description. Those features of the offender may be, to the virtuous person, unthinkable, unimaginable as real practical possibilities. Recognizing and appreciating the imperatives of justice and the conditions for genuinely civil society requires thoughtfully informed, properly proportional—and thereby constrained—resentment and punitiveness. Very bad offenders may be practically inaccessible—we find it impossible to fully, realistically take on their way of seeing things—and practically unreachable—they may take no interest in remorse or apology or even genuine acknowledgment of their wrongs *as* gratuitous, serious, inexcusable wrongs. Still, there are moral and epistemic reasons not to "write off" such persons if that implies that neither proportionality nor civility remain relevant.

Moreover, the morally intolerable conditions imposed on many incarcerated persons are an affront to their dignity as well as being causes of despondency and bitterness, and causing damage to their agential capacities. The paucity of meaningful activities, the often severe constraints on what sorts of interactions and cooperation are permitted, the morale-deadening tedium of so much prison life—these all mean that many prisoners have little opportunity to exercise the capacities and acquire the sorts of habits needed for reentering civil society successfully. There is substantial empirical evidence that many prisoners are *de-moralized* in the sense that their capacities for prudential self-determination and for civil interaction with others are severely eroded, lost through lack of exercise and impediments to exercise.[9] This, in turn, motivates distrust in criminal justice and stirs doubt regarding the legitimacy of criminal justice institutions, policies, and practices.

To be sure, many prisoners are dangerous, and for the safety of other prisoners and corrections personnel the liberties of such prisoners while incarcerated need to be very limited. But even when that is the case, spending months or years in solitary confinement; being denied access to books, news media, activities other than brief periods of exercise; and having no opportunities to do any purposeful work while in prison: Those all further erode prisoners' abilities to be accountable agents. They deepen distrust and hostility and cause despair, sometimes involving self-injury. The conditions in which large numbers of prisoners are forced to live impact psychological health, attitudes, and aspiration in ways that are steadily better understood; these are not mysteries. They are understood sufficiently to know that current practices have few good effects and many bad ones.

Large numbers of people, every year, face considerable difficulties reintegrating into society, overcoming substance-abuse, settling into stable, healthy relationships with intimates and responsibly looking after dependants, and other challenges and obstacles. The overall impact of this is a kind of indignity antithetical to the principles and values distinctive of a liberal democracy.

Perhaps the erosion of a stable, widely shared commitment to propriety (in the complex, morally interesting sense Smith intended) explains the comfort with incivility. Smithian propriety underwrites civility in a strong sense through the way that it reflects an effective concern for whether others can sympathize with our attitudes, motives, and reactions. Smith wrote:

> … the spectator must, first of all, endeavor, as much as he can, to put himself in the situation of the other, and to bring to himself every little circumstance of distress which can possibly

> occur to the sufferer. He must adopt the whole case of his companion with all its minutest incidents; and strive to render as perfect as possible, that imaginary change of situation upon which his sympathy is founded.
>
> (Smith 1982: 21)

Moreover, the spectator is to think of himself being spectated by the other. "The person principally concerned [the person the spectator watches] watches the spectator in the hope of sympathy, because the spectator's sympathy, which of course makes a difference to the spectator, no less makes a difference to the person principally concerned" (Broadie 2010: 81). Each person involved in the dynamic strives to bring his perception and judgment into alignment with that of the other, and it is in this way that we ascertain which responses to the situation are fitting. The effort to be fair and impartial is the effort by which we discover what propriety requires.

Negotiating this is not negotiation in the sense of any sort of bargaining; it is a process of mutual recognition (what Smith calls a "conversation" at 1982: 23) through which we attain command over our passions out of regard for what impartiality shows to be reasonable agreement in sensibility. This is a morality in which mutual respect is exhibited and made practically efficacious by a durable concern with civility, seeing each as an equal participant in a common moral order. Thus, "so it is the great precept of nature to love ourselves only as we love our neighbor, or what comes to the same thing, as our neighbor is capable of loving us" (Smith 1982: 25).

The legal and institutional arrangements of liberal democracy make possible the extent of liberty through which such civility is attainable and sustainable. It makes possible a moral community in which it matters to each participant whether his or her emotions and motives are in harmony as viewed "in this candid and impartial light" (Smith 1982: 22). "Though they will never be unisons, they may be concords, and this is all that is wanted or required" (Smith 1982: 22).

This does not require minimizing the pluralism of a genuinely liberal polity. It does not require narrow limits on the diversity and dynamism of civil society. It is true that the Scotland Smith lived in was a smaller, more homogeneous national community with a level of ethnic and cultural unity unlike that of the twentieth- and twenty-first-century United States. (However, there remained serious sectarian divisions in Scotland and also significant political fault lines and mixed attitudes toward being part of a united kingdom with England.) However, a greater degree of cultural diversity and value pluralism make a civil disposition and a willingness to see things in a "candid and impartial light" even more important.

We should not expect the love of our neighbor that is expressed by genuine forgiveness to have an extensive role in criminal justice. Even the kinds of reconciliation and restoration of trust and respect we should be able to expect may only figure on a modest scale. A great deal needs to be done, addressing myriad social, economic, and political issues, just to bring about the degree of civil disposition required for society to be genuinely civil.

Addressing issues of criminal justice needs to be thickly integrated with the other elements of that project. It is not a stand-alone context, and it is enmeshed with other issues as both cause and effect of them. Part of the task—though it concerns a large number of aspects of the issue—is to restore the civility of criminal justice, making it more humane, less disproportionately punitive, and diminishing official and unofficial obstacles to the reintegration of offenders. If efforts in that direction create conditions in which forgiveness is realized more fully, that will be beneficial. But issues of justice and issues concerning the character of civic culture and the dispositions and attitudes that most powerfully shape and orient it are more fundamental and will remain more fundamental. Moreover, they are issues regarding which not only are there significant "oughts," but those imperatives imply "can" in a way that is not as clearly the case regarding forgiveness. There are widely shared attitudes regarding criminal justice in the United States that diminish the civility of society. The toleration—or endorsement—of what are often terrible and inhumane conditions and practices is a moral scandal. The remedy, however, is not forgiveness; it is *civility*.[10]

Sentiments and civility

The responses most urgently needed involve making significant changes in the ways that criminal sanction is imposed and significant changes in how ex-offenders are regarded and treated. Additionally, steps that diminish the multiple kinds of unfairness in enforcement of the law and the operations of the justice system are needed. Remedies for those problems would better enable at least some victims to overcome bitter alienation from offenders and would help offenders overcome resentment and alienation from victims and the wider society. Such steps could encourage commitment to justice as a *shared* social concern. Currently, there are fissures of social and economic dis-integration creating rival social constituencies, which is a near-certain recipe for social tension, conflict, and distrust undermining what needs to be a shared conception of the legitimacy and soundness of criminal justice.

Punitiveness and resentment are among the sources of the excesses of suffering and degradation imposed by criminal justice. This results in far too many people thinking that anyone who has committed a crime is *nothing but a criminal* and that, by committing a crime one forfeits the regard and treatment distinctive of the civility of a liberal democracy.

That individuals should have equal standing before the law and that criminal sanction and the procedures of criminal justice should be morally intelligible and endorsable by those to whom they apply are among the elements of that civility. Smith's notion of the impartial spectator is a powerful conceptual resource for critically examining the sentiments and attitudes shaping the ways we see criminals and criminal sanction. Good faith employment of it would swiftly delegitimize many features of contemporary criminal justice chiefly by exposing degrees and forms of punitiveness and resentment inconsistent with the civility of civil society. No one could genuinely feel morally at home in the midst of the harms done to those who are punished, if being "at home" involved acknowledging that they could apply equally to oneself.

We can gain by considering the kind of sympathetic imagination to which Smith appealed in his project of explaining and justifying moral judgments. Whether or not we endorse its specific terms as an integral part of moral epistemology it is valuable for how it explicates the fundamental importance of sentiments and attitudes not just in the phenomenology of moral experience but also in regard to impartiality and the justification of moral judgments. Through representation of others' perspectives we are able to critically assess our own attitudes and responses. This involves taking seriously the fact that morally there is *nothing privileged about being me* or about me being *this one*, while at the same time recognizing one's sensibility and forms of concern as the materials out of which impartially endorsable moral reasonableness is fashioned. We need to be able to represent the reality of other people to ourselves in ways that are not distorted by contempt, animosity, or self-centered privileging of one's own interests and concerns.

Smith's contribution to understanding the civility of civil society integrates (i) the individual's concern with how one is acknowledged and regarded by others, with (ii) the love of virtue and what is praiseworthy, with (iii) the dignity of the individual person, with (iv) self-command and with (v) the enjoyment of fellow-feeling and having sentiments in harmony with those of others. This last matter is vitally important to the civility of civil society and to the enjoyment of being a participant in a common social world. When such a world is morally well ordered, the appreciation of that fact can itself be an important ingredient of individuals' happiness.

Though a "disagreeable" sentiment, resentment is actually part of the structure of mutual acknowledgment and regard that is crucial to the civility of civil society. The morally proper bases of resentment have to do with seeing oneself as one among others with equal moral status, each person an accountable agent capable of acting on the basis of reasons and capable of appreciating the morally relevant significance of action.

Because human beings are accountable, voluntary agents capable of appreciating the significance of desert, there are fundamental roles for resentment and gratitude in social and moral life. Those sentiments and the actions motivated by them shape some of the most important responses, actions, and practices shaping civil society. It is an outstanding strength of Smith's view that he does not wish away resentment, trying to minimize its impact and its role by bemoaning the errors and harms—real and serious enough—to which it can give rise. Instead, he sees it as a potent, persistent feature of our moral anthropology, and he shows how, when rightly regulated by sympathy and imagination seeking impartiality, it can serve justice, "the main pillar that upholds the whole edifice" (Smith 1982: 79) of civil life.

Notes

1 See Friedrich Nietzsche, *Beyond Good and Evil,* for his articulation of *ressentiment* and the way it can shape and sustain a system of values.

2 For an influential articulation of a retributive-communicative theory of punishment in which punishment is justified in part on the basis of how it can motivate genuine ethical reorientation and commitment to sound values, see R. A. Duff, *Trials and Punishments*, New York, NY: Cambridge University Press, 1986.

3 In *Deadly Vices,* Gabriele Taylor notes that Aquinas made a "distinction between righteous and sinful anger, for, he says, revenge may be desired both well and ill, hence which type of anger is experienced depends on the mode and object of the desire. Anger, like pride, concerns the relation between self and other, so in righteous anger we have got the relation right, in sinful anger we err in our own favour." *Deadly Vices*, New York, NY: Oxford University Press, 2006, 85. In Aquinas, see *Summa Theologiae*: 2a2ae, q. 158, art. 2. Taylor also notes a distinction Thomas Reid makes between anger that is a "blind, impulsive reaction to any kind of hurt" and "anger in response to a perceived injury from others." This latter type involves "thinking in terms of rights, dues, deserts, and so on ..." (*Deadly Vices:* 86). The relevant passages in Reid are in *Essays on the Active Powers of the Human Mind*, essay 3, section 4: "Of Malevolent Affection."

4 Some thinkers, such as Maimonides, argue that while there may be occasions on which it is appropriate to make a *show* of anger, perhaps for purposes of morally educating a child, it is wrong to *feel* anger. "Likewise, anger is an extremely bad character trait, and it is proper for a man to move away from it to the other extreme and to teach himself not to become angry" ("Laws Concerning Character Traits": ch. 2: 32). Anger causes a wise man's wisdom to depart from him; anger is one of two character traits with regard to which "a man is forbidden to accustom himself to the mean" ("Laws Concerning Character Traits": ch. 2: 31). The other trait is pride. At the same time, Maimonides held: "if someone sees his fellow man who has sinned or who follows a way that is not good, it is a commandment to make him return to the good and to make known to him that he sins against himself by his evil actions. As it is said: 'You shall surely rebuke your neighbor'" ("Laws Concerning Character Traits": ch. 6: 48). And, "the Torah was particularly concerned with grudge-bearing so that the wrong done be completely blotted out from a man's heart and he not remember it" ("Laws Concerning Character Traits": ch. 7: 52). Roughly, the view is, rebuke and punish, but without malice and without enduring resentment.

5 This is an issue I explore in "The Liberal Polity, Criminal Sanction, and Civil Society," in *Criminal Justice Ethics*, Vol. 32, No. 3, December 2013: 231–46. Also see my "From Bad to Worse: Crime, Incarceration, and the Self-Wounding of Society," in *Justice and Penal Reform*, S. Farrall, B. Goldson, I. Loader, A Dockley, (Eds.) Abingdon: Routledge, 2016.

6 I discuss some influential medieval conceptions of forgiveness in "Forgiveness and Perfection: Maimonides, Aquinas, and Medieval Departures from Aristotle," in *Ancient Forgiveness: Classical, Judaic, and*

Christian, ed. Charles Griswold, David Konstan, New York, NY: Cambridge University Press, 2011, 216–36.

7 See Jean Hampton's discussion of self-forgiveness and its relation to forgiving others in Jean Hampton, and Jeffrie G. Murphy, *Forgiveness & Mercy*, New York, NY: Cambridge University Press, 1988.

8 In "The Liberal Polity, Criminal Sanction, and Civil Society" I discuss the relation of mutual reinforcement between the liberal political/legal order on the one hand and open, dynamic civil society on the other. I argue that one of the most troubling aspects of current forms and terms of incarceration is that they damage prisoners' agential capacities, rendering them much less able to return to civil society successfully. This, in conjunction with the many impediments ex-offenders face, and the stigma that follows them, causes the civility of civil society to contract, with undesirable results concerning people's commitment to the values and principles of the liberal political/legal order.

9 See, for example, Craig Haney, *Reforming Punishment: Psychological Limits to the Pains of Imprisonment*, Washington, DC: American Psychological Association, 2006. Haney's own work and the many studies undertaken by others to which he refers, show that there is abundant evidence of many types for ways in which incarceration can cause lasting damage to prisoners in terms of suffering and in terms of eroded capacities.

10 Edward Shils's conception of civil society, as articulated in his *The Virtue of Civility*, ed. Steven Grosby, Indianapolis: Liberty Fund, 1997 has influenced my view. In large part this is on account of how Shils's conception understands the relation between a liberal political order and the character of civil society. I should note, also, that thinkers such as Smith and Hume are crucial figures in the development of a recognizable modern conception of civil society under a liberal rule of law. The relations between *The Theory of Moral Sentiments* and *An Inquiry into the Nature and Causes of the Wealth of Nations* and Hume's views, expressed in the works collected in *Essays: Moral, Political, and Literary*, contain complex and powerful insights and important analysis regarding the nature of the rule of law in a liberal polity, the character of governance, and the relations between those and the civic culture of a society. Along with the works of thinkers such as Montesquieu and Locke on the institutions of government and basic principles of political rights—works that have been hugely influential—Smith's and Hume's works contribute crucial elements of the understanding of modern civil society under a liberal rule of law.

Bibliography

Aquinas, T. (1998) *Thomas Aquinas: Selected Writings*, ed. and trans. R. McInenry, London: Penguin Books.

Broadie, A. (2010) 'Aristotle, Adam Smith and the virtue of propriety', *The Journal of Scottish Philosophy*, 8(1).

Casey, J. (1991) *Pagan Virtue*, Oxford: Clarendon Press.

Duff, R.A. (1986) *Trials and Punishments*, New York, NY: Cambridge University Press.

Hampton, J. and Murphy J. (1988) *Forgiveness & Mercy*, New York, NY: Cambridge University Press.

Haney, C. (2006) *Reforming Punishment: Psychological Limits to the Pains of Imprisonment*, Washington, DC: American Psychological Association.

Jacobs, J. (2011) 'Forgiveness and perfection: Maimonides, Aquinas, and medieval departures from Aristotle', in C. Griswold and D. Konstan (eds.) *Ancient Forgiveness*, New York, NY: Cambridge University Press.

Jacobs, J. (2013) 'The liberal polity, criminal sanction, and civil society', *Criminal Justice Ethics*, 32(3): 231–46.

Jacobs, J. (2016) 'From bad to worse: crime incarceration, and the self-wounding of society', forthcoming in A. Dockley, S. Farrall, B. Goodson and I. Loader (eds.) *Justice and Penal Reform: Re-shaping the Penal Landscape*, New York, NY: Routledge.

Maimonides, M. (1983) 'Laws concerning character traits', in C. Butterworth and R.L. Weiss (eds.) *Ethical Writings of Maimonides*, New York, NY: Dover Publications, Inc.

Moore, M. (2010) *Placing Blame: A Theory of Criminal Law*, Oxford: Oxford University Press.

Murphy, J.G. (2016) 'Last words on retribution', this volume.

Nietzsche, F. (1989a) *Beyond Good and Evil: Prelude to a Philosophy of the Future*, trans. W. Kaufmann, New York, NY: Vintage.

Reid, T. (2010) *Essays on the Active Powers of the Mind*, Edinburgh: University of Edinburgh Press.

Shils, E. (1997) *The Virtue of Civility*, ed. S. Grosby, Indianapolis, IN: Liberty Fund.

Smith, A. (1982) *The Theory of Moral Sentiments*, ed. D.D. Raphael and A.L. MacFie, Indianapolis, IN: Liberty Fund.

Taylor, G. (2006) *Deadly Vices*, New York, NY: Oxford University Press.

5

Eco-justice and the moral fissures of green criminology

Rob White

Introduction

To satisfy our primary needs, humans transform environments and utilise plants and animals in particular ways. In doing so there are necessarily consequences (negative and/or positive) for the individual areas, specimens, or creatures directly affected as well as potential impacts affecting particular species generally and wider eco-systems up to and including the Earth as a whole. Interacting in-and-with Nature means that humans have been and always will be implicated in the ongoing modification of Nature itself. That is, complex relationships and interdependencies – between Nature and Humans – continually reshape the terrain upon which and within which they emerge and exist. This is a simple but basic ecological proposition.

However, in transforming Nature, humans inevitably (it seems) do harm to others, both human and non-human. This is what brings ecology into the realm of criminology and in particular under the sustained scrutiny of 'green criminology' (White and Heckenberg 2014; South and Brisman 2013). Indeed, to whom or what we do harm, and under what conditions, are key moral questions that are fundamental to understanding emergent differences within green criminology, a rapidly growing area of criminological concern. Specifically, there are tensions between those who view the natural objects of the world as 'resources' for human use and exploitation and those who attribute certain intrinsic rights to specific eco-systems and animal species that preclude a simple or straightforward anthropocentric instrumentalism.

Matters pertaining to the conservation and protection of specific eco-systems, animals, and plants can be approached in a number of ways, including through diverse applications of instrumentalism and utility (for instance, future benefit depends upon careful management of resources now, benefit for the many depends upon marshalling of resources in an effective and equitable manner). Whatever the specific rationale, the law does allow for a modicum of protection for the non-human as well as the human as seen in legislation pertaining to endangered species (e.g., particular animals such as tigers) and to conservation more generally (e.g., in the form of national parks). Harm is central to these forms of social regulation; however, whether 'harm to the environment' is of consequence *unless* it is measured with reference to human values (e.g., economic, aesthetic, cultural) is of ongoing concern in regards to legal decision-making (see Lin 2006).

However, the argument herein is that environmental issues also need to be formulated in terms of justice and, as elaborated below, eco-justice specifically. For example, there is an argument that the inherent interests of 'natural objects' ought to be protected through legal actions by the objects themselves, with humans serving as their guardians or trustees (Stone 1972; Lin 2006). Similar arguments are put forward in relation to rights for non-human animals (Regan 2010). Justice is a complex concept with many different dimensions, some of which are explored in this chapter. Nonetheless, at its core is the notion of rights and in particular the rights to 'be' and to 'do'. A central contention of eco-justice is that such rights, in some form, ought to be attributed to (or in some interpretations, conferred upon) natural objects such as rivers and mountains and animals at both species-level and as individual creatures. According to Earth Law proponents and species justice advocates, these are precisely what lay at the heart of what constitutes 'justice' as this applies to the environment and its inhabitants (Cullinan 2003; Sollund 2012).

Specialist environment courts are likewise attempting to come to grips with how best to conceptualise and operationalise 'justice' in their responses to environmental crime (albeit starting within the framework of statutory provisions) (Walters and Westerhuis 2013; Westerhuis 2013; White 2013a). In doing so, they are concretising the seriousness of environmental harm by reference to specific ecological factors, which increasingly provide the substance of court deliberations (for example, through consideration of factors such as total area of land illegally cleared, the type of species impacted and whether or not they are vulnerable, and the number of plants and animals destroyed). They are also implicitly and explicitly (particularly through extra-judicial commentary) confronting more abstract problems that relate to, for example, victimisation (that is, how to be inclusive of non-human interests), ontology (determining the boundaries of the 'natural object'), expertise (who speaks for and on behalf of what or whom), and temporality (concepts of change, especially as this relates to remediation) (see White 2016). Justice as a form of judicial practice demands consideration of specific offences as set out in legislation, including examination of the rights of non-human victims (initially specified in the form of, for example, protected species laws and laws against illegal land clearance) in particular bounded circumstances. Determining the seriousness of environmental harm requires the court to delve into detailed classification schemes (to name is to know) and to draw upon various kinds of expertise (such as ecology, geomorphology, and Indigenous knowledge) in order to evaluate the nature and dynamics of harm in any given situation.

This chapter begins therefore by sketching the broad contours of eco-justice, an approach to justice that incorporates the human and non-human into consideration of ethical questions. The discussions to follow are largely based upon a longer work that explores these questions in greater depth and from a slightly different angle (White 2013b). Eco-justice acknowledges transgressions against humans (environmental justice), specific eco-systems (ecological justice), and animal and plant species (species justice) as the general domain of green criminology. However, this chapter asks the question 'whose justice' ought to prevail in situations where the needs, interests, and rights of the human, the environment, and the animal (and plant) come into conflict? This complex issue is discussed through consideration of the moral and pragmatic basis for the doing of justice, as informed by the overarching eco-justice perspective.

An eco-justice perspective

An eco-justice perspective refers to the broad orientation of green criminology directed at exposing different instances of substantive social and environmental injustice. From an eco-justice perspective, environmental harm is best framed in terms of justice, which in turn is based upon notions of human, ecological, and animal rights. A key issue is the weighing up of different kinds of harm and violation of rights, that involves stretching the boundaries of conventional criminology to include other kinds of harm than those already deemed to be illegal. Importantly, an essential aspect of green criminology is the prescription that the moral community ought to be extended to include non-human nature. By doing so, it is argued that this involves a new politics of obligation:

> In ecological thought, human beings have obligations to animals, trees, mountains, oceans and other members of the biotic community. This means that human beings have to exercise extreme caution before embarking upon any project which is likely to have the possibility of adverse effects upon the ecosystems concerned.
>
> (Smith 1998: 99)

This particular notion of moral community emphasises human obligations to all living things (and, indeed, to the non-living such as rivers) and the need to carefully assess the impacts of human activity across the human and non-human domains. It also incorporates notions of risk and taking precautions in order to minimise potential harm. However, such considerations are not without their challenges. The conceptualisation of 'rights', for example, is contentious when extended to the non-human, whether this refers to specific eco-systems or particular animals (Christoff 2000).

Within green criminology there are three broad approaches to justice, each with their own specific conceptions of rights and harm (see White 2008, 2013b). These include:

- *Environmental justice and human rights* – in which environmental rights are seen as an extension of human or social rights so as to enhance the quality of human life, now and into the future.
- *Ecological justice and ecological citizenship* – in which it is acknowledged that humans are merely one component of complex ecosystems that should be preserved for their own sake via the notion of the rights of the environment.
- *Species justice and animal rights* – in which environmental harm is constructed in relation to the place of non-human animals within environments and their intrinsic right to not suffer abuse, whether this be one-on-one harm, institutionalised harm, or harm arising from human actions that affect climates and environments on a global scale.

The first approach tends to put the emphasis on specific oppressed or exploited groups and frequently refers to allied concepts such as environmental racism and environmental inequality (see Bullard 2005; Agyeman and Carmin 2011). The quest for environmental equity alludes to attempts to reduce hazards, risks, and harms for all sections of the population and to ensure proportionate enjoyment of 'clean and green' environmental amenity. The second tends to prioritise places over people, and is focussed on issues of preservation and conservation. The third is concerned with animals rather than with humans or specific environments, with particular interest in animal welfare and animal rights. For many green criminologists the greatest threat to environmental rights, ecological justice, and non-human animal wellbeing are system-level structures and pressures that commodify all aspects of social existence, that are based upon the exploitation of humans, non-human animals, and natural resources and that privilege the powerful over the interests of the vast majority. Yet, while this proposition may be accepted at a highly abstract level by many green criminologists, at a grounded level of immediate policy and practice a series of ethical fault lines have appeared.

Conflicting views and moral dilemmas

For example, there are significant tensions between and within the three key justice-based approaches to the study of environmental harm. One such tension was signalled by Piers Beirne in the following observation:

> The [green environmentalists] rarely champion the sites of their concerns with rights talk, whereas for [animal rights advocates] their very focus is the criterion for moral standing and holding of rights. This crucial deep-seated difference is already present in green criminology in environmentalist notions such as 'fisheries' and 'harvests' and 'conservation', all of which are the stuff and fodder of animal welfare and sustainability but mostly anathema to animal rights.
>
> (Beirne 2011: 354)

To put it differently, some green criminologists view nature instrumentally, and harm is viewed through the lens of legality; others view the exploitation of nature, particularly in relation to animals, as intrinsically bad and harmful. How this 'moral fissure' is to be understood and whether or not it can be overcome is of major interest to the present chapter.

To position the debates and arguments to follow, it is useful to initially differentiate among three broad interpretations of the Nature-Human relationship. Although the philosophies employed to explicate the nature of the relation between the 'social' and the 'natural' worlds are numerous (see for example, Lane 1998; Halsey 2004), a useful analytical distinction can be made among anthropocentric (human-centred), biocentric (species-centred) and ecocentric (socio-ecological centred) perspectives (see Halsey and White 1998). The anthropocentric perspective emphasises the biological, mental, and moral superiority of *humans* over other living and non-living entities. Biocentrism views human beings as simply 'another species' to be attributed the *same* moral worth as such organisms as, for example, whales, wolves, and birds. Ecocentrism refuses to place humanity either above or below the rest of nature. However, the unique capacity of human beings to develop and deploy methods of production which have global consequences means that humans also have an explicit responsibility to ensure that such production methods do not exceed the ecospheric limits of the planet (White 2007). Moreover, this responsibility extends to human *and* non-human life.

Translated into a criminological framework, such philosophical considerations mean that environmental harm can be distinguished, variably depending upon perspective, on the basis of *who or what precisely is being harmed or victimised*. In part, the answer to this depends upon the (differential) valuing of the human and the non-human, as different perspectives will value the 'victim' in quite different ways. Extending 'value' to the non-human inevitably raises issues of 'rights' and 'justice' as these pertain to eco-systems, plants, and non-human animals. For example, in a discussion of the subject status of a natural object, such as a river or tree, Stone (1972) argues that some authoritative body needs to review the actions and processes of those who threaten it, but to make this count (i.e., to have its worth and dignity legally recognised in its own right), it is necessary:

- that the natural object can institute legal actions *at its behest*
- that in determining the granting of legal relief, the court must take *injury to it* into account
- that relief must run to the *benefit* of it. (Stone 1972)

In a similar vein, Cullinan (2003) points out that 'a fundamental river right (i.e., the riverine equivalent of a human right) would be the right to flow. If a water body couldn't flow it wouldn't be a river, and so the capacity to flow (given sufficient water) is essential to the existence of a river'. Therefore, 'from the perspective of the river, building so many dams across it and extracting so much water from it that it ceased to flow into the sea, would be an abuse of its Earth rights' (Cullinan 2003: 118).

A number of immediate questions arise, however. For example, trees and rocks and streams are not sentient beings capable of suffering, so where do they fit into the animal rights or environmental justice moral universe? Or, where do we draw the line when it comes to which animals should be conceptualised as having rights, and if there is a conflict between animal rights and the rights of humans? Very often, of course, conceptualisation and direct experience of environmental harm encapsulates the concerns of all three strands – protection of biodiversity within our forests is compatible with sustaining localised environments, protecting endangered species, and ensuring human happiness. Conversely, the clearfelling of old-growth forests can be highly problematic from the point of view of human enjoyment, nurturing of non-human animals, and conservation of complex eco-systems.

Schlosberg (2007) identifies the key categories or dimensions of environmental justice as including distribution, recognition, participation, and capability. The notion of justice as fairness is associated with questions of *distribution*. Justice, according to this conception, defines how we distribute various rights, goods, and liberties and how we define and regulate social and economic equality and inequality. What matters are the rules of distributive justice and how these are constructed. The rules may be procedure-based, such as providing equal opportunities for everyone to attain valued goods. Or they may be oriented towards consequentialist and substantive conceptions of justice that ensure equal outcomes. Differences of opinion occur over the principles governing those proposed distributions (e.g., need, desert, entitlement). Such principles are relevant to both human and non-human, particularly in the context of extending the notion of rights to environments and particular animals.

Recognition refers to the equal dignity accorded to all, as well as the politics of difference where everyone is recognised for his or her particular distinctiveness. It is observed that 'A lack of recognition in the social and political realms demonstrated by various forms of insults, degradation and devaluation at both the individual and cultural level inflicts damage to oppressed individuals and communities in the political and cultural realms' (Schlosberg 2007: 14). Derogatory language used in relation to animals provides one illustration of subordinated and disrespected identity as this applies to the non-human (see Beirne 2009). Here it is argued that contemporary practices of cultural domination are such that the rights, interests, and needs of eco-systems and animals are rendered invisible in ordinary life, and accordingly fewer legal, social, and economic resources are put into acknowledging, supporting, and respecting the non-human.

The need for *participation* is also defined as an important component of justice. Participation generally refers to a person's membership and engagement in the greater community, and is supported by the institutionalisation of democratic and participatory decision-making procedures. As applied to the non-human world, participation involves human advocacy, where the voice of animals or trees or eco-systems is 'heard' via the human third party. Humans speak 'on behalf of' that and those which cannot participate directly in human affairs that affect them.

Capability is important to justice as well. This refers to the ability to achieve valuable functionings within the context of one's essential character and setting. For humans, capabilities are about a person's opportunities to do and to be what he or she chooses in the context of a given society. Wellbeing is about 'doing' (activities) and 'being' (states of existence). Enhancing capability means concentrating on the opportunity to be able to have combinations of functionings and for the person to be free to make use of this opportunity or not (Schlosberg 2007). Translated into an eco-justice context, capability means that each thing should be able to flourish as the thing it is. What this means in practice is difficult to determine, however, since Nature by definition is complex, uncertain, interconnected, and ever changing. Capabilities (as possibilities) are therefore changing, open-ended, dynamic, and subject to ongoing deliberation.

Justice is not only concerned with 'what is/what ought to be', but 'what could be'. In other words, as described above, it encapsulates, as well, the idea of potentials – potentials that in many cases are stifled, prevented, or diminished by systemic pressures and limits of the society as a whole. Harm and injustice co-exist within the context of injurious social relationships that perpetuate wrongness.

Assigning worth

Yet, how 'rights' and 'harm' are conceived very much depends upon the yardstick by which worth is determined. To assess the severity of harm requires criteria linked to value, scale, and measure (White 2013b). A clear divide exists between instrumental value (e.g., harm measured in terms of human interests mediated by what happens to the environment, animals, and plants) and intrinsic value (harm measured according to criteria which says that certain things done to the environment and to animals and plants are inherently bad, from the point of view of environments, animals, and plants).

Moreover, assessment of 'worth' is partly dependent upon the scale at which evaluation occurs. The notion of scale is illustrated below:

Individuals	*Particular Species*	*Biotic Community and Abiotic Context*
e.g., person	e.g., homo sapiens	e.g., Arctic eco-systems
e.g., plant	e.g., hemp	e.g., grasslands eco-systems
e.g., animal	e.g., apes	e.g., mountain eco-systems

From the point of view of analysis and intervention, should the focus be on individual species or entire eco-systems? Should value also be applied to individual organisms, and if so, should this apply to every single plant and animal? Eco-systems incorporate the biotic (plants, animals) and the abiotic (water, soil) that, arguably, have value in their own right as self-maintaining and self-perpetuating systems. How does one determine the relative value of individual organisms, particular species and overarching biotic communities relative to each other?

To illustrate the practical or applied issues associated with scale, consider the following. As Cazaux (1999) has observed, consideration of human practices that are detrimental to the well-being of animals, such as loss and fragmentation of habitat, tend to focus on the effects regarding *animal populations* of a certain species (matters pertaining to the threat of extinction). Less attention is paid to the consequences of broad trends to the wellbeing of animals as *individual subjects*. The logic of species protection, over and above respect for the individual animal, means that in some instance animals are killed for no apparent reason or justification. In Norway, for example, efforts to protect the endangered species of polar fox, has nonetheless been accompanied by the killing of individual creatures which were guilty of the 'crime' of not fitting into the existing breeding programme (see Sollund 2012). Their deaths served no apparent purpose, but their value (or lack thereof) was reflected in the actions taken to put them down. Respect and acknowledgement of the right of these individual creatures to live is confounded by the human emphasis on collective survival.

A recent court case in New South Wales, Australia, provides another example of an approach to considering the impact of the environmental harm (in this case illegal land clearing) at several different levels. Where one draws the line in terms of scale is highly relevant not only to determining and assessing harm, but also to the possibilities of remediation. Assessment of environmental harm at the *local scale* indicated that the conservation value of the native vegetation was high and the clearing may have caused significant impacts on vegetation and fauna at this scale. Yet at the *landscape scale* the conservation value of native vegetation was considered low and its clearing unlikely to have caused significant impacts on the vegetation, fauna habitats, or habitat connectivity. This was because, at this larger scale, the vegetation communities on the land consist of three vegetation communities that are well represented in the region including within conservation reserves, and the clearing of the vegetation had impacted small areas of the vegetation communities that are well represented at a landscape level (see *Director-General, Department of Environment Climate Change* and *Water v Vin Heffernan Pty Ltd [2010] NSWLEC 200*).

Harms to specific eco-systems threaten all within them, human and non-human alike. Melting glaciers have implications for future flows of fresh water and thus affect many different biotic communities in diverse territories and climates. Interconnection and overlapping interests are as important to consider as discrete needs, rights, and concepts of justice. The value of human, eco-system and non-human species is reflected in how and why we measure harm. The 'why' of measuring harm may be informed by both intrinsic and instrumental criteria – a farmer's crops being contaminated by GMO products may combine elements of both considerations. The 'how' of measurement refers to efforts to put a value – monetary, ecological, aesthetic, cultural – on the harm. This involves attempts to make the harm visible and assess the magnitude of the harm (e.g., as minor, major, or catastrophic and in relation to what or whom). This can take the form of 'harm audits' (see Pemberton 2015). Key questions here are who is doing the valuing and what tools are utilised to assign value.

Weighing up the harm

There are concrete links among the health of natural environments, diverse human activity, and the exploitation of animals. Increasingly the language of rights is being used to frame responses to harm and abuse across the three areas of concern. As indicated above, this can sometimes lead to conflicts over which rights ought to take precedence in any given situation – human rights, rights of the environment, or animal rights (White 2007, 2013b). This necessitates moving beyond initial considerations of how to *define* harm ('what is harmful'?) to consider how we might best *debate* harm ('what is harmful relative to other harms'?). Defining harm is ultimately about philosophical frameworks as informed by scientific evidence, ethics, and traditional knowledge; debating harm is about processes of deliberation in the 'real world' and of conflicts over rights and the making of difficult decisions.

Overlapping and competing interests, in the context of 'real world' decision-making, alerts us to the need for a model of action that will enhance deliberations in cases where interests seem at cross-purposes. To put it differently, there is a need for a model that is 'open-ended', one that does not assume that we know the right or correct answers in advance. This recognises that in any discussion of harm (particularly within an eco-justice framework), there are always going to be conflicting interests and conflicting rights. These are exacerbated as conflicting conceptualisations of harm develop and positions become more clearly defined – as in the case of Beirne's (2011) sense of a moral fissure within green criminology.

It is not only different rights-claims that are contested (for example, between human rights and animal rights), generally over which ought to take priority in any given situation (Francione

2008). The notions of specific rights are themselves subject to contestation. For example, rivers are now being conceptualised as possessing rights in at least two different ways: firstly, in relation to stewardship populations, such as Indigenous people, in which there is a presumed unity of the river with the Indigenous population. In New Zealand, for instance, the Maori relationship with Nature has been expressed as follows:

> Indigenous peoples throughout the world have strong connections to the flowing freshwater of rivers. For instance, Maori – the Indigenous peoples of Aotearoa New Zealand – view many rivers as tupuna (ancestors) and invoke the name of a river to assert their identity. There is a deep belief that humans and water are intertwined as is encapsulated in common tribal sayings such as 'I am the river and the river is me' and 'the river belongs to us just as we belong to the river'.
>
> (Morris and Ruru 2010: 49)

In 2012, the Whanganui River was granted its own legal identity as part of an agreement between the government and the local Maori community (Shuttleworth 2012; Findlayson 2012).

Secondly, rivers may have rights conferred upon them via specific and targeted legislation that states that *this* river has protected status and certain rights by virtue of the legislation. For example, in Queensland, Australia the purpose of the *Wild Rivers Act 2005 (Qld)* was to (a) preserve the natural values of rivers that have all, or almost all, of their natural values intact and (b) provide for the preservation of the natural values of rivers in the Lake Eyre Basin. It was repealed in November 2014. *Wild Rivers* was supported by the Labor Party, scientists, and environmentalist groups such as the Wilderness Society but heavily contested by some local Indigenous leaders and communities who argued that it deprived Indigenous people of economic opportunities. As prominent Indigenous leader Noel Pearson (2014) stated: 'Traditional owners should decide whether they want conservation or a mixture of both. We don't want this unilaterally imposed on them by political deals in Brisbane' (see Fraser 2014; Rebgetz, Arthur, and Agius 2014).

There are then different types and points of contestation regarding justice and rights as these pertain to the environment, animals, and plants. As discussed elsewhere (White 2008), from a green criminology perspective the key questions are: how do we engender a system of regulation and human intervention that will provide the best outcome for human and non-human, and what criteria do we use to conceptualise the nature and value of harm arising from human actions? To answer these questions, we need to understand why it is that human societies simultaneously respect and protect certain creatures (especially animal companions such as dogs and cats) while allowing and even condoning the utterly dreadful treatment of others (as in the case of factory farming of battery hens to produce eggs) (see Beirne 2004, 2009). We need to understand why it is that we strive to preserve some environments (via creation of national parks), while at the same time devastating particular ecosystems (such as clearfelling of old-growth forests).

Responding to these issues demands some type of criteria to weigh up the interests, options, and consequences of particular courses of action. At a minimum it requires attention being given to the specific interests, harms, and rights involved. Put simply, there is a need to provide the basis upon which to privilege some interests over others, in given circumstances and situations (i.e., rather than all species being treated the same or as having in essence the same rights or worth). It may well be that there is no general, fixed criterion or method for ascertaining moral priority. But the necessity for judgement means that decision-making is best served by an awareness of why certain rights are contested, the competing interests that underpin such processes, and the paradoxes and unintended consequences of any choices that are made. A metaphorical balancing up of moral weight is always going to be complex and far reaching.

Dilemmas and choices

There are profound ethical and practical limitations on approaches that reinforce rigid definitions and absolutist positions, such as pronouncements that the Earth is more important than humans or animals, or that any harm to animals is bad. This kind of moral posturing tends to do two things. Firstly, it locks people into protagonist positions by declaring that there is no alternative to the position taken. Everything is 'black or white'. There is thus no shading or uncertainty when it comes to dealing with real-life situations requiring difficult and practical moral choices. Yet, in the end, someone or something will suffer the negative consequences of such sureties.

Secondly, taking such absolutist positions diminishes the centrality of humans – including precisely those of us writing about and advocating on behalf of these issues – in the greater scheme of things. Humans can be conceived as both destroyer and protector of all that we value and cherish. We are also the originators of the moral and ethical systems by which we judge ourselves and our behaviour. We are also the main actors in acting upon what we believe is right and good. The goat, the rose, and the river do not exercise this kind of volition, this sort of agency. This is what makes humans the most important participant in shaping the world.

Human interests in ecological context

From an environmental justice perspective, the point of human intervention is to protect and preserve particular environments and/or species for the 'greater good' of *humans*. But, should environmental rights be seen as an extension of human or social rights (e.g., related to the quality of human life, such as provision of clean water), or should human rights be seen as merely one component of complex eco-systems that should be preserved for their own sake (i.e., as in the notion of the rights of the environment) (see Thornton and Tromans 1999; Christoff 2000)? A narrow conceptualisation of environmental justice focuses predominantly on human welfare and interests. This translates into propositions such as, for instance, that present generations ought to act in ways that do not jeopardise the existence and quality of life of future generations.

Within this framework, environmental issues are thus examined in terms of effects on human populations, including the ramifications of certain practices on competing industries (e.g., negative impact of clearfell logging on tourism). The use of pesticides, to take another example, may have dramatic impacts on animal species (in that they seem to have coincided with the spread of a fatal tumour disease amongst the Tasmanian devil population in recent years) and on specific environments (the pollution of coastal waters in north eastern Tasmania). But the damage is often framed in terms of human loss (of a Tasmanian tourism icon; of the destruction of oyster farms), rather than biosphere or non-human animals per se. Not surprisingly, then, environmental justice movements are largely focussed on redressing the unequal distribution of environmental disadvantage and in particular on preventing environmental hazards being located in their local area.

The notion of *ecological justice* refers to the relationship of humans generally to the rest of the natural world and includes concerns relating to the health of the biosphere and also the plants and creatures that inhabit the biosphere. The main concern is with the quality of the planetary environment (that is frequently seen to possess its own intrinsic value) and the rights of other species (particularly animals) to live free from torture, abuse, and destruction of habitat. Analysis in this instance is directed at environmental harm that is directly linked to specific eco-systems.

Key questions that arise include which environments are destroyed and why, and which are not? There is, for instance, both selective destruction of eco-systems and biospheres (for example, the clearfelling of forests) and selective protection of such (for example, preservation of national parks and marine sanctuaries). Which eco-systems and biospheres are privileged or valued above others is an important consideration in critical evaluation of environmental harm as this pertains to ecological justice.

The notion of *sustainable development* reflects the human-centred idea that instrumental use of nature needs to be carried out in ways that ensure future exploitation as well as present entitlements. This can be contrasted with *ecological sustainability* that refers to eco-system needs rather than human needs. In the former, the strategic choices revolve around how best to manage natural resources in ways that help to alleviate outcomes such as loss of biodiversity, pollution of air and water, and land degradation because otherwise the whole system will be put into jeopardy. In the latter, the emphasis is on intrinsic values and protection of non-human nature for its own sake. This is sometimes expressed in the language of 'preservation', which implies a severing of human contact and un-interfered-with natural status quo, but more usually it alludes to conservation values which encapsulate the notion of continuous Nature-Human interaction that nonetheless maintains the basic ecological integrity of a region. Both the concept of sustainable development and ecological sustainability may be utilised in contemporary discussions of ecological wellbeing and health.

Specific practices and choices in how humans interact with particular environments present immediate and potential risks to everything within them. For example, the practice of clearfelling old growth forests directly affects many animal species by destroying their homes. Similarly, local natural environments, and non-human inhabitants of both so-called wilderness and built environments, are negatively impacted upon by human practices that destroy, re-channel, or pollute existing fresh water systems. If we pollute our rivers, streams, and waterways, we are not simply affecting human beings but also living creatures, such as the platypus. When we destroy the habitat of the platypus, we simultaneously destroy the biosphere.

Translated into the language of rights, it has been argued by Berry (in Cullinan 2003: 115) that every component of the Earth Community has three rights: 'The right to be, the right to habitat, and the right to fulfil its role in the ever-renewing processes of the Earth Community'. What this actually means in practice is difficult to determine, however, since any decision about a particular environmental issue very much depends upon situational factors, community norms and values, and available technologies and techniques. Even given the ambiguities of practice, however, what necessarily follows from an ecological perspective are notions of interconnectedness and human obligations to the non-human world around them. Eco-justice demands that how humans interact with their environment be evaluated in relation to potential harms and risks to specific creatures and specific locales as well as the biosphere generally. From this perspective, clearfelling of old growth forests, accompanied by the laying of poison baits to kill animals and the burning of remnants, is inherently wrong and deviant. But this is, of course, the 'easy' example.

By contrast are the 'hard' cases. Taking action on environmental issues always involves choices and priorities. Many communities who suffer from the 'hard end' of environmental harm feel that their wellbeing ought to take priority over particular natural environments or specific plants and animals as such (see Harvey 1996). For example, the reverence for and privileging of non-human nature sometimes translates into a concern for the 'righteous management' of nature and manifests in an agenda that advocates for the mass preservation of wilderness, protection of endangered non-human species, and restoration of disturbed areas towards a *pristine nature* or pristine condition (Devall and Sessions 1985). A key problem with this is that it implies a separation of humanity and nature as if this was and always has been, empirically, the case. The notion of 'pristine nature' implies precisely this kind of rigid separation, yet historical and cross-cultural study indicates exactly the opposite – namely, constant and continuous living in nature by humans (Plumwood 2004; Merchant 2005; Tsing 2005), including within the most inhospitable environments possible from a human perspective (Robin 2002).

Yet, some efforts to establish forest reserves or marine parks are based upon total exclusion of humans from these areas under any condition. This is based upon ideas that humans do not have an ethical right to alter the 'natural' integrity of forests or ocean spaces, or that they cannot be trusted to do the right thing when entering and experiencing such places. For traditional users especially, exclusionary policies ignore historical realities and are puzzling from the point of view of Earth care principles that often inform these historical relationships. On a global scale, such portrayals simultaneously reflect specifically Western notions of conservation, and frequently ignore a specifically colonial context within which such appropriation occurs (see Duffy 2010, 2014). For example, some interpretations of 'biodiversity' assume this means no people – thus biodiversity as an objective provides 'a rationale for the creation and maintenance of areas where wildlife is protected, but people are forced out' (Duffy 2010: 53). Translated into practice, this results in the creation of manufactured national parks which, among other things, are people-free wildernesses precisely made by the eviction of previous human occupiers who are then subjected to extreme violence to enforce this particular kind of order (Duffy 2014).

In such instances, issues of wilderness, wildlife and natural preservation are privileged over and above the interests and needs of humans, and especially those who are not members of elite groupings (see Brisman 2009; Duffy 2010; Rivers III and Gibbs 2011). Those who can afford to be ecologically virtuous or to push for causes that are oriented toward protecting and conserving 'nature' are portrayed as 'good' – those who express different interests or who cannot afford to take the most preferable ecological action are seen as part of the problem. In other words, conservation without acknowledgement of traditional human users, and their systemic contribution to biological diversity and ecological wellbeing, is oppressive and counter-productive.

Animal rights, human need and biological diversity

On another ethical front, the matter of animal rights and animal welfare is encapsulated in that work concerned with *species justice* (Benton 1998, Beirne 2007). This refers to the practice of discriminating against non-human animals because they are perceived as inferior to the human species in much the same way that sexism and racism involve prejudice and discrimination against women and people of different colour (Munro 2004). Animal rights supporters argue that there are two kinds of animals – human and non-human – and that both have rights and interests as sentient beings; they believe, however, that the dominant ideology of speciesism enables humans to exploit non-human animals as commodities to be eaten, displayed, hunted and dissected for human benefit.

Moral equivalence between species, however, can go against real, immediate needs of human communities. From an animal rights perspective the eating of the flesh of animals is problematic and is seen to constitute major social harm. In practical terms, though, what do we say to people who traditionally eat fish, for example, as their main source of protein? How realistic is veganism in regional environments such as Arctic tundra and Australian desert within which humans have survived for millennia by eating a wide range of protein sources including animals? One of the critiques of both conservation and animal rights movements is that they can privilege 'the need to save wildlife over the rights of people who live with it' (Duffy 2010: 82).

The tensions within eco-justice reflect a central debate within environmental philosophy 'between positions extending ethical concern only to (some) animals and positions emphasising ethical concern for ecological systems and all living things' (Plumwood 2004: 51). The latter position asserts that we must recognise the full diversity of people's lives in diverse cultures where the meaning of eating and using animals is variable. As Benton (1993) observes, humans are socially interdependent with animals and also ecologically interdependent. There is a material co-dependency of humans, animals, and environments which is grounded in time, place, and cultural space. Fundamentally, human cultural practices and the dynamics of natural environments are historically moulded in and by, and are part of, local ecologies. Rather than viewing humans as somehow 'outside nature', this particular perspective affirms an ecological universe of mutual use between humans and animals which necessarily varies in different ecological contexts and in which different cultures and individuals will have differing nutritional situations and needs (Plumwood 2004). In other words, there are contexts within which hunting (and fishing) should not be condemned since it is part and parcel of how humans 'live in nature' and are constituent parts of natural ecosystems.

This is particularly salient in regards to Indigenous people and their patterns of hunting and gathering food. Historically and for many people still today, the ways in which Indigenous people live in nature is informed by a particular value system and code of ethics. These are based on tenets of reciprocity and cyclical thinking that define responsibilities and ways of relating between humans and the world around them (e.g., by ensuring methods of harvesting resources that will not deplete supplies needed for survival). The notion that 'you take only what you need and leave the rest' is central to this. So, too, is the concept of 'reciprocity' that defines the relationship and responsibility between people and the environment (all parts – plants, animals, fish, rocks): 'This precarious balance still exists, and the relationship between plants, animals, the elements, the air, water, wind and earth are all equally and evenly placed within the whole' (Robyn 2002: 202). Integration of the ecological and the cultural, of nature and society, finds expression in all facets of life.

The specific relationship that humans have with nature requires a sense of complex relationships and that things do indeed change over time. Conventional animal rights proponents and mainstream conservationists have tended to place emphasis on only one part of the relationship between the human and the non-human. This is well captured in the following passage (Plumwood 2004: 56):

> Although each project has a kind of egalitarianism between the human and non-human in mind, their partial analyses place them on a collision course. The ecology movement has been situating humans as animals, embodied inside ecological systems of mutual use, of food and energy exchange, just as the animal defence movement has been trying to expand an extension to animals of the (dualistic) human privilege of being conceived as outside these systems. Many vegans seem to believe that ecology can be ignored and that the food web is an invention of hamburger companies, while the ecological side often retains the human-centred resource view of animals and scientistic resistance to seeing animals as individuals with life stories of attachment, struggle and tragedy not unlike our own, refusing to apply ethical thinking to the non-human sphere.

Animals eat animals; humans eat animals. The ethical issue is under what conditions and according to what justifications ought this to occur. The answer, according to Plumwood (2004), is to resituate humans in ecological terms, while simultaneously situating non-humans in ethical terms. But this must be done according to the specific context of both nature and culture. Similar conclusions are apparent in other discussions of these issues as well.

Ecological inclusion, for example, refers to the idea of establishing the foundations for a new interrelationship between humans and animals that is more respectful and caring on the part of humans from within the perspective of the ecological totality. Conflicts of interest – among environments, humans, and animals – ought to be evaluated not only from the point of view of moral criteria (such as animal rights or animal welfare), but also ecological criteria and by considering the total environment. The perspective is inherently contextual.

> The practical application of the concept of ecological inclusion will always be dependent upon place, time, and context and, therefore, solutions will vary. For example, killing domesticated animals that have escaped and established themselves in ecologically destructive nonendemic wild populations should only occur if it can be justified scientifically, culturally, ethnically, and morally. That justification is dependent on the protection of, for example, an endangered species in an area where that species has little chance of survival, and only upon ensuring that the non-human animals killed would not suffer in any way. Taking the life of any individual is in reality a denial of their intrinsic value, and denying such value in any individual should not be taken lightly.
>
> (Bennison 2010: 194–95)

Underpinning this concept is the idea that the entire planetary ecology must form part of the understanding we have of the relationship between humans and nature; that we are all a community of interdependent parts. Ecological inclusion implies respect for the entire ecological community that includes all biotic and abiotic elements. From soil to salamander, water to walrus, plant to platypus, the health and wellbeing of the individual resides in the health and wellbeing of the whole, and vice versa. All life forms have an intrinsic value, and even the non-living (i.e., rocks, waters) contribute to the greater whole. Thus, 'all individuals should have the right to have their inherent worth or intrinsic value up-held, whilst having the ability to pursue their individual ecological and evolutionary paths, as long as that does not impinge on the biological and ecological integrity of the greater whole (Bennison 2010: 197).

This is, of course, easier said than done. A big concern, from the point of view of human intervention, is what if any levels of management ought to be engaged in? Most commentators view intervention as a matter of contingency and 'doing the right thing' within specific social and ecological contexts (see Anderson 2004; an exception to this, see Francione 2008). In some cases, for example, it is argued that non-interference or hands-off management should be strictly adhered to, from the point of view of environmental ethics:

> Animals live in the wild, subject to natural selection, and the integrity of the species is a result of these selective pressures. To intervene artificially is not to produce any benefit for the good of the kind, although it may benefit an individual bison or whale.
>
> (Rolston 2010: 604)

This ethic may shift in cases where wild animals are affected by human-induced changes. It can change as well where an endangered species is involved: 'Duties to wildlife are not simply at the level of individuals; the ethic is that one ought to rescue individual animals in trouble where they are the last tokens of a type' (Rolston 2010: 605). In general though it is expected that individual animals living in the wild 'do not have a moral right to our direct protection and provision, even if they need it to survive', nor do they have a right to our assistance to protect them against animal predation (Anderson 2004: 284).

The rescue and protection of endangered species involves new types of ethical decisions and complex issues relating to individual and species harm.

> Wolves have recently been reintroduced to Yellowstone National Park, having been exterminated there early in this century. The restoration earned protests from some in the ranching community. Such restoration arises, according to most advocates, from a duty to the wolf as a species, coupled with the fact that the wolf was historically, and ought to be again, the top predator in the Yellowstone ecosystem. Conservationists also realize that problem wolves will have to be relocated, sometimes killed, and believe this is an acceptable killing of individuals in order to have the wolf species present. It removes wolves who turn to killing sheep or cattle, not their natural prey; it also protects ranchers against losses. In the recommended mix of nature and culture, if we are to have wolves, we must kill wolves
>
> (Rolston 2010: 605)

Such a view may seem to be anathema to animal rights advocates who believe in the sanctity of animal life as an absolute value rather than circumstantial privilege.

The debates over the ways in which 'feral' and 'sick' animals are approached also provide a useful summary of conflicting views pertaining to human intervention. Invasive species are seen as a threat to local species in the same way that ill animals are seen as a threat to local animal populations. More generally, from the perspective of humans, certain creatures are by their very nature hostile to human interests. As such, they demand action directed against them in order to protect ourselves. This applies to 'vermin, pests and parasites' that cannot adjust their behaviour and with which there is no possibility of communication or compromise. If left unchecked, they would create ecological havoc and harm to humans (Anderson 2004).

It is nonetheless acknowledged that 'Even vermin have some degree of moral considerability' (Anderson 2004: 289). A key debate when it comes to feral animals, therefore, is over 'what works' when it comes to methods of eradication and control. Animal welfare advocates generally express a concern about cruelty in the control regime, sparked by a sense of urgency in the light of the exemption of feral animals from the protections of animal welfare legislation and current eradication practices. They argue for 'humane' methods of numbers management in the face of methods such as use of poison bait, steel-jawed trapping, shooting from ground or helicopter, biological control with disease and exclusion fencing (McEwen 2008). As an alternative, it is argued that fertility control offers real hope as a long-term measure, a strategy that would involve a shift in emphasis from 'kill rate to birth rate' (McEwen 2008: 30).

Others argue that animals have an intrinsic right to life and as an expression of this, to reproduce (Coetzee 2008; see also Francione 2008). The implication is that we should let 'survival' be up to Nature, a principle that makes sense within specific social and ecological contexts (Anderson 2004) but not in others. This generalised stance is part of the basis for resistance to the idea of the badger cull in the United Kingdom, a strategy prompted by the transmission of illness within and from the badger population. Yet, this moral basis for inaction is countered by farmers' arguments that allowing infected animals to live is itself equally morally suspect. Enticott (2011: 206) refers to farmers rhetorically asking:

> Why should my cows be allowed to die from bTB when wild badgers are allowed to remain free? If conservationists cared about animal welfare then they would not complain about a badger cull because it would improve badger welfare.

Clearly there are many sides to each story when it comes to human decisions regarding when and how to intervene in regards to feral and sick animals. Again, this makes an absolutist position on these issues problematic at the level of complicated real-world problems and decisions. Animals have rights, but which and how these are enforced are variable depending upon natural and social contexts (Anderson 2004).

Ethical and moral dilemmas involving animals – in life and death situations – also extend to instances where individual animals of one species are sacrificed for the sake of the preservation of an entire other species, which can be either plant or animal. What is at stake here is an either/or choice, not one based upon simple human expediency, as with the case of the Norwegian polar fox.

> In a 1996 case, the U.S. Fish and Wildlife Service moved to poison 6,000 gulls at Monomoy National Wildlife Refuge off Cape Cod, in order to save 35 piping plovers, an endangered species. ... San Clemente Island, off the coast of California, has both endemic plant species and a population of feral goats, introduced by Spanish sailors two centuries ago. To protect plants numbering in the few hundreds, the Fish and Wildlife Service and the U.S. Navy have shot tens of thousands of feral goats.
>
> (Rolston 2010: 605–606)

This represents cases where the so called *ethic of species* has triumphed. The death of individual creatures has been weighed up against the potential demise of whole species. While objectionable from the point of view of killing animals, unless suitable alternatives for relocation are possible or available, there is a moral justification for such acts insofar as they allow future and more diverse life to flourish. The contemporary treatment of refugees offers a poignant human parallel to these kinds of decisions. Who suffers and who benefits is always complicated by immediate circumstance and longer term prospects.

At present and descriptively speaking, the 'value' of animals is thus largely constructed according to human interests, whether this is in regard to commercial benefit, psychological wellbeing, or safety and security. Indeed, the legitimacy of harm to animals is subject to specific contexts and circumstances. Harm is justified according to instrumentalism (e.g., food, trade, medicine, leisure), for the purposes of protection (e.g., animal attacks on humans), on the basis of national security (e.g., navy uses of sonar that have unintended harmful consequences for marine animals), and for ecological and biodiversity management purposes (e.g., invasive species, bio-security). The status of a particular animal may therefore also be subject to change. A dog that bites its master is no longer a trusted companion but a threat; a mouse that escapes the lab is now a pest to be eradicated not a tool in research; a racing horse that goes lame in the leg may be destined for the glue factory if not the stud farm. The situational use-value of an animal therefore determines its status – and frequently its individual fate.

At a pragmatic and concrete level, numerous dilemmas are posed by the unproblematic acceptance of the notion of human, ecological, and animal rights. If this is accompanied by the prescription to 'do no harm', then we have no moral compass to navigate muddied ethical waters involving human versus animal interests, animal versus animal interests, and animal versus plant interests. Who decides what, and on what basis, remain crucial considerations.

The study of environmental harm, including issues such as toxic discrimination involving humans, destruction of forests, and animal cruelty, is greatly influenced by the perspective one applies to the natural world generally and influences which issues ought to receive specific priority. This does not preclude collaboration and interaction with fellow travellers across the movement and theoretical divides (Beirne 2007), but the gulfs between those writing about environmental, ecological, and species justice can nonetheless be profound and troubling (Beirne 2011; Pellow 2013). Part of the problem is due to that fact that some analysis is pitched at too high a level of abstraction, which only reinforces rigid definitions and absolutist positions (e.g., humans come first; the earth is most important; any harm to animals is bad). This can preclude closely considered analysis of specific situations. For example, an absolutist approach may contend that humans should not, in any way, interfere with animals. This approach may be appropriate when dealing with a situation involving dingoes and kangaroos in the wilds of the Northern Territory in Australia but inappropriate when dealing with wandering polar bears in Churchill, Manitoba. The more specific and situational the problem, the more likely a reasonable solution and/or compromise can be worked out.

The working through of issues, however, is only 'successful' to the degree that participants are willing to talk with each other, appreciate alternative or opposing viewpoints, and listen to what is actually being said. This endeavour is frustrated by drawing hard lines in advance, thus prejudicing potential outcomes. Ideological rigidity (or moral steadfastness, depending on one's outlook) can create barriers within and across movements. Moreover, the emotive nature of the protection of human rights, eco-systems, and animals can serve to further entrench positions – love of one's neighbour, a tree, a dog can be a powerful motivator. It can also sway opinion on the basis of affective factors rather than science or rationality.

Conclusion

An eco-justice perspective draws upon some of the ideas ingrained in philosophical analysis of the Nature-Human relationship. It asks the question – '*justice for whom?*' and then attempts to distil the moral principles that can guide us in dealing with conflicting interests and contradictory situations (see White 2013b). What matters most is the ecological and cultural context within and through which animal welfare, eco-system requirements, and human needs are constituted. An interesting and significant implication of this type of analysis is that the value of the whole is greater than the joint value of the parts of the whole. If this is indeed the case, then it has major ramifications for how to view and respond to issues such as resource use and development, long-term economic planning, and the nature of ongoing relations among humans and animals, seas, rivers, mountains, and forests. If Nature is regarded as an organic whole (in both the sense of 'living' and 'more than the sum of its parts') and humans are part of this whole, the implications – and responsibilities – are enormous, especially in the context of climate change.

The fate of humans is inextricably bound up with that of eco-systems and the varied species that inhabit these. Criminal law and criminal justice need to reflect the importance of this. Yet, as the Council of Europe (2012: 12) recently observed, 'Currently, no comprehensive legally binding instrument for the protection of the environment exists globally'. Accordingly and in response, environmental activists, green criminologists, and international lawyers have called for the establishment of either a specific crime of "ecocide" and/or the incorporation of ecocide into existing criminal laws and international instruments (Higgins 2010, 2012). Ecocide has been defined as 'the extensive damage, destruction to or loss of ecosystems of a given territory, whether by human agency or by other causes, to such an extent that peaceful enjoyment by the inhabitants of that territory has been severely diminished' (Higgins 2012: 3). Where this occurs as a result of human agency, then it can be argued that such harm can be defined as a crime. The call for a new crime, ecocide, is premised on the idea of Earth stewardship. Paradigms of trusteeship, of stewardship, are very different to those based upon private property conceptions of ownership. As Walters (2011: 266) points out, 'Ownership implies that you can use land but don't have responsibility to others to care for it'. The Earth is seen to be, 'held in trust', and it is humans who have the responsibility to provide the requisite stewardship. Threats to Nature rights can be conceptualised as, in essence, a crime of ecocide, and thus punishable by law.

In the context of environmental harm as this pertains to humans, eco-systems, and animals, to maximise liberty is to maximise general functioning, the 'to be' and the 'to do' of life. This depends to a large degree on being recognised as being of worth and significant status (from the point of view of humans, since it is they who confer 'value' upon themselves and elements of the world around them). Supported and enhanced functioning requires the material necessities that allow for both subsistence and more-than-subsistence. This basically rests upon having an adequate habitat within which to flourish. Again, this is about the nature of home (i.e., quality of living) as well as finding a home in nature (i.e., being embedded in life-sustaining environments). Justice is about enhancing opportunities within the limits of what is possible to achieve within certain spaces.

Cases

Director-General, Department of Environment Climate Change and Water v Vin Heffernan Pty Ltd [2010] NSWLEC 200.

Bibliography

Agyeman, J. and Carmin, J. (2011) 'Introduction: environmental injustice beyond borders', in J. Agyeman and J. Carmin (eds.) *Environmental Inequalities Beyond Borders: Local Perspectives on Global Injustices*, Cambridge, MA: The MIT Press.

Anderson, E. (2004) 'Animal rights and the values of nonhuman life', in C. Sustein and M. Nussbaum (eds.) *Animal Rights: Current Debates and New Directions*, Oxford: Oxford University Press.

Beirne, P. (2004) 'From animal abuse to interhuman violence? A critical review of the progression thesis', *Society & Animals*, 12(1): 39–65.

Beirne, P. (2007) 'Animal rights, animal abuse and green criminology', in P. Beirne and N. South (eds.) *Issues in Green Criminology: Confronting Harms against Environments, Humanity and other Animals,* Devon: Willan Publishing.

Beirne, P. (2009) *Confronting Animal Abuse: Law, Criminology, and Human-Animal Relationships*, New York, NY: Rowman & Littlefield Publishers.

Beirne, P. (2011) 'Animal abuse and criminology: introduction to special issue', *Crime, Law & Social Change*, 55: 349–57.

Bennison, R. (2010) 'Ecological inclusion: unity among animals', in M. Bekoff (ed.) *Encyclopedia of Animal Rights and Animal Welfare*, Vol. 1, Santa Barbara, CA: Greenwood Press.

Benton, T. (1993) *Natural Relations: Ecological, Animal Rights and Social Justice*, London: Verso.

Benton, T. (1998) 'Rights and justice on a shared planet: more rights or new relations?', *Theoretical Criminology*, 2(2): 149–75.

Brisman, A. (2009) 'It takes green to be green: environmental elitism, "ritual displays", and conspicuous non-consumption', *North Dakota Law Review*, 85(2): 329–70.

Bullard R. (2005) 'Environmental justice in the twenty-first century', in Bullard R. (ed.) *The Quest for Environmental Justice: Human Rights and the Politics of Pollution*, San Francisco, CA: Sierra Club Books.

Cazaux, G. (1999) 'Beauty and the beast: animal abuse from a non-speciesist criminological perspective', *Crime, Law & Social Change*, 31: 105–26.

Christoff, P. (2000) 'Environmental citizenship', in W. Hudson and J. Kane (eds.) *Rethinking Australian Citizenship*, Melbourne: Cambridge University Press.

Coetzee, J. (2008) 'On the right to life', in *Animals Theme, Reform*, Sydney: Australian Law Reform Commission.

Council of Europe. (2012) *Manual on Human Rights and the Environment*, 2nd edn, Brussels: Council of Europe Publishing.

Cullinan, C. (2003) *Wild Law: A Manifesto for Earth Justice*, London: Green Books in association with The Gaia Foundation.

Devalle, B. and Sessions, G. (1985) *Deep Ecology: Living as if Nature Mattered*, Layton, UT: Gibbs Smith.
Duffy, R. (2010) *Nature Crime: How We're Getting Conservation Wrong*, New Haven, CT: Yale University Press.
Duffy, R. (2014) 'Waging a war to save biodiversity: the rise of militarized conservation', *International Affairs*, 90(4): 819–34.
Enticott, G. (2011) 'Techniques of neutralising wildlife crime in rural England and Wales', *Journal of Rural Studies*, 27: 200–208.
Findlayson, C. (2012) 'Whanganui River Agreement signed', beehive.govt.nz: The official website of the New Zealand Government, 30 August 2012.
Francione, G. (2008) *Animals as Persons: Essays on the Abolition of Animal Exploitation*, New York, NY: Columbia University Press.
Fraser, A. (2014) 'Cape York's Wild Rivers victory', *The Australian*, 18 June.
Halsey, M. (2004) 'Against "green" criminology', *British Journal of Criminology*, 44(6): 833–53.
Halsey, M. and White, R. (1998) 'Crime, ecophilosophy and environmental harm', *Theoretical Criminology*, 2(3): 345–71.
Harvey, D. (1996) *Justice, Nature and the Geography of Difference*, Oxford: Blackwell.
Higgins, P. (2010) *Eradicating Ecocide: Laws and Governance to Prevent the Destruction of Our Planet*, London: Shepheard-Walwyn Publishers Ltd.
Higgins, P. (2012) *Earth Is Our Business: Changing the Rules of the Game*, London: Shepheard-Walwyn Publishers Ltd.
Lane, P. (1998) 'Ecofeminism meets criminology', *Theoretical Criminology*, 2(2): 235–48.
Lin, A. (2006) 'The unifying role of harm in environmental law', *Wisconsin Law Review*, 3: 898–985.
McEwen, G. (2008) 'The challenge posed by feral animals', *Animals Theme, Reform*, Sydney: Australian Law Reform Commission.
Merchant, C. (2005) *Radical Ecology: The Search for a Livable World*, New York, NY: Routledge.
Morris, J. and Ruru, J. (2010) 'Giving voice to rivers: legal personality as a vehicle for recognising Indigenous peoples' relationships to water?', *Australian Indigenous Law Review*, 14(2): 49–62.
Munro, L. (2004) 'Animals, "nature" and human interests', in R. White (ed.) *Controversies in Environmental Sociology*, Melbourne: Cambridge University Press.
Pellow, D. (2013) 'Environmental justice, animal rights, and total liberation: from conflict and distance to points of common focus', in N. South and A. Brisman (eds.) *Routledge International Handbook of Green Criminology*, New York, NY: Routledge.
Pemberton, S. (2015) *Harmful Societies: Understanding the Production of Social Harm*, Bristol: Policy Press.
Plumwood, V. (2004) 'Gender, eco-feminism and the environment', in R. White (ed.) *Controversies in Environmental Sociology*, Melbourne: Cambridge University Press.
Rebgetz, L., Arthur, C. and Agius, K. (2014) 'Wild Rivers Legislation repealed in Queensland as new planning laws introduced to protect rivers', *ABC News*, 19 November 2014.
Regan, T. (2010) 'Animal rights', in M. Bekoff (ed.) *Encyclopedia of Animal Rights and Animal Welfare*, Vol. 1, Santa Barbara, CA: Greenwood Press.
Rivers III, L. and Gibbs, C. (2011) 'Applying a conservation-criminology framework to common-pool natural-resources issues', *International Journal of Comparative and Applied Criminal Justice*, 35(4): 327–46.
Robyn, L. (2002) 'Indigenous knowledge and technology', *American Indian Quarterly*, 26(2): 198–220.
Rolston, H. (2010) 'Wild animals and ethical perspectives', in M. Bekoff (ed.) *Encyclopedia of Animal Rights and Animal Welfare*, Vol. 2, Santa Barbara, CA: Greenwood Press.
Schlosberg, D. (2007). *Defining Environmental Justice: Theories, Movements, and Nature*, Oxford: Oxford University Press.
Shuttleworth, K. (2012) 'Agreement entitles Whanganui River to legal identity', *The New Zealand Herald*, 30 August 2012.
Smith, M. (1998) *Ecologism: Towards Ecological Citizenship*, Minneapolis, MN: University of Minnesota Press.
Sollund, R. (2012) 'Oil production, climate change and species decline: the case of Norway', in R. White (ed.) *Climate Change from a Criminological Perspective*, New York, NY: Springer.
South, N. and Brisman, A. (eds.) (2013) *The Routledge International Handbook of Green Criminology*, New York, NY: Routledge.
Stone, C. (1972) 'Should trees have standing? Toward legal rights for natural objects', *Southern California Law Review*, 45: 450–87.
Thornton, J. and Tromans, S. (1999) 'Human rights and environmental wrongs: incorporating the European convention on human rights: some thoughts on the consequences for UK environmental law', *Journal of Environmental Law*, 11(1): 35–57.

Tsing, A. (2005) *Friction: An Ethnography of Global Connection*, Princeton, NJ: Princeton University Press.

Walters, B. (2011) 'Enlarging our vision of rights: the most significant human rights event in recent times?', *Alternative Law Journal*, 36(4): 263–68.

Walters, R. and Westerhuis, D.S. (2013) 'Green crime and the role of environmental courts', *Crime Law and Social Change*, 59: 279–90.

Westerhuis, D. (2013) 'A harm analysis of environmental crime', in R. Walters, D.S. Westerhuis and T. Wyatt (eds.) *Emerging Issues in Green Criminology*, Hampshire: Palgrave Macmillan.

White, R. (2007) 'Green criminology and the pursuit of social and ecological justice', in P. Beirne and N. South (eds.) *Issues in Green Criminology: Confronting Harms against Environments, Humanity and Other Animals*. Devon: Willan Publishing.

White R. (2008) *Crimes against Nature: Environmental Criminology and Ecological Justice*, Devon: Willan Publishing.

White, R. (2013a) 'Environmental crime and problem-solving courts', *Crime, Law and Social Change*, 59(3): 267–78.

White, R. (2013b) *Environmental Harm: An Eco-Justice Perspective*, Bristol: Policy Press.

White, R. (2016) 'Four problems for specialist courts in dealing with nonhuman environmental victims', in T. Spapens, R. White and W. Huisman (eds.) *Environmental Crime in Transnational Context: Global Issues in Green Enforcement and Criminology*. Farnham, Surrey: Ashgate.

White, R. and Heckenberg, D. (2014) *Green Criminology: An Introduction to the Study of Environmental Harm*, London: Routledge.

6

Neurointerventions as criminal rehabilitation

An ethical review

Jonathan Pugh and Thomas Douglas

According to a number of influential views in penal theory,[1] one of the primary goals of the criminal justice system is to rehabilitate offenders. Rehabilitative measures are commonly included as part of a criminal sentence. For example, in some jurisdictions judges may order violent offenders to attend anger management classes or to undergo cognitive behavioural therapy as a part of their sentences. In a limited number of cases, *neurointerventions*—interventions that exert a direct biological effect on the brain—have been used as aids to rehabilitation. For instance, in certain jurisdictions drug-addicted offenders are required to take medications that are intended to attenuate their addictive desires.[2] In other jurisdictions, sex-offenders may receive testosterone-lowering drugs (sometimes referred to as "chemical castration") as a part of their criminal sentence or as required by their conditions of parole;[3] these interventions are intended to suppress the recipients' sex drive and thus reduce the risk of recidivism amongst this group of offenders.

This chapter reviews some of the ethical issues raised by the use of neurointerventions as aids to rehabilitation. It focuses specifically on cases in which the neurointerventions are administered to criminal offenders, in response to the commission of a particular crime, and under the provisions of the criminal law. We will refer to neurointerventions intended to aid rehabilitation as "neurocorrectives" when they are used in this way. Thus, we will have nothing to say about the use of neurointerventions as aids to offender rehabilitation within the context of ordinary medical or psychiatric care.

Whilst the use of neurocorrectives is currently rare, there are good reasons to take seriously the possibility that they might, in the future, be more widely used. Recent developments in behavioural and social neuroscience suggest that we may soon have a far wider range of neurointerventions that could be used to facilitate the rehabilitation of criminal offenders. For instance, recent research has suggested that pharmacological agents could be used to affect certain traits that are linked to criminal behaviour, such as aggression, impulsivity, and the willingness to inflict harm on others (Bond 2005; Crockett et al. 2008, 2010, 2013; Donovan et al. 2000; Khanzode et al. 2006; Nevels et al. 2010). It is also possible that deep brain stimulation (Lu et al. 2009), transcranial magnetic stimulation (Young et al. 2010), and neuro-feedback (Sitaram et al. 2009) could be used in similar ways.

Whilst such neurointerventions could potentially provide powerful new means of facilitating rehabilitation, it might be argued that they raise ethical problems that more traditional criminal justice interventions do not, and it is these problems that provide the impetus for this review.

Before beginning to outline these ethical problems, it is necessary to highlight a distinction that has important ramifications for the ethical debate regarding the use of neurocorrectives. The distinction pertains to the extent to which offenders have a choice about whether to undergo the neurocorrective. On the one hand, the neurocorrective might be imposed as a condition of parole or early release from prison. In such a scenario, the offender would essentially be given the option to agree to undergo the neurocorrective and serve less time in prison or to refuse to undergo the neurocorrective and to serve his original prison term. To date, this is the most common way in which neurocorrectives have been used.

On the other hand, a neurocorrective might be imposed as a *mandatory* part of a criminal sentence; in such a scenario, the offender would not be able to avoid undergoing the neurocorrective. Although uncommon, there is some precedent for this sort of use; for example, androgen deprivation therapy is mandated as part of the criminal sentence of certain sexual offenders in Florida.[4]

With this distinction in mind, we shall begin, in Section I, by assessing two ethical objections to what we will call "the neurocorrective offer": the offer of a choice between (i) undergoing a neurocorrective and receiving a reduced prison term and (ii) receiving the normal prison term without any requirement to undergo the neurocorrective. In assessing these objections, we will assume that the circumstances in which the neurocorrective offer is made are not coercive, or not coercive in a manner that would invalidate the offender's consent. In Section II, we shall consider an objection that challenges this assumption and that many have taken to be the most powerful objection to the neurocorrective offer. Finally, in Section III, we shall examine attempts to respond to this objection that deny that the offender's valid consent is required for the morally permissible use of neurocorrectives. We also consider the implications of such a denial for the moral permissibility of making neurocorrectives a mandatory part of criminal sentences.[5]

I Non consent-based objections to the neurocorrective offer

i) Slippery slope arguments

It might be argued that making the neurocorrective offer would be the first step on a slippery slope to the future use of neurocorrectives in more problematic ways. It is possible to distinguish two different 'slippery slopes' that might be invoked. First, it might be claimed that even if it would be morally permissible for the state to give offenders the option of undergoing a neurocorrective in return for a reduced sentence, this can be expected to lead to a situation in which the state begins to impose neurocorrectives as a mandatory part of criminal sentences. Second, it might be claimed that offering neurocorrectives that are safe and effective in facilitating rehabilitation can be expected to lead to unsafe or ineffective neurointerventions also being offered. The worry here is that the neurocorrective offer might be made to certain offenders, even though the neurointervention in question would either not aid their rehabilitation or pose excessive risks.[6]

The persuasiveness of any slippery slope argument depends in part upon the warrant that one has for claiming that the predicted bad outcome can be expected to occur once one has taken the first step on the putative slippery slope. In the arguments that we are considering here, we must assess our reasons for believing that the predicted bad outcomes mentioned above could be expected to follow from making the neurocorrective offer.

In relation to the first slippery slope argument mentioned above—the putative slippery slope to the mandatory imposition of neurocorrectives—it seems that there is little warrant for such a belief. To see why, it is illuminating to consider the fact that those who press this slippery slope argument as the sole basis for rejecting the neurocorrective offer believe that the neurocorrective offer *considered in itself* would be morally permissible. The reason they object to it is that they believe that making the neurocorrective offer would lead subsequently to the mandatory use of neurocorrectives in criminal justice. With this in mind, we might wonder why those who press this objection believe that the neurocorrective offer would not be objectionable (considered in itself), whereas the mandatory use of neurocorrectives would be.

It seems that the most plausible way to cash out this moral view is to appeal to the moral significance of the offender's consent; in the case of the neurocorrective offer, an offender's undergoing a neurocorrective would be *consensual*, whilst in the latter case it would be *involuntary*. This is a morally significant difference; in obtaining an agent's valid consent to some intervention, we are respecting his or her autonomous choice.[7]

Yet, if those who press this slippery slope objection appeal to the moral significance of consent in order to justify their initial claim that the neurocorrective offer is not morally problematic in itself, then their objection loses its force. If there is a morally significant difference between consensual and involuntary uses of neurocorrectives, then it is unclear why the former should lead to the latter.[8] Indeed, there is a clear and plausible moral principle that could be invoked against any such move, namely:

> *The Consent Requirement*: The provision of neurocorrectives to criminal offenders would be impermissible without the valid consent of the offender.
>
> (Douglas 2014: 107)

The consent requirement seems to provide us with a non-arbitrary moral principle that can allow us to clearly and consistently permit the neurocorrective offer whilst forbidding the mandatory imposition of neurocorrectives. Moreover, it is a principle that is in fact *likely* to be invoked, since it has the backing of a rich philosophical and political tradition. (This is not to say that it *ought* to be invoked. In Section III, we shall suggest that there may be ways of challenging the consent requirement.[9])

It might be objected, at this point, that the existence of a clear and principled ground for distinguishing two practices is not always enough to prevent a slippery slope from one to the other. In some contexts where slippery slope arguments are invoked, there is a fear that some morally acceptable practice might ultimately lead to a morally unacceptable practice because the difference between the acceptable and the unacceptable practice is merely one of degree. This raises the possibility that acceptance of the unacceptable practice might be made by a series of small steps, none of which will be significant enough to draw attention. Thus, though there is a moral difference between the two practices, this difference is not likely to attract sufficient attention to prevent the slide. However, in the case that we are considering here, the difference between offering a reduced prison term in return for agreement to undergo a neurocorrective and mandating a neurocorrective is a clear and qualitative difference, so we might expect any move from the former to the latter to attract attention.

Consider now the second slippery slope argument, according to which offering safe and effective neurocorrectives is likely to lead ultimately to the offering of unsafe or ineffective neurocorrectives. Given that the difference between a safe and effective intervention and an unsafe or ineffective one is often only a matter of degree (for example, it may consist in a difference in the dose of a drug), there is a possibility that the latter would be introduced by a series of small steps. There is also historical evidence that might be adduced in support of this argument: humanity has a disturbing track record of erroneously assuming the safety and effectiveness of purported neurotechnological "solutions" to criminality, with psychosurgery being only the most notorious example (Greely 2008).

These considerations suggest that the slippery slope argument adverting to the risk that neurointerventions will be used when unsafe or ineffective should be taken seriously. However, it should be noted that this argument cannot be fully assessed until we have a clear empirical understanding of the ways in which the use of neurocorrectives could be monitored and the likely success of these techniques in preventing unsafe or ineffective use. This is something we do not currently have.

ii) Neuro-interventions would not achieve the objectives of criminal justice

One of the main justifications for using neurocorrectives is that they promise to be highly effective in facilitating offender rehabilitation.[10] However, whilst rehabilitation might plausibly be claimed to be a central aim of the criminal justice system, it might be argued that the criminal justice system also has deterrent and retributive objectives. If this is right, then one might worry that even if the use of neurocorrectives might allow the criminal justice system to be more effective in facilitating rehabilitation, the use of such interventions may fail to achieve, or perhaps even run contrary to, the deterrent and retributive objectives of criminal justice.

One way to argue that neurocorrectives would fail to achieve the deterrent and retributive objectives of criminal justice is to claim that they would cause insufficient harm.[11] In order for an intervention to achieve the retributive and deterrent aims of criminal justice, that intervention must cause the offender a certain degree of harm. It might be feared that neurocorrectives—especially those with few side-effects—would not inflict sufficient harm to deter criminal offending by others. Furthermore, since retributivists believe that retribution requires punishing offenders in a manner that causes suffering *in proportion* to their desert, some (although, as we shall explain below, not all) retributivists might claim that neurocorrectives would fail to inflict enough suffering to adequately achieve the retributive objective of criminal punishment.

One problem with this objection is that it could arguably be avoided by purposely developing neurocorrectives that have, and are intended to have, serious negative side-effects; interventions with such effects would most appropriately be conceived as alternative punishments, rather than alternatives to punishment.[12] In response, though, it might be argued that there is something specific about the *kind* of harm inflicted by incarceration that makes it suited to realizing the deterrent or retributive goals of criminal justice.[13] Yet, it is not clear that this is the case; as Ryberg points out, "several retributivists accept that punishment need not consist only in imprisonment or fines" and can instead include sanctions such as "home detention, community service, and electronic monitoring" (2012: 240). Furthermore, even if incarceration were particularly well suited to achieving the retributive and deterrent objectives of criminal justice, concerns about insufficient retribution and deterrence would at most constitute a decisive objection to the use of neurocorrectives as the *sole* response to criminal offending. These concerns militate against the use of neuro-interventions alongside traditional punishments. Indeed, there might be certain advantages in using neurocorrectives to realise the rehabilitative goals of criminal justice while more traditional remedies are used to deter criminal behaviour and mete out deserved harm; separating rehabilitation from retribution and deterrence might allow these elements to be more closely tailored to the circumstances in a particular case.

As Ryberg notes, the above concerns regarding neurocorrectives causing *insufficient* harm only raise problems for so-called "positive retributivists" (2012: 239). Whilst both positive and negative retributivists claim that it is morally unacceptable to punish offenders more severely than they deserve, those who endorse positive retributivism also make the further claim that it is morally unacceptable to punish offenders *less* severely than they deserve. It is this latter requirement that was invoked above. However, the requirement that offenders not be punished more severely than they deserve might also be thought to ground an objection to the use of neurocorrectives. Both negative and positive retributivists might object to the use of neurocorrectives on the basis that they would cause *excessive* harm in the sense that they would constitute harsher punishment than the offender deserves.

How are we to ascertain the degree of harm that would be excessive for a punishment to cause? Of course, much will depend on the particular offense for which the punishment is being administered. However, one useful general comparison that can be made here is to the degree of harm caused by incarceration. If retributivists accept the assumption that the state may permissibly subject some criminal offenders to incarceration, then they cannot consistently claim that neurocorrectives that cause harms that are equal to (or less than) the harms caused by incarceration cause excessive harm in these cases. Indeed, it seems that the restrictions of movement and association entailed by incarceration reliably cause significant harms. They frequently damage existing personal relationships whilst making it difficult to form new ones; they seriously restrict sexual and reproductive freedoms; they make it impossible to pursue most careers; and they generally prevent the realization of many life-plans (Douglas 2014: 113–15). Yet retributivists often believe that prolonged incarceration is a punishment that is proportionate to desert in the case of certain offenders.

This suggests that one could not consistently object to the administration of *all* neurocorrectives on the grounds that they would inflict excessive harm, for many neurocorrectives would be substantially less harmful to offenders than incarceration. For instance, it seems plausible to suppose that the negative side-effects of many psychopharmaceuticals would be comparable in their quality, frequency, and severity to those of existing routinely used mind-active drugs such as fluoxetine (Prozac) and citalopram. Those effects are typically much less harmful than the effects of incarceration outlined above.

To these side-effects we also, of course, need to add the *intended* effects of the neurocorrective, which may also be somewhat harmful. For example, we can imagine that an aggression-lowering drug would cause harm to an individual to the extent that the individual enjoys and wishes to retain the aggressive urges that the drug attenuates. However, there seems no reason to suppose that the intended effects of all neurocorrectives would involve substantial harm. Consider a drug that attenuates only the most extreme impulses toward violent aggression, and suppose that it is imposed on an offender who dislikes and reflectively rejects those violent impulses. Such a drug could be expected to cause significantly less harm than incarceration. As such, it is not clear that a punishment that involved the use of neurocorrectives would cause suffering that is disproportionate to desert in all cases.

We shall return to the question of the harms that neurocorrectives might cause, and how they compare to the harms caused by incarceration, in Section III. To conclude our discussion of this objection though, it is worth noting that even if certain neurocorrectives on offer to offenders might cause harms that could appropriately be deemed excessive, we are considering this objection on the assumption that the offender could autonomously choose to reject the neurocorrective offer. Indeed, if we believe that the criminal justice system should respect criminal offenders as rational self-governing agents,[14] then we might plausibly claim that competent offenders should be free to make their own informed decision about whether the harms that a certain neurocorrective might cause outweigh the benefits of a reduced prison sentence.

II Consent-based objections to the neurocorrective offer

In the previous section, we suggested that one reason why imposing neurointerventions as a mandatory part of a criminal sentence might be deemed more problematic than making the neurocorrective offer is that the latter approach would allow the offender to consent to the use of a neurocorrective, whereas the former would not. Furthermore, we suggested that one of the primary reasons that consent is deemed to be morally significant is that, in obtaining an agent's valid consent to some intervention, we respect the agent's autonomy.

In medical ethics, it is often claimed that in order for an individual's consent to be valid (and reflective of autonomous choice), it must, amongst other things, be made in the absence of coercion (Beauchamp and Childress 2001; Faden and Beauchamp 1986). In their influential account of informed consent in medical ethics, Beauchamp and Childress claim that coercion occurs "if and only if one person intentionally uses a credible and severe threat of harm or force to control another" (2001: 94).

One possible objection to the neurocorrective offer is that an offender could not validly consent to undergo the neurocorrective because the offer is inherently coercive (Farah 2002). This sort of argument has commonly been raised against the practice of offering sex offenders chemical or physical castration in return for a reduced prison sentence, which we shall henceforth refer to as the "castration offer."[15] Since this offer is structurally similar to (and is indeed an instance of) the neurocorrective offer, it will be useful to consider the literature on the castration offer here.

Vanderzyl offers a clear statement of the objection under consideration in the following passage:

> … offering a convicted offender castration as an alternative to a lengthy prison sentence constitutes an inherently coercive practice rendering truly voluntary consent impossible.
> (1994: 140)

Proponents of this sort of argument are not always clear about *why* this sort of offer involves coercion. However, one justification that is sometimes suggested is that the dire circumstances that offenders facing incarceration find themselves in prevent them from making a free choice when they agree to undergo the castration. For instance, Green claims that in such a scenario:

> Freedom of choice is impossible because the convict's loss of liberty constitutes a deprivation of such a magnitude that he cannot choose freely and voluntarily, but he is forced to give consent to an alternative he would not otherwise have chosen. (1986: 16–17)

McMillan suggests that another way in which the castration offer might be coercive is if the offer were made to an offender with the intention that the operant reason for the offender's accepting the intervention would be the fact that the state will not release him if he refuses. Although the offer increases the range of options open to the sex offender, McMillan suggests that it may be understood to be coercive insofar as it "relies upon the undesirability of indefinite incarceration to coerce (the offender) into being castrated" (2014a: 587).

In this section, we shall consider two ways in which defenders of the neurocorrective offer might respond to the objection of coercion. The first response that we shall consider involves denying that the neurocorrective offer is coercive. One might begin to support such a denial by arguing that the explanations provided for why the neurocorrective offer is coercive are inadequate. For instance, many theorists have pointed out that one cannot claim that the offer is coercive simply by appealing to the offender's loss of liberty, because not all deprivations of liberty entail that the choices made in such circumstances are coerced (Bomann-Larsen 2013: 68; Rosati 1994: 161; Ryberg 2012: 236; Wertheimer and Miller 2014). The following example is commonly used to illustrate this point: Suppose that a patient suffering from a terminal illness is offered a high-risk, but potentially life-saving experimental operation; we believe that such a patient could validly consent to this offer, even though such a patient is making a choice between two unappealing alternatives from a position of severely restricted liberty. Ryberg and Petersen (2013) have also used this example to argue that McMillan's appeal to the state's intentions in making the castration offer cannot adequately explain why the offer is coercive. After all, a doctor who offered her patient the option of undergoing this operation might make the offer intending that the patient's "operant reason" for accepting it will be that he will die without the operation; yet, we do not seem to believe that this would make the offer coercive, as McMillan's argument seems to imply.

In response to this line of argument, defenders of the objection of coercion might seek to refine their analysis of why the neurocorrective offer is coercive, so that their view is no longer subject to counter-examples of this sort. However there may be a more robust way of arguing that the neurocorrective offer is not coercive: One could appeal to the conceptual claim that offers cannot, by their nature, be coercive. In the philosophical literature on coercion, it is often claimed that a necessary condition of coercion is that the coercer credibly *threatens* the victim (Nozick 1969: 83; Stevens 1988: 452). Indeed, Beauchamp and Childress invoke this sort of condition in their understanding of coercion, delineated above. Those who endorse such a view tend to endorse Wertheimer and Miller's claim that "genuine offers are inherently non-coercive and therefore cannot compromise consent qua coercion" (2014: 592).

If this is to be a satisfying reply to the objection of coercion, there will need to be a convincing account of the relevant difference between threats and offers that can explain why only the former can be coercive. There have been several different approaches to the distinction between threats and offers in the philosophical literature, and we lack the space to adequately explore them all here.[16] However, one account that has been particularly influential in this area that we shall briefly describe is the so-called "baseline" approach.

Both threats and offers announce an intention to bring about some outcome that is conditional on the recipient's actions. According to the "baseline" approach, threats and offers are to be distinguished by the relationship of the proposed outcome to the recipient's baseline state of affairs in the pre-proposal situation. Typically, threats announce a conditional intention to make the recipient worse off than the baseline state of affairs (think of a highwayman who threatens to shoot you if you do not hand over your wallet), whilst offers do not; indeed, in some cases, offers may announce an intention to make the recipient better off.

Theorists disagree about which baseline state of affairs should be relevant to our assessment of whether a proposal is a threat or an offer. On morally neutral baseline accounts, we might assess whether a proposal is an offer or a threat simply by considering whether it would make the recipient worse off than she is when the proposal is made.[17] The problem with such accounts is that the recipient's status quo situation might already include coercive elements. For instance, in his seminal essay on the topic of coercion, Nozick asks us to consider a slave owner who beats his slave each morning (for no reason connected to the slave's behaviour) and who one day proposes to the slave that he will not beat him on that day if he performs some task (1969: 450). Whilst the slave owner announces a conditional intention to make the slave better offer than he would normally be in this case, it nonetheless seems that the slave is being coerced here.

Partly in order to account for why this sort of example involves coercion, theorists have developed moralized baseline accounts, according to which the baseline state of affairs that is relevant to our assessment of whether a proposal is a threat or an offer is understood to incorporate certain moral conditions. For instance, on Wertheimer's moralized baseline account, a proposal amounts to a threat if the proposer announces the conditional intention to make the recipient worse off than the recipient *ought* to be, either by violating the recipient's rights or by failing to fulfil an obligation that the proposer has to the recipient. Such threats are coercive when the recipient has no reasonable choice but to comply with the proposal (Wertheimer 1989).

Indeed, Wertheimer and Miller (2014) have invoked this account of coercive threats in defence of the claim that the castration offer is not coercive. On the assumption that imposing the ordinary prison term would not violate the offender's rights, offering the offender a choice between that ordinary term and a shorter prison term plus castration cannot be coercive on Wertheimer's account, since it does not involve a threat to violate the offender's rights if he does not comply. If the offender does not agree to undergo the castration, he will simply face the prison term to which he has made himself liable through his criminal conduct. A similar claim could be made with regard to other instances of the neurocorrective offer.

However, it should be acknowledged that moralized baseline approaches to the distinction between threats and offers have been challenged on many counts.[18] For instance, Feinberg (1989: 218–28) and Cohen (1977) have suggested that moralized baseline accounts are not always congruous with our intuitions, whilst Zimmerman (1981) has suggested that moralized baseline accounts do not link up in the right way with the underlying idea that coercion is wrong because it undermines freedom.

Furthermore, these writers have also objected to the fundamental claim that only threats can be coercive, and suggested that offers can also sometimes be coercive. For instance, Zimmerman claims that a proposal amounts to an offer if the recipient would prefer to move from his normally expected (i.e., morally neutral) pre-proposal situation to the proposal situation. However, he claims that offers (as well as threats) can be coercive if the recipient of the offer would strongly prefer to move from his actual pre-proposal situation to some alternative, feasible pre-proposal situation that the proposing party is preventing the recipient from being in (Zimmerman 1981: 133). Meanwhile, Feinberg argues that offers are coercive if the proposer only gives the recipient a choice between different evils and if the "differential coercive pressure" of the offer (that is the difference in the comparative worth of the projected consequences of the recipient's refusing the offer and the recipient's accepting the offer) is sufficiently high (Feinberg 1989: 234).

There is room for debate on the question of whether the neurocorrective offer would qualify as a coercive offer on these accounts. For it to do so on Zimmerman's account, there would have to be a plausible sense in which the offender's most preferred pre-proposal situation (in which she is not incarcerated) satisfies Zimmerman's feasibility requirement. Similarly, on Feinberg's account, there might be scope to question whether the differential coercive pressure of the neurocorrective offer is sufficiently high for the offer to qualify as coercive.

Interestingly, Feinberg's account of coercive offers might be understood to suggest a second line of response to the objection of coercion. Whilst Feinberg claims that certain offers can be coercive (as explained above), he also suggests that not all coercive offers invalidate consent. In particular, he suggests that coercive offers in which the proposing party had no role in creating the recipient's pre-proposal circumstances of vulnerability (i.e., which represent one of the evil alternatives that the recipient may choose in an offer situation on Feinberg's account) very rarely invalidate consent (Feinberg 1989: 246). Accordingly, a second response to the objection from coercion that defenders of the neurocorrective offer could make is to argue that even if the offer is coercive, the offender's consent to undergo the neurocorrective can nevertheless be valid.

An initial problem with responding to the coercion-based objection to the neurocorrective offer in this way is that in order for an offer to be coercive without invalidating consent on Feinberg's account, the proposing party must have played no role in creating the recipient's pre-proposal circumstances of vulnerability. However, the neurocorrective offer does not meet this condition; after all, it seems most natural to understand the state as being the proposing party in this case, and the state has a clear role in creating the offender's pre-proposal circumstances of vulnerability, insofar as the state is responsible for incarcerating the offender. Arguably, though, one might circumvent this problem by weakening Feinberg's conditions on consent-preserving coercive offers, so that a coercive offer could qualify as preserving the validity of the recipient's consent if the proposing party did not violate the recipient's rights in creating the recipient's pre-proposal circumstances of vulnerability.

However, even if this is a plausible move to make, we might question whether Feinberg gives a convincing argument for the claim that some coercive offers do not invalidate consent. Moreover, even if such offers do not invalidate consent, one might wonder whether the neurocorrective offer could be wrong for reasons other than its coerciveness. For instance, Bomann-Larsen (2013) has argued that although the neurocorrective offer is not coercive, it is wrong because it fails to recognize the offender as a moral equal and violates his fundamental claim to moral respect.[19] In a similar vein, McMillan has suggested, following Feinberg's approach to coercion, that coercive offers that preserve consent can nonetheless cause the recipient "moral harm" (McMillan 2014b: 596). Finally, Shaw endorses Bomann-Larsen's criticism of the neurocorrective offer but also objects to it on the consequence-based grounds that offering neurocorrectives to offenders would "send out the message that all offenders who are offered the intervention stand in need of it, whether they consent to it or not" (Shaw 2014: 13).

Clearly, then, establishing that the neurocorrective offer is not coercive (or not coercive in a way that invalidates consent) will not settle the debate regarding the moral permissibility of making the offer. However, it should be acknowledged that whilst the wrongs associated with exploitation, inappropriate offers, and other moral harms may be significant, they are not readily understood as wrongs involving affronts to autonomy, unlike coercion. As such, the responses that we have so far considered may be understood as ways in which defenders of the neurocorrective offer might seek to move the debate away from autonomy-based objections. This is an important move for them to make, since violations of autonomy are often understood to be particularly egregious in contemporary bioethics, given the paramount value placed on autonomy in this context (Beauchamp and Childress 2001; Caplan 2006: 117; Gillon 2003).

Suppose, despite the above considerations, that it can be established that the neurocorrective offer is indeed coercive and that it is therefore not possible for an offender to validly consent to it. In order to defend the moral permissibility of the neurocorrective offer on this understanding, one would then have to refute the consent requirement that we introduced in our discussion of the first slippery slope argument, according to which neurocorrectives can only permissibly be provided with the valid consent of the offender who will undergo the intervention. In the final section, we shall turn our attention to arguments that have been used in an attempt to refute the consent requirement. Of course, such arguments also lend support to the claim that the *mandatory* use of neurocorrectives could also be morally permissible.

III Denying the need for valid consent

One way to argue against the consent requirement is to claim that the moral reasons we have to respect the offender's autonomy can be outweighed by other moral reasons. It seems plausible to claim that the state has strong consequence-based reasons to employ neurocorrectives. They could be highly effective at facilitating rehabilitation and preventing recidivism and might also be less costly than alternative means of realizing these goals, such as incarceration. As well as these good consequences for society in general, one might also point out that neurocorrectives might have beneficial consequences for the offenders themselves, either by allowing them to avoid more harmful corrective interventions or because their rehabilitation is itself beneficial (Day et al. 2004: 260–63; Ryberg 2012: 232).

However, this consequence-based argument against the consent requirement would be met with strong opposition, in view of the salience attributed to the principle of respect for autonomy in contemporary bioethics (as we briefly discussed above). There is some precedent within psychiatry and infectious disease control for the imposition of non-consensual medical treatments to competent adults; however, it is generally believed that an individual's right to refuse medical interventions (including neurointerventions) will outweigh any public interest or paternalistic case for imposing an intervention.

In any case, it is, as Ryberg argues, too simplistic to set up the debate as one in which we simply weigh autonomy-related concerns against the consequence-based reasons to allow these interventions. Ryberg (2013) argues that our moral judgment about the permissibility of coerced treatments in criminal justice should also incorporate penal-theoretic considerations. For instance, he points out that retributivists are likely to be unconvinced by consequence-based arguments in favor of the use of neurocorrectives if such interventions result in a penal reduction, assuming that offenders currently receive proportionate punishment. Having said this, if offenders currently receive punishment that is too severe, Ryberg suggests that there may yet be a retributivist argument in favour of using such interventions (2013: 10–11). These points are not intended to settle the debate about whether and when neurocorrectives may permissibly be used. Rather, the point is that the debate needs to be expanded to include penal-theoretic considerations.

Another factor that may complicate our moral judgment is that, somewhat paradoxically, one might also raise an autonomy-based *objection* to the consent requirement. One of the main reasons that valid consent is deemed to be of such moral importance is rooted in the principle of respect for autonomy. In view of this, one might argue that valid consent is not required for the imposition of neurocorrectives on criminal offenders if those interventions can be understood as enabling autonomy. There may well be scope for understanding certain interventions as having these autonomy-enhancing effects. For instance, Arthur Caplan has suggested that the mandatory treatment of drug addicts may be justified on these grounds, since such addicts "do not have the full capacity to be self-determining or autonomous because their addiction literally coerces their behaviour" (2006: 118). Douglas et al. (2013) have suggested that similar considerations might count in favour of offering sex offenders the option to undergo chemical castration regardless of whether they could validly consent to it, since the desires that motivate many sexual offences (and that are attenuated by chemical castration) would qualify as impediments to autonomy on most plausible theories of autonomy.

However, it is not clear that such considerations would be decisive; the claim that an individual's future autonomy can permissibly be enhanced even at the cost of disrespecting his present autonomy would be controversial. Moreover, it is unlikely that such an autonomy-based case for rejecting the consent requirement could be applicable to all criminal offenders (Douglas et al. 2013: 400–10). The argument seems plausible with respect to cases in which the offender feels alienated from the impulsive desires that motivated his criminal act. However, whilst most theories of autonomy would claim that an offender would lack autonomy with respect to those desires, many offenders may not feel alienated from their desires in this way and may instead endorse them. Most prominent theories of autonomy would claim that such offenders would be autonomous with respect to those desires.

Rather than objecting to the consent requirement by appealing to consequences or autonomy-based arguments, one might alternatively argue that consistency demands that we permit the non-consensual use of neurocorrectives in criminal justice. We tend to believe that the state may permissibly do things to criminal offenders without their consent that it could not permissibly do to others without (and in some cases with) consent (Douglas 2014: 105). The challenge that this observation raises for those who defend the consent requirement is to give an account of the moral difference between incarcerating an offender without consent and imposing a neurocorrective without consent that can explain why the former is morally permissible, but the latter morally impermissible.

One obvious difference is that neurocorrectives are likely to be physically invasive and thus may be said to violate the offender's right to bodily integrity in a way that incarceration does not. However, incarceration violates other important rights such as free movement and association; as such, in order to defend the consent requirement by appealing to the right to bodily integrity, it seems that one would need to defend the claim that this right is more robust than rights to freedom of movement and association, such that it would take more serious criminal offending for the rights to bodily integrity to lose their protective force than for the rights to free movement and association to lose theirs. One of us has recently argued that this claim is not as easy to defend as our intuitions might lead us to believe (Douglas 2014: 113–18).

Moreover, it might seem implausible that it is the bodily invasiveness of neurocorrectives that explains why, unlike incarceration, they may not permissibly be imposed without consent. The primary intended effects of neurocorrectives are *mental* rather than bodily. Indeed, some neurointerventions that might be used as neurocorrectives, such as transcranial electric brain stimulation, are only doubtfully or minimally physically invasive. It might thus seem more credible that the most significant moral difference between incarceration and neurocorrectives is to be located in the *mental* effects of the latter. Perhaps, then, the consistency argument should be resisted not by appealing to a right to bodily integrity, but by appealing to a right to *mental* integrity (Douglas 2014: 113–18).

Farah seems to implicitly appeal to this sort of concept in observing that neurocorrectives might deny offenders the "… freedom to think one's own thoughts and have one's own personality" (2002: 1126). However, there has been little research regarding whether there is a right to mental integrity or about what sorts of mental influences might violate it. Bublitz and Merkel have offered an initial exploration of this putative right, suggesting that such a right exists, or is, "as a tacit assumption, woven into law's structure" (2014: 60). They also argue that non-consensual interventions into other minds might violate this right if they substantially undermine mental self-determination by reducing the victim's mental control or by exploiting pre-existing mental weaknesses (2014: 68).

Furthermore, Bublitz and Merkel claim that there is an important moral difference between interventions that work directly on the brain (such as neurointerventions of the sort that we are considering) and indirect interventions that are perceived sensually and processed by psychological mechanisms. The two types of intervention differ morally, they claim, because indirect interventions may respect mental self-determination, whilst direct interventions circumvent it (Bublitz and Merkel 2014: 69–70).

Shaw (2014) has offered a similar account of the morally relevant difference between direct and indirect interventions. She suggests that certain direct interventions are problematic because they would serve to objectify offenders by rehabilitating them in a manner that fails to engage them in a rational moral dialogue.[20] She also suggests that permitting the use of neurointerventions in criminal justice would serve to widen the inequality of power between offenders and the state (Shaw 2014: 13).[21]

However, unlike Bublitz and Merkel, Shaw's account of why direct interventions are more morally problematic than indirect interventions does not rule out the possibility that some direct interventions might yet be morally permissible. Shaw claims that whilst direct interventions are problematic if they serve to change the offender's values in a manner that does not include the offender in a moral dialogue, non-consensual direct interventions may be permissible if they enable offenders to engage in a moral dialogue as part of their rehabilitation. For instance, she suggests that permissible interventions might include enhancing an offender's powers of attention, or the ability to delay gratification (Shaw 2014: 14–15).

It can be argued, however, that the question of whether the state may consistently permit the non-consensual incarceration of offenders without also permitting the non-consensual use of neurocorrectives remains open. Whilst the analyses considered above have laid important foundations for addressing this question, there is still a great deal of work to be done in this area; for instance, with respect to Bublitz and Merkel's analysis, one could question whether the fact that an indirect intervention engages the recipient's psychological processes is sufficient for establishing that the intervention respects the recipient's right to mental self-determination. Furthermore, we might also question whether some direct interventions might be permissible even if they bypass the offender's psychological processes, as Shaw suggests with regards to interventions that serve to enable the offender to participate in rational moral dialogue.

Notes

1 A number of theorists who advocate consequentialist views on punishment have claimed that punishment should contribute to the rehabilitation of the offender. (See, for example, Bentham 1890; Carlen 1989; Cullen 1982.) However, this claim is also supported by certain non-consequentialist views. For example, see Hampton 1984; Morris 1981.

2 For example, in the United Kingdom, methadone treatments have been imposed as part of Drug Treatment and Testing Orders imposed by the courts. See Eley et al. 2002; Hough et al. 2003.

3 For a discussion of medical interventions that have been used to prevent sexual recidivism, see Thibaut et al. 2010.

4 For discussion, see del Busto and Harlow 2011; Douglas et al. 2013: 396.

5 It should be acknowledged that in some US states the chemical castration of sex offenders is "mandated" not only in the sense that the law makes such interventions compulsory for these offenders, but also in the sense that the law does not allow judges discretion to exclude chemical castration from the sentence (*California Penal Code* 2012: 645(b)). In some statutes, the mandatory use of chemical castration is contingent upon a determination by a court-appointed medical expert that the offender is an appropriate candidate for such an intervention (*Florida Statutes Annotated* 2013: §794.0235; *Louisiana Revised Statutes* 2013: §14:43.6A). Whilst this practice raises other important moral issues, we shall not consider them in this chapter.

6 This objection has been raised in relation to the use of chemical castration as a criminal remedy (Lewis 1953: 229; Tancredi and Weisstub 1986).

7 In turn, the principle of respect for autonomy, which finds its roots in the philosophy of both Kant and Mill, is a cornerstone of liberal thought, as well as modern biomedical ethics. See Kant 2004; Mill 1991. See also Beauchamp and Childress 2001.

8 See Douglas 2010 for a related general objection to a class of slippery slope arguments.

9 Notice, though, that if the consent requirement can be challenged in this context, then, in the absence of another explanation, this may put pressure on the claim that the use of mandatory neurocorrectives would be an outcome that we have moral reason to avoid.

10 Whilst it is uncontroversial that neurointerventions could be effective in rehabilitating offenders in the superficial sense that the offenders will become less disposed to commit criminal offences, Vincent has argued that they may be unable to rehabilitate offenders into more responsible agents, since the way in which such interventions restore certain mental capacities might adversely affect other factors that undergird responsible agency, such as authenticity and personal identity. See Vincent 2014.

11 This is an objection that has been advanced by a US court against the use of chemical castration as a criminal remedy (Idaho Court of Appeals 1991: 120 Idaho 953, 821 P.2d 1008).
12 Jesper Ryberg develops this point (2012: 239–40).
13 Though see, for a response to this suggestion, Ryberg 2012.
14 See Murphy (1973) for a defence of this claim.
15 See European Committee for the Prevention of Torture and Inhuman and or Degrading Treatment or Punishment 2009; Green 1986; McMillan 2014a; Scott and Holmberg 2003; Vanderzyl 1994.
16 For a description and analysis of alternative approaches, see Anderson 2011.
17 As Feinberg suggests, there can be different interpretations of this. (See Feinberg 1989: 218–24.)
18 For Wertheimer's responses to some salient objections raised against his moralised baseline account, see Wertheimer 1989: 244–55.
19 For objections to Bomann-Larsen's account of why the neuro-intervention is morally problematic, see Ryberg and Petersen (2013).
20 Notice that in this paper, Shaw objects to Bublitz and Merkel's earlier work in which they endorse the claim that the moral difference between direct brain interventions and standard environmental influences is that the former involve a manipulator who takes over responsibility for the results of the intervention, whilst the latter type of influence does not. See Bublitz and Merkel (2009) and Shaw (2014: 8–12) for discussion.
21 Shaw (2014: 13) goes so far as to claim that the use of such interventions would not be permissible even if the offender requested them, on the grounds that doing so would affect society's stance toward offenders as a group.

Bibliography

Anderson, S., (2011) 'Coercion', in E.N. Zalta (ed.) *The Stanford Encyclopedia of Philosophy*, online. Available at: http:plato.stanford.edu/entries/coercion, accessed 25 March 2016.

Beauchamp, T.L. and Childress, J.F. (2001) *Principles of Biomedical Ethics*, 5th edn, Oxford: Oxford University Press.

Bentham, J. (1890) *Theory of Legislation*, 6th edn, London: Trübner.

Bomann-Larsen, L. (2013) 'Voluntary rehabilitation? On neurotechnological behavioural treatment, valid consent and (in)appropriate offers', *Neuroethics*, 6: 65–77. doi:10.1007/s12152-011-9105-9.

Bond, A.J. (2005) 'Antidepressant treatments and human aggression', *Eur. J. Pharmacol*, 526: 218–25. doi:10.1016/j.ejphar.2005.09.033.

Bublitz, J.C. and Merkel, R. (2009) 'Autonomy and authenticity of enhanced personality traits', *Bioethics*, 23: 360–74. doi:10.1111/j.1467-8519.2009.01725.x.

Bublitz, J.C. and Merkel, R. (2014) 'Crimes against minds: on mental manipulations, harms and a human right to mental self-determination', *Crim. Law Philos.*, 8: 51–77. doi:10.1007/s11572-012-9172-y.

California Penal Code. (2012).

Caplan, A.L. (2006) 'Ethical issues surrounding forced, mandated, or coerced treatment', *J. Subst. Abuse Treat,* 31: 117–20. doi:10.1016/j.jsat.2006.06.009.

Carlen, P. (1989) 'Crime, inequality and sentencing', in Carlen and Cook (eds.), *Paying for Crime*. Buckingham: Open University Press.

Cohen, G.A. (1977) 'Robert Nozick and Wilt Chamberlain: how patterns preserve liberty', *Erkenntnis*, 11: 5–23. doi:10.1007/BF00169842.

Crockett, M.J., Apergis-Schoute, A., Herrmann, B., Lieberman, M.D., Müller, U., Robbins, T.W. and Clark, L. (2013) 'Serotonin modulates striatal responses to fairness and retaliation in humans', *J. Neurosci.,* 33: 3505–13. doi:10.1523/JNEUROSCI.2761-12.2013.

Crockett, M.J., Clark, L., Hauser, M.D., Robbins, T.W. (2010) 'Serotonin selectively influences moral judgment and behavior through effects on harm aversion', *Proc. Natl. Acad. Sci.,* 107: 17433–38. doi:10.1073/pnas.1009396107.

Crockett, M.J., Clark, L., Tabibnia, G., Lieberman, M.D., Robbins, T.W. (2008) 'Serotonin modulates behavioral reactions to unfairness', *Science*, 320: 1739–39. doi:10.1126/science.1155577.

Cullen, F.T. (1982) *Reaffirming Rehabilitation,* Cincinnati, OH: Anderson Publishing Company.

Day, A., Tucker, K., Howells, K. (2004) 'Coerced offender rehabilitation – a defensible practice?', *Psychol. Crime Law*, 10: 259–69. doi:10.1080/10683160410001662753.

del Busto, E. and Harlow, M.C. (2011) 'American sexual offender castration treatment and legislation', in: D.P. Boer, R. Eher, L.E. Craig, M.H. Miner and F. Pfäfflin (eds.) *International Perspectives on the*

Assessment and Treatment of Sexual Offenders: Theory, Practice and Research, Oxford: Wiley-Blackwell, pp. 543–71.

Donovan, S.J., Stewart, J.W., Nunes, E.V., Quitkin, F.M., Parides, M., Daniel, W., Susser, E. and Klein, D.F. (2000) 'Divalproex treatment for youth with explosive temper and mood lability: a double-blind, placebo-controlled crossover design', *Am. J. Psychiatry* 157: 818–20.

Douglas, T. (2010) 'Intertemporal disagreement and empirical slippery slope arguments', *Utilitas,* 22: 184–97. doi:10.1017/S0953820810000087.

Douglas, T. (2014) 'Criminal rehabilitation through medical intervention: moral liability and the right to bodily integrity', *J. Ethics,* 18: 101–22. doi:10.1007/s10892-014-9161-6.

Douglas, T., Bonte, P., Focquaert, F., Devolder, K. and Sterckx, S. (2013) 'Coercion, incarceration, and chemical castration: an argument from autonomy', *J. Bioethical Inq.*, 10: 393–405. doi:10.1007/s11673-013-9465-4.

Eley, S., Gallop, K., McIvor, G., Morgan, K. and Yates, R. (2002) 'Drug treatment and testing orders: evaluation of the Scottish pilots', Scottish Executive Central Research Unit.

European Committee for the Prevention of Torture and Inhuman or Degrading Treatment or Punishment. (2009) Report to the Czech Government on the visit to the Czech Republic carried out by the European Committee for the Prevention of Torture and Inhuman or Degrading Treatment or Punishment (CPT).

European Committee for the Prevention of Torture and Inhuman or Degrading Treatment or Punishment. (CPT) (n.d.) Report to the German Government on the visit to Germany carried out by the European Committee for the Prevention of Torture and Inhuman or Degrading Treatment or Punishment (CPT) from 25 November to 7 December 2010 [WWW Document]. URL (accessed 10.24.13).

Faden, R.R., Beauchamp, T.L. (1986). *A History and Theory of Informed Consent,* New York, NY: Oxford University Press.

Farah, M.J. (2002) 'Emerging ethical issues in neuroscience', *Nat. Neurosci.*, 5: 1123–29. doi:10.1038/nn1102-1123.

Feinberg, J. (1989) *The Moral Limits of the Criminal Law, Vol. 3: Harm to Self* [electronic resource], New York, NY: Oxford University Press.

Florida Statutes Annotated. (2013).

Gillon, R. (2003) 'Ethics needs principles – four can encompass the rest – and respect for autonomy should be "first among equals"', *J. Med. Ethics,* 29: 307–12. doi:10.1136/jme.29.5.307.

Greely, H.T. (2008) 'Neuroscience and criminal justice: not responsibility but treatment', *Univ. Kans. Law Rev.*, 56: 1103–38.

Green, W. (1986) 'Depo-Provera, castration, and the probation of rape offenders: statutory and constitutional issues', *Univ. Dayt. Law Rev.*, 12: 1.

Hampton, J. (1984) 'The moral education theory of punishment', *Philos. Public Aff.*, 13: 208–38.

Hough, M., Clancy, A., McSweeney, T. and Turnbull, P. (2003). *Impact of Drug Treatment and Testing Orders on Offending: Two-Year Reconviction Results,* London: Home Office.

Idaho Court of Appeals. (1991) *State v. Estes.*

Kant, I. (2004) *Critique of Practical Reason,* Mineola, NY: Dover.

Khanzode, L.A., Saxena, K., Kraemer, H., Chang, K. and Steiner, H. (2006) 'Efficacy profiles of psychopharmacology: Divalproex Sodium in conduct disorder', *Child Psychiatry Hum. Dev.*, 37: 55–64. doi:10.1007/s10578-006-0019-4.

Lewis, C.S. (1953) 'Humanitarian theory of punishment', *The. Res Judicatae,* 6: 224.

Louisiana Revised Statutes. (2013).

Lu, L., Wang, X. and Kosten, T.R. (2009) 'Stereotactic neurosurgical treatment of drug addiction', *Am. J. Drug Alcohol Abuse,* 35: 391–93. doi:10.3109/00952990903312478.

McMillan, J. (2014a) 'The kindest cut? Surgical castration, sex offenders and coercive offers', *J. Med. Ethics,* 40: 583–90. doi:10.1136/medethics-2012-101030.

McMillan, J. (2014b) 'Surgical castration, coercive offers and coercive effects: it is still not about consent'. *J. Med. Ethics,* 40: 596–96. doi:10.1136/medethics-2013-101507.

Mill, J.S. (1991) 'On Liberty', in J. Gray and G.W. Smith (eds.) *J.S. Mill, On Liberty, in Focus,* New York, NY: Routledge.

Morris, H. (1981) 'A paternalistic theory of punishment', *Am. Philos. Q.,* 18: 263–71.

Murphy, J.G. (1973) 'Marxism and retribution', *Philos. Public Aff.*, 2: 217–43.

Nevels, R.M., Dehon, E.E., Alexander, K. and Gontkovsky, S.T. (2010) 'Psychopharmacology of aggression in children and adolescents with primary neuropsychiatric disorders: a review of current and potentially promising treatment options', *Exp. Clin. Psychopharmacol.*, 18: 184–201. doi:10.1037/a0018059.

Nozick, R. (1969) 'Coercion', in S. Morgenbesser, P. Suppes and M. White (eds.) *Philosophy, Science, and Method: Essays in Honor of Ernest Nagel,* New York, NY: St. Martin's Press.

Rosati, C.S. (1994) 'Study of internal punishment', *A. Wis. Law Rev.*, 1994: 123.

Ryberg, J. (2012) 'Punishment, pharmacological treatment, and early release', *Int. J. Appl. Philos.*, 26: 231–44. doi:10.5840/ijap201226217.

Ryberg, J. (2013) 'Is coercive treatment of offenders morally acceptable? On the deficiency of the debate', *Crim. Law Philos.*, 1–13.

Ryberg, J. and Petersen, T.S. (2013) 'Neurotechnological behavioural treatment of criminal offenders—a comment on Bomann-Larsen', *Neuroethics*, 6: 79–83. doi:10.1007/s12152-011-9146-0.

Scott, C.L. and Holmberg, T. (2003) 'Castration of sex offenders: prisoners' rights versus public safety', *J. Am. Acad. Psychiatry Law*, 31: 502–509.

Shaw, E. (2014) 'Direct brain interventions and responsibility enhancement', *Crim. Law Philos.*, 8: 1–20. doi:10.1007/s11572-012-9152-2.

Sitaram, R., Caria, A. and Birbaumer, N. (2009). 'Hemodynamic brain-computer interfaces for communication and rehabilitation', *Neural Netw. Off. J. Int. Neural Netw. Soc.*, 22: 1320–28. doi:10.1016/j.neunet.2009.05.009.

Stevens, R. (1988) 'Coercive offers', *Australas. J. Philos.*, 66: 83–95. doi:10.1080/00048408812350261.

Tancredi, L.R., Weisstub, D.N. (1986) 'Technology assessment: its role in forensic psychiatry and the case of chemical castration', *Int. J. Law Psychiatry*, 8: 257–71.

Thibaut, F., De La Barra, F., Gordon, H., Cosyns, P. and Bradford, J.M.W. (2010). 'The World Federation of Societies of Biological Psychiatry (WFSBP) guidelines for the biological treatment of paraphilias', *World J. Biol. Psychiatry Off. J. World Fed. Soc. Biol. Psychiatry*, 11: 604–55. doi:10.3109/15622971003671628.

Vanderzyl, K. (1994) 'Castration as an alternative to incarceration: an impotent approach to the punishment of sex offenders', *North. Ill. Univ. Law Rev.*, 15.

Vincent, N.A. (2014) 'Restoring responsibility: promoting justice, therapy and reform through direct brain interventions', *Crim. Law Philos.*, 8: 21–42. doi:10.1007/s11572-012-9156-y.

Wertheimer, A. (1989) *Coercion*, 1st Princeton pbk. edn, Princeton, NJ: Princeton University Press.

Wertheimer, A. and Miller, F.G. (2014) 'There are (STILL) no coercive offers', *J. Med. Ethics*, 40: 592–93. doi:10.1136/medethics-2013-101510.

Young, L., Camprodon, J.A., Hauser, M., Pascual-Leone, A. and Saxe, R. (2010) 'Disruption of the right temporoparietal junction with transcranial magnetic stimulation reduces the role of beliefs in moral judgments', *Proc. Natl. Acad. Sci. U. S. A.*, 107: 6753–58. doi:10.1073/pnas.0914826107.

Zimmerman, D. (1981) 'Coercive wage offers', *Philos. Public Aff.*, 10: 121–45.

Part II

Criminalization, decriminalization, and punishment

7

Retributive desert and deterrence

How both cohere in a single justification of punishment

*Douglas Husak**

My objective is to sketch a theory to justify state punishment that combines principles of retributive desert with considerations of deterrence and crime control. Any acceptable theory, I believe, *must* incorporate these distinct components. But how? My first of two sections identifies several background assumptions that I hope are acceptable but for which I cannot argue. My second and final section presents the theory itself and the reasons I believe it to be preferable to alternatives.

I Background to a theory of justified punishment

Legal philosophers since at least the time of Plato have struggled to justify state punishment. Anyone who is familiar with the voluminous literature on this topic must be struck by the enormous discrepancy between the kinds of approach that are favored by theorists from different disciplines. Obviously, generalizations about these matters are perilous. Abolitionism—the position that punishment *cannot* be justified and thus the state must find alternatives that do not rely on penal sanctions, to deal with offenders—is becoming somewhat more respectable among academic commentators in the United States. In my judgment, no alternative is less problematic than punishment itself. In any event, fundamental differences persist in distinct disciplines among theorists who continue to believe that state punishment *can* be justified. In what follows, I will use a very broad brush to characterize these differences. I hope that my (admittedly oversimplified) description is useful not only to illustrate the conflict between disciplines, but also to identify the challenge that any acceptable theory must meet.

Many and probably most legal philosophers are broadly sympathetic to the *retributive* tradition. Legal philosophers disagree profoundly about how retributivism should be characterized. According to my preferred account, retributivism refers loosely to a family of theories that award a central and indispensable place for *desert* in their efforts to justify state punishment. Particular retributive theories differ depending on the exact role that desert should play. By contrast, many and probably most criminologists and economists are likely to favor a utilitarian or consequentialist framework. Punishment is justified if its imposition produces better results than its absence—and better than any alternative means to respond to persons who commit crimes. Most consequentialists hold that punishment is justified if it is the optimal means to deter criminality, although several lesser objectives of punishment are frequently alleged to enter into its rationale. As these crude sketches indicate, the prevention of crime seemingly plays no role in the thought of legal philosophers, while desert is conspicuously absent from the perspective of criminologists and economists. The wide chasm between the justificatory strategies invoked within these disciplines seems insurmountable.

Legal philosophers have a hard time understanding why criminologists tend to attach so little significance to desert. I regard the most significant challenge to a consequentialist approach to be as follows. Any respectable theory of punishment must explain why the commission of a crime by the individual to be punished should be needed before a penal sanction is justifiably imposed. Utilitarian theories fail to satisfy this basic desideratum. If better consequences could be achieved by punishing those known to be innocent—if crime could thereby be reduced more effectively—why insist that those to be punished must actually be guilty? Legal philosophers are likely to take seriously the Kantian worry about using persons as a mere means to achieve a greater good. Kant regarded any such use as a paradigm instance of immorality. Although philosophers disagree about exactly how the Kantian constraint should be analyzed and applied, it seems to clearly prohibit the infliction of penal sanctions on innocent persons as a means to reduce crime. But if those to be punished *deserve* their treatment, sanctions can plausibly be imposed without disregarding the Kantian constraint.

Of course, criminologists are equally baffled by the presuppositions of legal philosophers. The most straightforward reason requires no deep philosophical sophistication. Desert, if it exists at all, is gained solely because of what someone has done in the past. Can it really be true that the attainment of future goods in general, and the reduction of crime in particular, plays no role whatever in an adequate defense of punitive sanctions? Only philosophers would seem to think that an acceptable theory of punishment could afford to ignore prevention altogether. The apparent commitment to this extraordinary position is further evidence that philosophers are detached from reality and unresponsive to problems that arise in the real world. This divide may seem intractable, but my primary objective in what follows is to sketch a way to bridge it. Of course, I am not alone. Much of the recent history of efforts to justify state punishment can be interpreted as an attempt to incorporate both desert and deterrence within a single framework. *Mixed* theories of punishment seek to provide a role for both backward-looking conceptions of desert as well as forward-looking goals of deterrence. The problem, of course, is that no one has clearly succeeded in explaining exactly how these two components can be combined intelligibly. Many of the most well-known attempts to do so are ad hoc, incomplete, rest on simple confusions, have peculiar implications, or do not really solve the problem they were meant to address. In this part I mention only one such failed effort, although I return to a second familiar attempt in Part II.

For example, some theorists celebrate a distinction between *negative* (or *weak)* and *positive* (or *strong*) forms of retributivism.[1] Any justification of punishment must accept limitations on what it will allow to be done to achieve social benefits. Almost no one openly approves of brutal torture, for example, even if it could be shown to be effective in reducing crime. Negative retributivists hold that the pursuit of worthwhile objectives such as crime reduction must be limited by a demand that the innocent not be punished: Only the guilty are eligible for penal sanctions. As so construed, retributive desert provides only a limitation on what may be done when an affirmative reason to punish is given. The rationale for observing this constraint—like the rationale for precluding torture—is independent of the justification for reducing crime. Positive retributivists, by contrast, hold that a reason to punish is to dispense retributive justice to those who deserve it—those who are culpable for perpetrating criminal offenses without justification or excuse. Although this distinction itself is relatively unproblematic, it should be apparent that negative retributivism, as so construed, is not really a theory of punishment at all. Negative retributivists explicitly deny that desert provides any reason to punish. Thus it purports to tell us not when to punish, but when not to punish. All the real justificatory work is done by the pursuit of valuable objectives such as crime control.

Moreover, the conception of desert contained in negative retributivism is peculiar and incompatible with what most of us are inclined to say about desert in other contexts. If the desert of the offender simply limits what we are allowed to do to achieve our objectives, desert turns out not to be a reason-giving property. More precisely, desert is not a property that gives anyone a reason to take any positive action. Normally, however, when we claim that a person deserves to be treated in a given way, we imply at least that someone has a reason to provide the treatment in question. It would be odd, for example, to say that a person deserves a reward for providing some notable service, but then to add that no one has the slightest reason to reward him.

If the distinction between negative and positive retributivism is not especially helpful to justify punishment, how *should* both backward-looking judgments of desert and forward-looking considerations of deterrence be integrated into a single theory of punishment? I seek to answer this question in Part II. In order to do so, however, I must make several background assumptions. First, I presuppose a definition of punishment itself. We must be able to recognize when given treatments are instances of punishment rather than other kinds of sanctions (e.g., taxes, compensatory damages, quarantines) with which punishments are easily confused. In the absence of an adequate definition, we are bound to be uncertain about what it is we are trying to justify. In my view, a response amounts to a punishment when it deliberately expresses condemnation or stigma and imposes a deprivation or hardship. Each of these components is crucial. A treatment is not punitive because it *happens* to deprive and stigmatize. In order to qualify as a punishment, the very *purpose* of a response must be to inflict a hardship and to condemn. That is, punishments *intentionally* impose condemnation and deprivation. Armed with this definition, we can clarify the exact question to be addressed. The question of why the state is justified in punishing criminals is identical to the question of why the state is justified in deliberately stigmatizing and imposing a deprivation on persons who commit crimes.

Next, I presuppose that the state implements (an approximation of) the correct theory of criminalization so that the offender whose punishment we seek to justify will have breached a statute that is legitimately contained within its criminal code. With this assumption in place, it becomes accurate to refer to these individuals as *culpable wrongdoers.* I will return briefly to this assumption later, when trying to explain the central role of the *state* in imposing punishment. I mention it here because it is almost certainly an indispensable (but surprisingly neglected) ingredient of *any* account of justified punishment. We cannot hope to justify punishment in the absence of commitment about what it is imposed *for.* A theory should not be faulted for failing to justify the punishment of persons who breach statutes that our best theory of criminalization would not have allowed us to enact in the first place.

In addition, I assume that offenders who commit such crimes without justification or excuse can have negative desert, that is, can be deserving of something bad. This assumption is huge, and I cannot defend it here. I suspect it will be denied mostly by *desert skeptics,* that is, by philosophers who deny the existence of desert altogether. Some such skeptics do not reject the existence of desert per se, but only the allegation that the suffering inherent in punishment can be among those things that persons might deserve.[2] I make no effort to respond to desert-skeptics, but not because their worries are immaterial to my project. Instead, I neglect them because it is exceedingly difficult if not impossible to devise persuasive arguments on one side or the other. In what follows, I will assume without argument that desert is sensible despite requiring explication and analysis. Like obligation and responsibility, desert is part of the moral furniture of the world.

This latter claim, like many comparable claims about moral concepts, is notoriously difficult to defend.[3] I confess that I find myself unable to convince or to produce non-question-begging arguments against nihilists who deny the intelligibility of *all* moral discourse.

Moreover, I recommend that we avoid commitment about whether the stigmatizing deprivation of a deserved punishment is *intrinsically valuable*. All we really need to affirm is that desert provides a reason to treat persons as they deserve. My suggestion is designed to avoid what some philosophers have regarded as the most barbaric and counterintuitive implication of retributivism: that a world that includes more deprivation could contain more value than a world with less. Indeed, this implication *is* worrisome. My *suspicion,* however, is that the state of affairs in which people are treated as they deserve *does* have intrinsic value—that is, contains more value than the state of affairs in which people are not treated in accordance with their desert. Perhaps giving offenders what they deserve precludes, negates, or changes the valence of what would otherwise be an intrinsic *dis*value, so it is not intrinsically bad when offenders receive their just deserts. If we had just one "happiness pill" we were allowed to distribute, and we could give it either to someone with positive desert or to someone with negative desert, we would create more intrinsic value by making the former choice, even though the amount of happiness in each world is identical. Or, if we had just one "unhappiness pill" we were forced to distribute, and we could give it either to someone with positive desert or to someone with negative desert, we would create less intrinsic disvalue by making the latter choice. I am unsure whether any of these suspicions is defensible, but I think both are widely shared. In any event, I deny that the adequacy of my view depends on them.

Like the existence of desert itself, claims about what is intrinsically valuable are extraordinarily hard to support. The difficulties of defending judgments about intrinsic value are compounded when we introduce *impersonal* goods into our calculus—as we must. No one knows how to balance these impersonal goods—goods that are not good *for* anyone—against personal goods—goods that are good *for* persons. Nonetheless, philosophers persist in trying to assess retributivism by reference to its supposed commitments about intrinsic value. Intuitions about hypothetical cases are routinely solicited to support (and to challenge) these alleged commitments. I will mention one such example later. For now, suffice it to say that most of these cases are hard to imagine, so we should lack confidence in whatever intuitions we report.[4] And even if we are confident about our intuitive response, we may be hard-pressed to decide that whatever value we think is achieved is intrinsic or merely instrumental. Thus we should try to escape from this morass. In light of the difficulties philosophers encounter when addressing these hypothetical cases, it would be preferable if we did not need to resolve disputes about intrinsic value at all. I hope that we only need believe that desert is a reason-giving property; it provides a moral reason to treat persons as they deserve. The weight of this reason, as I will indicate, is typically minimal and probably has substantial force only when the most monstrous crimes are perpetrated. We need not decide whether or not intrinsic value is produced when we conform to this reason.[5] Maybe it is; maybe it is not; maybe the answer depends on further details of given examples.

I believe desert provides something approximating a *necessary* condition for justified punishment. But if the strength of the reason supplied by desert is minimal—as I believe it to be—the *absence* of this reason might not seem to be so crucial either. Why *not* punish the innocent? This question is yet another example of an issue that need not detain us. One response is that the reason *not* to punish that applies to those who do not deserve to be punished is much more stringent than the reason *to* punish that applies to those who *do* deserve their treatment. This claim is not *ad hoc*. The negative public reaction to the punishment of the innocent is much stronger than the negative public reaction to the failure to punish the guilty, and all non-consequentialists recognize a weighty deontological constraint against punishing those who lack negative desert.[6] Still, it is inevitable that any system of penal justice in the real world will punish innocent persons. The inevitability of this injustice does not show that a rationale for punitive sanctions cannot be built upon the foundation of desert.[7] At the end of the day, theorists should be willing to bite the bullet about the morality of punishing the innocent. If the instrumental value of punishment is sufficiently great, it may well be permissible, all things considered, to falsely accuse and convict someone who lacks negative desert.[8] This concession is not as startling as it may appear. As I will indicate, we are unlikely to know that the conditions in the familiar thought-experiments designed to give us pause—which typically stipulate supreme confidence that the injustice will never be detected—obtain in the real world.[9] Finally, hard questions about the moral status of punishing the innocent should be posed to all theorists, regardless of the jurisprudential tradition to which they belong. We should not suppose that difficulties that plague all theories of justified punishment raise special problems for attempts to defend a desert-based account.

II How to combine retribution and deterrence

With these background assumptions in place, I move now to my preferred strategy for combining retributive desert with deterrence in a coherent justification of state punishment. To do so, I will discuss each of the premises and inferences in the following argument:

1. Criminal C deserves punishment p.
2. Someone has a reason to give p to C.
3. The state has a reason to give p to C.
4. The state has an all-things-considered reason to give p to C.

A *justification* of an imposition of state punishment, as I construe it, had better support (4). As we will see, the centerpiece of my theory—the part that mixes retribution and deterrence—involves a novel way to bridge the chasm between (3) and (4). First, however, I discuss some of the earlier premises.[10]

Premise (1) suffices to make my theory a version of retributivism. As we will see, desert plays an indispensable role in my overall justification. By starting here, it should be clear that I begin my inquiry somewhere in the middle. I do not pretend that a complete defense of (1) would be trivial or straightforward. Obviously, it is neither. As I have indicated, I make no effort to respond to desert-skeptics. I also admit that even if we accept some claims about desert as true, and some claims about deserved punishments as true, we are bound to be uncertain about how to instantiate the variable p. Judgments of desert are notoriously vague and imprecise. Critics of retributivism never tire of pointing out the difficulties of identifying the *cardinal* desert of a given offender—the exact quantum of punishment she deserves for committing her particular offense. Generally, I concur that the severity of the punishments imposed upon most offenders in the United States in recent years is grossly disproportionate to the extent of their desert. It is unfair to blame retributivism for our epidemic of over-incarceration. Because it is difficult to substantiate this belief, however, I remain non-committal on exactly what punishment given offenders deserve and simply represent this quantum of punishment as p.

Let us see how a defense of (1) might get off the ground, although my own attempt will be incomplete and inconclusive. Recall that punishment, by definition, involves two crucial components: hard treatment or deprivation and stigmatization or condemnation. A separate rationale is required to show why an offender deserves each; together, these rationales would show why an offender deserves *punishment*. Of the two, condemnation is the easier to defend. I contrast three analytically distinct stages through which responses to wrongdoing might (and often do but need not) pass. Suppose Harry knowingly, unjustifiably, and inexcusably rapes Sally. I assume without argument that a set of Strawsonian reactive attitudes are apt or appropriate for Sally. As Strawson famously indicates, normal individuals feel indignation and resentment toward those who wrong them.[11] What is fitting and appropriate for Sally is a *feeling* and/or an *attitude.*[12] The fact that persons have these feelings and attitudes, it seems to me, is the clearest and least controversial part of what wrongdoers deserve. That is, Harry deserves that Sally feels resentment and indignation toward him (and almost certainly much more) in virtue of the rape he has perpetrated. I think we should say—although Strawson himself did not express the matter quite this way—that it is fitting and appropriate for Sally to judge Harry to be *blameworthy* for what he has done. Still, Sally might decline to share her feelings and attitudes with anyone, regardless of how fitting and appropriate they may be. Thus, a second stage through which her response to wrongdoing might pass takes place when she expresses her feelings and attitudes through verbal or non-verbal behavior. She might confide in her friends or therapist, for example. If and when Sally moves to this second stage, we might say that she no longer merely judges Harry to be *blameworthy;* she *blames* him.

Next, these feelings and attitudes might be conveyed or somehow made known to the wrongdoer himself. The expression of Sally's feelings and attitudes *to Harry* represents yet a third contingent stage in her response to his act. Blame expressed to the wrongdoer himself might be called *directed blame.*[13] Does Harry deserve the blame Sally directs to him? I think so. We are not simply interested in how *victims* are entitled to feel or the judgments they are entitled to make about those who wrong them. More importantly, we want to know what *wrongdoers* deserve. Presumably, part of what Harry deserves is that he be made aware of the feelings and judgments it is appropriate for others to have and to make. The easiest way for him to gain such awareness is for Sally to direct her blame at him. If Harry possesses a normal psychology, he doubtless will experience a loss of utility when he becomes aware that others blame him and that their judgments are appropriate. Moreover, persons with a normal psychology feel guilt and remorse when they recognize the gravity of their wrongs. These feelings are also unpleasant. The resultant disutility Harry can be expected to experience is part of what I believe him to deserve. This disutility might be called *suffering,* but this term might mislead us into thinking that physical pain is involved. Disutility is probably the more neutral and thus the preferable term.

Notice that no mention has yet been made of the role of the *state* in expressing condemnation and stigma, and for good reason. The rationale for allowing or requiring the state to create formal institutions that convey blame exceeds anything that has been said thus far. The case for state action is not simply that Harry deserves such state action to take place. When Harry has been stigmatized and condemned by victims and others who learn about his offense, it is hard to see how anything more must be done to him in order to treat him as he deserves. Of course, state punishment is the institution legal philosophers must try to justify. I will briefly turn to the role of the state in discussing premise (3).

In any event, criminal punishment necessarily involves a second component I have characterized as *hard treatment*—some *extra* deprivation or loss of rights. How is *this* component of punishment deserved? This question is even more difficult than its predecessor; only two kinds of answers are available. The first is that this extra hardship is justified in terms of desert itself. Criminal defendants deserve not only to be made aware of the condemnation of others and to feel the guilt and remorse (or disutility) such awareness almost inevitably causes, but also deserve an additional deprivation. The second alternative is that this additional hardship is not justified in terms of desert, but depends on some other objective—in all likelihood, on instrumental goals. Deterrence and crime control are the most plausible candidates for these instrumental goals. Additional deprivations are imposed on criminals not because they deserve it, but because they are used for the greater good of public safety and crime reduction. This latter alternative, however, does not represent much progress in explaining how punishment can be deserved. The deprivations imposed by penal sanctions such as imprisonment are problematic because they seem to treat persons in ways that violate their rights and contravene the Kantian principle against treating persons merely as a means. Desert provides a promising rationale for infringing (rather than violating) rights or for allowing persons to be treated as a mere means; as we have seen, it is the basis for condemnation that is appropriately directed. This second alternative, however, explicitly denies that the additional hardship imposed is justified in terms of desert. Thus, it represents little headway in producing an adequate justification of punishment. Hence the first alternative would make punishment easier to defend than the second would.

Return, then, to the first kind of answer. Why *might* criminals deserve the additional deprivation or hardship imposed when they already experience a loss of welfare or utility due to the guilt and remorse they feel (and ought to feel) in response to their wrongdoing and the condemnation directed against them? To my mind, this is the single most difficult question to answer in constructing a defense of punishment based on desert. One possible answer is that remorse and guilt are necessarily inadequate. The loss of welfare or utility such feelings cause is less than the loss of welfare or utility wrongdoers deserve to experience when they are blamed. The lacuna is filled by inflicting an extra hardship.

John Kleinig makes a different attempt to show that criminals deserve hard treatment. He alleges that "more than [censure, rebuke, and condemnation] is deserved. For though such expressions of blame constitute some kind of practical response to wrongdoing, they fail to 'embody' it. That is why desert defensibly requires not merely a response, but a proportionate one. One cannot separate out the 'blame' from something more."[14] If an additional deprivation is not imposed, wrongdoing is not taken sufficiently seriously. In describing why "something more" than condemnation is required, Kleinig invites us to shift our perspective: "To think otherwise is to make the same mistake as would be involved were someone to take the view that appropriate responses of gratitude to benefaction could always consist of sincere expressions of thanks."[15] Kleinig's argument invites the rejoinder that positive and negative desert may be asymmetrical. Persons who perform exceptionally good deeds might deserve more from their benefactors than praise, but persons who perform extraordinarily bad deeds may not deserve more from their victims than condemnation. After all, the challenge is to explain how the loss of welfare and disutility that results from hard treatment *can* be deserved. Apart from the possible asymmetry of punishments and rewards, however, Kleinig's observation is trenchant. Although good deeds sometimes are said to be their own reward, something is deficient about a response to a massively generous act that consists solely in a verbal expression of gratitude. If the beneficiary is *really* as grateful as he claims to be, some additional benefit—a gift or a return favor of roughly comparable value—is required to supplement the expression itself. Otherwise, he might add, the benefactor has not been treated as he deserves.

So much for (1). If we concede (1) to be true, the transition to (2) is straightforward. As I have suggested, if criminal C deserves punishment p, then *someone* has a reason to give p to C. But further elaboration on (2) is helpful. Retributivists should not be content merely to argue that someone has a reason to treat offenders as they deserve. They must also try to identify the *weight* or strength of this reason in a world in which persons have countless reasons for and against alternative courses of action. We lack a vocabulary to quantify the precise strength of given reasons. Nonetheless, most reasons play little role in practical deliberation. After all, we have a reason to relieve the pain of suffering rodents and even to eat our cars for the valuable minerals they contain.[16] But these reasons have minimal strength and are easily outweighed by conflicting demands. In many cases, the reason anyone might have to treat offenders as they deserve is vanishingly small. Thus, the contested issue is not only *whether* someone has a reason to treat offenders as they deserve (or *whether* such treatment has intrinsic value), but *how much weight* (or *how much* intrinsic value) this reason exerts. I allege that the reason to give (or the intrinsic value, if any, of giving) offenders what they deserve is small—perhaps even miniscule.

But the strength of the reason created by desert is not constant across all offenses. *Ceteris paribus*, the weight of this reason varies with the seriousness of the crime. If the offender and the offense are sufficiently heinous, the overall case for inflicting punishment becomes more compelling. This characteristic of desert accounts for a (weak) intuition I tend to share and that many philosophers take to represent the ultimate test of whether a respondent holds retributive sympathies: The affront to retributive justice many of us would feel if Hitler or Stalin managed to escape the punishments they deserved for their terrible crimes. According to the famous thought-experiments, Hitler has evaded capture, has never paid for his crimes, and is found to be living a happy and tranquil life on some island paradise. It is stipulated that nothing done or not done to Hitler will ever be known to outsiders and thus will not deter future wrongdoing or promote any other instrumental benefits.[17] Does anyone have a reason to punish him? Would intrinsic value be produced thereby? I tend to reply affirmatively, but I do not think we should have any certainty in our answer. In my judgment, our intuitions about this hypothetical case should not be given a great deal of credence. I mention this hypothetical case example to point out that we might well concede it without applying our conclusion to more ordinary crimes. Massive culpable wrongdoing creates massive desert and thus generates a stronger reason to impose deserved punishment.

We should resist the tendency to draw too general a lesson from this weak intuition about how the state should treat the worst fiends in history. Many retributivists have failed to appreciate that the reason to punish—to give criminals what they deserve—is not very weighty in the overwhelming majority of cases and can only be sufficient in the most extreme examples. Retributivists should know better than to make this mistake. No retributivist can be heard to claim that we have a *pro tanto* reason to permit crimes rather than to prevent them because their occurrence allows us to add intrinsic value through prosecution and punishment. Nor do retributivists complain that we miss opportunities to increase the quantity of intrinsic goodness in the universe because the state fails to apprehend and prosecute more garden-variety offenders. This sentiment is expressed (and is respectable) only when villains like Osama Bin Laden remain at large.

Some support for my position about the weight of the reason to punish comes from our attitudes about *positive* desert. When a person performs a socially valuable act that displays exceptional virtue, he deserves an appropriate recognition and reward. Again, however, few theorists seem to believe that a significant injustice is perpetrated when the deserved response is not forthcoming. The best explanation of this belief is that the reason created by positive desert is nearly always weak—too weak to support the all-things-considered judgment that we should undertake the effort of actually bestowing the reward or recognition. Of course, the overall case for commemorating truly astounding accomplishments is much stronger; an injustice would be done if Aristotle or Newton were not honored in some tangible way. In any event, the same conclusions apply, I think, when desert is negative.

Do the foregoing claims simply assume what I have admitted to be most controversial: that some amount of intrinsic good, however small, is produced when culpable wrongdoers are made to experience disutility? Perhaps. As I have indicated, I would prefer to bypass questions of value altogether and simply rely on what reason we have to perform or not perform given actions (e.g., impositions of punishment). Our best theories of intrinsic goodness are so controversial and under-developed that few implications of an account should be regarded as sufficiently counter-intuitive to lead us to reject them on that ground alone. So the disutility inherent in deserved punishment probably *is* intrinsically valuable—to a tiny degree. If I am forced to express my position in terms of intrinsic value and to explain how disutility can ever be good, I offer the following response on my behalf. Much of the sting of this position can be eased by returning to my earlier position about how a responsible moral agent (e.g., Harry) ought to *feel* when he commits a serious wrong for which he is culpable. Typically, this person should recognize the wrong he has done and ought to feel shame and remorse for having done it. Subtleties aside, he should feel *bad* about his deed. Others in an appropriate relation are permitted to *blame* him for his culpable act. A person who is blamed by others, admits he is a legitimate target of blame, and recognizes the gravity of the wrong he has perpetrated but does not feel awful about what he has done is a curious creature indeed. I strongly suspect that something is defective about the psychology of the culpable wrongdoer who does not feel bad under these circumstances. Those who deny my claim must posit a peculiar human psychology, deny that these feelings produce disutility, or offer a solely instrumental account of why such persons should experience shame and remorse. I believe that any of these alternatives is less plausible than my original contention that these feelings of culpable wrongdoers are good and appropriate despite causing disutility.

But how should we move from (2) to (3)? That is, by what rationale does the reason to punish come to vest in the *state*? According to some approaches, this question can be very difficult. For those who rely solely on utilitarian, consequentialist considerations, the answer can only be instrumental. That is, the state should impose punishment because it does a better job of punishing than any competing alternative. Perhaps these theorists are correct about the relative advantages of state punishment over its competitors, but one wonders why they should be so confident. Few alternatives have been given a sufficient trial to be deemed as failures. In any event, my answer to this question is not wholly instrumental but returns to my prior claims about the importance of identifying what persons are justifiably punished *for*. According to my theory of criminalization, the state enters the picture of what it can justifiably punish in two related places. First, the state may enact penal statutes only to punish *public wrongs*. The state neither does nor should punish *all* wrongs—even when these wrongs are egregious.[18] Instead, the state should proscribe only public wrongs, that is, wrongs that properly concern the whole polity and not merely those victims who have been wronged.[19] Second, the state must have a *substantial* state interest in proscribing conduct and in subjecting offenders to state punishment.[20] The requirement that the state interest must be substantial is designed to support the intuition that trivial state interests, however real, do not warrant a punitive response. If I am correct about these two claims, it follows that a theory of the state—in particular, a theory of which wrongs concern it and to what extent—is needed to decide what crimes the state may enact and enforce through the infliction of punishment. Thus a theory of justified criminal law and punishment cannot be derived solely from moral philosophy, but is intimately connected to a political theory of the state. No legal philosopher can hope to provide an adequate theory of the former in the absence of normative presuppositions about the latter.

More importantly for our present purposes, the foregoing claims make it relatively easy to understand why the state has the authority to punish crime. Since any conduct the state is justified to proscribe must concern it (as well as its direct victims)—and also implicate a substantial interest of the polity—the authority of the state to impose punishment is no more mysterious than the authority of any person or institution to deliberately impose a stigmatizing deprivation on those who commit wrongs against it. Schools, for example, may punish their students who break the rules of a competition by using banned substances just as Sally may punish Harry for raping her. Admittedly, *all* punishments require a justification, whether or not they are imposed by the state. My point is not that punishment itself is easy to justify, but that the authority of the state to punish criminals is no more in need of explication than the authority to punish in these other kinds of case.

Finally, what about the transition from (3) to (4)? The defense of this step involves the most original part of my theory and identifies the place where consequentialist goods such as crime-reduction play a necessary role in what is otherwise an unmixed retributive account. Even though someone has a reason to punish Harry, and this reason might be vested in the state, it hardly follows that the state is actually justified in punishing, all things considered. Like other persons and institutions, the state has several reasons to do many things. In order to defend an all-things-considered reason for the state to punish, it must conclude that it is *important* to treat people as they deserve, that is, to conform to the reason it has to punish. Thus separate considerations are needed to show why political systems should go to the tremendous effort and expense of creating institutions that are designed to give offenders what they deserve.

Most thoughtful philosophers acknowledge the gap between (3) and (4). I believe, however, that this gap involves a chasm. Recall that the crucial feature of my version of retributivism is that the weight of the reason created by negative desert is usually minimal. Countless considerations come into play in most or all moral disputes, and it is always easy to identify several reasons that the state should *not* give p to C, even though C deserves p. Desert may be all that is needed to justify punishment in a divine realm, but it provides an extraordinarily weak reason to create earthly institutions that treat persons as they deserve. In the real world—the world in which we seek to justify punishment—at least three reasons invariably militate *against* giving p to C. I will only summarize these reasons here.[21] Punishment is extraordinarily expensive, prone to error or mistake, and subject to tremendous abuse. In nearly all cases, a plethora of additional reasons against giving p to C can be found. The collateral consequences of punishment, especially its impact on third parties such as friends and family, provide additional considerations. When all of the reasons on both sides are identified and balanced, it frequently turns out to be impermissible, all things considered, for the state to give criminals the punishments they deserve.

Since the weight of the reason created by desert is small and significant countervailing reasons can always be found on the other side, in all but the most extreme cases the state requires additional reasons to treat criminals as they deserve. What reasons will suffice? Of the many possible reasons that might be adduced, only the prospects of general deterrence are sufficiently important to bridge the chasm between (3) and (4). Admittedly, a few of the reasons that allow us to move from (3) to (4) —and to actually permit the infliction of punishment on the deserving—are not solely instrumental. Additional deontological factors—norms of fairness and equality, for example—come into play in deciding whether to impose punishments. Still, on my theory, deterrence is by far the most prominent of the reasons to actually give run-of-the-mill criminals the punishments they deserve. Thus deterrence is essential to a complete justification of punishment. It shows why the state should actually (all things considered) go to the enormous trouble of creating penal institutions and employing them to actually give offenders the punishments they deserve.

My position may seem reminiscent of the well-known approach adopted by H.L.A. Hart, but the differences are important. Hart famously argued that different normative questions about punishment should be contrasted and that distinct moral principles should be invoked to answer them.[22] In particular, questions about the *general justifying aim* of punishment should be contrasted to questions of how punishment should be distributed, that is, from questions about who should be punished and to what extent. The general justifying aim of the institution of punishment, Hart contended, is crime-prevention and deterrence. But matters of distribution should be governed by separate considerations that reflect retributive principles. I am skeptical that Hart's approach is defensible.[23] In any event, my own approach differs in assigning weight to retributive principles even at the level of what Hart called the general justifying aim of punishment. On my account, *contra* Hart, the institution of punishment should not be created unless the state has a reason to treat offenders as they deserve. Typically, however, the reason to give offenders what they deserve is extraordinarily weak and cannot justify real-world institutions with all of the disadvantages systems of penal justice are known to have. States should go to the enormous trouble and expense of actually conforming to its reason—that is, to create institutions to give offenders what they deserve—only if consequentialist objectives, most notably crime-prevention and deterrence, are thereby achieved.

Deterrence may enter into the complete justificatory story at other places as well. Fines and imprisonment are the most familiar modes of deprivation, but other kinds of hardships might be imposed on offenders. Decisions about the particular mode of deprivation provide yet another opportunity to ensure that punishments attain instrumental objectives such as crime reduction. Unless some other deontological constraint is violated, the determination to impose one kind of punishment rather than another should be made after examining empirical evidence about which of the available alternatives is likely to achieve our instrumental goals most efficiently. Again, legal philosophers who hope to justify the actual inflictions of punishment in the real world cannot afford to neglect the criminological data that bears on these matters.[24] Even if hard treatment itself is deserved, the *form* it should take need not be governed by desert.

I do not know whether the theory I have sketched qualifies as a "mixed" theory. In any event, I hope the foregoing sketch of a theory of justified state punishment provides a plausible way to combine retributive considerations with deterrence in a coherent justification of state punishment. Like any philosophical theory, my view has its weaknesses, and quite a few details remain unfilled. The challenge, however, is to present a less problematic alternative that combines the ingredients of retributive desert with deterrence in a single theory of punishment. Unless we become abolitionists, a competitive theory would need to be defended before I would be persuaded to reject my own theory.

Notes

1 See David Dolinko: 'Some thoughts about retributivism', 101 *Ethics* 537 (1991).

2 See, for example, Derek Parfit, *On What Matters* (Oxford: Oxford University Press, Volume One, 2011), 263–72.

3 For empirical evidence that "the bare retributive norm is a basic, independent part of our moral worldview" and is among those "norms [that] retain normative legitimacy even if they have no independent justification," see Shaun Nichols, 'Brute retributivism', in Thomas A. Nadelhoffer, *The Future of Punishment* (Oxford: Oxford University Press, 2013), 25, 32, 43.

4 For a nice discussion, see Jakob Elster, 'How outlandish can imaginary cases be?' 28 *Journal of Applied Philosophy* 241 (2011).

5 For further speculation, see Douglas Husak: 'Retributivism in extremis', 32 *Law and Philosophy* 3 (2013).

6 The importance of not punishing those who lack desert provides a plausible normative defense for the presumption of innocence in Anglo-American law. See the symposia in 8 *Criminal Law and Philosophy* 283–525 (2014).

7 For possible worries about the moral ramifications of punishing the innocent, see George Schedler: 'Retributivism and fallible systems of punishment', 30 *Criminal Justice Ethics* 240 (2011).

8 I avoid considering whether the false conviction qualifies as a *punishment* as I have characterized it. The contested issue, after all, is not conceptual, but normative: whether framing persons known to be innocent can be justified by good consequences.

9 The debate on this point goes back decades. See, for example, T.L.S. Sprigge: A utilitarian reply to Dr. McCloskey', 8 *Inquiry* 264 (1963).

10 I present some of this material in Douglas Husak: 'What Do Criminals Deserve?' in Kimberly Ferzan and Stephen Morse, eds.: *Legal, Moral, and Metaphysical Truths: The Philosophy of Michael S. Moore,* Oxford: Oxford University Press, 2016.
11 Peter F. Strawson: 'Freedom and Resentment', 48 *Proceedings of the British Academy* 1 (1962).
12 These feelings and attitudes are effectively beyond our control. As Hume observed, "the mind of man is so formed by nature that, upon the appearance of certain characters, dispositions, and actions, it immediately feels the sentiment of approbation or blame.... [T]hese sentiments are not to be controlled or altered by any philosophical theory or speculation whatsoever." *An Enquiry Concerning Human Understanding*, ed. Eric Steinberg, Indianapolis, IN: Hackett, 1977, 68.
13 See Michael McKenna: 'Directed blame and conversation', in D. Justin Coates and Neal A. Tognazzini, eds.: *Blame: Its Nature and Norms,* Oxford: Oxford University Press, 2013, 119.
14 John Kleinig: 'What does wrongdoing deserve?, in Michael Tonry, ed.: *Retributivism Has a Past. Has It a Future?,* Oxford: Oxford University Press, 2011, 46, 54.
15 *Id.,*.54. Kleinig attributes his argument to Terrance McConnell: *Gratitude,* Philadelphia, PA: Temple University Press, 1993.
16 See the discussion of reasons in Mark Schroeder: 'The negative reason existential fallacy', (forthcoming).
17 A nice discussion of these hypothetical cases is offered in Michael Moore: 'Closet retributivism', in Michael Moore, ed.: *Placing Blame,* Oxford: Clarendon Press, 1997, 83.
18 See Leo Katz: 'Villainy and felony', 6 *Buffalo Criminal Law Review* 100 (2003).
19 See R. A. Duff: 'Towards a Modest Legal Moralism', 7 *Criminal Law and Philosophy* (2013).
20 See Douglas Husak: *Overcriminalization,* Oxford: Oxford University Press, 2008.
21 See Douglas Husak: 'Why Punish the Deserving?', 26 *Nous* 447 (1992). Reprinted in Douglas Husak, ed.: *The Philosophy of Criminal Law,* Oxford: Oxford University Press, 2009, 393.
22 H. L. A. Hart: 'Prolegomenon to the Principles of Punishment., in Hart: *Punishment and Responsibility,* Oxford: Oxford University Press, 2d. ed., 2008, 1.
23 See Douglas Husak: 'A framework for punishment: what is the insight of Hart's *Prolegomenon*?" in Christopher G. Pulgram, ed. *Houndmills*, Basingstoke: Palgrave Macmillan, 2014, 91.
24 See Raymond Paternoster: 'How much do we really know about criminal deterrence?', 100 *Journal of Criminal Law & Criminology* 765 (2010).

Bibliography

Dolinko, D. (1991) 'Some thoughts about retributivism', *Ethics,* 101(3): 537–59.

Duff, R.A. (2013) 'Towards a modest legal moralism', *Criminal Law and Philosophy*, 8: 217–35.

Elster, J. (2011) 'How outlandish can imaginary cases be?', *Journal of Applied Philosophy*, 28: 241.

Hart, H.L.A. (1975; 2nd edn 2008) 'Prolegomenon to the principles of punishment,' in H.L.A. Hart *Punishment and Responsibility*, New York, NY: Oxford University Press.

Husak, D. (1992) 'Why punish the deserving?', *Nous*, 26: 447; reprinted in *The Philosophy of Criminal Law* (2009), Oxford: Oxford University Press.

Husak, D. (2008) *Overcriminalization*, New York, NY: Oxford University Press.

Husak, D. (2013) 'Retributivism in extremis', *Law and Philosophy,* 32: 3–31.

Husak, D. (2015) 'What do criminals deserve?', in K. Ferzan and S. Morse (eds.) *Legal, Moral, and Metaphysical Truths: The Philosophy of Michael S. Moore,* Oxford: Oxford University Press.

Husak, D. (2014) 'A framework for punishment: what is the insight of Hart's prolegomenon?' in C. Pulgram (ed.) *Houndmills,* Basingstoke: Palgrave Macmillan.

Katz, L. (2002) 'Villainy and felony: A problem concerning criminalization', *Buffalo Criminal Law Review,* 6: 451–82.

Kleinig, J. (2011) 'What does wrongdoing deserve?' in M. Tonry (ed.) *Retributivism Has a Past. Has it a Future?* Oxford: Oxford University Press.

McConnell, T. (1993) *Gratitude*, Philadelphia, PA: Temple University Press.

McKenna, M. (2013) 'Directed blame and conversation', in D. Coates and N. Tognazzini (eds.) *Blame: Its Nature and Norms*, Oxford: Oxford University Press.

Moore, M. (1997) 'Closet retributivism', in M. Moore (ed.) *Placing Blame*, Oxford: Clarendon Press.

Nichols, S. (2013) 'Brute retributivism', in T.A. Nadelhoffer (ed.) *The Future of Punishment,* Oxford: Oxford University Press.

Parfit, D. (2011) *On What Matters,* Vol. 1, Oxford: Oxford University Press.

Paternoster R. (2010) 'How much do we really know about criminal deterrence?', *Journal of Criminal Law & Criminology,* 100: 765.
Schedler, G. (2011) 'Retributivism and fallible systems of punishment', *Criminal Justice Ethics,* 30: 240.
Schroeder, M. (2007) 'The negative reason existential fallacy', unpublished paper, available in PDF format at: http://www-bcf.usc.edu/~maschroe/research/Schroeder_Negative_Reason_Existential_Fallacy.pdf.
Sprigge, T.L.S. (1963) 'A utilitarian reply to Dr. McCloskey', *Inquiry*, 8: 264.
Steinberg, E. (1977) *An Enquiry Concerning Human Understanding*, Indianapolis, IN: Hackett Publishing.
Strawson, P.F. (1962) 'Freedom and resentment', *Proceedings of the British Academy,* 48: 1.

8

The ethics of criminalisation

Intentions and consequences

Jill Peay and Elaine Player

Introduction

When enacting a new criminal offence to what extent is attention paid to ethical questions concerning the balance to be struck between harm reduction and harm creation? And what might these questions be with respect to that process? Is harm even the most relevant criterion by which to judge the ethical basis of the process? This chapter strives to explore some of the parameters and perimeters of that balancing process. In particular, it examines the extent to which attention is paid to the differential impact of legislation on identifiable groups. For whilst legal egalitarianism is not contentious, namely, the principle under the rule of law that all – regardless of status – are equally subject to it (Bingham 2010; Dicey 1915), actually ensuring that the law has an equal impact on offenders is much more problematic. There is an extensive literature on the field of impact in sentencing (see, for example, Ashworth and Player 1998; Piper 2007; Easton 2008), but there are also issues about the abilities of different identifiable groups to comply with legislation, or, indeed, to bear the impact of criminalisation and thus the consequential adverse effects of negative labelling. For example, those with the requisite financial resources are more able to facilitate a fresh start by moving from an area where knowledge of their wrongdoing is widespread. The question that arises is whether any of these factors should be a relevant consideration in designing new criminal laws? For if the consequential harms of criminalisation are predictable, more thought ought to be given to developing a coherent ethical framework to guide that necessary process.

We do not underestimate the difficulties of this task. Others have struggled much more authoritatively than we are able to do here; and the work of Duff, Farmer, Marshall, Renzo, and Tadros on their Scottish criminalisation project[1] is impressive, extensive, and on-going (see, for example, Duff et al. 2014). In short, criminal sanctions have been used to both punish and deter harmful behaviour and thereby protect potential victims from future harm and the offender from future self-harming activities. Law can be both protective and paternalistic, protecting citizens from the harms which may be done by others and from the harms that they do to themselves. The latter, as in laws against drug taking, are much more controversial than the former, but some criminal prohibitions, for example the laws on drunk driving, achieve both objectives at the same time. However, punishment itself is in part harm-producing. So a balance needs to be struck between an intervention where there may be good motives, but variable outcomes; and non-intervention, where the state may fail to protect citizens, but in so doing maximally preserve individual autonomy. Thus, ethical issues concerning harm prevention and distribution do not all point in the same direction. And where there are major inequalities with respect to power and poverty, the process of criminalization ought, if it is to strive for an ethical balance, to be at least cognizant of the consequences of criminal labelling.

The criminal law protects both individual interests and public interests; examples of the latter would include environmental crimes and those aimed at preventing corporate corruption, for example, by placing burdens on lawyers to check the identity of their clients for money laundering purposes. As Ashworth (1995: 50–51) has illustrated, threats of punishment can be 'a relatively cheap, convenient, and swift means of reinforcing a system of regulation' making it an attractive option. Moreover, much of the supervision of offenders in the community now operates through essentially privatised mechanisms. Indeed, both the probation service, where over 70 per cent of offenders are now supervised by the private and voluntary sector, and the system of electronic tagging, lie outwith the state criminal justice system.[2] It is a complex picture.

Adding into this brew the issue of longer-term consequences makes the task even more challenging. Offenders exist in a network of relationships which may both draw them into crime, and whose members may suffer the indirect consequences of punishment. The impact on families should not be underestimated (Condry 2007). Whilst for many offences the harm that is caused to others will manifestly outweigh the potential harm arising from a criminal justice intervention, most criminal offences fall into a substantially less serious bracket. Indeed, the bulk of criminal offences are offences of strict liability where no *mens rea* is required on the part of the offender, or the prosecution is relieved of the burden of proving some element of *mens rea* in relation to the conduct element of the offence (Ashworth and Blake 1996).[3] Although one might argue that such offences rarely if ever attract sentences of imprisonment, and their consequences for offenders are accordingly less harmful, imprisonment does sometimes follow. And in any event, for some offenders the stigma of the conviction (or possibly even the stigma of a mere allegation) can destroy their reputation and, in certain cases, ruin a career. Criminalisation then, in some contexts for some individuals, can be devastating.

This chapter accordingly examines the process of criminalisation, explores in part some of the existing normative frameworks for an ethical structure, examines in detail one hard example and considers decisions at the margins of the framework. In so doing it concludes that the context of the act of criminalisation is the key to understanding its arguably incoherent and ethically problematic application. But before doing this, it briefly reviews the extent of criminalisation.

The extent and nature of criminalisation

Although there is doubt about the precise extent of the expansion of criminalisation in the UK since 1997, no one doubts that there has been a significant increase in the reach of the criminal law (Chalmers and Leverick 2013; Law Commission 2010) and that this continues.[4] Indeed, as Chalmers and Leverick (2013: 50) put it 'we face a crisis of over-criminalisation'. Just how new this phenomenon of over-criminalisation is, is contested (Chalmers, Leverick and Shaw 2015), but its presence is readily recognised.

Decriminalisation, the active repealing of provisions which criminalise, is a notably rarer event. High profile examples, such as laws on abortion, homosexuality, and suicide, can be cited, but the political imperative to decriminalise is rarely as insistent a response to a social problem. In contrast, the positive desire that 'something must be done' lies behind much of the resort to the criminal law as a perceived solution. Yet there is an evident tension between a moral approach which argues in favour of the criminalisation of wrongs, and which stems from an anxiety that without law there would be anarchy; and an approach which favours individual autonomy, the freedom to make bad choices and a recognition that criminalising otherwise lawful activities can be counterproductive. The avoidance of doing too much or doing too little is the challenge.

This tension is writ large in the heated debates over the decriminalisation of various aspects of our drug laws. Thus, opposition to decriminalisation persists despite evidence from theorists, scientific and practitioner sources, and now policy-makers, that the link between criminal penalties and lowered drug use may be spurious (Husak 2002; Nutt 2010, 2013; Nutt et al. 2013; Home Office 2014). Indeed, the political response to a Home Office drugs study (2014), a study notably published without conclusions, only reinforces the message that decriminalisation is much more problematic than criminalisation.[5] For politicians worried about the prospect of re-election, sustaining the status quo, rather than striving towards a more ethically rigorous approach, appears to have been the default position.

A much less contentious issue, the decriminalisation of television licence evasion (a criminal offence under s.363 of the *Communications Act* 2003) is currently under review; it signally illustrates why decriminalisation can be so problematic. The proposal has wide support; criminalising licence evasion undoubtedly disproportionately affects the destitute, the illiterate and those simply confused by the licence requirements.[6] In 2012–2013 it resulted in almost 200,000 prosecutions and 50 people were sent to prison for non-payment of fines. Yet the BBC will assuredly argue that having a criminal penalty ensures high compliance with the law; in turn compliance, brought about in part by the activities of a privatised enforcement agency, produces some 74 per cent of the BBC's income, enabling them to provide a service to all. Whether the ethical balance is properly struck between harm to the vulnerable few and benefit to the compliant masses, some of whom would have the capacity to pay more, or who might be prepared to pay more, is hard to determine without an established framework for so doing.

Decriminalisation by default – either through the use of sunset clauses or by the passive failure of some forces to investigate some kinds of crime – also occurs (HMIC 2014). But this is probably less of an ethically informed strategy and more an arbitrary response to resource constraints. But at a time when police numbers are being reduced, the balance between law enforcement and non-enforcement becomes ever more subject to police discretion. All acts of criminalisation have the potential for a widening application of their remit.[7] Similarly, at a time of heightened anxiety about risk, existing legislation can be applied in novel ways.[8] Crime enforcement may also suffer in other areas. And effectively asking victims to investigate the crimes to which they have been subject by placing greater reliance on them to produce evidence of offending, as the HMIC Report (2014) implies, in turn brings its own ethical problems and challenges the claims of a criminal justice system to treat all equitably.

Understanding how and in what ways our criminal law has expanded exponentially is not our purpose. The Law Commission has already reported on the evidence in graphic terms 'more than 2 and a half times as many pages were needed in Halsbury's Statutes to cover offences created in the 19 years between 1989 and 2008 than were needed to cover the offences in the 637 years prior to that' (2010: para 1.17).[9] No doubt Lacey (2014) is correct to assert that much of this expansion arises from the attractions of legislating against a strong policy context where there has been a political consensus over being 'tough on crime'; some pandering to the increased feelings of insecurity and vulnerability that have arisen in recent years (Ramsay 2012); and a growing inequality which has reinforced both of these tendencies.

To reiterate, this chapter is concerned with the ethical issues that are relevant to the process of criminalization; and the context of criminalization is key to understanding why this can be so ethically problematic. However careful the legislature might be about the generation of new offences, and we argue that sufficient ethical care about their likely consequences is not always taken, the extent of those consequences through the application of the law will invariably be subject to a series of unintended events. As the chapter progresses we will consider a number of normative frameworks which could underpin an ethical structure and consider why the predictable consequences of criminalization ought to be a relevant factor when the intention to criminalize is being formed. But we start with a brief detour into a recent development in the process of criminalization in England and Wales, which begins to illustrate the problematic nature of this enterprise.

The process of criminalisation

The extent of criminalisation and its process are not entirely divorced. Whether, how, and in what contexts behaviour becomes the subject of criminal sanctions is highly contingent, not only on the prevailing political consensus, but also on the confidence that any government has in its own programme of law reform. However, one notable initiative links the extent and process, as highlighted by Chalmers and Leverick (2013); namely, the recent establishment of a gateway mechanism by the Ministry of Justice; a mechanism which appears to recognise that criminalisation should be used sparingly.[10]

This gateway mechanism arises out of the Law Commission's (2010) work on *Criminal Liability in Regulatory Contexts*. Its focus on regulatory contexts led it naturally, albeit not exclusively, to the less serious end of the criminal offences spectrum, but the consultation paper did recommend some principles for setting limits on criminalisation generally (2010: para. 8.1). Some 15 provisional proposals were made in the context of a 254 page document: the three general principles are worth setting out in full.

> 8.1 PROPOSAL 1: The criminal law should only be employed to deal with wrongdoers who deserve the stigma associated with criminal conviction because they have engaged in seriously reprehensible conduct. It should not be used as the primary means of promoting regulatory objectives.
>
> 8.2 PROPOSAL 2: Harm done or risked should be regarded as serious enough to warrant criminalisation only if, (a) in some circumstances (not just extreme circumstances), an individual could justifiably be sent to prison for a first offence, or (b) an unlimited fine is necessary to address the seriousness of the wrongdoing in issue, and its consequences.
>
> 8.3 PROPOSAL 3: Low-level criminal offences should be repealed in any instance where the introduction of a civil penalty (or equivalent measure) is likely to do as much to secure appropriate levels of punishment and deterrence.

In addition to these general principles the Commission also stressed a number of other important factors. Namely, the need for criminal offences to be created or amended only through primary legislation; the need for unfettered recourse to the courts where someone is subject to a regulatory (civil) penalty; the need for regulators to facilitate process fairness by having a duty to warn potential offenders that they are subject to liability; and for courts to have the power to stay proceedings in appropriate cases until after non-criminal regulatory steps have been taken. The Commission's tone is in keeping with Ashworth's (2011a) discussion of the role of ignorance in the criminal law: in short, if governments choose to impose sanctions on citizens for breach of the criminal law they should properly undertake the role of giving fair warning to citizens of their obligations under the law. So far, so good.

In November 2010 the Coalition government accordingly established the gateway mechanism to scrutinise all legislation containing criminal offences as part of its commitment 'to prevent the proliferation of unnecessary new criminal offences' (Ministry of Justice 2011: 1). The Ministry of Justice document asserts 'The Criminal Offences Gateway considers the case for proposed new offences and whether they are sufficiently tightly drawn. New behaviour is not criminalised lightly' (Ministry of Justice 2011: 2). Notably, the gateway mechanism does not apply to new criminal offences outside of England and Wales and hence does not apply to Scotland's devolved administration. And as Chalmers and Leverick (2013: 551) note 'the rate of creation of new criminal offences applicable to Scotland … was much higher in 2010–11 than in England and Wales'. Although the authors are cautious about coming to the obvious conclusion, entering the caveat that much more longitudinal data would be required, the fact that there were almost twice as many offences applicable to Scotland compared to England and Wales could suggest that the gateway mechanism was having some effect. But it remains the case, as they illustrate, that new offences with substantial maximum periods of imprisonment are implemented by means of statutory instrument. Here, effective parliamentary scrutiny will be all but non-existent and ethical scrutiny potentially vanishingly small.[11] Legislation introduced by statutory instrument is subject to a variety of parliamentary procedures, much of which can be described as 'light touch'.[12] Whilst there is formal scope for ethical scrutiny, in a parliamentary democracy where one party holds a majority it is hard to be confident that a balanced approach is achieved.[13]

The gateway document (Ministry of Justice 2011) asserts, in the section 'How will your proposals be assessed?' that the Secretary of State will only approve proposals where he is satisfied they are necessary. Amongst the factors noted are whether there are

> any particular drivers behind your proposals (e.g. strong public interest in change, ministerial commitments, case law, or practical drivers such as cross-border enforcement issues or resource implications that weigh in favour of criminal offences);
>
> whether the behaviour is sufficiently serious to merit the stigma associated with a criminal conviction;
>
> where you are creating a hierarchy of enforcement mechanisms, such as a system of informal advice, civil notices, other non-criminal sanctions and criminal offences, whether the offences will be a sanction of last resort and how that is achieved (for example, by restricting criminal offences to the most serious or persistent breaches, guidance for prosecutors);

and notably:

> where you have consulted on enforcement mechanisms, the views of interested parties, in particular whether business is supportive of your approach;

and that

> A wide range of civil sanctions might be employed to create a proportionate and targeted hierarchy of enforcement mechanisms, for example improvement or compliance notices served to secure compliance with particular obligations, voluntary undertakings or civil monetary penalties.

The initiative is admirable in its intentions. Alongside the publication of annual statistics on the number of new criminal offences, it may do much to restrain the easy attractions of criminalisation. However, it does not explicitly ask proponents of new offences to consider the ethical impact of such initiatives, but rather focuses on whether the objectives can be achieved through less draconian and expensive routes. This is notable for being an approach to criminalisation based in part on a last resort thesis – and one which Husak reluctantly rejected as a principled theoretical basis for restraint. He concluded (2004: 235)

> The need to identify principles to limit the reach of the criminal sanction is more urgent than ever. One might reasonably expect that a last resort principle could play this role. Unfortunately, I am unable to defend a plausible interpretation of this principle that will be helpful in reversing our pernicious tendency to criminalise too much and punish too many.

Insofar as 'last resort' is a limiting principle, it is unlikely to be effective, as is illustrated by the discussion below of parents failing to ensure their children attend school regularly. Paradoxically, the real danger may lie in the downgrading of criminal offences with resort to criminal-civil hybrids which simultaneously net-widen and undermine the protections associated with the criminal process (Morgan 2011). For example, the use of Anti-Social Behaviour Orders, which could be applied for in the Magistrates' court on the basis of behaviour which did not infringe a criminal provision, could then be followed by a criminal sanction where the order preventing the (non-criminal) behaviour was breached (Ramsay 2004).

So why the seeming avoidance of any ethical reflection? And what might the relevant ethical framework look like?

Reviewing some normative frameworks: What is the proper subject of a criminal offence?

As documented above, criminalisation has been easy and popular; decriminalisation much more problematic. Being seen to be doing something about a social problem favours the former not the latter. But there can be little dispute that criminalisation implies more than the formal regulation of behaviour and conveys a distinctively moral message of disapproval that is rarely communicated in the realm of civil laws.[14] Whilst it functions to set the boundaries between acceptable and unacceptable behaviour, it also serves to identify conduct that is wrongful and deserving of censure. In this, the voice of the criminal law is authoritative and uncompromising, issuing specific prohibitions and threatening punitive consequences for disobedience. Being labelled as a criminal carries negative consequences that do not arise in the resolution of civil disputes. A criminal record imposes a status of disrepute that is all-embracing of the person and capable of subjugating all other identities. Its stigmatising effects can have far-reaching and long-lasting social consequences for the offender himself and sometimes for people associated with him. Most obviously this can occur where loss of employment consequent upon a conviction causes hardship for an offender's family whose lives are disrupted and material living conditions substantially reduced. In this way criminalisation alone, independent of the threat of any formal sanctions imposed by the courts, has the potential to deter offending behaviour. However, the coercive and stigmatising powers of the criminal law can themselves cause dysfunctional and often unintended consequences that undermine and subvert the purposes they purport to serve. In societies that value individual liberty the legitimacy of the state to criminalise has traditionally rested upon principled arguments that limit the reach of the criminal law by upholding 'a presumption in favour of liberty' (Feinberg 1984: 9). These aim to balance each citizen's moral claim to be free to pursue his or her own interests, against the duty to respect and not interfere with the freedoms of others. The criminal law, then, aims both to limit and to protect individual liberty.

In setting these parameters in liberal democratic states, the starting point is typically defined by John Stuart Mill's Harm Principle, which states that 'the *only* purpose for which power can rightfully be exercised over any member of a civilised community against his will is to prevent harm to others' (Mill 1859: ch. 1, para. 9). Of course, as Monahan (1977: 24) carefully observes, the quotation fails to do justice to the complexity of Mill's argument and the caveats he offers; for example, with respect to those without 'the ordinary amount of understanding'. Consistent with this more nuanced approach it is clear that not all such harms are covered, only those which have been *wrongfully* imposed. In principle, the criminal law is entitled to step in where there is culpability and insufficient justification or excuse. Substantial personal injury and attacks upon private property are central to many criminalised behaviours across the globe. Yet the reasons which justify or excuse such conduct may be variously interpreted. For example, the extent to which householders are criminally liable for the injuries they inflict on burglars found trespassing in their homes, raises fundamental questions about the balance which the law must strike between upholding people's freedom to protect their property and fulfilling the legitimate role of the state to protect all individuals from being victimised by the use of excessive force. In liberal democracies the principle of proportionality, which may be variously interpreted, tends to determine whether defensive retaliation is deserving of criminal prohibition. As a result, the parameters of the criminal law inevitably shift to reflect prevailing concerns and attitudes.

But the criminal law is concerned not only with the immediate harms that one individual can cause another, it engages also with the indirect and remote harms that can adversely affect individuals' interests. Feinberg (1990:13) draws attention to 'exploitative injustices' where one individual gains an unfair advantage over others, but does so without causing them discernible harm. Minor tax evasion, for example, may be viewed as a moral wrong but its criminalisation is not immediately justified under the Harm Principle because the harm caused to the economy is imperceptible. However, if other people also engaged in doing the same, the harm would soon become evident. Hence, individual wrongdoing which only becomes harmful when committed *en masse* may be criminalised for the indirect harm that is risked. A different illustration is found in cases where motorists are convicted of speeding violations regardless of whether other road users or pedestrians have been harmed by their behaviour. The justification for this rests on the knowledge that serious road accidents are reduced when speed restrictions are applied. Enforcement of the law in such cases therefore restricts individual freedom not on the ground that direct harm has been caused but that public safety has been indirectly enhanced. The criminal law, therefore, fulfils a preventive function which not only builds on Mill's original formulation but also facilitates significant additional discretion in the application of law (Ashworth and Zedner 2014: 42–44); a development which may be antithetical to a mature ethical system and one to which we will return when considering strict liability offences.

Another development of the Harm Principle relates to the prohibition of behaviours that are harmless in themselves but which may facilitate remote harm. Selling prohibited drugs or firearms may not directly harm those who choose to buy them but the transaction enables harm to be caused at a later stage. The shift from actual to potential harm raises particular difficulties when the harm to others rests upon the criminal choices of third parties. A key question for criminalisation in these circumstances is whether the initial actor can be held responsible for the consequences that arise from the behaviour of others. The shopkeeper who sells a kitchen knife that is subsequently used in a fatal assault is hardly responsible for the harm that is caused, albeit that in keeping with the expansive development of the criminal law, inchoate offences are progressively embraced.[15] Simester and von Hirsch (2011: 47) emphasise that penal censure should focus upon wrongful behaviour and should not be invoked where an individual has 'no ability to control the potential harmful choices' of another and where their own behaviour has not 'sought to assist or encourage those choices'.

A not dissimilar extension of the Harm Principle has been used to justify criminalisation where the harm stems not from the act itself but from the reaction of others to it. Here the argument for criminalisation rests on the claim that harm will be caused if the action is *not* criminalised (Gardner and Shute 2000: 216). For example, a fascist rally in an ethnically mixed neighbourhood may be prohibited to avoid the risk of public disorder. Such use of the criminal law raises questions about the extent to which individuals' freedom can be restricted when the harm to be avoided is caused by third parties. Simester and von Hirsch (2011: 48) argue that aside from some general duties of citizenship, the responsibility to prevent remote harms should only be allocated on a role-related basis where there is a specific duty of care. Such duties may attach to those who have a responsibility to protect the interests of individuals or groups who occupy positions of dependence or specific vulnerability, such as those responsible for the care of children or prisoners.

One of the most controversial uses of the criminal law relates to the control and prohibition of behaviours that do not inflict harm in the usual sense but which cause *offence* to others. A wide range of conduct can be considered which directly offends the sensibilities of others, causing affront to their moral sense of decency. The most obvious examples relate to the regulation or prohibition of particular sexual acts, especially if performed in public and to behaviour that denigrates or disrespects religious beliefs or practices. Arguably, those who are affronted by such behaviour are not harmed in the same way as those who are the victims of violence or who suffer loss or damage to their property. An important distinction drawn by Simester and von Hirsch (2011: 108–9) between harmful and offensive actions is that the former involves a setback to a person's interests, whereas an act that is 'merely' offensive does not entail any future consequences for a person's enjoyment of the good life, even though it can generate unpleasant emotional states such as embarrassment and humiliation, disgust and revulsion, anger, shame and even fear. In some instances behaviour can be both offensive and harmful; for example, where someone suffers a series of sexist insults that negatively affect their mental and physical health or where the routine use of racist language induces third parties to undermine equal opportunities and treat minorities unfairly. In the absence of such longer term consequences the risk of extensive criminalisation of conduct that is merely offensive is particularly problematic for a liberal state, even if the behaviour does cause widespread affront and displeasure. One significant attempt to limit the reach of the criminal law in this respect is developed by Simester and von Hirsch who emphasise the need for offensive conduct to be wrongful before it can be considered criminal. What is needed is a reason why a particular behaviour is objectionable. They propose that offensive behaviour is wrong when it demonstrates a lack of due consideration and respect for the interests of others. Hence obtrusive behaviour such as playing loud music in a public place may be wrongful not because the noise is unpleasant but because it disrupts or reduces the ability of other people to pursue their own activities in peace. Liberal states, however, require citizens to extend a degree of tolerance towards the behaviour of others and to invoke the criminal law only when such behaviour breaches the limits of what should reasonably be endured. The task of balancing these competing freedoms when not mediated by the Harm Principle and reliant only upon the perception of offensiveness, raises some of the most important ethical questions concerning the differential use of criminal legislation to control the activities of identifiable groups.

Feinberg (1985) argues that there should be a presumption against the criminalisation of purely offensive conduct and that the decision should weigh not just the degree of public disapproval but also the extent to which the conduct is reasonably avoidable by those who object to it. Hence, the appropriateness of the criminal law to regulate offensiveness is more difficult to justify when concerned with behaviours occurring in a private rather than public context. But Feinberg also argues that the decision to criminalise or not should take some account of the importance of the conduct to a particular way of life. Where this utility can be shown the case for outright prohibition is weakened and greater weight may be given to permitting participation subject to certain regulations and restrictions. But such judgements are inevitably shaped by prevailing values and conventions: some groups will have greater power than others to establish their own social mores as normative standards, and consequently some lifestyles will be deemed more deserving of protection than others. The exercise of restraint advocated by Feinberg in his support of the Offence Principle has proven to be difficult to protect in the face of alternative political preferences. Liberal concepts of tolerance struggle to survive when political decisions are guided principally by utilitarian values that sacrifice individual freedoms in order to promote the 'greater good'. The courts of England and Wales, for example, have been given wide discretionary powers to impose Anti-Social Behaviour Orders, with severe criminal penalties for breach, on those whose behaviour falls short of existing criminal prohibition.[16] One illustrative example has been the growing intolerance displayed towards rough sleepers and beggars, by the revitalisation of the *Vagrancy Act* 1824, introduced to remove the homeless from sleeping and begging in public places. Although having fallen into disuse by the mid-twentieth century, it has been recalled into active service in the new millennium, producing a 70 per cent increase in prosecutions for vagrancy offences in England and Wales between 2012–2013 and 2013–2014. A range of hybrid orders, imposed under civil law but prosecuted as crimes if violated, such as Public Spaces Protection Orders,[17] provide recent additional opportunities to criminalise beggars and rough sleepers in public places.[18] In England and Wales historical and contemporary legal frameworks have exercised a preference to uphold the freedom of individual citizens to move about in public space without any interference or solicitation from impoverished strangers, over the freedom of those impoverished individuals to ask strangers for financial assistance. Although it may be argued that the offence concerns aggressive begging, this distinction is not mandatory and is, in practice, open to variable interpretation. But most importantly from our perspective, the criminalisation of begging does not have an equal impact across society, even though it may apply to all members equally. Those who are homeless and destitute are inevitably less able than more affluent individuals to comply with the legislation. Even Simester and von Hirsch's requirement for criminal offensiveness to be limited to wrongful behaviour does not resolve the ethical problem of negative labelling attaching more easily to those who possess the fewest social resources. Arguably any claim to the legitimacy of criminalisation in this area must rest on a presumption that beggars are expressing a distinct preference to beg for a living over other more conventional alternatives and are indifferent to the 'detrimental consequences' and offensiveness they generate. In our view, the wealth of research on social exclusion and poverty (Lansley and Mack 2015; Maine and Bradshaw 2014) undermines the plausibility of any such claim.

Closely linked to the offence principle as a justification for criminalisation is the concept of legal moralism, which extends the criminal law beyond the prohibition of behaviours that directly victimise an unwilling third party to those that affect only the perpetrator himself or those who have consented to his actions. Although often claiming to affront moral sensibilities, the dominant arguments for their criminalisation rest principally on the proposition that the state should protect individuals from damaging their own interests. John Stuart Mill was less persuaded and argued from the principle that every adult with mental capacity should be treated as an autonomous being, capable of rational thought, and consequently the best judge of what is and what is not in his best interests. He maintained that even if damaging consequences arise from the life-choices that are made, the value of choice itself is independent of the wisdom embodied in the decision. But the caveat remains that the choice requires 'understanding'. Legal paternalists, however, would disagree and argue for the state to exercise a duty of care that offers a degree of protection against self-harm. The law that requires all motorcyclists to wear a helmet clearly undermines their liberty in favour of more paternalistic considerations that protect them from exercising a flawed judgement. But Gerald Dworkin (1971: 182) notes that 'almost any piece of legislation is justified by several different kinds of reasons' even if it can be shown to have been introduced for strictly paternalistic motives. Riding without a motorcycle helmet may therefore be criminalised not only on the ground that it reduces the risk of serious injuries and therefore serves the best interests of motorcyclists, but also because it supports a broader public interest by reducing the burdens placed upon health and other public services. Dworkin makes a case for a limited form of legal paternalism whereby criminal prohibition can be justified if the individual risks causing himself irreversible and far-reaching harm. In this way it would be legitimate to prohibit sado-masochistic acts or the use of psychotropic drugs if these behaviours were destructive of mental and physical capacities that impaired a person's ability to make reasoned decisions in the future. However, in restricting the reach of paternalistic criminalisation he sets out two limiting principles: the first is that the burden of proving the magnitude of harm would lay with the state, and it would not be for the individual to demonstrate a lack of harmful consequences and secondly, any paternalistic law would need to show that alternative, less restrictive means to achieve the desired end were not available, irrespective of their financial costs.

Whilst the ethical framework sketched out here broadly reflects the structure of the contemporary criminal law in England and Wales, it does not determine its content. Indeed, Husak (2011: 97), whilst arguing that 'a theory of criminalization provides the set of conditions under which the state is entitled to resort to punishment', recognises that this is a starting point. It does not generate a comprehensive list of conditions that must be satisfied before punishment is warranted. Much as he would like to achieve this, if anything he appears despairing of the viability of the project of limiting criminalisation in this way. So much depends upon the historical, cultural, and political context in which these decisions are taken and the prevailing power relations that shape their substantive content.

We would argue that in creating the criminal law each of the ethical dilemmas described above is subject to a final adjudication to determine its legitimacy. This may be rooted in specific and long-standing moral arguments or rest on pragmatic solutions to immediately pressing social circumstances, or indeed, a combination of the two The criminalisation of murder, for example, is embedded in powerful moral arguments about the wrongfulness of intentionally taking human life. However, the extent to which these claims justify the continued criminalisation of euthanasia and assisted suicide is in many Western jurisdictions hotly contested. In the absence of legislative change the senior judiciary and the Director of Public Prosecutions are adopting pragmatic solutions that take account of shifting public attitudes and new challenges created by scientific advances.[19] In addition, the weight of an argument is not always distributed consistently. Compare, for example, the paternalistic protection of motorists and motorcyclists who are respectively required to wear seatbelts and helmets, with the more laissez-faire approach adopted towards other activities such as horse riding or participating in 'contact' sports such as boxing or rugby. Or consider the contrast between the *regulation* of alcohol *consumption* with the *prohibition* of *possessing* other mood altering drugs. And there are other areas of harm-creation in which the state has abandoned virtually all paternalistic inclinations; notably, those that arise from the unequal impact of the criminal law on the rights and freedoms of particular social groups.

One telling example would be that the criminalisation of prostitution has consequential effects that exacerbate the risks to an already vulnerable group, primarily comprising women. There are a number of models employed in different jurisdictions for the regulation of prostitution (Honeyball Report 2014). The model adopted in England and Wales has been broadly condemned for its consequential failure to protect prostitutes whilst exacerbating the potential harms associated with this trade. And whilst soliciting for prostitution is not an imprisonable offence, failure to pay the resulting fines is. Equality issues are therefore writ large.

The risk of discrimination arguably reaches beyond the uneven exposure of some groups to particular legislation and includes the ways in which punishment itself can exacerbate existing inequalities. For example, in reviewing the empirical evidence of the impact of mass imprisonment in the United States, Muller and Wildeman (2013: 170) point to the difficulty of 'distinguishing the effects of prison from the effects of being the *type of person likely to go to prison*'. They caution against reliance on simple correlations and the need for more research on the mechanisms that drive the relationship between imprisonment and social inequality. But notwithstanding these reservations they conclude that:

> ... having ever been incarcerated is associated with lower socio-economic status, disruption of family life, poor health (with important short term exceptions) and higher levels of political and social exclusion than would be expected based on the observed characteristics of adult men. (180)

In addition they emphasise that these associations affect not only the offender him or herself, but appear to 'extend to the families, communities and states of the incarcerated' (181). In the US the strong association between mass imprisonment and social inequality has led some to question the balance of welfare and penal policies in the lives of the poor. Muller and Wildeman maintain that how the balance is struck 'is at least as important as estimating any effects of the institution itself' (181–82).

A final paradox is that although the prevailing ethical model emphasises the principle that criminal behaviour should not only be harmful but also wrongful, the criminal law has been significantly expanded by strict liability legislation which enables criminalisation without any proof of fault. Here the individual is held responsible for his actions even though he did not intend to offend and did not possess a 'guilty mind'. Examples include many motoring offences, such as speeding, as well as statutory rape, which criminalises sexual intercourse with a minor irrespective of the offender's knowledge or state of mind. The justification for this expansion of criminalisation highlights some important issues discussed earlier in relation to the protection of individual interests from the tyranny of utilitarian claims in favour of the 'greater good'. It is to the consideration of these issues that we now turn.

But before we do so we should reiterate that one should never underestimate the power of state condemnation through conviction, not only in respect of its immediate consequences for the offender convicted, but also through the longer-term consequences for the offender and his or her family, friends and associates. This emerges clearly from the case study below. Offenders exist in a network of relationships. If, as seems progressively likely, childhood experiences have real consequences in later life (see, in another context, Bentall 2014[20]) then it ethically behoves the state to ensure that before conviction all necessary protections for the alleged offender are upheld in the preceding processes (see Ashworth and Zedner 2008). Moreover, as the Law Commission's Proposal 2 begins to imply, criminalisation of behaviour should be confined to those harmful activities that would justify either imprisonment or, in the cases of companies, an unlimited fine. In short, criminalisation should be used sparingly.

An illustrative case

S. 444(1) of the *Education Act* 1996 (and this has been part of the relevant legislation since 1944) creates a criminal offence where a parent fails to ensure that a child attends school regularly. The offence is curious since it punishes the parent for the child's non-attendance, and yet it applies to children up to the age of 16; that is, well beyond the age of criminal responsibility.[21] It is an offence of strict liability and attracts a maximum sentence of a fine not exceeding level 3.[22] In 2000 s. 72(1) of the *Criminal Justice and Courts Services Act* added a new offence under s.444(1A). That offence is defined as follows: 'If in the circumstances mentioned in subsection (1) the parent knows that his child is failing to attend regularly at the school and fails without reasonable justification to cause him to do so, he is guilty of an offence'. The offence is more serious than the s.444(1) offence, entailing as it does proof of knowledge on the part of the parent and an absence of reasonable justification. The maximum penalty is a fine not exceeding level 4 and/or imprisonment for a term not exceeding three months.[23] This new provision complies with the Law Commission's stricture on criminalisation, that the harm done or risked should be sufficiently serious to merit imprisonment, with the seriousness element here deriving in part from the additional *mens rea* requirement. Quite why a new criminal offence was thought necessary is less clear, given the longstanding strict liability offence, but that is another issue. However, one can imagine that a government faced with the perceived social problem of persistent truanting saw the employment of a bigger stick preferable to the use of a juicier carrot, which would arguably have required more innovation on their part.

The case we will examine (*Barnfather v Islington Education Authority* [2003] EWHC 418 (Admin)) concerns the prosecution of a mother under the strict liability offence of s.444(1). Regular attendance at school fulfils a number of social purposes and unauthorised absences are a persistent and worrying problem. As Sheila Scales[24] observed, unauthorised absences severely affect young people's life chances and are inextricably linked to educational under-attainment. Citing a survey from 2002 by the Youth Justice Board, she noted that such children are less likely to remain in education, training, or employment after leaving school and are twice as likely to offend as those who attended regularly. Whilst one can see that there were potentially conflicting rights under the European Convention on Human Rights (ECHR) with respect to the right to a family life and the right to be protected against discrimination, the case turned on the much narrower point of whether s.444(1) was compatible with the ECHR. The High Court ruled that it was, since Article 6(2) – the presumption of innocence before proof of guilt – of the ECHR had no role in determining the legitimacy of substantive law, its remit was confined to matters of procedure.[25]

The court's reasoning, however, is of interest here, since it went further than dealing solely with the narrow substantive point, to consider whether, if Article 6(2) had a role, was s.444(1) contained within reasonable limits and proportionate? The judges were divided, with Maurice Kay J. deeming it proportionate and Elias J. being much more sceptical. Maurice Kay J. noted

> Against this background it cannot be disputed that the offence prescribed by section 444(1) seeks to achieve a legitimate objective. ... The more difficult question is whether the imposition of criminal liability without a fault requirement goes further than is necessary to achieve that legitimate objective (para. 27).

He concluded that s.444(1) was proportionate, since proceedings could *only* be brought by the local education authority, that they had to consider first whether to apply for an education supervision order for the child which could head off the criminal proceedings, and because the maximum penalty was relatively low. But Elias J. questioned whether, just because this was a convenient mechanism for local authorities to meet an important objective, whether that in turn justified the strict liability offence. He asked, if the parent cannot avoid liability irrespective of the rigour of the measures they take to avoid bringing about the prohibited consequence, what was the incentive to take any measures? So did the strict liability offence positively discourage compliance? Moreover, he noted,

> there is none the less a real stigma attached to being found guilty of a criminal offence of this nature. It suggests either an indifference to one's children, or incompetence at parenting, which in the case of the blameless parent will be unwarranted. … Justice is not served by prosecuting the innocent. If they ought not to be prosecuted, neither in my view ought there to be legislation permitting them to be. (para. 57)

Had the question needed an answer, he would have concluded that s.444(1) was disproportionate.

It is, of course, ironic, that had the legislature not also newly enacted the fault based s.444(1)(A) then the strict liability offence might not have been interpreted so strictly. And it also raises the question as to what view the court might have taken with respect to s.444(1)(A). If one increases the penalty but imports a *mens rea* element what does that do to questions of proportionality? If the stigma is avoidable in principle (because of the need to prove *mens rea*) but highly problematic to do so in practice (because parents, particularly single parents, may find it exceedingly difficult to get a wilfully truanting child to school) where does the ethical balance lie?

In the event Mrs Barnfather was fined £75 with £50 prosecution costs. However, in the face of considerable media attention putting a value on her stigmatisation as a 'bad parent' is altogether more difficult to quantify. Thus, the social context of a strict liability offence can raise its punitive aura beyond that which may have been intended, depending, of course, on the variable susceptibilities of the offender to that response.

Pragmatists might argue that no parent would be unaware that their child was not attending school, since compulsory registers mean that schools are quickly aware of absentees and as quickly inform their parents. Accordingly only those who are at fault would, in practice, be prosecuted under the lesser strict liability offence. So the strict liability offence both protects a legitimate public interest (in educating children) and is used (only) against those at fault.[26] In addition, others might argue that criminal prosecution in these circumstances is the approach of last resort, when all other interventions have been tried and failed, including the use of education supervision orders.

But what of Mrs Barnfather's ability to comply with her parental duties? Assuming that she was aware and, knowing nothing about the details, one is led to the conclusion that either she did not appreciate the consequences of non-compliance (and then there is a debate to be had about the role of ignorance in the criminal law; see Ashworth, 2011a) or that she was unable to get her child to comply (since we must give her the benefit of the doubt that she shared the state's view of the importance of education). And for the sake of argument, what chance does a parent have against a truculent and determined 15-year-old who refuses to go to school?

Is it the case that these provisions on non-attendance were always much more likely to affect the ill-educated and ill-equipped, who may already be struggling with chaotic lives? And, given the preponderance of female single parents as primary caretakers, are there implications under equality legislation? The public sector duty provided under s149 of the *Equality Act* 2010, effectively requires all public authorities to exercise their functions in ways that aim to eliminate sex discrimination and advance equality of opportunity for men and women. It includes indirect discrimination resulting from rules or arrangements that put someone with a protected characteristic at an unfair disadvantage. But although sex is a protected characteristic, socio-economic position is not included. In practice, however, recent statutory guidance issued by the Department for Education in relation to school attendance and the enforcement of parental responsibilities, omits any reference to the equality duty despite referring to seven other pieces of primary legislation and four sets of statutory regulations (Department of Education 2015: 3). What does a punitive response achieve, and why has an inducement-based approach seemingly not been tried?[27] Indeed, whether the enhanced s.144(1)(A) would have made it through the gateway mechanism is now a moot point.

Subsequent to the prosecution the *Anti-Social Behaviour Act* 2003 was passed, section 23 of which empowers designated local authority (LA) officers, head teachers, and the police to issue penalty notices in cases of unauthorised absence from school.[28] These fixed penalty notices are designed to supplement the criminal offence under the *Education Act* 1996. The issuing of penalty notices must, of course, conform to all requirements of the *Human Rights Act* 1998 and equal opportunities legislation. However, it is again an open question as to whether the provisions conform not merely in substance but also in their application. Fixed penalty notices raise problematic issues of justice in themselves (Ashworth 2013). There is no statutory right of appeal against educational penalty notices, the sum of £60 must be paid within 21 days, or £120 within 28 days. And non-payment can then invoke fast track prosecution under s.144 of the *Education Act*.[29] Again, parents (women) whose lives are sufficiently chaotic not to be able to get their children to attend school regularly look like prime candidates for failing to meet the 21 day deadline: or even not to have the wherewithal to pay the penalty and thereby incur prosecution.

Conclusions

Exploring the relationship of criminalisation, enforcement and non-enforcement, and their ethical context, is a demanding task. We are painfully aware of the complexity of the issues and breadth of scholarship that characterise debate in this field; not least the important stream of work by Duff and his colleagues (2014) cited earlier. Our endeavours in this chapter represent a modest introduction that aims to unpack some of the relevant ethical issues in relation to existing normative frameworks and to consider their intentions and practical consequences. It is well established that the criminal law is highly contingent – a product of its time and place. And powerful interests shape the normative values and substantive content of the law. Indeed, we would argue that context is paramount, so achieving a universal ethical framework is problematic. Timing can also be critical, so even if a comprehensive framework could be achieved it is unlikely to be stable over a extended time-frame. This is, of course, a slightly troubling conclusion since one might presuppose that ethical values have a timeless and unequalled quality, indeed, a quality that some might regard as transcendent. However, it may be easier to assert transcendence than to descend to the tricky contested territory as to which values, and which values deriving from which cultural and national traditions, should underpin the demands of laws fairly enacted and fairly applied in specific contexts. Disagreements about the realization of these objectives are likely to be much more taxing than simply agreeing that a process based on ethical considerations is one that all would support.

Serious harm, where direct and immediate physical, psychological, or material injury is caused to others clearly deserves a punitive response; but, beyond that, much is tenuous. Issues of remote harm, harm to the perpetrator, victimless crimes, behaviour that is offensive but harmless are subject to a process of evaluation and subjective judgement by those with the discretion and power to define, interpret, and enforce the law. Those with the fewest resources to resist negative labelling are those who are most efficiently regulated by the criminal law. Conversely, those who retain the power to resist negative labelling are least affected. As many commentators have illustrated (Silvestri 2011; Ashworth 2011) these themes also straddle the divide between the criminal law's responses to individuals and its response to corporations. The latter naturally prefer, and the law seemingly facilitates, a process of compliance and conciliation, rather than prosecution and punishment. And these issues take on new meaning in the emergent context of transnational wrongdoing, which is less readily addressed by national criminal laws.

The gateway document, whilst an admirable start, is clearly insufficient as a basis for an ethical framework of the nature we have been discussing. We would endorse its cautious approach to the expansion of the criminal law but encourage the development of a document more reflective of some of the issues of inequality. Indeed, as times change certain behaviours shift from the criminal to the non-criminal sphere, such as those concerning consenting homosexual conduct, whilst others become the focus for future criminalisation. For example, changing cultural values have extended the relevance of criminal prosecution to instances of domestic abuse. In December 2014 the Home Secretary, Theresa May, announced the intended creation of a new domestic abuse offence of 'coercive and controlling behaviour', which will carry a penalty of up to five years imprisonment and a fine. The new offence will outlaw 'sustained patterns of behaviour that stop short of serious physical violence, but amount to extreme psychological and emotional abuse' and is thought to be necessary because such behaviour in relationships can be 'tantamount to torture'.[30] Yet some remain unconvinced that this is a suitable case for criminalisation and question its feasibility given the difficulty of providing evidence to satisfy criminal standards. Clearly tricky questions arise about what thresholds to apply whilst still holding on to an important political message.

The creation of criminal laws requires not just a clear statement of the degree and/or probability of harm that is required to qualify for inclusion. Other issues arise. Are offensiveness and harmfulness on a sliding scale, or are they categorically different? Should mere offensiveness ever justify prosecution? Or should offensive conduct only qualify for criminalisation if a demonstrable wrong is also evident? We would broadly support the notion of a sliding scale, but that does not resolve just how harmful offensiveness has to be before it crosses the threshold for criminalisation; or just how serious 'serious harm' has to be. We do not profess to have definitive answers; we merely urge that an ethically informed framework ought, at the very least, to require that these issues be explicitly considered.

Notes

1 http://ukcatalogue.oup.com/category/academic/series/law/crim.do.

2 See http://ampp3d.mirror.co.uk/2014/03/31/the-privatization-of-the-probation-service-will-it-work/e http://www.crimeandjustice.org.uk/resources/coming-probation-privatisation-disaster and http://www.g4s.uk.com/en-GB/What%20we%20do/Services/Care%20and%20justice%20services/Electronic%20 monitoring/.

3 Whilst Ashworth and Blake's study was confined to offences triable in the Crown Court, where they note that some 40% of offences include legal burdens or defences operating against the defendant, they cite the wider earlier Justice study, which identified some 7,200 offences, of which just over half (3,500) could be regarded as offences of strict liability. Three quarters of offences could only be tried in the Magistrates' courts.

4 In the 12 months ending May 2013, new criminal offences were contained in 60 pieces of legislation; this compares to 52 legislative provisions in the 12 months to May 2012; 327 new criminal offences were created, representing a 12% increase compared with the preceding 12 months (Ministry of Justice 2014) https://www.gov.uk/government/uploads/system/uploads/attachment_data/file/300241/new-criminal-offences-england-and-wales-2009-2013-revision.pdf.

5 The political response being, essentially, a non-response. http://www.theguardian.com/society/2014/oct/30/drug-laws-international-study-tough-policy-use-problem.

6 http://www.theguardian.com/society/2014/sep/24/in-court-non-payment-tv-licence-television-desperate-cases.

7 For example, the police use of s.14 notices under the *Public Order Act* 1986 to deal with peaceful fracking protesters in 2013 has been criticised. The cases, including that against the Green Party MP Caroline Lucas, were dismissed by Magistrates as they did not satisfy the requirement that a 'senior police officer … reasonably believes that it may result in serious public disorder. …' (s.14 (1)(a)).
8 For example s. 132 of the *Serious Organised Crime and Police Act* 2005 was passed to ban unauthorised protests within half a mile of Westminster (a law introduced to deal – unsuccessfully as it turned out – with the long-time peace campaigner Brian Haw). Maya Evans was convicted under it and given a conditional discharge for reading out at London's Cenotaph in Whitehall the names soldiers killed in Iraq. http://news.bbc.co.uk/1/hi/england/london/4507446.stm.
9 But see Chalmers et al. (2015) at p. 178 for a more nuanced account.
10 For details of the Ministry of Justice Response see http://lawcommission.justice.gov.uk/docs/criminal-offences-gateway-guidance.pdf.
11 See also Chalmers et al. (2015) at p. 186.
12 http://www.parliament.uk/documents/commons-information-office/l07.pdf.
13 See, for example, s.2 of the *Legislative and Regulatory Reform Act* 2006.
14 The development of hybrid legislation, such as Anti-Social Behaviour Orders, represent an interesting exception, being imposed as civil orders but attracting a criminal response if breached.
15 See *Serious Crime Act* 2007.
16 *Crime and Disorder Act* 1998 ss1–4; *Anti-Social Behaviour Act* 2003.
17 The *Anti-social Behaviour Crime and Policing Act* 2014 ss59–61.
18 See Chambliss (1964) for an historical analysis of vagrancy laws.
19 See for example, *Airedale N. H. S. Trust v Bland* [1993] A.C. 789 and Policy for Prosecutors in Respect of Cases of Encouraging or Assisting Suicide issued by the Director of Public Prosecutions (2014) http://www.cps.gov.uk/publications/prosecution/assisted_suicide.html.
20 Bentall and his team have found specific kinds of social adversity and specific types of symptoms, with, for example, disruption of early attachment relationships being a particular risk factor for paranoid symptoms. See also Bentall et al. (2014).
21 In England, Wales and Northern Ireland the age of criminal responsibility is 10: but there are variations across international jurisdictions, and across time.
22 Currently up to £1,000.
23 Level 4 fines are currently up to £2,500.
24 A civil servant in the Department of Education and Skills, submitting a witness statement on behalf of the Secretary of State; at para. 27 of the judgment.
25 The case in the High Court concerned a preliminary issue, determined in the Crown Court, namely whether a strict liability offence was compatible with the presumption of innocence guaranteed by Article 6(2) of the ECHR, since no proof of fault on behalf of the accused was necessary. The High Court determined that Article 6(2) only provided a criterion against which matters of evidence and procedure could be tested, and not matters of substance, and therefore the Court could not use Article 6(2) to make a declaration of incompatibility. In so doing they arguably avoided the key issue of substance.
26 Even if the terms of a statute don't strictly require this; see, in the context of health and safety legislation, Richardson (1987).
27 Historically, some LAs did pay a daily attendance fee; it is certainly an approach which works in other contexts (see, for example, the House of Lords).
28 *The Education (Penalty Notices) (England) Regulations* 2004 came into force on 27 February 2004, and have been much amended since, most recently in 2013 (see Department of Education 2015).
29 See http://www.haringey.gov.uk/fixed_penalty_notice.htm There is a Code of Conduct for issuing penalty notices, but failure by a parent to pay a fixed penalty notice can only be responded to by the local authority by prosecution or withdrawal of the notice.
30 See http://gu.com/p/44agq/sbl.

Bibliography

Ashworth, A. (1995) *Principles of Criminal Law,* Clarendon Law Series, Oxford: Oxford University Press.

Ashworth, A. (2011a) 'Ignorance of the criminal law, and duties to avoid it', *Modern Law Review,* 74: 1–26.

Ashworth, A. (2011b) 'Avoiding criminal justice: diversion and sentencing', in *Lessons for the Coalition: An End of Term Report on New Labour and Criminal Justice,* London: Centre for Crime and Justice Studies.

Ashworth, A. (2013) 'Penalty notices for disorder and summary justice', Editorial, *Criminal Law Review,* 869–70.

Ashworth, A. and Blake, M. (1996) 'The presumption of innocence in English criminal law', *Criminal Law Review,* 306–17.

Ashworth, A. and Player, E. (1998) 'Sentencing, Equal Treatment and the Impact of Sanctions' in Ashworth, A. and Wasik, M. (eds) *Fundamentals of Sentencing Theory* Oxford, Clarendon Press 251–272.

Ashworth, A. and Zedner, L. (2008) 'Defending the criminal law: reflections on the changing character of crime, procedure and sanctions', *Criminal Law and Philosophy,* 2: 21–51.

Ashworth, A. and Zedner, L. (2014) *Preventive Justice,* Oxford: Oxford University Press.

Bentall, R. (2014) 'The social determinants of psychosis', Presentation to the 3rd Bergen International Conference on *Forensic Psychiatry: Treatment and Management of Psychosis,* 17th-19th September 2014.

Bentall, R., Sousa, P., Varese, F., Wickham, S., Sitko, K., Haarmans, M. and Read, J. (2014) 'From adversity to psychosis: pathways and mechanisms from specific adversities to specific symptoms', *Social Psychiatry and Psychiatric Epidemiology,* 1011–22.

Bingham, T. (2010) *The Rule of Law,* London: Allen Lane, Penguin Group.

Chalmers, J. and Leverick, F. (2013) 'Tracking the creation of criminal offences', *Criminal Law Review,* 543–50.

Chalmers, J., Leverick, F. and Shaw, A. (2015) 'Is formal criminalisation really on the rise? Evidence from the 1950s', *Criminal Law Review,* 177–91.

Chambliss, W. (1964) 'A sociological analysis of the law of vagrancy', *Social Problems,* 12(1): 67–77.

Condry, R. (2007) *Families Shamed: The Consequences of Crime for Relatives of Serious Offenders,* Collumpton, Devon: Willan Publishing.

Department for Education. (2015) *School Attendance Parental Responsibility Measures: Statutory Guidance for Local Authorities, School Leaders, School Staff, Governing Bodies and the Police.* https://www.gov.uk/government/uploads/system/uploads/attachment_data/file/401467/parental_responsibility_measures_for_school_attendance_and_behaviour.pdf.pdf (Accessed 1 June 2015).

Dicey, A. (1915) *Introduction to the Study of the Law of the Constitution,* 8th edn, London: Macmillan and Co.

Duff, R.A., Farmer, L., Marshall, S.E. Renzo, M. and Tadros, T. (eds.) (2014) *Criminalization: The Political Morality of the Criminal Law,* Oxford: Oxford University Press.

Dworkin, R. (1971) 'Paternalism' in R.A. Wasserstrom (ed.) *Morality and the Law* Belmont, CA: Wadsworth.

Easton, S. (2008) 'Dangerous waters: taking account of impact in sentencing', *Criminal Law Review,* 105–20.

Feinberg, J. (1984) *The Moral Limits of the Criminal Law Vol. 1: Harm to Others,* Oxford: Oxford University Press.

Feinberg, J. (1985) *The Moral Limits of the Criminal Law Vol. 2: Offense to Others,* Oxford: Oxford University Press.

Feinberg, J. (1990) *The Moral Limits of the Criminal Law Vol. 4: Harmless Wrongdoing,* Oxford: Oxford University Press.

Gardner, J. and Shute, S. (2000) 'The wrongness of rape', in J. Horder (ed.) *Oxford Essays in Jurisprudence,* Oxford: Oxford University Press.

Home Office. (2014) *Drugs: International Comparators,* October 2014. https://www.gov.uk/government/uploads/system/uploads/attachment_data/file/368489/DrugsInternationalComparators.pdf (Accessed 1 June 2015).

Honeyball Report. (2014) *Report on Sexual Exploitation and Prostitution and Its Impact on Gender Equality (2013/2013 (INI)).* Committee on Women's Rights and Gender Equality, European Parliament.

Husak, D. (2002) *Legalize This! The Case for Decriminalising Drugs,* London: Verso.

Husak, D. (2004) 'The criminal law as last resort', *Oxford Journal of Legal Studies,* 24: 207–35.

Husak, D. (2011) 'Reservations about overcriminalization', *New Criminal Law Review,* 14: 96–107.

HMIC. (2014) *Core Business: An Inspection into Crime Prevention, Police Attendance and the Use of Police Time.* A Report by Her Majesty's Inspectorate of Constabulary, London, http://www.justiceinspectorates.gov.uk/hmic/publication/core-business/ (Accessed 1 June 2015).

Lacey, N. (2014) 'The state of freedom in Britain', http://www.lse.ac.uk/newsAndMedia/videoAndAudio/channels/publicLecturesAndEvents/player.aspx?id=2499 (Accessed 1 June 2015).

Lansley, S. and Mack, J. (2015) *Breadline Britain: The Rise of Mass Poverty,* London: Oneworld.

Law Commission. (2010) *Criminal Liability in Regulatory Contexts: A Consultation Paper,* no. 195 http://lawcommission.justice.gov.uk/docs/cp195_Criminal_Liability_consultation.pdf (Accessed 1 June 2015).

Maine, G. and Bradshaw, J. (2014) *Child Poverty and Social Exclusion: Final Report of 2012 PSE Study*, Economic and Social Research Council, http://www.poverty.ac.uk/sites/default/files/attachments/PSE-Child-poverty-and-exclusion-final-report-2014.pdf (Accessed 1 June 2015).

Mill, J.S. (1859) *On Liberty*, London: John W. Parker & Son.

Ministry of Justice. (2011) *Criminal Offences Gateway Guidance*, http://lawcommission.justice.gov.uk/docs/criminal-offences-gateway-guidance.pdf (Accessed 1 June 2015).

Ministry of Justice. (2014) *Revision New Criminal Offences England and Wales*, Statistics Bulletin, 3 April 2014, https://www.gov.uk/government/uploads/system/uploads/attachment_data/file/385537/new-criminal-offences-june-2009-may-2014.pdf (Accessed 1 June 2015).

Monahan, J. (1977) 'John Stuart Mill on the liberty of the mentally ill: a historical note', *American Journal of Psychiatry*, 134(12): 1428–29.

Morgan, R. (2011) 'Austerity, subsidiarity and parsimony: offending behaviour and criminalisation', *Lessons for the Coalition: An End of Term Report on New Labour and Criminal Justice*, London: Centre for Crime and Justice Studies.

Muller, C. and Wildeman, C. (2013) 'Punishment and inequality' in *The Sage Handbook of Punishment and Society*, London: Sage Publishing Ltd.

Nutt, D. (2010) 'Science and non-science in UK drug policy', *Addiction*, 105: 1154.

Nutt, D. (2013) 'Beyond prohibition: putting science at the forefront of drug and alcohol policy', *Drug and Alcohol Review*, 32: 3.

Nutt, D.J., King, L.A. and Nichols, D.E. (2013) 'Effects of Schedule I Drug Laws on neuroscience research and treatment innovation', *Nature Reviews Neuroscience*, 14: 577–85.

Piper, C. (2007) 'Should impact constitute mitigation? Structured discretion versus mercy', *Criminal Law Review*, 141–55.

Ramsay, P. (2004) 'What is anti-social behaviour?', *Criminal Law Review*, 908–25.

Ramsay, P. (2012) *The Insecurity State: Vulnerable Autonomy and the Right to Security in the Criminal Law*, Oxford: Oxford University Press.

Richardson, G. (1987) 'Strict liability for regulatory crime', *Criminal Law Review*, 295.

Silvestri, A. (2011) 'Tough on corporate crime? Negligence, death and the Corporate Manslaughter and Corporate Homicide Act 2007', in *Lessons for the Coalition: An End of Term Report on New Labour and Criminal Justice*, London: Centre for Crime and Justice Studies.

Simester, A. and Von Hirsch, A. (2011) *Crimes, Harms and Wrongs: On the Principles of Criminalisation*, Oxford: Hart Publishing.

Waugh, R. and Pidd, H. (2014) 'Begging prosecutions increase dramatically across England and Wales', *The Guardian* 30 November 2014, http://www.theguardian.com/society/2014/nov/30/begging-prosecutions-increase-england-wales.

9

De-moralising retributivism

Agency, blame, and humanity in criminal law theory and practice

Matt Matravers

Mapping the landscape

Writing in 1969 in a standard text on justifications of punishment, the philosopher Ted Honderich commented that 'there no longer are defenders of the traditional retributive theory. ... At any rate, there are no defenders writing in the usual places' (1969: 148). In this, across the USA and UK (as well as elsewhere), theory reflected practice.[1] The use of indeterminate 'public protection' sentences was common, and the Model Penal Code that had been adopted by the American Law Institute in 1962 gave as the general purposes of "the sentencing and treatment of offenders":

(a) to prevent the commission of offenses;
(b) to promote the correction and rehabilitation of offenders;
(c) to safeguard offenders against excessive, disproportionate or arbitrary punishment;
(d) to give fair warning of the nature of the sentences that may be imposed on conviction of an offense;
(e) to differentiate among offenders with a view to a just individualization in their treatment ... (American Law Institute 1962 (1985): 1.02(2)).

Over the following half century, things changed dramatically. Beginning with work in the mid 1970s – including John Kleinig's *Punishment and Desert* (1973) and Andrew von Hirsch's *Doing Justice* (1976) – by the 1984 revision of Honderich's text book a postscript was needed dealing with the 'new college industry [which] turns out theories of retribution' (1984: 10). Again, theory reflected practice. Indeterminate sentences had given way to more rigid sentencing guidelines, and in many cases to mandatory minimum sentences. The transformation seemed complete when the 2007 revision to the Model Penal Code gave primacy to proportionality in relation to blameworthiness and explicitly relegated the other concerns of sentencing to a subservient role. The general purposes now being:

(i) to render sentences in all cases within a range of severity proportionate to the gravity of the offences, the harms done to crime victims, and the blameworthiness of offenders;

(ii) *when reasonably feasible*, to achieve offender rehabilitation, general deterrence, incapacitation of dangerous offenders, restoration of crime victims and communities, and the reintegration of offenders into the law-abiding community, *provided these goals are pursued within the bounds of proportionality* [as specified above] (American Law Institute 2007: 1.02(2), emphasis added).

As we will see, in penal practice this picture of a landscape transformed from a consequentialist/preventive to a retributive criminal justice system was never fully descriptively accurate. However, in penal theory it is possible to delineate the contours of a broadly retributivist understanding of punishment that remains in the ascendancy in the Anglo-American world.

Contemporary retributivism

> Begin with the proposition that the rationale for the criminal law is to provide for the conviction and punishment of those who culpably do serious public wrongs, the distinctive technique being to declare those wrongs, to provide for the public censure of those who commit them … and to provide for punishment up to a proportionate maximum.
>
> (Ashworth 2011: 129)

As Ashworth notes, the distinctiveness of the criminal law lies – or is often presumed to lie – in its *censuring* and *punishing*. Its legitimacy depends on its punishing only those who deserve censure to the degree proportional to the censure that is deserved. Moreover, in some leading retributive thinking – and in the minds of many in the general public – the justification of the system of criminal sanctions is to be found in its overlap with morality. We are justified in punishing those who have committed morally wrong acts (at least those that fall in the subset of morally wrong acts that are also serious public wrongs) to the degree proportional to their moral blameworthiness.

This commitment to a broadly retributivist account of punishment has generated wide agreement on two key themes: that the punishment of a particular individual expresses blame (censure) for the serious public wrong done and that both the blame and the sanction that follows must be proportional to that wrong and to the culpability of the offender where culpability 'tracks' (in some sense) the offender's responsibility. These themes are in turn reflected in two growing literatures. One on what is properly *criminal* (what are – and, perhaps more important, what are not – the serious public wrongs that ought to be the concern of the criminal law) (Husak 2008; Duff, Farmer et al. 2010; Duff, Farmer et al. 2012). The other on what kinds of persons, with what kinds of capacities, are rightly held responsible, and what kinds of circumstance excuse or reduce culpability (where the literature is now vast).

The broad conclusions that flow from these literatures follow from the key themes: the criminal law ought to be reserved only for serious public wrongs and blame and sanctions reserved only for those offenders whose actions can be properly attributed to their voluntary choices (an agent who has 'the general capacity to understand and to be guided by reasons … or the general capacity to understand the law's commands and the consequences for violating them' and who is not non-culpably irrational such that s/he 'is unable rationally to comprehend the facts that bear on the morality of his action or is unable rationally to comprehend the applicable moral or legal code that provides the good reason not to breach') (Morse 2013: 121).

This broadly retributive picture is of course not uncontroversial – and retributivist theories continue to come in a variety of guises[2] – but it nevertheless captures something of the spirit of the age in both theory and practice. It also, for those who endorse it, provides the template against which contemporary policies are to be judged. That said, criminal law theory and practice do not map easily onto this retributivist picture for at least three reasons. First, the transformation of the criminal justice landscape was never as complete as some accounts of the rise of retributivism would have it. With respect to the key claims above, second, criminalization and the criminal law have continued to expand in ways that have increased the gap between retributive theory and the phenomenon which it is meant to theorise. Third, the notion of agency and responsibility – the culpable person presumed by retributive theory – has continued to prove problematic. It is worth saying a little about each of these as a way of setting up the debate and motivating the responses to that debate.

The report of the death of preventive justice was an exaggeration

Although it is accurate to describe retributive thinking as having the ascendancy since (roughly) the mid 1970s, elements of the other rationales of punishment have not of course completely disappeared in that time. Concern for prevention, reform, rehabilitation, and so on, have continued to inform policy-making and penal practice. For example, §142 of the British Government's Criminal Justice Act of 2003, lists five 'purposes of sentencing':

> 1. Any court dealing with an offender in respect of his offence must have regard to the following purposes of sentencing—
>   (a) the punishment of offenders,
>   (b) the reduction of crime (including its reduction by deterrence),
>   (c) the reform and rehabilitation of offenders,
>   (d) the protection of the public, and
>   (e) the making of reparation by offenders to persons affected by their offences.[3]

These multiple purposes are reflected in penal practice. Diversion programmes (drug courts and the like) and attempts at treatment and rehabilitation (in particular through Cognitive Behaviour Therapy) have continued and to these have been joined practices of restorative justice. Beyond these familiar rehabilitative measures, there has also been significant growth in preventive policies to control those deemed 'dangerous'. This in part reflects the rhetorical division promoted by populist politicians and media between the law-abiding 'us' and the dangerous 'them' – rhetoric that was fuelled by the attacks of 9/11 on New York and 7/7 on London and more generally by the rise of global terrorism – and in part the growth of a 'risk society' in which the management of risk becomes the predominant concern (for a classic statement on the 'risk society', see Beck 1992; for application to criminal justice see Hudson 2003). These 'dangerousness' policies include statutes to increase dramatically the sentences for repeat offenders (most notoriously 'three strikes' rules); sex-offender registers and so-called 'Megan's Law' statutes; sentencing guidelines that increase the penalty for those perceived as a future risk to others; and 'sexual predator' laws that allow the continued detention of those considered to present a continuing danger to the public on completion of their penal sentence.

The criminal law's wrongs

As noted above, the retributive model has at its core the idea of censuring those who do moral and legal wrongs in proportion to the harm done and to their blameworthiness in performing those wrongs. However as Vincent Chiao notes, this looks increasingly out of touch with the reality of the law both 'on the books' and as practiced 'on the ground'. As Chiao puts it, 'if we look at actually existing institutions it becomes quite implausible to describe those institutions as exclusively, or even, for that matter, primarily, devoted to censorious punishing of prejusticial wrongs' (Chiao: 8; these ideas are discussed further in Chiao Forthcoming, Chapter 2). The basis for Chiao's assessment lies in a number of empirical observations.

'On the books', US Federal Law is estimated to contain over 3,000 distinct offences only a tiny minority of which could possibly be described as serious moral wrongs. Moreover, the figure of 3,000 does not include the thousands of regulatory offences created by governmental agencies of various kinds.

'On the ground', arrests for drug offences, property offences, public order offences, and misdemeanours far exceed those for the 'core' of serious assault, rape, homicide, and so on. In short, large parts of the criminal justice systems of both the USA and UK resemble more a system of rules for co-operative living than they do a system for censuring and sanctioning those who culpably commit serious moral wrongs.

The criminal law's persons

Finally, there is an increasing gap between the retributive model of the offender – a responsible agent whose voluntary choices determine his culpability – and the target of criminal law. This gap is evident in three ways. First, in the growth of strict liability offences (offences in which at least one element is strict). On the retributive model such offences ought to be outliers or even, as H.L.A. Hart put it, compromises that if not justified by some important policy goal render strict liability 'an odious and useless departure from proper principles of liability' (2008: 34). Yet, far from being outliers – or thought 'odious' – strict liability is now a commonplace across the criminal law (for a discussion of its prevalence in English and Welsh criminal law see Ashworth and Blake 1996). Second, and as mentioned above, the criminal law and criminal 'punishments' are increasingly used not to censure people for their past wrongs, but to control and prevent people from performing future wrongs. This is not merely a matter of the extension of inchoate offences, but includes additional punishment for 'dangerousness', sex-offender registers, and the other policies described above. For some of those who fall under these regimes, the accompanying rhetoric is one that is, from the retributive point of view, deeply confused. The 'sexual predator', for example, is *both* a culpable agent who deserves punishment for his past act *and* a continuing menace who cannot help himself and who thus needs incapacitating in one way or another. Third, and finally, the default view of the person as an agent who acts voluntarily in response to reasons such that it is fair to blame him for his actions is coming under increasing pressure given the realities of crime and punishment and from various disciplines that offer explanations of human behaviour.

With respect to crime and punishment, the sad reality of criminal offending does not reflect the neat abstractions of choosing agents guided by reasons. Instead, the unemployed, the socially and economically disadvantaged, members of minority racial groups, those from communities in which crime is rife and commonplace whose options are few and whose position is often desperate, make up the bulk of those processed by an impersonal criminal justice system that is far removed from the model of a respectful dialogue through which to bring the offender to an awareness of the moral wrong he has done.

With respect to the pressures that arise from causal explanations of human behaviour, of course some psychiatrists and social scientists – and now neuroscientists – have long pressed their claims that human action is caused in ways that render judgements of praise and blame illegitimate so the point should not be pushed too far. Nevertheless, the basic legitimating story on which retributivism depends – that punishment is only of the blameworthy in proportion to their blameworthiness – is one that has been both subject to criticism from the outside (by, for example, neuroscientists; Greene and Cohen 2004) and to a degree accommodated from within (by, for example, developments in defences for 'battered women' and so-called 'cultural defences') in ways that threaten to render the default position unstable.

Two further features

It is worth adding two features to the landscape; features that challenge retributive and other theorists alike (albeit in different ways). First, the aim of much of the retributive work done in the 1970s was to criticise, and to find an alternative to, indeterminate sentencing. The goal was to *reduce* the use of prison (as well as to try to ensure greater equality in the treatment of offenders of different classes and races). However, by promoting proportionality in the language of desert these theorists unwittingly played into the hands of populist politicians who colonised the language of retributivism to promote harsher penalties, mandatory minimum sentences, and other draconian policies (see Matravers 2011). The result, nearly half a century later, is a staggering increase in the prison populations of the USA and UK.[4]

Second, to repeat the point part made above, most crimes (other than those for which high levels of education or status are required) are carried out by young men who are disproportionately drawn from the ranks of the disadvantaged. Their lives will already have been blighted by limited opportunity, unemployment, and disadvantage, and there is a good chance that the same will apply to their victims. Crime and punishment do not exist in a vacuum sealed from the facts of socio-economic and racial injustice. However, it is also worth noting that most will stop offending – 'desist' – as they grow older. Being a 'criminal' may well be a social state from which many offenders never escape, but being someone who commits crime, for many individuals, is a transitory state that may have begun in their early teens and that they will grow out of by their mid to late twenties.

Responding to the landscape

The gulf between the retributive theory of the criminal law and the actual state of the criminal law is something that ought to concern retributivist theorists. As Nicola Lacey reminds us, philosophers who are 'engaged in theorizing social phenomena which have a "real" existence' bear a special responsibility, insofar as their 'philosophical account is ... in some sense answerable ...' to the contours of that social phenomena (Lacey 2007: 138). Of course, Lacey does not mean that philosophical theories ought to bend uncritically to accommodate what is happening in the world. Many theories – not merely of the criminal law, but for example, of justice – have as an important function to provide ideals not only to which we should aspire, but that allow us to see how far short of ideal is the world we inhabit. What kind of challenge, then, is it that taken as a whole our systems of criminal justice so little resemble retributive theory?

One possibility is as mentioned: that retributive theory correctly articulates the ideal system and provides the basis on which to challenge existing non-retributive practices. This might be done wholesale or in part. Amongst 'wholesale' theorists Michael Moore stands out as insisting that 'we are justified in punishing because *and only because* offenders deserve it' (1997: 91, emphasis added). For Moore, then, although crime reduction might be a happy side effect of justified punishment, criminal law practice ought to be brought into line with strict retributivist principles.

For others, there is no need to deny that punishment can have other aims, or effects, than 'doing justice'. For example, in different ways both Andrew von Hirsch and 'Limiting

Retributivists' such as Norval Morris and Michael Tonry allow that penal hard treatment can aim at prevention but insist that this can only be done in ways consistent with the demands of justice. In the language of the Model Penal Code 2007, all other goals must be 'pursued within the bounds of proportionality' (Morris 1974; Morris and Tonry 1990; von Hirsch 1993).[5] Finally, there are those such as Stephen Morse and Paul Robinson for whom the issue is one of the distinct purposes of *criminal* justice as against *preventive* justice. For Morse and Robinson, the aim of preventing future harm is an acceptable one, but it is distinct from the aim of punishing past wrongdoing (Morse 1999; Robinson 2001).

The differing responses of the 'wholesale' and 'in part' retributivists reflect to some degree their willingness to include the prevention of future crimes amongst the overall purposes of the criminal justice system. For Moore, criminal justice exists only to give offenders the punishment that they deserve. Similarly, for Duff, it exists only to censure offenders and to allow them the opportunity and vehicle for penance. Others, like von Hirsch and Morris and Tonry, accept that the overall purpose – in H. L. A. Hart's famous phrase, 'the general justifying aim' (Hart 2008: 4) – of the system of criminal justice includes the prevention of future crimes, but insist that proportionality (understood strictly or within limiting retributivism) is always a side constraint when pursuing this goal. For these theorists, the task is to mediate the potentially different demands of prevention and proportionality and, looking at the landscape as it is, to distinguish between those initiatives that are consistent with their position and those that are not.[6]

What follows does not engage point by point with retributivist theory with a view to revising or rebutting it. Rather, what is offered is a sketch of an alternative vision of criminal law and punishment. It will be clear in what ways the sketch differs from retributivism (in short, what is offered below is robustly political and institutional rather than moral), but there is no decisive argument in favour of the account or against the retributive one. As this is a relatively unusual way for a philosophical argument to proceed it is worth saying something about what does (and does not) motivate it.

Although the sketch below is offered as a better fit with the realities of criminal justice presented above, it is not an attempt to justify or rationalise current criminal and penal policy. The extensions of criminal law and their disproportionate application to those already disadvantaged are rightly the subject of severe criticism.

That said, partly what motivates the account is a certain frustration with the existing state of the debate. Philosophers have offered sophisticated arguments in good faith for and against retributive and consequentialist accounts of punishment for years and in the meantime criminal law and criminal justice practices have continued to fail to adhere to either paradigm. Politicians and legislatures – often pushed by actual or perceived public opinion – extend the scope of the criminal law and add to penal severity in the name of 'keeping us safe', 'protecting the law-abiding', and 'giving offenders what they deserve', as it suits them (and their electorates).

Aligning retributive arguments with moral theory exacerbates this problem and has, to a large degree, left retributivist penal theorists shouting (sometimes entirely apt) denunciations of penal policy from the side lines (consequentialist theorists can at least engage with the 'what works?' agenda on the basis of empirical research). Perhaps this is in part a result of believing that the alternatives are mutually exclusive. In Stephen Morse's terms, that the alternatives are 'desert jurisprudence' or 'disease jurisprudence' (or sometimes 'the justice model' or 'the treatment model') (Morse 2000, 2013) and that any move away from the justice model will result in a slide towards the treatment model. If this were right, then we have good reason to be careful. Being a criminal is not a disease, and it is important that the state treats its (sane adult) citizens as responsible agents. However, as the metaphor of 'sliding' suggests, there is conceptual space between 'desert' and 'disease'. Finally, there is the possibility that political philosophy just is a suggestive discipline. That it progresses not by 'proof' and 'refutation', but by the suggestion that looking at a certain thing in a certain way might shed on it a different and potentially more interesting light. In any event, that is the hope in what follows.

Constructing the criminal law

The chapter began with a retributive account in which the criminal law is concerned with offences that involve a moral wrong done by a responsible agent in virtue of which that agent deserves blame in a sense that brings with it deserved sanctions. The demands of agency and responsibility are intimately tied to the idea of deserved sanctions. On this picture it is legitimate to use the power of the criminal law to punish only and because the responsibility of the offender underwrites her deserving the sanction. However, as we have seen, neither criminal practice nor theory fully accords with this picture. In practice, many things are criminalized that are not moral wrongs and the law fails to track responsibility. Moreover, non-desert based, non-proportional practices continue to flourish. These variations from the retributive norm can be deliberate and explicit, as in the case of strict liability with respect to responsibility and therapeutic jurisprudence in the management of offenders, but are often neither as in the case of 'three-strikes' laws and sexual predator statutes.

What follows is recognisably a 'mixed theory' in that it accords place to both the thought that the whole edifice of criminal justice, law, and punishment must have something to do with reducing future offending and the thought that 'punishment' must be 'of an offender for an offence' (Hart 2008).

The starting point for many mixed theories is with the values 'in the mix' (for example, with prevention and desert). This then structures what follows, which is to deploy philosophical resources to show how these values can both be realised in one scheme. What this threatens to miss is that it is *the state* that criminalises and punishes. As T.M. Scanlon puts it, 'Governments owe it to their citizens to affirm their rights by condemning serious rights violations (whether or not this makes those violations less likely to occur). They also owe it to their citizens to discourage violations by condemnation and, insofar as this is necessary, by threatening wrongdoers with forms of hard treatment' (Scanlon 2013: 103).

Thus, before we can ask about the justifiability of punishing this or that offender to this or that degree, we have to ask what justifies the existence of a set of state rules that have attached to them the threat of sanctions for those who culpably disobey those rules. The values to be affirmed need to be understood in the light of this question as do the particular features of the criminal law and state punishment.

A 'contract' heuristic

In a liberal democratic state, political power – 'coercive power backed by the use of sanctions' – is 'ultimately the power of the public, that is, the power of free and equal citizens as a collective body' (Rawls 2005: 136). It is a power that we impose upon ourselves. A heuristic question can then be put, 'under what circumstances and for what reasons would I, together with others, agree to a set of coercive rules which have attached to them the threat of sanctions for those who disobey?'

Heuristic devices of this kind – particularly those that use the language of 'contract' – can arouse suspicion, so it is worth being clear as to its purpose here. The point is simply to try to make the steps in the argument clear; to illustrate how reasoning in a certain way from a certain position gives rise to certain results (different reasons and/or different positions would of course result in different results).[7]

The circumstances of justice

The circumstances in which the question of punishment arises cannot be entirely abstract. However, we can borrow from Rawls's account of the circumstances of justice (itself borrowed from Hume). Amongst what Rawls calls the 'objective circumstances' are that 'many individuals coexist together at the same time on a definite geographical territory'; the capacities of these individuals are roughly similar so that 'no one among them can dominate the rest'; each is 'vulnerable to attack, and all are subject to having their plans blocked by the united force of others'; and society is characterized by a moderate scarcity such that 'natural and other resources are not so abundant that schemes of cooperation become superfluous, nor are conditions so harsh that fruitful ventures must inevitably break down'.

Amongst the 'subjective circumstances of justice' are that persons have their own 'plans of life'. These plans are 'in various ways complementary' so that living together with others is both possible and advantageous, but nevertheless people have 'different ends and purposes', and they 'make conflicting claims on the natural and social resources available'. Finally, 'we suffer from various shortcomings of knowledge, thought, and judgment'. Our 'knowledge is necessarily incomplete, [our] powers of reasoning, memory, and attention are always limited, and [our] judgment is likely to be distorted by anxiety, bias, and a preoccupation with [our] own affairs.' As Rawls notes, 'some of these defects spring from moral faults ...', but many are simply features of our imperfect natures (Rawls 1971: 126–27).

Regulating our lives together

Given the circumstances of justice there is a need for co-ordination and regulation. To give a simple example, we all have an interest in getting around quickly and safely; we have roads and cars, so we need a rule for whether we drive on the right or the left as well as many (formal and informal) conventions governing how we indicate to each other our intentions, allow one another to pass, and so on. Our lives are regulated in a wide variety of ways – from rules of etiquette to the criminal law – and of the nature and scope of these we can always ask 'under what circumstances and for what reasons would I, together with others, agree to them?'[8]

What circumstances could give rise to the need for a system of criminal law and punishment? First, like any regulative system, there is the 'declarative' need identified by Ashworth. The criminal law needs to identify what must not be done (sometimes what must be done). This is so that people can adjust their behaviour as needed so as to live together successfully. In this, the criminal law is no different from, for example, the conventions that regulate discussion in a seminar. If everyone were to speak simultaneously and as a result no-one was able to hear anything other than babble, discussion would not work. By 'declaring' that one person speaks at a time, participants know what to do and what not to do, and there is a chance of effective discussion.

In a formal setting like a university seminar, the tutor may attach sanctions to the rules of discussion. For example, that if a participant persistently interrupts, then he will be barred from speaking for 15 minutes. The circumstances that would motivate such a move are of course disputed by retributivists and their opponents (the debate does not disappear – and nor should we expect it to – when we use a heuristic device to shed light on it). A consequentialist will argue that what explains the attaching of a sanction is the risk of interruptions and the need to deter those who are, or would be, motivated to interrupt. Should there be no such risk, there would be no reason to sanction. By contrast, the focus of the retributivist is on the need to sanction the person who interrupts. That person has done something wrong, and there is a need to mark that wrong by sanctioning him.

That said, if there were no great need for seminar discussions – or for conversation generally (perhaps because human beings developed the ability to communicate silently by reading each other's minds) – we surely would not need to bring the rules of discussion into existence merely so that we could sanction interrupters when necessary. The need to sanction, where it exists, is a *consequence* of having systems of regulation, which are themselves a consequence of the structures of social interaction, not a reason to bring such systems into existence.

Regulating through the criminal law

To pinpoint the circumstances that could give rise to the need for a system of criminal law and punishment requires that we identify some characteristics of a *criminal,* rather than any other, system of regulation. Begin with those on the table: the criminal law is distinctive because of the way in which it sanctions in the quantitative sense that its sanctions are severe and in the qualitative sense that they express a particular form of public censure.

The 'circumstances of criminal justice' borrow from the 'circumstances of justice'. Given that we have reason to live together, we need systems of regulation. Some of those systems will govern activities that are vitally important because, for example, they include aspects of our lives that are essential to our individual plans of life (such as our bodily or sexual integrity) or because they include interactions that are essential to the functioning of the system as a whole (such as rules of property ownership).[9] Thus the criminal law declares that citizens ought not to infringe on others' sexual integrity without consent and that they ought not to steal from one another (and so on). In designating these things as *criminal* wrongs it adds weight to the declaration.

Sanctions

The grounds on which to add sanctions to the regulations of the criminal law are that there is a risk that its injunctions will not be obeyed. This risk arises in a number of ways. There are those who will disobey in any case. There are those who will only disobey if there is no sanction (elsewhere (Matravers 2016), I have called this group 'potential direct offenders'). In addition, there are those whose obedience is conditional on their being assured that others are obeying and that they are not the victims of free-riding ('potential assurance offenders'). Finally, it is worth recalling Rawls's subjective circumstances of justice. We are all (to greater and lesser degrees) subject to various 'shortcomings of knowledge, thought, and judgment' and our reasoning 'is likely to be distorted by anxiety, bias, and a preoccupation with [our] own affairs.' Any one of us, then, might disobey the reasonable demands of the criminal law through momentary bad judgement.

Attaching sanctions to the rules mitigates these risks in different ways. For example, there are those who absent sanctions would conceal their incomes so as to avoid paying tax (potential direct offenders). There are those who would not do this if they believed others were complying, but who would do so if they came to believe that tax avoidance was widespread and that they were the victims of others' free riding. Finally, there are those who might be generally obedient, but whose reasoning is prone to letting them down (who think, for example, that paying tax is an obligation with which one ought to comply, but who then think that it will not 'really matter' if in their particular case they do not declare some bit of unexpected income).

If these risks did not exist, and (enough) citizens would obey the criminal law in the absence of any sanctions, then there would be no reason to attach sanctions to the declarations of the criminal law. If the risks do exist and the threat of sanctions is effective, then there is reason to attach sanctions, but of course were the threat of these entirely successful, then they would never need to be used.

At this point, the wholesale retributivist demurs. For him, the rules and their associated sanctions are needed in order to punish those who do (serious public) moral wrongs. That is no part of this picture. The performance of moral wrongs may rightly elicit moral criticism, but criminal regulation and sanctions represent a discrete form of regulation whose rationale lies in the need for regulation if we are to live together successfully.[10]

However, that still leaves blame. So far, what has been offered is a purely instrumental account of sanctions – as needed to render the system of criminal regulation effective – with no mention of blame. If we return to our heuristic device, under what circumstances and for what reasons would we incorporate blame as an essential element in the system of criminal regulation to which we subject ourselves individually and as a public body?

Blame

Consider again the example of a seminar discussion. Imagine that one person (call him Bill) consistently interrupts and generally shows disregard for the conventions that regulate such discussions. Assuming that Bill is an adult and does not suffer from some kind of disorder that renders him unable to control his behaviour or unable to recognise normal social cues, it is likely that this will trigger in the other participants certain 'reactive attitudes' such as resentment (Strawson 1962). In these circumstances, the other participants might criticise Bill and challenge him for his behaviour and, at the end of the seminar, they might not extend to him the invitation to join the group in continuing the discussion in the pub. In doing these things, the group may have no intention of making Bill suffer (although of course it is possible that he may feel uncomfortable at being criticized). Rather, they wish to mark their disapproval of his conduct, call him to account for it, and perhaps give him the opportunity to explain or to apologise.[11]

This example suggests two reasons for the inclusion of blame in the system of criminal regulation. First, there is the possibility that 'strong feelings produced by … crimes … would remain unassuaged' and that 'revenge would be the only source of the indispensable comfort now provided by criminal justice' (Gross 2012: 2). This argument – that the criminal law is needed to avoid a society plagued by private justice and vendettas – has a long history (dating back to Athena's taming of the Furies), and to a large degree its importance depends on the empirical matter of what might in fact satisfy our need to blame and to punish (such as it is).

Second, and far more important, is the claim that by engaging with Bill and subjecting him to criticism the group treats him as a responsible agent. They would not, for example, behave the same way had they been interrupted by a crying infant. Of course, this does not mean that the group always has decisive reason to voice their criticism or to exclude Bill from the pub (perhaps it is someone's birthday and there is a desire not to spoil the atmosphere), but there is a *prima facie* reason for so-doing, and it would certainly be inappropriate for the group to treat him as if he were a child rather than a responsible adult.

For Strawson, the reactive attitudes and the conduct that goes along with them constitute what it is to treat one another as responsible adults. In a further step, he argues that the withdrawal of good will that accompanies the reactive attitudes can involve 'modification of the general demand that another should, if possible, be spared suffering' and a 'preparedness to acquiesce in that infliction of suffering on the offender which is an essential part of punishment' (Strawson 1962: 90), but nothing underwrites that claim (cf. Scanlon 2013: 108). The idea that you are appropriately the subject of criticism cannot ground a separate claim that it is appropriate that you be made to suffer (other than the suffering felt as a result of being criticised).

We need not commit to this Strawsonian picture of responsibility to find a place for blame in the account. If there is reason to regulate some aspects of our lives together through the criminal law, that regulation will plausibly need to be backed up by the threat of sanctions. In addition, *given* the existence of the system of regulation those who culpably violate the rules can be appropriately criticised for so-doing. Of course, insofar as the regulations of the criminal law govern particularly important matters for us as individuals and as members of a society, we should expect their content to overlap extensively with moral regulations, but it is as a criminal not a moral wrongdoer that the offender is called to account.

This leaves of course the question of how to integrate sanctions and censure into a coherent account. Although the appropriateness of being liable to criticism cannot underwrite or ground liability to suffering, it might be the case that the way in which serious criticism is expressed is through the imposition of suffering. If so, the deterrence and censure rationales could contingently come together. Attaching sanctions to criminal rules both serves the consequentialist function of reducing violations of those rules and simultaneously provides the vehicle for expressing society's criticisms. This neat solution has been pioneered by Andrew von Hirsch (1993) with the important difference that the offender is censured for his moral failings as revealed in his offending. This incorporation of morality puts pressure on the account as the degree of proportional moral censure can often differ from the degree of sanction needed to contribute effectively to crime prevention. By making both aspects of criminal regulation, this pressure can be relieved.

Agency, blame, and the criminal law

It is worth bringing together the various strands of the argument. The question is 'under what circumstances and for what reasons would I, together with others, agree to a set of coercive rules which have attached to them the threat of sanctions for those who disobey?' It is important that this question is understood from an individual's perspective. That is, in favouring sanctions for reasons of reducing future offending I am not arguing that the 'general good' or 'total utility' is to be maximised, but rather that each of us has reason to agree to rules that have attached to them the threat of sanctions in circumstances where temptation, the lack of assurance, or mistakes of reason and judgement will give rise to levels of disobedience such as to render social life unstable. In addition, we have reason to attach to this system an idea of blame or censure where appropriate as a means of marking the responsibility of the agent (and possibly of assuaging the reactive attitudes of others).

In one sense that completes the sketch by providing an alternative vision of the grounds of criminal regulation to that given by the retributivist with which the chapter began. However, and although there is no possibility of filling out the account in any great detail, this section pushes the argument a little further in part by returning to the landscape of the criminal law described earlier.

The heuristic method remains the same, but for this section more detail is needed (put another way, having given a general account of the circumstances that give rise to the need for, and the rationale of, criminal regulation, the question arises as to its shape and for this it is not enough merely to know the circumstances of (criminal) justice).

In reflecting on the general shape of criminal regulation, (at least) three additional factors matter.[12] First, the criminal law and criminal sanctions are the most powerful weapons in the state's arsenal (at least with respect to domestic policy). Even at their best they impose significant burdens on the punished. At their worst (as is often the case), criminal sanctions are blunt tools whose impact is not limited to the offender. They often are, as Hyman Gross puts it (2012: 5), 'a terrible source of human misery' that can and often do disrupt and ruin the lives of those punished and of their families and dependents.

Second, precisely because of the seriousness of criminal sanctions, and the element of blame that accompanies them, the agreement to have a set of coercive rules of criminal law will be conditional on a set of protections such as due process, the presumption of innocence, a high burden of proof that falls on the accuser and not the accused, and so on. This in turn means that the investigative process itself will often be burdensome and invasive. Together with the costs of sanctions, it will also be expensive. In short, in reflecting on the existence of the criminal law and asking under what circumstances and for what reasons one would endorse it, the case needs to be compelling. Criminal justice is hugely burdensome and expensive for the guilty and innocent alike.

Finally, criminal liability can befall anyone. We are all susceptible to temptation and all capable of mistakes of judgement. If one is lucky, one's lapses of judgement will lead to nothing (as when one drives over the speed limit, but arrives home without incident) or to no more than a social *faux pas* and slight embarrassment. In others (as when speeding and hitting a child who has stepped into the road from behind a parked car) it may lead to criminal prosecution and punishment (the effects of) which might last a lifetime.

The range of criminal liability

Given the above, there is reason to endorse a criminal law of a limited range.[13] There are many forms of regulation of social behaviour. To fail to behave in accordance with their demands may make one liable to criticism and to certain social costs. Some, like the rules governing corporate finance, are very important and the penalties involved may dwarf those routinely imposed in the criminal law. Nevertheless, there are some individual interests and elements of co-operative living that are sufficiently central to our lives and to living together to make it sensible to give these the imprimatur of 'crime' and to threaten as sanctions not merely financial or other penalties, but both censure and potentially severe sanctions such as imprisonment. Precisely what these are will depend on the social meanings of the society in which they are to be applied, but given human nature (and biology) they are likely to include serious attacks on, and endangerments to, the person. Given current socio-economic arrangements, they will also include some aspects of property rights, and so on.[14]

Given this, the account here joins forces with the retributivist in criticising the current range of offences. Much that is currently criminal – for example, in England the failure to buy a television licence – needs regulating, but does not need to be included in the criminal law. It would be enough to penalise those who fail to buy a television licence (perhaps by increasing its cost by a small percentage for each month during which the person had watched television without a licence) to provide the incentive needed to potential direct offenders and the assurance needed by potential assurance offenders. In the end, the criminal law might be required as a backstop, but then the offence would not be the failure to buy a licence, but the failure (after repeated opportunities) to obey the law.

The scope of criminal liability

Under 'scope' is included those aspects of criminal liability that are not covered by the cases above. In particular, inchoate offences and criminal complicity (Ashworth and Horder 2009: 6). In many cases, the argument here will again support the retributive critique. Consider the offence (in England and Wales) of 'publishing a statement that that is likely to be understood as glorifying acts of terrorism, intending to encourage others or reckless as to whether others are encouraged to commit or prepare for such acts' (Terrorism Act 2006: s1(2); Ashworth and

Horder 2009: 41). This has been rightly criticised as it does not require that any encouragement is actually given, any harm (or preparation for harm) done, or that one intends to encourage others (recklessness is sufficient). Moreover, given the general law of attempts, the creation of this offence extends the scope of criminal liability still further by creating an associated attempt offence.

What has gone wrong is not just the extension of the scope of criminal liability, but the thinking behind the offence that implicitly assumes a 'good guys/bad guys' or 'them and us' view of the criminal law. That is, the assumption is that the enforcement agencies and those who make decisions over prosecution will distinguish between, for example, an academic writing on 'the war on terror' and the dangerous terrorist doing the same. The former can be assured that she has nothing to fear while the latter is swept up by the legislation. This is incompatible with the reasoning captured by the heuristic device. Each citizen must endorse (or be able reasonably to endorse) the proposal to institute criminal regulation of a certain shape (and each must be cognisant of the risk of themselves falling foul of criminal regulations).

What of other offences in which the harm is remote or need not have resulted for their being complete? In at least some of these cases, focussing on the fallibility of agents' knowledge and reasoning opens up a set of reasons that risks being obscured by the retributivist. Consider offences of possession of firearms, knives, or other weapons. A standard and important justification of these is that they 'promote an environment the enjoyment of which is not fraught with the risk of harm, unless running that risk of harm is integral to an activity with important value' (Ashworth and Horder 2009: 333). That is right, but what it misses is that an agent considering whether to endorse such rules has an additional reason to do so grounded in recognition that we might all fall foul of temptation and mistakes of judgement. Put crudely, if I am on a night out and I am not carrying a knife, I significantly reduce the risks of a momentary lapse of judgement ruining my life.

This line of reasoning empowers the state to enact legislation designed in part to save me from myself. This raises fears of paternalism, but paternalism imposed by a public power understood as 'the power of free and equal citizens as a collective body' need not be objectionable (for example, we might endorse taxation to provide health services and pensions because we know that left to our own devices we tend to discount the future in irrational ways and so are unlikely to make adequate provision for our elderly selves. Similarly, we might endorse 'cooling off' periods on certain kinds of financial commitments given that we know our first judgements are not always our best ones).

This argument is not meant as a defence of the recent expansion of the scope of criminal liability and, of course, it is not by itself enough to distinguish the justified from the unjustified elements of that expansion. Rather, it stresses a way of thinking about the criminal law that risks being forgotten in the standard analysis. The criminal law not only regulates all of us, but it threatens all of us, and given our everyday fallibility we have good reason to protect ourselves from falling into its clutches.

The conditions of criminal liability

The conditions of criminal liability refer to the fault requirements and ultimately to the nature of agency in the criminal law. As we have seen, this is an area that has come under pressure from three directions. First, the expansion of strict liability, which requires no fault. Second, the expansion of preventive legislation designed not to punish for past offences, but to control 'dangerous' persons from committing offences in the future. Third, the greater sophistication of explanatory accounts of human behaviour that threaten the idea of the responsible agent whose acts can be unproblematically assigned to his voluntary choices.

In one sense the account given here – which stresses, on the one hand, the political and institutional nature of the criminal law and, on the other, the fallibility of persons' knowledge and judgement – has little to differentiate it from the retributive account when delineating the conditions of criminal liability. Given the seriousness of criminal sanctions, we have reason to be wary of strict liability. One ought always to have what H. L. A. Hart calls the 'fair opportunity' to avoid criminal liability (I have tried to develop an account of preventive justice along these lines in Matravers 2013).

However, that does not necessarily render strict liability 'odious' or unjustified. Rule of strict liability might sometimes be justified as ways of putting one on one's guard that one is entering risky territory. For example, discussing strict liability in relation to an adult engaging in sexual activity with a child under a specified age, Antony Duff comments 'if part of the rationale for such stipulations is that citizens should not trust themselves to make such substantive judgements as whether their intended sexual partner is mature enough, the child's age becomes a guiding reason to which the would-be sexual partner should pay careful attention' (Duff 2007: 259).

In relation to dangerousness: as noted above legislation driven by dangerousness has greatly expanded the reach of the criminal law. Moreover, much of this has been done under the guise of criminal law and punishment. Nothing in the above argument adds or detracts from the retributive critique of this.

There are people who present a continuing significant danger to others. If they can be identified with an acceptable degree of certainty, we have reason to incapacitate them (using the least intrusive measures possible). However, this is not punishment. The grounds and legitimacy of the system of punishment are entirely different, and both are undermined by the pretence that the situation is otherwise (Robinson 2001).

More generally, the account defended here has as one aim that we should remember that criminal law and punishment are expensive, invasive, and often have terrible consequences not only for those who are subject to it, but also for their families and communities. It ought to be a last resort in enabling us to live together given the circumstances of (criminal) justice. The concerns of 'dangerousness' detached from the idea of 'the dangerous person' – that is, understood as concerns to reduce future serious violations of rights – are genuine, but they are best and most effectively addressed by regulative systems other than the criminal law. In short, and to state the obvious, if our concern is with reducing future harms we have reason to invest in situational crime control and even before that in education and social justice.

It is with respect to blame and agency – to the responsible agent – that the retributive account and the one articulated here come apart in interesting ways. As we have seen, the retributive model stresses the moral culpability of the agent. The offender has performed a moral wrong for which he deserves censure in proportion to his culpability. The pressures that result from making criminal blame a species of moral blame appear in a number of places and underwrite the concerns of those who worry that the legitimacy of the criminal law – which depends on punishing only those who are blameworthy – is threatened by explanatory accounts of human behaviour. Consider two examples that push in slightly different directions.

First, impossible attempts. In a much used example, a committed believer in the power of voodoo pushes pins through the heart of a wax doll of his victim intending to kill the victim and confident that the method chosen will achieve this end. Such a person is surely morally culpable, but there is something odd about deploying the criminal law in a case where the harm is not merely remote, but impossible (for a clear account of this position, see Robinson 2001).

The institutional account, which stresses the regulative purposes of the criminal law in enabling us to live together, suggests an answer in which the moral culpability of the agent is orthogonal to the issue of whether to criminalise. Although the agent clearly embodies homicidal

intent, there is no reason to criminalise actions that could not under any circumstances cause harm (for a sophisticated discussion of impossible, and other, attempts see Duff 1996).
Second, consider a case of what I will call 'no wonder' criminal activity.

> Imagine an eighteen-year-old male gang member who was brought up in a disorganized, broken family living in a dirty, dangerous, disorganized, deprived community. Assume that the gang member is of average or below-average intelligence and does not have much education, but he is not cognitively disabled. Perhaps he is even functionally illiterate. From his pre-teen days, family, school, and church life had little emotional hold on him, but the gang in his neighborhood recruited him. The gang offered him the sense of identity, belonging, structure, meaning, and self-worth that his family and community failed to provide. Starting at an age when he was not a fully responsible moral agent – say, as early as ten or eleven – the gang encouraged him with its emotional leverage and perhaps threats to engage in various forms of antisocial conduct. He complied, and by age eighteen, he is a hard guy whose allegiance is firmly to the gang. Now, the gang asks him to execute a rival gang member. The gang no longer needs to threaten him or in any other way to manipulate him. He is committed to the gang and its projects, and he carries out the request, perhaps even proudly.
> (Morse 2000: 148)

As Morse notes, following Watson, our reaction to cases such as this need not be that 'it had to be' or 'it was determined to be', but rather 'no wonder' (cf. Watson 2004: 242). Given the background as described, no doubt some people would have resisted the gang's demand to execute a rival, but some will not and 'no wonder'.

Such cases can be accommodated within the retributive picture of the criminal law. Unless gang membership has genuinely undermined the agent's capacity to appreciate right and wrong, the agent is criminally liable. He is not insane, and he does not face an intolerable hard choice. The issue, though, is not whether this or that agent is properly held responsible within the criminal law, but whether the criminal law (as understood by the retributivist) meets its own legitimacy condition. Is it *fair* to blame this agent for his conduct and to ignore the story that accounts for how he came to be the person he now is?

To a degree, the retributivist tries to have it both ways. Yes, the agent is responsible and so can be found guilty of murder. But, the sentencing scheme available to the judge ought to allow that the degree of his culpability is recognised in the sentence he receives. Given his background, we might think he is less culpable and so deserving of a lesser sentence (although quite why these kinds of consideration can make such a significant difference to the penalty whilst being completely excluded from the earlier question of criminal liability is left unanswered).[15]

In what way will the account sketched here differ from this? Clearly, there are good reasons to criminalise murder and good reasons to treat the gang member as an agent (not as a child or a dangerous animal). The difference lies in the nature of the blame communicated to the offender. The example above is a particularly extreme one, but the pressures of life it describes are all too common amongst many of those who regularly fall within the purview of the criminal justice system. Ours is a complicated world scarred by distribute injustice. Against that background, the language and practices of moral blame fit very uneasily. Moreover, they are unnecessary. Our task is to respond to a criminal wrong in a way that characteristically marks the harm done to the victim and accords respect to the offender as an agent. That can be done in ways that resist moral blame and yet do not reduce to the treatment model.

One possibility would be to do without blame entirely. But, as noted above, blame can operate as an important marker of responsibility. When a free and equal citizen co-participant in the project of living together acts in ways that are justifiably criminalised, the public institution of the criminal law holds him to account not only to affirm the rights that he has violated, but as a responsible citizen who is answerable to himself and others. The issue is not whether to blame or not, but how and for what blame is conveyed.

As noted above in the discussion of rude Bill, our immediate reactions to wrongdoing are often hostile, and we feel that they are deserved by the offender in virtue of his wrongdoing. This is what Nicola Lacey and Hanna Pickard characterise as 'affective blame' (Lacey and Pickard 2013: 3) and Scanlon as 'blame as sanction' (Scanlon 2008: Chapter 4).

There is nothing wrong with affective blame, and there are occasions on which it is the only appropriate response. If one reads, and sees pictures, of Nazi extermination camps it is morally fitting to feel 'hatred, anger, resentment, indignation, disgust, disapproval, contempt and scorn' (Lacey and Pickard 2013: 3).

In some cases that will also be the appropriate *moral* reaction to more ordinary criminality, but other than in exceptional cases it is not the appropriate legal reaction. The state's role is to mark the violation of rights and to hold the violator to account as a responsible agent for his legal failing. It can do this 'through the simple judgement' of blameworthiness, which Lacey and Pickard (2013: 19) characterise as 'detached blame' (and Scanlon calls 'blame as evaluation').

Separating punishment from the hostile elements of affective blame does not of course resolve the question of whether it can ever be fair to punish (given that we are all products of causes that stretch back to points before we were born). Rather, it speaks, on the one hand, to the appropriate role of political institutions and, on the other, to the awareness we should all have that 'what separates us' from those who find themselves subject to the criminal law is 'not just, as we would like to think, that we behave better and choose more wisely, but also our luck in being the kind of people who respond in these ways' (Scanlon 1998: 294).

Finally, in adopting a more neutral stance with respect to blame, the opportunity arises to *use* the attribution of responsibility as a rehabilitative tool. Most offenders wish to escape the treadmill of disadvantage, offending, and punishment – 'to turn their lives around'[16] – and it is in this spirit rather than in a retributive one that punishment should be imposed. In practice, this will require greater use of meaningful community penalties, but also where custodial sentences are necessary, they should allow offenders to learn to read and write (where they cannot do so), to gain skills that might enable them to get jobs on release, and to help them with drug and alcohol addictions, and so on (cf. the report of the then Chief Inspector of Prisons for England and Wales, which was imaginatively titled 'Doing Time or Using Time', Great Britain 1993).

This is not to embrace 'an objectifying stance of treatment' (Kelly 2013) or a dystopian vision of a state that uses criminal justice to 'fix' people. It is rather to endorse a humane system of punishment fashioned in the light of the twin demands of living together and our own fragile natures.

Conclusion

This chapter began with the observation that the dominant model of criminal law theory was not descriptively accurate and has argued that it is also not normatively adequate. Using the heuristic tool of asking under what circumstances and for what reasons each of us has reason to endorse a system of criminal law and punishment – given that we understand ourselves as jointly constituting a society whose public power is simply the power of its members – it has offered an alternative vision of the nature and place of the criminal law in modern pluralistic societies. The vision, like so many visions, is short on detail, but the intention of the chapter was not to provide a blueprint. Rather, its purpose is suggestive. Once we think of the criminal law as one amongst a number of regulative systems that allow us to live together, and detach it from moral judgement, it becomes easier to map the theory onto practice and, in particular, to map the deep imperfections of any system of criminal law onto the deep imperfections in ourselves and our societies. Throughout, then, the focus has been on the criminal law as a necessary political institution and on imperfect citizens whose flaws in both knowledge and judgement might at any time render them liable to its reach.[17]

Notes

1 Throughout the chapter, reference is made to the theory and practice of the criminal law. There is of course no such thing as *the* criminal law, but only the criminal laws of different jurisdictions (and even within jurisdictions what is criminal might be difficult to determine). The focus in this chapter is on what Hyman Gross calls 'a composite of convenience that might be called the Anglo-American legal system' (Gross 2012: vii).

2 Famously, John Cottingham distinguished nine varieties of retributivism in his 1979 paper, which was enough to make him doubt the usefulness of the term (Cottingham 1979).

3 The Sentencing Guidelines Commission subsequently addressed this seeming jumble of purposes by giving priority to a proportionality principle found in §143, which requires that 'in considering the seriousness of any offence, the court must consider the offender's culpability in committing the offence and any harm which the offence caused, was intended to cause or might foreseeably have caused' (Ashworth 2010: 78).

4 Although the political systems in the USA and UK are very different, Nicola Lacey argues that the electoral systems, which promote an adversarial approach in which political parties can become locked in an 'arms race' of escalating policy on being 'tough on crime', makes them particularly susceptible to this issue (Lacey 2008).

5 There are significant differences between von Hirsch's 'proportionality model' and Morris and Tonry's 'limiting retributivism'. Von Hirsch demands a fairly strict proportionality scale that leaves relatively little room for discretion. Limiting retributivists allow for a wider range of 'not unjust' sentences within which the sentencer can choose based on other values. From the perspective of the argument here what matters is that both are clear that should the demands of proportionality conflict with other demands, proportionality must triumph (they disagree, of course, about how often such conflicts will arise).

6 For example, habitual offender statutes that significantly increase the sentence for recidivist offenders on the grounds that a prior record is an indicator of future dangerousness are clearly illegitimate. This contrasts with a legitimate policy in which a first offender receives a modest discount that is reduced by each subsequent offence until it runs out (see von Hirsch and Ashworth 2005: 148–55).

7 It is not a criticism of this kind of contract account – although it might be of an overambitious contract theorist – that the outcomes are determined by the choice situation (that is the point) (see Rawls 1971: 41–2, 138).

8 For complicated reasons, I think this question is often better asked in the negative form of 'under what circumstances and for what reasons have I decisive reason to reject such regulation', but that is not relevant here (for discussion see Matravers 2000: Chapter 7).

9 Note, these are contingent claims. It is possible to imagine a society in which sexual integrity was not particularly valued by its members, and there are societies in which property ownership is relatively unimportant.

10 I am aware that this is not an *argument* against the wholesale retributivist position. As noted above, the method here is only to present an alternative vision of criminal law and punishment, not to try to rebut retributivism. That said, in this instance the retributive position strikes me as implausible. We are surely not required to bring into existence 'the institution of property' so as 'to punish thieves' (to borrow an example from Rawls 1971: 313).

11 In an important contribution to penal theory, Antony Duff has built an account of the criminal trial and punishment as centrally involving censure of this kind. The offender has violated the law and is called to account. Assuming he is fit to answer, he may deny that he did it, or offer an excuse or justification, or he may plead guilty. If he is guilty, he is appropriately censured. As noted above, the difference between Duff's account and that being sketched here is that for Duff the criminal law and criminal sanctions exist in order to provide the opportunity to censure, and the vehicle for

penance for, those who commit serious public moral wrongs (which are, for Duff, the substance of the criminal law).

12 Of course, were one to try to reason to particular features of a given criminal code, far more factors would need to be included.

13 The language of 'range', like that of 'scope' and 'conditions' below is taken from Ashworth and Horder's *Principles of Criminal Law* (2009: 5–7, 17).

14 In other times and places, they might have included, for example, attacks on, or endangerment to, personal honour (a matter we would now consider one for private law). That is not to say that 'anything goes' and these are entirely matters for social meanings and conventions. Our reasoning must be coherent in light of the best evidence and reasons available.

15 In some jurisdictions the illegitimate confusion of dangerousness and punishment will render him more 'culpable' in that his gang membership and enculturation will be aggravating factors (based on predictions of likely future dangerousness).

16 I have borrowed this phrase from Anthony Bottoms, who used it in a discussion of 'desistance'. Although a common phrase, it seems to me to capture something very important about both the majority of those who are swept by the criminal justice system and how we ought to respond to them.

17 I am grateful to the editors of this volume for inviting me to participate in it and to Jonathan Jacobs in particular for comments on an earlier draft. As will be clear from the text, I am deeply indebted to Andrew Ashworth, Antony Duff and Nicola Lacey from whom I have learned an enormous amount (although they will think 'clearly not enough'). I am also grateful to the Independent Social Research Foundation for a Mid-Career Fellowship award, which allowed time for the thinking underpinning this piece.

Bibliography

American Law Institute, The. (1962 [1985]) *The Model Penal Code: Official Draft and Explanatory Notes*, Philadelphia, PA: The American Law Institute.

American Law Institute, The. (2007) *Model Penal Code: Sentencing, Tentative Draft No. 1*, Philadelphia, PA: The American Law Institute.

Ashworth, A. (2010) *Sentencing and Criminal Justice*, Cambridge: Cambridge University Press.

Ashworth, A. (2011) 'Attempts', in J. Deigh and D. Dolinko (eds.) *The Oxford Handbook of Philosophy of Criminal Law*, Oxford: Oxford University Press, pp. 125–46.

Ashworth, A. and Blake, M. (1996) 'The presumption of innocence in English criminal law', *Criminal Law Review*, pp. 306–17.

Ashworth, A. and Horder, J. (2009) *Principles of Criminal Law*, Oxford: Oxford University Press.

Beck, U. (1992) *Risk Society: Towards a New Modernity*. London: Sage.

Chiao, V. (2014) *What is the Criminal Law For?* http://www.law.utoronto.ca/utfl_file/count/documents/chiao/WPS%202014-05.pdf.

Chiao, V. (Forthcoming). *Criminal Law in the Age of the Administrative State*, New York, NY: Oxford University Press.

Cottingham, J. (1979) 'Varieties of retribution', *Philosophical Quarterly*, 29: 238–46.

Duff, R.A. (1996) *Criminal Attempts*, Oxford: Oxford University Press.

Duff, R.A. (2007) *Answering for Crime: Responsibility and Liability in the Criminal Law*, Oxford: Hart Publishing.

Duff, R.A., Farmer, L., Marshall, S., Renzo, M. and Tadros, V. (2010) *The Boundaries of the Criminal Law*, Oxford: Oxford University Press.

Duff, R.A., Farmer, L., Marshall, S., Renzo, M. and Tadros, V. (2012) *The Structures of the Criminal Law*, Oxford: Oxford University Press.

Great Britain, H.M.P.S. (1993) *HMCIP Review of Regimes: Doing Time or Using Time? The Prison Service Response*, H.M. Prison Service.

Greene, J. and Cohen, J. (2004) 'For the law, neuroscience changes nothing and everything', *Philosophical Transactions of the Royal Society London B: Biological Sciences*: 1775–85.

Gross, H. (2012) *Crime and Punishment: a Concise Moral Critique*, Oxford: Oxford University Press.

Hart, H.L.A. (2008) *Punishment and Responsibility: Essays in the Philosophy of Law*, Oxford: Oxford University Press.

Honderich, T. (1969) *Punishment: The Supposed Justifications*, London: Hutchinson.

Honderich, T. (1984) *Punishment: The Supposed Justifications*, Harmondsworth: Penguin.

Hudson, B. (2003) *Justice in the Risk Society: Challenging and Re-affirming Justice in Late Modernity,* London: Sage.
Husak, D. (2008) *Overcriminalization: The Limits of the Criminal Law,* Oxford: Oxford University Press.
Kelly, E. (2013) 'Beyond blame (reply to Fried)'. Retrieved 28/07/2015 from http://www.bostonreview.net/forum/beyond-blame/blame-corrupts-criminal-justice-system.
Kleinig, J. (1973) *Punishment and Desert,* The Hague: Martinus Nijhoff.
Lacey, N. (2007) Interview. *Legal Philosophy: 5 Questions.* M. Nielsen, Automatic Press: 125–41.
Lacey, N. (2008) *The Prisoners' Dilemma: Political Economy and Punishment in Contemporary Democracies,* Cambridge: Cambridge University Press.
Lacey, N. and Pickard, H. (2013) 'From the consulting room to the court room? Taking the clinical model of responsibility without blame into the legal realm', *Oxford Journal of Legal Studies,* (1): 1–29.
Matravers, M. (2000) *Justice and Punishment: The Rationale of Coercion,* Oxford: Oxford University Press.
Matravers, M. (2011) 'Is twenty-first century punishment post-desert?', in M. Tonry (ed.) *Retributivism Has a Past: Has it a Future?,* New York, NY: Oxford University Press.
Matravers, M. (2013) 'On preventive justice', in A. Ashworth, L. Zedner and P. Tomlin (eds.) *Prevention and the Limits of the Criminal Law: Principles and Policies,* Oxford: Oxford University Press.
Matravers, M. (2016) 'Punishment, suffering and justice', in S. Farrall, B. Goldson, I. Loader and A. Dockley (eds.) *Justice and Penal Policy,* New York, NY: Routledge.
Moore, M. (1997) *Placing Blame: A General Theory of the Criminal Law,* Oxford: Oxford University Press.
Morris, N. (1974) *The Future of Imprisonment,* Chicago, IL: University of Chicago Press.
Morris, N. and Tonry, M. (1990) *Between Prison and Probation: Intermediate Punishments in a Rational Sentencing System,* New York, NY: Oxford University Press.
Morse, S.J. (1999) 'Neither desert nor disease', *Legal Theory,* 5: 265–309.
Morse, S.J. (2000) 'Deprivation and desert', in W.C. Heffernan and J. Kleinig (eds.) *From Social Justice to Criminal Justice: Poverty and the Administration of Criminal Law,* New York, NY, Oxford: Oxford University Press, pp. 114–60.
Morse, S.J. (2013) 'Compatibilist criminal law', in T. Nadelhoffer (ed.) *The Future of Punishment,* Oxford: Oxford University Press, pp. 107–31.
Rawls, J. (1971) *A Theory of Justice,* Cambridge, MA: Harvard University Press.
Rawls, J. (2005) *Political Liberalism: Expanded Edition,* New York, NY: Columbia University Press.
Robinson, P. (2001) 'Punishing dangerousness: Cloaking preventive detention as criminal justice', *Harvard Law Review,* 114(5): 1428–56.
Scanlon, T.M. (1998) *What We Owe to Each Other,* Cambridge, MA: Harvard University Press.
Scanlon, T.M. (2008) *Moral Dimensions: Permissibility, Meaning, Blame,* Cambridge, MA: Harvard University Press.
Scanlon, T.M. (2013) 'Giving desert its due', *Philosophical Explorations,* 2: 101–16.
Strawson, P. (1962) 'Freedom and resentment', *Proceedings of the British Academy,* 48: 1–25.
von Hirsch, A. (1976) *Doing Justice: The Choice of Punishments: Report of the Committee for the Study of Incarceration,* New York, NY: Hill and Wang.
von Hirsch, A. (1993) *Censure and Sanctions,* Oxford: Oxford University Press.
von Hirsch, A. and Ashworth, A. (2005) *Proportionate Sentencing: Exploring the Principles,* Oxford, New York:, NY Oxford University Press.
Watson, G. (2004) 'Responsibility and the limits of evil: reflections on a Strawsonian theme', in G. Watson (ed.) *Agency and Answerability: Selected Essays,* Oxford: Oxford University Press, pp. 219–59.

10

Justice, but not as 'we' know it

Anticipatory risk, pre-emption, and ethics

Gabe Mythen and Sandra Walklate

Introduction

This chapter focusses on the ethical questions posed for criminal justice systems by the processes of security regulation that have swept across the West in the early twenty-first century. The 2001 terrorist attacks in the United States produced a range of institutional responses which have produced sizeable effects on criminal justice and human rights. The so-called '9/11 effect' (Roach 2011) has been both broad and wide, ranging from tiers of domestic counter-terrorism legislation to international military interventions. One of the remarkable features of this recent phase of securitization has been the interventionist and activist nature of policy-making. Following the tone set by George W. Bush in the aftermath of 9/11, a strong emphasis has been placed on pre-emptive methods of regulation designed to avert an attack of such scale in the future by proactive intervention. Bolstered by the 9/11 Commission's (2004) summation that 'the most important failure was one of imagination', the logic of anticipatory risk has driven a range of new modes and techniques of regulation, from Internet data mining to electronic tagging and biometric scanning. In a world in which the terrorist threat is pronounced, pre-emptive methods of intervention may seem eminently sensible. If the threats are grave, the risk of inaction is sizeable. Thus, intelligence and security services need to intervene, even in circumstances in which the evidence may be patchy and incomplete. Thus, the 9/11 effect has involved a tangible shift in the calculus of risk, away from post hoc probabilistic assessment to pre hoc imaginings of upcoming threats. What Vedby-Rasmussen (2004) has alluded to as the 'presence of the future' in considerations about domestic and international security has produced profound consequences.

Rather than being drawn into an otherwise important discussion about the efficacy and the effects of 'activist' military strategies, here we wish to map out some of the consequences of the 'pre-emptive turn' in criminal law, for criminal justice policy and policing practices. Given the potential range of such an inquiry, we will be drawing on counter-terrorism initiatives in the United Kingdom as a means of engaging with some of the broader issues that have arisen around the ethics of 'doing' security in uncertain and troubled times. While the solutions to these problems are beyond our ambit, we will be suggesting some conceptual apparati that can enable us to understand some of the prominent ethical problems and issues that have arisen in this area.

The chapter falls into four parts. In the first, drawing on recent criminological literature, we offer an understanding of pre-emption. In the second, we consider what the role of the criminal justice system might be in setting a context in which ethical policies and practices are formulated. Here we start from the presumption that criminal justice is a public good from which all members of any society are intended to benefit. We recognise that such a position is open to contestation. However, the nature of this contestation is not the central purpose of this discussion; consequently, this is not the place to engage in those debates. In the third part, using the policing of counter-terrorism in the United Kingdom as our example, we illustrate the kinds of policies and practices that have been put in place under the principles of pre-emption. In the final part of the chapter, we offer some theoretical tools that can enable us to reflect on the emergent issues posed by this particular pre-emptive moment in time.

Making sense of pre-emption

Pre-emption is more than prevention. Pre-emption is firmly rooted in anticipating the risks rather than acting on the known risks. As Hudson and Ugelvik (2012: 9) observe: 'unlike the normal logic of risk management, precautionary logic does not entail actuarial calculations of the likelihood of the disastrous event occurring, its mere possibility is sufficient to bring forth preventive actions'. Indeed Zedner (2007: 259) notes, the pre-emptive moment takes place prior to concrete identification of harm and thus occurs at a point at which threats may be inexact and uncertain. Rather than asking the question 'what is?' pre-emptive logics instead move more readily into the speculative terrain of 'what if?' questions (see Walklate and Mythen 2015). Under the logic of pre-emptive risk, early action is justified with an eye on the potential scale of the threat and the need to protect the majority. Thus, pre-emption is effectively something of a risk trade-off. It refers to the institutional preference for early intervention – even if this results in the reduction of the civil liberties of a minority – on the basis that inaction may pose a larger threat to public safety (see Maras 2013: 127). This logic of trading-off the loss of individual liberties in favour of greater collective security has been routinely inscribed in policy in the UK. The National Security Strategy (2012: 23), for instance, states: 'to protect the security and freedom of many, the State sometimes has to encroach on the liberties of a few: those who threaten us'. Thus, while neo-liberal states may still pride themselves on a commitment to secure the safety of citizens, it is clear that these pledges are increasingly conditional rather than absolute. What statements like this make explicit is a distancing of the state from guaranteeing fundamental rights for all, whilst simultaneously sanctioning a reduction in rights for some as a necessary measure for the protection of all. This effort to create a cloudless divide between an 'us' worthy of protection and a 'them' who are considered to be less worthy of protection, redefines what might be understood as 'justice'.

Public goods, criminal justice and ethics

As the discussion above implies, the increasing presence of pre-emption in informing policy and practice has proceeded by making particular assumptions about the relationship of justice, liberty, and security. Of course in any society rooted in principles that address the interests of all of citizens, security and liberty are interdependent (see Hudson 2012). Moreover, there are always tensions in the relationship between liberty and security, and these are by no means new in liberal democracies. Nonetheless, if we start from a presumption that they exist in a symbiotic relationship with one another rather than a separate one, the delivery of criminal justice can be framed in a particular way, which raises specific issues. This assumption of interdependence raises the issue of what constitutes a safe and fair society. How can the principle of 'public goods', and this chapter starts from the position that criminal justice is a public good, be sustained in in the context of a criminal justice system which inflects towards pre-emption as a solution for insecurity? Before we respond to this question we should first be clear about our terms. Following Waldron (1993: 358) we would concur that a public good is 'something which is said to be valuable for human society without its value being adequately characterisable in terms of its worth to any or all of the members of society considered one by one'. The value of public goods is thus not reducible to their aggregate value for each member of society, but rather what they are worth collectively. In other words public goods represent something more than their economic value and are irreducibly *social*. Following Loader and Walker (2007), we might go on to suggest that security and justice can be conceived as 'thick' public goods. In other words, they contribute to, 'a state of well*being* – a state in which we are able to live – and live together – securely with risk' (Loader and Walker 2007: 169). Indeed, as Cook (2006: 21) posits, in many senses, the value of public goods in general, but security and justice in particular, stems from the capacity to guarantee the dignity and rights of all citizens:

> If a society cannot guarantee 'the equal worth of all its citizens', mutual and self-respect and the meeting of basic needs, it cannot expect that all citizens will feel they have an equal stake in abiding by the law, and it cannot dispense justice fairly and enhance confidence in the law.

So far as ethics are concerned, any criminal justice system is a key component in delivering this sense of equal worth. In this sense, criminal justice is intimately connected with social justice. In other words it is a process in which we all have an interest, particularly in terms of appropriate delivery, whether or not 'we' are the ones on the receiving end of such delivery processes. This position poses moral questions for the criminal justice system in the round and, in a more focussed fashion, for those charged with the delivery of security practices and initiatives. All this said in theory, just what public goods mean and represent *in practice* remains both uncertain and unclear. Furthermore, such questions are heightened by economic considerations, particularly in austere times, when cost-cutting initiatives in the United Kingdom and elsewhere have impacted heavily on the criminal justice system in general and policing in particular. This context adds further to the already existing complex and blurred boundaries between the public and private delivery of security and justice (see Bowling and Sheptycki 2012). Exposure to the economic pressures of the neo-liberal market has provided a space in the delivery of justice which has been partially filled by what might be termed 'security entrepreneurs', within both the public and private domains. Of course, the extent to which such entrepreneurs have wider collective interests – or indeed the delivery of justice – as their primary focus is a moot point. There are, however, other complexities here.

Loader and Walker (2007) ask whether or not it is actually possible, amidst this complexity, to even conceive of a 'transnational public interest' which the post 9/11 context appears to have put to the fore. The presence of over 40 political leaders from a wide range of constituencies joined in solidarity in Paris on January 11th, 2015, suggests that such an interest might be possible. Whether or not such events offer promise for future dialogue about transnational justice is a moot point. Nevertheless, what the incidents in France – like the terrorist attacks in New York, Madrid, and London before them – have triggered is a demand for more extensive pre-emptive security powers including the extension of surveillance and data mining practices and interception of communications (see Watt 2015). Just whose interests are served by these developments and how effective they may be in reducing the threat is far from evident. Yet the critical voices are invariably scotched and shouted down by those that join in the chorus of 'more security'. It is at this point, when security is presumed to be an end point, that the question of collective social good becomes silenced. In the insistent search for a security utopia, sight is lost of the social value of the criminal justice system and its wider moral purpose for the domestic sphere.

Thus, contemporarily searching for a sense of wellbeing in which we can all live together securely with risk is multi-layered and multi-faceted. In any particular social context how those layers manifest themselves will be a reflection of the particular ways in which criminal justice and social justice are intermeshed in the delivery of security for every member of that society. In any society the delivery of security involves a wide range of actors and points of intervention whose everyday practices might coalesce with 'ordinary pre-emption' (Simon 2012) or risk profiling (Leese 2014) to government-led directives that frame such practices, such as risk registers (Hagmann and Cavelty 2012). It also involves more specific criminal justice centred policies. It is to these policies that we shall now turn, using developments in the United Kingdom as our example. In the spirit of recognising that criminal justice is multi-layered and multi-faceted, three features of this complexity and its expression in relation to pre-emption will be considered: criminal law, criminal justice policy, and criminal justice practices.

Pre-emption: Impacting law, policy and practice

The criminal law

Given the historical presence of the 'troubles' in Northern Ireland, the extant legislative powers to combat terrorism in place in the UK were already stringent prior to 9/11. Following on from the Terrorism Act (2000), the Anti-Terrorism, Crime and Security Act (2001), the Prevention of Terrorism Act (2005), the Terrorism Act (2006) and the Counter-Terrorism Act (2008) all added to existing tiers of legislation and extended the remit of criminal law. Within these tiers new pre-emptive modes of regulation have proven to be the most controversial, including the introduction of Control Orders, extensions to detention without charge, acts preparatory to terrorism and the offence of incitement (see Kibbe 2012; Miller and Sabir 2012). Taken together these examples are indicative of efforts by the state to intervene earlier to prevent would-be terrorists from launching attacks. Naturally, the extension of precautionary powers has been welcomed by senior police officers and intelligence agents who believe that pre-emptive measures are necessary to combat the threat and to enhance public safety (see Parker 2013). Measures such as these assume that reducing liberties for a minority (defined as dangerous) is an acceptable trade off if it enables the safety of the many. Aside from the implicit erroneous zero-sum assumption, it is the section in brackets that we might want to focus on and the extent to which the dangerous have – or indeed can be – clearly defined.

The rafts of legislation recounted above mark the consolidation of what Hudson and Ugelvik (2012: 8) describe as a 'preventive state'. This is a state that has cast aside the presumption of innocence – a presumption that is in our collective interest – in favour of pre-emptive intervention, a presumption that accepts and supports particular interests. Within the spectrum of pre-emptive legislation introduced in the UK, extensions to detention without charge and the enforcement of control orders have proven to be highly controversial. Prior to the 2005 terrorist attacks in London, the UK already had extensive powers to detain individuals without charge in cases in which they were suspected of involvement of terrorism. Despite this, after the 7/7 attacks, the British Prime Minister Tony Blair campaigned to extend the period from 14 to 90 days, having already doubled the allowable period from 7 to 14 days in 2003. In 2006 legislation was passed to extend such detention to a period of 28 days without the need for charges to be levelled. Given that the introduction of new offences of glorification and incitement considerably reduced the threshold for terrorism related charges, the setting of 28 days of permissible detention without charge provoked widespread disquiet. In effect, detention without charge renders the ancient right of *habeas corpus* void and shifts the presumption of innocence until proved guilty to a presumption of guilt unless innocence can be proven (see Zedner 2009). Having reviewed the legislation passed through parliament by the former Labour government, the present Conservative-Liberal coalition amended the Terrorism Act, reducing the maximum allowable period of pre-charge detention to 14 days under The Protection of Freedoms Act (2012). It is worth noting that 14 days remains exceptional and is one of the longest periods of pre-charge detention that exists in any comparable liberal democracy. In the United States the limit is two days, in Italy it is four, and in Canada just 24 hours (see Liberty 2015).

The long-standing and cherished principles of justice and freedom threatened by detention without charge were similarly undermined by the regime of control orders. Formally introduced in the Prevention of Terrorism Act (2005) to restrict the activities of terrorism suspects, control orders allowed a range of restrictions on liberty, including restrictions on communications, possessions, employment, residence, and travel. Further, those under control orders were subjected to electronic tagging, passport surrender, and frequent police visits. Despite being rarely utilised, control orders caused something of a storm amongst lawyers, human rights groups, academics, and civil liberties campaigners. Given their impact on basic rights and freedoms, control orders are tantamount to house arrest and akin to imprisonment without bars. The much-maligned system of control orders – deemed in 2006 by the High Court to be incompatible with the European Convention on Human Rights – was repealed in 2011 and replaced by Terrorism Prevention and Investigation Measures (TPIMs).

What is common in the criminal law examples above is the application of anticipatory risk in the interests of collective security. Yet defending against an imagined catastrophic future ultimately permits the curtailment of basic rights and freedoms for all, not just the targeted few. One commonly used justification for this kind of legislative response has been the 'ticking bomb scenario'. The Senate Intelligence Committee Report on the use of torture made public in December 2014 has certainly challenged the efficacy of that scenario. Nonetheless, it has served as a powerful metaphor in defending various 'states of exception' ranging from secret surveillance to torture. History illustrates that what begins as an exception soon becomes the norm (see McCulloch and Pickering 2009), and the legislation referred to above is indicative of a normative pre-emption creep in policing and surveillance. The consequences of which, as shall be argued, are profound, not only for the ways in which the rights of those deemed 'risky' are curtailed, leaving the rest of 'us' safe (in theory), but also for the ways in which this legislative framework infringes upon what might be considered to be the public good of criminal justice: something that is in our collective interest.

Criminal justice policy

The forms of counter-terrorism legislation referred to above are indicative of a long-standing political imperative to 'think security' (see de Lint and Virta 2004). In the UK this imperative is epitomised by CONTEST, the British State's overarching counter-terrorism strategy. CONTEST comprises four interconnected strands of activity: Pursue, Prevent, Protect, and Prepare. The first two of these four strands are configured around the principle of pre-emption. Whilst elements of the Pursue strategy have been documented, it is the Prevent initiative that is worthy of further comment. Prevent (2011) constitutes the UK government's policy response to the threat of extremism and is constituted by five goals. The first is to challenge violent extremism by recruiting moderate voices to challenge extremist ideology. The second is to disrupt extremism and to challenge the promotion of it. The third is to extend support to individuals deemed susceptible to extremism. The fourth is to increase local communities' resilience to extremists and the fifth to tackle the grievances felt by local communities. The policy initiatives designed to counter radicalisation that comprise Prevent have been extremely controversial since its introduction in 2007–2008 (see Heath-Kelly 2012; Kundnani 2009; Thomas 2012). Although the present iteration of the Prevent strategy formally seeks to address all kinds of extremism – including that of the far right – in translation it has predominantly been areas with large Muslim populations that have been subjected to interventions under this initiative. The underlying aspiration is to encourage Muslims in particular to proclaim violence as illegitimate and align with core British values, thus discouraging religious extremism, preventing radicalisation, and promoting moderate forms of Islam.

This strategy has been widely criticised (see Miller and Sabir 2012: 21) not least because of the presumptive starting point that Muslim communities do not align with core British values to begin with. The attention given to Muslim communities under Prevent – at a time at which it is evident that far right extremism is flourishing in some white working class areas – is highly questionable (see McGhee 2010: 36). Prevent has sought to co-opt individuals within and without Muslim communities, to survey those communities, and to promote behavioural change in those that may be attracted to extremism (see Kundnani 2009). These processes of data-gathering have resulted in infringements on civil liberties, with the Channel project in particular causing consternation. The Channel project was a pre-emptive initiative – through which youth workers, teachers, and religious leaders were invited to gather and share personal data about young people, including their friendship groups, sexual preferences, and religious commitments – has been heavily criticised, both in terms of the rationale for intervention and its effects on the individuals targeted by it. In excess of 2,600 people have been referred through Channel for exhibiting signs of worrying behaviour that may lead to extremism, with 750 of this number being school children (see Whitehead 2013). Aside from the dubious grounds on which judgements regarding extremism and/or future radicalisation are being made, critics such as Heath-Kelly (2012) have pointed out that the logic of anticipatory risk in such policies is being stretched to the extreme, with young people being targeted not so much because they are risky, but because they are 'at risk of being risky'.

Some of the problems with these earlier iterations of Prevent have been acknowledged by the government (Dodd 2010), yet newer versions have continued to accent surveillance and ideational change, while the support for the maintenance of community cohesion appears to have slipped away (see Awan 2013; Thomas 2012). Thus, a salient question, given the concerns of this chapter, that follows on from these observations is: what impact do pre-emptive policies such as Prevent have and on whom? As Spalek and Lambert (2008: 181) observe, policies such as Prevent place Muslims in a challenging and uncomfortable social position:

> Muslims' responsibilities as active citizens have increasingly been framed by anti-terrorist measures that encourage internal community surveillance so that the responsible Muslim citizen is expected to inform the authorities about the activities, suspicious or perceived to be suspicious, of their fellow community members, and actively help deal with any potential extremism.

This process of responsibilisation (Garland 2001) has ramifications for both the community and the self, throwing out contradictory and mixed messages about the security and protection of minority groups in contemporary society. Indeed, there is some empirical evidence to support the nature and extent of this contradiction and its impact on individuals and specific communities (see Kundnani 2009; Mythen, Walklate, and Khan 2013). Put simply, these policies are rooted in a conception of Muslim communities as suspect communities. In so doing they reflect implicit assumptions about whose security counts and, as a consequence, whose access to justice counts. Thus, instead of ensuring the self-worth of all members of society, these policies are only concerned to deliver that self-worth for some sections of society: 'us' not 'them'. Simultaneously such policies are also blinkered and curtail the capacity to think differently about the delivery of security and justice.

For example, Dalgaard-Nielsen's (2010) review of the available literature on radicalisation points out that, despite a panoply of policies being launched to counter extremism, the evidence base for these policies is extremely thin. When all is said and done, we actually know very little about what the process of 'radicalisation' actually looks or feels like. As Borum (2013: 106) cautions:

> Assuming that radicalisation is the key to understanding and predicting terrorism is a grave misapprehension. Investigators must be mindful that terrorism does not always follow a linear process where a vulnerable person is inducted into a particular ideology, and adherence to those ideas escalates until the individual inevitably is driven to commit acts of violence. Sometimes terrorism evolves that way, but not often enough, perhaps, even to be considered 'typical'.

Given that some of the explanations that now deceased Islamist terrorists have given for their attacks relate to material and institutional processes – oppressive foreign policy, military interventions in Muslim countries, economic and cultural imperialism – attempting to tackle extremism by focussing solely on the de-radicalisation of individuals would seem to be as short-sighted as it is partial. As we will argue, the potential for misinformed or even misguided policies to backfire is present, and this may only result in further alienation for those communities routinely subjected to such interventions.

Criminal justice practices

Clearly, there are deep connections between criminal law, policy, and practices. In the realm of counter-terrorism, the laws passed by parliament set in place policies and practices that are implemented by a range of institutional actors, not least the police force. To illuminate this connectivity, we wish to focus on the operationalisation of Section 44 of the 2001 Terrorism Act, recently superseded by Section 47A. At this juncture, it should be noted that police stop and search powers have a long and chequered history in Britain. Stop searches were introduced under the Police and Criminal Evidence Act (1984) in direct response to the problems associated with the use of the 'sus' laws (a colloquial reference to legislation that permitted police officers to detain people on the basis of suspicion rather than evidence) that were implicated in a series of disturbances in British cities in the early 1980s. Building on these initial powers, Section 60 of the subsequent Criminal Justice and Public Order Act (1994) allowed a police officer to stop and search a person 'in anticipation of violence' provided that the search took place in an area pre-authorized by the police as dangerous or in which violence has occurred or appears likely to occur. Unsurprisingly, widespread complaints have been raised concerning the use of these forms of intervention on black and minority ethnic individuals since their enshrinement in law (see, Bowling and Phillips 1998; Pantazis and Pemberton 1999; Weber and Bowling 2012). The debate continues amongst criminologists concerning the use of these powers. That debate has particularly focused on whether or not the use of these powers is proportional with the ethnic composition of the population as a whole, or whether or not they are used in proportion to the population available for such interventions, for example, young people who may spend time on the streets (see Parmar 2011; Waddington et al. 2004). This debate notwithstanding, the statistics on the rate of stop and search under Section 60 shows that Black people are, on average, around 11 times more likely to be stop searched than Whites (Runnymede Trust 2010). Section 44 of the Terrorism Act (2000) went a step further than the existing Section 60 powers, permitting police officers to search individuals without recourse to 'reasonable suspicion' that an offence either has been committed or being planned. Under Section 44, permission was granted to stop and search any person in a designated zone without requiring grounds for so doing. Various data sets indicate that these powers have been inordinately deployed against Black and Asian people, particularly those from Pakistani and Bangladeshi communities (see Kundnani 2009; Pantazis and Pemberton 2009). Uneven application of this legislation by the police has led to claims that the deployment of Section 44 powers has been by racial profiling which criminalizes populations and communities.

Moreover, beyond the formal goal of countering terrorism, political protestors, photographers, journalists, and tourists have all been stop searched under these powers. Interestingly, it was ultimately a case brought to the European Court of Human Rights by Kevin Gillan and Pennie Quinton – a journalist and a peace activist respectively – that led to these powers being declared illegal. Following this judgement, a Counter-Terrorism Review that was commissioned by the Home Office in 2010 reported that Section 44 should be repealed. In response in March 2011, the Government introduced a temporary Remedial Order as a temporary measure which replaced Sections 44 to 47 of the Act with a new Section 47A. Under these revised powers, stops and searches without 'reasonable suspicion' of the individuals in question can still take place, but with tighter safeguards. Further to this in 2012, Section 44 was replaced by the Protection of Freedoms Act which permits a senior police officer to designate an area for stop and search without suspicion only if it can reasonably surmised that an act of terrorism is likely to occur. While statistics published by the Home Office in June 2013 indicate an overall reduction in the number of stops and arrests under the terrorism legislation, pre-emptive practices such as these have put a strain on relations between the police and ethnic minority groups (see Spalek and Lambert 2008). Further, the capacity to increase tension rather than decrease the potential for violence should not go unheeded (see Diprose et al. 2008). The damaging effects that stereotypical assumptions have on populations so policed need to be recognised. Further, as Hillyard (2009: 142) sagely notes, the interconnected use of criminal justice through law, policy and practice, is not unique to the contemporary British government, suggesting the broader formation of states that routinely rely on otherwise extraordinary measures:

> Increasing use of a wide range of personnel in the exercise of informal control, intensified surveillance of the population, and the widespread shift away from the ordinary criminal law to the use of 'counter-terror' law are all essential elements of an exceptional State.

In terms of the evidence discussed here it would be hard not to find agreement with Hillyard's (2009) synopsis. The implications of this for criminal justice and its wider ethical foundations are far-reaching.

Pre-emption and (in)security: Dilemmas for criminal justice

Having considered the role and functions of criminal justice and flagged some of the broad impacts and effects of pre-emptive security policies on the idea and the nature of justice, we wish to end by drawing together some key ethical dilemmas. In so doing, we will be proposing a conceptual apparatus that can assist us in understanding some of the risks that arise in this search for security. Our examination of the use of pre-emption in the area of counter-terrorism reveals a layered presence in the criminal justice system, from the framing of the law to the practices of criminal justice professionals. We have argued that, in each of these layers, the impact on those who have been both the subject and the object of practices of pre-emption (Muslim minority groups) has been profound. However, there are also major issues at stake for the criminal justice system itself that impact on its wider moral role in contributing to the wider social good. In grappling with these issues, we offer three interlinked conceptual devices that can enable us to understand some of the problems that pre-emptive modes of regulation generate: the loss of the principle of innocent until proven guilty; the deployment of the law under a condition of 'states of exception' (Agamben 1995); and the law of inverse consequences (the resulting effect of an intervention producing the opposite of that intended).

Liberal democracies have not only favoured the principle of innocent until proven guilty but also fought to defend it as a cornerstone of the criminal justice system. If there is any element of doubt in this regard at a jury trial, the jury is advised by the judge to acquit the defendant. It has already been observed above that the practices of pre-emption, by their very nature, undermine this principle. The tension between guaranteeing civil liberties for all and targeting those thought to be problematic for everyone's civil liberties is of vital importance in contemporary society. In considering the kinds of developments since 9/11 discussed above, Hudson (2003: 74) remarks:

> The balancing of rights has gone: the only rights that matter for most people are the safety rights of selves and loved ones. The sense of shared risk, shared responsibility has also gone: we cope with risk by a constant scanning of all with whom we come into contact to see whether or not they pose a threat to our security, and the only way we can operate this scanning is by adopting stereotypes of safe and risky kinds of people.

As discussed earlier, the logic of trading individual liberties in favour of greater collective security has been a common feature of recent security policy. The discussion above has elucidated some of the problems that this trade-off has engendered for those at the sharp end of policy whose human rights are eroded. These observations ostensibly indicate an unreasonable struggle for liberty for suspected minorities. Yet this struggle in and of itself implies a process of *collective* loss. In the intermeshing of the legal policies and practices outlined here, justice for all of us is also compromised. This does not only impact on the few, it also impacts on the many. As Smart (1990) cogently argued some time ago, the law, once changed, can serve purposes other than those for which it was intended. We have given several examples of this form of transference here. At a wider level, the bending – and in some cases the violation of – fundamental principles of justice such as *habeus corpus* is tantamount to the production of what Ericson (2008) has called 'counter-laws' that are contrary to the very values that laws seek to uphold. While the search for security through pre-emptive policy has produced deleterious consequences for 'the few', the collective loss belongs to us all.

As Lomell (2012) points out, the substitution of a presumption of guilt for a presumption of innocence prior to any act having been committed can result in two other problems: the problem of false positives and false negatives and the problem of intent. The first of these can result in the conviction of an innocent person, and the second can result in a guilty person remaining free. Nonetheless, underpinning each of these scenarios, once the presumption of innocence has been compromised, is the potential for 'errors', bureaucratic or otherwise, that may end in imprisonment. The compromise of this principle, of course, impacts on all, not just those deemed problematic. The second of these problems, the problem of intent, denies individuals the capacity to change their minds. Clearly, this is not the place to engage in a knotty legal discussion of intent. Suffice it to say that in order to deem someone guilty it is necessary to establish both *mens rea* (intent to commit an act) and *actus reus* (the act having been committed that is against the law). The link between these two is an essential component in order to evidence guilt or innocence. One or the other is not enough. Moreover before any crime is committed (*actus reus*), an individual can choose to behave otherwise. However, under a pre-emptive regime, these principles are effectively denied. Again, this possibility is one which is denied for all of us, not just those defined and treated as dangerous.

Aside from challenges to the principle of *habeus corpus*, it is clear that the role of the state in administering 'justice' has been transformed in the last two decades. Further, the aspirations and objectives of governments have increasingly informed and shaped criminal justice policy. In reviewing the complex interplay of the different layers of criminal justice, the 'suspectification' of particular ethnic populations is a marked feature particularly in the UK but not solely confined to this context (for a more detailed discussion of this see Walklate and Mythen 2015). This is a process of demarcation that in political and policy terms has been and continues to be justified and explained with reference to the 'exceptional' circumstances in which we live. Thus, we, the public, are frequently reassured that – given the scale of the threat faced – the price paid by the few is in the interests of the many. The risks to us all are exceptional, so exceptional responses become necessary. Yet, as McCulloch and Pickering (2009) have observed, as time moves on, such exceptional power becomes normalized along with the security practices associated with them (see also Zedner 2009: 122). The question remains: how valid and viable is this kind of response? In addressing this issue, critical legal scholars have looked to Agamben's (1995: 169) notion of the 'state of exception':

> The state of exception, which was essentially a temporary suspension of the rule of law on the basis of a factual state of danger, is now given permanent spatial arrangement, which as such nevertheless remains outside the normal order.

Agamben's notion of the exceptional has been used to understand how it has been possible to create responses to threats that are neither legal nor non-legal – but ensure the continued legal projection of power (Whyte 2010: 150). He goes on to point out:

> In advanced capitalist societies, the state of exception has a range of simultaneous functions: as ideological or propaganda supports, as means of expanding or enhancing state security apparatuses, legitimizing colonial reach externally, and so on. But of those functions it is those that are connected to the preservation or deepening of a social order that continually seeks to expand its capacities for capital accumulation.
>
> (Whyte 2010: 150)

It is at this juncture that the messy boundaries between the role of the state and the role of the security industries, in the form of security entrepreneurs, re-emerge. Moreover it is no great surprise to find that those subjected to the processes under discussion here are those who invariably find themselves at the lower end of the socio-economic pile. Indeed, the 'exceptional' powers of the state have contributed to the construction of them as 'police property' – perhaps better read as 'state property' – without recognising the embedded presumptions that such constructions entail, and with little heed to their impact (Walklate and Mythen 2015: 139). There is nothing exceptional in this for those so targeted. As Hillyard

(1993) opines, it was ever thus. However, when overlaid with a state-endorsed loss of civil liberties accompanied by a legally endorsed presumption of guilt rather than innocence, the capacity for criminal justice to ensure the moral culture required for its own sustainability is also severely curtailed.

In addition to considering the imperilment of democratic rights and liberties for all raised by the introduction of exceptional measures, we also have to ask what the impact of pre-emptive security policies is likely to be on the populations that are targeted. Do the extending tentacles of the state discipline populations and deter would-be offenders or do they serve to marginalise and alienate? When examining the effectiveness of criminal law in general and counter-terrorism measures in particular, it is the capacity to enhance collective security in the long-term which is crucial. Of course, those in the intelligence services are quick to remind us of their successes in keeping the public safe through revealing foiled plots and thwarted attacks (see Parker 2013). Yet it is clear that particular forms of pre-emptive intervention have served to further frustrate and alienate Muslim minority groups leading to a decline in trust and a fracturing of community relations (see Kundnani 2009; Mythen, Walklate and Khan 2013; Spalek and Lambert 2008). Such circumstances do not make for fertile grounds for information sharing that may help in the fight against terrorism, nor do they bode well in terms of reducing grievances. As Daalgard-Nielsen (2010: 800) reasons, 'the question of whether anti-terrorism laws have in themselves become a significant factor in violent radicalization in Europe remains an open question – a question with obvious policy implications'. In the light of the thousands of citizens born and brought up in European countries presently choosing to travel to Syria to fight with radical Islamic militia, finding answers to this question becomes all the more pressing. What must be more firmly factored into future discussions about policy-making around the terrorist threat is the possibility that interventions can aggravate rather than reduce the situation and thus increase rather than decrease the risk. Borrowing from the natural sciences, we have alluded previously to such iatrogenic effects as the 'law of inverse consequences' (Walklate and Mythen 2015).

Conclusion

In the turn to pre-emption in security policy what is at stake is more than a trade-off between the liberty of the few for the security of the many. Rather, the dilemma is to what extent is it acceptable that the principles of justice for all of us, and by implication the social good of the criminal justice system, be compromised in the interest of states that must be seen to be doing something. The diminishing of this social good for us all has been lost in the concern for justice for the few. Terrorist attacks are always a provocation, but it is the response to this provocation which is critical. As Hillyard (1999) observed some time ago, rather than the prevention of terror, dominant responses by the state seem to have generated the inverse effect: the terrors of prevention. In this chapter, we have been concerned to address the ethical implications of the pre-emptive turn in responding to the terrorist threat for criminal justice.

We have taken the view that criminal justice is a thick public good in which we all have vested interests, particularly in terms of how it is delivered, in order to ensure social justice for us all. Etzioni (2007: 7) reminds us that most people most of the time do what they do in ways that sustain social order, 'because they believe it is right and just'. In this sense, any criminal justice system performs a vital role in sustaining that moral culture. Arguably such moral culture is the value-glue that binds us all together, socio-economic differences notwithstanding. Criminal justice as a 'thick' social good, as suggested at the start of this chapter – along with other institutional features of any society – in terms of its ethics can contribute to or undermine that moral culture. The tendencies we have documented here can, and do, threaten that potential contribution and afford the space in which such moral glue becomes differently informed. It is justice, but not as 'we' would like to know it.

Bibliography

Agamben, G. (2005) *State of Exception*, Chicago, IL: University of Chicago Press.

Awan, I. (2013) 'Let's prevent extremism by engaging communities not by isolating them', *Public Spirit*. December Edition. Viewable at: http://www.publicspirit.org.uk/the-importance-of-local-context-for-preventing-extremism. Accessed 23 January 2014.

Borum, R. (2013) 'Informing lone-offender investigations', *Criminology and Public Policy*, 12(1): 103–12.

Bowling, B. and Phillips, C. (1998) *Violent Racism: Victimization, Policing and Social Context,* Oxford: Clarendon.

Bowling, B. and Sheptycki, J. (2012) *Global Policing,* London: Sage.

Change Institute. (2008) *Studies into Violent Radicalization; Lot 2. The Beliefs, Ideologies and Narratives,* London: Change Institute.

Cook, D. (2006) *Criminal and Social Justice*, London: Sage.

Dalgaard-Nielsen, A. (2010) 'Violent radicalization in Europe: what we know and what we do not know', *Studies in Conflict & Terrorism*, 33(9): 797–814.

de Goede, M., Simon, S., and Hoijtink, M. (2014) 'Performing pre-emption', *Security Dialogue*, 45(5): 411–22.

de Lint, W. and Virta, S. (2004) 'Security and ambiguity: towards a radical security politics', *Theoretical Criminology*, 8(4): 465–89.

Diprose, R., Stephenson, N., Mills, C., Race, K. and Hawkins, G. (2008) 'Governing the future: the paradigm of prudence in political technologies of risk management', *Security Dialogue*, 39(2): 267–88.

Dodd, V. (2010) 'MPs demand investigation into Muslim spy allegations against prevent', *The Guardian*, March 30: 3.

Equality and Human Rights Commission. (2013) *Stop and Think Again*, London: EHRC.

Ericson, R. (2008) 'The state of pre-emption: managing terrorism through counter law', in L. Amoore and M. de Goede (eds.) *Risk and the War on Terror,* London: Routledge, pp. 57–76.

Etzioni, A. (2007) *Security First: For a Muscular Foreign Policy*, New Haven, CT: Yale University Press.

Garland, D, (2001) *The Culture of Control,* Oxford: Oxford University Press.

Hagmann, J. and Cavelty, M.D. (2012) 'National risk registers: security scientism and the propagation of permanent insecurity', *Security Dialogue*, 43(1): 79–96.

Heath-Kelly, C. (2012) 'Reinventing prevention or exposing the gap? False positives in UK terrorism governance and the quest for pre-emption', *Critical Studies on Terrorism*, 5(1): 67–85.

Hillyard, P. (2009) 'The "exceptional" state', in R. Coleman, J. Sim, S. Tombs and D. Whyte (eds.) *State, Power, Crime*, London: Sage, pp. 129–44.

Hudson, B. (2003) *Justice in the Risk Society: Challenging and Reaffirming Justice in Late Modernity*, London: Sage.

Hudson, B. (2012) 'Who needs justice? Who needs security?', in B. Hudson and S. Ugelvik (eds.) *Justice and Security in the 21st Century*, London: Routledge, pp. 6–23.

Hudson, B. and Ugelvik, S. (2012) 'Introduction: new landscapes of security and justice', in B. Hudson and S. Ugelvik (eds.) *Justice and Security in the 21st Century*, London: Routledge, pp. 1–5.

Kibbe, J. (2012) 'Conducting shadow wars', *Journal of National Security Law and Policy*, 5: 373–92.

Kundnani, A. (2009) *Spooked! How Not to Prevent Violent Extremism*, London: Institute of Race Relations.

Kundnani, A. (2012) 'Radicalisation: the journey of a concept', *Race and Class*, 54(2): 3–25.

Leese, M. (2014) 'The new profiling: algorithms, black boxes, and the failure of anti-discriminatory safeguards in the European Union', *Security Dialogue*, 45(5): 494–511.

Liberty. (2015) 'Extended pre charge detention', viewable at: https://www.liberty-human-rights.org.uk/human-rights/countering-terrorism/extended-pre-charge-detention. Accessed January 25 2015.

Loader, I. and Walker, N. (2007) *Civilising Security*, Cambridge: Cambridge University Press.

Lomell, H. M. (2012) 'Punishing the uncommitted crime: prevention, pre-emption, precaution and the transformation of criminal law', in B. Hudson and S. Ugelvik (eds.) *Justice and Security in the 21st Century*, London: Routledge, pp. 83–100.

Maras, H. (2013) *Counterterrorism*, New York, NY: Jones and Burlington.

McCulloch, J. and Pickering, S. (2009) 'Pre-crime and counter terrorism: imagining future crime in the war on terror', *British Journal of Criminology*, 49(5): 628–45.

McGhee, D. (2010) *Security, Citizenship and Human Rights*, Basingstoke: Palgrave Macmillan.

Miller, D. and Sabir, R. (2012) 'Counter-terrorism as counterinsurgency in the UK war on terror', In S. Poynting and D. Whyte (eds.) *Counter-terrorism and State Political Violence,* London: Routledge, pp. 12–32.

Mythen, G. (2012) 'Who speaks for us? Counter-terrorism, collective attribution and the problem of voice', *Critical Studies on Terrorism*, 5(3): 1–16.

Mythen, G. and Walklate, S. (2008) 'Terrorism, risk and international security: the perils of asking what if?', *Security Dialogue*, 39(2): 221–42.

Mythen, G. and Walklate, S. (2010) 'Pre-crime, regulation, and counter-terrorism: interrogating anticipatory risk', *Criminal Justice Matters*, 81(1): 34–36.

Mythen, G., Walklate, S. and Khan, F. (2013) 'Why should we have to prove we're alright? Counter-terrorism, risk and partial securities', *Sociology*, 47(2): 382–97.

9/11 Commission Report. (2004) Washington: Viewable at http://www.9-11commission.gov/report/911Report_Exec.htm. Accessed 17 January 2015.

National Security Strategy Report. (2010) *A Strong Britain in an Age of Uncertainty*, London: HMSO.

Pantazis, C. and Pemberton, S. (2009) 'From the old to the new suspect community: examining the impacts of recent counter-terrorist legislation', *British Journal of Criminology*, 49: 646–66.

Parker, A. (2013) Speech by the head of MI5 to the Royal United Services Institute. October 8. Viewable at http://www.rusi.org/events/past/ref:E5254359BB8F44. Accessed 25 January 2014.

Parmar, A. (2011) 'Stop and search in London: counterterrorist or counterproductive?', *Policing and Society*, 21(4): 369–82.

Prevent Strategy. (2011) London: HMSO.

Roach, K. (2011) *The 9/11 Effect: Comparative Counter-terrorism*, Cambridge: Cambridge University Press.

Runnymede Trust. (2010) 'Stop and search powers'. Viewable at: http://www.runnymedetrust.org/events-conferences/econferences/ethnic-profiling-in-uk-law-enforcement/the-report/young-people-and-section-60/section-60-stop-and-search-powers.html. Accessed December 3 2013.

Simon, S. (2012) 'Suspicious encounters: ordinary pre-emption and the securitization of photography', *Security Dialogue*, 43(2): 157–73.

Smart, C. (1990) *Feminism and the Power of Law*, London: Sage.

Spalek, B. and Lambert, R. (2008). 'Muslim communities, counter-terrorism and counter-radicalization: a critically reflective approach to engagement', *International Journal of Law, Crime, and Justice Studies*, 36(4): 257–70.

Thomas, P. (2012) *Responding to the Threat of Violent Extremism*, London: Bloomsbury.

Vedby-Rasmussen, M. (2004) 'It sounds like a riddle: security studies, the war on terror and risk', *Millennium: Journal of International Relations*, 30(2): 381–95.

Watt, N. (2015) 'David Cameron pledges anti-terror law for Internet after Paris attacks', *The Guardian*, January 12: 1.

Waddington, P., Stenson, K. and Don, D. (2004) 'In proportion: race and police stop and search', *British Journal of Criminology*, 44: 889–914.

Waldron, J. (1993) *Liberal Rights: Collected Papers 1981–91*. Cambridge: Cambridge University Press.

Walklate, S. and Mythen, G. (2015) *Contradictions of Terrorism: Security, Risk and Resilience*, London: Routledge.

Weber, L. and Bowling, B. (eds.) (2012) *Stop and Search: Police Power in Global Context*, London: Routledge.

Whitehead, T. (2013) 'Hundreds of children identified as extremism risk', *The Telegraph*, 22 July: 1.

Whyte, D. (2010) 'The neo-liberal state of exception in occupied Iraq', in W. Chambliss and R. Michalowski (eds.) *State Crime in the Global Age*, Collumpton, Devon: Willan Publishing, pp. 134–53.

Zedner, Z. (2007) 'Seeking security by eroding rights: The side-stepping of due process', in B. Gould and L. Lazarus (eds.) *Security and Human Rights*, Portland, OR: Hart.

Zedner, L. (2009) *Security*, London: Routledge.

11

The moral psychology of penal populism

Leonidas K. Cheliotis and Sappho Xenakis

Scholarship has paid due recognition to the excessive overuse of harsh criminal justice measures such as imprisonment in a large and growing range of jurisdictions around the world over the last four decades or so. What has yet to receive sufficient attention in this regard is the relationship between criminal justice policy-making and public attitudes. More specifically, there is little clarity as to whether publics tend to disapprove of government decisions but are practically ignored by elites in office, or popular preferences are more or less reflected in government decisions, with any discordances pertaining only to particulars. In addition, to the extent that the level and nature of penal policies are thought to be reflective of popular preferences, it is commonly left unclear whether government elites engage in what Bottoms (1995) terms "populist punitiveness" or rather deploy strategies of what Roberts et al. (2003) call "penal populism"; that is, whether they merely respond to punitive public opinion (or, at least, what they believe public opinion to be) or, conversely, feign responsiveness to punitive public attitudes that they have previously largely incited themselves.[1]

Although it was not originally developed with this analytic goal in mind, the concept of penal populism fits well within the recently rejuvenated field of the political economy of punishment. This is especially the case with politico-economic accounts of neo-Marxist lineage that focus on the symbolic role of penal force against weak minorities in eliciting majority support for elites failing to meet their expected responsibilities on the socio-economic front. But whilst such accounts have shed light on the drivers of penal policy-making, not least by extending our understanding of the interests underlying penal populism beyond electoral success as such, they are nevertheless in need of further development in at least three important respects: first, in terms of identifying the array of factors that work, both independently and in tandem, to heighten public susceptibility to ideological manipulation; second, in terms of revealing the deep psychological grounding of each of the factors in question; and third, in terms of explaining the psychological processes that make it possible for governing elites themselves to manipulate public opinion and promote private, in-group, and affiliate interests without compromising their self-perceived legitimacy.

The aim of this chapter is to help address these gaps in terms of both method and substantive insights. We begin by situating our discussion in the context of key broader arguments regarding the ways in which ideology contributes to the maintenance and strengthening of social order and political domination. We then proceed to discuss the role culture is often thought to play in the emergence of punitive ideas and ideals amongst the public before explaining why a political economy approach is necessary and then issuing a call for a blending of the extant literature on the political economy of punishment with psychosocial perspectives on human attitudes and with Erich Fromm's work in particular. We conclude with a few short remarks as to the role politico-economic scholarship and especially Frommian critique may play in countering the excesses of the penal system.

Ideological domination and physical force

This chapter is situated squarely within the age-old debate over why people submit to objectively failing and unjust authorities. More precisely, if subordination to authorities is a form of action, and insofar as the undertaking of any action presupposes that actors deem it accordant with commonly shared principles of rationality and morality, the analytical task is to locate and deconstruct the defenses people evoke to justify their subordination to authorities that use their powers irrationally and immorally if judged by the very principles they purport to share in common with subordinates. To this extent, one needs to grapple with the theory of ideology broadly conceived; namely, with the genus of claims that power inequalities require the kind of consciousness which prevents subordinates from behaving as their interests and values could otherwise dictate.

It should be clarified from the outset that we consider rationalism to be insufficient to provide an alternative to the theory of ideology as an account of the voluntary acceptance of *prima facie* illegitimate social orders. If humans are endowed with a constant ability to exercise pure reason and an unyielding motivation to optimize positive gain, they should swiftly awaken to instances where the gains of submission weigh less than the attendant burdens (Cheliotis 2011). Equally, we are not convinced that submission is likely to derive simply from the negative will to avoid sanctions of physical force. This is partly due to the inherent deficiencies of organizational structures meant to ensure physical control over supernumerary subordinates and partly due to the capacity of human individuals to act on their own accord, especially in disguised ways (see, e.g., Scott 1990).

To be sure, the formation of ideological consciousness is far from a straightforward matter. The effectiveness of political myths employed to this end is commensurate with an array of factors, not least the environment within which the narrative is communicated and the substantive content of the narrative itself. In an attempt to salvage the conceptual value of physical force, Gaventa (1980) suggests that the overhanging threat to punish disobedience, a threat reinforced through regular exhibitions of pure force against deviant others, creates itself a context that renders subordinates vulnerable to ideological manipulation. Yet one cannot but wonder why intimidation by the mere threat of force should be so vital to the process of ideological incorporation when intimidation by the actual exercise of force proves inadequate to generate resignation.

A plausible reply is offered by Wrong (1979). Compared to the exercise of force as such, Wrong argues, the threat and fear of force are more likely to produce consent because they afford subordinates the illusion of participation in the ensuing relationship of authority. What is not clear in this case is the nature of the motive behind the illusion of participation. At any rate, unless one deals with individuals unable to elude the shackles of physical domination (for example, because they fail to recognize or exploit windows of opportunities for dissent), it is superfluous to search for explanations in a common tendency to treat as beneficial and just arrangements that are or appear to be unavoidable.

It would nevertheless be a mistake to dismiss in a wholesale fashion all those accounts of ideological manipulation that identify a facilitative role for physical force. Rather than seeking to explain susceptibility to ideological narratives by reference to the fearful prospect of personal subjection to force, we ought to shift the focus of attention to narrative contents that make the use of force seem necessary, if only against third parties. These are narrative contents that target coercive state intervention against particular subgroups of subordinates as the means by which to preserve or restore corporeal and ontological security (that is, feeling secure as to one's physical existence and identity, respectively) amongst the rest. Tyrannical rule is thereby recast as legitimate and turned into an object of attachment.

Other things being equal, however, myths about urgent extra-state dangers that lie beyond the layman's own control and require authorities to purge the group of culprits, are insufficient to sustain the acceptance of unequal or otherwise illegitimate social orders. This is, on the one hand, because individuals never cease assessing the rationality and morality of their actions, and, on the other hand, because yardsticks for assessment vary according to the particular circumstances of the moment. "Internal conversations," as Archer puts it, "are continuous; they always take place in the present tense, but that, of course, is always situated at some specific historical time" (Archer 2003: 113). It seems likely, moreover, that the frequency and depth of inner dialogue increase with the practical, psychological, and moral weight of the object under scrutiny. The successive concessions implicit in alarmist political myths are just such weighty objects, from bestowing the mandate to rule on powerful authorities to consenting to the violent exclusion of others (or even, on occasion, making practical and active sacrifices like becoming subject to generalized policing measures and partaking oneself in surveillance activities, respectively). Thus, despite an initial stage of concurrence, concessions are inevitably liable to regular and thorough testing against the contrary calls of lived reality. Order begins to shatter as soon as subordinates grasp the rational incongruity of subordination and the immoral nature of the authority at issue (Cheliotis 2013).

This is why one needs to take a reflective step back and resume the quest for particular contextual conditions that may boost the appeal of political myths.[2] Resolution is found in what at first sight resembles tautological or circular reasoning. Indeed, a constant discovery in pertinent scholarship is that humans exhibit greater susceptibility to mythical narratives when feeling trapped in situations of intense insecurity as to their actual life prospects—when there are objective reasons to fear death. This, as Cassirer writes, "[is] the natural soil upon which political myths [can] grow up and in which they [find] ample nourishment" (Cassirer 1946: 278; see further Bottici 2007). Such being the case, the function of political myths that themselves promulgate danger, is not to explain away pragmatic problems of existence, but to displace their original source onto artificial supplements. Myth thus becomes a powerful tool in the hands of political leaders who wish to abdicate personal accountability for failing to care for their constituents.

Below we explore these themes with specific reference to the relationship between state and public punitiveness. In so doing, we pay particular attention to the recently renewed field of the political economy of punishment and efforts made in this vein to describe and explain the processes of political production of public support for increased investment in penal institutions despite not only declining crime rates but also the array of known counterproductive effects penal institutions commonly have, in terms, for example, of reduced job opportunities for offenders, the social disorganization of communities, increased psychological and financial burdens on prisoners' families, and a stronger likelihood of future criminal activity (see further Travis and Visher 2005).

The culture of punitiveness

The ways in which individuals understand, feel about, and ultimately respond to the problem of crime are usually unrelated to first-hand, sensory experiences of victimization. To begin with, although comparatively few people actually fall victims of crime, the general public typically exaggerates the prevalence and seriousness of criminal behavior. Moreover, whilst public opinion usually favors the use of custodial sanctions, underestimating both the degree to which they are meted out already and their harshness, victims of crime are not necessarily supportive of harsh or retributive punishment for offenders (see, e.g., Mattinson and Mirlees-Black 1998; Hough and Roberts 1998; Roberts 2002; Tufts and Roberts 2002). It should therefore come as no surprise that, whereas rates of crime have been following a downward trend on both sides of the Atlantic over recent decades, levels of fear of crime and punitiveness have remained disproportionately high amongst the public (see further Farrall et al. 2009; van Dijk et al. 2007; King and Maruna 2009; Johnson 2009; Enns 2014).

It may be tempting to try to explain such public attitudes as the manufactured product of political discourse and political discourse alone. Elites, after all, have historically tried to dominate subordinates by employing scaremongering myths that incite aggression against third parties. But it is one thing to recognize, foretell, or promise to cure danger, and it is quite another thing to actually manage to draw the masses into genuinely consensual subordination by way of distortive diagnoses, predictions, or therapies (Cassirer 1949). To solve the emerging riddle, several scholars have developed functionalist accounts specifically contextualized in the manner of Émile Durkheim.

At the end of the nineteenth century, Durkheim (1893/1964) argued that the force and general direction of punishment emanate from such psychological reactions as outrage, commonly felt by the majority when cherished beliefs about right and wrong are violated. At the same time as allowing psychic energy to be released against deviants, punishment reaffirms the moral order of the day and promotes social cohesion. With a view to accounting for the evolution of punishment, Durkheim asserted two further propositions: first, that the severity of punishment is inversely proportional to the level of social development; and second, that "as social development proceeds, deprivation of liberty, varying in time with the severity of crime, tends to become the normal and sole means of penal control" (Cotterrell 1999: 79). What is important here is not whether history has proved Durkheim right or wrong, or the role he attributes to crime as such, but his methodological choice to link the nature and functions of punishment to the general structure of society and its cultural dimensions in particular.

More recently, leading thinkers such as David Garland (2001) and Zygmunt Bauman (2000) have stretched their focus on culture beyond majoritarian moral sentiments to include the ever-spreading insecurities of contemporary life as well. These range from job insecurity under conditions of neoliberalism to the ontological insecurities of "the open, porous, mobile society of strangers that is late modernity" (Garland 2001: 165). Garland writes in *The Culture of Control*, for example, that "[o]utrage and anger are the culture's antidotes to fear and anxiety, and the open expression of these emotions is part of the consolation and therapy it offers. The sentiments we now see expressed are quite specific ones, grounded in definite features of our social organisation rather than in some timeless punitive instinct" (145; see further Garland 2006; Karstedt 2002).[3] Hollway and Jefferson (1997) help elaborate this kind of argument by specifying what makes the fear of crime discourse so appealing in today's "risk society." They suggest that, in contrast with other late-modern risks (e.g., radioactive waste, nuclear fission, the greenhouse effect, and genetically modified food), crime-related risks refer to identifiable others who are so powerless that they cannot escape labeling. The figure of the "criminal" thus becomes a convenient folk devil and the fear of crime discourse a satisfying location for anxieties generated more widely.

Just as public attitudes are never formed in a cultural vacuum, however, so too culture is never the product of parthenogenesis. Our point here is that cultural accounts of punishment in the contemporary Anglo-American world suffer from what one might call a "political" or "strategic deficit." Punishment, they tell us, serves to remedy anxieties and satisfy wants that exist already as the inevitable by-products of an abstract, disembodied culture. (Garland [2001: 164] also makes the controversial claim that in "late-modern" societies high crime rates have become a "normal social fact," so much so that the "trauma of powerlessness in the face of fear prompts the demand for action" at both the state and community levels.) When ruling elites deploy punishment as a means to their own, chosen will, it follows, they only do so inasmuch as their will may appear congruent with the popular beliefs and understandings that define command-obedience relationships "from below"; a phenomenon that, as mentioned earlier and discussed in more detail later, pertinent scholarship terms "populist punitiveness."

Although cultural accounts accept that culture is never really immune to political and other pressures, they still assign overwhelming causal priority to the former over the latter. Garland, for instance, argues that "the ways of thinking and feeling which have grown around crime and insecurity … are cultural adaptations to predicaments that are, *in turn*, conditioned by the field of social forces in which the relevant actors are operating" (2006: 437; emphasis added). Contemporary culture is thus viewed as inviting emotivism and the emphatic expression of feeling, thereby pushing political discourse about crime and punishment in that direction (Garland 2001: 144–45). It is also in culture that Garland locates the origins and political appeal of what he terms the "criminology of the other," a deeply illiberal and decidedly anti-modern pseudo-discipline that dramatizes crime and attributes it to "the bad choices of wicked people" (Garland 2001: 185). Hollway and Jefferson (1997) make a similar argument when they treat the role of "independent" criminological knowledge in fueling fear of crime and related attitudes as a cultural happenstance well-suited to the ceaseless attempts of the state to impose social order in an age of uncertainty.

The "political" or "strategic" deficit inherent in cultural accounts is counterbalanced by the recently renewed tradition of the political economy of punishment and its neo-Marxist strand in particular. To elaborate this point, below we discuss Loïc Wacquant's *Punishing the Poor* as the most well-known recent example of such scholarship.[4]

The political economy of punitiveness

Wacquant's goal is to demonstrate that "the penal state has become a potent cultural engine in its own right, which spawns categories, classifications, and images of wide import and use in broad sectors of government and civic life" (Wacquant 2009: 288). Of the various anxiety-provoking trends Garland (2001) describes under the catchall term "late modernity," i.e., the advent of neoliberal capitalism, shifts in the structure of the family and the household, changes in social ecology and demography, the coming of electronic mass media, and the "democratisation" of social life and culture, including unrestrained individualism and hedonistic consumerism—of these trends, Wacquant singles out for scrutiny the first. To narrow the focus to neoliberalism is not to exaggerate one of many distinctive features of "late modernity," Wacquant explains. It rather springs from the need for a different explanatory model of contemporary punishment, one centered specifically around the role of the economy and its repercussions, social as well as psychological, for the people. Attesting to this need, according to Wacquant, is the fact that state punitiveness has been, and continues to be, at its most acute not in the countries most thoroughly affected by the transformative dynamics of "late modernity" (e.g., Finland, Denmark, Sweden), but those where neoliberalism has known the greatest expansion.

Neoliberalism, as defined succinctly by Wacquant, is a transnational political project that aims to remake the nexus of market, state, and citizenship "from above." It is carried out by a "new global ruling class in the making," spanning the heads and senior executives of transnational firms, high-ranking politicians, state managers, and top officials of multinational organizations (e.g., the World Bank and the European Union), as well as cultural-technical experts in their employ (e.g., legal and media experts). Wacquant elaborates that neoliberalism entails not only the reassertion of the dynamic of capitalist production and market exchange, but the articulation of four institutional logics: economic deregulation; the withdrawal of welfare protection; the cultural trope of individual responsibility; and an ever more expansive penal apparatus. Rather, then, than being a deviation from neoliberalism, penality is one of its essential components.

More specifically, at the same time as publicly repudiating intervention in economic and social matters to ensure national competitiveness on the global stage, neoliberal states promote the "new 'punitive common sense' forged in the United States" (Wacquant 2009: 162), which is to say that they elevate criminal insecurity and punishment to the frontline of governmental priorities. The underlying aim is to manage the social reverberations of "advanced social insecurity" that neoliberal policies generate amongst the lower and middle classes. At the bottom of the class structure, punishment works to contain the disorders caused by the "objective insecurity" of flexibilized wage labor and social-welfare retrenchment (Wacquant 2009: 93). Concurrently, punishing the poor creates a convenient outlet for the "subjective" insecurity experienced by the middle classes, "whose prospects for smooth reproduction or upward mobility have dimmed as competition for valued social positions has intensified and the state has reduced its provision of public goods" (300). As such, punishment of the nether regions of social space compensates for the deficit in legitimacy suffered by state leaders on the economic and social fronts.

Wacquant, then, concurs with Garland (2001) that punitive penal policies would not have reached their contemporary ascendancy had it not been for the stereotypical perceptions and the consent, silent or otherwise, of the professional middle classes. But—and here Wacquant's argument parts company with cultural penology—the origins of public attitudes are to be traced in the political struggle over the capacity to legitimate and spread particular visions of the social world. No doubt the cultural context within which this struggle takes place is important; successful myth-making, for example, rests on familiar descriptive idioms and widespread ideas about causation and methods of evaluating the world, the acceptability of which helps further justify what would on closer scrutiny turn out to be irrational. But here the role of culture is facilitative, not causal.

Albeit justly influential, Wacquant's political economy of contemporary punishment is essentially based upon a Foucauldian conception of power relations, whereby, as Butler notes, "power imposes itself on us, and, weakened by its force, we come to internalise or accept its terms." For "'we' who accept such terms are fundamentally dependent on those terms for 'our' existence" (Butler 1997: 2). This is a common tendency amongst critical students of power. To borrow again from Butler: "[t]o underscore the abuses of power as real, not the creation or fantasy of the subject, power is often cast as unequivocally external to the subject, something imposed against the subject's will" (1997: 20). Yet the fact that the subject is formed in subordination, that human agency is initiated and sustained under conditions of dependency, assumes a specific psychoanalytic valence when we consider that what power shapes and exploits is the basic human need for corporeal and ontological security (or, indeed, that agents with divergent biographical trajectories are similarly prone to ideological incorporation and subordination in times of adversity).

At least at its beginnings, the formation of subjects in subordination may be said to emerge as the result of a primary, innate vulnerability to external influences. To make this argument is not necessarily to adopt psychologism and its determinist assumptions. And it is neither to exonerate the abuses subjects suffer at the hands of the established order, nor to imply their inevitability. It is rather a call for moving the study of why people submit to objectively failing and unjust authorities beyond a dialectic between social structures and individual cognitive templates and toward a trialectic that also takes into account the innermost psychic bases of domination and submission—indeed, a trialectic that grounds both social structures and individual cognition in what is always there already: "first nature."

The moral psychology of punitiveness

The trialectic approach is best exemplified in Erich Fromm's "materialistic psychoanalysis," whose method and findings became highly influential in both psychoanalysis and the social sciences in the Western world and beyond between the 1940s and late 1960s, and which has been undergoing steady resurgence in recent years. Fromm's general premise is that utilitarian and moral motives are in significant measure the rationalized expression of the libidinal substructure, and that both the libidinal substructure and its rationalized expression are molded under the influence of socio-political factors and the overarching economic "superstructure" (Fromm 1970). Fromm pays particular attention to what he terms the "social character" and to the innate narcissistic forces that are formed and find outlet therein.

More specifically, Fromm contends that at their most basic level, or at what one may term "first-order" level, human attitudes and actions are driven by private corporeal needs, such as securing food and shelter. But—and here basic or "first-order" needs assume an additional, ontological dimension—humans "could not remain sane even if [they] took care of all [their] material needs, unless [they] were able to establish some form of relatedness to others that allows [them] to feel 'at home,' and saves [them] from the experience of complete affective isolation and separateness" (Fromm and Maccoby 1970: 14). Other fundamental ontological needs consist of happiness, rootedness, and transcendence (see, e.g., Fromm, 1962/2006).

Fromm elaborates that basic or "first-order" needs, be they corporeal or ontological, are built in the instinctual apparatus, and specifically in the "narcissistic core" of the psyche. All individuals, he argues, are born into a state of narcissism; that is, in the belief that the whole world revolves around them, that the whole world *is* them. This implies that the general directions of basic or "first-order" needs, as well as their tenacity, intensity, and universal spread, are biological givens. Fromm adds, however, that the specific content of narcissism, and thus of basic or "first-order" needs, is highly modifiable. In the process of maturation, personal narcissism may be transformed into group or social narcissism, even though the individual must always retain a sense of individuality within a collectivity, just as it may come to revolve around different objects (Fromm 1964; see further Cheliotis 2011).

Importantly, Fromm argues that narcissism also forces individuals to constantly evaluate and try to ensure the legitimacy—that is, the rationality and morality—of their attitudes and actions. It follows that the search for a clear conscience, which is an ontological need in and of itself, makes it imperative that satisfaction of corporeal and other ontological needs be sought in legitimate or, at least, legitimizable ways. Whichever the case, and insofar as motivations are concerned, self-perceptions of legitimacy are epiphenomena of what may be termed a "second-order" narcissistic need—a need relating to the quality of the specific content and type of resolution of basic or "first-order" narcissistic needs (see further Cheliotis 2011, 2013).

What determines whether narcissistic needs acquire a corporeal or an ontological direction in the sense of greater urgency; what determines the specific content needs assume and the particular group that appears preferable to the individual for the purposes of belonging; what defines the precise ways in which needs are to be satisfied and the attendant consequences for the individual and society as a whole; what shapes the general techniques and particular ideals and ideas that are employed to legitimate the struggle for the satisfaction of needs in given ways, including who or what may be viewed as posing threats to corporeal survival and identity—all these issues are typically dependent on the "social character" that is predominant at a given historical moment. Operating as a reciprocal mediator between the economic superstructure, the ideals and ideas prevalent in society, and the narcissistic needs of the individual, the social character transforms "general psychic energy into specific psychosocial energy" (Fromm and Maccoby 1970: 18). Fromm's point here is not merely that socialization serves subtly to align mass desires and their pursuit with the interests of powerful economic elites and their political allies. This alignment, he argues further, requires that socialization work simultaneously to misguide people into actively accepting the legitimacy of the desires and pursuits prescribed for them.

Whilst, in other words, narcissistic urges inescapably set in motion the process of continuously assessing the legitimacy of one's own attitudes and actions, there are no guarantees as to whether engagement in this process will bring about objectively rational and moral outcomes. This is because the concrete standards, the knowledge resources, and the cognitive operations by which attitudes and actions are evaluated commonly derive from one's social existence and especially from the unfolding of the economic environment. Thus, insofar as the social character promotes ideological incorporation through control of culture, it plays a key role in the maintenance of unjust civil orders and their economic foundations (Fromm 1962/2006).

What Fromm terms the "hoarding" character orientation, for instance, privileges a puritan approach to work and accumulation of wealth. The hoarding character was the backbone of nineteenth-century capitalism, because the "combination of a stable world, stable possessions, and a stable ethic gave the members of the middle class a feeling of belonging, self-confidence, and pride" (Fromm 1949/1986: 81). By contrast, *homo consumens* develops in capitalist societies that nurture the greed for consumption by tying it to symbolic recognition of distinction and success in life (Fromm 1976/1997). "Our economy," Fromm was writing of the US back in the 1960s, "would face a severe crisis if people—the working and the middle classes—were not to spend most of their income on consumption, rather than to save it" (Fromm 1962/2006: 63).

Nevertheless, as Fromm is quick to recognize, the growth of contradictions in society threatens to provoke a "revolutionary" mode of thinking on a mass scale, which would dissolve the social character in place, including any justifications this provides for ongoing and growing social contradictions, and shake the economic order to its roots (Fromm 1970). Resolution, Fromm explains, tends to be found for the ruling establishment in the nurture of new character orientations that are neither alternative to the old nor necessarily mutually exclusive of one another. At the furthest extreme of such resolution lies the "authoritarian character," the person who "admires authority and tends to submit to it, but at the same time ... wants to be an authority himself and have others submit to him" (Fromm 1941/1994: 162).

Here the ruling establishment displaces mass anger onto out-groups scapegoated as dangerous, and activates an aggressive striving to dominate over them, thereby producing the "legitimate" need for authoritarian action that the establishment is both specially equipped and amply willing to undertake. To achieve domination over scapegoated others, the people must submit to, and identify with, their otherwise failing rulers. It is not simply that "[b]y this symbolic participation in [rulers' lives], man has the illusion of acting, when in reality he only submits to, and becomes a part of, those who act" (Fromm 1964: 31). It is also that this illusion of power facilitates "the development of economic forces even if those forces contradict the economic interests of [one's own] class" (Fromm 1941/1994: 295). Fromm's preferred example is the rise of Fascism in antebellum Germany, and particularly the way in which the lower middle classes were drawn into Nazi ideology amidst a climate of widespread socio-economic insecurity, itself the outcome of mass unemployment, hyperinflation, and a severe crisis in the stock market (see further Fromm 1973/1984; also McLaughlin 2007).[5]

The means by which particular social characters are cultivated consist of such agencies of socialization as the family, educational establishments, and the mass media, themselves also subject to the "meta-structure" of the economy (see, e.g., Fromm 1941/1969, 1955/2006). The social function of education, argues Fromm, "is to qualify the individual to function in the role he is to play later on in society; that is, to mould his character in such a way that it approximates the social character, that his desires coincide with the necessities of his social role." Parents, too, apply the educational patterns of the society in which they live, whilst also representing in their own personalities the social character of their society or class (Fromm 1941/1969: 284). And so the longevity of class rule is due not only to economic necessities under capitalism or the threat of physical force, but also to

> certain moral principles which entice the poor to suffer rather than to do wrong, and which lead them to believe that the purpose of their life is to obey their rulers and do their duty. Even these ethical conceptions, which are so important for social stability, are the products of certain affective and emotional relations to those who create and represent such norms.
> (Fromm 1970: 159)

Seen in this way, ties to rulers may well be a repetition or continuation of the child's attitude toward parents, especially toward the father. Just as children exhibit "a mixture of admiration, fear, faith, and confidence in the father's strength and wisdom, briefly, an affectively conditioned reflection of his intellectual and moral qualities," so "we find the same in adults of a patriarchal class society *vis-à-vis* the members of the ruling class" (Fromm 1970: 159).

Crucially for our discussion, Fromm does not view criminal justice as an instrument of crime control; he is, in fact, well aware that custodial punishment routinely fails to achieve deterrence. Nor does Fromm consider criminal justice as a means of open, brute oppression based upon the rational interests of the people. He rather includes criminal justice in the cultural apparatus that serves to solidify the social character—indeed, what Fromm describes in subsequent work as the "authoritarian character"—by directing infantile attitudes of obedience toward rulers. Fromm articulates this thesis in two articles he published in the early 1930s, during his tenure at the Institute for Social Research in Frankfurt (now better known as the Frankfurt School), though several years before Georg Rusche and Otto Kirchheimer (1939), also of the Frankfurt School, published *Punishment and Social Structure*, a book considered by most contemporary penologists as the founding text in the political economy of punishment.

Fromm's articles raise and provide imaginative clues to issues such as the symbolic facets of punitiveness under capitalism, which still remain under-studied today. His overall aim there is to deconstruct the twofold manner in which "the fear of crime and the role of the state in repressing crime support and legitimate the existing capitalist order" (Anderson 2000: 83). The state elite, Fromm suggests, uses the criminal justice system to project itself as a father figure (*Vaterimago*) in the unconscious of the dominated classes, not only claiming the capacity to "protect society from the criminal and to reform or correct him," but also highlighting the "fact that the father can punish, that the child is defenceless because of the father's physical superiority. … Criminal justice is like the rod on the wall, which is supposed to show even the well-behaved child that a child is a child, and a father a father" (Fromm 1930/2000: 126). Caught in between the Scylla of perceived vulnerability to criminal victimization and the Charybdis of feeling weak in the face of state-sanctioned punishment, the child-citizen has little choice but to transform into admiring worship his or her aversion toward the punitive father-ruler. All the while, punishment of criminals provides the masses with an outlet upon which to unleash the resentment caused by the instinctual deprivations of daily life under conditions of capitalist exploitation, principally on the front of economic wellbeing. No wonder "it is very important to the rulers that these impulses be diverted from them and onto another subject" (Fromm 1930/2000: 126). "Only from this point view," Fromm concludes, "can we understand the contradiction that has appeared between the ineffectiveness of the criminal justice system and the holding on to it both by eminent experts in criminal law and by politicians concerned with crime" (Fromm 1931/2000: 147; see further Anderson 2000; Cheliotis 2013).

Bringing Frommian psychoanalysis to bear upon insights produced by cultural as well as politico-economic studies of contemporary punishment, one of the authors of this chapter has sought to trace the ways in which the expanded use of imprisonment allows governing elites in the US and the UK today to manage public insecurities under conditions of neoliberal capitalism. The focus of this work has been on the symbolic role of physical penal control over socio-economically weak segments of the population in eliciting support from the middle classes for elites failing to meet their expected responsibilities on the socio-economic front. In this context, it is argued, the use of imprisonment against weaker others lends itself as an outlet for the continuous cathartic discharge of stubborn middle-class anxieties, whilst these anxieties are channeled to the resolution provided by imprisonment in large part through the vehicle of heightened concerns over violent street crime. The fact that governing elites themselves often claim that the state has failed to control violent street crime is because ineffectiveness on the part of the criminal justice apparatus is a necessary ingredient of that form of state domination which is heavily predicated upon displacing substantive public anger and insecurities and discharging them against weak out-group minorities. Such domination cannot materialize on a steady footing without the persistence or continuous emergence of problems fit to rationalize and moralize the repeated violent resolution of esoteric psychic conflicts (see further Cheliotis 2013).

More generally, Fromm's psychosocial approach helps to explain why susceptibility to political myths that promulgate danger and call for harsh reaction by the state increases when people feel tangled in situations of intense insecurity as to their actual life prospects. It also helps to account for the appeal of the illusion of participation in a relationship of authority that is actually based on the fear or threat of force against oneself, the latter being itself a theme as yet under-studied in the political economy of punishment. Equally, Fromm's psychosocial approach allows one to appreciate that state authority may stand in inverse proportion to lasting or even accruing insecurities amongst the people and that policy failure may be politically convenient insofar as it carries unconsciously positive symbolisms, a crucial point commonly missed given that policy is typically evaluated strictly by reference to the principles of "instrumental rationality." Below we conclude our chapter by discussing how Fromm applies his approach to those elites who seek and manage to draw the people into ideological incorporation, one more theme that the political economy of punishment has left more or less unexplored to date.

The moral psychology of penal populists

Our analysis so far has proceeded on the assumption that political elites bear fundamental responsibility for punitive public attitudes. In discussing such responsibility, pertinent literature typically employs one of two rival if often conflated interpretations. These we may term, respectively, a "passive" version of elite responsibility and a "proactive" alternative.

The "passive" version of elite responsibility for punitive public attitudes is widely referred to as "populist punitiveness" and sees "politicians tapping into, and using for their own purposes, what they believe to be the public's generally punitive stance'"(Bottoms 1995: 40). Here political elites are not thought to manufacture public punitiveness, yet they do nothing to reverse it. Green evokes opinion research to issue the caveat that public attitudes are not uniformly or equally punitive and that "politicians *should* know better by now" (2008: 21; original emphasis). To the extent that such evidence goes ignored, one may argue further, it may be because politicians need to retain a favorable self-image, putting the blame for punitive policies on what they directly or indirectly portray as an almighty and stubbornly regressive public. Implicit in this resolution, however, is that politicians would actually prefer it, or find it convenient, if the broader public were monolithically punitive, which opens up the possibility of ideological manipulation as the means of generating such attitudes.

This brings us to the second, "proactive" version of elite responsibility for public punitiveness, best encapsulated by the notion of "penal populism." Politicians, in this case, are said strategically to misrepresent reality in ways that stir up punitive sentiments amongst the public. The harsh policies adopted against criminals in turn (e.g., mandatory sentencing) may well fail to meet basic standards of fairness and effectiveness, but are nevertheless electorally attractive (Roberts et al. 2003). It is not difficult to see how the concept of penal populism fits with a politico-economic approach to state and public punitiveness, even if it was not originally developed with this analytic goal in mind. Yet there are insufficient grounds for asserting that politicians would consciously act as manipulative cynics, much as their actions may serve individual, in-group, and affiliate goals according to a plan that is rationally manipulative in the objective sense of the term.

As Fromm explains, the elites are not driven by "an overwhelming greed for power, money, or prestige. To be sure, such motives exist, too; but the people in whom this is the all-consuming motive are the exception rather than the rule" (Fromm 1962/2006: 83). Fromm's counter-argument is that whilst exploitative elites are typically driven by a "first-order" narcissistic greed for power, pay, or status, they are no less subject to the "second-order" narcissistic need to keep one's own conscience satisfied, which impels them to legitimate their position and decisions to themselves and to their immediate circle at least as much as to masses they govern.

What Fromm puts forward is, in effect, a combination of the Weberian and Marxist models of accounting for manipulative elite action. For Weber, it may be recalled, inherent to the acquisition and exercise of power is a normative conception of self-respect, combined with the stakes and consequences of losing it. Drawing on Weber's account, Barker (2001) has recently argued that statesmen cannot view themselves as usurpers or tyrants, which is why they tend to legitimate their position and power to themselves and to their immediate staff at least as much as to the people they govern. What Barker alludes to, but does not name, is that every legitimating account derives from the universal narcissistic need to keep one's own conscience satisfied. It may thus be the case that criticisms from dissatisfied subordinates regarding their situation are criticisms which power-holders address to themselves. The rejection of criticisms, however, may prove profoundly irrational in the sense of being rationally or scientifically indefensible (Kronman 1983).

Marx and Engels (1976) take the analysis one step further when they rebuke historians who presume that ideas determine the course of history independently of materialist class interests. Not that the powerful "lie for pay," Marx and Engels explain, but personal materialist interests mold personal beliefs, especially beliefs concerning one's own self. In the 1800s, for example, British manufacturers insisted on claiming that a reduced, 10-hour workday would bring about the collapse of the British industry, although they had ample evidence to the contrary. But they held a genuine belief in what they were saying. "[T]heir belief was based on their interest in persuading others of this proposition, together with the normal interest in avoiding the mental pain of lying" (Miller 1991: 76; see also Mannheim 1971; Pareto 1968/2006).

There is, then, an unmistakable Weberian-cum-Marxist tone in Fromm's contention that the standards, knowledge, and methods by which elites gauge their moral performance follow directly from their social existence and the unfolding of the economic mode of production in particular.

> They consider their way of organisation and the values that are implied in it as being in "the best interests of man"; they have a picture of human nature which makes this assumption plausible; they are hostile to any idea or system which questions or endangers their own system; they are against disarmament if they feel that their organisations are threatened by it; they are suspicious and hostile of a system in which their class has been replaced by a different and new class of managers. Consciously, they honestly believe that they are motivated by patriotic concern for their country, duty, moral and political principles, and so on. … The motivating factor is that their social function forms their consciousness, and hence their conviction that they are right, that their aims are justified and, in fact, beyond doubt'.
>
> (Fromm 1962/1983: 83)

Fromm himself did not apply these observations to penal policy-making elites, and as far as we know, no systematic account of this kind has been produced to date. There is, however, research to suggest that there is significant mileage to a psychosocial approach to the enactment of penal populism. It has been argued, for example, that political leaders may choose of their own accord to be surrounded by sycophantic and similarly minded advisors, including status-seeking experts welcomed in the corridors of power to lend a veneer of scientific rationality to unfair and failing criminal justice measures already adopted on grounds other than the "problem" of crime (Bigo 2002; Wacquant 2009). It has been found, conversely, that governing elites may rush to dismiss empirical criminological evidence that doubts the necessity of their chosen policies, regardless of whether the evidence in question has been produced in accordance with the methodological directions of the establishment itself (Hope 2004). Also, as argued by Roberts et al. (2003: 7), penal populists may consciously account for their "tough on crime" discourse as being a "small compromise with populism" forced upon them by populist opposition parties; unless one compromises with populism, so the logic goes, one may "lose power—and along with it the chance of making improvements to the criminal justice system."

Oddly, perhaps, criminologists have long sought to attribute to criminals the propensity to neutralize lawbreaking (see further Maruna and Hopes 2006) yet have usually withheld that affirmation from those responsible for harsh and ineffective penal policies, including policies that stand in contravention of domestic and international human rights legislation (see, e.g., Simon 2014).

Concluding comments

Several important implications flow from our analysis thus far. To begin with, insofar as penology aspires to put a halt to the excesses of the penal system, it needs to intervene in the field of symbolic politics and engage directly in public debate. The substantive aim of such intervention should be to help correct the fallacies underpinning, and reveal the hidden functions served by, state punitiveness, and this in turn may reorient public attention hitherto unduly paid to issues of crime and punishment toward politico-economic change. Fromm's psychosocial approach is particularly useful in this respect. Not only does it shed light on the psychological roots and functions of illegitimate forms of social arrangements, without knowledge of which any account must be incomplete. It does so, moreover, by refraining from fatalistically blaming human nature while avoiding the alienating castigation of individuals or groups for their complicity in irrational and immoral phenomena. Instead, it draws attention to the social, cultural, political, and economic factors under the influence of which all humans may come to hold attitudes and engage in actions they would otherwise reject.

Notes

1 Exceptions here include Beckett (1997), Chambliss (1999) and, as discussed later on in the chapter, Wacquant (2009).

2 Other factors, such as the symbolic capital of the narrator and the media and channels of communication, are also arguably important. That we do not discuss them in this chapter is due to reasons of space (but see further Kearney 2002).

3 Such accounts resonate with research findings that mortality salience and ontological concerns (relating, for example, to social status, community cohesion, or future generations) are strong predictors of punitiveness (see further Pyszczynski et al. 2003; Gaubatz 1995; Tyler & Boeckmann 1997; Maruna & King 2004; Unnever et al. 2007).

4 For an overview of the literature on the political economy of punishment, see De Giorgi (2006).

5 Notwithstanding some obvious similarities, Fromm's concept of the authoritarian character should not be mistaken for its conceptual cousin that is the "authoritarian personality," put forward 10 years later by Adorno and a research team he led at the Frankfurt School. The goal of their study was to trace a complex of personality characteristics shared by individuals holding right-wing authoritarian views in the US in the 1950s. It is thus doubtful whether the authors of *The Authoritarian Personality* ever actually grappled with the authoritarian personality *per se*, for they ignored both left-wing authoritarianism and the "traditionalist authoritarianism" found in agrarian settings. More fundamentally, and unlike Fromm, their primary focus was on interpersonal psychological factors of Freudian inspiration, particularly on oedipal experiences during early childhood, and far less on socio-economic class (see further Cheliotis 2011).

Bibliography

Anderson, K. (2000) 'Erich Fromm and the Frankfurt School critique of criminal justice', in K. Anderson and R. Quinney (eds.) *Erich Fromm and Critical Criminology: Beyond the Punitive Society*, Urbana and Chicago, IL: University of Illinois Press, pp. 83–119.

Archer, M. S. (2003) *Structure, Agency, and the Internal Conversation*. Cambridge: Cambridge University Press.

Barker, R. (2001) *Legitimating Identities: The Self-Presentations of Rulers and Subjects,* Cambridge: Cambridge University Press.

Bauman, Z. (2000) 'Social uses of law and order', in D. Garland and R. Sparks (eds.) *Criminology and Social Theory*, Oxford: Oxford University Press, pp. 23–45.

Beckett, K. (1997) *Making Crime Pay: Law and Order in Contemporary American Politics,* New York:, NY Oxford University Press.

Bigo, D. (2002) 'Security and Immigration: Toward a Critique of the Governmentality of Unease', *Alternatives* 27(Special Issue): 63–92.

Bottici, C. (2007) *A Philosophy of Political Myth*. Cambridge, NY: Cambridge University Press.

Bottoms, A.E. (1995) 'The philosophy and politics of punishment and sentencing', in C.M.V. Clarkson and R. Morgan (eds.) *The Politics of Sentencing Reform*, Oxford: Clarendon Press, pp. 17–49.

Butler, J. (1997) *The Psychic Life of Power: Theories in Subjection,* Stanford, CA: Stanford University Press.

Cassirer, E. (1946) *The Myth of the State*. New Haven, CT: Yale University Press.

Chambliss, W.J. (1999) *Power, Politics and Crime,* Boulder, CO: Westview Press.

Cheliotis, L.K. (2011) 'For a Freudo-Marxist critique of social domination: rediscovering Erich Fromm through the mirror of Pierre Bourdieu', *Journal of Classical Sociology*, 11(4): 438–61.

Cheliotis, L.K. (2013) 'Neoliberal capitalism and middle-class punitiveness: bringing Erich Fromm's "Materialistic Psychoanalysis" to penology', *Punishment & Society*, 15(3): 247–73.

Cotterrell, R. (1999) *Emile Durkheim: Law in a Moral Domain,* Stanford, CA: Stanford University Press.

De Giorgi, A. (2006) *Re-Thinking the Political Economy of Punishment,* Aldershot: Ashgate.

Durkheim, E. (1893/1964) *The Division of Labour in Society,* New York, NY: Free Press.

Durkheim, E. (1914/1973) 'The dualism of human nature and its social conditions', in R.N. Bellah (ed.) *Emile Durkheim on Morality and Society,* Chicago, IL: University of Chicago Press, pp. 149–63.
Enns, P.K. (2014) 'The public's increasing punitiveness and its influence on mass incarceration in the United States', *American Journal of Political Science*, 58(4): 857–72.
Farrall, S., Jackson, J. and Gray, E. (2009) *Social Order and the Fear of Crime in Contemporary Times.* Oxford: Clarendon.
Fromm, E. (1929/1984) *The Working Class in Weimar Germany: A Psychological and Sociological Study.* Leamington Spa: Berg.
Fromm, E. (1930/2000) 'The state as educator: on the psychology of criminal justice', in K. Anderson and R. Quinney (eds.) *Erich Fromm and Critical Criminology: Beyond the Punitive Society*, pp. 123–28. Urbana, Chicago, IL: University of Illinois Press.
Fromm, E. (1931/2000) 'On the psychology of the criminal and the punitive society', in K. Anderson and R. Quinney (eds.) *Erich Fromm and Critical Criminology: Beyond the Punitive Society*, Urbana, Chicago, IL: University of Illinois Press, pp. 129–56.
Fromm, E. (1941/1994) *Escape from Freedom,* New York, NY: Henry Holt & Company.
Fromm, E. (1949/1986) *Man for Himself,* London: Ark.
Fromm, E. (1955/2006) *The Sane Society,* New York, NY: Rinehart.
Fromm, E. (1955/1992) *The Dogma of Christ and Other Essays on Religion, Psychology, and Culture,* New York, NY: Henry Holt & Company.
Fromm, E. (1956/2000) *The Art of Loving,* New York, NY: Perennial.
Fromm, E. (1962/2006) *Beyond the Chains of Illusion: My Encounter with Marx and Freud,* New York, NY: Continuum.
Fromm, E. (1964) *The Heart of Man: Its Genius for Good and Evil,* New York, NY: Harper & Row.
Fromm, E. (1970) *The Crisis of Psychoanalysis: Essays on Freud, Marx, and Social Psychology,* New York, NY: Holt, Rinehart & Winston. London: Cape.
Fromm, E. (1973/1984) *The Anatomy of Human Destructiveness,* Harmondsworth: Penguin.
Fromm, E. (1976/1997) *To Have or to Be?* New York, NY: Continuum.
Fromm, E. (1981) *On Disobedience and Other Essays,* New York, NY: The Seabury Press.
Fromm, E. and Maccoby, M. (1970) *Social Character in a Mexican Village: A Sociopsychoanalytic Study,* Englewood Cliffs, NJ: Prentice-Hall.
Funk, R. (1978/1982) *Erich Fromm: The Courage to be Human,* New York, NY: Continuum.
Garland, D. (2001) *The Culture of Control: Crime and Social Order in Contemporary Society,* Oxford: Oxford University Press.
Garland, D. (2006) 'Concepts of culture in the sociology of punishment', *Theoretical Criminology* 10(4): 419–447.
Gaubatz, K.T. (1995) *Crime in the Public Mind.* Ann Arbor, MI: University of Michigan Press.
Gaventa, J. (1980) *Power and Powerlessness: Quiescence and Rebellion in an Appalachian Valley,* Urbana, IL: University of Illinois Press.
Green, D. (2008) *When Children Kill Children: Penal Populism and Political Culture,* Oxford: Clarendon.
Hollway, W. and Jefferson, T. (1997) 'The risk society in an age of anxiety: situating fear of crime', *British Journal of Sociology*, 48(2): 255–66.
Hope, T. (2004) 'Pretend it works: evidence and governance in the evaluation of the reducing burglary initiative', *Criminology & Criminal Justice*, 4(3): 287–308.
Hough, M. and Roberts, J. (eds) (1998) *Attitudes to Crime and Punishment: Findings from the British Crime Survey*, Home Office Research Studies 179. London: HMSO.
Johnson, D. (2009) 'Anger about Crime and Support for Punitive Criminal Justice Policies', *Punishment & Society* 11(1): 51–88.
Karstedt, S. (2002) 'Emotions and Criminal Justice', *Theoretical Criminology* 6(3): 299–317.
Kearney, R. (2002) *On Stories.* London and New York, NY: Routledge.
King, A. and Maruna, S. (2006) 'The function of fiction for a punitive public', in P. Mason (ed.) *Captured by* the Media: Prison Discourse in Popular Culture, Cullompton: Willan, pp. 16–30.
King, A. and Maruna, S. (2009) 'Is a Conservative Just a Liberal Who Has Been Mugged? Exploring the Origins of Punitive Views', *Punishment & Society* 11(2): 147–169.
Kronman, A.T. (1983) *Max Weber,* Stanford, CA: Stanford University Press.
Lijphart, A. (1997) 'Unequal participation: democracy's unresolved dilemma', *American Political Science Review*, 91(1): 1–14.
Maccoby, M. (1976) *The Gamesman: The New Corporate Leaders,* New York, NY: Simon and Schuster.

Mannheim, K. (1929/1936) *Ideology and Utopia*. London: Routledge.

Marx, K. and Engels, F. (1976) *German Ideology*. New York, NY: International Publishers Co.

Maruna, S. and King, A. (2004) 'Public opinion and community penalties', in A. Bottoms, S. Rex and G. Robinson (eds.) *Alternatives to Prison: Options for an Insecure Society*, Cullompton: Willan, pp. 83–112.

Maruna, S., Matravers, A. and King, A. (2004) 'Disowning our shadow: a psychoanalytic approach to understanding punitive public attitudes', *Deviant Behavior*, 25(3): 277–99.

Mattinson, J. and Mirrlees-Black, C. (1998) *Attitudes to Crime and Criminal Justice: Findings from the 1998 British Crime Survey*, Home Office Research Findings 111. London: Home Office.

Mayhew, P. and van Kesteren, J. (2002) 'Cross-national attitudes to punishment', in J. Roberts and M. Hough (eds.) *Changing Attitudes to Punishment: Public Opinion, Crime, and Justice*, Cullompton: Willan, pp. 63–92.

McLaughlin, N. (2007) 'Escape from Evidence? Popper, Social Science, and Psychoanalytic Social Theory', *Dialogue* 46(4): 761–780.

Miller, R.W. (1991) 'Social and Political Theory: Class, State, Revolution', in T. Carver (ed.) *The Cambridge Companion to Marx*, pp. 55–105. Cambridge: Cambridge University Press.

Pareto, V. (1968/2006) *The Rise and Fall of Elites: An Application of Theoretical Sociology*. New Brunswick, NJ: Transaction Publishers.

Pyszczynski, T., Solomon, S. and Greenberg, J. (2003) *In the Wake of 9/11: The Psychology of Terror*. Washington, DC: American Psychological Association.

Roberts, J. (2002) 'Public Opinion and the Nature of Community Penalties: International Findings', in J. Roberts and M. Hough (eds) *Changing Attitudes to Punishment: Public Opinion, Crime and Justice*, pp. 33–62. Cullompton: Willan.

Roberts, J.V., Stalans, L.J., Indermaur, D. and Hough, M. (2003) *Penal Populism and Public Opinion: Lessons from Five Countries*, New York, NY: Oxford University Press.

Scott, J. C. (1990) *Domination and the Arts of Resistance: Hidden Transcripts*. New Haven: Yale University Press.

Simon, J. (2014) *Mass Incarceration on Trial: A Remarkable Court Decision and the Future of Prisons in America*, New York and London: The New Press.

Travis, J. and Visher, C. (eds.) (2005) *Prisoner Reentry and Crime in America*, New York, NY: Cambridge University Press.

Tufts, J. and Roberts, J. (2002) 'Sentencing Juvenile Offenders: Public Preferences and Judicial Practice', *Criminal Justice Policy Review* 13: 46–64.

Tyler, T. R. and Boeckmann, R. J. (1997) '"Three Strikes and You are Out", but Why? The Psychology of Public Support for Punishing Rule Breakers', *Law & Society Review* 17(1): 21–45.

Unnever, J. D., Cullen, F. T. and Fisher, B. S. (2007) '"A Liberal is Someone Who Has Not Been Mugged": Criminal Victimisation and Political Beliefs', *Justice Quarterly* 24(2): 309–334.

van Dijk, J., R. Manchin, J., van Kesteren, S. Nevala and G. Hideg (2007) *The Burden of Crime in the EU*. Brussels: Gallup Europe.

Wacquant, L. (2009) *Punishing the Poor: The New Government of Social Insecurity*, Durham, NC and London: Duke University Press.

Wrong, D.H. (1979/1988) *Power: Its Forms, Bases, and Uses*, New Brunswick, NJ and London: Transaction.

Wrong, D.H. (1994) *The Problem of Order: What Unites and Divides Society*, Cambridge, MA: Harvard University Press.

12
The retribution heuristic

Stephen Koppel[1] and Mark R. Fondacaro[2]

Introduction

Among the four generally accepted justifications of punishment—retribution, rehabilitation, incapacitation, and deterrence—retribution is aberrant in that it rejects consequential reasoning. Although there are various conceptions of retribution,[3] each holds that wrongdoing should be punished proportionately, *regardless* of practical consequences. "Do justice though the heavens may fall," as a proponent of retributivism would have it. Despite efforts to root criminal justice policy in empiricism, this peculiar feature of retribution has been left largely unchallenged. This is surprising since retribution's indifference to consequences makes it unfit for empirical scrutiny, for without concern for consequences, measuring the effectiveness of retributive punishment is not possible. For some perspective on how unusual this is in the realm of policy-making, consider your reaction to the following proposals: a health care intervention wholly unconcerned with medical outcomes; a fiscal plan with no tangible economic indicators of success; a military intervention whose purpose is not to improve national security but to give another country what it deserves, no matter the result. But perhaps retribution's abiding relevancy is due to the fact that retributive urges—the rush of emotion a person feels when he or she has been wronged—are so familiar to us all. That these emotions are universal, however, also points to the possibility that retribution is more concerned with consequences than it at first seems.

Cognitive heuristics are mental shortcuts that enable quick and efficient decision-making. Several converging lines of research suggest that retribution reflects one of these rule-of-thumb heuristics—what we term a retribution heuristic—that answers the question of how to respond to wrongdoing. Such findings belie the claim that retribution is unconcerned with consequences: Like all hard-wired cognitive heuristics, the retribution heuristic can be assumed to reflect an adaptive logic that at one time enhanced survival. What's more, though such cognitive heuristics can generally be relied upon to produce sound judgments, research shows that they can lead us to systematically commit errors of judgment known as cognitive biases. Perhaps this is because many rules-of-thumb were codified in environmental conditions that differ significantly from today. This leads to the question of whether the retribution heuristic can also be demonstrated to produce errors of judgment?

Section I of this chapter will provide neurobiological and psychological evidence for a retribution heuristic. Section II will explore recent discoveries in psychology showing that a number of cognitive heuristics produce errors of judgment. Section III will situate the retribution heuristic among these other cognitive biases and show its tendency to produce fundamental retribution errors that are shaped and influenced by cultural and social factors over time. Section IV will draw conclusions about the link between the retribution heuristic and the imposition of overly harsh, unjust, and ineffective criminal sanctions.

I The retributive heuristic

In *Sociobiology: The New Synthesis*, E. O. Wilson, a renowned evolutionary biologist, advances the controversial hypothesis that our sense of morality is rooted in biology and has been shaped by natural selection (1975). But if biology lies behind morality, then what of the great cerebrations of ethical philosophy? Wilson argues that ethical philosophy is limited in that it treats the human mind as a "black box" and then assumes that emanations from it reflect a "direct awareness of right and wrong that it can formalize by logic." The problem with this, he claims, is that ethical philosophers fail to consider the "biological or ecological" implications of their arguments. His solution: snatch ethics temporarily from the hands of philosophers and "biologize" it. While philosophers continue to cogitate about right and wrong, scientists have been making progress toward prying open the black box to reveal morality's neurobiological and psychological underpinnings.

The language of disgust is commonly used to describe moral transgressions: Immoral acts leave us feeling dirty; unfair prices tags are obscene; the legal doctrine requiring a plaintiff to enter a suit free of unfair conduct is "clean hands." Could this be something more than metaphor? Hypothesizing that the clean/dirty metaphor indicates a connection between moral disgust and more primitive forms of disgust related to toxicity and disease, researchers searched for similarity in the facial motor activity elicited by unpleasant tastes, basic disgust elicited by photographs of contaminants, and moral disgust elicited by unfair treatment in an economic game. They found that all three evoked an identical facial response: activation of the levator labii muscle region of the face (Chapman et al. 2009).

The results suggest a biological link between disgust and moral judgments. Researchers believe that this can be explained by an evolutionary phenomenon known as exaptation, whereby a physical trait previously shaped by evolution is co-opted for a new use (Gould and Vrba 1982). A classic example of exaptation is the shift in use of bird feathers from temperature regulation to their present role in flight. Evolutionary biologists posit that exaptations have also occurred at the psychological level. The exaptation of language out of brain structures that previously served a different function is one plausible candidate (Gould 1991). That the faculty for moral evaluations appears to have exapted from disgust of environmental toxins suggests a similar role in a different context—judging conduct to be right or wrong in order to avoid future harm (Hoffman 2014). This raises the question: If through evolutionary pressures we have become hard-wired to recoil from certain environmental toxins, are we also hard-wired to have moral aversions to certain conduct?

With advanced neuroimaging technology, cognitive psychologists have been able to probe the underlying biology of moral decision-making. One such investigation carried out by Joshua Greene and Jonathan Cohen was designed to reveal the parts of the brain engaged while faced with a moral dilemma: the runaway trolley problem. The trolley problem generally includes two scenarios: Scenario #1 in which subjects are asked if they would pull a lever to divert a trolley that fatally threatens five people onto another track where it only threatens one; Scenario #2 is identical, only now subjects are asked if they would physically push a person in front of the trolley for the same purpose. Typically, people approve of pulling the lever in order to save five lives in exchange for one but disapprove of pushing a person despite the identical result. What accounts for the differences? When asked, participants have difficulty justifying their inconsistent responses.

With the aid of neuroimaging, though, researches can examine the neurobiology that underlies such moral reasoning. By doing so, they have identified several areas of the ventral medial pre-frontal cortex (VMPFC) and medial front and posterior gyri of the insula—regions associated with emotion—that are significantly more active during contemplation of Scenario #2 (Greene et al. 2004). That these areas of the brain are more engaged in Scenario #2 suggests that the thought of pushing a person triggers an intuitive moral aversion that overrides the cost-benefit reasoning displayed in Scenario #1. The researchers theorized that "the thought of pushing someone in front of a trolley elicits a prepotent, negative emotional response that drives moral disapproval." In the absence of a prepotent emotional response, though, they found that "utilitarian reasoning" prevails. When the same experiment was conducted on individuals with a disorder characterized by damage to the emotional center of their brain, frontotemporal dementia (FTD), they found further support for this view (Mendez, Anderson, and Shapira 2005). Like healthy individuals, subjects with FTD approved of pulling the lever in order to save five lives. However, unlike healthy individuals, they exhibited little reluctance to push a person in order to achieve the same goal: Without the countervailing brain area responsible for moral aversion, cost-benefit reasoning prevailed.

On research conducted with babies, cognitive psychologists have found evidence that humans enter the world with a sophisticated moral schema. Though babies clearly lack the capacity to communicate moral judgments, their preferences can be discerned indirectly by measuring attention. In a study conducted by a team of Yale psychologists, babies were presented a puppet show in which a climbing puppet struggled to ascend a hill (Hamlin, Wynn, and Bloom 2007). On some occasions a puppet came along and helped the climber up. On others a second puppet came along and swatted the puppet down. Then, researchers placed the helper and hinderer puppets in front of the babies. When babies expressed their preference by way of choosing a puppet to play with, they were significantly more likely to prefer the helper puppet. The results, according to the investigators, suggest that the capacity of individuals to express moral preferences on the basis of social interactions is "universal and unlearned."

To determine whether a mental process is rational and under conscious control, as opposed to intuitive, automatic and outside conscious awareness, cognitive psychologists use a robustly validated experimental method called cognitive loading. Under a heavy cognitive load—such as holding in working memory a string of arbitrary numbers—people have been demonstrated to have a diminished capacity for controlled mental processes. Thus, if performance suffers while carrying a cognitive load, controlled processes can be inferred. If performance remains unchanged, though, an automatic process is implicated. In an experiment designed to test whether moral judgment is affected by cognitive load, researchers found no difference in performance when participants were carrying a cognitive load (Haidt 2012). These results suggest an important role for automatic mental processes in the evaluation of moral problems.

In the struggle for survival among animals, what can be characterized as punishment is routinely imposed by animals that are subjected to harm or threatened with harm. From an evolutionary perspective, this type of eye-for-an-eye strategy makes sense. In certain species, though, punishment goes beyond eye-for-an-eye retaliation: It's imposed by third parties in the presence of moral transgressions. In humans, this model of third-party punishment parallels formal systems of criminal justice, where members of the community (judges and/or jurors) sit in judgment of a defendant who has committed an offense against some other member of society or a social norm. Evolutionary biologists observe that third-party punishment, where "animal A punishes animal B for violating norm C," occurs exclusively in highly cooperative species. For example, chimpanzees attack allies that do not support them in third-party conflicts, and queen naked mole rats will attack workers that they judge to be lazy. Punishment of this kind, referred to as altruistic punishment, has been identified as a key factor accounting for the extraordinary degree of cooperation displayed by humans (Seymor, Singer, and Dolan, 2007). According to game theorists, this is because altruistic punishment mitigates against the free-rider problem—caused by individuals reaping the rewards of cooperation without contributing—and thereby increases the likelihood that a cooperative equilibrium will emerge (Yamagishi and Sato 1986).

Using a laboratory task designed to elicit acts of altruistic punishment among human volunteers, cognitive psychologists appear to have identified the complex processes driving this behavior (Knutson 2004). During the task, subjects played a single game involving real money with a series of partners. In each game, subjects would give their partners money, which was then quadrupled by the investigators. Then, the recipients were given a chance to reciprocate. If they failed to do so, subjects could choose to administer a monetary punishment against the non-cooperator. During the act of imposing punishment, the subjects' brains were scanned. The researchers found that imposing punishment activates a subcortical region of the brain called the striatum. The striatum has been shown to be associated with reward-processing in similar studies looking at the areas of the brain activated during anticipation of non-social rewards such as monetary gains and pleasant tastes. Thus, the researchers interpreted the findings to indicate that punishing a defector activates brain regions related to feeling good about punishment, rather than bad about a violation.

What are the implications of these findings? The picture that begins to emerge is of a highly complex, biologically hard-wired network of regions in the brain, shaped by evolution so as to produce automatic moral assessments, and when a moral wrong has occurred, to engender retributive emotions that promote a punishment response. Like all other products of evolutionary pressure, the utility of this intuitively guided behavior is readily identifiable: to increase fitness for survival by deterring future harm and fostering cooperation.

II Folk reasoning and inevitable bias and mistake in judging others

Without understanding Newton's laws of physics, a center fielder in pursuit of a fly ball can quickly calculate its trajectory. This intuitive grasp of physical laws is an example of folk physics. Folk physics serves us quite well. In many domains, though, our intuitions about the physical world fail us miserably. In fact, quantum mechanics runs so counter to intuition that one of its leading scientist famously quipped, "If you think you understand quantum mechanics, then you don't understand quantum mechanics" (Dawkins 2009). And nevertheless, it works: Quantum mechanics has been demonstrated through empirical testing to be one of the most reliably accurate theories in the history of science.

A growing body of evidence suggests a similar phenomenon in the psychological domain of common sense or folk reasoning. Research suggests a gap between folk reasoning and reality. Like folk physics, folk reasoning appears to be useful—up to a point. In some situations, however, it has been shown to predictably produce errors of judgment. The following are a number of empirically studied examples of cognitive heuristics that are based on folk reasoning and can lead to erroneous and biased judgments.

The first example is the confirmation bias, which results from the tendency to search for or interpret information in a way that confirms one's preconceptions. Put differently, people tend to focus on results that support their position and ignore the rest. For example, researchers showed a confirmation bias in subjects who held strong views on capital punishment (Lord, Ross, and Lepper 1979). In that study, subjects were divided into groups based on whether they favored or opposed capital punishment and were then each given descriptions of two studies—one in support and one in opposition to capital punishment. They were then asked whether their opinions had been swayed by the studies. Next, they were given a more detailed account of the studies and were told whether one study was written in support of or in opposition to capital punishment.

Though subjects were initially influenced by the descriptions, their original preconceived opinions re-emerged upon learning more information about the research. When asked to justify their views, the subjects invoked the supporting research. In response to questions regarding contradictory research, though, the subjects were apt to cast doubts on its validity.

A similar study was conducted during the 2004 presidential elections (Westen et al. 2006). Subjects were given three statements from three individuals: the Republican candidate, George Bush, the Democratic candidate, John Kerry, and Tom Hanks. The first two statements from the candidates were patently contradictory. The third statement attempted to reconcile the conflict between statements one and two. For example, the first statement by George Bush indicated support for Kenneth Lay; the second a clear criticism of Kenneth Lay; the last an attempt to give a reason for the contradiction, for instance, that George Bush was betrayed by Kenneth Lay or was sincerely disappointed by his alleged conduct at Enron. The subjects were significantly more likely to find the statements of the candidate from the opposing party inconsistent, whereas statements from the political party with which they identified were seemingly reconciled by the third statement.

Another cognitive heuristic with potential to bias decision-making is the framing bias. Research in this area has shown how the presentation of like things in different formats can significantly affect the decisions people make. Experiments performed by Tversky and Kahneman, for instance, showed that framing influenced participants' responses to questions regarding disease prevention (1981). In that experiment, subjects were informed that an outbreak of a rare Asian disease was imminent and would result in the death of 600 people. They were then given the option to decide between two alternative programs to combat the disease. The first group was presented two programs: option 1) 200 people will be saved or option 2) There is a 1/3 probability that 600 people will be saved and a 2/3 probability that no one will be saved. The second group was presented two programs: option 1) 400 people will die or option 2) There is a 1/3 probability that no one will die and a 2/3 probability that 600 people will die.

Plainly, saving 200 lives is the same as 400 people dying. Even so, when the participants were asked to choose a treatment, option 1 was favored over option 2 by 72 percent of participants when it was presented with positive framing ("saves lives"), and fell to 22 percent when the same choice was presented with negative framing ("people will die"). Simply framing a decision in either positive or negative terms had a significant effect on the outcome.

The overconfidence bias is another common phenomenon anchored in folk reasoning in which individuals subjectively overestimate their abilities relative to objective criteria. This bias has been confirmed in various ways; for example, in a poll drivers were asked to rate their competence at driving in relation to others, nearly 93 percent reported to be above average (Svenson 1980).

The availability bias is a cognitive tendency in which people make predictions about the rate of an event based on available information. For example, in a study in which subjects were asked to judge whether a word randomly chosen from an English text was more likely to begin with K or have K as its 3rd letter, significantly more participants were found to believe that there are more words that begin with the letter K (Tversky and Kahneman 1973). According to the researchers, this was because such words like kid, kick, and kiss are more readily available to our minds than ask, bike, and joke, and so we are biased toward thinking that there are more of these words. Tversky and Kahneman have shown that this availability heuristics produces errors of judgment in a variety of settings.

Finally, the fundamental attribution error (FAE) is the tendency, when forming impressions of others, to overestimate the importance of dispositional factors (e.g., aggressiveness) in the person being judged and to underestimate the importance of the situation in which the observed behavior is occurring (Ross 1977). Using a mock TV quiz show, Ross and his colleagues demonstrated the tendency to commit fundamental attribution errors (Ross, Amabile, and Steinmetz 1977). In that study, participants were assigned to play the role of the questioner, contestant, or spectator. In front of the spectators, the questioners were then instructed to come up with 10 questions from their own general knowledge to pose to the contestants. Contestants answered roughly 40 percent of the questions correctly. When spectators were asked to rate the questioners' and the contestants' general knowledge, they rated the questioners as above average and the contestants as below average. In doing so, they attributed the results to an essential characteristic rather than the important fact that questioners held a distinct advantage—naturally they knew the answers to their own questions.

The systematic bias in judgment detailed above raises concerns regarding the consequences of folk decision-making. If folk reasoning is so shot through with bias, then what type of bad outcomes might it produce? And what happens when people learn of the error in their judgment? Do they simply self-correct? One reason to believe that the implications of folk reasoning are even worse than they appear comes from the now famous chicken-claw experiment conducted on split-brain patients: people whose corpus callosum, the channel of communication between the two brain hemispheres, is severed. In the experiment, researchers showed a split-brain patient two pictures: The patient's left hemisphere saw a chicken claw, and his right saw a snow scene. Then, from an assortment of pictures that were visible to both hemispheres, the patient was asked to choose two that matched. Appropriately, he chose a chicken to go with the claw and a shovel to go with the snow. Next, the researchers asked him to explain why he chose those items. "The chicken goes with the chicken claw," he replied. This was no surprise given that his left hemisphere, the region responsible for language, had seen the chicken claw and was able to explain the decision to choose a chicken to go along with it. The left hemisphere, though, was completely unaware of the snow scene, which was seen only by the right hemisphere. Still, when asked to articulate why he chose the shovel, the man's left hemisphere simply fabricated an answer: "And you need a shovel to clean out the chicken shed." His brain had done something astonishing: It created a coherent story in order to justify the decision it had unconsciously made. For this reason, Dr. Gazzaniga, the scientist who designed the experiment, dubbed the left-brain hemisphere responsible for the story the "interpreter."

On the basis of his work on split-brain patients, Gazzaniga characterizes the left hemisphere as the brain's "story-teller," whose role is to create a coherent narrative to support one's perception of behaving intentionality and purposefully, even when that's not the case. These stories that people tell themselves, he notes, are likely to be based on "post-hoc explanations using post-hoc observations with no access to non-conscious processing" (Gazzaniga 2011). With regard to the various cognitive heuristics, this ability of the interpreter to read intentionality into and justify decisions would seem to make honest self-assessment and correction unlikely.

What's more, research by Heider and Simmel suggests a similar tendency to read intentionality into the behavior of *other* people (1944). For example, they found that when subjects were asked to describe the movement of geometric figures (a small circle and triangle and a larger circle), they typically characterized the figures as animated persons. And when asked to interpret the movement of the figures as human actions, they typically ascribed internal motives and said things like the big circle is "bullying" the little triangle. Thus, like the stories the "interpreter" tells about oneself, there seems to be a tendency for people to read intentionality into others' behavior.

Together, these two tendencies—to concoct intentional and coherent stories about one's own decisions and those of others—raise serious concerns with respect to the retribution heuristic and the judgments to which it leads. That's because one way to determine proportional punishment—and the approach our modern criminal justice systems has adopted—is to measure culpability by retrospectively reading the mental state of the accused at the moment of the crime. Specifically, the question of criminal liability under this approach turns on whether a person's mental state ("mens rea") actuated a criminal act ("actus reus"). The Model Penal Code ("MPC"), for instance, ascribes criminal responsibility only if it can be shown that a criminal act was carried out with a negligent, reckless, knowing, or purposive mind, with each step up representing an increase in the amount of punishment an individual deserves. Thus, under the MPC the difference of a crime committed negligently as opposed to recklessly or purposefully can amount to years of incarceration. That we are prone to read intentionality into others' behavior raises serious doubts about the accuracy and reliability of such judgments of criminal responsibility.[4] And that we are prone to tell ourselves make-sense stories about such judgments, blind to the non-conscious processes behind them, raises concerns about our capacity to identify and correct our own automatic and, at times, erroneous decision-making. What type of errors might we expect the retributive heuristic, which underlies this assessment of criminal responsibility, to produce? It is to this question that we will turn in the following section.

III Fundamental retribution errors

As we have seen, punishment appears to be an intuitive response to moral transgressions (Darley 2009). Given that intuitive folk reasoning has been shown to produce various errors of judgment, the following concern arises: Does folk reasoning lead us to make fundamental retribution errors? On retribution's own terms, establishing an error of judgment is difficult. That's because the retributive justification is facially indifferent to punishment's effects—so there is no empirical criterion against which to judge outcomes. Also, the only remaining criterion by which to judge the appropriateness of retributive punishment—whether punishment is commensurate with a crime—is vague and very difficult if not impossible to assess with an acceptable degree of confidence. Nevertheless, if it can be shown that punishment severity is influenced by factors wholly irrelevant to any reasonable assessment of proportional deserts, this would constitute persuasive evidence of fundamental retribution errors (Dripps 2003). The following research showing how irrelevant factors can influence judgments of punishment provides such evidence.

Relying on evidence that the cognitive process underlying moral disgust stems from physical disgust, researchers hypothesized that moral judgment could be affected by taste perception. In a study testing this idea, participants were given a sweet beverage, a bitter beverage, or water and then asked to rate a variety of moral transgressions. Results showed that there was a relationship between taste and moral judgments—specifically, physical disgust elicited significantly greater feelings of moral disgust. In a similar study, researchers sprayed a nearby trash can with commercially available fart spray to induce disgust in their participants (Schnall et al. 2008). Investigators found that participants exposed to strong and mild stink conditions made harsher judgments on a variety of moral transgressions (e.g., sex between first cousins) than did participants in a no-spray condition.

Using the framework of terror management theory, which posits that reminders of mortality cause individuals to invest in and defend their cultural beliefs, the effect of mortality salience on punishment severity has been investigated in several studies. Postulating that law constitutes a central part of a judge's worldview, one study conducted with 22 municipal court judges examined the effect of mortality salience on judgments against a transgressor (Rosenblatt et al. 1989). The judges were presented with a hypothetical defendant held on a charge of prostitution. Following a mortality salience induction, the judges imposed an average bond of $455 on the defendant, compared to an average bond of $50 from judges in the control group.

A similar study was conducted in which students were first given an assessment of their attitude toward prostitution and then asked to set a bond amount for the alleged prostitute (Rosenblatt 1989). Among those who were subjected to heightened mortality salience, only those with a relatively negative view of prostitution recommended particularly high bonds.

Factors that influence neurotransmitter levels can also affect the strength of individuals' retaliatory responses to a perceived transgression. For example, serotonin, a neurotransmitter involved in communication between brain cells, is thought to play a significant role in emotional responses to unfairness. Researchers posit that serotonin does so by modulating impulsivity via emotional regulation mechanisms. The function of these emotional mechanisms during social interactions has been studied with the Ultimatum Game (Nowak, Page, and Sigmund 2000). The rules of the game are simple: One player (the offeror) is given money and is told to split it with another player (the responder). Should the responder accept, both players are paid; if the responder rejects, neither player is paid.

Researchers investigated the effects of manipulating serotonin on rejection behavior in the Ultimatum Game. Using a procedure called acute tryptophan depletion, investigators temporarily lowered the serotonin levels of the subjects. Participants then played the role of responder in the Ultimatum Game. The researchers found that simply by temporarily lowering serotonin levels in participants they could increase their retaliatory response to perceived unfairness.

Evidently we do judge books by their covers. For example, researchers have consistently found an attractive-leniency effect: people recommend less severe punishment for defendants with physically attractive features (Sigall and Ostrove 1975). This effect has been found in experimental studies, where attractiveness is manipulated through the use of defendants' photos, as well is in the court room, where observers were asked to rate the attractiveness of defendants standing trial (Stewart 1985). Similarly, researchers have found that people recommend harsher punishments for defendants perceived to have stereotypical black facial features. In one study, participants were asked to rate the degree to which images of black defendants who were convicted of murdering white victims had stereotypically black faces. After controlling for other factors, researchers found that defendants whose appearance was perceived as more stereotypically black were more likely to have been executed. In the study, only 24 percent of black defendants classified in the bottom half of the black stereotype scale were executed; those classified in the top half did not fare as well: 58 percent were executed (Eberhardt et al. 2006).

With legal realism in mind—particularly the idea that a judge's decision is likely to turn on something as arbitrary as what he or she ate for breakfast—investigators sought to test whether a judge's food breaks influenced his or her decision to grant or deny parole (Danziger, Levav, and Avnaim-Pesso 2011). Relying on earlier research demonstrating that repeated judgments tend to deplete executive functioning, investigators hypothesized that food breaks would restore executive decision-making capacity. Granting a request for release was further hypothesized to require heightened executive functioning compared to a continuation of the status quo (i.e., ongoing detention). In the study, two food breaks were used to divide a judge's day into three deliberation sessions. Researchers found that during the course of a typical session the percentage of rulings to grant parole dropped from roughly 65 percent to zero toward the end of a session and then returned abruptly to 65 percent after a break.

Glitchy computers and websites are not held morally responsible for the psychic harm that they wreak. That is because they lack the capacity to choose. Humans, on the other hand, are held morally responsible for our actions for the opposite reason: We are perceived to have free will. But as recent discoveries in neuroscience cast more and more doubt on humans' capacity for free choice, researchers have begun to question whether moral determinations of punishment are influenced by the strength of a person's conviction in the notion of free will. To test the relationship between free-will belief and retributive punishment, researchers compared the severity of punishment chosen by participants after reading a passage in which free will is rejected in favor of a mechanistic view of human behavior, against a control group that read a neutral passage (Shariff, Greene, et al. 2014). Researchers found that the participants whose belief in free will had been weakened by the anti-free-will passage recommended roughly half the length of imprisonment compared with the control group.

Judgments of morality and punishment are susceptible to influence by extraneous factors. Contrary to the perception of such judgments as based on scrupulous weighing of relevant factors, the evaluation process works more like an erratic scale: now adding because of a foul odor, now subtracting on account of a fetching face, now adding because of a reminder of mortality, now subtracting on account of a muffin, now adding due to a drop in serotonin, now subtracting because of a loss of belief in free will. Susceptibility to such factors would not be so problematic if there were a feed-back mechanism to separate the good reasons from the bad. Decisions by scientists in the lab, to be sure, are also subject to any number of extraneous influences. The difference is that the scientific method compels them to put their ideas to the empirical rack to test their validity. Proponents of consequential justifications of punishment can do the same by testing, say, whether a rehabilitative program reduces recidivism and by how much or whether a sanction deters crime and by how much. The results could then inform decisions to continue or discontinue such policies. Justifications rooted in retribution, by contrast, are beyond the reach of empiricism. As we have seen, this is because retribution is rooted in a cognitive heuristic whose consequential aims are shrouded in retributive reasoning.

IV Conclusion

What are the effects of relying on a cognitive heuristic to dispense justice? As a recent report by the US National Research Council observed, retribution is one of the "main impulses" behind the United States' punishment problem: perennially the highest rates of incarceration in the industrialized world; incarceration patterns that suggest invidious discrimination; the use anachronisms like capital punishment (Travis, Western, and Redburn 2014). Nonetheless, the Council goes on to endorse the "normative values" that underlie retributive incarceration. And though the Council rightly criticizes recent criminal justice policy discourse premised on cost-benefit calculations that "mask strong but hidden normative assumptions," it fails to recognize the opposite problem: normative assumptions that mask strong but hidden, and often erroneous, calculations that occur outside the conscious mind.

The research presented in this chapter sheds light on these normative values. It suggests that judgments of morality and punishment have neural correlates in the emotional centers of the brain, that the behaviors produced by these areas are largely biological, automatic, and apt to have at one time played a key adaptive role in avoiding harm and improving cooperation.

Like folk physics, having a quick, intuitive response to questions of crime and punishment has proven useful. But research also shows that intuition can often lead us astray. Cognitive psychologists have demonstrated that intuitive folk reasoning can lead to erroneous judgment in a wide range of contexts. And, in thinking about crime and punishment particularly, can lead to fundamental retribution errors. The potential harm of punishment policy based on such faulty intuitions should prompt us to ask why retribution is still taken seriously at all.

Several arguments in favor of retribution can be anticipated. First, Robinson and Kurzban purport to find empirical support for retribution (2006). But their work, which they have dubbed "empirical deserts," merely demonstrates that intuitions with regard to punishment are roughly consistent among lay people. This is no surprise, since retribution appears to be rooted in our common biology and our common cultural milieu. But in no way does this undermine the argument made here that retribution is not empirical in the sense that it fails to produce testable hypotheses about the effects of punishment. To continue with the analogy above from astronomy, by their definition of "empirical," a poll showing that most people believed that the earth was at the center of the universe would provide support for a geocentric universe.

Second, Cass Sunstein, though he agrees that retribution stems from a cognitive heuristic, contends that retribution should not be dismissed because it may nonetheless be the right approach (2013). This argument fails to appreciate that science is a corrigible and collective enterprise that depends on individuals showing their work. Sure, as far back as ancient Greece there were people who intuited the process of evolution. But real progress in our understanding of evolution did not get underway until Darwin carefully collected data to support the theory, which was later corroborated and fine-tuned by countless other researchers. In the same way, even if retribution is the right approach, the inability to operationalize it would prevent us from examining and improving upon punishment policies.

Finally, Steven Pinker defends retribution on the grounds that, if the criminal justice system were to become too narrowly consequentialist, people would learn to "game it" (2003). Retribution, he argues, may ultimately serve as a deterrent against this contingency. But there is no reason an exclusively consequentialist criminal justice system that fails to deter crime couldn't self-correct for exclusively consequentialist reasons—in fact, it would have every reason to do so—without resorting to the notion of retribution. Pinker's argument, it seems, equates consequentialism with leniency, which needn't be the case.

One final thought. Careful empirical research represents our best tool for overcoming the cognitive limitations outlined here. In the case of physics, the shift from intuition to empiricism was pivotal; without it our understanding of the physical universe might still be stalled in the fifteenth century. Criminal justice punishment policy, on the other hand, does in many ways seem to be stuck in another epoch. One of the reasons for this is that the principal justification for punishment—retribution—still lies beyond the reach of empirical scrutiny. In order to move criminal justice policy forward, it will therefore be necessary to de-legitimate retribution as a justification of punishment. Otherwise, we are liable to continue to equate doing justice with dispensing harsh punishment, though the heavens—and the criminal justice system—may collapse.

Notes

1 Stephen Koppel, JD is a PhD candidate in the Doctoral Program in Criminal Justice at the CUNY Graduate Center and John Jay College of Criminal Justice.

2 Mark R. Fondacaro, JD, PhD is Professor and Director of the Psychology & Law Doctoral Training Area at John Jay College of Criminal Justice and the Graduate Center of the City University of New York.

3 For a discussion of several conceptions of retribution, *see:* Robinson (2008). 'Competing conceptions of modern desert: vengeful, deontological, and empirical'. *The Cambridge Law Journal*, *67* (01): 145–75.

Robinson distinguishes three types of retribution based on their metric of proportional punishment: Vengeful retribution measures proportional punishment based on the extent of harm; deontology on the degree of moral blameworthiness; and empirical deserts on a community's shared intuitions of justice. Since this paper is concerned with reliance on retribution in contemporary criminal justice policy, its focus is the deontological form. This is because considerations of moral blameworthiness figure prominently in penal codes such as the Model Penal Code; for instance, the assignment of varying degrees of criminal responsibility on the basis of mental states perceived to evince more or less evil. Also, note that Robinson justifies "empirical deserts" on the basis of consequential reasons, such as shaping societal norms and promoting compliance. The challenge to retribution posed in this paper thus does not apply to Robinson's conceptualization of empirical deserts. That said, while we agree that, contrary to other conceptions of retribution, empirical deserts is in principle testable, we disagree that evidence of shared intuitions regarding punishment provides support for retributive punishment. For that, Robinson would have to offer evidence that punishment effectively advances empirical desert's stated purposes. A second way conceptions of retribution differ is on their view of whether wrongdoing may or must be punished. Mandatory, positive, and pure retribution all hold that wrongdoing must be punished; permissive retribution holds that it may be punished.

4 Researchers have found that, whether or not given legal instructions on mental state definitions, laypeople were generally unable to agree on their judgments of past mental state, with the exception of the difference between the least (criminal negligence) and most (criminal intent) culpable states (Severance, Goodman, & Loftus 1992). In a more recent study of the mental states used in the Model Penal Code, researchers found that, although subjects were generally able to distinguish among purposeful, negligent, and blameless conduct, they fared poorly in distinguishing knowing and reckless conduct (Shen et al. 2011).

Bibliography

Chapman, H., Kim, D., Susskind, J., Anderson, A. (2009) 'In bad taste: evidence for the oral origins of moral disgust', *Science*, 323: 1222.

Danziger, S., Levav, J. and Avnaim-Pesso, L. (2011) 'Extraneous factors in judicial decisions', *Proceedings of the National Academy of Sciences*, 108(17): 6889–92.

Dawkins, R. (2009) *The God Delusion*, New York, NY: Random House.

Darley, J.M. (2009) 'Morality in the law: the psychological foundations of citizens' desires to punish transgressions', *Annual Review of Law and Social Science*, 5(1): 1–23.

Dripps, D.A. (2003) 'Fundamental retribution error: criminal justice and the social psychology of blame', *Vanderbilt Law Review*, 56: 1383.

Eberhardt, J.L., Davies, P.G., Purdie-Vaughns, V.J. and Johnson, S.L. (2006) 'Looking deathworthy perceived stereotypicality of black defendants predicts capital-sentencing outcomes', *Psychological Science*, 17(5): 383–86.

Eskine, K., Kacinik, N., Prinz, J. (2011) 'A bad taste in the mouth: gustatory disgust influences moral judgment', *Psychological Science*, 22: 295–99.

Gazzaniga, M. (1989) 'Organization of the human brain', *Science*, 245: 947–52.

Gazzaniga, M. (2011) *Who's in Charge. Free Will and the Science of the Brain*. New York, NY: Ecco.

Greene, J., Nystrom, L., Engell, A., Darley, J. and Cohen, J. (2004) 'The neural bases of cognitive conflict and control in moral judgment', *Neuron*, 44: 289–400.

Gould, S.J. (1991) 'Exaptation: a crucial tool for evolutionary psychology', *Journal of Social Issues*, 47: 43–65.

Gould, S. J. and Verba, E.S. (1982) 'Exaptation-a missing term in the science of form', *Paleobiology*, 4–15.

Haidt, J. (2012) *The Righteous Mind: Why Good People are Divided by Politics and Religion,* New York, NY: Vintage Books.

Hamlin, J, Wynn, K. and Bloom, P. (2007) 'Social evaluation by pre-verbal infants', *Nature*, 450: 557–60.

Heider, F. and Simmel, M. (1944) 'An experimental study of apparent behavior', *American Journal of Psychology*, 57: 243–59.

Hoffman, M.B. (2014) *The Punisher's Brain: The Evolution of Judge and Jury,* Cambridge: Cambridge University Press.

Knutson, B. (2004) 'Sweet revenge?', *Science*, 305: 1246–47.

Lord, C., Ross, L. and Lepper, M. (1979) 'Biased assimilation and attitude polarization: the effects of prior theories on subsequently considered evidence', *Journal of Personality and Social Psychology*, 37: 2098–2109.

Mendez, M., Anderson E. and Shapira, J. (2005) 'An investigation of moral judgment in frontotemporal dementia', *Cognitive Behavioral Neurology*, 18: 193–97.

Nowak, M., Page, K. and Sigmund, K. (2000) 'Fairness versus reason in the ultimatum game', *Science*, 8: 1773–75.

Pinker, S. (2003) *The Blank Slate: The Modern Denial of Human Nature*, New York, NY: Penguin.

Robinson, P.H. and Kurzban, R. (2006) 'Concordance and conflict in intuitions of justice', *Minn. L. Rev.*, 91: 1829.

Rosenblatt, A., Greenberg, J., Solomon, S., Pyszczynski, T. and Lyon, D. (1989) 'Evidence for.

terror management theory: the effects of mortality salience on reactions to those who violate or uphold cultural values', *Journal of Personality and Social Psychology*, 57: 681–90.

Ross, L. (1977) 'The intuitive psychologist and his shortcomings: distortions in the attribution process', *Advances in Experimental Social Psychology*, 10: 173–220.

Ross, L., Amabile, T. and Steinmetz, J. (1977) 'Social roles, social control, and biases in social-perception processes', *Journal of Personality and Social Psychology*, 35: 485–94.

Schnall, S., Haidt, J., Clore, G. and Jordan, A. (2008) 'Disgust as embodied moral judgment', *Personality and Social Psychology Bulletin*, 34: 1096–1109.

Seymor, B., Singer T. and Dolan, R. (2007). 'The neurobiology of punishment', *Nature Reviews Neuroscience*, 8: 300–11.

Shariff, A.F., Greene, J.D., Karremans, J.C., Luguri, J.B., Clark, C.J., Schooler, J.W., … and Vohs, K.D. (2014) 'Free will and punishment: a mechanistic view of human nature reduces retribution', *Psychological Science*, 0956797614534693.

Shen, F.X., Hoffman, M.B., Jones, O.D., Greene, J.D. and Marois, R. (2011) 'Sorting guilty minds', *New York University Law Review*, 86.

Sigall, H. and Ostrove, N. (1975) 'Beautiful but dangerous: effects of offender attractiveness and nature of the crime on juridic judgment', *Journal of Personality and Social Psychology*, 31(3): 410.

Stewart, J.E. (1985) 'Appearance and punishment: the attraction-leniency effect in the courtroom', *The Journal of Social Psychology*, 125(3): 373–78.

Sunstein, C.R. (2013) 'Is deontology a heuristic? On psychology, neuroscience, ethics, and law', *On Psychology, Neuroscience, Ethics, and Law (August 1, 2013).*

Svenson, O. (1980) 'Are we all less risky and more skillful than our fellow drivers?', *Acta Psychologica*, 47: 143–48.

Travis, J., Western, B. and Redburn, S. (eds.) (2014) *The Growth of Incarceration in the United States: Exploring Causes and Consequences,* Washington, DC: National Academies Press.

Tversky, A. and Kahneman, D. (1973) 'Availability: a heuristic for judging frequency and probability', *Cognitive Psychology*, 5: 207–32.

Tversky, A. and Kahneman, D. (1981) 'The framing of decisions and the psychology of choice', *Science*, 211: 453–58.

Westen, D., Pavel, B., Harenski, K., Kilts, C. and Hamann, S. (2006) 'Neural bases of motivated reasoning: an fMRI study of emotional constraints on partisan political judgment in the 2004 U.S. Presidential Election', *Journal of Cognitive Neuroscience*, 18: 1947–58.

Wilson, E.O. (1975). *Sociobiology,* Cambridge, MA: Harvard University Press.

Yamagishi, T. and Sato, K. (1986) 'Motivational basis of the public goods problem', *J. Pers. Soc. Psychol.*, 50: 67–73.

13

Punishment and forgiveness

Justin Tosi and Brandon Warmke

1 Introduction

There is, we suspect, a widely held assumption that forgiveness and punishment are crucially linked. Our sense is that many people think that if a victim forgives her wrongdoer then the victim gives up her right to punish the wrongdoer, or at least that if the victim *were* to punish someone she had forgiven, then she would have done something morally inappropriate. Such a view likely seems intuitively correct to many. We will argue that upon inspection it is not so appealing.

A number of philosophers have claimed that there is an important link between punishment and forgiveness. In *Leviathan*, for example, Hobbes drew a connection between forgiving and the facility to pardon in his sixth Law of Nature: "A sixth Law of Nature is this, 'that, upon caution of the future time, a man ought to pardon the offences past of them that, repenting, desire it'" (1969 [1651]). Remarking on this law, Bernard Gert writes, "This virtue, which Hobbes calls having the facility to pardon, one can also call being forgiving" (2010: 98). In a similar vein, Leo Zaibert has recently argued that to forgive is "deliberately to refuse to punish" (2009: 368). David Londey tells us that that a "clear" condition on forgiveness is that "in forgiving you I remit *any* penalty or sanction that your wrongdoing would otherwise bring on your head" (1986: 4–5, italics original).[1] Nicholas Wolterstorff writes that one of the "main components" of forgiveness "is the foregoing of retributive punishment" (2009: 203). Relatedly, Richard Swinburne has claimed that "if I forgive you for some act, I ought not subsequently to punish you for that act" (1989: 87 fn. 8). Psychologists have also linked forgiveness and punishment. According to Robert Enright and his colleagues, forgiveness involves "the casting off of deserved punishments" (1992: 88). On these sorts of *punishment-forbearance* views of forgiveness, forgiving crucially implicates, in one way or another, the forbearance of punishment.[2]

If these theorists are right about forgiveness, there could be important consequences for criminal justice ethics. Consider the following passage from Anthony Bash:

> Suppose W, a wrongdoer, defames V, a victim. The wrongdoing is actionable in the courts. Rather than go to court, V chooses to forgive W, because W and V are long-standing friends and because W is sorry about what she has done. By forgiving W, V implicitly declares

> (among other things) that W has wronged her and that she is setting aside the right to take legal proceedings against W for the wrongdoing. Legally, V can still sue W for the wrong (as her legal rights are unchanged); however, as I have said [earlier], it is contrary to what is implicit in what it means to forgive if V pursues her legal rights against W. (2015: 53)

Suppose that Bash is correct that there is such a relationship between forgiveness and punishment: If one forgives, one should not press one's legal rights against and seek punishment of one's wrongdoer. This claim raises a number of practical issues. For example, if a wrongdoer has been forgiven by her victim, should this be taken into account when it comes to questions of what counts as a just punishment? If it was widely believed that if one forgives a wrongdoer, the wrongdoer should not be punished, would this have deleterious effects on the justice system? Would victims, for example, be less willing to testify in court or file charges if they believed that doing so is wrong because they have forgiven? Can states that are in a position to punish criminals also "forgive" them? And more generally, what relationship should forgiveness have to criminal justice systems in the first place?

In this paper we shall not attempt to answer all of these questions. We will, however, provide a basic philosophical framework for thinking about the moral relationship between forgiveness and punishment.[3] In Section 2, we will develop and motivate the kind of punishment-forbearance view we target in this paper: the claim that if one forgives a wrongdoer for some bit of conduct, one should not subsequently punish her for it. In Section 3, we turn to critically assess the arguments for this view. We conclude that none succeeds and that we have good reason to deny that forgiving a wrongdoer must make punishing her morally inappropriate. In Section 4, we turn to the issue of institutional forgiveness: can entities like states forgive individuals? We argue that to the extent that this is possible at all, such "forgiveness" will largely be a matter of simply issuing a pardon. We conclude in Section 5 by reflecting on the differences between forgiveness and acts of mercy.

2 Punishment and forgiveness

In this section we explain and motivate one way of thinking about how forgiveness and punishment are crucially linked. Specifically, we will be exploring what kind of relationship forgiveness has to the *forbearance* of punishment. By "forbearance of punishment" we have in mind two things. First, to forbear punishing a wrongdoer is to commit not to punish her or to deliberately refuse to punish her. Second, by forbearing punishment, one also actually abstains from punishing. To forbear punishing a wrongdoer, then, is both to deliberately refuse to do so and then actually to refrain from punishment. This way of putting the matter makes clear that the victim who forbears punishment does so purposefully. She does not just, say, forget to punish; rather, her not punishing the wrongdoer is intentional. This also makes clear that one's forbearing punishment is not *just* to commit not to or refuse to punish; it is also to abstain from punishing the wrongdoer. Naturally enough, there are numerous other ways of exploring the relationship between punishment and forgiveness, but for now, we shall simply focus on the possible moral connections between forgiveness and the forbearance of punishment. We will suggest a few ways of arguing for some interpretation of the claim that forgiveness requires forbearance from punishment.

To begin, consider just one way of construing the relationship between forgiveness and the forbearing of punishment. According to this view, the relationship is a moral one, not a metaphysical or conceptual one.[4] In other words, this view makes no claims about, for example, whether forgiving *itself* involves forbearing punishment. Rather it makes a moral claim: forgiving a wrongdoer makes it morally inappropriate to punish her, and so if one forgives, one should forbear punishment. We might put the claim this way:

> If agent A forgives agent B for B's conduct X, then *ceteris paribus* A should forbear punishing B for X.

What would motivate such a view? Why might forgiving a wrongdoer make it morally wrong or inappropriate to punish her? Here, we explore three kinds of motivations.[5]

First, consider the fact that it is widely held that forgiving requires one to forswear both retributive attitudes like resentment as well as retributive behaviors. From this view, it is not a great leap to the thought that when one forgives one forfeits any right to visit unpleasant consequences upon the wrongdoer on the basis of what she did. After all, the right to make life unpleasant for the wrongdoer seems no longer to be something the forgiving agent will want to stand on. Punishment is (minimally) the visiting of unpleasant consequences in response to a wrong.[6] So, forfeiting the right to punish is simply a part of forgiveness. Well, quite obviously, once one has forfeited the right to punish a wrongdoer, one cannot rightly punish that wrongdoer for what she has done. To insist that one retains the right to punish in this case is simply to misunderstand what forgiveness involves. Therefore, to punish a wrongdoer when one has forgiven her would be wrong—one should forbear punishment instead. Call this the *forfeiture argument*.

Second, one plausible way of understanding forgiveness is as an abandonment of certain reasons for action. By abandonment we mean something like a dismissal or disavowal of the justifying force of those reasons. Once I abandon a reason, I can no longer appeal to it as a justification for my actions. Indeed, this is the very sort of thing that many think happens in the case of forgiveness and blame. When we forgive, we still judge that the wrongdoer is *blameworthy* and that we could have the *right* to blame the wrongdoer. And yet when we forgive, we forswear blame—we commit to not blame, we abandon justifying reasons to blame.

So perhaps when we forgive, we abandon all justifying reasons for punishment and so to punish anyway would be inappropriate. Note that this argument does not depend on the success of the forfeiture argument. One may retain the right to punish and still have no good reason to do so. To punish without a good reason for doing so—a justifying aim—would be truly perverse.[7] Since punishment imposes costs, and often significant ones, on another person, it is not something we should do without a morally important goal in mind. But if forgiveness involves abandoning the reasons that could serve as justifying aims of punishment, then what we are left with in punishment is pointless and cruel treatment of another. Therefore, forgiving has the consequence that (barring exceptional circumstances) one is not permitted or justified in punishing someone that one has forgiven.[8] One should instead forbear punishment. Call this the *no justification argument*.

Third, it might also be argued that when we forgive, we enter into a new kind of relationship with the wrongdoer. We are to some degree reconciled and typically seek still further reconciliation. We welcome the wrongdoer back into the moral community. We endeavor to treat and regard her with love and good will, seeking to repair the relationship as much as possible. In light of this new orientation, however, punishment will be out of place. If you are seeking to *repair* a relationship—to put it back on something approximating equal moral footing—then punishing the wrongdoer is manifestly *not* the way to go about doing so. On this sort of view, punishment is morally inappropriate given the kind of relationship that one has to the wrongdoer when one forgives her. It may be perfectly appropriate to punish the wrongdoer *before* one has forgiven, one might argue. But once you have forgiven, you've set the course for the relationship going forward, a course that ought not to involve punishing the wrongdoer for the wrongdoing in question. Again, you should forbear punishment. Call this the *new relationship argument*.

3 Some objections

Before treating the individual arguments canvassed above, we should note some general worries about punishment-forbearance views of forgiveness. First, usually when we are wronged, we are not at liberty to punish our wrongdoers. We might be able to blame them, or take revenge upon them, but neither of those is the same thing as punishment (see, e.g., McKenna 2012; Warmke 2013). We generally think of punishment as something institutions do—particularly, the state. Interpersonal punishment seems to be restricted to personal hierarchical relationships, as between a parent and child or a teacher and a student. Some political philosophers think that there is a natural right to punish wrongdoers, held by all, but those who hold this view generally think that we, as members of civil society, transfer it to the state upon leaving the state of nature.[9] We suspect, then, that talk of interpersonal punishment between equals within civil society will probably strike many readers as odd. So in order to get this view off the ground, we will suppose that punishment-forbearance theorists must take a wide view of what counts as punishment, so that it includes informal social sanctions in response to wrongdoing. Thus, ostracizing a wrongdoer, kicking her out of your home, breaking off personal ties, or perhaps even spreading the news of her wrongdoing far and wide—all of these acts would (or at least could) count as punishment.[10] Without a very inclusive conception of interpersonal punishment, we think it is very difficult even to get punishment-forbearance views off the ground.[11] For the purposes of this paper, then, we shall adopt a liberal view of what can count as punishment.

Second, we think that many conflate punishment with related but importantly different moral phenomena. For instance, we suspect that when many people use the word "punishment" in discussions of forgiveness, they have in mind either something like overt moral blame (e.g., certain forms of censure, denunciation, reproach, withdrawal of friendly relations)[12] or instead revenge. However, we distinguish between all of these: These phenomena come apart, both conceptually and in practice. Now if defenders of the forbearance view thought that what they call punishment really just is (what we would call) overt blame or revenge, then we could agree that forgiveness is crucially linked to those phenomena: Forgiveness typically does rule out overt blaming and revenge, and the forgiveness literature is in general agreement about this.[13] If by "punishment" the defender of this view just meant, say, overt blaming behaviors, then we will be the among the first to agree that forgiveness typically involves forbearing such reactions to the wrongdoer and also makes such reactions to the wrongdoer morally inappropriate. But thinking (as we do) that forgiveness typically rules out blame and revenge does not vindicate the defender of the punishment-forbearance view unless she *just equates* interpersonal punishment with either overt blame or revenge. In what follows, we will assume that the defender of punishment-forbearance views *does* think that punishment is something *distinct* from overt moral blame and revenge, and that they are not simply making a claim about a phenomenon of the forbearance of blame or revenge.

How might we distinguish among overt blame, revenge, and punishment? If forgiveness typically rules out blame and revenge, but not punishment, how would one go about showing this? One strategy would be to give full accounts of each of these phenomena. That is obviously beyond the scope of this paper or any paper. Another strategy would be to articulate certain key differences between the phenomena without giving full accounts. That way, we could differentiate between phenomena by asking whether they have certain key features. One of us (Warmke 2013) attempted this strategy elsewhere, and we shall not rehearse those arguments here. We shall pursue a different tack. Instead of trying to distinguish these phenomena, we shall simply argue that forgiveness does not have the tight relationship to forbearing punishment that punishment-forbearance theorists claim. What we shall argue is that in many cases of forgiveness, there are behaviors that are morally compatible with forgiveness that can plausibly be taken to be forms of punishment. Of course, our critic might wish to argue that those behaviors we claim are sometimes morally compatible with forgiveness are not actually forms of punishment, and so cut no ice against their theory. We invite them to make those arguments. We take this to be an opening salvo.

With these initial points in mind, let us turn to the arguments we canvassed above. In what follows, we hope to raise serious doubts about the view that forgiving rules out punishment. While we do not take our arguments to be decisive objections, we think that they identify the sorts of considerations that punishment-forbearance theorists of forgiveness must contend with if they hope to vindicate their view.

We first considered the forfeiture argument. There is something appealing to the main idea of this argument, which is that in forgiving a wrongdoer, we forfeit our liberty right to punish her (or at least to do so any further).[14] If we have forfeited this right, then it is no longer morally permissible to punish the wrongdoer (for the wrong for which she was forgiven).

The problem with the forfeiture argument, however, is that it is easy to come up with cases in which it looks like while an agent has forgiven a wrongdoer, she has not forfeited her right to punish her. We can imagine a child who lies to her parent (a clear violation of house rules) and does so in front of her siblings. The mother reprimands the child and the child apologizes and expresses sadness and regret over her poor choice. The mother then says the following: "I love you very much, and it hurts me when you lie to me. I'm glad you apologized, though, and I forgive you. However, you know the punishment for lying in this house, so please go to your room for the next hour. I'll let you know when you can play with your toys again."[15] It seems to us that in such a case, the mother can both forgive and yet retain her right to punish the child. If so, then it is not the case that one necessarily relinquishes one's right to punish, thereby making one's punishment of the wrongdoer morally inappropriate.[16]

Turn now to the no justification argument. The crucial claim of this argument is that to forgive one's wrongdoer entails that (among other things) one has dismissed the fact that she wronged you *as a reason* to punish her. The defender of this argument might concede that when we forgive we do not forfeit the *right* to punish. But from this it does not follow that punishment is morally appropriate. For when we forgive, we decide not to act on certain classes of reasons. We take certain reasons for action "off the table," as it were, even if, strictly speaking, we retain a right to act for those reasons.[17] Upon forgiving, then, one lacks justification to punish because one has disavowed the kinds of reasons that would naturally motivate one to punish a wrongdoer. Having those reasons for punishment undercut, punishment becomes inappropriate.

There is something attractive about this argument, too, as it is natural to think of forgiveness as a way of deciding no longer to be swayed by a certain class of reasons. In so doing, it seems plausible that agents who forgive might let go of reasons that would have otherwise motivated them to punish their wrongdoers. Perhaps the desire to "get even" will evaporate entirely, relying as it does on a kind of personal indignation toward one's wrongdoer. Minimally, such desires will be disavowed and not endorsed—not seen as acceptable reasons for action.

We think, however, that the no justification argument depends on a mistakenly narrow view about what can count as justifying reasons to punish a wrongdoer. For it seems that one can let go of one's feelings of anger, hurt, personal protest, bitterness, or rancor toward the wrongdoer, and yet insist upon punishing her out of other moral considerations. For one simple way of seeing this, consider two ways of expressing a moral complaint. One might say to a wrongdoer "you lied to me." This couches the complaint in personal terms and emphasizes one's indignation at having been wronged by this person—as having done something to *this relationship* (see, e.g., Scanlon 2008). On the other hand, one might say to the same person "you lied." This is an impersonal, or general, expression of a moral complaint (even though the wrong was done to the one making the complaint).[18] The general expression of the complaint seems to place the wrong in a sphere of broader concern: it casts the wrong as a kind of offense against everyone (or perhaps against God or the moral order or whatever). The general form of the complaint emphasizes not the directional feature of the wrong (i.e., "to me"), but the fact of the wrongdoer's having committed it. Most importantly, for our purposes, the general complaint seems to be much more in line with forgiveness than does the personal complaint.[19] Thus, you might forgive the wrongdoer for lying *to you*, yet still permissibly persist in regarding or treating her as someone *who lied*.

The deep moral point behind all this is that there are many kinds of moral reasons. Even if we grant that forgiveness nullifies the motivation for making the *personal* form of a moral complaint (that would typically be at issue when we blame *as victims* of wrongdoing), it leaves intact the fact that the wrong occurred and so does not interfere with the grounds of the *general* moral complaint (the kind of complaint that third parties who were not victims of the lie could *share* with victims). And if the general complaint stands, then it can also serve to motivate and justify punishment of the wrongdoer. And so even if the victim of wrongdoing lets go of her grounds to make personal complaints against the wrongdoer, this would not entail that she has also let go of her grounds of making general or impersonal complaints, complaints that could be shared by anyone for whom indignation can be an appropriate response. These general grounds for complaint could then persist through forgiveness: by letting go of one's personal complaint, then one need not also let go of any and all justifications to punish.[20]

For another type of response to the no justification argument, we can consider the standard justifications of punishment. These are typically advanced as defenses of institutional punishment, of course, but the same reasons behind them may apply to cases of interpersonal punishment (whatever we think of the wisdom of actually attempting to apply them). For each justification, we can ask whether the fact of the victim having forgiven her wrongdoer interferes with the justification for punishment. If the justification for punishment remains, then that is some evidence that, by forgiving, a victim need not be understood as disavowing or taking such reasons "off the table."

Take first consequentialist justifications of punishment. The aim of punishment on these views is to bring about good consequences and especially to deter further wrongdoing from either the wrongdoer herself or other prospective wrongdoers. Forgiving a wrongdoer does not seem to remove the need to deter further wrongdoing, by her or others.[21] It might be objected that if the victim forgives the wrongdoer, then there will be no need for further deterrence (at least in the wrongdoer's own case), as perhaps the victim is well-positioned to know whether the wrongdoer needs to be deterred or has really reformed.

In reply, we note that on the theory of punishment under consideration, either punishing a wrongdoer in order to deter her from wronging again is the optimal action in terms of consequences or it is not. If it is, then we have a justification for punishing her, and whether she has been forgiven is irrelevant to whether punishing her is optimal. On the other hand, if punishing her is not optimal, then whether she should be punished or not does not have anything to do with whether she has been forgiven.[22] The upshot is that on this view of punishment, one's forgiveness need not be tied to forbearing punishment. The matter of punishment is simply tied to the matter of promoting good consequences and deterring bad ones. These reasons can remain for a victim, we claim, even if she forgives.

Consider next the communicative account of punishment.[23] On this family of views, punishment is a communicative act that, roughly, sends a message to the wrongdoer, victim, and broader community that the victim did not deserve to be wronged and that the wrongdoer is culpable for doing so. It seems to us that on this view, forgiveness makes punishment all the more morally urgent. After all, the victim risks sending the message that it is acceptable to mistreat her if she simply forgives her wrongdoer without some accompanying message to make clear the fact that the wrong was unacceptable.[24] Perhaps it will be objected that coupling forgiveness with an expression of commitment to punishment sends a mixed, or even incoherent, message.

To this we reply that the message need not be mixed or incoherent. Recall the mother-child case from above, in which the mother says: "I love you very much, and it hurts me when you lie to me. I'm glad you apologized, though, and I forgive you. However, you know the punishment for lying in this house, so please go to your room for the next hour. I'll let you know when you can play with your toys again." It seems to us that in such a case, the mother is not sending mixed messages. While she need not deploy something as complicated as the communicative theory of punishment in her explanation to her child, the child can understand that, while she is forgiven for her lie, she is being punished for breaking the house rules (the corresponding punishments for breaking we can imagine being justified by communicative theories).

For retributivists, the purpose of punishment is to give wrongdoers their just deserts.[25] Retributivists therefore need to specify a desert-basis—an answer to the question of what makes a person deserve punishment to a certain degree. The desert basis could plausibly be argued to be any number of things—the degree of culpability of the wrongdoer's choices, the extent of harm she causes, or even the degree of wickedness of the wrongdoer's character. One thing that could not plausibly determine what wrongdoers deserve, however, is the degree of resentment harbored against them by their victims that is discharged upon forgiving. Of course, we might hope that rational people could make reasonable assessments of what their wrongdoers deserve, but then of course the assessments themselves would be at best a proxy for the appropriate moral considerations. And even if the victims were uniquely situated to determine accurately the degree of deserved punishment, it is implausible to hold that a victim's assessment itself *determines* the answer.[26] So, since the desert-basis must be something other than the degree of victim resentment (or whatever other kind of attitudes taken up by the victim) that is discharged upon forgiving, the fact that a victim forgives a wrongdoer need not undermine one's justification for punishing that wrongdoer.

The restitution model of punishment might seem to lend support to the punishment-forbearance view of forgiveness.[27] The purpose of punishment, on that model, is not for the wrongdoer to suffer unpleasant consequences, but rather for him to restore the victim as best as possible to the condition she was in before he wronged her—in other words, to pay a debt to victim. So it could be that if the victim forgives the wrongdoer, she also absolves the wrongdoer of any debt. And since punishment consists solely in the repayment of the debt arising from a wrong, there is no remaining justification for punishing the wrongdoer.

However, we see two problems with this line of argument. First, even if I, as a victim, forgive your interpersonal moral debt to me, this does not entail that *all* of your debts that you incurred by your wrongdoing have been canceled. There may be debts remaining that I as the victim do not even have the standing to cancel through my forgiveness. To hold that the debt is owed only to the victim is to construe the nature of wrongdoing rather narrowly, as a purely private affair. It seems more plausible to us that wrongdoers also typically incur a more general debt to the moral community, so that the victim is not the only party with a claim against the wrongdoer. A wrongdoer might pose a similar risk to others, or his action could be understood as a wrong against all those who follow the rules of the moral community.[28] If the victim sometimes has the standing to punish the wrongdoer because of these remaining debts, then even if forgiveness involves the cancellation of certain kinds of personal moral debts, this would not require the victim to forbear punishing the wrongdoer, so long as she has standing to do so. (Of course, if the victim does not have the standing to punish in order to secure payment of these outstanding debts, then the question of the permissibility of punishment after forgiveness has already been settled, and the explanation will have nothing to do with having forgiven her.)

The second problem is that, even if we focus on the debts that can be canceled by the victim of the wrongdoing, we need not think that, by forgiving, the victim necessarily cancels *all* debts the wrongdoer owes to her. Perhaps forgiveness cancels some kinds of interpersonal debts, but not others. You might, in a fit of rage, drop a can of paint on your neighbor's living room carpet. Your neighbor might forgive you for this mean act, but still be, we think, within her rights to ask you to replace her carpet. That debt to her still might remain. The point, then, is that if forgiveness does not necessarily cancel *all* debts incurred because of a wrong, then some of those debts that remain might be ones that can justify punishing the wrongdoer. The defender of the view under consideration must claim, by contrast, that interpersonal forgiveness cancels any and all debts that could plausibly serve as a justification for punishment according to restitution theories of punishment.

Next, consider the moral education account of punishment. On this view, the purpose of punishment is to reform the character of the wrongdoer. Presumably no one would think that forgiveness itself will necessarily cause a wrongdoer's moral reform—though perhaps it could humble some wrongdoers and start them on a path to redemption. And so despite being forgiven, a wrongdoer may still require further reform-based punishment.[29] If so, then there would be reasons to punish that need not be disavowed when one forgives. Someone could object that forgiveness is only appropriate when a wrongdoer has fully reformed. But if forgiveness requires that the wrongdoer already be reformed, then it would be wrong to punish a fully reformed person whether she has been forgiven or not. The justification for her punishment would disappear along with her vicious character, and this disappearance would have nothing to do with first being forgiven.

Finally, take the new relationship argument. This argument casts forgiveness as a way of morally repairing a relationship. If forgiveness is (at least in part) about reconciliation with one's wrongdoer, then it does seem a bit odd to say that you forgive someone who has wronged you, yet continue to punish her all the same. How serious could you be about reconciliation, after all, if you take one step toward repair and then immediately jump backwards? To this argument we answer that people seem to have no trouble doing exactly this in practice, and it seems sometimes to be a great relief to both victim and wrongdoer. It would not be unusual to hear of someone asking for nothing more than forgiveness, even if it is granted that the relationship will never be the same, or that victim and wrongdoer will never see each other or speak again. Yet, if we insist that forgiveness require forbearance from punishment, because forgiveness must always involve seeking reconciliation, these requests become difficult to understand, amounting as they do to asking for forgiveness while leaving punishment in place. While forgiveness is typically aimed at full or partial reconciliation, there is no quick, easy path from forgiveness to reconciliation, and in some cases, there may be no clear path at all.

Here is a second practical counter-argument. Forgiveness is generally not regarded as an outrageous thing to request. It is a part of every 12-step program. It is often (and ideally) asked for with a great deal of humility. Yet, if asking for forgiveness necessarily includes asking for forbearance from punishment on the grounds that the victim should not do anything that does not directly promote reconciliation, then it is not hard to see that asking to be forgiven would often be a truly outrageous request.[30] Far fewer people would have the temerity to ask for it, and they and their victims would miss opportunities for a partial moral repair that many see as something worth wanting. So it turns out that far from being odd, we have a great deal of practical use for forgiveness if it requires only a partial moral repair, and relatively little use for it if it must require avoiding anything that could impede reconciliation, such as subsequent punishment.

A third reply rests on pointing out an implied assumption in the new relationship argument: Punishment cannot be an important means to reconciliation. But why think that? Indeed, being punished may not always feel in the moment as if it is promoting reconciliation—it hurts. But getting a rabies vaccine hurts, too. This does not rule out the vaccine being a necessary means to future health. Punishment, too, might not rule out future reconciliation—indeed, it might be a very important (perhaps even necessary) stopover on the long road to reconciliation. If that is correct, then punishment might itself be a vital part of the new post-wrongdoing relationship inaugurated between victim and wrongdoer.

In this section we have argued that the forfeiture argument, the no justification argument, and the new relationship argument each fail to vindicate the claim that forgiving a wrongdoer morally requires one to forbear punishing her. This is so even if we grant that punishment is something individuals commonly have the standing to do in their interpersonal relationships. If correct, we think this undermines at least some obvious strategies for arguing that forgiveness makes subsequent punishment impermissible. It is worth noting that this result does not directly cut against the claim that forgiving *itself* involves something like the forswearing or forbearing of punishment. To argue against the moral claim that forgiveness morally requires forbearing punishment is not to argue against the claim that to forgive *is* (in part or whole) the forbearance of punishment. Of course, these views are connected: If it is false that forgiveness makes punishment morally impermissible, then that would be very good evidence that it is also false that, as a necessary condition on forgiveness, one must forbear punishment.

4 Institutional forgiveness?

We noted earlier that punishment is a practice that we generally associate with institutions and that it is thus odd to think of forgiveness as requiring one to forbear punishment, as if this was typically an option for individuals. We made sense of the view by introducing an expansive interpretation of punishment, which included interpersonal punishment. But perhaps the punishment-forbearance view is best studied in a different context. Suppose we maintain a more limited, institutional view of punishment, but also think of forgiveness as something that institutions can do. In fact, some theorists have done exactly that (Digeser 2001). Perhaps thinking of forgiveness at the institutional level will reveal something about the concept of forgiveness that is not immediately clear when we think about interpersonal forgiveness.

The first institution that comes to mind when one thinks of punishment is the state. If the state were to forgive a wrongdoer, what would that involve? Issuing a pardon, and so foreclosing the possibility of further punishment for the wrong in question, is one obvious possibility. But might the state do less and still be said to have forgiven the wrongdoer? Suppose that some public official responds to a wrongdoer's request for clemency by issuing a statement expressing sympathy for her plight and a warm assessment of her improved character but nonetheless reaffirms the plan to punish her. One possible assessment of the case is to say that this is not forgiveness at all, as it might be a pure political move made in response to pressure from some interest group. But suppose we specify that the official's order is only made as a result of rethinking the state's relationship to the wrongdoer, in isolation from political-careerist concerns.

Is this a case of forgiveness? Issuing such a statement seems, at least to us, like an odd thing for the official to do. Perhaps we can make progress by asking whether the statement described is something the wrongdoer would value. If she would value the statement, then that would suggest that her relationship with the institution of the state is something she values apart from any punitive consequences attached to it. And if she does so value the relationship, then that suggests that we have a practical use for an understanding of institutional forgiveness that does not include forbearing punishment. But unless she either has a close relationship with the public official or is civic-minded in a way not commonly seen in modern states, the answer is likely "no." In general, we suspect that practically anyone in a position to be forgiven by the state is interested only in punishment-forbearance.[31]

Can this feature of state forgiveness be generalized to any other plausible forms of forgiveness? We think not. It cannot be generalized to interpersonal forgiveness, because, as we have already argued, people do typically have a practical interest in forgiveness in interpersonal relationships that does not include punishment-forbearance. More plausibly, we might consider the possibility that there are different kinds of forgiveness for different kinds of agents.[32] It might be thought that institutional forgiveness in general (and not just by the state) includes punishment-forbearance. But this also seems false. It may be odd to think that citizens of modern states would value forgiveness without punishment-forbearance, but things may have been different when people's identities were more closely bound up with their political community. And states are hardly the only institutions that can engage in punitive behavior. A person might plausibly care about being forgiven by a religious organization, charity, hospital, or any number of other kinds of institutions with which she might have fallen out. So if we want to hold out the possibility of forgiveness from these sorts of institutions, we should note that punishment-forbearance does not seem necessary.

We close this section by asking whether state forgiveness is a useful concept at all. Perhaps it is, but it does not seem to add anything to our familiar way of talking about state pardons. In fact, the idea of forgiveness seems rather out of place in the context of talking about a type of institution to which few have deep emotional connections akin to personal relationships. Ironically, it is this lack of emotional depth in the citizen-state relationship that makes the requirement of punishment-forbearance in "state forgiveness" plausible in the first place: Without it, there would be very little state action that is even in the neighborhood of forgiveness. So it turns out that there is a lesson to be learned by considering the possibility of institutional forgiveness that is relevant to interpersonal forgiveness, but it is not the kind of lesson for which punishment-forbearance theorists might have hoped. This discussion suggests that punishment-forbearance accounts of forgiveness are most plausible when we remove the emotional complexity of interpersonal relationships. But we worry about the prospects for a claim about forgiveness if the claim is made most plausible in contexts that have very little in common with the interpersonal relationships in which forgiveness is typically thought to find its paradigmatic instantiations.

5 Forgiveness and mercy

Thus far, we have argued against a conception of forgiveness that requires one to forbear punishment. Of course, we do not mean to argue that if one forgives, one *must* punish one's wrongdoer (assuming such a thing is even possible in non-hierarchical relationships). All we mean to have shown is that forgiveness can be morally consistent with punishment. Naturally, however, one might wish to forbear punishment of one's wrongdoer—and this may or may not be concomitant with one's forgiving the wrongdoer. In other words, forbearing punishment might be an act of mercy, but this act of mercy is separable, conceptually and morally, from having forgiven the wrongdoer. We conclude, then, by reflecting briefly on some key differences between forgiveness in particular, and acts of mercy in general.

First, manifestations of mercy, but not forgiveness, are essentially overt. To extend or show mercy to someone who has acted badly is to engage in some overt behavior: A governor may show mercy by commuting a guilty criminal's sentence, or a parent may lessen a guilty child's punishment. In any such cases, however, the act of mercy is overtly expressed. Forgiveness, however, is not necessarily overt. It is possible to forgive privately; indeed, philosophical discussions of forgiveness have focused predominantly on its private manifestations.

Second, mercy is third-personal in a way that forgiveness is not. Forgiveness is paradigmatically a second-personal enterprise, whereby the only person in a position to forgive S for S's wronging of P is P herself. As some philosophers have suggested, there are perhaps exceptions to this general rule, but even so, these cases are clearly non-paradigmatic.[33] Mercy, on the other hand, is very often shown third-personally. A governor need not be the victim of a criminal's offense in order to show mercy and commute a sentence. A parent may abate Little Tommy's punishment even though Tommy's offense was to hit his sister. A boss may reprimand an employee for telling an inappropriate joke in the lunchroom even though termination would be justified and the boss herself is not personally offended by it. In all of these cases, a third-party shows mercy and does so (we may presume) justifiably. This is not to say that mercy *must* be third-personal. After all, the boss herself might have been personally offended by a joke aimed specifically at her. But forgiveness, if it is ever third-personal, is not third-personal in *this* way. Barring exceptional circumstances, you cannot forgive me for the offense I caused to a co-worker—you simply lack the standing to forgive me for my offense to *her.* Mercy is not paradigmatically second-personal in this way.

Third, mercy is often (if not always) connected to authority in a way that forgiveness is not. Indeed, our examples above were instances of mercy shown by individuals in positions of legal, parental, and occupational authority. It is natural to think that in order for S to show mercy to P, S must be in *some* kind of position of authority over P. You might even be justifiably offended if someone who is *not* in a position of authority over you was to communicate her desire to show you mercy for something you had done—you might take her comment as an implicit assertion of her authority over you, something you might justifiably resent if she is your equal. Interpersonal forgiveness, however, is tied to no such authority structures: Peasants may forgive kings.

Whatever similarities they possess on the surface, forgiveness and mercy are clearly distinguishable phenomena. Mercy is essentially overt, paradigmatically third-personal, and tied to authority. Forgiveness, however, is possibly private, paradigmatically second-personal, and independent of authority.

6 Conclusion

We began by speculating that there is a common folk view that forgiveness and punishment are somehow linked, such that one should not punish a person after forgiving her. We think that the discussion above presents a strong *prima facie* case for rejecting that view. Forgiveness, acts of mercy, the withdrawal of blame, the forbearance of revenge, and the forbearance of punishment are indeed moral phenomena that reside in the same neighborhood. It is understandable that some might draw strong connections between any or all of them. Indeed, we think that some of them are in fact connected. Though we have not argued for it here, we do think that forgiveness typically morally requires one to forbear revenge and most (if not all) acts of moral blame. But even if this is so, it does not follow that forgiveness also morally requires one to forbear punishment. Indeed, we have tried to show that even if victims do indeed have the authority to punish, there can be plenty of justifying reasons for a victim to punish her wrongdoer after forgiving her. Further, forgiving itself need not involve the forfeiture of a liberty right to punish. And even further, the fact that one has forgiven does not entail that subsequent punishment violates the normative standards of a post-forgiveness relationship. Of course, it goes without saying that we are not claiming that just *any* kind or measure of punishment can be appropriate after forgiveness. It seems to us, however, that the moral relationship that punishment-forbearance theorists claim holds between forgiveness and punishment is not as strong as advertised.[34]

Notes

1 Londey clarifies his use of the phrase "penalty or sanction" to "include moral censure as well as more tangible punishments" (1986: 5).

2 Claims like these just adumbrated are usually made in passing and are not given defense. One exception is Zaibert (2009). Because one of us has discussed that view elsewhere (Warmke 2011), we shall not pursue it here. We shall instead be concerned with what kinds of defenses *could* be marshaled for these claims, and with how plausible those arguments could be.

3 While punishment-forbearance views of forgiveness have not received systematic treatment, discussions of forgiveness and punishment can be found in Mabbott (1939), Morris (1968), Duff (1986: 216–17), Haber (1991), Griswold (2007: 32–33), Murphy (2003: 101), O'Shaughnessy (1967), Swinburne (1989), Garrard and McNaughton (2002), Zaibert (2009), Warmke (2011, 2013), Pettigrove (2012), and Jacobs (this volume).

4 Here are two other ways of thinking about the relationship between punishment and forgiveness. One is a necessity claim: Agent A forgives agent B for B's conduct X only if A forbears punishing B for B's having done X. The other is a sufficiency claim: Agent A forgives agent B for B's conduct X if A forbears punishing B for B's having done X. These statements make a metaphysical or conceptual claim about the relationship, and not, in the first instance, a moral claim. We shall not be addressing these other claims in this paper.

5 While, as we noted above, it is sometimes claimed that punishment is linked to forgiveness, it is a claim that is rarely argued for. Hence we shall try to construct three plausible motivations for certain kinds of punishment-forbearance views.

6 The definition of punishment is an extremely controversial topic. This brief statement is arguably not sufficiently ecumenical, but it is roughly accurate, and should be sufficient for our purposes. It is loosely adapted from Hart (1968: 4–6). For an extensive recent discussion of the definition of legal punishment, see Boonin (2008: 3–28).

7 We do not mean to claim here that the justification of punishment must be consequentialist. The term "justifying aim" is borrowed from Hart (1968: 8–11) and may refer more broadly to the purpose of the act of punishing itself rather than merely to its consequences.

8 Why the caveat? It may turn out that in exceptional circumstances, even though it would be wrong for a victim to punish someone she has forgiven (as such), the balance of reasons might weigh strongly in favor of punishing anyway. If punishing is the only way to save a village of children, then it may be, all things considered, permissible to punish even if there are strong *pro tanto* reasons against punishing.

9 Cf. Wellman (2009), though see Simmons (1991).

10 Does forbearing punishment require one to "undo" one's previous punishment (or perhaps blaming) of her? Suppose you punish your child for smoking dope in his bedroom by kicking him out of the house. Does forbearing punishment require inviting him back into the house? Is that "undoing" his punishment or ceasing his punishment? As best we can tell there is no good general answer to these questions, and they must be considered on a case-by-case basis.

11 Strictly speaking, one could perhaps consistently claim that we forbear punishment when we forgive (or that we must not punish if we forgive), *even if* we are rarely if ever able to punish (because we lack standing to do so). That we cannot do something, one might argue, does not show that we cannot forbear doing it. Even granting this point, the view would be a vacuous one and not worth discussing. We will assume then, that whatever view of punishment is at issue, it must be something that could be at issue in common cases of interpersonal forgiveness.

12 Though a full treatment of blame (in both its private and overt varieties) would take us far afield, in our view, overt blame is private blame's outward manifestation. Private blame is a manifestation of a disposition to *regard* the wrongdoer in a certain way (cf. McKenna 2012). According to a very popular view, the relevant kind of regard involves the manifestation of a "reactive attitude," such as resentment, indignation, or disapprobation (e.g., Fischer and Ravizza 1998, Russell 1995, Wallace 1994, and Strawson 1962). Overt blame, then, is a manifestation of a certain kind of disposition to *treat* the wrongdoer in a certain way, such as the examples given above. We should be clear that in our view, to blame someone

is not the same as to judge someone blameworthy. One might judge someone blameworthy without being disposed to blame him or manifest such a disposition (see McKenna 2012). Consequently, in our view, forgiving does not require one to give up a judgment of blameworthiness.

13 On forgiveness typically ruling out both overt blaming and revenge, see, e.g., Butler (1846), Garrard and McNaughton (2002), Murphy (2003), Griswold (2007), Pettigrove (2012), and Warmke (2011, 2013, 2015). Forgiveness probably also makes many or all forms of *private* moral blame inappropriate as well. But because no one would ever confuse punishment (an essentially overt activity) with private blame (an essentially private activity), we will set aside the matter of private moral blame.

14 A liberty right to do X is generally understood as a "cluster right," as it contains both a permission to do X and a claim right against interference in doing X. See Thomson (1990: 53–56).

15 Hughes (1993) suggested such a case in a different context, and Warmke (2013) gave another version of it.

16 It might be objected that this case relies on a hierarchical relationship between mother and child and that we had taken ourselves to be widening our discussion of punishment to ordinary interpersonal cases where such hierarchical relationships need not exist. Even supposing we grant the point, what follows from it? If one can forgive without forfeiting one's right to punish when one has the right, does it matter to the forfeiture argument whether the relationship is a hierarchical one or not? We cannot see how, at least not according to the current construal of the forfeiture argument.

17 Cf. Waldron (1981).

18 We do not claim that no one would express a general moral complaint by uttering dispassionately "you lied to me." But these seem to us typical ways of expressing the two forms of complaint.

19 Another way of expressing the point might be to say that forgiveness ought not be thought of as a matter of justice, but that punishment should (see Griswold 2007: 32–33).

20 Paul Hughes (1993) appears to have a similar sort of thought in mind: The fact of wrongdoing as such can remain as a grounds for punishment, even when we forgive.

21 This may be true even if the justification for moral blame is also consequentialist (e.g., Vargas 2013), for the aims of each of these practices may be to secure different kinds of ends.

22 Whether the wrongdoer has been forgiven is, of course, even less relevant to whether punishing her would be an efficient method for deterring wrongdoers in general.

23 See, e.g., Duff (2001).

24 There is, of course, a concern that the message need not be delivered specifically through punishment, but that is a general quibble with the communicative view of punishment and not one raised specifically by cases of forgiveness.

25 See, e.g., Moore (1987), Morris (1968), and Murphy (1973).

26 It would be much more plausible to hold that the morally appropriate level of resentment felt by a victim tracks the degree of fitting punishment. But then it is not the victim's resentment that determines the degree of fitting punishment (if any), but whatever makes that resentment morally appropriate.

27 The most prominent defender of this view is Barnett (1977).

28 The idea of a general debt to society is useful, and perhaps indispensable, for explaining crimes without individual victims. Cf. Dagger (1980, 1991).

29 Cf. Duff (2001: 107–109).

30 "Listen, I know I stole your car, slept with your brother, and ran up $100,000 in credit card debt in your name, but my sponsor says I have to ask, so how about we pick up where we left off?"

31 It might be objected that just because the wrongdoer has no interest in being forgiven, this does not mean that she is not forgiven, or that such phenomena should not count as a kind of forgiveness. After all, even in ordinary, interpersonal cases of forgiveness, sometimes the wrongdoer has no interest in being forgiven, either because she thinks she did nothing wrong, or because she does not value her relationship with the putative victim of her wrongdoing. But the difference between these cases, we think, is that, generally speaking, people *do* care about being forgiven in ordinary interpersonal contexts, whereas generally, people would not usually care about being "forgiven" by the state (or a representative thereof) unless that forgiveness involved pardon or something similar. So while we grant that this "value argument" does not show that states cannot forgive over and above simply forbearing punishment, it does draw a disanalogy between state forgiveness and ordinary forgiveness that should give pause.

32 Digeser distinguishes between "ordinary forgiveness" and "political forgiveness" (2001: 28).

33 See, for example, Griswold (2007: 117–19).

34 We thank Jonathan Jacobs for his excellent comments on a previous draft of this chapter. Support for BW's work on this paper was funded in part by a grant from the Templeton World Charity Foundation. The opinions expressed in this paper are my own and do not necessarily reflect the views of the foundation.

Bibliography

Barnett, R.E. (1977) 'Restitution: a new paradigm of criminal justice', *Ethics*, 87(4): 279–301.

Bash, A. (2015) *Forgiveness: A Theology*, Eugene, OR: Cascade Books.

Boonin, D. (2008) *The Problem of Punishment*, New York, NY: Cambridge University Press.

Butler, J. (1846) *Fifteen Sermons Preached at Rolls Chapel*, in S. Halifax (ed.) *The Works of the Right Reverend Father in God, Joseph Butler, D.C.L., Late Bishop of Durham*, New York, NY: Carter.

Dagger, R. (1980) 'Restitution, punishment, and debts to society', in J. Hudson and B. Galaway (eds.) *Victims, Offenders, and Alternative Sanctions*, Lexington, MA: Lexington Books, pp. 3–14.

Dagger, R. (1991) 'Restitution: pure or punitive?', *Criminal Justice Ethics*, 10(2): 29–39.

Digeser, P.E. (2001) *Political Forgiveness*, Ithaca, NY: Cornell University Press.

Duff, R.A. (1986) *Trials and Punishments*, Cambridge: Cambridge University Press.

Duff, R.A. (2001) *Punishment, Communication, and Community*, New York, NY: Oxford University Press.

Enright, R.D., Eastin, D.L., Golden, S., Sarinopoulos, I. and Freedman, S. (1992). 'Interpersonal forgiveness within the helping professions: an attempt to resolve differences of opinion', *Counseling and Values*, 36: 84–103.

Fischer, J.M. and Ravizza, M. (1998) *Responsibility and Control: A Theory of Moral Responsibility*, Cambridge: Cambridge University Press.

Garrard, E. and McNaughton, D, (2002) 'In defence of unconditional forgiveness', *Proceedings of the Aristotelian Society*, 103(1): 39–60.

Gert, B. (2010) *Hobbes: Prince of Peace*, Cambridge: Polity.

Griswold, C.L. (2007) *Forgiveness: A Philosophical Exploration*, New York, NY: Cambridge University Press.

Haber, J.G. (1991) *Forgiveness*, Lanham, MD: Rowman and Littlefield.

Hart, H. (1968) *Punishment and Responsibility*, Oxford: Oxford University Press.

Hobbes, T. (1651[1969 edition]) *Leviathan*, Menston, England: The Scholar Press Limited.

Hughes, P.M. (1993) 'What is involved in forgiving?', *Journal of Value Inquiry*, 27: 331–40.

Jacobs, J. (2016) 'Resentment, punitiveness, and forgiveness: an exploration of the moral psychology of punishment', this volume.

Londey, D. (1986) 'Can God forgive us our trespasses?', *Sophia*, 25: 4–10.

Mabbott, J.D. (1939) 'Punishment', *Mind*, 48(190): 152–67.

McKenna, M. (2012) *Conversation and Responsibility*, Oxford: Oxford University Press.

Morris, H. (1968) 'Persons and punishment', *The Monist*, 52: 475–501.

Murphy, J.G. (1973) 'Marxism and retribution', *Philosophy and Public Affairs*, 2(3): 217–43.

Murphy, J.G. (2003) *Getting Even: Forgiveness and Its Limits*, New York, NY: Oxford University Press.

Moore, M.S. (1987) 'The moral worth of retribution' in F.D. Schoeman (ed.) *Responsibility, Character, and the Emotions: New Essays in Moral Psychology*, Cambridge: Cambridge University Press, pp. 179–219.

O'Shaughnessy, R.J. (1967) 'Forgiveness', *Philosophy*, 42(162): 336–52.

Pettigrove, G. (2012) *Forgiveness and Love*, Oxford: Oxford University Press.

Russell, P. (1995) *Freedom and Moral Sentiment. Hume's Way of Naturalizing Responsibility*, Oxford: Oxford University Press.

Scanlon, T.M. (2008) *Moral Dimensions: Permissibility, Meaning, and Blame*, Cambridge: Belknap Press.

Simmons, A.J. (1991) 'Locke and the right to punish', *Philosophy and Public Affairs*, 20(4): 311–49.

Strawson, P.F. (1962) 'Freedom and resentment', in G. Watson (ed.) *Free Will: Second Edition*, Oxford: Oxford University Press.

Swinburne, R. (1989) *Responsibility and Atonement*, New York, NY: Oxford University Press.

Thomson, J.J. (1990) *The Realm of Rights*, Cambridge, MA: Harvard University Press.

Vargas, M. (2013) *Building Better Beings: A Theory of Responsibility*, New York, NY: Oxford University Press.

Waldron, J. (1981) 'A right to do wrong', *Ethics*, 92(1): 21–39.

Wallace, R.J. (1994) *Responsibility and the Moral Sentiments*, Cambridge, MA: Harvard University Press.

Warmke, B. (2011) 'Is forgiveness the deliberate refusal to punish?', *Journal of Moral Philosophy*, 8(4): 613–20.

Warmke, B. (2013) 'Two arguments against the punishment-forbearance account of forgiveness', *Philosophical Studies*, 165(3): 915–20.

Warmke, B. (2015) 'The economic model of forgiveness', *Pacific Philosophical Quarterly*.

Wellman, C.H. (2009) 'Rights and State Punishment'. *Journal of Philosophy*, 106(8): 419–39.

Wolterstorff, N. (2009) 'Jesus and forgiveness', in P. Moser (ed.) *Jesus and Philosophy: New Essays*, Cambridge: Cambridge University Press.

Zaibert, L. (2009) 'The paradox of forgiveness', *Journal of Moral Philosophy*, 6(3): 365–93.

Part III

Institutions, policies, and practices

14

Enabling and constraining police power

On the moral regulation of policing

Ben Bradford and Jonathan Jackson

Dubber (2005) describes the police power as unlimited, and while he was referring to a concept of police much broader than the uniformed public police service that is our focus here, it is certainly true that the police remit is both broad in terms of its potential objects (threats to the stability of established social order) and wide in the set of means available to achieve its aims (up to and including the use of deadly force). The extent of the power vested in police, the fact that most officers operate in low visibility settings, and the discretion many of them wield – all of these factors create significant problems of oversight, governance, and inevitably, ethics. That policing tactics and techniques are often only loosely constrained in law and/or are unavailable to other actors (Brodeur 2010) serves only to make these issues more pertinent and more pressing.

Our goal in this chapter is to consider some of the ethical challenges inherent in the regulation of discretionary police power. The ability to address a situation either formally (evoking legal categories) or informally (using situated problem solving), discretion is central to police policy and practice. It also provides a level of freedom that opens up the space for injustice and inequity, as seen most vividly in recent debates about unfairness and racial profiling in the distribution and experience police stops in the US and UK. Police are able to use a huge range of tactics to address the problems they encounter, yet the low visibility and high discretion granted to street-level officers ensures that only relatively rarely will these solutions be 'second-guessed' by supervisors or, more pertinently, external review processes. This is arguably a characteristic of all police, but these issues pose particular problems in liberal democratic states where the power of the state over citizens is, at least from an ideological perspective, constrained. In such contexts, police indeed remain something of an exceptional power – one that poses a significant threat to liberties many would consider both well-established and inviolable.

How to regulate discretionary power, to channel it in ethically desirable directions, is a challenging question, and this is especially so in the context of practices like stop-and-search/stop-and-frisk. The ability to stop people in the street and question them is central to policing as it is understood in many liberal democracies, but under conditions of unfairness and questionable efficacy – when the application of this particular police power appears unethical as well as ineffective – one can reasonably ask whether the power should be dropped or curtailed, and if curtailed, how this would work in practice. Changing the legal landscape may help, particularly as it relates to racial profiling. One solution to the problem of inequitable policing outcomes may be to make the practices that produce them illegal and then enforce such laws with established and/or new or novel mechanisms. But the empirical fact that police need to be able to deal at least provisionally with the huge range of problems with which they are confronted limits this possibility in important ways. Police officers are the first, and often only, responders to a huge variety of situations and events; they require an ability to react to and (re)direct these events; that is – due to the significant freedom and discretion required – by definition difficult if not impossible to codify within a set of legal rules. What is the 'right thing' to do, in a given situation, cannot be determined in such a manner.

How might these policies and practices be regulated? Whether the onus comes from a change in the legal landscape or from other cultural, social, and political pressures, there are in our minds three main ways in which the ethical curtailment – or perhaps more precisely re-direction – of stop-and-search/stop-and-frisk practices might be achieved 'on the ground.' First, the visibility of police activity could be increased – something that is already occurring as a result of the uptake of camera phones and other mobile technologies, the work of 'citizen journalists' and others, and policy movement towards officers using and wearing video cameras. Yet, while the importance of such developments should not be understated, they are unlikely to provide a panacea; the camera can lie, and there will always be a limit to what can and should be recorded.

Second, in a related but wider sense, extrinsic modes of bureaucratic regulation can be utilized that motivate either individual officers or police organizations to behave in a more ethical fashion, by which we mean acting in line with established norms of probity and right, in ways that respect the rights of citizens to be as free from intrusive state power as possible, being honest and transparent, and so forth. By extrinsic, we mean authority structures and processes either within police organizations, aimed at directing officer practice (e.g., reward and disciplinary schemes) or outside police organizations, aimed at directing the activity of the organization as a whole (e.g., civilian oversight, police and crime commissioners. etc.).

This is, by and large, the 'traditional' approach to corralling the power of the police and directing it in normatively desirable directions. It has claimed some success, with police practice in many developed countries changing for the better over the years as a result of regulatory change and related factors. While it may be impossible to come up with a definitive list of things police can and cannot do (see above), particular behaviours (such as aggressive interrogations) can be, and have been, curtailed and often prohibited. Such change has frequently been associated with extrinsic pressure on police organizations to change their practices or suffer a loss of material or symbolic capital.

Yet, despite these developments, present-day police practice is plainly still far from ideal – witness, precisely, the ongoing scandals about police stop practices in contexts as diverse as Scotland (Murray 2014), Spain (Añón et al. 2013), and the United States (Tyler et al. 2014). Simply banning (making illegal) particular practices does not mean they do not take place, and as we describe below there are two important reasons for the continued failure of regulatory change to rein in the power of the police and direct police activity in more desirable directions. Not only do external modes of regulation continuously run into the twin problems of discretion and (in)visibility, but most are premised on instrumental understandings of human motivation that, evidence suggests, are not particularly well-suited to explaining the ways people actually behave in social settings.

Third, intrinsic modes of regulation can be encouraged or enhanced. Our central theme in this chapter is the idea that the legitimacy police command and require, both externally and internally, may be pivotal to this process. On the one hand, police at the organizational level are engaged in a continuous process of establishing and reproducing their legitimacy among those they police; this means that they must – to some extent – be responsive to, and in tune with, the communities they serve. Police cannot, in other words, simply do what they want. Legitimacy is founded in public perceptions of fairness, probity, honesty and lawfulness (although the situation in some developing countries may provide an interesting counterpoint, where effectiveness may be relatively or absolutely more important – Karakus 2015; Jackson et al. 2014; Bradford et al. 2013; Tankebe 2009; although see Akinlabi 2015; and Kochel et al. 2013) and the need for legitimacy acts as an empirical constraint on police power. If police wish to reproduce their legitimacy they are channelled towards behaving within certain limits; actions outside established normative frameworks will undermine legitimacy, and these limitations are likely to correlate closely with established ethical values – particularly in relation to notions of fairness.

On the other hand, legitimacy within police organizations can motivate officers to behave in certain ways. The argument here is that:

(a) Organizational justice encourages identification with the organization.
(b) Identification with the organization leads to legitimation of its practices and processes and internalization of its values and goals.
(c) Legitimation and internalization motivates compliance with organizational rules and values.
(d) This process encourages officers to see themselves as legitimate, strengthening self-confidence, and opening up the possibility for positive policing styles.

Police organizations that have the right goals, communicate these goals to staff, and treat staff in organizationally fair ways may be able to motivate internal processes of legitimacy that are themselves constitutive of a check on police power or at least will tend to channel it in desirable directions.

It seems to us that – in the absence of fundamental change to the role of police in liberal democracies (which is not quite as far-fetched as it might seem if contractual, private-sector type arrangements gain even greater traction than is currently the case) – and given the intractable problems associated with the application of extrinsic constraints on officer behaviour, questions of legitimacy should take centre-stage in efforts to exert constraints on police discretionary power and encourage ethical policing. In particular, the internal notion of legitimacy seems to offer significant possibilities, not least because it can bypass currents in public opinion inimical to limits on police power (at least when this is directed at denigrated out-groups and 'others') yet is at the same time amenable to external influence from, for example, democratically elected oversight bodies. Which is to say, in addition, that legitimacy backed up by extrinsic modes of regulation (and greater visibility) is likely to be a particularly effective strategy. However, as we describe below, this is not an entirely one-way street, and it is entirely possible that legitimacy also opens up the space for unethical behaviours.

In the following pages we consider the three strategies outlined above in the context of regulating stop and search/frisk and similar policing tactics. This is an example of the sort of police activities that raise questions about individual rights, of structural racism, procedural and distributive justice, and the limits of police power and legitimacy (and which many believe need to change). To set the scene we first introduce the issue of stop and search/frisk. We focus primarily on the UK given the context in which we both work – but much of what follows will be relevant in other Anglophone contexts as well, perhaps, as more widely still.

Stop and search/frisk

The power to stop, question, temporarily detain, and search people 'on the streets' is one of the most controversial powers vested in the police in the UK, the US, and increasingly elsewhere (e.g., Open Society Justice Initiative 2009). Legally speaking, this police power is often relatively constrained, albeit wide-ranging. In most circumstances police cannot simply decide to 'randomly' stop and/or search people. But there are important exceptions in some contexts. In England and Wales, for instance, various forms of the power are enshrined in law, the most important of which is Section 1 of the Police and Criminal Evidence Act 1984, otherwise known as PACE. PACE applies a reasonable suspicion test, meaning police must have a justifiable reason for stopping someone with a view to searching him or her. But other pieces of legislation do not, notably s60 of the Criminal Justice and Public Order Act 1994, which allows officers to search a person without suspicion. Searches under these powers, although they occur in public spaces, can be relatively invasive; individuals stopped are required by police to stay for the duration of, and acquiesce to, any search that follows, and officers can use force to ensure they do so.

Despite the existence of legal constraints, the conduct of street stops is a classically low visibility, high discretion, police activity. Street-level officers get to decide whom to stop, when and where, with very little possibility of external oversight (of individual stops – the overall number of stops is a potential target for external regulation, and police can be, and often are, encouraged to increase/decrease the number of stops they conduct). The importance of discretion here is magnified by the fact that police have a range of what might be termed sub-legal powers to 'stop' people and question them in the street. In some countries, such as Scotland, it is known that the use of 'consent' searches is widespread, since many are recorded by police (Murray 2014). Elsewhere, the use of 'consent' as an enabler of police activity is assumed to be wide spread, but its extent remains largely hidden (Dixon 2008). Sub-legal tools available to police to garner consent for a stop range from the inherent authority they command in relation to significant numbers of people – to whom a simple question from a police officer may be experienced as requiring a response – to their ability to draw upon other informal sources of power and influence to direct behaviour. Moreover, in continental Europe and elsewhere the ability of and often requirement to conduct ID checks offers a further range of opportunities for police to interdict and question people.

In a general sense, a power to stop, question and search people that is short of a full arrest is useful for both police and policed (in the latter case mainly because of the well-known negative implications arising from being arrested – it is often argued that if police did not have the power to stop and search they would turn to the more invasive power of arrest as a means to achieving the same ends). Yet, public encounters with the police provide moments in which the legitimacy of the police is asserted, tested, and all too often undermined (Tyler and Fagan 2008; Jackson et al. 2012a; Mazerolle et al. 2012; Geller et al. 2014; Tyler et al. 2014; Slocum et al. 2015). Whether governed by statute or based on the sociological power of police to intervene in people's lives, stop and search/frisk encounters can take place in almost any of the contexts within which police and public interact. Officers conducting a stop are, implicitly or explicitly, making a claim as to the rightfulness of the authority vested in them. As a key part of the police 'voice' in the legitimacy 'dialogue' envisioned by Bottoms and Tankebe (2012), every stop and search encounter involves a claim that police are empowered to treat citizens in this way; that the nature and extent of this power is defensible; and that the ability of police to wield coercive force to ensure compliance is itself justified. The people stopped make judgements about these claims, asking whether the actions of the police were justified in this and similar cases; whether the officer acted proportionately and with the right intentions, or whether he or she motivated by bias or prejudice; whether the laws on which this method of policing is based themselves justified, in terms of the aims they embody and the fairness with which they are applied; and whether it is right that this officer can forcibly detain one if one resists.

Stop and search remains a highly charged, contested and in many ways deeply problematic aspect of police practice. The proximate reason for this is ethnic and other disproportionalities in the experience of police such activity. Stop and search has been a controversial issue for many years, in part because it is a mode of police practice that seems consistently to be unevenly applied: socially, geographically and, particularly, ethnically (Smith and Gray 1985; Keith 1993; Bowling and Philips 2002; Medina Ariza 2014; Bradford and Loader 2016). People from some ethnic minority groups are more likely to experience this form of police contact than their majority-group counterparts, a phenomena which has, we should note, been identified well beyond the UK (see Weber and Bowling 2012). Black people living in England and Wales are stopped at a rate around 6 times that which their proportion in the general population would suggest is appropriate, for example (Shiner and Delsol 2015). This is a practice intimately caught up in the debate around institutional and other forms of racism within the police service, and with wider currents of ethnic and racial exclusion and oppression.

Despite the underlying desirability of granting to police an investigatory tool that stops short of arrest, then, the wide-ranging power vested in officers to initiate stop and search encounters poses problems for both parties involved. Police lose legitimacy when its use of power seems misdirected; the policed are dragged at least to the threshold of the criminal justice system; all lose when trust in the police is undermined. And these questions are made all the more pressing by the weight of evidence that the power stop and search/frisk can be, and is, misused and sometimes abused. There is the issue of ethnic disproportionality: racial profiling, and equally implicit bias and stereotyping, violate foundational principles of equality and citizenship, and such behaviours on the part of police serve as part of what Epp et al. (2014: 5) call a 'broad, continuing pattern in which racial minorities are disproportionately subjected to suspicious inquiries without any particular basis or justification.' Other disproportionalities have also been identified – by gender, age, social class and across other markers of exclusion (Bradford and Loader 2016) – and the typically low proportion of stop/searches that result in arrests is also an issue. The London Metropolitan Police Service (MPS), for example, has recently *improved* its 'hit rate' (the proportion of stops resulting in an arrest) to around 20 per cent, from previous rates as low as 9 per cent. But this means that something like four out of five searches in London do not result in an arrest (although a further proportion do lead to some other criminal justice outcome, such as a drug warning). There is a constant concern that this implies a misuse of invasive police power.

In sum, stop and search is a police power both necessary and in need of ethical constraint. While it is generally desirable that police have available to them investigatory powers that fall short of arrest it is important that their use of these powers is restrained, appropriate and proportionate. Yet, evidence from a wide variety of contexts frequently suggests a lack of restraint, inappropriate application, and disproportionate outcomes.

Finding the balance: Enabling and constraining discretionary power

All this raises a number of important questions about the legitimacy of the power and the wider set of police practices it represents (proactive, police-led, coercive criminal justice interventions, see Tyler et al. 2015; Bowling and Philips 2007; Delsol and Shiner 2006; Jackson et al. 2012b; Miller and D'Souza 2015). How can the practice be effectively regulated such that it is wielded in a more ethically sustainable manner? What mechanisms can be put in place to encourage (if not, in the final analysis, to ensure) restraint, appropriateness, and proportionality?

In the rest of the chapter we consider some of the ways in which constraint might be provided for, while at the same time recognizing that the existence of constraints on police activity also, perhaps paradoxically, enable the use of power – including in an unethical manner. In what follows we are interested in the regulation of police activity in its widest sense, as well as stop and search in particular, where much of this activity – including 'police stops' – occurs in settings either not governed by explicit law or, at least, where the police are given very significant discretion in how to apply the law. By regulation, we refer to setting the goal of an activity, monitoring it, and realigning it if it is found to be misapplied or misdirected (Sanders 2008: 51) – of these, monitoring and realignment figure most prominently in the discussion – but, equally, we are concerned with the question of how to promote and maintain ethical standards within police organizations in a wider sense. By what mechanisms can police officers be encouraged to 'do the right thing'?

Limiting police discretion through changing the law

Most police stops occur as and when officers, individually or in small groups, decide whom to stop and for what reason – of course, the decision on whom not to stop is equally discretionary – albeit such practice can also be directed by organizational policies and priority setting. Indeed, the extent of discretion available to police in this area seems likely to be one of the key factors driving ethnic and other disproportionalities in stop and search/frisk activity, not least because discretion – the ability to make decisions – enables and even motivates biased and stereotyped decision-making. Officers are often making differentiating or categorizing decisions at very short notice in low-information settings – it would hardly be surprising if they based these decisions on stereotypes or were subject to implicit biases when doing so (Glaser 2015; Legewie 2016).

On the face of it, one way to realign police activity in this and related areas would be to place legal limits on officer discretion. It might seem, at first glance, relatively easy to come up with a list of circumstances within which stop and search could and could not be used. But such a task would likely fail, for the simple reason that, as noted by Bittner (1974: 35, quoted in Reiner 2010: 144), the job of the police is to produce contingent solutions 'to an unknown problem, arrived at by unknown means'. The task of policing is so diffuse and wide-ranging that is impossible to come up with an a priori list of possible problems, the corollary being that potential solutions might be applied in an almost limitless set of circumstances. Discretion on what solution to use and when to use it is fundamental to the practice of police, and to limit it would not only fundamentally alter the nature of policing but would also make it less effective. As an important tool of policing, not least because it is less invasive than arrest, stop and search provides a potential 'solution' to an extremely large number of 'problems', and the ethics of its use – whether or not it is the right thing to do – will vary on an almost case-by-case basis.

Police discretion is also vital for another reason: it is impossible to enforce all laws, all of the time; or even for a fraction of the time (Goldstein 1963). Police are constantly engaged in the process of deciding when, where, and on whom the law should be applied, and for all that this is a highly imperfect process (the law is misapplied, the 'wrong' people are targeted) it is also inevitable. As Goldstein pointed out, it is, first, simply not feasible to enforce all laws or sanction their transgression in every case, not least because resources are limited. Second, police have other aims, such as 'keeping the peace' and assisting people in need, which can and do conflict with any requirement to enforce the law. To return to the example at hand, it might be argued that police should be required to stop and search an individual when, for example, they have a strong suspicion of drug use, and that this requirement might be offset by raising the 'reasonable suspicion' bar in some way, such that discretion is limited at the top and the bottom of the scale. But to impinge on discretion in this way would create more problems than it solved, as when, for example, a 'required' search might increase the risk of public disorder. Police officers are constantly engaged in balancing these types of competing demands.

We do not, then, focus on legal solutions in this chapter. This is not because we believe that the law has no place in regulating the power of the police, but rather because we take seriously the findings of 50 years of police research that has found legal regulation to be only one factor among many influencing police activity and, many would claim, a relatively minor one at that (Bittner 1990; Ericson 1982; Reiner 2010). We ask, instead, how and by whom can stop and search be effectively scrutinized, and how can change be effected, if its use is found to be out of kilter with norms of probity and justice. We discuss three possible ways that stop and search practice – and by extension other police activity – might be brought into and maintained within a set of ethical standards or constraints: (a) increased visibility; (b) extrinsic motivation of individuals and organizations; and (c) legitimacy and procedural justice inside and outside the police. These three headings are intended as heuristic rather than determinative categories, not least because there will plainly be significant overlap and interaction among them. They do, however, provide for a relatively wide-ranging set of possibilities. It is important to reiterate that legal proscription will have a part to play here, but it will inevitably be just one element of a wider process that, we might further suggest, will often exert pressure on police via one or more of the pathways we explore below.

Increased visibility

There is little doubt that policing is becoming more and more visible, in the sense that technological advances such as mobile phone cameras and Internet connections mean that police activity that was previously visible only to those 'at the scene' can now be recorded, uploaded, and viewed online more or less in real time (Goldsmith 2010). Social media ensure that the existence of any such recordings can be rapidly propagated, and there is an ever-increasing blurring of the lines between 'traditional' and 'new' media that can trigger significant repercussions from particular events, as witnessed most dramatically in the furore surrounding many recent police shootings in the United States. Sanders' (2008) call for 'anchored pluralism' in the regulation of police resonates with the idea that multiple actors can and should be involved in the monitoring of police via enhanced visibility. Whether policing is made visible by change within the service, via body worn video or similar technology, or outside the service via citizen 'sousveillance' (Mann et al. 2003) of the police, this process may provide for more effective monitoring of police and constitute a lever through which to exert pressure for change.

Considering the full effect of these developments on police behaviour is beyond the scope of this chapter. In a general sense, though, we concur with the argument that the advent of new communication technologies means it is "highly probable that the new capacities for surveillance of policing inherent in these technologies may increase the police's accountability to the public, while decreasing their account ability" – that is, their ability to provide definitive accounts of events that cannot effectively be challenged by other participants (Goldsmith 2010: 915). It is hard to imagine that such developments will not, to some extent at least, curtail and channel the power of police in new and in all likelihood more ethically desirable (less aggressive, more conciliatory) directions. As proponents of deterrence theory have long emphasized (Ariel et al. 2015: 516), even the suggestion of being watched can influence behaviour, for example if the revelation of non-compliance risks reputational damage or punishment. Yet new communication technologies do not offer a panacea, as the recent (at the time of writing in November 2015) string of recordings of aggressive, violent and lethal police actions in various parts of the United States attests. Being recorded on someone's mobile phone does not always deter police malpractice. Moreover, police often retain the ability to shape perceptions (most pertinently, in court) of what was reasonable or unreasonable to do in a given situation regardless of whether it happened to be caught on video or not (Brucato 2015).

One specific example of technological change is worthy of a little more consideration, however, precisely because it often *is* presented as a panacea (Ariel et al. 2015: 510) that will resolve deep-seated issues in the relationship between police and publics – body worn video cameras (hereafter, BWV). These devices are increasingly being taken up by police organizations in the United States, United Kingdom, and elsewhere (Jennings et al. 2014), and they have been welcomed by police and activist groups alike as a tool that will increase visibility and transparency and thus enhance accountability (Brucato 2015) via a new system of monitoring mechanisms that was simply unavailable a decade ago. In terms of our example in this chapter, one claim would be that stop/searches recorded by the police are less likely to escalate – since both parties are aware they are being recorded and adapt their behaviours to bring them in line with established behavioural norms in relation to, for example, fair process (Ariel et al. 2015) – and if encounters do become more problematic as a result of the behaviour of either party, a record of what transpired will exist to aid any subsequent investigation.

Again, this idea has face validity and seems likely to have some explanatory power. It would seem perverse to argue that the greater visibility provided by BWV will have no positive implications whatsoever. However as Brucato (2015) and others (e.g., Ledderman 2014) have argued there is significant danger in over-emphasizing their potential benefits. First and most obviously, the people wearing the cameras choose when to turn them on and off. The decision on what to record and for how long will rest with individual officers, and while guidelines or more formal rules will obviously play some role (Kitzmueller 2014) the discretion vested in those officers will still grant them significant control over what gets recorded. Yet this is just one example of what Brucato (2015) argues is a much wider problem – the use of mobile recording technology does not obviate, and may even strengthen, the symbolic and actual power of police to 'frame' what is recorded, both literally (events recorded on BWV are by definition shown from the officer's perspective) and figuratively. Despite increased challenges to their authority over recent years, police remain 'legitimate namers' (Loader and Mulcahy 2001), with a significant ability to define events and shape their resolution. To reiterate the point made above, this means that recordings from BWV are likely to be viewed from a police perspective and in a way that favours police interpretations of what transpired.

In sum, BWV and other ways of recording police activity are indeed likely to have made the activity more transparent and accountable, and possibly also more compliant with established norms of probity and fairness. However they do not constitute a magic wand, since they neither undermine the fundamental power of police to define events nor shift officer motivations much beyond reaction to a greater risk of being called out for inappropriate, undesirable or illegal behaviour. This last point is central. Almost all discussion of the influence of BWV and other recording technology on police officers has revolved around rational choice and deterrence theory – the presence of cameras deters them from behaviours they might otherwise have engaged in simply because the cameras increase the risk of censure and sanction. The emphasis is, then, on extrinsic motivations for behaviour that, we argue below, are not necessarily particularly strong or efficacious. On this basis alone increased surveillance of police is unlikely to solve on its own the problems thrown up by stop and search (and many other practices besides).

Extrinsic motivation of individuals and organizations

Extrinsic motivations relate in essence to enticements and punishments. Rational choice (risk and reward) models of human behaviour appear as dominant in the human resource departments of police organizations as they are in many other public- and private-sector organizations (Kohn 1999; Tyler 2011). Rewards (such as performance-related pay) and punishments (such as fixed limits on sickness absence) are frequently used to motivate staff. The core idea is that individual officers can be motivated to modulate or realign their behaviour by external pressures. First, they will comply with rules, or conform to priorities when they believe they will be punished in some way if they do not. Stop and search might be encouraged or discouraged, for example, by threatening front-line officers with sanction if they conduct too many, or not enough. Second, they will respond to the promise of reward, and comply and cooperate when they feel they will gain from doing so. Organizations can of course be influenced in cognate ways – by the threat of disapproval, opprobrium, or sanction from external actors who are symbolically, economically, or legally relevant, or by the promise of financial or other rewards from the same sources.

Tyler (2011: 27) contrasts such extrinsic motivations with intrinsic motivations that stem from personal values and moral beliefs (see below), and the efficacy of extrinsic motivations in relation to individuals is contested, despite the fact that their potential relevance in a hierarchical and quasi-military organization such as the police cannot be doubted. Police officers do act, and do refrain from acting, because they fear the threat of sanction or punishment. Perhaps more importantly, though, it seems almost certain that police organizations are open to influence via, in particular, the threat of sanction or disapproval from legally or politically relevant actors – particularly those with control legislation and/or budgets.

An example of just such a process has been observed in London in recent years precisely in the arena of stop and search. Following a peak in the numbers of stop and searches around 2010/11, and a corresponding upsurge in the level of dispute around the practice – some of which was shaped by the aftermath of London riots in 2011 – the Home Secretary Theresa May made a number of highly critical comments about the Metropolitan Police's (MPS) use of the power, which she repeated on numerous occasions over the next few years. In April 2014, for example, she said in Parliament that 'if the numbers do not come down, if stop and search does not become more targeted, if those stop-to-arrest ratios do not improve considerably, the government will return with primary legislation to make those things happen' (Guardian 2014). In the face of threats of an enforced change to its practice – and perhaps equally importantly in reaction to the stigma associated with such a threat – it appears the MPS made significant changes in relation to the use of stop and search; or, at least, it encouraged its officers to do so. Over 468,000 stop and searches under PACE section 1 and associated powers were conducted in London in 2011/12;[1] by the calendar year 2014 this had fallen to less than 200,000.[2] As noted above, arrest rates increased over the same period. It is important to note here that the use of power was not changed by legislation, but, apparently, by the mere threat of legislation, and the political pressure exerted by police not only by the Home Secretary but by activist groups as well (e.g., Release 2014).

Despite such apparent successes, however, it is unlikely that extrinsic motivations in relation to either officers or organization will be enough on their own to maintain an appropriate level of constraint on police power – or of ethical practice – in this or any other area. Notably, there was a previous reduction in the use of stop and search, and in ethnic disproportionality, in England and Wales around the time of the Stephen Lawrence enquiry in 1999. It is generally hypothesized that this reduction reflected, at least in part, a change in police practice in the face of significant public and political scrutiny in the wake of the scandal the enquiry uncovered (e.g., Shiner and Delsol 2015). However, as the political agenda changed and shifted focus in the early years of the new millennium the use of stop and search, and ethnic disproportionality, increased significantly. By the middle of the decade both had surpassed previous levels.

Extrinsic motivations are by nature short-lived and even transitory. Individuals shift back to previous behaviour patterns once threats and rewards lose salience. This is a key criticism of, for example, performance related pay (Frey and Osterloh 2012; Perry et al. 2009) – it does not motivate long-term change to attitudes and behaviours. It seems organizations are much the same. Moreover the overall effect of even fundamental changes to the legal framework around stop and search – that might be expected to generate changes in practice by shifting structures of risk – is contested. Sanders (2008) claims, for example, that the introduction of PACE actually did little to affect street-level police practice, certainly as the 'shock' of its introduction receded. Of course, we might also note that there have been few if any convictions or other sanctions of officers for breaking the PACE guidelines (c.f. HMIC 2013) and, of course, that many 'police stops' occur entirely outside the framework it established.

Legitimacy and procedural justice inside and outside the police

Our third set of possible ways to regulate the power of the police and motivate ethical practice revolves around the relationship the police have with the policed, and the ways in which officers behaviour affects this relationship. In our view, the need for police to retain a certain level of legitimacy among the populations they serve provides an important empirical constraint on their behaviour and, moreover that processes of legitimation within the police may be critical for understanding how officers behave in relation to citizens.

The most important understanding of the relationship people have with police and other legal authorities is currently provided by work conducted under the banner of procedural justice theory. Developed by Tom Tyler and colleagues in the US (Sunshine and Tyler, 2003; Tyler 2006; Tyler and Blader 2000; Tyler and Huo 2002) and increasingly applied in contexts across the world (e.g., Hinds and Murphy 2007; Tankebe 2009; Hasisi and Weisburd 2011; Huq et al. 2011; Murphy and Cherney 2012; Factor et al. 2013; Mazerolle et al. 2012; Jackson et al. 2014; Bradford et al. 2014; Slocum et al. 2015; Pennington 2015; Cheng 2015; Saarikkomäki 2015; Akinlabi 2015; Van Damme 2015; Wolfe et al. 2015; Mclean and Wolfe 2015; Reisig and Bain 2015; Bieijersbergen et al. 2015; Murphy et al. 2016), procedural justice theory stresses the social connection between criminal justice agencies and the populations they serve. Studies of the general population have found that people regard the police as legitimate when and if they believe officers exercise their authority through fair and impartial means – that is, when they behave in a procedurally just manner (Sunshine and Tyler 2003a; Tyler and Huo 2002; Jackson et al. 2013).

There is also some evidence of procedural justice effects among what might be termed 'offender populations' (Paternoster et al. 1997; Papachristos et al. 2012; Murphy et al. 2016) and in relation to other criminal justice agencies, for example prisons, which unlike the police deal primarily with such populations (Sparks et al. 1996; Robinson and McNeil 2008; Liebling 2004; Brunton-Smith and McCarthy 2015). It seems that the associations between experiences of policing, trust and legitimacy described above are found among social groups or categories of individual who might be expected to be alienated from the police and thus uninterested in the expressive aspects of police behaviour, although this is not of course to claim that procedural justice effects are in any sense universal.

Procedural justice is marked and demonstrated by transparency and fair, equitable, and respectful treatment, following correct procedure and not exhibiting bias, as well as a feeling of control over the processes through which people interact with authorities. People place particular value on voice (Hirschman 1970) and neutrality on the part of the authority; they like to be treated with respect and dignity, and they value a sense of trust. The term 'procedural justice' refers neither to process in a technical sense – for example, court process or police protocol – nor to justice in a normative or philosophical sense. Rather, what is at stake is individuals' subjective judgements about the quality of interpersonal interaction with police officers and the openness of police decision-making processes that affect them. Treatment that is experienced as fair, decent and respectful encourages people to trust the police; a general perception that police behave in a fair way promotes a similar sense of trust. Despite the lack of formal correspondence between 'procedural justice' and more legally informed notions of 'fair process' it is an interesting feature of procedural justice theory that there is a significant overlap between lay understandings of the way criminal justice agencies should behave and institutional and legal structures intended to govern their behaviour – what in the US might be termed 'due process' and a respect for individual's rights, for example – which are themselves oriented toward objective criteria of justice and probity.[3]

Importantly, research has failed to find consistent links between perceptions of the instrumental effectiveness of police and legitimacy (ironically, perhaps, if police officers believe that their legitimacy is earnt by effectiveness and not procedural justice; see Nix, 2015). While in some contexts, such as developing countries (Bradford et al. 2014; Tankebe 2009), it may be that efficacy and efficiency are strongly linked to legitimacy, studies conducted in developed countries regularly find only weak associations between measures of police effectiveness (for example in dealing with crimes or maintaining order) and measures of legitimacy (for an overview of the European context see Hough et al. 2013). Just as it seems that deterrence – the demonstration of effectiveness – has relatively little direct influence on offending (although it can have some), effectiveness has relatively little direct association with legitimacy (although, again, it can have some).

The work of legitimacy

Police rely on the legitimacy they command to operate effectively (Tyler 2003, 2004). If procedural justice theory is correct that legitimacy is founded most importantly in the use of fair process, then the constant need to establish and reproduce legitimacy may serve as an important check on police power (Sunshine and Tyler 2003; Tyler 2006; Hough et al. 2013). While such power may, in a conceptual sense, be 'unlimited' – since the police are the arm of that the state charged with confronting all possible internal threats to its integrity and effective functioning (see Dubber 2005) – it is limited in an empirical sense by the need for police to ensure they do not behave in ways that consistently challenge their legitimacy and which might, in the long run, undermine or even remove it. Should this occur, the very existence of the organization would be called into question – the ultimate extrinsic motivation, perhaps. What this means is that police cannot simply 'do what they want', despite the extent of the power vested in them, and this is for reasons less to do with the law (although the law will of course be relevant in some circumstances) and more to do with the fact that every interaction they have with citizens is a moment in which legitimacy is tested, proved, or undermined (Tyler 2011).

There are, however, some important provisos to this argument. First, it is obvious that police organizations can and do act in ways that run against dominant norms of probity and fairness without necessarily undermining their legitimacy in any fundamental sense. There are too many examples to count, but one is the continued over-use and even abuse of stop and search/frisk, which all available evidence suggests has been used unjustly on many occasions in the UK and elsewhere. Not only has the legitimacy of the police not collapsed as a result of this; public support for the use of stop and search remains, in a general sense, high.

Second, and relatedly, police behaviour that runs counter to norms of procedural justice can be, and is, tolerated by some individuals and groups if it is directed at denigrated or excluded out-groups. Indeed, since procedural justice is not the only factor shaping legitimacy, there may be significant numbers of people who might in fact respond positively to police 'cracking down' on out-groups and grant legitimacy on that basis, at least to some degree (c.f. Harkin 2014).

Third, it is likely that legitimacy can create the possibility for acting beyond established norms, or against community wishes, since it creates a reservoir of good will on which police can draw and against which they may discount specific transgressions; a notion akin to Easton's

(1965) concept of diffuse support. There are historical resonances here, in that police abuses in the past were almost certainly facilitated by the unquestioning adherence of large sections of the population to the legitimacy of the police (see, for example, Royal Commission on the Police 1962): high levels of legitimacy created the space in which police malpractice could flourish. However, as the history of policing in a country such as the UK shows, this reservoir can be drained, not least by reports of police misbehaviour and corruption (Bradford 2011).

Fourth, the external notion of legitimacy positions the organizational need for legitimacy as a kind of 'natural' constraint on police power because this legitimacy rests on citizens' experiences of the fairness of police activity. However, to the extent that the police do not rely on the policed for legitimacy (i.e., where it is granted directly by the state or by some other authority), the need to reproduce legitimacy will provide much less of a constraint on behaviour.

Encouraging legitimate policing

Provisos aside, it can be argued that the need to establish and reproduce legitimacy serves, at least in a country such as the UK, as an important check on police power. Because abiding by established norms of fairness is such an important factor shaping legitimacy, police have a strong motivation to engage in ethically desirable practice; yet this raises an important question. How can officers be encouraged to behave in ways that produce and reproduce legitimacy? It is highly unlikely that such behaviour will simply arise organically, not least because of the well-known disconnect between the 'police culture' emphasis on crime-fighting and thief-taking and the prioritization of procedural justice among large sections of the population (Jonathan-Zamir et al. 2014). It seems that for many police, the way to generate legitimacy is to demonstrate firm effectiveness and not to treat people with procedural fairness. Equally, the pressures and conflicting priorities under which most police operate might seem inimical to the development of relationships with the policed based on fairness and shared interests – to police, that is, procedural justice often seems nice to do but not essential (Foster et al. 2010). And if legitimacy as a motivating factor remains extrinsic, tied to external forces to which police merely respond, then as argued above it is likely to provide only a weak check on practice in the long run. An upswing in public concerns about fairness might affect police practice in the short term, but once the spotlight of media and/or political attention turns elsewhere things are likely to return to the status quo ante.

There is, however, an emerging body of evidence that police activity – the actions of individual police officers and the values that underpin them – can be influenced by procedural justice within the organization. Just as members of the public value fairness, openness, honesty, and respect in their interactions with police, so officers value these same features of their relationships with their superiors (Bradford et al. 2013; Bradford and Quinton 2014; Haas et al. 2015; Myhill and Bradford 2013; Tankebe 2011; Wolfe and Piquero 2011). Research has shown that 'organizational justice', a term generally assigned a meaning very close to that of procedural justice (Colquitt et al. 2001; Colquitt et al. 2008), can enhance positive forms of identification with the police organization and promote commitment to organization goals and norms and is associated both with positive views about procedural justice and community based modes of policing and lower levels of misconduct.

While little research thus far has directly addressed the issues at hand, it seems that one possible way to regulate the power of the police is to ensure that those wielding this power – street-level officers – are treated in as organizationally just a manner as possible by their managers and superiors. Particularly striking is research that suggests fairness within police organizations is associated with greater 'buy-in' to organizational goals (Bradford et al. 2013; Bradford and

Quinton 2014; Myhill and Bradford 2013; Tankebe 2011), and a diminished adherence to problematic beliefs and behaviours (Wolfe and Piquero 2011). On these accounts, if police organizations set the correct goals – for example in relation to the appropriate use of powers such as stop and search – and communicate these to staff effectively, then compliance with them would be promoted by the use of fair processes within the organization. At one level, this appears as a version of social exchange theory – the 'reward' of fair treatment (as a form of emotional resource) is linked in a reciprocal relationship with behaviours that actors believe will stimulate the reward in the future. Much work on organizational justice, however, shares with procedural justice theory (e.g., Bradford et al. 2014) the idea that fairness at the hands of group authorities – in this case superiors within a work setting – promotes identification with the organization as a social group and, over time, internalization of its aims and values (Tyler and Blader 2000, 2003).

Organizational justice – and the positive identification with the police organization that it engenders – has also been directly linked to processes of internal legitimacy development (Bottoms and Tankebe 2012; Bradford and Quinton 2014). Processes of legitimation are intimately linked with processes of identification (Barker 1991), and those with power and authority in a particular context are constantly engaged in generating a narrative that both justifies their power – turning it into authority in their own minds – and elides the difference between the self and the role. 'Self-legitimacy', in these terms, is an important motivator of behaviour, enabling actions by providing them with direction and meaning. Behaviour that fits a self-legitimating narrative reinforces the feeling of justified authority that is required by those in power if they are to maintain an appropriate image of themselves and confidence in their own authority. This narrative also helps constitute a set of claims to legitimacy and is a key part of the legitimacy dialogue envisaged by Bottoms and Tankebe (2012).

Bradford and Quinton (2014) found that identification with the police organization was very strongly correlated with officers' confidence in their own authority (their sense that their use of power was justified), and that both identification and self-legitimacy predicted attitudes towards policing means, such as the appropriate use of force, and ends, such as protecting suspects' rights. Working with a sample of police officers from an English constabulary, they argued that identification with the police force promoted 'buy-in' to its values, and promoting or acting on these values became an important part of the officers' construction of self and understanding of themselves as figures of authority in society.

There is a possibility, therefore, that there is a virtuous circle that links organizational justice within the police organization, through officer's identification as police, to their sense that their power and authority are justified. Identification and legitimation motivate attitudes and behaviours that 'fit' with the narrative of justified authority of which they are part. The obvious problem is that identification and legitimation within police organizations might, absent a clearly expressed and honestly held set of ethical goals and criteria for success, encourage officers to behave in ways different to those outlined above. That is, the narrative of policing has to be based on a more or less clearly expressed set of ends and means, and these have to be the right ends and means in an ethical sense for the above process to be considered 'virtuous'. Police organizations need to communicate clearly to staff about how they are expected to behave and why, if organizational justice is to lead to or promote ethical behaviour 'on the streets'. Because officers internalize the values the organization expresses to them as part of the process of identification and legitimation, it follows that if these are the wrong values then behaviours that reinforce the narrative of self-legitimacy might look rather different.

Stop and search again provides a useful example of this latter kind of process. As suggested above police organizations all too often over-stress, to both internal and external audiences, the need for and desirability of instrumental effectiveness in relation to crime over other aspects of police work, such as its more service- and even social service-related aspects (Punch 1979). Based in some of the classic elements of 'police culture', such as the thin blue line ideology and the emphasis on 'thief-taking' (Reiner 2010) and also the continued dominance of deterrence-based thinking in police policy and political discourse, this emphasis communicates to officers that what is really important is 'getting results'. This in turn becomes a value and an aim, working towards which is integrated into their identity as police officers and their sense of their own legitimacy. Stop and search practice – more or less pro-active policing aimed at solving or preventing crimes and asserting order on the streets – may then be an important element in officers' self-legitimacy and the legitimation claims they make to others. Despite the problematic history of stop and search, this is a power that can nevertheless represent the activity of policing in important ways, its chance for success and the place of police in wider society. Stop and search may serve as a mechanism through which legitimacy is claimed; the need to make such claims, and the types of benefits they might bring for police if successful, may provide one set of reasons for its continued use.

It is also undoubtedly the case that there is significant support for stop and search – and pro-active and even aggressive policing styles more generally – among the general public, certainly in a general sense and, on occasion, in specific instances (Fitzgerald et al. 2002). Pro-active, and sometimes aggressive, policing is popular among a significant proportion of the population, at least as long as it is not aimed at them (Girling et al. 2000), and it is not entirely unreasonable for police managers to respond to such preferences by encouraging officers to use stop and search. In other words, as well as pressure from within the service that can be both cultural and managerial, there are external factors that may encourage police to believe increased, or at least continued, use of stop and search is not only acceptable but desirable and supported by the communities they serve. Responding to community priorities is central to legitimation processes, at least in as much as these are embedded in discursive or dialogical forms of legitimacy, and we should not imagine that such community priorities revolve only around procedural justice. Most obviously, significant numbers of people in many social settings will, as noted, wish police to target and control 'difficult', 'recalcitrant', or simply different population groups, and the extent to which they grant police legitimacy will be based, in part, on the perceived success or failure of such efforts.

The key to ethical practice in this area would thus seem to be promotion of organizational structures and processes that encourage appeals to notions of fairness, dignity, and respect that cross the boundaries of the police organization (i.e., that are important both within it and in its relationship with external actors) while at the same time minimizing the valence of more atavistic strands of public opinion. Stop and search stands for a much wider set of police powers, practices, and policies situated in the nexus formed by these competing forces. Indeed, providing at least a provisional reconciliation of these forces – charting a course between the need to be responsive to the desires and wishes of the policed and the need to resist some of those desires – is, arguably, a key task of the police: albeit one it often fails to live up to.

Some closing words

Our discussion in this chapter has emphasized the need for those at the top of police organizations to promote ethical policing practice that will, in as much as it is based on fair process, serve to bolster legitimacy. Equally, the reconfiguration of internal structures along the lines of organizational justice should motivate individual officers to internalize such values and enact them in their day-to-day activity. These processes can and indeed possibly do place ethical constraints around the exercise of discretionary police power, and we have considered in this chapter the idea that legitimacy inside and outside the police provides a useful source of moral regulation – particularly when the need or desire to reproduce legitimacy is operative within a context marked by high levels of visibility around policing.

Yet, while the quest to win and maintain legitimacy through fair, neutral, and equitable policing may be an important constraint on police power, its usefulness relies to a significant degree on the extent to which police (a) understand and act on what people 'really want' from policing but also (b) are operating according to a set of normatively justifiable set of ends and means. The empirical legitimacy of the police is not an absolute limit on the exercise of police power; the extent to which (the need for) legitimacy constrains police action is conditioned on the criteria used by the policed to assess the police. In as much as their assessments revolve around principles of procedural justice, police power will be constrained and channelled in ethically desirable directions. Where other factors become more important, this restraint may be attenuated and even removed. One obvious conclusion here is, unsurprisingly, that recourse to normative concepts of legitimacy is needed to 'ground' this relationship in a set of objective criteria against which police can be judged. It will not be enough to claim, or even demonstrate, that there is widespread public support for police activity – this activity must also be held up against ethical and legal norms that establish its legitimacy in a quite different sense.

Of yet more concern is the possibility that legitimacy also enables malpractice. Our claim that it is a useful constraint on police power is empirical rather than normative, and it is easy to envisage situations where there is 'too much' legitimacy, a state of affairs that would seem likely to open up space for, allow, and even encourage normatively undesirable police activity. As noted above, there is much to suggest that, historically, a broadly unquestioned legitimacy allowed the British police to get away with if not necessarily murder then often something very close. Which is to claim that there is a significant, and probably irreconcilable, tension – or even paradox – at the heart of our argument. Police need legitimacy to survive, and are thus constrained in their use of power by the need to demonstrate procedural and other forms of fairness. But legitimacy also enables police to wield their power, provides a reservoir of support in the face of individual malpractice, and possibly even mandates problematic modes of policing. The interplay between these countervailing factors, and their particular configuration at any point in time, is likely to have a significant effect on practices such as stop and search events – the ends towards which they are directed, how they are conducted, and the ways they are experienced by the policed.

Notes

1 http://www.stop-watch.org/your-area/area/metropolitan.
2 'MPS stops and searches monitoring mechanism', January 2015. Available at: http://www.met.police.uk/foi/pdfs/priorities_and_how_we_are_doing/borough/mps_stop_search_mon_report_january2015.pdf.
3 Although we note, of course, that these regulations are often honoured more in the breach than in the observance, and that criminal justice agencies often behave in ways that are subjectively and objectively unfair.

Bibliography

Akinlabi, O.M. (2015) 'Young people, procedural justice and police legitimacy in Nigeria', *Policing and Society Online First*, pp. 1–20.

Añón, J.G., Bradford, B., Sàez, J.A.G., Cuenca, A.G. and Ferreres, A.L. (2013) *Identificación policial po perfil étnico en España*, Valencia: Tirant lo Blanch.

Barker, R. (2001) *Legitimating Identities*, Cambridge: Cambridge University Press.

Barragan, M., Sherman, N., Reiter, K. and Tita, G. E. (2015) '"Damned if you do, damned if you don't" perceptions of guns, safety, and legitimacy among detained gun offenders', *Criminal Justice and Behavior*, 0093854815611707.

Beijersbergen, K.A., Dirkzwager, A.J. and Nieuwbeerta, P. (2015) 'Reoffending after release: does procedural justice during imprisonment matter?', *Criminal Justice and Behavior*, 0093854815609643.

Bittner, E. (1974) 'Florence Nightingale in pursuit of Willie Sutton: a theory of the police', in H. Jacob (ed.) *The Potential for Reform of Criminal Justice*, Beverly Hills, CA: Sage Publications, pp. 17–40.

Bittner, E. (1990) *Aspects of Police Work*, Boston, MA: Boston University Press.

Bottoms, A. and Tankebe, J. (2012) 'Beyond procedural justice: a dialogic approach to legitimacy in criminal justice', *Journal of Criminal Law and Criminology*, 102(1): 119–70.

Bowling, B. and Phillips, C. (2002) *Racism, Crime and Justice*, Harlow: Pearson Education.

Bowling, B. and Phillips, C. (2007) 'Disproportionate and discriminatory: reviewing the evidence on police stop and search', *Modern Law Review*, 70: 936–61.

Bradford, B. and Loader, I. (in press) 'Police, crime and order: the case of stop and search', in B. Bradford, B. Jauregui, I. Loader and J. Steinberg (eds.) *The SAGE Handbook of Global Policing Studies*, London: Sage.

Bradford, B. and Quinton, P. (2014) 'Self-legitimacy, police culture and support for democratic policing in an English Constabulary', *British Journal of Criminology*, 54(6): 1023–46.

Bradford, B., Huq, A., Jackson, J. and Roberts, B. (2014) 'What price fairness when security is at stake? Police legitimacy in South Africa', *Regulation and Governance*, 8(2): 246–68.

Bradford, B., Murphy, K. and Jackson, J. (2014) 'Officers as mirrors: policing, procedural justice and the (re)production of social identity', *British Journal of Criminology*, 54(4): 527–50.

Bradford, B., Quinton, P., Myhill, A. and Porter, G. (2013) 'Why do "the law" comply? Procedural justice, group identification and officer motivation in police organizations', *European Journal of Criminology*, 11(1): 110–31.

Brodeur, J.-P. (2010) *The Policing Web*, Oxford: Oxford University Press.

Brucato, B. (2015) 'Policing made visible: mobile technologies and the importance of point of view', *Surveillance & Society*, 13(3/4): 455.

Brunton-Smith, I. and McCarthy, D.J. (2015) 'Prison legitimacy and procedural fairness: a multilevel examination of prisoners in England and Wales', *Justice Quarterly* (ahead-of-print): 1–26.

Cheng, K.K.Y. (2015) 'Prosecutorial procedural justice and public legitimacy in Hong Kong', *British Journal of Criminology*, azv106.

Colquitt, J. (2008) 'Two decades of organizational justice: findings, controversies, and future directions', in C. Cooper and J. Barling (eds.) *The Sage Handbook of Organizational Behavior,* Newbury Park, CA: Sage, pp. 73–88.

Colquitt, J., Conlon, D., Wesson, M., Porter, C. and Ng, K. (2001) 'Justice at the millennium: a meta-analytic review of 25 years of organizational justice research', *Journal of Applied Psychology*, 86: 425–45.

Delsol, R. and Shiner, M. (2006) 'Regulating stop and search: a challenge for police and community relations in England and Wales', *Critical Criminology*, 14: 241–63.

Dixon, D. (2008) 'Authorise and regulate: a comparative perspective on the rise and fall of a regulatory strategy', in E. Cape and R. Young (eds.) *Regulating Policing. The Police and Criminal Evidence Act 1984: Past, Present and Future*, Oxford: Hart, pp. 21–44.

Dubber M. (2005) *The Police Power. Patriarchy and the Foundations of American Government,* New York, NY: Columbia University Press.

Easton, D. (1965). *A Systems Analysis of Political Life,* Chicago, IL: University of Chicago Press.

Epp, C.R., Maynard-Moody, S. and Haider-Markel, D.P. (2014) *Pulled Over: How Police Stops Define Race and Citizenship*, Chicago, IL: University of Chicago Press.

Ericson, R.V. (1982) *Reproducing Order: A Study of Police Patrol Work,* Toronto: University of Toronto Press.

Factor, R., Mahalel, D., Rafaeli, A. and Williams, D.R. (2013) 'A social resistance perspective for delinquent behavior among non-dominant minority groups', *British Journal of Criminology*, 53(5): 784–804.

Fitzgerald, M., Hough, M., Joseph, I. and Querish, T. (2002) *Policing for London,* Cullompton: Willan.

Foster, J. and Jones, C. (2010) '"Nice to do but not essential": neighbourhood police officers' views on community engagement and citizen focus in an English police force', *Policing: An International Journal of Policy and Practice.*

Frey, B.S. and Osterloh, M. (2012) 'Stop tying pay to performance. The evidence is overwhelming: it doesn't work,' *Harvard Business Review,* January–February.

Geller, A., Fagan, J., Tyler, T.R. and Link, B. (2014) 'Aggressive policing and the mental health of young urban men', *American Journal of Public Health*, 104(12): 2321–27.

Girling, E., Loader, I. and Sparks, R. (2000) *Crime and Social Change in Middle England*, London: Routledge.

Glaser, J. (2015) *Suspect Race. Causes and Consequences of Racial Profiling,* Oxford: Oxford University Press.

Goldsmith, A.J. (2010) 'Policing's new visibility', *British Journal of Criminology*, 50(5): 914–34.

Goldstein, H. (1963) 'Police discretion: the ideal versus the real', *Public Administration Review*, 23(3): 140–48.

Guardian. (2014) 'Theresa May announces reform of police stop-and-search powers', *The Guardian*, London, 30 April 2014.

Haas, N.E., Van Craen, M., Skogan, W.G. and Fleitas, D.M. (2015) 'Explaining officer compliance: the importance of procedural justice and trust inside a police organization', *Criminology and Criminal Justice*, 1748895814566288.

Harkin, D. (2014) 'The police and punishment: understanding the pains of policing', *Theoretical Criminology*, 19(1): 43–58.

Hasisi, B. and Weisburd, D. (2011) 'Going beyond ascribed identities: the importance of procedural justice in airport security screening in Israel', *Law and Society Review*, 45(4): 867–92.

Hinds, L. and Murphy, K. (2007) 'Public satisfaction with police: using procedural justice to improve police legitimacy', *Australian and New Zealand Journal of Criminology*, 40: 27–42.

Hirschman, A.O. (1970) *Exit, Voice, and Loyalty: Responses to Decline in Firms, Organizations, and States,* Cambridge, MA: Harvard University Press.

HMIC. (2013) *Stop and Search Powers: Are the Police Using them Effectively and Fairly?*, London: Her Majesties Inspectorate of Constabulary.

Hough, M., Jackson, J. and Bradford, B. (2013) 'The governance of criminal justice, legitimacy and trust', in S. Body-Gendrot, R. Lévy, M. Hough, S. Snacken and K. Kerezsi (eds.) *The Routledge Handbook of European Criminology*, Oxon: Routledge, pp. 243–65.

Huq, A.Z., Tyler, T.R. and Schulhofer, S.J. (2011) 'Mechanisms for eliciting cooperation in counterterrorism policing: a study of British Muslims', *Journal of Empirical Legal Studies*, 8(4): 728–61.

Jackson, J., Asif, M., Bradford, B. and Zakar, M.Z. (2014) 'Corruption and police legitimacy in Lahore, Pakistan', *British Journal of Criminology*, 54(6): 1067–88, doi: 10.1093/bjc/azu069.

Jackson, J., Bradford, B., Hough, M., Myhill, A., Quinton, P. and Tyler, T.R. (2012). 'Why do people comply with the law? Legitimacy and the influence of legal institutions', *British Journal of Criminology*, 52(6): 1051–71.

Jackson, J., Bradford, B., Stanko, E.A. and Hohl, K. (2012), *Just Authority? Trust in the Police in England and Wales*. London: Routledge.

Jackson, J., Huq, A.Z., Bradford, B. and Tyler, T.R. (2013) 'Monopolizing force? Police legitimacy and public attitudes towards the acceptability of violence', *Psychology, Public Policy and Law*, 19(4): 479–97.

Jonathan-Zamir, T. and Harpaz, A. (2014) 'Police understanding of the foundations of their legitimacy in the eyes of the public: the case of commanding officers in the Israel National Police', *British Journal of Criminology*, 54(3): 469–89.

Karakus, O. (2015) 'Instrumental and normative pathways to legitimacy and public cooperation with the police in Turkey: considering perceived neighborhood characteristics and local government performance', *Justice Quarterly*: 1–30.

Keith, M. (1993) *Race, Riots and Policing: Lore and Disorder in a Multi-Racist Society*, London: UCL Press.

Kitzmueller, M. (2014) 'Are you recording this? Enforcement of police videotaping', *Conn. L. Rev.*, 47: 167–196.

Kochel, T.R., Parks, R. and Mastrofski, S.D. (2013) 'Examining police effectiveness as a precursor to legitimacy and cooperation with police', *Justice Quarterly*, 30(5): 895–925.

Kohn, A. (1999) *Punished by Rewards,* Boston, MA: Houghton Mifflin.

Lederman, R. (2014) *More copwatchers! Less cops w cameras!* March 13, 2014. http://wecopwatch.org/police-camerasquick-fix-for-police-misconduct-or-counter-surveillance-tool/ (Accessed 9 March 2016).

Legewie, J. (2016) 'Racial profiling and use of force in police stops: how local events trigger periods of increased discrimination', working chapter, NYU.

Liebling, A. (2004) *Prisons and Their Moral Performance: A Study of Values, Quality and Prison Life,* Oxford: Oxford University Press.

Loader, I. and Mulcahy, A. (2001) 'The power of legitimate naming. Part I—Chief constables as social commentators in post-war England', *British Journal of Criminology*, 41(1): 41–55.

Mann, S., Nolan, J. and Wellman, B. (2003) 'Sousveillance: inventing and using wearable computing devices for data collection in surveillance environments', *Surveillance and Society,* 1(3): 331–55.

Mazerolle, L., Antrobus, E., Bennet, S. and Tyler, T.R. (2012) 'Shaping citizen perceptions of police legitimacy: a randomized field trial of procedural justice', *Criminology*, 51(1): 33–64.

McLean, K. and Wolfe, S.E. (2015) 'A sense of injustice loosens the moral bind of law specifying the links between procedural injustice, neutralizations, and offending', *Criminal Justice and Behavior*, 0093854815609655.

Medina Ariza, J.J. (2014) 'Police-initiated contacts: young people, ethnicity, and the "usual suspects"', *Policing and Society*, 24(2): 208–23.

Miller, J. and D'Souza, A. (2015) 'Indirect effects of police searches on community attitudes to the police: resentment or reassurance?', *British Journal of Criminology*, azv068.

Murphy, K. and Cherney, A. (2012) 'Understanding cooperation with police in a diverse society', *British Journal of Criminology*, 52(1): 181–201.

Murphy, T., Bradford, B. and Jackson, J. (2015) 'Motivating compliance behavior among tax offenders: procedural justice or deterrence?', *Criminal Justice & Behavior*, 43(1): 102–118.

Murray, K. (2014) *Stop and Search in Scotland: An Evaluation of Police Practice.* SCCJR Report 01/2014.

Myhill, A. and Bradford, B. (2013) 'Overcoming cop culture? Organizational justice and police officers' attitudes toward the public', *Policing: An International Journal of Police Strategies and Management*, 36(2): 338–56.

Nix, J. (2015) 'Do the police believe that legitimacy promotes cooperation from the public?', *Crime and Delinquency,* On-line first.

Open Society Justice Initiative. (2009) *Ethnic Profiling in the European Union: Pervasive, Ineffective and Discriminatory,* New York, NY: Open Society Institute.

Papachristos, A.V., Meares, T.L. and Fagan, J. (2012) 'Why do criminals obey the law? The influence of legitimacy and social networks on active gun offenders', *Journal of Criminal Law and Criminology*, 102(2): 397–440.

Paternoster, R., Brame, R., Bachman, R. and Sherman, L.W. (1997) 'Do fair procedures matter? The effect of procedural justice on spouse assault', *Law and Society Review*, 163–204.

Pennington, L. (2015) 'A case study approach to procedural justice: parents' views in two juvenile delinquency courts in the United States', *British Journal of Criminology*, 55(5): 901–920.

Perry J.L., Engbers T.A. and Jun S.O. (2009) 'Back to the future? Performance-related pay, empirical research, and the perils of persistence', *Public Administration Review,* January/February: 39–51.

Punch, M. (1979) 'The secret social service', in S. Holdaway (ed.) *The British Police,* London: Edward Arnold.

Reiner, R. (2010). *The Politics of the Police,* 4th edn, Oxford: Oxford University Press.

Reisig, M.D. and Bain, S.N. (2015) 'University legitimacy and student compliance with academic dishonesty codes: a partial test of the process-based model of self-regulation', *Criminal Justice and Behavior*, 0093854815611165.

Release. (2014) *The Numbers in Black and White: Ethnic Disparities in the Policing and Prosecution of Drug Offences in England and Wales.* London: Release.

Robinson, G. and McNeill, F. (2008) 'Exploring the dynamics of compliance with community penalties', *Theoretical Criminology*, 12(4): 431–49.

Royal Commission on the Police. (1962) *Final Report.* London: HMSO. Cmnd 1728.

Saarikkomäki, E. (2015) 'Perceptions of procedural justice among young people: narratives of fair treatment in young people's stories of police and security guard interventions', *British Journal of Criminology*, azv102.

Sanders, A. (2008) 'Can coercive powers be effectively controlled or regulated? The case for anchored pluralism', in E. Cape and R. Young (eds.) *Regulating Policing. The Police and Criminal Evidence Act 1984: Past, Present and Future,* Oxford: Hart, pp. 45–74.

Shiner, M. and Delsol, R. (2015) 'The politics of the powers', in R. Delsol and M. Shiner (eds.) *Stop and Search: The Anatomy of a Police Power,* Basingstoke: Palgrave MacMillan, pp. 31–57.

Slocum, L.A., Wiley, S.A. and Esbensen, F.A. (2015) 'The importance of being satisfied: a longitudinal exploration of police contact, procedural injustice, and subsequent delinquency', *Criminal Justice and Behavior*, 0093854815609069.

Smith, D. and Gray, J. (1985) *Police and People in London: A Survey of Londoners,* London: Policy Studies Institute.

Sparks, J.R., Bottoms, A. and Hay, W. (1996) *Prisons and the Problem of Order,* Oxford: Clarendon Press.

Sunshine, J. and Tyler, T.R. (2003) 'The role of procedural justice and legitimacy in shaping public support for policing'. *Law and Society Review*, 37: 513–48.

Tankebe, J. (2009) 'Public cooperation with the police in Ghana: does procedural fairness matter?', *Criminology*, 47(4): 1265–93.

Tankebe, J. (2010) 'Public confidence in the police: testing the effects of public experiences of police corruption in Ghana', *British Journal of Criminology*, 50(2): 296–319.
Tankebe, J. (2011) 'Explaining police support for use of force and vigilante violence in Ghana', *Policing and Society*, 21(2): 129–49.
Tyler, T.R. (2006) *Why People Obey the Law* 2nd edn, New Haven, CT: Yale University Press.
Tyler, T.R. (2011) 'Trust and legitimacy: policing in the US and Europe', *European Journal of Criminology*, 8(4): 254–66.
Tyler, T.R. and Blader, S. (2000) *Cooperation in Groups: Procedural Justice, Social Identity, and Behavioral Engagement,* Philadelphia, PA: Psychology Press.
Tyler, T.R. and Blader, S. (2003) 'Procedural justice, social identity, and cooperative behavior', *Personality and Social Psychology Review*, 7: 349–61.
Tyler, T.R. and Fagan, J. (2008) 'Why do people cooperate with the police?', *Ohio State Journal of Criminal Law*, 6: 231–75.
Tyler, T.R., Fagan, J.A. and Geller, A. (2014) 'Street stops and police legitimacy: teachable Moments in young urban men's legal socialization', *Journal of Empirical Legal Studies*, 11(4): 751–85.
Tyler, T.R. and Huo, Y.J. (2002) *Trust in the Law: Encouraging Public Cooperation with the Police and Courts*, New York, NY: Russell-Sage Foundation.
Tyler, T.R. and Jackson, J. (2014) 'Popular legitimacy and the exercise of legal authority: motivating compliance, cooperation and engagement', *Psychology, Public Policy and Law*, 20(1): 78–95.
Tyler, T.R., Jackson, J. and Mentovich, A. (2015) 'On the consequences of being a target of suspicion: potential pitfalls of proactive police contact', *Journal of Empirical Legal Studies*, 12(4): 602–36.
Van Damme, A. (2015) 'The impact of police contact on trust and police legitimacy in Belgium', *Policing and Society* Advance Access.
Weber, L. and Bowling, B. (eds.) (2012) *Stop and Search: Police Power in Global Context,* London: Routledge.
White, M.D., Mulvey, P. and Dario, L.M. (2015) 'Arrestees' perceptions of the police exploring procedural justice, legitimacy, and willingness to cooperate with police across offender types', *Criminal Justice and Behavior*, 0093854815602501.
Wolfe, S.E. and Piquero, A.R. (2011) 'Organizational justice and police misconduct', *Criminal Justice and Behaviour*, 38(4): 322–53.
Wolfe, S.E., Nix, J., Kaminski, R. and Rojek, J. (2015) 'Is the effect of procedural justice on police legitimacy invariant? Testing the generality of procedural justice and competing antecedents of legitimacy', *Journal of Quantitative Criminology*, 32(2): 253–282.

15

Agency slack and the design of criminal justice institutions

Aziz Z. Huq[1]

Introduction

Crimes are investigated, prosecuted, and adjudicated by agents of the state such as the police, prosecutors, judges, and juries. In all jurisdictions, the legal authority exercised by each of these agents is circumscribed by constitutional rules, statutes, regulations, or internal guidelines. These legal constraints are intended to ensure that individual suspects' constitutional and human rights are not violated. But it is tolerably clear that agents do not always observe the letter or spirit of those constraints. Police, for example, can and do target suspects on the basis of impermissible criteria, such as race, class, perceived sexuality, or religion. They occasionally employ unlawful methods for extracting information, such as illegal searches or coercive interrogations. And when a criminal offense comes to be adjudicated, prosecutors, judges, and juries may violate legal rules due to bad motives, negligence, or simple ignorance. The result of such abuse, neglect, and error is the impairment of highly esteemed constitutional and human rights to privacy, equality, and liberty from arbitrary state action.

This chapter analyzes the problem of *remedies* for state wrongs in criminal justice institutions. The problem of remedies is analytically distinct from questions of what the substantive rules should be in the first instance. Jurisdictions differ in how much authority they assign to police, prosecutors, and other key actors in the criminal justice system. French prosecutors, for example, have considerably more discretion when it comes to interrogations and searches than their American or British counterparts (Bradley 2001). Even if the scope of legal constraint bears on how much a remedial mechanism is needed, it is nonetheless analytically feasible to bracket the substance of legal rules and to focus narrowly on the distinct problem of remedies, and in particular how remedies for state wrongs are appropriately built into the design of criminal justice institutions. Due to my own unfortunate parochialism, I will draw largely, albeit not exclusively, on examples from the American context to explore this question, although the general framework offered here should be portable across national borders.

To be clear at the threshold, my concern here is not with any and all sorts of errors that occur in criminal justice's administration. I am not, for example, concerned with routine bureaucratic inefficiencies and errors. Like any other large bureaucracy, a criminal justice system must develop regularized administrative systems to triage information and correct administrative problems

(Gaines and Worrall 2011). At times, the breakdown of this administrative system can lead to violations of individual rights, for example, when paperwork errors lead the police to target the wrong person (e.g., *Herring v. United States* 2009). I do not address the very real problems of sound administrative design in criminal justice systems here. Nor am I directly concerned with the development of rational, evidence-based policing strategies (Sherman 2013), although these too might have a large effect on rates of abuse and neglect.

I am also not concerned here with instances of *comprehensive* political failure at the system designer level. Democracies and, more commonly, autocrat regimes often fail to install formally robust protections of basic rights in their criminal justice systems (see, e.g., Trevaskes 2007). It is also possible that a polity enacts rights into formal law but then systematically and persistently lacks the political will to enforce those rights. Indeed, it may well be that *most* Western jurisdictions are characterized by a large chasm between the formal content of legal constraints on the states and the median voter's beliefs and desires about how strictly those rules should be followed. Legal constraints on police, that is, may not embody aspirations in fact held by the polity as opposed but rather comprise Potemkin-like charades—the lies that liberal polities tell themselves to sleep better at night.

There is no serious question that such political failures raise complex and difficult problems—problems that likely warrant political solutions. But such problems are distinct from the phenomenon of institutional difficulties that arise when serious efforts are made to enforce existing rules. My focus here is the latter, not the former. To bring them into crisp focus, I therefore limit my analysis to liberal democracies in which a democratic principal (e.g., a parliament or a legislative coalition acting in tandem with a chief executive) wishes to secure public safety but, at the same time, ensures that its agents do not engage in serious forms of official malfeasance and neglect leading to rights violations. To the extent that democratic polities entrench rights in formal law, for example through constitutionalization, but falter in their implementation for practical reasons rather than any endemic want of political will, it is quite plausible to talk of a rights-remedy gap and to conceptualize the problem using the economic terminology of principal-agent relationships. Under these circumstances, it can be said that there is a democratic principal that seeks to reduce *agency slack* among criminal-justice agents (Moe 1984). This, for example, may entail minimizing rates of illegal searches, coercive interrogations, discriminatory policing and prosecutions, and serious violations of due process. The question of how means solving an agency problem. The analysis that ensues, focusing on the scope and superintendence of delegations to agents, can then draw on a conceptual toolkit employed routinely in economics (Tirole 2009), political science (Goodin 1998), and law (Vermeule 2007).

While my analysis sets to one side systematic political dysfunction, I do assume that the democratic principal has strictly limited time, energy, and will power to devote to monitoring. Its goal, therefore is not the elimination of agency costs—an ambition that may be elusive—but rather an arrangement that tolerably, but not exactly, balances the cost of designing institutions, agency slack, and monitoring. In decision theoretical terms, I ask what a *satisficing* democratic legislative would do (Byron 1998). For American readers, this perspective should seem familiar: The US Supreme Court crafts rules for police and other government actors when interpreting provisions of the US Constitution's Bill of Rights. Like my analytic perspective, the Court's rule-making is superficially styled as somewhat *sub specie aeternitatis*, rather than the product of distinct historical interest groups and ideas. At least ideally, the Court is supposed to weigh how best to install remedies for constitutional violations, given not only the likely responses of state agents within criminal justice systems, but also its own institutional limitations.

To take this posture toward criminal justice institutions, and to ask about how best to remedy serious violations of the law, is to reject the view, famously associated with Oliver Wendell

Holmes, that the law simply is a prediction of the legal consequences of an act (1897). On the Holmesian view, to speak of rights and remedies as distinct is incoherent: The observed pattern of official behavior is all there is, and complaining about the law being unobserved is whistling in the wind. This is neither a necessary nor an appetizing view of the law here. Instead, it is clear that the law can meaningfully specify a behavioral desideratum related to individual rights, such as an absolute ban on torture or racial profiling, even if that rule is not observed in every case (or even most cases). Such law reflects an independent normative judgment about what sort of official behavior is desirable. Even if violated, law can still serve as a lodestar for institutional designers. It can, for example, mitigate the stresses imposed by the transient preferences of legislators suffering from occasional lapses of political will. It can also influence unelected officials' selection, incentives, and beliefs (Besley 2007; Shleifer and Vishny 1993; Tirole 2009).

The analysis presented here cleaves into roughly two halves. In the first half of the chapter, I investigate why criminal justice institutions should include remedies for serious malfeasance and neglect in the first instance. Why do these rights violations even provide a cause for remedial design expenditures? I identify both consequentialist and deontic grounds for acting. But even assuming such grounds matter, I consider why we need *institutional design* solutions, as opposed to *political* solutions, or other responses exogenous to the structure and basic operation of criminal justice institutions. In the second half of the chapter, I then define and explore two pivotal institutional design choices that a democratic principal must make. First, should policy responses or remedies be *ex ante* or *ex post*? And second, should they be public or privatized? After showing that all four combinations of these two choices exist in practice, I explore the strengths and weaknesses of each approach. That analysis suggests, at a bare minimum, that some mix of remedial features is probably warranted in the criminal justice context, although the precise mix will vary with local circumstances.

I Why does institutional design matter in criminal justice?

Agency slack—malfeasance, neglect, gross error, and other species of lawlessness—is in all likelihood endemic within not just most criminal systems, but also most governmental entities to greater or lesser degrees. That fact alone does not mean that an institutional designer must include mechanisms to impose formal, legal consequences when legal rules are violated and important individual rights are infringed. Indeed, there are two reasons for withholding such institutionalized responses to serious rule-breaking. First, it may be that there is no welfarist or other normative justification for the provision of such remedies. Second, although a remedy might well be justified, it may not need to be a formal, legal one, given the existence of alternative channels for corrective action, in particular in the political domain. Both reasons might lead to a rationing of remedial responses, as well as outright elimination of remedies. Neither of these reasons suffices, though, to vitiate the need to consider remedies in the design of criminal justice institutions.

A Normative justifications for institutionalizing remedies

Foundational legal instruments such as the UN Convention on Civil and Political Rights and the US Constitution reflect a belief in universally held individual entitlements against certain kinds of state action, including torture, rape, discrimination on the basis of race, religion, or gender, and arbitrary deprivations of somatic liberty. These entitlements rest upon an overlapping consensus amongst consequentialist and deontic normative theories rooted in different cultural and religious contexts (Rawls 1989). All are at least imperiled, if not necessarily impinged, when the state exercises its Weberian monopoly on force to achieve public order and minimize violence. From this simple fact flows the need to design criminal justice institutions with agency slack in mind and remedies to hand.

It is not adequate, moreover, to postulate that if these rights are indeed foundational and the object of an overlapping consensus, then there will be no need to build a remedial architecture since criminal justice institutions, being necessarily embedded in society, will respect those values. This fails to account for the hardly improbable scenario in which individual police and prosecutors have preferences at odds with legal norms. Nor does it address the possibility that they may simply not wish to exert the necessary effort to ensure that rights are respected, or the possibility that rights violations might be an illicit means to achieve some otherwise legitimate end, such as success in the electoral process. Unanimity over social ends, in short, does not refute the possibility of divergence over means.

But perhaps such rights violations are, as Wilson (1968) intimates, simply the price of maintaining order. On this view, it suffices to focus on crime-control goals, while writing off rights violations as regrettable, but necessary, costs of "doing business" as a Weberian state. For a number of reasons, this view is not persuasive. At a minimum, state agents who use authority in a discriminatory fashion, or who brutalize rather than investigate, are not as a consequence engaged in efficient law enforcement. It would, in short, be a mistake to assume that there is necessarily a simple trade-off between public order and individual rights.

Further complicating the relationship between public order and rights is the large empirical literature showing that expected compliance with legal rules is primarily a function of the public's perceptions of state legitimacy. This literature defines legitimacy as a normative judgment derived from an evaluation of whether state agents comply with norms of procedural justice (Tyler 2006; Tyler and Huo 2002). Contra rational-actor models, it also suggests that normative evaluation of the state provides a more powerful predictor of future conformity to law than expected sanctions. As a correlative, empirical research in Britain demonstrates that decreasing police legitimacy is associated with increasing acceptance of private violence (Jackson et al. 2013). Given these externalities from official law breaking, the costs of rights violations are not well captured by a narrow focus on the discrete state-citizen transaction.

Especially powerful evidence that official malfeasance can have corrosive spillover effects derives from evidence of how race and policing interact in the American context. The US criminal justice system is characterized by large racial disparities at both the policing stage (Epps et al. 2014) and the incarceration stage (Western 2007). Whether motivated by individual bad motives or structural forces, pervasive patterns of racially disparate policing and incarceration powerfully communicate a message of social stigma and hierarchy, one that resonates with America's long and recent history of racial subordination (Epps et al. 2014; Goffman 2014). That message, at least one study suggests, may have criminogenic effects (Unnever et al. 2009). Stigmatic and demoralization effects have been identified as following from the disparate treatment of other ethnic minorities (Tyler et al. 2010).

Racial disparities in criminal justice do not merely impede public order goals. In the US, they also have large collateral repercussions on social outcomes. Those disparities have been found to deepen economic inequalities by systematically limiting blacks' access to employment (Pager 2007) and by diminishing income over the life course (Kerley et al. 2004). As a result, disparate enforcement of the criminal law also impoverishes black communities in particular (Clear 2009) and leads to political disenfranchisement through subtle demoralization effects, not just due to incarceration but also due to contact with police (Lerman and Weaver 2014). Perhaps most troublingly, those disparities reproduce and deepen historical patterns of social and economic inequalities across generational lines. The one in four black children within a cohort born in the 1990s who experienced paternal incarceration suffered sharp increases in infant mortality, mental and behavioral problems, and rates of homelessness, all as a probable result of their father's incarceration (Wakefield and Wildeman 2013). Finding effective remedies for racial discrimination in law enforcement therefore has the potential to generate not only a more just state, but also gains in public order and social equity.

B Alternatives to institutionalizing remedies

The second strategy for resisting formal legal remedies in the design of criminal justice institutions would not deny either the deontic or the consequentialist case for respecting rights against state violence and discrimination. It would instead insist that the solution for these problems is exogenous to the design of criminal justice institutions. Rather, given the absence of any comprehensive democratic failure (of the kind not addressed in this chapter), the democratic framework of elections provides ample opportunity for retrospective accountability exercised through the ballot. Just as voters use the franchise to punish other occasional abuses of state power, so too they deploy their votes to discipline criminal justice actors. This is a serious argument. Impressive theoretical and experimental evidence supports the underlying hypothesis of retrospective voting (see, e.g., Powell and Whitten 1993; Woon 2012; but see Berry and Howell 2007 for some cautionary countervailing evidence). In the US Constitution, one key element of constitutional design—the sweeping power of presidents to pardon crimes, perhaps even their own (Kalt 1996)—also implies a general reliance on retrospective voting, rather than tailored remedies, as a strategy for controlling intermittent agency slack in criminal justice. Should not the same hold for police, prosecutors, and their ilk?

Some have suggested that the availability of retrospective accountability in the democratic sphere already inflects the operation of criminal justice institutions. Barkow (2008), following Davis's canonical treatment (1980), points out that prosecutors in the American context possess a uniquely large measure of discretionary authority. Barkow notes that this discretion might be viewed as normatively unproblematic because prosecutors are uniquely subject to democratic control via elections. In other work, however, Barkow has rejected this idea and suggested that Davis's normative concerns are indeed engaged by the breadth of prosecutorial discretion (2009a, 2009b, 2013). In light of Barkow's work, it is worth considering whether electoral accountability of prosecutors should suffice as a mechanism to regulate rights violations in criminal justice.

A threshold reason for skepticism of political responses to discrete wrongs in criminal justice administration is a mismatch in scale between the problem and the putative solution. That is, rights violations in the criminal justice context are usually individualized in effect, and dispersed in space and time. Political accountability mechanisms, and especially elections, are by contrast periodic and bundled in nature: An electoral is asked to evaluate many policy decisions via a single vote (Gersen 2010). Public-order maintenance is often the responsibility of city mayors, who are typically responsible for a heterogeneous array of distinct policies. It is certainly possible to point to examples in which violations by criminal justice officials furnish the central point of contention in an election: Consider the New York City election of 2013, where the "stop and frisk" policy of the New York Police Department (NYPD) was a pivotal object of public debate, but such instances seem the exception rather than the rule. At a minimum, the all-or-nothing character of democratic elections means that electorates have no way to punish low to moderate rates of rights violations.

Stepping back and accounting for the historically contingent aspects of politics only deepens the case against any reliance on electoral checks. At least in pervasively racially divided societies such as the United States, where minorities bear a disproportionate share of the costs from public-order maintenance (Alexander 2012), it is hardly clear that majoritarian institutions can be relied upon to generate sufficient remedies. To the contrary, in the US context at least, recent empirical work suggests that the polity may be all too content that the costs of crime control fall on groups widely viewed as less deserving of compassion and solicitude (Enns 2014). Unnever and Cullen (2010), for example, demonstrate that public preferences for punitive policies are predicted by negative views of racial minorities and not fear of crime. Similar factors predict punitive sentiment in the British context (King and Maruna 2009). The problem of electoral bias is compounded by systematic epistemic deficiencies in public policy debates. Pettit (2012) shows that the young, low-skill black men who are overrepresented in the criminal justice system, are also "categorically and systematically" excluded from the data used to frame social policy. Finally, Garland's (2002) pathmarking analysis of the ideological framings of crime policy implies that majoritarian institutions will not respond rationally to perceived crime risk in ways that mitigate effectively the rights-related consequences of criminal justice. The democratic politics of crime, that is, may be distinctively (if not uniquely, see Gilens 1999) opaque to non-racial conceptions of justice.

These objections to reliance on political remedies hinge on the distinctive role of race in the criminal justice context. Another argument, developed by Marie Gottschalk (2008, 2014), focuses instead on the path-dependent development of "carceral politics" in the United States. Gottschalk points out that punishment-related policies in the American context are characterized by a positive feedback effect. This dynamic both entrenches existing punitive policies against reform and also catalyzes the subsequent adoption of even more punitive policies. The positive feedback loop arises from the complementary operation of two dynamics. On the one hand, she points out, prison unions and the prison industry have become increasingly powerful lobbies. On the other hand, legislative appointment rules that assign prison populations to districts with prisons, rather than districts of original residence, deflate urban communities' influence at the expense of rural communities' power. This political economy means that correcting excessively punitive policies, to say nothing of discrete rights violations, becomes more difficult with time, even as the scale of criminal justice institutions—and thus the numerical volume of related errors and abuses—expands. It is worth noting that Gottschalk's powerfully pessimistic argument for the positive feedback loops in the carceral state competes with more optimistic prognoses (Clear and Frost 2013).

The argument developed here against reliance on political checks in the criminal justice context might be pressed even further, so that it yields a critique of my analytic strategy in this chapter. The critique, which has a familial resemblance to the Holmesian position rejected earlier, goes as follows: If democratic mechanisms are inadequate responses to retail rights violations in the criminal justice context, it is because there is never sufficient democratic will to mitigate them. And if that is so, then the whole project of institutional design to minimize such costs is misbegotten. It will always be the case that majoritarian preferences prevail and minorities fold, by dint of the sheer weight of numbers (an argument anticipated most eloquently in Stephen 1873). The strong do what they can, and the weak bear what they must.

I do not think this critique ought to succeed for several reasons but delineate here only one response: Even if elective democratic institutions are not persistently attentive to the rights-related costs of crime control, this does not mean they are *never* so responsive. It seems plain that there are at least moments of broadly shared concern. Moreover, it also seems plausible to think that in those moments elective institutions *may* choose to install durable institutional responses to agency slack and abuse in criminal justice. Without succumbing to whiggish fantasia of inexorable progress, it is surely plausible to think that *sometimes* we the public work improvements in our institutions.

In the American context, the task of institutional repair fell first and foremost to the US Supreme Court under Chief Justice Earl Warren, which installed a suite of rights under the Bill of Rights to the US Constitution through path-marking rulings in the 1950s and the 1960s (Amar 1998). To be sure, these rulings have proven to be vulnerable to erosion and backlash (Steiker 1996), and may have had the counterintuitive effect of legitimating a certain volume of rights violations (Seidman 1992). Any institutional remedy can be limited by legislation, or it can be defunded to the extent it depends on the public fisc. But an institutionalized remedy coupled with some backsliding may still be more desirable than no institutionalized remedy at all. To foreclose the possibility of democratically catalyzed responses to the agency and abuse problems of crime control is either to succumb to a Nirvana fallacy or to adopt a mistakenly static view of political institutions. One can, in short, be generally pessimistic about democratic institutions, while still insisting upon, and perhaps working to realize, their occasional capacity for deep and enduring good.

There is a second way of arguing against the need for formal legal institutional responses to agency slack and abuse in the criminal justice system. Setting to one side the electoral mechanisms of control and sanctioning discussed above, it might be argued that formal legal remedies of the sort considered below are unnecessary if the correct mechanisms are used for selecting criminal justice officials. That is, assuming the correct sorts of screening and selection mechanisms are in place, the task of the democratic principal designing criminal justice institutions is at an end.

Yet again, this alluringly easy response is also insufficient. To begin with, it seems clear that selection, as well as retention and promotion, rules will play an important part in any institutional strategy to address agency slack, lawlessness, and error. An institution that persistently hires individuals who are unable or unwilling to account for important goals is unlikely to achieve these goals. Nevertheless, there are several reasons to resist the temptation to rely exclusively on personnel-related instruments. As discussed below, criminal justice systems (police, prosecution offices, and courts) tend to be large organizations. As the size of an organization expands, the more costly and difficult it is at the margin to find good personnel. At the outer margin of organizational growth, it is likely to become increasingly difficult to hire effective personnel. Simply put, it is easier to find the first good police officer than the one thousandth.

In addition, employment decisions are characterized by asymmetric information, and, as a result, a need for employees to find a signal that separates good from bad types in the candidate pool. This signal is a quality good types find less expensive to acquire than bad types (Spence 1973). At least with respect to the propensity to violate rights, it is not clear what that signal would be. One possibility, at least for prosecutors, is that lawyers who had been more successful in legal education and during the early stages of their legal careers are more likely to be highly motivated and hence effective prosecutors. Empirical studies of prosecutorial choice in the US context create complications for this account by demonstrating that prosecutorial ambition tends to distort charging decisions, by eliciting indictments that are likely to gain public attention rather than social gains (Rasmusen et al. 2009; Glaeser et al. 2000)

Finally, even if there is a signal that can be employed to sort employees who will respect rights from those less likely to do so, that signal may be undermined or distorted by other dynamics within the hiring process. Consider here the example of police. Generally, police officers will be permitted to use force in situations in which individuals are not so allowed (Harmon 2008). That is, electing to join the police is a way of enlarging one's right to use force. There is likely variance within the populace in respect to the taste for violence. An implicit wage of police employment is the license to use violence that would otherwise be unlawful (see Heywood et al. 2007 for the concept of an implicit wage). It follows that police employment will be more attractive—because it carries a larger net explicit and implicit wage—for those in the population who have more of a taste for violence. Of course, whether this implicit wage effects hiring, or whether it is offset by other factors (e.g., the implicit cost accepted by police of entering stressful and abusive situations), is an empirical question. Resolution of that question will nevertheless at least complicate, and perhaps seriously distort, the operation of signaling in the job market for police.

Finally, it is worth noting here that conduct rules for state actors might also interact with efforts to select good types only for criminal justice institutions. Rules for the use of force, for example, may influence the composition of police departments (Vermeule 2005). That is, the larger the margin of discretionary authority police have to use force, therefore, the larger the net wage differential between those with and those without a taste for violence. The more discretion police have to use force, therefore, the more the job will disproportionately attract those least inclined to use it wisely. The ensuing tension is perhaps sharpest when a jurisdiction faces significant public order problems.

In short, it is not persuasive to write off abuse, neglect, and malfeasance as merely the price of engaging in crime control. Nor is it sufficient to relegate the management of those costs to the democratic political process or to hope that the right people will somehow always fill critical posts. Instead, just as in the corruption context (Shleifer and Vishny 1993), there is a need for more particularized attention to institutional design and the role of remedies therein.

II The institutional circumstances of criminal justice remedies

If institutional rather than political remedies are warranted, then what form should they take? There is likely no global answer to this question. The political, sociological, and historical circumstances of criminal justice diverge widely from jurisdiction to jurisdiction. The ensuing variance precludes across-the-board responses. Rather, the best way to understand how a democratic principal might go about regulating her criminal agents so as to limit rights violations is to specify the institutional circumstances that characterize criminal justice in ways that are salient to remedial design. With these firmly in view, we can start to think most clearly about remedy-related design choices.

Most importantly, the delivery of criminal justice is almost always a highly dispersed phenomenon. Unlike other state functions such as legislating or fashioning monetary policy, the delivery of criminal justice necessarily occurs in a large number of geographically dispersed sites. This is most obviously the case with policing, which is necessarily decentralized down to the street level. But it is also true of the prosecutorial and adjudicative functions. In the United States, for example, most prosecutions are initiated by state and local actors, not federal US attorneys (Glaeser et al. 2000). Each county or city may have its own prosecutor, one who often serves only upon election, as well as its own system of criminal courts. The next result is a great deal of necessary variance in the preferences and behavior of prosecutors and criminal judges across a wide variety of physical sites for the delivery of criminal justice outcomes. In addition to this, theories of policing emphasize the need for only "loose coupling" between an agency's goals and the day-to-day actions of its officers (Crank 2003). Given this complexity and unpredictability, that is, a space between instruction and application is almost inevitable.

Geographic dispersion and decentralization have a number of implications. As a threshold matter, a democratic principal cannot easily maintain ongoing surveillance over its agents in the criminal justice domain. Agency relations are almost always characterized by informational asymmetries (Moe 1984). But the epistemic gap in the criminal justice context will tend to be especially large for a number of reasons. Most importantly, many criminal justice encounters occur with only agents of the state and putative victims present. If a legal violation occurs, it is usually brief or instantaneous but at the same time generates evidence that will endure into the adjudicative process. That enduring evidentiary trace, however, usually does not indicate whether it was secured through illegal means. Determinations of what happens when police use force—or when a confession is elicited in the station-house or when prosecutors squeeze out a plea deal—require an evaluation of competing testimonies from state agents and putative victims. Those determinations, even if reached through the formalized mechanism of the individual criminal trial, must often be based on systematically untrustworthy information. As a result, it will almost never be enough simply to announce a rule and expect it to be self-executing: The likelihood of detection—which is the main determinant of deterrence effects (Nagin 2013)—is inevitably small or practically nonexistent.

Worse, variation in local conditions means that observed fluctuations in official behavior cannot always be immediately characterized in positive or negative terms. For example, American jurisdictions close to the Mexican border often have "fast track" programs with streamlined procedures and reduced punishments for immigration-related offenses. These programs are responses to a local problem. They may be ranked as either pragmatic accommodations or problematic deviances from the law, depending on one's baseline (Bibas 2005). The need for this sort of judgment renders the identification of legally problematic behavior especially onerous.

Decentralization has other implications for the institutional context of criminal justice, particularly in large polities such as the United States. There, geographic variation is associated with wide fluctuations in fiscal arrangements. As Thacher (2011) has demonstrated, there can an order-of-magnitude difference in the fiscal resources available to police in a given US jurisdiction. Further, in many jurisdictions, law enforcement budgets are a function of the magnitude of assets seized pursuant to criminal forfeiture laws (Baicker and Jacobson 2007). Again, the presence of these mutable background conditions of policy implementation likely impinge on officials' incentives and also complicate efforts to identify certain forms of official behavior as per se problematic, at least on an *ex ante* basis.

In summary, criminal justice presents a particularly acute epistemic problem from the perspective of a democratic principal due to decentralizations, wide variation in local conditions, and weak epistemic signals. These are not the only constraints on monitoring in law enforcement. For example, Richman (2003) has pointed out that prosecutors and law enforcement agents in the United States often operate in collaborative teams. This implies the existence of a team production problem for a principal, where the bundled nature of outputs renders it difficult to reach separate judgments about each participant in the team (Holmstrom 1982). Even without accounting for these additional concerns, it should be tolerably clear that any mechanism to identify and remedy abuse and neglect in the criminal justice system faces considerable epistemic hurdles.

III Two design decisions in institutionalizing remedies

The acute epistemic difficulties a democratic principal faces in designing remedies in the criminal justice context render two distinct institutional choices especially critical: the election between *ex ante* and *ex post* remedies and the distinction between public enforcement mechanisms and their private analogs. These design margins matter because selecting between them can dramatically alter the magnitude and accuracy of information available for remedying abuse and neglect. Altering these parameters furthermore has implications for the efficacy of a remedial regime. To illuminate these diverse implications, I first set forth the two design margins and then identify some consequences of the choices they imply. As will become clear, most of the examples I supply from the American context concern remedying *police* misconduct for the simple reason that American law does not bring sufficient institutional resources to bear on the problem of *prosecutorial* or *judicial* misconduct for us to understand their incidence, let alone think about cogent responses (Barkow 2009b). In response to that shoal of wrongs, American law rather maintains a profound silence.

A Ex ante versus ex post remedies

Consider first the choice between *ex ante* and *ex post* remedial mechanisms. American law resorts to both options. On the one hand, the Fourth Amendment to the US Constitution requires warrants for most home searches. The warrant rule is a procedural check: It does not directly speak to the scope of the search or to the evidentiary justification required before an officer can proceed. Instead, it operates as a sort of licensing scheme, inserting an independent magistrate before a legal violation occurs rather than after the fact (Stuntz 1991). The prophylactic effects of licensing emerge, to be sure, partly from the evidentiary and explanatory burdens imposed on police by the warrant rule. But the warrant system also helps limit illegal searches because it operates as a "costly screen" (Milgrom and Roberts 1986). In simple terms, it imposes an effort tax on police, forcing them to "stop and think" whether a search is really appropriate, lawful, and needful (Bar-Gill and Friedman 2012). That cost incentivizes police to choose among potential searches and to proceed only with those that are truly worthwhile. Another *ex ante* remedy is the requirement that a suspect be permitted to have legal representation prior to being included in a post-charge police line-up (*Wade v. United States* 1967). In the interrogation context, counsel does not need to be provided, but suspects are given a warning of their right to have counsel present, as well as their right to remain silent without that being used against them at trial (*Miranda v. Arizona*, 1966).

Ex post remedies come in at least three flavors under US law. First, policing illegality often has consequences at trial. Starting in the United States, but increasingly across the world, physical and testimonial evidence obtained in violation of the law will be excluded from a subsequent criminal trial. This is done at least in part to elicit compliance with *ex ante* rules such as the warrant requirement. Bradley (2001) argues that the main difference between the US rule and that of other jurisdictions is the latter's mandatory character (*Mapp v. Ohio* 1961). Recent expansions to a "good faith" exception to the exclusionary rule in the American context (see, e.g., *Davis v. United States* 2011), however, may be narrowing that gap. Another class of illegality that has a trial remedy is courtroom misconduct by prosecutors, which is often addressed through the use of the, arguably fictive, curative function of instructions from judge to jury (Sklansky 2013).

Second, federal law provides a damages remedy for individuals whose constitutional rights are violated. Damages actions against state actors proceed under a late nineteenth-century statute, now codified as 42 U.S.C. § 1983, while the damages action against federal officials has been recognized as a matter of constitutional common law (*Bivens v. Six Unknown Named Agents* 1971). The law of constitutional torts is complicated by the existence of "qualified" immunity, which police enjoy, and "absolute" immunity, which prosecutors often and judges always enjoy (Rudovsky 1989). Under qualified immunity doctrine, liability does not attach unless it would be very clear to a reasonable officer that he or she was violating a constitutional norm. Under absolute immunity, even the most egregious errors do not generate liability. In consequence, prosecutors and trial judges can almost never be held liable for money damages, even for the most egregious and harmful species of constitutional violations. Even in fairly extreme instances of discrimination and abuse rising to the level of torture, monetary relief therefore tends to be only rarely available (Huq 2009).

Finally, American law has adopted the English common-law remedy of *habeas corpus* and transformed it into a vehicle for the post-conviction review of criminal convictions for constitutional error. A prisoner seeking *habeas* relief identifies a constitutional error in his or her trial and seeks a *vacatur* of the conviction or (in capital cases) the sentence. Most frequently, the prisoner will focus upon alleged trial errors such as defense counsel that failed to meet constitutionally required standards of competence or prosecutorial failures to produce exculpatory evidence. The state then faces the option of releasing the prisoner or retrying him or her. Since the 1970s, post-conviction *habeas* has accrued a positively baroque encrustation of procedural rules that operate to titrate out in small increments (for a summary, see Huq 2014). For example, police violations of *Miranda* can be raised on *habeas*, but unlawful searches and seizures cannot. The net result of these rules, which are a product of both legislative hostility to prisoners and judicial hostility to the *habeas* caseload, is that federal courts must assign a large amount of effort applying complex procedural rules to pro se prisoner pleadings, some of which might be meritorious. At the same time, those same rules virtually guarantee that the rate of merits success will be *de minimus*. Hence, it is hard to see how the institution of post-conviction review, at least as currently constituted, can stand on a rational or defensible footing.

B Private versus public enforcement

The second important design margin is the election between private and public remedies. All of the aforementioned *ex post* remedies, except for suppression motions, are privatized in the sense that it is a private individual (typically the person who has suffered constitutional harm), who must file suit and prosecute a case against the state. It is also possible to imagine an *ex ante* private remedy in the form of an injunction, sought on behalf of a given individual or a class, against a certain kind of state conduct, and enforced via contempt sanctions. As a matter of practice, *ex ante* private remedies are rarely observed. In 1983, the US Supreme Court held that a person lacked "standing" (i.e., a constitutional right to sue) to enjoin a police chokehold policy in the absence of sufficient evidence that he would be subject to a future chokehold (*City of Los Angeles v. Lyons* 1983). Because police and prosecutors tend not to announce whom they intend to target with illegal measures before the fact, the 1983 decision in *Lyons* staunched the flow of private *ex ante* challenges. After *Lyons*, therefore, class actions against police and prosecution offices are rare, although, as recent litigation challenging the NYPD's stop-and-frisk policy shows as racial discrimination, not impossible (Kalhan 2014; Steiker 2013; Geller and Fagan 2010).

A key characteristic of all private remedies is that their use turns on the initiative—and by implication the legal, epistemic, and fiscal resources—of the individual harmed by the state. Given inequalities in the distribution of legal knowledge and resources across the populations, in practice this means that the ability to deploy a private remedy turns on the quality of counsel that a person can obtain or the state furnishes. American law permits some contingent fee arrangements and occasionally imposes fee shifting, but distributional factors remain salient.

A public remedy, by contrast, is one sought and administered by the state. *Ex ante* state intervention and supervision of a sort is at stake in warrant rules. It is possible to read the US Supreme Court's rules requiring warrants for some classes of searches as a departure from the text of the Fourth Amendment, which seems to limit the use of warrants rather than requiring them for any class of cases (Amar 1998). On that view, the Court *suo moto* has delegated to the judiciary at large responsibility for policing the state's use of search authority *ex ante*. That delegation is public in character because it comprises a requirement by one state actor imposed on another state actor, operationalized without any triggering by a private party. As with any other delegation, there is an attendant risk of agency slack.

Ex post public remedies, at least of a certain kind, are more common. On the one hand, civil and criminal suits against individual police or prosecutors for constitutional violations are technically available but in practice are rarely observed (Barkow 2009b; Harmon 2008). Perhaps unsurprisingly, prosecutors are not disposed to investigate or charge peers or law enforcement colleagues. The recent failure of state and federal prosecutors to bring charges against the police officer responsible for the shooting death of Michael Brown in Ferguson, Missouri, is symptomatic of this. More generally, there are remarkably few instances in which police or prosecutors are subject even to internal discipline for either constitutional violations or culpable obfuscation of such violations.

On the other hand, a powerful and even more wide-ranging public remedy is available: the "pattern or practice" lawsuit that the federal Department of Justice can lodge against a municipal or county police department (Harmon 2008). Enacted in 1994, the statute, located at 42 U.S.C. § 14141, allows the federal government in effect to place police departments in receivership in the wake of repeated serious constitutional violations and to impose new management, training, and internal rule-making. §14141 requires the Department of Justice to maintain statistics on rates of police violence and excessive force. The ensuing suits, if relatively rare, can force local municipalities to prioritize policing investments, install ongoing monitoring mechanisms to elicit rule-compliance from frontline officers, and provide police leadership with political cover for reform.

As a final caveat, the public/private distinction refers to ideal types. Public defenders, who are funded by the state but tasked with acting on behalf of private individuals, arguably reflect a hybrid category. In practice, it is also possible to imagine yet other mixtures of private and public enforcement. For example, notionally private law suits seeking institutional reform can in practice operate as sites for negotiation and joint action by both private and public actors aimed at reforming problematic criminal justice institutions (Sabel and Simon 2004). Extending those possibilities, Gilles (2000) argues that § 14141 should be modified to allow for the delegation of enforcement powers to private individuals, who could sue in lieu of the Department of Justice.

IV Trade-offs in remedial design in criminal justice administration

How should a democratic principal select between the diverse options—public versus private and *ex ante* versus *ex post*—developed here? To anticipate my conclusion, there is no one right answer: In most instances, some mix of remedial pathways will instead be desirable. Not all pathways, however, will be utilized, and under inevitable conditions of institutional scarcity, some remedies must be prioritized over others. But which? A starting point for analysis is how different remedial strategies measure up to the distinctive epistemic problem faced by a democratic principal in the criminal justice context.

Consider first that distinctive *ex ante* and *ex post* remedies have different epistemic strengths and weaknesses. On the one hand, it would seem obviously true that *ex post* remedies will be epistemically superior to *ex ante* remedies: The action in question has occurred and hence can be investigated and clarified when the remedy is *ex post*. In the *ex ante* context, the regulator or judge must necessarily guess at the consequences of a state action. But this may not be so. Official decision-makers may suffer from cognitive biases that cause them to make persistent Type I errors. For example, in American law the *ex post* regulation of illegal search occurs in the context of pretrial suppression hearings in which a judge is confronted with illegally obtained, but inculpatory, evidence. Even aside from the judiciary's likely inclination to align itself with other official actors such as the police, judges will tend to view the suppression question through a cognitive lens distorted by hindsight bias, which presses toward the conclusion that police action was surely reasonable because it did, in fact, yield good evidence (Stuntz 1991). Worse, police may be inevitably tempted in suppression hearings to at best color their testimony to render their own actions seemingly lawful or, worse, engage in outright perjury so as to prevent a perceived offender from walking free. Given these systematic distortions in the *ex post* remedial context, the *ex ante* device of warrants may in fact be preferable even if epistemically more pinched.

The choice between *ex ante* and *ex post* rules also has selection effects, especially when the *ex post* remedy is available only in the criminal trial context. A thoroughgoing *ex ante* system for intrusive and coercive—say, an action that required a warrant or some other sort of approval, whether from a judge or a departmental superior—operates equally in cases where the object of state attention is innocent or guilty. Indeed, the very purpose of a costly screen is to elicit the decision-maker to leverage more fully available information to determine when an intrusive state action is in fact warranted (Milgrom and Roberts 1986). *Ex ante* screening may also prevent actions that would otherwise have been illegal, without any large spillover deterrence on lawful searches. The net result of an *ex ante* regime, therefore, will tend to a lower rate of Type I errors, at least in comparison to a world without remedies. Further, the suppression remedy used *ex post* for illegal searches and coercive interrogations selects for only the guilty objects of state attention, while leaving innocent objects of police attention without a remedy. Faced with a stream of culpable and unsympathetic victims of state depredation, a judge may be ill-disposed to fashion capacious privacy or dignity protections. That same judge, however, will never see the stream of cases in which innocent citizens are subject to state harassment or coercive prosecution threats. Exclusive reliance on *ex post* remedies, therefore, may both yield a distorted body of law and a radically incomplete remedial landscape.

Similarly, the choice between public and private remedies is not as clear as it might at first seem. On the one hand, the geographically dispersed operation of criminal justice institutions means that information about law violations reposes in the first instance in private hands (although it remains to be seen whether the emergence of algorithmic "big data" tools could change that). Private remedial litigation affects a kind of Hayekian aggregation function. Moreover, individuals have stable and strong incentives to pursue remedies at least once a violation has occurred. The epistemic advantage of private enforcement tools, on the other hand, may be outweighed by distortive wealth effects. Invocation of adversarial corrective mechanisms turns on the availability of fiscal and cognitive resources on the victims' part. Where background allocations of such resources are unequal, an adversarial mechanism is likely to yield highly uneven and even inequitable results (Deffains 2008; Stuntz 2008). Where background inequalities in resources correlate with racial or ethnic stratification, as in the United States, it may well be that reliance on private enforcement has a perverse effect, especially where publically funded defense counsel tend to be under-resourced: This would mean that the expected rate of corrective process when an African-American's rights are violated would be lower than when a Caucasian person's rights are violated. Under these (rather too plausible) conditions, private enforcement mechanisms create a tax that presses officials *away* from racially equitable policing.

Yet the case in favor of public enforcement is not without significant weaknesses either. Public enforcement renders corrective process vulnerable to "capture" by interest groups hostile to subordinated groups that may be more frequently targeted for wrongful criminal justice attention. That is, well-organized interest groups such as law enforcement may expend resources gaining control over oversight mechanisms. Hence, it is perhaps no surprise that former prosecutors numerically dominate federal bench (Kalhan 2014). Even in the absence of such capture, public enforcement may be vulnerable to the political cycle and the associated fluctuations in public priorities. Some administrations, often on the right of the political spectrum, are likely to be less sympathetic to the classes of individuals who tend to suffer more frequently from legal violations in criminal justice contexts. But there is no reason to believe that partisan cycles of officeholders will correspond to peaks and troughs in the demand for remedies in the criminal justice context. To the contrary, reliance on public enforcement alone may be perversely countercyclical, if administrations most prone to remedial under-enforcement are also most prone to violations in the first instance.

Conclusion

The bottom line of this analysis is simple: Institutionalized remedies for serious abuse and neglect in the criminal justice context are necessary yet difficult, costly, and bound to fail in some proportion of cases. On the one hand, political and selection-based remedies are limited in their effects. On the other hand, any effort to embed remedial resources within the criminal system faces substantial epistemic challenges given the dispersed and hard-to-monitor ways in which police, prosecutors, and trial courts work. In that regulatory enterprise, a democratic principal must select among *ex ante* and *ex post* options and also between public and private remedies. A pure strategy—i.e., one that is all public or all private or one that is all *ex ante* or all *ex post*—is likely to fail. Each such approach has substantial drawbacks standing alone. In consequence, a mixed approach that draws in diverse tools in response to the observed distribution of abuse and neglect, as well as the expected responses by regulated actors, is likely necessary. The framework articulated in this chapter may guide the analysis of a mixed approach, but it cannot resolve the local question of the satisfactory mix for a given jurisdiction—let alone the problem of how to install that mix by legislation or court decision. On these counts, the design of remedies in the criminal justice context necessarily presents persistently difficult questions to which no clear or quick response is feasible. Of course, this is no reason to desist in the effort to craft such responses—it is rather a spur to invest more, try harder, and engage creatively with the onerous social task of overcoming agency slack in the administration of criminal justice.

Note

1 Professor of Law and Herbert and Marjorie Fried Teaching Scholar, University of Chicago Law School. Thanks to Mike Seidman for helpful comments.

Bibliography

Alexander, M. (2012) *The New Jim Crow: Mass Incarceration in the Age of Colorblindness,* New York, NY: The New Press.

Amar, A.R. (1998) *The Constitution and Criminal Procedure: First Principles,* New Haven, CT: Yale University Press.

Baicker, K. and Jacobson, M. (2007) 'Finders keepers: forfeiture laws, policing incentives, and local budgets', *Journal of Public Economics,* 91(11–12): 2113–36. doi:10.1016/j.jpubeco.2007.03.009.

Bar-Gill, O. and Friedman, B. (2012) 'Taking warrants seriously', *Northwestern University Law Review,* 106: 1609.

Barkow, R.E. (2008) 'The ascent of the administrative state and the demise of mercy', *Harvard Law Review,* 121(5): 1332–65.

Barkow, R.E. (2009a) 'Organizational guidelines for the prosecutor's office', *Cardozo Law Review,* 31: 2089.

Barkow, R.E. (2009b) 'Institutional design and the policing of prosecutors: lessons from administrative law', *Stanford Law Review,* 61(4): 869–921.

Barkow, R.E. (2013) 'Prosecutorial administration: prosecutor bias and the department of justice', *Virginia Law Review,* 99(2): 271–342.

Beckett, K. (2000) *Making Crime Pay: Law and Order in Contemporary American Politics,* Oxford: Oxford University Press.

Berry, C.R. and Howell, W.G. (2007) 'Accountability and local elections: rethinking retrospective voting', *The Journal of Politics*, 69(3): 844–58.
Besley, T. (2007) *Principled Agents? The Political Economy of Good Government*, Oxford: Oxford University Press.
Bibas, S. (2005) 'Regulating local variations in federal sentencing'. *Stanford Law Review*, 58(1): 137–54.
Bingham, P.G. Jr., and Whitten, G.D. (1993) 'A cross-national analysis of economic voting: taking account of the political context', *American Journal of Political Science*, 37(2): 391–414. doi:10.2307/2111378.
Bradley, C.M. (2001) 'Mapp goes abroad', *Case Western Reserve Law Review*, 52: 375.
Byron, M. (1998) 'Satisficing and optimality', *Ethics*, 109(1): 67–93. doi: 10.1086/233874.
Clear, T.R. (2009) *Imprisoning Communities: How Mass Incarceration Makes Disadvantaged Neighborhoods Worse*, Oxford: Oxford University Press.
Clear, T. R. and Frost, N.A. (2013) *The Punishment Imperative: The Rise and Failure of Mass Incarceration in America*, New York, NY: NYU Press.
Crank, J.P. (2003) 'Institutional theory of police: a review of the state of the art', *Policing: An International Journal of Police Strategies & Management*, 26(2): 186–207. doi:10.1108/13639510310475723.
Davis, K.C. (1980) *Discretionary Justice: A Preliminary Inquiry*, Westport, CT: Greenwood Press, Reprint.
Deffains, B. and Demougin, D. (2008) 'The inquisitorial and the adversarial procedure in a criminal court setting', *Zeitschrift Für Die Gesamte Staatswissenschaft*, 164(1): 31–43.
Epp, C.R., Maynard-Moody, S. and Haider-Markel, D.P. (2014) *Pulled Over: How Police Stops Define Race and Citizenship*, Chicago, IL, London: University Of Chicago Press.
Gaines, L.K., and Worrall, J.L. (2011) *Police Administration*, Boston, MA: Cengage Learning.
Garland, D. (2002) *The Culture of Control: Crime and Social Order in Contemporary Society*, Chicago, IL: University of Chicago Press.
Geller, A. and Fagan, J. (2010) 'Pot as pretext: marijuana, race, and the new disorder in New York City street policing', *Journal of Empirical Legal Studies*, 7(4): 591–633. doi:10.1111/j.1740-1461.2010.01190.x.
Gersen, J.E. (2010) 'Unbundled powers', *Virginia Law Review*, 96(2): 301–58.
Gilens, M. (2009) *Why Americans Hate Welfare: Race, Media, and the Politics of Antipoverty Policy*. Chicago, IL: University of Chicago Press.
Gilles, M.E. (2000) 'Reinventing structural reform litigation: deputizing private citizens in the enforcement of civil rights', *Columbia Law Review*, 100(6): 1384–1453. doi:10.2307/1123570.
Glaeser, E.L., Kessler, D.P. and Morrison Piehl, A. (2000) 'What do prosecutors maximize? An analysis of the federalization of drug crimes', *American Law and Economics Review*, 2(2): 259–90. doi:10.1093/aler/2.2.259.
Goffman, A. (2014) *On the Run: Fugitive Life in an American City*, Chicago, IL, London: University of Chicago Press.
Goodin, R.E. (ed.) (1998) *The Theory of Institutional Design*, Cambridge: Cambridge University Press.
Gottschalk, M. (2008) 'Hiding in plain sight: American politics and the carceral state', *Annual Review of Political Science*, 11(1): 235–60. doi:10.1146/annurev.polisci.11.060606.135218.
Gottschalk, M. (2014) *Caught: The Prison State and the Lockdown of American Politics*. Princeton, NJ: Princeton University Press.
Harmon, R.A. (2008) 'When is police violence justified?', *Northwestern University Law Review*, 102: 1119.
Heywood, J.S., Siebert, W.S. and Wei, X. (2007) 'The implicit wage costs of family friendly work practices', *Oxford Economic Papers*, New Series, 59(2): 275–300.
Holmes, O.W. (1897) 'The path of the law', *Harvard Law Review*, 10(8): 457–78. doi:10.2307/1322028.
Holmstrom, B. (1982) 'Moral hazard in teams', *The Bell Journal of Economics*, 13(2): 324–40. doi:10.2307/3003457.
Huq, A.Z. (2014) 'Habeas and the Roberts Court', *The University of Chicago Law Review*, 81(2): 519–608.
Huq, A.Z. (2009) 'Against national security exceptionalism', *The Supreme Court Review*, 2009(1): 225–73.
Jackson, J., Huq, A.Z., Bradford, B. and Tyler, T.R. (2013) 'Monopolizing force? Police legitimacy and public attitudes toward the acceptability of violence', *Psychology, Public Policy, and Law*, 19(4): 479–97. doi:10.1037/a0033852.
Kalhan, A. (2014) 'Stop and frisk, judicial independence, and the ironies of improper appearances', *Georgetown Journal of Legal Ethics*, 27: 1043.
Kalt, B.C. (1996) 'Pardon me? The constitutional case against presidential self-pardons', *The Yale Law Journal*, 106(3): 779–809. doi:10.2307/797310.
Kerley, K., Benson, M., Lee, M. and Cullen, F.T. (2004) 'Race, criminal justice contact, and adult position in the social stratification system', *Social Problems*, 51(4): 549–68. doi:10.1525/sp.2004.51.4.549.

King, A. and Maruna, S. (2009) 'Is a conservative just a liberal who has been mugged? Exploring the origins of punitive views', *Punishment & Society,* 11(2): 147–69. doi:10.1177/1462474508101490.

Lerman, A.E. and Weaver, V.M. (2014) *Arresting Citizenship: The Democratic Consequences of American Crime Control,* Chicago, IL, London: University of Chicago Press.

Milgrom, P. and Roberts, J. (1986) 'Price and advertising signals of product quality', *Journal of Political Economy,* 94(4): 796–821.

Moe, T.M. (1984) 'The new economics of organization', *American Journal of Political Science,* 28(4): 739–77. doi:10.2307/2110997.

Nagin, D.S. (2013) 'Deterrence in the twenty-first century', *Crime and Justice,* 42(1): 199–263. doi:10.1086/670398.

Pager, D. (2007) *Marked: Race, Crime, and Finding Work in an Era of Mass Incarceration,* Chicago, IL: University of Chicago Press.

Pettit, B. (2012) *Invisible Men: Mass Incarceration and the Myth of Black Progress,* New York, NY: Russell Sage Foundation.

Rasmusen, E., Raghav, M. and Ramseyer, M. (2009) 'Convictions versus conviction rates: the prosecutor's choice', *American Law and Economics Review,* July, ahp007. doi:10.1093/aler/ahp007.

Rawls, J. (1989) 'The domain of the political and overlapping consensus', *New York University Law Review,* 64: 233.

Richman, D. (2003) 'Prosecutors and their agents, agents and their prosecutors', *Columbia Law Review,* 103(4): 749–832. doi:10.2307/1123778.

Rudovsky, D. (1989) 'The qualified immunity doctrine in the Supreme Court: judicial activism and the restriction of constitutional rights', *University of Pennsylvania Law Review,* 138(1): 23–81. doi:10.2307/3312179.

Sabel, C.F. and Simon, W.H. (2004) 'Destabilization rights: how public law litigation succeeds', *Harvard Law Review,* 117(4): 1015–1101. doi:10.2307/4093364.

Seidman, L.M. (1992) 'Brown and Miranda', *California Law Review,* 80(3): 673–753. doi:10.2307/3480711.

Sherman, L.W. (2013) 'The rise of evidence-based policing: targeting, testing, and tracking', *Crime and Justice,* 42(1): 377–451. doi:10.1086/670819.

Shleifer, A. and Vishny, R.W. (1993) 'Corruption', *The Quarterly Journal of Economics,* 108(3): 599–617. doi:10.2307/2118402.

Sklansky, D.A. (2013) 'Evidentiary instructions and the jury as other', *Stanford Law Review,* 65: 407.

Spence, M. (1973) 'Job market signaling', *The Quarterly Journal of Economics,* 87(3): 355–74. doi:10.2307/1882010.

Steiker, C.S. (1996) 'Counter-revolution in constitutional criminal procedure? Two audiences, two answers', *Michigan Law Review,* 94(8): 2466–2551. doi:10.2307/1289832.

Steiker, C.S. (2013) 'Terry unbound', *Mississippi Law Journal,* 82: 329.

Stephen, Sir J.F. (1967) *Liberty, Equality, Fraternity,* Cambridge: Cambridge University Press.

Stuntz, W.J. (1991) 'Warrants and Fourth Amendment remedies', *Virginia Law Review,* 77(5): 881–943. doi:10.2307/1073442.

Stuntz, W.J. (2008) 'Inequality and adversarial criminal procedure: comment', *Journal of Institutional and Theoretical Economics (JITE) / Zeitschrift Für Die Gesamte Staatswissenschaft,* 164(1): 47–51.

Stuntz, W.J. (2013) *The Collapse of American Criminal Justice,* Boston, MA: Belknap Press.

Thacher, D. (2011) 'The distribution of police protection', *Journal of Quantitative Criminology,* 27(3): 275–98. doi:10.1007/s10940-010-9125-3.

Tirole, J. (2009) 'Motivation intrinsèque, incitations et normes sociales', *Revue Économique,* 60(3): 577–89.

Trevaskes, S. (2007) 'Severe and swift justice in China', *The British Journal of Criminology,* 47(1): 23–41.

Tyler, T.R. (2006) *Why People Obey the Law,* Princeton, NJ: Princeton University Press.

Tyler, T.R. and Huo, Y. (2002) *Trust in the Law: Encouraging Public Cooperation with the Police and Courts,* New York, NY: Russell Sage Foundation Publications.

Tyler, T.R., Schulhofer, S. and Huq, A.Z. (2010) 'Legitimacy and deterrence effects in counterterrorism policing: a study of Muslim Americans', *Law & Society Review,* 44(2): 365–402. doi:10.1111/j.1540-5893.2010.00405.x.

Unnever, J.D. and Cullen, F.T. (2010) 'The social sources of Americans' punitiveness: a test of three competing models', *Criminology,* 48(1): 99–129. doi:10.1111/j.1745-9125.2010.00181.x.

Unnever, J.D., Cullen, F.T., Mathers, S.A., McClure, T.E. and Allison, M.C. (2009) 'Racial discrimination and Hirschi's criminological classic: a chapter in the sociology of knowledge', *Justice Quarterly,* 26(3): 377–409. doi:10.1080/07418820802506180.

Vermeule, A. (2005) 'Selection effects in Constitutional law', *Virginia Law Review,* 91(4): 953–98.
Vermeule, A. (2007) *Mechanisms of Democracy: Institutional Design Writ Small,* Oxford, New York, NY: Oxford University Press.
Wakefield, S. and Wilderman, C.J. (2013) *Children of the Prison Boom: Mass Incarceration and the Future of American Inequality.* New York, NY: Oxford University Press.
Western, B. (2007) *Punishment and Inequality in America,* New York, NY: Russell Sage Foundation Publications.
Whitman, J.Q. (2005) 'The comparative study of criminal punishment', *Annual Review of Law and Social Science,* 1(1): 17–34. doi:10.1146/annurev.lawsocsci.1.041604.115833.
Wilson, J.Q. (1968) 'Dilemmas of police administration', *Public Administration Review,* 28(5): 407–17. doi:10.2307/973756.
Woon, J. (2012) 'Democratic accountability and retrospective voting: a laboratory experiment', *American Journal of Political Science,* 56(4): 913–30.

Cases

Bivens v. Six Unknown Named Agents, 403 U.S. 388 (1971).
City of Los Angeles v. Lyons, 461 U.S. 95 (1983).
Davis v. United States, 564 U.S. 229 (2011).
Herring v. United States, 555 U.S. 135 (2009).
Mapp v. Ohio, 367 U.S. 643 (1961).
Miranda v. Arizona, 384 U.S. 436 (1966).
United States v. Wade, 388 U.S. 218 (1967).

16

Mercy and the roles of judges

Adam Perry

Introduction

Suppose that a person has been convicted of a crime and comes before a judge to be sentenced. This person has had a hard life, and the judge feels compassion for him. At first she is tempted to show mercy and impose a light sentence. She resists this temptation, though, and imposes a heavier but just sentence instead. Did the judge act rightly? When, if ever, ought judges to show mercy during sentencing? After the judge imposes her sentence, the criminal asks the head of state (or the appropriate executive body) to pardon him. Moved by the criminal's plight, the head of state shows mercy and grants his request. The criminal is not free yet, however. His victims go to the judge and ask her to rule that the pardon is invalid. On what basis ought judges to evaluate—or, as lawyers say, "review"—a decision by a head of state to grant (or withhold) mercy?

The first set of questions concerns the judge in her role as sentencer. The second set concerns the judge in her role as reviewer. When thinking about mercy in the criminal justice context, philosophers and criminal law scholars have tended to focus on judges as sentencers. Public law scholars, who on the whole have had less to say about mercy, have focused on judges as reviewers. There has been little dialogue between these groups of scholars, but I want to show we can better understand how judges ought to act in each of their roles by considering them alongside each other and alongside the roles of other institutional actors, particularly heads of state. Most of the discussion below is pitched at a general enough level to be relevant to any legal jurisdiction. When the discussion becomes more specific, I will confine my remarks to common law jurisdictions.

What is mercy?

Philosophers disagree as to the proper analysis of many concepts, but the disagreement is especially fierce when it comes to mercy. Some scholars have tried to explain why there is so little consensus about what mercy is; unfortunately, even they disagree.[1] This is not the place to propose another analysis of mercy, and I am not able to review, let alone assess, all of the existing ones. What I shall do instead is set out a common core of mercy then add to it by making several somewhat controversial assumptions. This will give me an account that few would accept without qualification but that captures what is often meant by mercy. This chapter is best read not as a defense of any understanding of mercy, but as a reflection on the implications for judges of one possible understanding of mercy.

The core of mercy

Everyone accepts that, for you to now be merciful to me, several conditions must be met. They are that (i) there are two acts *A* and *B* you can now perform; (ii) you perform *A*; and (iii) your performing *A* harms[2] me less than your performing *B* would have harmed me.

Permissibility and justice

Conditions (i)-(iii) are often satisfied even when no act of mercy has been performed. Suppose that a maniac roams the street with a gun in his pocket. Spying me waiting at a traffic light, he decides I will be his first victim. He approaches with the gun in his hand. Before he shoots, he changes his mind and moves away. Conditions (i)-(iii) are met in this scenario, but the maniac has clearly not acted mercifully. What is missing? When you show mercy, you choose not to impose a harm even though doing so is, *in a certain sense*, permissible. The difficult question is what this "certain sense" is.[3] Indeed, this may be the most difficult issue mercy poses. We do not need to resolve it to know that the maniac has not acted mercifully, because it is hard to imagine *any* notion of permissibility that would sanction killing me in cold blood. But we do need to know what the relevant notion of permissibility is to understand mercy in a general way.

Here I shall make my first somewhat controversial assumption. I shall assume that the relevant notion of permissibility is permissibility according to *justice*, such that (iv) your performing *B* would have been just. By "justice" I mean justice according to morality, not (necessarily) justice according to law. I assume that justice in this sense fixes the relevant notion of permissibility for two reasons. First, it is consistent with how most philosophers now think about mercy. Alwynne Smart set the tone for much of the contemporary discussion of mercy when she wrote that a person who shows mercy "decides that a particular punishment would be appropriate or just, and then decides to exact a punishment of lesser severity than the appropriate or just one."[4] Second, even if mercy does not always pose a challenge to justice, it does in the cases that create real dilemmas for judges, and these cases are my concern here.

Compassion

It is uncontroversial that mercy and compassion are closely connected, but the precise nature of that connection is controversial. One view is that compassion is essential to any merciful *act*, such that you act mercifully toward a person only if you act out of compassion for that person. Another view is that compassion is essential to a merciful *character*, such that you are a merciful person only if you are disposed to act mercifully out of compassion for others. If you act out of self-interest, then according to the first view, you have not acted mercifully; according to the second view, you might have acted mercifully, but you will not have shown yourself to be a merciful person. I find the second view more attractive because it explains why a person can act mercifully without being a merciful person. I cannot argue for that view here, however, so I shall assume in what follows that compassion is relevant to whether a person is merciful, not to whether she acts mercifully.[5]

Duty and grace

Some philosophers treat its normative status as part of the concept of mercy; others separate the two issues. I shall take the latter approach for the sake of simplicity. To act mercifully is to act in a way that is (at least *prima facie*) morally good. This is consistent with either of two possibilities: that mercy is supererogatory or that mercy is the subject of a moral duty. A person who never performs a supererogatory act is not, for that reason, morally blameworthy. By contrast, a person who never acts mercifully is, for that reason, morally blameworthy. So mercy must be the subject of a moral duty.[6]

There are different kinds of moral duties. Some moral duties give you a degree of discretion or latitude as to when, how often, in what manner, or with respect to whom you must perform some act (or perhaps latitude along other dimensions); others give you no latitude at all. This is the distinction between *imperfect* and *perfect* moral duties. Which is the duty to act mercifully: imperfect or perfect? Were the duty to act mercifully a perfect duty, a person would be (at least *prima facie*) morally blameworthy for not performing a particular merciful act. As George Rainbolt has pointed out, though, this is not how we think about mercy.[7] We think people can be criticized for never acting mercifully, but not for failing to act mercifully on this or that occasion. So it would seem that mercy is the subject of an imperfect moral duty, one that requires us to act mercifully some of the time but not all of the time.

There is another reason to think of mercy as the subject of an imperfect moral duty. Mercy is commonly thought to be a "gift" or an act of "grace."[8] It is up to you whether to act mercifully on a particular occasion. No one has a moral right that you show mercy to him specifically; no one may demand mercy, only ask for it. This is exactly what we would expect if mercy is the subject of an imperfect moral duty, given the latitude it confers.

Genuine mercy and royal mercy

Almost all legal jurisdictions give the head of state (or another executive body[9]) the power to pardon criminals, i.e., to remit all or part of a criminal's sentence. In the United Kingdom and some other jurisdictions, this pardoning power is called the "royal prerogative of mercy," and lawyers and legal scholars in these jurisdictions understandably tend to describe any granting of a pardon as an act of "mercy." Let us call the grant of a pardon an act of "royal mercy."

An act of royal mercy always meets conditions (i)–(iii). The head of state will have two acts open to her: granting or refusing a pardon. When she grants a pardon, she harms a criminal either not at all or less than she would have by refusing the pardon. Condition (iv) is more difficult. If a judge has sentenced a criminal to a just punishment, then refusing a pardon to the criminal would be consistent with justice. Condition (iv) is then met. If the head of state pardons the criminal anyway (as in the example in the introduction), then the head of state shows royal mercy *and* genuine mercy. A judge may impose an unjust sentence, however. (This may not be the judge's fault. The law may not permit the morally just sentence.) In such a case, for the head of state to refuse a pardon would be inconsistent with justice. So, by granting the pardon, the head of state shows royal mercy but *not* genuine mercy. In short, if judges have acted justly, then royal mercy will be genuine mercy but otherwise not. In what follows, my concern shall be acts of royal mercy only insofar as they are also acts of genuine mercy.

Judges as sentencers

Suppose the law allows a judge to sentence a thief to either 1 or 2 years in prison. A sentence of 2 years would be just. A sentence of 1 year would be unjust, so imposing that sentence would be merciful. Which sentence ought the judge to impose?

Conflicting duties

It is often said that a judge has a duty to do justice within the law. This does not mean that a judge has a duty to do justice all the time. She has a duty to do justice while acting as a judge. Doing justice is part of a judge's "job description," to use Jeffrie Murphy's phrase.[10] In the role of sentencer, a judge has a duty to impose just sentences, i.e., to sentence criminals to just punishments as far as the law allows. Now, I take it to be intuitive that a judge has a *duty* to act justly and a more specific *duty* to sentence justly. (If you are sceptical, though, I ask you to wait until the next section when I give some reasons for these claims.)

As I said, there is also a duty to act mercifully. The duty to act mercifully applies to everyone, so it applies to judges. A judge is not under a duty to act mercifully because she is a judge (or, at least, not only for that reason[11]). She is under a duty to act mercifully because she is a human being. Thus, with this personal duty in mind, Antony Duff writes that "[m]ercy … is not a virtue of sentencers, qua sentencers; it is not a virtue internal to the role of sentencer within a system of criminal law. It is, rather, a virtue of the human beings who fill that role."[12] A judge who imposes a merciful sentence is guided not by the demands of her office but by her emotions toward the person before her, whom she treats "simply as a suffering fellow."[13]

So, judges have two duties: a role-based duty to sentence justly and a non-role-based or personal duty to act mercifully. In cases like the one above, these duties conflict. Which sentence the judge ought to impose—the 2-year just sentence, or the 1-year merciful sentence—depends on how this conflict is resolved.

Resolving the conflict

Some conflicts between duties are resolved based on the relative importance of the duties. Some other conflicts can be resolved by the availability of alternative ways of fulfilling one of the two duties—and this is usually the case when it comes to the conflict between a judge's role-based duty in justice and a judge's personal duty in mercy.

To fulfill her duty to sentence justly, a judge must impose a just sentence on *every* criminal she sentences. If she sentences even one criminal unjustly, she violates her duty. The judge's duty to sentence justly gives her no latitude as to whom to treat justly, or on what occasions. Her duty to sentence justly is a perfect duty. Her duty to act mercifully, by contrast, is an imperfect duty. The different character of these duties is crucial, because it means a judge can fulfill both duties. All she needs to do is to always impose just sentences, thereby fulfilling her duty to sentence justly, and to perform a considerable number of merciful acts in her personal life, thereby fulfilling her duty in mercy. Although a judge must sometimes choose between justice and mercy in her role as sentencer, she need not choose between fulfilling her duty to sentence justly and fulfilling her duty to act mercifully.

As a general principle, you ought to act in a way that fulfills two duties rather than in a way that fulfills only one of them.[14] This suggests that a judge ought to always impose just sentences, even when they are merciless. In short, a judge ought to do justice at work, reserving mercy for her personal life. In terms of the example, above, this would mean that the judge ought to sentence the thief to 2 years. She is acting mercilessly by doing so, but she can make up for it by acting mercifully on other occasions, in her personal life.

To be clear, this is not an argument to the effect that a judge's role-based duty to sentence justly is more important than her personal duty to act mercifully. The argument is that her duty to sentence justly takes priority because there is an alternate, equally good way for the judge to fulfill her duty in mercy, but no alternate, equally good way for the judge to fulfill her duty in justice.

Other duties

The "general principle" that a person ought to fulfill two duties rather than just one of them is merely that—a generalization, which may not always hold true. In particular, it may not hold true when there are more than two duties in play.[15] A judge might restrict mercy to her personal life to avoid violating her duty in justice, only to find that she cannot act mercifully in her personal life without violating some other duty (e.g., a promissory duty). In such a case, what ought the judge to do?

Without trying to answer this question definitively, there are a few points that stand out. First, these cases will be unusual. Judges have roughly as many opportunities to show mercy in their personal lives as the rest of us, and we do not tend to find it impossible to reconcile our duty in mercy with our other duties. Second, asking "what ought the judge do?" amounts to asking "which duty ought the judge violate?" The answer to that question will depend on which duty is least important. Third, the least important duty may be neither the judge's duty in mercy, nor her duty in justice, but rather her "third" duty, i.e., the duty she cannot fulfill while acting mercifully in her personal life. In that case it will be unnecessary to decide whether her duty in mercy or justice is more important.

If the judge's choice comes down to fulfilling her duty in mercy or her duty in justice, there is at least one reason to think she ought to prioritize her duty in justice. Were the judge to do otherwise and give priority to her duty in mercy, she would be using the powers and discretion entrusted to her by the public not for the public good, but to fulfill her *personal* duty. Normally, we condemn that kind of act as an "abuse of power." Suppose, by way of comparison, that a friend of the judge's comes before her for sentencing. She can fulfill her duty in friendship, or she can impose the just sentence. To my mind, there is no genuine dilemma here: The judge's public duty comes first. As it is with friendship, so it would seem to be with the judge's other personal duties—including mercy.

Judges in context

I have been taking it as given that a judge's only duty to act mercifully is the duty we all have to act mercifully. In other words, I have been taking it as given that a judge does not have any additional, role-based duty to act mercifully. Maybe that is wrong, though. Suppose a judge defends her merciful sentencing like this:

> It is true that everyone has a duty to act mercifully and that I am no different in this respect. It is true, too, that I ought not to let my personal duty in mercy interfere with my duties as a judge. But it is wrong to set mercy in opposition to the official role of a judge and to imply in this way that by passing a merciful sentence I am failing to act as a judge qua judge ought to act. For it is not only individuals who should act mercifully. The state should, too. The state should temper justice with mercy—and as an agent of the state, so should I. Therefore, by showing mercy, I am not putting a personal duty ahead of a professional one; I am recognizing that justice does not define the whole of my duty as a judge.

The idea is that the state should sometimes act mercifully, and a judge should act to advance or fulfill this aim or duty by sometimes acting mercifully herself. In that case, justice would not exhaust a judge's official duties, nor could mercy properly be confined to a judge's personal life. A judge qua judge would properly be guided by considerations of both justice and mercy.

One objection might be that, contrary to what the judge has argued, in fact the state should always act justly, never mercifully. Some philosophers do say this, but it seems doubtful to me.

It would mean that the state had a duty to punish (that is, to serve justice by giving wrongdoers the hard treatment they deserve), whereas what the state seems to have is a *right* to punish, which it can waive if it wishes. Moreover, there seem to be strong reasons for the state to waive this right and to act mercifully. Those reasons are similar to the reasons we as individuals have for acting mercifully: to reduce human suffering, to show an awareness of human frailty and weakness, and to show that we are strong enough not to need to react to every wrong.[16] This is not to say the state should act mercifully in all cases. That would lead to too much injustice, for one thing. Instead the state should strike a balance between justice and mercy.

These remarks are sketchy, and the relationship between justice and the state is a core concern of political philosophy. So in what follows I shall assume that the state should sometimes act mercifully and consider what other objections to the judge's argument might be made.

Institutional design

A second objection is that, even assuming the state should sometimes act mercifully, it is not the case that *judges* should sometimes act mercifully on behalf of the state. For this objection to be sound, there must be some other official who should act mercifully on behalf of the state instead. I think there is, and it is the head of state. I say that for four reasons.

First, even when the state shows mercy to a criminal, it should make known that punishing him would have been just. Otherwise, people might think the state treated the criminal justly, rather than unjustly but mercifully. The state would be seen as condoning the criminal's behaviour instead of condemning and forgiving it. These are very different messages to send. Moreover, by making the just punishment known, the state indicates what treatment people can expect from it in similar cases in the future, when mercy may not be forthcoming.

There are different ways the state can communicate what justice requires even when it ultimately shows mercy, but some ways are more effective. A judge might decide that a just punishment for a thief is 2 years imprisonment, decide that justice should yield to mercy, and order the thief to be released. We can find out that the just punishment was 2 years—but only by reading the judge's reasons. Instead, the judge could sentence the thief to 2 years, and the head of state could pardon him. Here we have two legal orders made by two legal institutions. Dividing responsibilities in this way allows the state to more clearly communicate the different demands made by justice and mercy.

Second, giving the job of deciding what is just to one institution and the job of deciding between justice and mercy to another institution has symbolic value. It shows clearly that there is a tradeoff between justice and mercy. In the time between the judge sentencing the criminal and the head of state pardoning him, the criminal's fate is clearly in the hands of the state; he is at the state's mercy. We do not want the state to revel in its power over us. But we do want it made clear that mercy cannot be expected. Justice should be reliable; mercy should be exceptional. When different officials perform justice and mercy at different times using different procedures, it draws attention to the difference in what the state is doing.

Third, an institution needs different legal powers when its job is to decide what is just than when its job is to decide between justice and mercy. Judges may have discretion to decide on a just punishment, but their discretion is usually limited. In Canada, for example, a judge must sentence a person convicted of second-degree murder to between 10 and 25 years in prison. The judge can show mercy (by imposing a sentence of 10 years), but only up to a point. By contrast, the Governor General, who represents Canada's head of state, can grant even a convicted murderer a full pardon. In common law jurisdictions generally, sentencing judges are able to show mercy to a lesser degree than heads of state. On the other hand, heads of state are unable to *increase* the punishment a judge has ordered, even when it would be just to do so. Both facts suggest that sentencing judges have the better tools with which to do justice and heads of state the powers more suited to showing mercy.

There is a fourth and more subtle reason that heads of state are better suited than judges to decide when to give priority to mercy. One way the state can act mercifully is by not insisting that a criminal serve his just punishment. But the state can act mercifully in other ways, too. To give just two examples:

(i) Some former students are burdened by large student loans. It will take them decades to pay these loans back, if not longer, and their lives are harder as a result. By "forgiving" these debts, the state would show mercy.
(ii) During the recent housing crisis, many people ended up with mortgages they could not hope to pay back. When states were not legally obligated to forgive them, but did so anyway, they showed mercy.[17]

In the same way that an individual has a duty to act mercifully sometimes but not always, the state should act mercifully sometimes but not always. The state should show mercy often enough, but not too often. So, there are two points: The state has opportunities to show mercy outside the criminal justice context, and the state should not act on all of its opportunities to show mercy.

As a result, a state needs to somehow *coordinate* or *ration* its merciful activity. The state's merciful activity in one context must be set against its merciful activity in other contexts to ensure that, overall, it acts mercifully often enough but not too often. Thus, the more often the state acts mercifully in other contexts, the less often it needs to act mercifully in the criminal justice context and vice versa. This may sound too calculating, but the idea is a familiar one: Just as an individual should decide whether she is acting mercifully enough by considering all aspects of her life, the state should decide whether it is acting mercifully often enough by considering all aspects of its activity.

The most obvious way for the state to coordinate its merciful activity is by centralizing much of its merciful activity in one institution. That institution will not be the judiciary. Judges do not have opportunities to show mercy as officials except in the courtroom. They are deliberately kept separate from the rest of government. The executive, by contrast, has many opportunities to show mercy beyond the criminal justice context. Indeed, in many states, the acts in (i) and (ii) would be overseen by the executive.

I have given several reasons judges should leave mercy to the executive. I should add that this is often exactly what judges do. Consider the Canadian case of *R v. Latimer.*[18] Latimer had killed his severely disabled daughter for (he said) compassionate reasons. After his conviction for second-degree murder, the trial judge imposed a sentence of 10 years, which was the minimum sentence the law allowed. The trial judge also recommended that the executive consider showing Latimer mercy. The Supreme Court, which upheld the sentence, said:

> [T]he prerogative [of mercy] is a matter for the executive, not the courts. The executive will undoubtedly, if it chooses to consider the matter, examine all of the underlying circumstances surrounding the tragedy of Tracy Latimer that took place … some seven years ago. Since that time Mr. Latimer has undergone two trials and two appeals to the Court of Appeal for Saskatchewan and this Court, with attendant publicity and consequential agony for him and his family.[19]

The Supreme Court is clearly of the opinion that Latimer's suffering and the suffering of his family are relevant to whether he should receive mercy. Equally clearly, the Court thinks these are factors for the *executive* to consider, because it is the executive that ought to decide whether to show Latimer mercy.[20]

In the last section I said that a judge should not use her public office to fulfill her personal duty in mercy. One of my arguments was that she had an alternative way to fulfill her personal duty. My argument for why judges should not seek to show mercy on behalf of the state has a parallel structure. Judges should not try to show mercy on behalf of the state because there is an alternate and better way for the state to show mercy, namely, through the executive. In short, judges should not act mercifully as sentencers because mercy should be given over to other spheres of their lives and to other state officials.

Institutional realities

Suppose that the executive announces a policy that says, in effect—no pardons, no exceptions. The executive keeps all of its powers and capabilities, but it refuses to issue any more pardons. Judges know that if they do not show mercy to criminal wrongdoers, no one will. Now, we would need to know more to be sure (including why the executive refused to issue pardons), but it seems that the argument I outlined for why judges should stick to doing justice no longer holds true. The executive should show mercy on behalf of the state, and if it does, judges should not. But if the executive is unwilling to do its job, then it seems to be better that judges do it for them than that no one does.

In the scenario in the last paragraph the executive says it will *never* show mercy. That is unrealistic.[21] But is easy to imagine that the executive will show mercy in the criminal justice context less often than it should. Alex Tuckness and John M. Parrish have described a "decline of mercy in public life," including a decline in the number of executive pardons in the United States. They write:

> Perhaps the most stunning contemporary use of the power to pardon and commute sentences was the decision of Governor Ryan of Illinois to pardon or commute the sentences of all 171 inmates on the state's death row shortly before he left office. To put this into perspective, that one act was more than four times the number of pardons and commutations in death penalty cases by all American governors combined over the previous twenty years.[22]

There are no doubt many causes of the decline in the number of pardons, and it may be that this decline is to be welcomed. That depends on how often the state should be merciful. But if the executive is not acting mercifully as often as it should, as Tuckness and Parrish seem to believe, perhaps judges should ensure the state continues to show mercy to criminal wrongdoers.

Judges as reviewers

Even if judges should let the executive show mercy on the state's behalf, this does not mean that judges have no role relevant to mercy. They do—the role of reviewer. At this point we move from the domain of the criminal law to that of public law. What follows is a brief sketch of the relevant basics of public law.

The executive is given legal authority to make certain decisions, but this authority comes with conditions attached. A decision that does not meet these conditions is "invalid," i.e., without legal effect. Judges have the responsibility to determine the validity of the executive's decision, an activity that is known (in many but not all common law jurisdictions) as "judicial review." The "grounds of review" are the conditions a decision must meet to be valid.

With respect to executive decisions to grant or refuse pardons, judges traditionally exercised a very light touch review. This is still the case in the United States. Elsewhere in the common law world, though, things are changing. Judges in Canada,[23] England and Wales,[24] India,[25] Northern Ireland,[26] Singapore,[27] and other jurisdictions are now willing to review pardoning decisions on a range of grounds. It would take more space than I have to discuss the different approaches these jurisdictions have taken. So I shall focus on the ground of review that raises the most interesting philosophical issues, namely, consistency.

Suppose there are two convicted thieves, Thief 1 and Thief 2, their cases alike in all relevant respects. Each has been sentenced to a just punishment of 5 years in prison. The head of state shows mercy to Thief 1 and grants him a full pardon but refuses Thief 2's request for a pardon. Thief 2 asks a judge to review the head of state's decision. His argument is simple. There was no more reason for the head of state to show mercy to the other thief than to him. The head of state has acted inconsistently and hence arbitrarily. And this, the thief says, she should not be permitted to do.

The thief's argument raises an ancient problem regarding mercy. The thief's objection is to inconsistent *legal* mercy, but St. Anselm had much the same concern with seemingly inconsistent *divine* mercy. Anselm wrote:

> But if it can be comprehended in any way why you can will to save the wicked, yet by no consideration can we comprehend why, of those who are alike wicked, you save some rather than others, through supreme goodness; and why thou dost condemn the latter, rather than the former, through supreme justice.[28]

How, Anselm asked, could it be right to show mercy to some of those who deserve punishment, but not to others who are equally deserving?

Perhaps an answer can be found with respect to divine mercy, as Anselm thought. In the legal context, however, courts are often hostile to inconsistent acts of mercy by heads of state. In India, for example, the Supreme Court has long held that pardoning decisions are reviewable for arbitrariness.[29] In Northern Ireland, the Court of Appeal has been willing to conduct detailed comparisons of pardoning decisions to see if they have been made in an "unequal" or "inconsistent" way.[30] Courts in England have been willing to invalidate pardoning decisions if they are not based on "relevant" factors or are based on "irrelevant" factors.[31]

The question for us is, *should* courts review pardoning decisions for inconsistency? The answer will be "yes" only if it is objectionable to make pardoning decisions inconsistently. Intuitively it seems that it must be. Yet it turns out to be hard to say what exactly the objection is.

Let us start with justice. Some philosophers, including Joel Feinberg, say that there are two kinds of justice.[32] Non-comparative justice requires that people be treated as they deserve. Comparative justice, by contrast, requires that people similarly situated be treated similarly. Punishing Thief 2 is comparatively unjust, given that Thief 1, similarly situated, was let free. That makes the head of state's decision to refuse a pardon to Thief 2 objectionable, in a sense. But we should not condemn her decision yet. Letting Thief 2 go free might be comparatively just, but it would be non-comparatively unjust (because he deserves a punishment of 5 years in prison). There is a conflict between non-comparative and comparative justice. There is no dilemma here, though, because as Feinberg says, "injustice by noncomparative standards tends to be a much more serious thing than comparative injustice."[33] When they conflict, non-comparative justice prevails over comparative justice. So, even assuming there are two kinds of justice, justice does not favor pardoning Thief 2 in an overall sense.[34]

Another possible objection is based on rationality. Rationality is often said to require like cases to be treated alike. Were this indeed what rationality requires, the head of state would have acted irrationally by showing mercy to Thief 1 but not to Thief 2. This is not what rationality requires, however. Suppose there is a bowl of red and green jellybeans, and you have a reason to take any two. You take a red one, then you take a green one. You have acted "inconsistently," but not irrationally. What rationality requires is for you to respond appropriately to your reasons. When a choice is undetermined by your reasons, as the choice of jellybeans is, you act rationally whichever choice you make. The state has a reason to sometimes show mercy. But it has no greater reason to show mercy to one wrongdoer than to another. As long as the state shows mercy to enough people, it responds appropriately to the reason mercy provides it with. So, the state can show mercy inconsistently without acting irrationally.[35]

We might instead object to the head of state's inconsistency on practical grounds. If the head of state makes consistent decisions, then her decisions will be easier to predict. In general, predictability in legal decision-making is valuable, because it allows citizens to plan their lives better. However, as Andrei Marmor points out, this general point does not apply with equal force in all contexts.[36] It is important that tax decisions be made consistently because people should be provided with a stable basis on which to plan their economic lives. But the value of predictability is less obvious with respect to criminal punishments and less obvious still when it comes to mercy. What valuable plans are likely to be disrupted or inhibited by unpredictable pardoning decisions?

There is a second and stronger practical objection to inconsistent pardoning decisions. Suppose you, as a private individual, only show mercy to people who pay you to do so. There is something wrong here, but the fault lies not with what you have done but with you, and specifically your character. To act mercifully is one thing; to be a merciful person is another. To be a merciful person means being disposed to act mercifully out of love or compassion. By only showing mercy for money, you show yourself not to be a merciful person, and that is grounds for criticizing you. Just as we care about a private individual's motives for acting mercifully, we care about the state's motives for acting mercifully. We want the state to not just act mercifully, but to be merciful. That is to say, we want the state to act mercifully out of compassion or sympathy for us, its citizens. If the head of state's pardoning decisions are the result of improper motives like nepotism, racism, or corruption, instead of compassion, the head of state and the state she represents are open to criticism. If pardoning decisions are made inconsistently, even taking into account the features of cases that properly evoke compassion, then people may tend to believe that the inconsistency is the result of improper motives. If it is valuable to avoid such suspicions, then it may be valuable to ensure that pardoning decisions are made consistently.

This seems to me to be a sound, but limited, objection to inconsistent pardoning decisions. It is limited because, while a requirement of consistency is one way to avoid suspicions of impropriety, there might be other, even better ways. For example, the process of making pardoning decisions could be made highly public. Or, heads of state could be required to prepare guidelines setting out the kinds of factors they will consider. Or, judges could simply ask whether pardoning decisions have been made for improper purposes—as judges in some jurisdictions in fact do.[37] It would be worthwhile to compare these alternatives in detail. For now, the somewhat surprising result is that there seems to be nothing wrong with arbitrary pardoning decisions in themselves. If they are objectionable, it is because they are a symptom of other problems.

Summary

Discussions of judges and mercy have tended to focus narrowly on sentencing. I have discussed sentencing, but I have also widened the focus to include judges' personal lives and the opportunities they present for showing mercy; the institutional context within which judges operate; and judges' power to review the merciful decisions of the executive. My major claims are, first, judges should not fulfill their personal duties to act mercifully by imposing merciful sentences. Second, judges should not try to act mercifully on behalf of the state. They should let the executive do that job. But a possible exception is if the executive is unwilling to do that job. Finally, there is reason to think that judges are entitled to review the executive's pardoning decisions for consistency as a means of avoiding the appearance of improperly motivated pardons.

Notes

1 See, e.g., Alex Tuckness and John M. Parrish, *The Decline of Mercy in Public Life* (Cambridge: Cambridge University Press 2014) c 9 (arguing that mercy is a family resemblance concept); K. Bell, 'Mercy and criminal justice' (unpublished PhD manuscript) (arguing that there are actually two concepts of mercy).

2 I am using 'harm' in a broad sense to mean hard or undesirable treatment, such that even deserved punishments count as harms.

3 See N. Markosian, 'Two Puzzles about Mercy' (2013) 63 *Philosophical Quarterly* 269 for an excellent discussion of the different notions of permissibility that have featured in debates about mercy.

4 A. Smart, 'Mercy' (1968) 43 *Philosophy* 345, 350. See also J. Murphy, 'Mercy and legal justice', in J. Murphy and J. Hampton, *Forgiveness and Mercy* (Cambridge: Cambridge University Press 1990); A Duff, 'Mercy' in J. Deigh and D. Dolinko (eds.), *Oxford Handbook of the Philosophy of Criminal Law* (OUP 2011) 480.

5 Others have argued for this view, e.g., A. Brien, 'Mercy, utilitarianism and retributivism' (1995) 24 *Philosophia* 493, 498–99.

6 As far as I know, this argument was first made in G. Rainbolt, 'Mercy: an independent, imperfect virtue' (1990) 27 *American Philosophical Quarterly* 169, 171.

7 G. Rainbolt, 'Mercy: in defense of caprice' (1997) 31 *Nous* 226, 231–36. Others who have claimed that mercy is an imperfect duty include S. Garvey, 'Is it wrong to commute Death Row? Retribution, atonement, and mercy' (2004) 82 *North Carolina Law Review* 1319, 1331–1334; S. Kershnar, 'Mercy, retributivism, and harsh punishment' (2000) 14 *International Journal of Applied Philosophy* 209.

8 That mercy is an act of grace is a common theme in literature. It is often expressed in the law, too. See, e.g., *United States v Wilson*, 2 U.S. (7 Pet.) 150 (1883) at 160; *Reckley v Minister of Public Safety and Immigration (No 2)* [1996] AC 527 at 540.

9 In some states, including the United States, the head of state has the legal power to issue pardons, and exercises real discretion as to the exercise of that power. In other states, including the United Kingdom, the head of state has the legal power to issue pardons, but de facto and indeed constitutional control over the exercise of that power lies with the government. To avoid awkward constructions, I shall write as if the decision lies in law and in fact with the head of state.

10 J. Murphy, 'Mercy and legal justice' in J. Murphy and J. Hampton, *Forgiveness and Mercy* (Cambridge: Cambridge University Press 1990) 175.

11 I consider whether showing mercy is part of a judge's responsibilities as a judge in the next section.

12 A. Duff, 'Mercy' in J. Deigh and D. Dolinko (eds.), *Oxford Handbook of the Philosophy of Criminal Law* (Oxford: Oxford University Press 2011) 480.

13 Ibid. 479.

14 S. Hale, 'Against supererogation' (1991) 28 American Philosophical Quarterly 273, 276 ('when the demands of a perfect duty conflict with the demands of an imperfect duty, it is morally forbidden to neglect the demands of the perfect duty; whereas, the demands of the imperfect duty are not neglected in a morally permissible manner by acting on the perfect duty rather than on the imperfect duty'). For a similar 'principle of conflict resolution' with respect to reasons, see J. Raz, *Practical Reason and Norms* (Princeton, NJ: Princeton University Press 1990) 188.

15 A point made by J. Raz, *Practical Reason and Norms* (Princeton University Press 1990) 188.

16 G. Rainbolt, 'Mercy, justice and the death penalty' (unpublished manuscript).

17 This example is from Alan Tuckness and John M. Parrish, *The Decline of Mercy in Public Life* (Cambridge: Cambridge University Press 2014) 3.

18 *R v. Latimer* [2001] 1 SCR 3.

19 Ibid. [89].

20 Ultimately Latimer did not apply for mercy.

21 Apparently only one regime has officially abolished pardons, and that was for a short time, during the French Revolution of 1789. See K. Moore, *Pardons: Justice, Mercy, and the Public Interest* (New York: Oxford University Press 1989) 24–25.

22 Alan Tuckness and John M. Parrish, *The Decline of Mercy in Public Life* (Cambridge: Cambridge University Press 2014) 2. The authors add that, by contrast, in many European countries pardons and amnesties remain common.

23 *Thatcher v Attorney General of Canada* [1997] 1 FC 289 (reviewable for procedural and substantive unfairness).
24 *McGeough v Secretary of State for Northern Ireland* [2012] NICA 28 (inconsistency).
25 *Maru Ram v Union of India* [1980] INSC 213 (arbitrariness, bias); *Epuru Sudhakar v Government of Andhra Pradesh* [2006] INSC 638 (relevancy, failure to exercise discretion).
26 *R v Secretary of State for the Home Department, ex p Bentley* [1994] QB 349 (error of law); *R (Page) v Secretary of State for Justice* [2007] EWHC 2026 (Admin) (relevancy).
27 *Yong Vui Kong v Attorney General* [2011] SGCA 9 (procedural impropriety).
28 St. Anselm, *Proslogium* XI (translated by SN Deane, Chicago: Open Court 1903).
29 *Maru Ram v Union of India* [1980] INSC 213 at [62].
30 *McGeough v Secretary of State for Northern Ireland* [2012] NICA 28.
31 See, e.g., *R (Page) v Secretary of State for Justice* [2007] EWHC 2026 (Admin).
32 J. Feinberg, 'Noncomparative justice' (1974) 83 *Philosophical Review* 297.
33 Ibid. 317.
34 Another response would be that this kind of example shows that the distinction between comparative and noncomparative justice is flawed, and that Thief 2 has not been treated unjustly in any meaningful sense: see P. Montague, 'Comparative and noncomparative justice' (1980) 30 *Philosophical Quarterly* 131, 133.
35 For a related argument, see J. Tasioulas, 'Mercy' (2003) 103 *Proceedings of the Aristotelian Society* 101, 129–130.
36 A Marmor, 'Should like cases be treated alike?' (2005) 11 *Legal Theory* 27, 33–34.
37 See, e.g., *Epuru Sudhakar v Government of Andhra Pradesh* [2006] INSC 638 (invalidating a pardon given to a person for being 'a good Congress worker', at [55]).

Bibliography

Bell, K. 'Mercy and criminal justice', unpublished PhD manuscript.

Brien, A. (1995) 'Mercy, utilitarianism and retributivism'. *24 Philosophia,* 493: 498–99.

Duff, A. (2011) 'Mercy', in J. Deigh and D. Dolinko (eds.) *Oxford Handbook of the Philosophy of Criminal Law,* Oxford: Oxford University Press, p. 480.

Epuru Sudhakar v Government of Andhra Pradesh [2006] INSC 638.

Feinberg, J. (1974) 'Noncomparative justice', *Philosophical Review,* 83: 297.

Garvey, S. (2004) 'Is it wrong to commute death row? Retribution, atonement, and mercy', *North Carolina Law Review,* 82: 1319, 1331–1334.

Hale, S. (1991) 'Against supererogation', *28 American Philosophical Quarterly,* 28: 273, 276.

Kershnar, S. (2000) 'Mercy, retributivism, and harsh punishment', *International Journal of Applied Philosophy,* 14: 209.

Markosian, N. (2013) 'Two puzzles about mercy', *Philosophical Quarterly,* 63: 269.

Marmor, A. (2005) 'Should like cases be treated alike?', *Legal Theory,* 11: 27, 33–34.

Maru Ram v Union of India [1980] INSC 213.

McGeough v Secretary of State for Northern Ireland [2012] NICA 28.

Moore, K. (1989). *Pardons: Justice, Mercy, and the Public Interest,* Oxford: Oxford University Press.

Montague, P. (1980) 'Comparative and noncomparative justice', *Philosophical Quarterly,* 30: 131, 133.

Murphy, J. (2011) 'Mercy and legal justice' in J. Murphy and J. Hampton *Forgiveness and Mercy,* New York, NY: Cambridge University Press.

Rainbolt, G. (1990) 'Mercy: an independent, imperfect virtue', *American Philosophical Quarterly,* 27: 169, 171.

Rainbolt, G. (1997) 'Mercy: in defense of caprice', *Nous,* 31: 226, 231–236.

Rainbolt, G. 'Mercy, justice and the death penalty', unpublished manuscript.

Raz, J. (1990) *Practical Reason and Norms*: Princeton, NJ: Princeton University Press, p. 188.

R v Latimer [2001] 1 SCR 3.

R (Page) v Secretary of State for Justice [2007] EWHC 2026 (Admin).

R v Secretary of State for the Home Department, ex p Bentley [1994] QB 349.

Reckley v Minister of Public Safety and Immigration (No 2) [1996] AC 527 at 540.

Smart, A. (1968) 'Mercy' *Philosophy,* 43: 345, 350.

Tasioulas, J. (2003) 'Mercy', *Proceedings of the Aristotelian Society,* 103: 101, 129–130.

Thatcher v Attorney General of Canada [1997] 1 FC 289.

Tuckness, A and Parrish, J. M. (2014) *The Decline of Mercy in Public Life,* Cambridge: Cambridge University Press, c 9.

United States v Wilson, 2 U.S. (7 Pet.) 150 (1883) at 160.

Yong Vui Kong v Attorney General [2011] SGCA 9.

St. Anselm, *Proslogium* XI (translated by SN Deane, Chicago: Open Court 1903).

17

The ethics of innovation in criminal justice

Hannah Graham and Rob White

Introduction

This chapter presents a bounded analysis of the nature and impact of innovation in criminal justice contexts. Implicit within this reflexive critique are some evocative questions. What constitutes innovation, and who or what is being reformed? What makes advances in criminal justice just? According to whom and to benefit whom? Calls for criminal justice reform and public service innovation continue to saturate public, professional, and academic discourses in many jurisdictions. Yet, while support for change in principle may be widely observed, it is not matched by a commensurate level of consensus regarding the forms and directions changes might take in practice, and why.

In this chapter, we present one possible schema whereby innovation in criminal justice contexts can be analysed in a more systematic fashion. Specifically, after describing 'social innovation' as the central concept of interest here, we start to test its possibilities by interrogating it in terms of what Siedman (2010) calls strategies of amelioration, disruption and transformation, and accommodation. In doing this, we reflect on the extent to which creative and pioneering forms of social innovation may be used not only to benefit the people involved, but also the extent to which they ameliorate, disrupt and transform, or accommodate macro-processes of mass supervision and hyper-incarceration.

Against the backdrop of contemporary criminal justice systems and penal cultures, we use this schema to demonstrate that innovation is not morally or politically neutral. In other words, not all that is 'innovative' is necessarily good or just (Graham and White 2014). Questions about the forms and functions ('what', 'where', and 'how') of innovation in criminal justice should not be divorced from questions about its architects and beneficiaries, including their intentions and ideologies ('who' and 'why'). Attention is drawn to issues of power and politics in considering which 'innovative' justice initiatives are genuinely predicated on a logic of reform and which paradoxically propagate the status quo or mask the sources and effects of the carceral problems they are supposed to resolve.

To preface these discussions, it is necessary to clarify the terrain that lies beyond the scope of our analysis. This chapter does not focus on new developments in electronic monitoring and surveillance technologies, psychological rehabilitation programmes, or the next generation of criminogenic risk assessment tools. Although prominent features of contemporary criminal justice, in many senses these represent the *status quo* rather than something particularly innovative or creative. Similarly, routine features of offender management processes (e.g., monitoring and compliance) and the labelling of people by risk, diagnosis, or crime type are largely peripheral to the line of inquiry pursued in this chapter. Rather, we wish to highlight social justice and social change as integral to our notion of innovation and the ethics and efficacy of its use in advancing positive penal and social change.

Social innovation – forms and functions

It is striking how little critical reflection there has been within criminology on the meaning and consequences of innovation. In part, this has made the task of developing this chapter that much harder, insofar as while it purports to consider the ethics of innovation in criminal justice, there is limited theoretical and empirical scholarship upon which to draw from within the field of criminology. While terms such as 'innovative' and 'creative' are increasingly used to denote a plethora of new developments in criminal justice, their meaning and use in this chapter is imbued with an emphasis on *social innovation*. This is similar but different to the more widely used general term 'innovation', which carries multiple connotations deriving from its intellectual origins in business and science.

Social innovation (SI) is premised on being a response to a need, problem, or issue of social justice. Examples include food poverty, sexism and gender inequality, cyber-bullying, lack of infrastructure in war zones, sanitation issues, or climate change. Informing our analysis of SI here is the definition put forward by the Stanford Center for Social Innovation (2013):

> A novel solution or pioneering approach to a social problem that is more effective, efficient, sustainable, or just than present solutions and approaches, and where the value and benefits of these are social in the sense of collective.

Social innovation has the capacity to result in change and produce social value beyond the individual personalities and organisations that might have been instrumental in instigating or initiating it (Stanford Center for Social Innovation 2013; Graham and White 2015). Similarly, in articulating what is meant by 'social value', Phills, Deiglmeier and Miller (2008: 39) explain that it is 'the creation of benefits or reductions of costs for society – through efforts to address social needs and problems – in ways that go beyond private gains … [these benefits] may accrue to both disadvantaged or disenfranchised segments of society or society as a whole.' Swapping the term 'social problems' for the alternative of 'social needs', Murray, Caulier-Grice, and Mulgan (2010: 3) define social innovation as:

> New ideas (products, services and models) that simultaneously meet social needs and create new social relationships or collaborations. In other words, they are innovations that are both good for society *and* enhance society's capacity to act.

Notwithstanding the imprecision and contestability of the criterion of being 'good for society', this definition is similar to the first in that they are both implicitly relational and humanitarian in their orientation towards processes of social change.

Social innovations, as such, are exceptionally diverse in the forms and functions they may take. They often involve community groups, social enterprises, cooperatives, and charitable and civil society organisations in their implementation; however, private firms and public institutions are increasingly partnering with others to enable social innovations to thrive. Social innovations often recognise and tap into the capital of citizens and civil society, inspiring people's interest and mobilising their time and resources, in ways that state policies may struggle with or fail to do. Where there is a complementarity between policies and innovations, the latter are more likely to arise where policies *enable* their development; however, state policy is rarely their catalytic starting point. Innovations are more often nested in what is increasingly being referred to as 'eco-systems' of social innovation in recognition of the constellation of factors and actors that are often involved. Social innovations can be local or structural, ranging in scale and impact from 'grassroots'-level initiatives that tend to assist vulnerable people or particular communities of interest, through to systemic initiatives, which are catalysts for fundamental shifts in attitudes, values, strategies and policies, organisational structures, markets and economies, and systems (Bureau of European Policy Advisors [BEPA] 2011).

Examples of grassroots and community-level innovations include innovative education and digital social innovation technology initiatives that engage different groups of people (e.g., youth, prisoners) in response to issues of inequality and discrimination, such as exclusion from or discrimination in labour market participation and digital society. The 'Girls Who Code' (2015) initiative provides young women with intensive computer science education and matches them with female mentors from leading technology companies with the aim of challenging stereotypes and addressing gendered workforce inequalities in technology industries. In a prison context, The Last Mile (2015) program trains male and female prisoners as computer programmers, giving them access to cutting-edge technology and supporting their reintegration and post-release employment prospects in the fields of entrepreneurship and digital industries.

A different form of a community-level social innovation is 'time banking', where time is the central element or currency that can be traded or exchanged through a localised cooperative or community-level 'time banking' scheme. Each member's time and capacity to help is considered to be worth the same amount in a time bank, regardless of whether the individual is offering specialised professional skills or undertaking menial tasks. Time banking is 'a unique transaction-based system for mutual aid and assistance that fosters economic opportunities, social inclusion, community self-help and enhances civic engagement among often marginalised community members' (Marks 2012: 1230). Importantly, it can also enhance civic engagement among more influential actors and agencies in civic society. Time banks can be based on a 'person-to-person' model or a 'person-to-agency' model (Murray et al. 2010: 201), the latter of which can involve all sorts of stakeholders (e.g., including individual citizens, social housing services, local authorities, transport services, schools, trades and commercial services) and time volunteered can become a substitute or form of co-payment alongside money for things like bus fares or rent in social housing. There are existing time banking initiatives involving children, young people and families involved with youth justice and child welfare services (see Drakeford and Gregory 2010; Marks 2012), as well as with prisoners.

Examples of systemic or larger scale social innovations include: the Fair Trade movement advancing ethics and equality in global supply chains; digital social innovations (DSI), which harness the Internet and design new technologies and digital platforms to help overcome geographical, cultural, and social barriers (see European Union 2015); and progressive, participative environmental initiatives which tackle issues of sustainability and climate change. These range from 'eco-villages', to cooperatively owned renewable energy plants, through to emissions trading schemes that seek to influence market dynamics (see Murray et al. 2010). Some social innovations incorporate a strong socio-political element, assisting social movements and counter-hegemonic activism seeking social change.

Social innovation in criminal justice in an era of mass supervision and hyper-incarceration

In essence, social innovation is responsive, participative, and solution-focussed in nature. At every level of analysis, it is concerned with ethical and sustainable change. The aforementioned definitions emphasise the pursuit of social innovation as being premised on the acknowledgement of some kind of social problem or need. While theoretical and political debates about crime and justice continue to evolve in Western neoliberal jurisdictions, the characterisation of crime as a social problem attracts a moderate degree of public consensus (see Roberts and Hough 2002). Thus, social innovations that offer solutions and responses to the costs and harms of crime appear less likely to be rebuffed at face value as unfounded. Social innovation can be harnessed to serve community or collective interests, with its responses amenable to being targeted towards the immensely popular but imperfect ideal of reducing recidivism rates, without necessarily posing a challenge to the dominance of public protection agendas.

With regard to criminal justice, provocative questions linger. How might social innovation be rationalised in light of the costs and harms of crime control and criminal justice, especially in an era of fiscal constraint? The economic, social, moral and human costs and pains of incarceration and probation are well-documented (see, for example, Clear 1996; Durnescu 2010; Henrichson and Delaney 2012). Incisive critiques draw attention to the contributions of 'mass supervision' (that is, the burgeoning growth of community-based penal sanctions) and 'mass incarceration' or 'hyper-incarceration' (that is, spiralling incarceration rates, encompassing a racialised and gendered impact) to crime, social inequality and injustice (Clear 1994; Cunneen et al. 2013; Garland 2001a, 2001b; McNeill and Beyens 2014; Miller 2013, 2014; Simon 2000; Wacquant 2001, 2009; Wakefield and Uggen 2010). The inference that criminal justice policies and practices are as much of a social problem as the social problem they purport to address (crime) remains controversial but should not be disregarded. To accept policies and practices as neutral and unproblematic is to belie the social determinants and structural mechanisms that influence who does and who does not become subject to them. This, in turn, carries implications for who does and who does not need to participate in or become a beneficiary of a social innovation in criminal justice contexts.

Can social innovation be justified as a legitimate response to the proliferation of punishment? We believe it can. In most Western jurisdictions, crime rates are falling, and this trend is consistent over time (see Tonry 2014). The specific populations in which rates of criminal offending are *not* falling are those who have been subject to disproportionate rates of penal sanction, especially incarceration. It would therefore be more apt to ask whether the forms and functions of social innovation are better placed to respond to the needs and reintegration of people, individually and *en masse*, who have been subject to penal intervention? The rise of critical carceral studies and notions of hyper-incarceration add a certain level of credence to this purpose, insofar as the subjects of punishment are, more often than not, individuals and groups who live with social inequality, exclusion, and victimisation before, during and after criminal justice intervention (see Wacquant 2009; Cunneen et al. 2013).

If innovation in criminal justice is to accomplish ethical and effective impact, extending from the level of the individual (e.g., supporting desistance, reintegration, agency, and equality) through to the level of society (e.g., reducing mass supervision and hyper-incarceration, more creative responses to injustice), a considerable amount of theoretical and empirical work needs to be done. Others, such as Fox and Grimm (2015) and Grimm et al. (2013), have started to consider the ways in which social innovation in criminal justice might challenge neoliberal ideologies and policies. Similarly, it is our hope that the preliminary analysis incorporated in this chapter and in our 'Innovative Justice' international research findings elsewhere present a modest but helpful starting point to inform wider discussions (Graham and White 2014, 2015; Graham 2015a, 2015b, 2016; Graham, Graham, and Field 2015; White and Graham 2015). In particular, we are interested in using ethical critiques of the *status quo* from critical criminological scholars alongside visions of change from the field of social innovation. The remainder of this chapter is structured around this interest.

Innovative strategies of disruption: Moving beyond mass supervision and hyper-incarceration

In an excellent and aptly named piece on 'hyper-incarceration and strategies of disruption', Siedman (2010) envisions three types of strategies which have the potential to tackle the problem of hyper-incarceration in the United States, with particular emphasis on issues of racism and racial justice. Siedman (2010) categorises the three types of strategies for change as:

- the politics of amelioration;
- the politics of transformation and disruption; and
- the politics of accommodation.

Siedman (2010) focuses on penal change and its potential catalysts but does not cover the topic of innovation. In this chapter, we adapt and expand upon his three categories of strategies and apply them to a series of examples of social innovation, in order to consider the potential implications within and beyond criminal justice.

The three types of strategies differ in scope and temporal dimensions of the change and reform they seek to produce. Pragmatic and participative in style, 'ameliorative' ideas and approaches seek to realise improvements in the here-and-now, helping those most affected by crime and punishment (Siedman 2010). Conversely, 'accommodation' ideas and approaches involve a certain level of acceptance of existing penal cultures and practices that, in part, produce mass incarceration or hyper-incarceration, while incrementally seeking their adaptation to achieve more positive, or at the very least less harmful, outcomes. This type of 'solution' may not immediately appear to be innovative or to differ from normative approaches, yet it has the capacity to realise incremental change from the inside (Seidman 2010). By way of contrast, 'transformative' ideas and approaches reject and disrupt the *status quo*, and often entail alternatives to and/or extensive relinquishment of existing orders of penal power and social stratification. This type of strategy is less predictable in its impact: it may spark revolutionary and wide-reaching effects, which make it difficult to return to what was before, or it may amount to utopian but inchoate visions, which do little to mobilise the actions needed to realise them, either in part or in their totality (Seidman 2010). These three categorisations are not mutually exclusive; a moderate degree of overlap and hybridisation exists, as will become apparent in the discussions that follow.

Innovation as amelioration? Pragmatic, creative, and compassionate initiatives in criminal justice

The arts and creative practices in criminal justice

Above and beyond criminal justice contexts, the arts are more universally accepted as a medium for expression and enrichment, benefiting individuals as well as having the capacity to change environments and cultures. The longstanding history of the arts in criminal justice settings around the world precludes claims that their use is innovative in and of itself. However, specific applications of the arts and creative practices in criminal justice are being used in participative and progressive ways, which make them a form of social innovation. In prison and probation contexts, these include: choirs, orchestras and bands, story-telling forums, and writing groups, as well as books and poetry production, documentary film making and film clubs, graphic design, theatre, dance and choreography, photography, art exhibitions and fine arts, textiles and fashion design (see Cheliotis, 2012 and Graham and White, 2015).

Arts-based social ventures in criminal justice tend to take the form of social enterprises, charities, or cooperatives that collaborate with prison or probation personnel. For example, Fine Cell Work (2015) is a successful social enterprise that has been operating in English prisons for more than two decades. It trains prisoners in paid, skilled needlework, making bespoke hand-stitched products which are purchased by customers in the community. Fine Cell Work offers prisoner participants opportunities for income generation, a creative and productive avenue for making use of daily in-cell time, pro-social connections with community volunteers, training and learning, developing self-esteem in achieving a high standard of workmanship, and fostering positive identity change in the desistance process (Graham and White 2015). This initiative is particularly ameliorative for prisoners who face approximately 17 hours a day in their cell with few other meaningful activities available to them. One of the fascinating aspects of the achievements of this social enterprise is the ways in which it supplants stereotypes (e.g., traditional gender stereotypes about sewing) and respectfully defies the overarching risk-averse preoccupation of the closed institutions in which its creative practices occur (e.g., access to needles and thread in prison cells) (Graham and White 2015). Fine Cell Work represents just one example among many arts-based ventures doing positive work in correctional settings.

In terms of community-based initiatives, new forms of participative 'forum' theatre are emerging and give voice to the lived experience of social problems; they engage participants to think and act in ways that seek their amelioration and resolution. In Brazil, Augusto Boal has developed the 'Theatre of the Oppressed', where actors and non-actors play out stories of oppression, speaking through images, reflecting on issues (e.g., crime and victimisation, such as family violence) and emotions, and offering participants the ability to re-write the stories, collaboratively co-producing responses and alternative endings (Murray et al. 2010: 32). Participative forum theatre positions marginalised people and their experiences of social injustice as central, offering a potential emancipatory vehicle for healing and being heard. While participative and compassionate in *response* to injustice, this creative approach remains limited in its capacity to *reduce* or *prevent* the occurrence of oppression and the social issues it highlights. As such, its impact is important at the level of individuals and social networks, but is less likely to have a systemic impact extending to the level of affecting policies, sentencing trends, institutions, or the social determinants of crime and injustice.

In conceptualising the arts as ameliorative, it is tenuous, if not naïve, to presume a direct association between the two, as though the arts and creative practices will necessarily be catalysts for cultural, institutional, and systemic change. Cheliotis' (2012, 2014) incisive critique of the arts in prisons demonstrates how they may be used in different ways to pursue very different ends. He draws on the seminal theoretical work of Cohen (1985) to argue that the State uses the arts to 'empower' and 'rehabilitate' prisoners, yet such 'good stories' can constitute 'decorative justice', conveniently masking the instrumental functions of the arts as tools of control and denial of the injustices of incarceration (Cheliotis 2014: 24). Similarly, it would be entirely possible for a government to commission 'Theatres of the Oppressed' participative forum theatre to engage and 'consult' marginalised citizens (including people with convictions and histories of victimisation), without having to make any real commitment to action in response to the social issues and injustices raised.

Conversely, Cheliotis (2012, 2014) also affirms the capacity of the arts to be used by people with convictions and others as creative tools of resistance and emancipation, giving voice and mobilising momentum for reform. To avoid uncritical uptake and moral reification of arts initiatives in criminal justice as inherently 'good', he argues that empirical investigations of arts initiatives must not ignore 'the socio-political dimensions of their context, content, conduct and consequences' (Cheliotis 2014: 16). Questions of power and epistemology—*who* can know and say if the arts 'work' or help, and to what end—remain relevant in appraising their ameliorative and emancipatory capacity in criminal and community justice.

Animals in criminal justice

Another area where ameliorative strategies can be observed is the increasing use of animals for creative and therapeutic purposes in criminal justice institutions. Elsewhere, we discuss our research findings regarding the positive developments associated with using trained assistance dogs in mainstream and therapeutic treatment courts, policing, forensic interviews, victim services and child advocacy centres, and prisons (see 'Animals and Therapeutic Justice' chapter in Graham and White 2015). The remarkably positive work being orchestrated by the Courthouse Dogs Foundation (2015) with community and criminal justice partners in the United States, Canada, Chile, and Finland illustrates the capacity for the place of animals in court innovation to benefit victims (including child victims of sexual abuse) and their families, defendants, and offenders (especially in mental health, drugs and veterans courts), and practitioners (including court staff, the judiciary, lawyers, police, and forensic investigators). Additionally, animal foster care and training is increasingly common in prison settings (see Britton and Button 2005; Bachi 2013). Emergent research indicates positive benefits for prisoners, as well as indirectly for the institution, in terms of fostering self-worth and empowerment through generative giving, the development of new knowledge, and pro-social identity (see Graham and White 2015). However, many animal-based therapeutic programmes are selective in which prisoners are allowed to participate, and the logic of incarceration may not be fundamentally challenged just because such initiatives help to realise positive changes at the levels of individuals and institutions.

In summary, ameliorative innovations may lessen the pains of incarceration or probation and advance rights, creativity, and quality of life. However, their impact is more likely to be at the micro- and meso-levels and unlikely to make a dent or lessen macro-level processes of mass supervision or hyper-incarceration. By way of contrast, the next section canvasses ideas and strategies that extend much further in envisioning change.

Innovation as disruption? Transformative approaches and different visions of justice

In the field of social innovation, the concept itself is routinely conceptualised as 'disruptive' and game-changing, unsettling traditional thought and established orders to make way for new, more creative, and sustainable ideas (Nicholls 2006). Influential forerunner Joseph Schumpeter drew attention to the 'creative destruction' associated with entrepreneurship and social change (in Phills et al. 2006: 37). More recently, extensive theoretical work has been devoted to understanding 'disruptive innovation' and leading social change (see Christensen 2000). Here, we only have space to canvass a few social innovations that pertain to criminal justice: justice reinvestment, restorative justice, and microfinance.

Justice Reinvestment (JR)

As the name 'justice reinvestment' (JR) suggests, a portion of the public funds that would have been spent on covering the significant costs of imprisonment are meant to be diverted to local communities that have a high concentration of people subject to criminal justice intervention. The money is invested in community initiatives, services, and networks that are aimed at addressing the underlying causes of crime and social disadvantage in those communities (see Gooda 2010; Murray, Caulier-Grice and Mulgan 2010). As is often the case in regards to the development and implementation of social and criminal justice policies, justice reinvestment takes different forms, and these find application in different ways in different jurisdictions due to unique and variable local characteristics (of offenders, of crimes, of communities) (see La Vigne et al. 2014). One approach, for instance, places the emphasis on re-directing money from funding for prisons to *individuals* who are non-violent and need to access drug rehabilitation services. A key issue here pertains to the selectivity involved in who gains assistance, and the abrogation, yet again, of dealing with the 'hard' and risky cases (i.e., those needing the most support and attention) within criminal justice.

The more favoured and well-known model, however, is based upon the idea of re-directing money from prisons to those *communities* where prisoners predominantly come from. Geographical and socio-economic analysis is undertaken, and strategies are devised as to how best to redirect funds and resources back into those communities (see for example, Gooda 2012, and Australian Youth Affairs Coalition 2013; see also Allard et al. 2013). The intention is to engage in community development and social inclusion as preventative measures to forestall future offending and marginalisation and to diminish the possibilities of repeat offending for those leaving criminal justice supervision. There is evidence that, in some American states where JR has been introduced, there has indeed been a significant reduction in the number of (especially young) people being sent to prison (Murray et al. 2010).

However, by adopting a focus on specific communities in this way (that is, in a manner that, explicitly or implicitly, portrays them as dysfunctional and deviant), the door is open for further stigmatisation of both the communities and the individuals within them and for the widespread legitimation of coercive 'outside' intervention in these same communities. In this way, it may unintentionally contribute to racialised and spatialised (i.e., in the poorest areas) welfare interventions that run parallel to hyper-incarceration. Moreover, the JR focus on reinvestment as crime prevention and as a decarceration strategy may unintentionally obscure broader social justice issues centring on access to employment, education, and other opportunities that underpin much adult and youth offending to begin with.

In the Australian context, Justice Reinvestment has had particular resonance in relation to Indigenous young people and their relationship to juvenile justice. In some instances, and in some communities, allocations of funding away from youth detention to community building 'makes sense' to local populations and communities that are already struggling to come to grips with severe disadvantage. Rather than a general panacea or response to mass incarceration, as in the United States (see La Vigne et al. 2014), JR is seen in Australia to be most relevant to specific groups of young people, and such approaches have garnered significant political support within Indigenous communities and advocacy bodies precisely because of the dire nature of the contemporary policies and practices affecting Indigenous people across the country (see Gooda 2012; Australian Human Rights and Equal Opportunity Commission 2009). Interpreted as a social innovation – that is, informed by social justice considerations and collective social impact – justice reinvestment offers the promise of change based upon a logic of penal abolition, decarceration, and community development.

Restorative Justice (RJ) and Restorative Practices (RP)

In a similar vein, the spread of restorative justice (RJ) and the wider restorative practices (RP) movement around the world have generated and reflected widespread support for non-adversarial and inclusive options for conflict resolution. Such initiatives take many different forms and can be highly selective as well, sometimes thereby excluding those who might best benefit on the basis of risk (Cunneen and White 2011). Nonetheless, non-adversarial justice of this kind does include interesting and creative restorative practices in prisons and offender supervision. Restorative justice has recently garnered significant attention for new innovative applications in response to sexual violence (Centre for Innovative Justice 2014). Some RJ initiatives tend to reflect in a more ameliorative way as strategies (insofar as they focus solely or predominantly on the victim and repairing harm), but ultimately, the philosophy of restorative justice and restorative practices is mostly transformative because it seeks to move towards healing and redemption, to advance liberal democratic notions of citizenship, and move away from a reliance on traditional adversarial and exclusionary approaches.

Microfinance

At a societal or, indeed, a global level, the foremost paragon of social innovation is microfinance – the provision of financial services (including savings accounts, small loans, and insurance) to people and small businesses affected by poverty and inequality, enabling them to generate capital and their capacity to benefit from their own labour. Its most internationally recognised pioneer is social entrepreneur Muhammad Yunus who, in 2006, was awarded the Nobel Peace Prize with the microfinance and community development Grameen Bank he founded.

Microfinance is an active, social ecological type of response to poverty, in contrast to more passive one-directional forms of charity that offer the immediacy of ameliorative emergency relief but do not constitute a sustainable avenue for change in the future. In the last 15 years, microfinance initiatives and services have grown exponentially with transformative social impact, with recent estimates indicating that approximately 1 billion people access microfinance services globally (Roodman 2011; Kemp 2014). Internationally, microfinance is reputed to spur relatively rapid social change, including shifts in the structures and dynamics of financial markets and the economy, as well as making progress in pursuit of things like social cohesion, citizenship, and labour market participation.

Microfinance is raised briefly here for its transformative potential in response to systemic issues of discrimination and exclusion faced by people with convictions. A significant number of people leaving prison and other people with criminal records do not have access to a bank account, let alone credit or financial services. A recent report by Evans (2014), aptly titled 'The Debt Penalty', underscores the extensive costs and harms of criminal justice and legal involvement, and the financial barriers that people with convictions face in the process of reintegration. Access to microfinance-related supports for people with convictions may not only yield positive results for individuals and their families, but may redress some of the harms and costs associated with their criminal justice involvement in the hope of reducing or preventing further offending. Little empirical literature exists in this area currently (see Rainford 2010; and on microenterprise, see Lindahl 2007), however, and more research is needed.

Innovation as accommodation? Incremental approaches and paradoxes in pursuit of penal reform

Just as punishment is not morally or politically neutral, social innovation in penal contexts is not either. As with many facets of criminal justice, there are frequently helpful, unhelpful, and even deeply paradoxical applications associated with particular innovations and diverse motivations for their introduction.

For example, some advocates for restorative justice see it as revolutionary in potential scope – in effect, as a replacement ideology and set of practices to conventional retribution-based criminal justice. Others, however, view it as having a distinctly circumscribed application, as an add-on to existing systems of punishment which will, over time, result in incremental shifts and the greater use of diversion. In Australia, for example, every jurisdiction has some form of restorative justice based 'juvenile conferencing'. Yet generally these are reserved for first time offenders and those who commit trivial offences. In this instance, the social impact of restorative justice is thus muted and variable. We nonetheless maintain that the very idea of 'restorative justice' serves to provide an important counterweight theoretically and practically to punitive discourses and retributive practices. RJ can be both an accommodation to the system (a component of a larger complexity) and present a challenge to it (insofar as it embodies principles, such as repairing harm, citizenship, participation, and forgiveness that are intrinsically subversive of retributive agendas and traditional approaches to crime control).

In some jurisdictions, penal reform agendas and promising ideas have been adapted in ways that are not necessarily ethical, effective, or innovative. Two examples are illustrative of the paradoxical tensions and the range of mixed motives and, consequentially, mixed results. The first example is that of the 'greening justice' movement, where criminal justice institutions are increasingly advancing policies and practices, in partnership with others, that focus on environmental sustainability and resource conservation. In a recent international review of 'greening justice' initiatives, a wide range of motivations and purposes were identified (White and Graham, 2015). Top of the list for administrators and policy-makers is fiscal objectives, that is, saving money by cutting energy, saving water, and recycling materials and waste. Even so, there was, in many cases, simultaneously a genuine commitment to eco-friendly practices, and for some initiatives this translated into more benign and engaged forms of policing, more socially inclusive courts, and more empowering approaches to prisoner rehabilitation.

However, there were certainly instances of 'decorative justice' (Cheliotis 2014) as well. Being 'green' does not always translate into being 'good' and can constitute more of a case of greenwashing than any association with progressive reform. Nowhere is this more evident than the appropriation of the 'green' mantra by the United States government in proclaiming the green credentials and environmental sustainability of the prison and other facilities at Guantanamo Bay in Cuba. Wind turbines, recycling, and bicycle-riding traffic police do little to diminish the trauma and injustices that occur within that carceral regime (White and Graham, 2015).

Our view is that, overall, such initiatives can be seen as paradoxical in that positive developments can co-exist with and be seen to be accommodating of quite brutal institutional regimes and with those that entrench exciting new forms of social innovation. An understanding of context, nuanced practice, and complexity, as well as critical evaluation of tendencies and consequences, is central to exposing the limitations and possibilities of 'greening justice' initiatives and restorative justice projects. Through such assessments, it is possible to better appreciate why it is that, in some instances, the transformative logic is one of decarceration and abolitionism (social innovation = social justice), while in others the system logic is one of cost-saving and continued penal expansion (innovation = instrumentalism in support of the status quo).

The area of correctional industries illustrates the need to differentiate creative and effective ideas and approaches that, when taken on face value, appear similar, but upon closer reflection, reveal ethical divergences. As in other places around the world, in the American State of California, prisoners are used as firefighters. Again, we wish to highlight the mixed motives and substantive differences in the benefits for participants (the prisoners) and the benefits for the state derived from this seemingly innovative initiative. The socially valued role of fighting fires can tap into feelings of accomplishment and 'giving back' on the part of many prisoners and hence may act as a prelude to their rehabilitation and desistance. Yet issues remain regarding the place of prison labour, in particular instances of its exploitative forms and functions, within criminal justice. Moreover, in recent years lawyers for the state have resisted court orders to expand parole programmes because to do so would reduce the pool of inmates available to undertake prisoner industries. By employing inmates at $2–3 a day to fight fires, working firefighting shifts of up to 24 hours a day (Barford 2015), the State of California saves more than $80 million per year (Californian Department of Corrections and Rehabilitation in Barford 2015). This means that any overarching policy that expands parole simultaneously reduces the number of inmates available to fight wildfires (Flatow 2014). There is thus a built-in systemic financial disincentive to let prisoners out on parole early (Flatow 2014), even though prisoner firefighters are able to obtain 'day for day' credits for good behaviour that help to 'accelerate' their release by discounting time from their sentence (Barford 2015). Despite the good results it does achieve, this type of initiative accommodates the norms and factors that continue processes of mass incarceration and enables the state to use 'good news stories' as decorative justice to belie ulterior motives that are ultimately at odds with efforts towards decarceration and the promotion of the human rights of prisoners as citizens.

Mainstreaming innovation: Legitimacy, procedural justice and sustainability

A significant opportunity and challenge in establishing social innovation is the struggle for legitimacy, especially in jurisdictions where the backdrop is one of volatile penal politics. Literature in the international field of social innovation demonstrates that, the more radical and disruptive a social innovation is, the greater its initial struggle for legitimacy. The same applies to the architects and change agents who initiate social ventures. New innovations tend to unsettle and threaten established social orders and in this case the established dynamics of penal power and carceral regimes. To some extent, it affects the capacity of the idea or venture to become mainstream.

> Cognitive legitimacy is played out in normative isomorphic pressures that demand a fixed organisational position within the broader socio-structural architecture as a precursor to a venture having a basic right to exist for the wider population. However … social entrepreneurs disrupt these structures and work most effectively outside of established organizational patterns. As such – and in common with many innovative organizations – social entrepreneurship typically lacks cognitive legitimacy, but rather than this be a barrier to effective operations it, in fact, becomes a means towards greater impact.
>
> (Nicholls and Cho 2006: 115)

Architects and leaders of social innovation often differ from others in criminal justice contexts in terms of their character traits, values, and behaviours. For example, commonly celebrated traits include boldness, ambition, persistence, unreasonableness, relationship building and brokering, and an entrepreneurial ability to leverage resources (Elkington and Hartigan 2008; Moore and

Westley 2011; Phills et al. 2008). A fascinating anomaly can be observed in noting that these types of people may be celebrated as pioneers achieving change with and within penal institutions while thinking and acting in ways that do not necessarily always complement or comply with the nature and intent of penal cultures and practices (Graham 2016). This is sometimes described as 'intrapreneurship.'

Social innovation literature suggests that one of the key barriers to the development and mainstreaming of social innovations include 'traditional risk-averse cautious organisational cultures of administrations, [and] closed systems which favour single issue solutions developed within clusters of organisations lacking mutual awareness … and trust' (BEPA 2011: 11). Unfortunately, this seems an apt description of the state of many prison and probation services in Western jurisdictions and is not unrelated to the conditions that give rise to mass supervision and mass incarceration. Just as the more radical and disruptive visions of social innovation and change struggle for legitimacy in their adaptation and uptake in the mainstream, so too do the more radical and disruptive visions of liberal reformism and penal abolition – many of which stem from critical criminological schools of thought and desistance scholarship.

Critical questions about capital, resources, and sustainability from those in the criminal justice establishment should not be dismissed as unreasonable or unfounded, for two related reasons. The first reason is the sheer number of social start-ups that, irrespective of the calibre of ideas on which they are premised, fail and fold within the first few years. A significant number of pilot projects or trials associated with social ventures struggle to upscale and integrate. In criminal justice institutions, a moderate degree of power is conferred to senior decision-makers who have a legally binding duty of care to examine the fine-grain detail of a proposed innovation for how it will potentially impact on different stakeholders. Issues of potential failure usually become bifurcated along the lines of those proposing social innovations as 'outsiders', compared to the hegemonic logic of those who are powerful actors within the penal establishment. Hypocritical differences can be observed in the extent to which start-ups or new initiatives have to fight to rationalise their efficacy and ethics, often facing extensive scrutiny and bureaucratic hurdles just to be able to start. Yet, the risks and lack of justification of failed penal policies and practices of the State, and the collateral consequences of such failure, do not attract similar levels of scrutiny and reflexivity.

The second reason is to underscore the fact that procedural justice and legitimacy matter in ground-breaking social ventures, cooperatives, or alliances, even where they are initiating new things. As discussed earlier, social innovations are just that, *social*. Perceptions of procedural justice and legitimacy are related to the development of trust, cooperation, and the flourishing of creativity – between those leading and participating in the innovative initiative, and in achieving valorisation and trust between those involved and the wider system and communities in which it exists (see Tyler and Blader 2003; Luo 2005; Streicher et al. 2012; Sabatini et al. 2014; Graham 2015a, 2015b). Therefore, some limits are placed on the nature and scope of rule-breaking and counter-normative behaviour by those pioneering new initiatives; otherwise, without boundaries, infractions on justice and the potential of failure are possible, if not likely. A key challenge for people leading social innovations in criminal justice is dealing with people and issues in contexts where there is a lot at stake.

Conclusion

What becomes clear in our analysis of the three types of strategies outlined in this chapter is that they should not be reified as universal solutions, nor are they as discrete and disparate as they might initially seem. Context matters, as claims of being ethical and effective are contingent upon those making them and the multi-faceted implications they carry.

Some innovative social ventures succeed precisely because they are tailor made for people in prison or community-based sanctions. A key example of this is new forms of arts or employment-based social enterprises, which aim to assist prisoners' community reintegration and desistance processes (see Lindahl 2007; Graham 2015b). However, many other social ventures are effective because access to and participation in them are open to a variety of people in the community, including but certainly not limited to people with convictions. Examples of this are the networks of people involved in community time bank initiatives.

Much of this chapter has been oriented towards influencing meso- and macro-level processes in criminal justice and society, namely the impact of innovation to realise change in an era of mass supervision and hyper-incarceration. It is at the intersection of personal, penal, and social change that the full arc of ethical implications, and the exigency of penal reform, becomes most apparent. It is our hope that these discussions will stimulate the thoughts and responses of others, including the development of empirical agendas, to co-produce new knowledge from the interfaces of social innovation and justice.

Bibliography

Bachi, K. (2013) 'Equine-facilitated prison-based programs within the context of prison-based animal programs: state of the science review', *Journal of Offender Rehabilitation,* 52(1): 46–74.

Barford, V. (2015) 'The prisoners fighting wildfires in California' *BBC News Magazine,* 24 September 2015. Accessible online: http://www.bbc.co.uk/news/magazine-34285658 (Accessed 26/09/2015).

Britton, D. and Button, A. (2005) 'Prison pups: assessing the effects of dog training programs in correctional facilities', *Journal of Family Social Work,* 9(4): 79–95.

Bureau of European Policy Advisors [BEPA]. (2011) *Empowering People, Driving Change: Social Innovation in the European Union,* Luxembourg: European Union.

Centre for Innovative Justice. (2014) *Innovative Justice Responses to Sexual Offending.* Melbourne: RMIT. Available at: http://mams.rmit.edu.au/qt1g6twlv0q3.pdf.

Cheliotis, L. (ed.) (2012) *The Arts of Imprisonment: Control, Resistance and Empowerment,* Surrey: Ashgate Publishing.

Cheliotis, L. (2014) 'Decorative justice: deconstructing the relationship between the arts and imprisonment', *International Journal for Crime, Justice and Social Democracy,* 3(1): 16–34.

Christensen, C. (2000) *The Innovator's Dilemma: When New Technologies Cause Great Firms to Fail,* Cambridge, MA: Harvard Business Review Press.

Clear, T. (1994) *Harm in American Penology: Offenders, Victims, and Their Communities,* Albany, NY: State University of New York Press.

Clear, T. (1996) 'Backfire: when incarceration increases crime', *Journal of the Oklahoma Criminal Justice Research Consortium,* 3: 7–18.

Cohen, S. (1985) *Visions of Social Control: Crime, Punishment and Classification,* Cambridge: Polity.

Courthouse Dogs Foundation. (2015) www.courthousedogs.com (Accessed 3 January 2015).

Cunneen, C., Baldry, E., Brown, M., Brown, D., Schwartz, M. and Steel, A. (2013) *Penal Culture and Hyper-Incarceration: The Revival of the Prison,* Surrey: Ashgate Publishing.

Cunneen, C. and White, R. (2011) *Juvenile Justice in Australia,* South Melbourne: Oxford University Press.

Drakeford, M. and Gregory, L. (2010) 'Transforming time: a new tool for youth justice', *Youth Justice,* 10(2): 143–56.

Durnescu, I. (2010) 'Pains of probation: effective practice and human rights', *International Journal of Offender Therapy and Comparative Criminology,* 55(4): 530–45.

Elkington, J. and Hartigan, P. (2008) *The Power of Unreasonable People: How Social Entrepreneurs Create Markets that Change the World,* Boston, MA: Harvard Business Press.

European Union. (2015) *Growing a Digital Social Innovation Ecosystem for Europe,* Brussels: European Union. Available at: http://issuu.com/digitalsocialinnovation/docs/dsireport-forwebsite-print.

Evans, D. (2014) *The Debt Penalty: Exposing the Financial Barriers to Offender Reintegration,* New York, NY: Research and Evaluation Center John Jay College of Criminal Justice.

Fine Cell Work. (2015) http://www.finecellwork.co.uk/ (Accessed 1 February 2015).

Flatow, N. (2014) 'California tells court it can't release inmates early because it would lose cheap prison labor', http://thinkprogress.org/justice/2014/11/17/3592964/how-californias-program-to-have-inmates-fight-wildfires-could-be-keeping-people-behind-bars/ (Accessed 19 November 2014).

Fox, C. and Grimm, R. (2015) 'The role of social innovation in criminal justice reform and the risk posed by proposed reforms in England and Wales', *Criminology and Criminal Justice,* 15(1): 63–82.

Garland, D. (2001a) *The Culture of Control: Crime and Social Order in Contemporary Society,* Chicago, IL: University of Chicago Press.

Garland, D. (ed.) (2001b) *Mass Imprisonment: Social Causes and Consequences,* London: SAGE Publications.

Girls Who Code. (2015) http://girlswhocode.com/ (Accessed 3 January 2015).

Gooda, M. (2010) 'Justice reinvestment: a new solution to the problem of indigenous over-representation in the criminal justice system', ANTaR NSW Seminar - Juvenile Justice Strategy: A Better Way, Sydney Mechanics School of Arts NSW. Available at: https://www.humanrights.gov.au/news/speeches/justice-reinvestment-new-solution-problem-indigenous-over-representation-criminal.

Graham, H. (2015a) 'On knowing and being known: trust and legitimacy in co-producing desistance', Co-producing Desistance blog, 8 May 2015, http://www.coproducingdesistance.org.uk/on-knowing-and-being-known-trust-and-legitimacy-in-co-producing-desistance-by-hannah-graham/.

Graham, H. (2015b) 'Reproducing co-production and upscaling innovation: the growth of forums supporting desistance' Co-producing Desistance blog, 22 May 2015, http://www.coproducingdesistance.org.uk/reproducing-co-production-and-upscaling-innovation-the-growth-of-forums-supporting-desistance-by-hannah-graham/.

Graham, H. (2016) *Rehabilitation Work: Supporting Desistance and Recovery,* London: Routledge.

Graham, H., Graham, S. and Field, J. (2015) 'Returning citizens: a quiet revolution in prisoner reintegration', *Scottish Justice Matters,* 3(1): 32–33.

Graham, H. and White, R. (2014) 'Innovative justice – according to whom?', in K. Lumsden and A. Winter (eds.) *Reflexivity in Criminological Research: Experiences with the Powerful and the Powerless,* Basingstoke: Palgrave Macmillan.

Graham, H. and White, R. (2015) *Innovative Justice,* London: Routledge.

Grimm, R., Fox, C., Baines, S. and Albertson, K. (2013) 'Social innovation, an answer to contemporary societal challenges? Locating the concept in theory and practice', *Innovation: The European Journal of Social Science Research,* 26(4): 436–55.

Henrichson, C. and Delaney, R. (2012) 'The price of prisons: what incarceration costs taxpayers', *Federal Sentencing Reporter,* 25(1): 68–80.

Kemp, R. (2014) 'Social innovation as an emerging phenomenon', Seminar paper presented on 26 November 2014 at the Australian Innovation Research Centre at the University of Tasmania, Hobart, Australia. Available online at: http://www.transitsocialinnovation.eu/blog/social-innovation-as-an-emerging-phenomenon.

La Vigne, N., Bieler, S., Cramer, L., Ho, H., Kotonias, C., Mayer, D., McClure, D., Pacifici, L., Parks, E., Peterson, B. and Samuels, J. (2014) *Justice Reinvestment Initiative State Assessment Report,* Washington, DC: The Urban Institute and Bureau of Justice Assistance, US Department of Justice.

Lindahl, N. (2007) *Venturing beyond the Gates: Facilitating Successful Re-Entry with Entrepreneurship,* New York, NY: Prisoner Reentry Institute, John Jay College of Criminal Justice.

Luo, Y. (2005) 'How important are shared perceptions of procedural justice in cooperative alliances', *Academy of Management Journal,* 48(4): 695–709.

Marks, M. (2012) 'Time banking service exchange systems: a review of the research and policy and practice implications in support of youth in transition', *Children and Youth Services Review,* 34: 1230–36.

McNeill, F. and Beyens, K. (eds.) (2014) *Offender Supervision in Europe,* Basingstoke: Palgrave Macmillan.

Miller, R.J. (2013) 'Race, hyper-incarceration, and US poverty policy in historic perspective', *Sociology Compass,* 7(7): 573–89.

Miller, R.J. (2014) 'Devolving the carceral state: race, prisoner re-entry and the micro-politics of urban poverty management', *Punishment & Society,* 16(3): 305–35.

Moore, M. and Westley, F. (2011) 'Surmountable chasms: networks and social innovation for resilient systems', *Ecology and Society,* 16(1): 5–17.

Murray, R., Caulier-Grice, J. and Mulgan, G. (2010) *The Open Book of Social Innovation,* London: The Young Foundation and NESTA UK.

Nicholls, A. (ed.) (2006) *Social Entrepreneurship: New Models of Sustainable Social Change,* Oxford: Oxford University Press.

Nicholls, A. and Cho, A. (2006) 'Social entrepreneurship: the structuration of a field', in A. Nicholls (ed.) *Social Entrepreneurship: New Models of Sustainable Social Change,* Oxford: Oxford University Press.
Phills, J., Deiglmeier, K. and Miller, D. (2008) 'Rediscovering social innovation', *Social Innovation Review,* 6(4): 34–43.
Rainford, W. (2010) 'Crime, social development and correctional social work', in J. Midgley and A. Conley (eds.) *Social Work and Social Development: Theories and Skills for Developmental Social Work,* Oxford: Oxford University Press.
Roberts, J. and Hough, M. (eds.) (2002) *Changing Attitudes to Punishment: Public Opinion, Crime and Justice,* Cullompton: Willan Publishing.
Roodman, D. (2011) *Due Diligence: An Impertinent Inquiry into Microfinance,* Baltimore, MD: Centre for Global Development and Brookings Institution Press.
Sabatini, F., Modena, F. and Tortia, E. (2014) 'Do cooperative enterprises create social trust?', *Small Business Economics,* 42: 621–41.
Siedman, L. M. (2010) 'Hyper-incarceration and strategies of disruption: is there a way out?', *Georgetown Public Law and Legal Theory Research Paper No. 10 – 76:* 1–31.
Simon, J. (2000) 'The "society of captives" in the era of hyper-incarceration', *Theoretical Criminology,* 4(3): 285–308.
Stanford Center for Social Innovation. (2013) 'Social innovation'. Available at: http://csi.gsb.stanford.edu/social-innovation.
Streicher, B., Jonas, E., Maier, G., Frey, D. and Spießberger, A. (2012) 'Procedural fairness and creativity: does voice maintain people's creative vein over time?', *Creativity Research Journal,* 24(4): 358–63.
The Last Mile. (2015) https://thelastmile.org/ (Accessed 3 January 2015).
Tonry, M. (2014) 'Why crime rates are falling throughout the Western world', in M. Tonry (ed.) *Why Crime Rates Fall and Why They Don't [Crime and Justice, Vol. 43],* Chicago, IL: University of Chicago Press.
Tyler, T. and Blader, S. (2003) 'The group engagement model: procedural justice, social identity and cooperative behavior', *Personality and Social Psychology Review,* 7(4): 349–61.
Wacquant, L. (2001) 'Deadly symbiosis: when ghetto and prison meet and mesh', *Punishment & Society,* 3(1): 95–134.
Wacquant, L. (2009) *Punishing the Poor: The Neoliberal Government of Social Insecurity,* Durham, NC: Duke University Press.
Wakefield, S. and Uggen, C. (2010) 'Incarceration and stratification', *Annual Review of Sociology,* 36: 387–406.
White, R. and Graham, H. (2015) 'Greening justice: examining the interfaces of criminal, social and ecological justice', *British Journal of Criminology,* 55(5): 845–65.

18

Deliberating racial justice

Toward racially democratic crime control

Geoff Ward and Peter A. Hanink

Introduction

The pursuit of racial justice and equality within the United States remains mired in contradiction, contention, and largely symbolic intervention. While growing numbers of white Americans acknowledge the persistent inequality their non-white counterparts have long recognized (Lauter and Pearce 2015; but see Norton and Sommers 2011), substantive remedial commitments and strategies remain unclear (Berrey 2015). American criminal justice—long central to the reproduction of white advantage rooted in non-white disadvantage and thus a focus of opposition (see Muhammad 2011; Ward 2012)—is at the forefront in this contemporary awakening and search for viable solutions. Facing devastation wrought by racialized mass incarceration and its collateral group consequences (Alexander 2010; Travis et al. 2014) and confronted by a series of police killings of people of color across the US, civic leaders and public officials have increasingly called for changes to this crime control system, including greater racial and ethnic group representation.

We argue that such remedies should prioritize a more deliberative understanding of representation, viewing participatory parity in crime control as a *practice* of racial justice. The question of representation among legal authorities is of course not new, but is often reduced to a narrow distributive challenge, while substantive participation demands deliberative inclusion. Recent news stories and reports lament low and declining percentages of non-white police and prosecutors (Ashkenas and Park 2015; Fandos 2015; Bies et al. 2015), framing proportionality as a proxy for group power or influence. While status group presence is obviously important to group influence, the two are not one in the same. Indeed, despite significant percentage increases in the ranks of formal legal authorities, most notably in metropolitan police departments and prison systems, such authorities and institutions continue to be viewed by racial and ethnic minorities with suspicion, fueling calls for greater representation and accountability.

Far from being limited to the United States, calls for inclusion in crime control processes resound worldwide, historically and today (see, e.g., Brogden and Shearing 2005; Rowe 2012; Anderson and Killingray 1992). At base, such demands reflect normative expectations of respect, representative government, and participation within ostensibly democratic societies. In nation-states torn by histories of racial and ethnic conflict and inequality, this struggle for recognition is intensified and so too are hopes that representative systems of social control might advance racial justice (Ward 2012; Smith 1993). In theory, a multi-racial and ethnic polity governed by similarly constituted deliberative bodies will generate relatively supportive and inclusive crime control policies and practices, at least in comparison to historically racially and ethnically hostile and exclusionary systems. Worldwide, racial and ethnic group domination of legal authority—through legislation, within courts, in policing, and among influential associations—has proven a fundamental mechanism of oppression and domination, that is, a practical means by which groups defined by race have been denied self-realization and societal participation.

While the idea of inclusion and reality of its denial are relatively clear, less straightforward is how substantively representative systems might be formed and function, especially as to supplant norms of institutions with long histories of racial exclusion. We celebrate pioneering legislative and legal officials, and aggregate these actors in diversity studies, but give little consideration to their representative mandate or experiences within actual deliberative milieus where crime control priorities, policies, and practices take shape. On those occasions when we do check back in on these ostensible representatives of previously excluded group interests—for example, to assess how historically under-represented police or judges experience incorporation within police or court organizations and whether those organizations are changing—the evidence is often discouraging. Empirical studies reporting "no effect" of variable racial and ethnic group representation among police or other legal actors typically interpret this as evidence of the substantive irrelevance of workforce diversity, rather than a more likely sign of legal cultures and institutions resisting change (see, e.g., Lawton 2007; McCluskey and Terrill 2005; McElvain and Kposowa 2004).

At least in the US, and likely elsewhere, there is a sort of bipolar discourse around racially representative crime control practices, with, often uncritical, celebrations of diversity inattentive to actual inclusion, on one hand, and indifference or opposition to the idea of actual racial and ethnic group recognition, on the other. For some, these reactions co-exist as a merely symbolic investment in diversity. They mark a momentous occasion of formal inclusion such as the election of Barack Obama as a sign of social progress, while contesting that President's assertion of racial or ethnic identity or claim to group representation. This dissonance plagues the idea and practice of *inclusion*.

We seek to clarify and push this debate by advancing an ideal of deliberative racial justice in crime control processes, as a theoretical and practically useful alternative to diversity initiatives. We consider a number of the claims, implications, and challenges attendant to this approach. Our description of the form and function of this model of inclusion draws on sources in history, socio-legal scholarship, and political theory, with emphasis on Iris Young's (2000) *Inclusion and Democracy*. We contrast this deliberative ideal with narrower empirical, policy, and public discourses on "diversity" in legal professions, which rarely broach the complex relational notion of racial and ethnic group representation. Finally, we stress the role of political culture in regulating the discussion and functioning of inclusion, including how "color-blind" racial ideology contributes to the dissonant pursuit of diversity without representation, undermining the realization of "deeply democratic" (Young 2000) criminal social control.

We begin with an assessment of what racially democratic crime control describes, requires, and offers. This discussion examines how inter-locking notions of *recognition*, *representation*, and *participatory parity* relate to this process and outcome of deliberative racial justice. We close with a discussion of objections and theoretical and practical challenges when considering the future prospects of racially democratic crime control, particularly in the United States.

The promise of racially democratic control

The pursuit of equal racial and ethnic group representation within the ranks of legal and law enforcement authorities is long-standing and widespread. The effort to achieve freedom and equality in the US by black American and other racial and ethnic groups has prioritized inclusion among arbiters of justice. In 1852, on the eve of the potential incorporation of full black citizens, early civil rights leader Martin Delaney (1852) noted that, "No people can be free who themselves do not constitute an essential part of the ruling element of the country in which they live" (209). The recognition promised by Emancipation was violently denied instead, and generations of civic leaders have since fought to dismantle a structure of racial tyranny in law enforcement systems. In these movements, representation among legislators, judges, lawyers, police, and other authorities—and throughout associated deliberative milieus that authorize representatives and hold them accountable (e.g., among voters, jurors, civilian review boards, etc.)—is idealized as a means to secure and maintain equal rights of citizenship.

Historically, efforts to advance recognition have been countered by measures to *deny* representative social control. This opposition sought to maintain white societal domination by either preserving monopolistic control over legal authority and influence or severely restricting the authority of token non-white representatives. Reconstruction, a reform period during which black Americans experienced dramatic but short-lived advances in representation among legal authorities, was followed in the 1890s by a concerted effort to reverse these gains. "To extinguish the memories of black jurors, judges, police and legislators during Reconstruction was to make clear the undisputed and permanent authority of whites," Leon Litwack (1998) writes. "The entire machinery of justice—the lawyers, the judges, the juries, the legal profession, the police—was assigned a pivotal role in enforcing these imperatives ... underscoring in every possible way the subordination of black men and women of all classes and ages" (249).

Decades later, when the first black American officers were recruited to police forces in the 1930s and '40s, their authority was severely constrained. In many cities, black officers were forbidden from detaining or testifying against white Americans in court and were not issued weapons or uniforms for concern that these signs of authority would be gravely offensive to whiteness (Dulaney 1996). Black and other non-white legal authorities have as often been employed to *preserve* status quo race relations, including white domination, as to change them. This is clearly conveyed in a 1912 *Harper's Weekly* article on the exploits of Native American police, "Who maintain the peace on the reservations, often at risk of life and dishonor among their own people." The article celebrates a "peace" preserved by native police killing a Crow Indian leader behind a popular rebellion. "It took more than purely physical courage to enforce the law in an Indian reservation setting," the article notes, "it took moral stamina to stand behind white men's rules that were unpopular with the policeman's own people" (Chapman 1912).

There are many more recent illustrations of fraught diversity initiatives in the realm of crime control. In 2003, the US Department of Justice (DOJ) under the Republican administration of President George W. Bush and Attorney General John Ashcroft, announced an initiative to increase diversity among (federal) US Attorneys. The effort illustrates the celebratory tones of contemporary diversity discourse and its more clearly symbolic than substantive commitments, which Ellen Berrey (2015) aptly calls the "halo and haze" of diversity (42). The episode also underscores the need for closer theoretical, empirical, and public policy attention to representative social control.

The Justice Department's "New Diversity Program," no doubt related to the literal prosecution of a growing War on Terror, was introduced with a press release touting the importance of participatory parity in the US justice system. The statement declares:

> Our pursuit of justice is stronger, and fulfillment of our national mission more effective, when we bring to bear the experience, judgment, and energy of colleagues from a wide spectrum of racial, ethnic, economic, and geographic backgrounds. … To succeed fully in our mission, we must earn and retain the trust and confidence of all Americans in how we fulfill our responsibility as custodians of justice. And that … is a function of the American people's understanding that [the DOJ] draws on the finest legal talent from every quarter of this great nation. (US Dept. of Justice 2003)

The program got off to an inauspicious start. It began with a commissioned study of diversity in the ranks of US attorneys, the findings of which seem to have so displeased the administration that the report was shelved until congressional black and Latino caucuses forced its release. When the department complied in distributing its 186-page report, half of the content was redacted, including the entire report summary (Lichtblau 2003).

An un-redacted version of the report was eventually generated and circulated by a self-described "information archaeologist," revealing pervasive race and sex-based harassment, reprisal, and other discrimination allegations. Non-white and women lawyers (esp. non-white women) lamented exclusion from positions of influence, hostile work environments, and other forms of marginalization, notwithstanding their formal inclusion (Johnston and Lichtblau 2003). The matter cast doubt on the administration's actual commitment to participatory parity, while illustrating the significance of inclusion among legislators whose modest intervention had altered the visibility and trajectory of this effort.

Efforts to deny, expand, and contain participation in systems of social control belie both the importance and challenge of accessing legal authority, historically and today. Whether in the case of historical policing or contemporary federal courts, these examples further illustrate how a broader political culture devaluing and denying racial and ethnic group recognition can not only limit *statistical* inclusion, but also constrain and alter the *substantive* meaning of numerical presence to representative government.

Deliberating racial justice: Recognition, participation, and equal representation

An absence of societies organized by principles of deliberative racial justice compels us to imagine what such a world would look like, a task for which political philosophy is well suited (see Rawls 2001: 1–5). In envisioning racially democratic crime control, it is useful to employ related language expressing values in the present political culture, beginning with the idea of inclusion. While inclusion is most often deployed in a minimalist sense, to relay a statistical presence, we reject this interpretation and offer one instead rooted in a deliberative ideal of democratic participation. Whereas inclusion is often viewed as a finite *outcome* (e.g., proportional representation), a deliberative ideal of racial justice regards inclusion as an ongoing participatory *process* reflecting racial and ethnic group recognition, participation, and dominion.

Diversity rhetoric tends to assume that as historically excluded groups officially join the ranks of formal and informal authorities (e.g., as officials of various sorts or registered voters), they claim influence in these deliberative realms. Ample evidence exists to refute this assumption. For example, notwithstanding formal political equality, political scientists have observed that, particularly when dealing with broader problems of social and economic equality, federalism—i.e., the sharing of power between local and central governments—limits representative social control. In a study of the politics of gun control in the US, Miller (2008: 4) finds that, "Policies widely supported by local officials and citizen alliances [in poorer and minority urban communities] are sometimes thwarted by legislators representing much larger constituencies with little or no connection to local problems and much less connection to serious crime."

Miller (2010: 834–35) notes three major challenges posed by a federal division of power. First, a federal system lends itself to a "decoupling" of criminal justice issues from other socio-economic inequalities. Second, a federal system adds "several layers" between the overwhelmingly poor (minorities who experience the worst of these inequalities) and the overwhelmingly wealthy (white formal authorities tasked with addressing them). Finally, a federal system forces urban areas to compete, rather than cooperate, for scarce state and federal resources. This disjoint is no mere inefficiency in the case of gun control. In this case, a constituency most vulnerable to lethal gun violence has diminished ability to translate that interest into public policy limiting gun ownership.

Various practices related to selection, professional socialization, and the organization of decision-making have also been shown to undermine potential for claims-making, relegating formal representatives of historically excluded groups to positions from which they are less able to influence deliberations. The rise of actuarial decision-making (e.g., risk assessment or sentencing guidelines) is one example (see Ward 2008, 2012; Ward, Farrell, and Rousseau 2009). *Standardizing* use of discretion runs counter to an "integration and learning" perspective (Ely and Thomas 2001), which values diverse outlooks and experiences as organizational (i.e., decision-making) resources.

The principle of "bleached out professionalism" (Wilkins 1998) in legal ethics is another case in point. The ideal of "bleached out" or "pure" professionalism envisions the legal actor as one whose identity becomes totally subsumed by professional legal norms and expectations, ostensibly rendering other aspects of identity (e.g., race and ethnicity, gender and sexuality, etc.) irrelevant to legal practice. Of course, legal realists have long recognized the myth of objectivity in law and legal institutions, which are encoded by centuries of selective status group inclusion (esp. elite, white, male). As Wilkins (1998) writes, "feminist scholars have argued that the rigid, detached, hierarchical, and adversarial character of traditional notions of lawyer professionalism reflect a distinctly 'male' identity," and critical race theorists have similarly noted the racial encoding of law and the legal profession (1519–1520). As such, "bleaching-out" seems more accurately understood as accommodation of dominant group norms and expectations. Insofar as this normative notion remains influential in legal education and professions, it conditions the substantive meaning of increased statistical inclusion.

As these wide-ranging examples of "after inclusion exclusion" (Carbado et al. 2008) illustrate, even when historically excluded groups gain increased presence among arbiters of justice, institutional cultures and practices condition and often diminish the actual standing and influence of marginalized constituencies, limiting actual *recognition*, *representation*, and *participatory parity*.

Recognition

Representative social control incorporates a number of ethical claims, the most basic being that all members of a society should enjoy moral and political standing, where respect includes a recognition of legitimate interests (Young 2000: 23). Racially democratic control builds upon this normative foundation, envisioning racial and ethnic groups engaged in an inclusive, communicative democracy. Within that deliberative milieu, diverse values, interests, and experiences around crime and its control would be duly expressed, acknowledged, and reconciled with one another.

This has never been the case. Those in power have long excluded certain groups—whether due to race, sex, ethnicity, creed, or class—from deliberative milieus of criminal social control, as well as other realms of policy (e.g., education, health, civil law, etc.). Exclusion has been rationalized in part by rejecting these groups' basic moral claims to respect and thus their human and civil rights (see Mills 1997; Dayan 2011). Disrespect rooted in alleged inhumanity or fundamental moral and intellectual inferiority works to deny democratic inclusion, framing subjects as beings to be ruled (i.e., controlled) rather than engaged or incorporated in governance (see, for example, Ward 2012: 38–44).

Such arguments were often used in the nineteenth- and twentieth-century US to justify exclusions of black Americans and others in an idealized white democracy. The sentiment was enshrined in law in *Dred Scott v. Sanford* (1857), in which the US Supreme Court held that black Americans had long been "regarded as beings of an inferior order, and altogether unfit to associate with the white race, either in social or political relations; and so far inferior, that they had no rights which the white man was bound to respect." By establishing race (i.e., whiteness) as a determinant of basic respect and democratic standing, the court formalized non-white exclusion from the polity to whom "obligations are owed, to whom rules apply, and whose injuries call for [amends]" (Foner 1998: 74–75; see also Mills 1997; Dayan 2013), or severely abridged such obligations.

Overt disregard of ethical and political claims based on race or ethnic group membership is relatively rare today, particularly in public discourse and policy. Yet similar ordeals of invisibility and degradation linger (see Dayan 2013: 133–35), including through negations of claims to representation. Evidence in policing is especially illustrative and disconcerting. Several studies point out that non-white police struggle to endure and challenge white-dominated police cultures, so as to transform institutions through inclusion. These studies note, for example, routine racist hazing of black, Latino and Asian police in Europe and North America, where being subjected to racist jokes, epithets, and other abuse shapes rituals of socialization in white-dominated police organizations (see Cashmore 2001; Bolton and Feagin 2004; also see Chow 1991).

Non-recognition more commonly manifests today as avoidance and selective engagement. Though color-blind racial ideology—which, as we discuss further below, disavows the significance of race and objects to race consciousness—is the most extreme expression of this non-recognition, substantively hollowed-out diversity discourse is an analogous manifestation. While academics and policy-makers might lament the lack of diversity in legal and law enforcement fields and celebrate the presence of under-represented actors in policing, courts, or legislatures, few engage the specific matter of *group recognition* in conceptual or practical depth. When diversity agendas are expressed, little attention is typically paid to envisioned or actual cultural and institutional change. Discussions or acts of substantive recognition are often met with opposition.

In essence, symbols of inclusion are celebrated while substantive recognition is downplayed and contested. When it was noted that US Supreme Court Justice nominee Sonia Sotomayor had ties to a "Latino advocacy group" and publicly opined that a "wise Latina women with the richness of her experiences" would enrich the rule of law, her celebration as a potential statistical first gave way to considerable unease, disparagement, and opposition (Sotomayor 2009; Oliphant and Savage 2009). Relationships with civil society organizations—voluntary and self-governing associations that exist outside of the governmental and for-profit sectors (Salamon et al. 2003: 8)—are essential to a deliberative ideal of representation, as we elaborate further below, yet are used here and in other cases to question professional qualifications and integrity.

Similarly, Judge Ashley Tabaddor, an American immigration judge of Iranian descent, was recently ordered to recuse herself from cases involving Iranians, after accepting an invitation to attend a White House roundtable with Iranian-American community leaders (Associated Press 2014). The Department of Justice reportedly ordered her recusal on grounds that this roundtable participation, where she joined with other prominent Iranian Americans in a community outreach meeting hosted by the White House, created an impression of impropriety. The sanction seems to contradict previously noted Department of Justice claims regarding the importance of inclusion to the effective pursuit of justice and fulfillment of national interests, again betraying a lack of commitment to substantive group representation or actual participatory parity.

Critics were quick to note contradictions and concerns about precedent. In Judge Tabaddor's case the National Association of Immigration Judges observed that, "While the government once sought to appoint judges who reflected the country's racial and ethnic diversity, the [DOJ] order deters those same judges from participating in their communities" (Associated Press 2014). The Public Affairs Alliance of Iranian Americans asked, if she cannot hear cases involving Iranians, "Can an African American judge hear an employment discrimination lawsuit involving African Americans? Can a female judge hear a sex discrimination lawsuit? Can a gay judge hear a case relating to the rights of gay citizens?" Answering in the affirmative, they cite a 1974 opinion by black US District Judge A. Leon Higginbotham (*Pennsylvania v. Local Union* 542), who asserted, "So long as Jewish judges preside over matters where Jewish and Gentile litigants disagree; so long as Protestant judges preside over matters where Protestants and Catholic litigants disagree; so long as white judges preside over matters where white and black litigants disagree, I will preside over matters where black and white litigants disagree" (Austin and Shehabi 2015).

The irony of Judge Tabaddor's discrimination lawsuit was not lost on a writer for *The National Review,* a conservative publication that seized the occasion to ridicule the liberal administration and its contradictory diversity discourse. "U.S. Attorney General Eric Holder, whose department is charged with the alleged discrimination, has spoken at great length about how his life experiences as a black man influence his view of justice," Lovelace (2014) writes. "But [Holder] has not so far commented on what, if any, insights he might have, as a non-white person, into the unique Iranian-American experience."

Representation

Having outlined the basic problem of recognition and its bearing on inclusion, we turn our focus to more practical matters of representation, including what it means to represent others and to enjoy democratic participation, in the system of participatory parity envisioned as racially democratic crime control.

Representation references a number of cultural and institutional processes. These include framing or constructing meaning (e.g., through language, visualization, or other rendering), which is a constitutive rather than descriptive act (Hall 1997). Social phenomena such as "crime" have no pre-existent, fixed, objective meaning; their meaning is constantly rendered or constituted by those whose voices are represented. Though the term is more commonly invoked to describe political participation, especially through the influence of political representatives, both uses are critical to the idea of deliberative racial justice, where participatory parity in justice processes is expected to generate inclusive constructions (i.e., ideas and practices) of justice.

The contrast between diversity and inclusion mirrors that between aggregative and deliberative conceptions of democratic participation. In *Democracy and Inclusion* (2000), political theorist Iris Young distinguishes between these two models of democracy in terms of their normative ideals of inclusion. The *aggregative* model locates democracy in the aggregation of citizen preferences in selecting public officials and policies. With this "allowance for the expression of and competition among preferences," the democratic process amounts to a market in which, "aggregations of the strongest or most widely held preferences" win more shares of representation (19).

By contrast, *deliberative* representation focuses on participation in ongoing dialogues comprising democratic decision-making. This view of a representative democratic process prioritizes actual "discussion of problems, conflicts, and claims of need and interest," viewing the aggregation of public sentiment in selecting official "deciders" as an insufficient model of inclusion. The deliberative view, a more actively inclusive ideal of democratic participation, expects collective agreement to be developed through the expression of the best arguments or reasons. In a "deeply democratic" society this inclusive democratic dialogue and reasoning is commonplace and widespread, culturally and institutionally (Young 2000: 5).

The agenda of increasing statistical diversity among formal legal authorities is most consistent with an aggregative notion of democratic participation. In a narrow, aggregative sense, additional non-white police or court officers, for instance, are expected to shift "influence shares" to those racial and ethnic groups and to signify the legitimacy of these legal institutions by their numerical (e.g., proportional) presence. Diversity is seen as an institutional additive, blended into the mix of existing legal authority (norms, policies, etc.) in order to substantively incorporate constituent preferences and symbolize the inclusivity of the social control apparatus.

Yet deliberative democratic representation demands more concrete and active representational bonds between representatives and constituents. We have seen in the earlier examples of Justice Sotomayor and Judge Tabaddor how ties to the associational life of civil society are invoked as evidence of bias and impropriety. Against the ideal of a "bleached out professional" (Wilkins 1993), these actors have "gone too far" in their embrace of identity and by maintaining such bonds have compromised their objectivity and integrity. Of course, these active bonds are critical to the "authorization" of potential representatives—establishing an *actual representative relationship*—and to maintaining the "accountability" of representative actors to those constituencies whose plural claims they are expected to help voice (see Young 2000: 128–33).

What substantive difference would racial and ethnic diversity in the judiciary or another legal field make if these actors did not maintain ties to civil society organizations where diverse group concerns, ideas, and preferences are expressed? These ties are key to representative relationships. As Young (2010) writes, "[R]epresentation systems sometimes fail to be sufficiently democratic not because the representatives fail to stand for the will of the constituents, but because they have lost connection with them" (128). She explains,

> The process of authorization and accountability that constitute the representative function should not be confined to official government bodies. … Free associative life of civil society contributes to the formation and expression of interests and opinions … [and] the consolidation and expression of social perspectives. Organization and agitation in the public spheres of civil society … are among the best methods of maintaining connections between representatives and constituents, and insisting that representatives be accountable. (153)

This broad participatory feature of communicative democracy is thus crucial to deliberative racial justice. In *The Black Child Savers: Racial Democracy and Juvenile Justice*, for example, Ward (2012) found that formal inclusion of black Americans among juvenile justice authorities contributed to a deactivation of civic initiative around issues of juvenile social control, leaving these representatives isolated from black civil society. The resulting loss of connection weakened vital relationships, including access to culturally informed service resources, means of maintaining legal professional accountability, and leverage to influence future directions in juvenile justice policy. This loss of connections upon which substantive representation would depend helped render these authorities less reliable and effective as advocates of group interests, diminishing their relevance to group representation, notwithstanding their increased presence.

In a more recent example, Cornell Williams Brooks, the President of the National Association for the Advancement of Colored People (NAACP), stressed the value of associational ties to the federal government's response to police violence and other racially disparate crime control today. "We are the nation's primary care physicians when it comes to civil rights," Brooks claimed, emphasizing NAACP work behind the scenes to advance racial justice, including by providing information facilitating government action. "Whether or not CNN or MSNBC follow what we do, we do it day in and day out. Let's look at Missouri, where the Department of Justice issued a scathing report describing profound racial disparities in Ferguson, an unholy trinity of courts, police, and city hall. Where did this evidence come from?" he asked, "From a 2014 state racial profiling law co-written by the NAACP" (Seligson 2015: 48).

As these and other examples help illustrate, representation arises through sustained exposure to constituencies, in exchanges where priorities are expressed and strategies take shape in narrative traces that inform representative actions (e.g., around policy preferences, funding allocations, tactics, etc.). Engagement is particularly vital to continual authorization of representatives and to maintaining accountability, limiting the likelihood of selective stakeholder representation (e.g., black middle class), of drift into established and often antagonistic police or court organizational culture, or loss otherwise of an ability or inclination to represent the plurality of group interests.

Participatory parity

A final point of distinction regarding racially democratic crime control concerns its broader meaning and challenge of *equal* group representation. In this framework, equal representation in crime control implicates a wide range of contexts and relationships where ideas, priorities, and practices of justice take shape. Such milieus are many, spanning formal and informal institutions, and a diverse array of civil society organizations. Equally important here are the substantive relationships between representatives and constituencies and substantive relationships among constituents and representatives within specific community and institutional or organizational contexts.

What does it mean in this context for racial and ethnic groups to be represented equally, and how is that representation achieved? The notion of "participatory parity" summarizes the equitable outcome and practice envisioned as deliberative racial justice. Political theorist Nancy Fraser (2005: 87) describes democratic justice and participatory parity as mutually entwined and co-implicated aspects of inclusion, explaining:

> On the one hand, the principle of participatory parity is an outcome notion, which specifies a substantive principle of justice by which we may evaluate social arrangements: the latter are just if and only if they permit all the relevant social actors to participate as peers in social life.
>
> On the other hand, participatory parity is a process notion, which specifies a procedural standard by which we may evaluate the democratic legitimacy of norms: the latter are legitimate if and only if they can command the assent of all concerned in fair and open processes of deliberation, in which all can participate as peers.

Participatory parity represents an important departure from a common emphasis on "proportionality" as both a mechanism and indicator of equal representation. This distributive frame envisions authorities standing in for status groups they represent and idealizes proportionality among representatives, relative to population percentage. Yet this formulation rests on a problematic, essentialist notion of racial and ethnic group identity. If we accept the basic proposition that all black Americans (or white Americans, etc.) are not the same, a one-to-one match between black population percentage and that of police, judges, and so on does not ensure recognition or representation of this plurality.

Young's (2000) solution to this problem of essentialism is to frame representation instead "as a differentiated relationship among plural actors," where equity resides not in proportional balance but in the richness of these relationships. This helps to resolve the implausible notion that an individual (e.g., a black male police officer) can stand in for the experience and opinions of "black people," since "[t]here is no single will of the people that can be represented" (127). Drawing on Derrida's work on temporality, this notion of democratic inclusion foregrounds "a process involving a mediated relation of constituents to one another and to a representative." Young explains:

> The representative function of *speaking for* should not be confused with an identifying requirement that the representative *speak as* the constituent would, to try to be present in their absence.... [C]onceiving representation under the idea of différance means describing a relationship between constituents and the representative, and among constituents, where the temporality of past and anticipated future leave their traces in the actions of each. (127)

Rather than expect authorities to stand in for the status groups they represent, locating equity in proportionality, equal representation is contingent upon the active maintenance of relationships with various publics, through which the authority gains shared understanding of constituent ideas and preferences (i.e., authorization), and greater responsibility to express them (accountability).

Whatever their representational ties to social life, if formal representatives are marginalized within legal institutions, then the robustness of these ties to constituents will be trivialized accordingly. Recall how women and non-white US attorneys claimed to be denied access to positions of influence, which undercut their representative potential, blocking "traces" of constituent influence that might otherwise influence federal crime control policy and practice. Patterns of racial segmentation—such as the concentration of non-white actors in less powerful legal fields (see Ward 2006), and other noted ordeals of "after inclusion exclusion" (Carbado et al. 2008), where new forms of marginalization arise amid formal access—clearly diminish racial and ethnic group recognition and participation, notwithstanding visible diversity.

The obligations posed by this deliberative idea of equal representation are not only upon the state (i.e., to increase access) or particular legal institutions and official actors (i.e., to engage civil society), but also civic actors, who are challenged to cultivate and sustain means of authorization and accountability. The resulting "inclusive communicative democracy" would involve an ongoing, productive, and likely contentious "process of anticipation and recollection flowing between representative and constituents' participation in activities of authorization and accountability" (Young 2000: 125). Whereas legal and law enforcement authority is often prone to set itself apart from the people, and particularly marginalized groups, the public can and often does challenge this distance (e.g., through protest, calls for civilian review, etc.) and thus renegotiates these terms of participation in representative social control. Whatever the racial and ethnic or other/intersecting status group in question, it represents a heterogeneous democratic voice vying for influence over ideas and practices of crime control, through the activity of communicative democracy.

Objections, challenges, and prospects facing deliberative racial justice

In the previous section we discussed the promise of racially democratic control within modern multi-ethnic societies, focusing on a deliberative notion of racial justice rooted in a norm of recognition and practice of participatory parity. We are not so naïve as to consider this likely in the near future and realize the challenges are tremendous. In the US, for example, there is increasing concern that a merely flawed democratic political system has given way to oligarchic concentration of power among the elite that effectively prevents the representative ideals we advocate. Nevertheless, if only to escape the illusion that diversity equals inclusion, we advance this alternative understanding of racially democratic social control. In the interest of entertaining its practical potential, we turn our attention in this closing section to more proximate ethical and political objections to a race-based agenda of participatory parity and to other challenges and prospects facing racially democratic crime control.

Objections to racial logic

Racially democratic control envisions participatory parity within and across all deliberative milieus of crime control, with emphasis on substantive racial and ethnic group inclusion in this communicative democracy. Participation must go beyond formal authorities (e.g., police, courts, and legislatures) to include informal authorities (e.g., political parties, neighborhood groups, and other civil society organizations) and their collective engagement in processes of representative government. We contrast this deliberative ideal of racial justice with a more symbolic and essentialist *distributive* idea of representational diversity, arguing that it offers a means of more substantive inclusion.

A basic objection to this idea of democratic social control is that racial and ethnic groupings are illegitimate bases of political recognition. The objection casts such representational notions as trappings of a benighted past, the legacy of which we as a society must shrug off by disavowing race. Color-blind racial ideology represents an extreme, conservative version of this argument.

In his dissent in *Plessy v. Ferguson*, Justice Harlan declared, "Our Constitution is color-blind." In the century that followed, "color-blindness" came to stand for the idea that the "races are formally and legally equal," such that "neither substantive inequality, nor past or present forms of racial oppression change how the law should treat racial groups or individual members of such groups" (Harris 2000). This is often translated to mean "race has all but disappeared as a factor shaping the life chances of all Americans" (Bonilla-Silva 2006) and that "being blind to race will lead to racial equality" (Obasogie 2013). Beyond contending that the US is *already* post-racial, color-blindness attributes lasting conflict and inequality to racial provocations of liberal or progressive activists and intellectuals and to alleged "pathologies" of non-whites (see Brown et al. 2005).

Color-blindness obviously challenges an agenda of racially and ethnically representative governance. In particular, it restricts the pursuit of inclusion to a narrow "discrimination and fairness" perspective (Ely and Thomas 2001), providing only a negative right to be spared discrimination while denying positive rights to group recognition, representation, and participatory parity. Senate confirmation hearings for US Supreme Court Justices Clarence Thomas and Sonia Sotomayor put color-blind ideology and these implications for representation on political theatrical display. In 1991, white, Republican senators rallied to Thomas's defense against what he termed a "high-tech lynching for uppity blacks who in any way deign to think for themselves," while disregarding African Americans who questioned Thomas's credibility as a representative black leader, given his political conservatism. Two decades later, many of these same white, Republican senators mocked and criticized Sotomayor for her suggestion that a "wise Latina" might provide a different, and useful, perspective to the Court. According to the ideology of color-blindness, Thomas's deployment of race was "proper," as he argued that his race was being used as a "barrier" and the only proper role for government is the removal of explicit racial barriers. Yet Sotomayor's reference to race or ethnicity was castigated as "improper" as she asserted her own recognition of racial and ethnic group differences, in reference to her personal and professional identity and the relevance of her candidacy to a more inclusive legal culture.

Color-blindness is not alone in disavowing race discourse. A contrasting, and perhaps more compelling version of this argument advocates abandoning racial logic, whatever the remedial intent, to avoid reifying its ideological and political destruction (Montagu 1974; Miles 1989; Darder and Torres 2004). This line of argument is generally critical of what "knowledge production, in general, and the social sciences, especially, have done ... to create, authorize, legitimate, and license the figures of racial otherness, [and perpetuate the] fabrication of racial selves and social objects" (Goldberg 1993: 208).

In their book *After Race* (2004), Darder and Torres insist, "we must disconnect from 'race' as it has been constructed in the past, and contend fully with the impact of 'race' as ideology on the lives of all people." This in part means that "the everyday use of 'race' for symbolic and political purposes has to be uprooted," (2–3) and replaced by what they call historical materialist analyses attentive to racisms, yet divested of racial logic. "In order to analyze ... new racialized relations," they write, "we do not need to employ a concept of 'race.' Indeed, its retention is a significant hindrance" (Darder and Torres 2004: 46). Similar arguments have been made by a number of scholars who critically examine racism while objecting to racial discourse (see Miles 1989).

These progressive interventions have generated valuable alternative frameworks, such as "Cultural Citizenship," as a way of describing interests in inclusion but without reference to race (Rosaldo 1994). Similar to our agenda, cultural citizenship "seeks to understand differences significant to people along a continuum, in the hope of disrupting the racialized discourse of the Other" Darder and Torres (2004) write, yielding "a political strategy [meant] not only to establish a collectivity in which no one is left outside the system, but to extend the rights of first-class citizenship to all people" (23).

Our interest in participatory parity in crime control (and beyond) aligns with this progressive vision but specifies the need for substantive racial and ethnic group inclusion for what we consider pragmatic reasons. Most of all, we specify a deliberative theory of racially and ethnically representative crime control to counter a commonplace distributive notion of inclusion, which limits recognition, representation, and participation. By advocating *democratic crime control* in what are presently racialized social systems, in which exclusions align in part with racial and ethnic group status, we are not invested in the perpetuation of racial structures. We make no assumptions regarding either the lasting significance of race in these societal contexts, or any claim to universal application, irrespective of specific racial histories. Moreover, we expect a practice of deliberative racial justice to generate new structures of racial meaning, by weakening white racial dominance (ideological and structural) in particular.

We consider racially democratic crime control an anti-racist strategy aimed at what Goldberg (1993) describes as "dissolving in theories and in practice both the institutions of exclusionary power and the powers of exclusionary institutions." As a theoretical frame and prospective practice, it involves an assumption of more substantive power within crime control systems, "the power of the racialized, of the racially excluded and marginalized, to articulate for themselves and to represent for others who they are and what they want, where they come from, how they see themselves incorporated into the body politic, and how they see the social body reflecting them" (Goldberg 1993: 237). In theory, deliberative racial justice has the potential to negotiate a world where exclusionary racial politics dissipate and social justice flourishes.

Challenges of intersectionality, geopolitical scale, and racial endogeneity

Countless other conceptual and practical challenges lie in the way of racially democratic crime control. These include intersectionality, globalization, and racial endogeneity to name only a few. While this list is neither exhaustive nor addressed comprehensively here, we note these examples to acknowledge their practical importance, and to encourage further engagement in theoretical and empirical research.

Intersectionality refers to the ways in which status characteristics such as gender and race interact to shape multiple dimensions of experience (Crenshaw 1989, 1991). These complexities become obscured in various cultural and institutional contexts, such as social movements and law, with the effect of eliding and reproducing some forms of subordination. For example, an initiative focused on increasing the presence of women and non-whites among police or court authorities might neglect representational interests of women of color if these statuses are not understood as intersecting. While focusing on intersections of race and gender, Crenshaw's foundational analyses fueled engagement with other categories of difference, such as class, age, and sexual orientation, which further complicate an idea of racially democratic control.

We have provisionally acknowledged this challenge by emphasizing the need for a more plural orientation toward racial and ethnic group experiences and interests, in contrast to the essentialism characteristic of diversity discourse. As Young (1989) notes,

> No one can claim to speak in the general interest, because no one of the groups can speak for another, and certainly no one can speak for them all. Thus the only way to have all group experience and social perspectives voiced, heard, and taken account of is to have them specifically represented in the public. (262–63)

Rather than speaking as "black America," as if with a singular voice, the black official authorized by and accountable to black *communities* (young and old, rich and poor, women and men, LGBTQ and not) and diversity within these collectivities, becomes better able and inclined to speak with this multitude in mind. If representatives limit engagement to select constituencies, for example, by engaging civil society organizations with particular ideological orientations or dominated by elites, their authorization and accountability will be limited accordingly.

Ultimately, intersectionality reminds us that representative social control must involve the expression of the "needs and points of view" arising from complex, overlapping, and dynamic societal constituencies. This is a considerable practical challenge, given the uneven expression of constituent interest within associational life, and presents an important issue for further theoretical and empirical investigation.

Related to this, we should acknowledge considerable geopolitical challenges facing the idea of racially democratic crime control. Namely, at what geopolitical levels or targets should representative social control be aimed, and how is this accomplished? While our discussion up to this point has focused on national and local levels, we have left unaddressed issues of transnational and international representation. As laws passed in one country increasingly impact the lives in others, a deeply democratic view would require that voices of those who would be most affected would be heard, not just in their own nation-states, but also in other nations and by international bodies.

Consider the obvious example of immigration law and resulting immigration control policies and practices. Numerous scholars observe transnational racial and ethnic group interests in immigration, including how US policies criminalizing immigrants simultaneously impact populations within and beyond the borders of the United States (see Menjivar and Abrego 2012; Zilberg 2004; Heyman 2002). If "[r]epresentation should be designated whenever the group's history and social situation provide a particular perspective on the issues, *when the interests of its members are specifically affected*, and *when its perceptions and interests are not likely to receive expression without that representation*" (Young 1989: 265–66, emphasis added), how is substantive representation mapped onto these problems of justice? The examples not only defy national boundaries and governance structures but also seem to exponentially increase status group intersections (e.g., ethnicity/gender/class/age interacting with nationality/citizenship) requiring representation.

Populations ethnically defined in the US as Hispanic, Latino, or Asian have some intersecting experiences and interests with counterparts elsewhere in the Latin or Asian diaspora (and with other women and men, young and old, etc.), but these are certainly limited. Mexican American authorities or civil society organizations cannot sufficiently represent the plurality of experiences and interests among Mexican nationals, in the case of US immigration control and otherwise, let alone those of other Latinos within and outside the United States (e.g., El Salvadorian Americans, El Salvadorian nationals in the United States, and citizens of El Salvador), who are still further distinguished by status group differences.

As Young's analysis concludes, a project of democratic inclusion must ultimately come to terms with such realities of globalization. This presents substantial conceptual and practical challenges we cannot resolve here, but we acknowledge the uncertain meaning and plausibility of "participatory parity" in the case of such an obviously transnational issue as immigration control and likely many others less obvious to us.

Racial endogeneity

Finally, work on racial endogeneity—noting that practical meanings of race (including racial group representation) are constituted *within* various milieus rather than established from *without*—points to the roles of these constructions in conditioning the meaning of inclusion (see Carbado et al. 2008). One implication of this line of work is that an official or policy embrace of the deliberative ideal of representation we advocate is no assurance of an actual practice of deliberative racial justice in particular contexts.

Organizational behavior research on "diversity perspectives" as a mediator of the substantive importance of statistical diversity is illustrative here. In a qualitative study of three culturally diverse organizations, Ely and Thomas (2001) observed several distinct perspectives on workforce diversity, which vary in terms of their rationale for diversifying, the value placed on cultural identity, the connection between diversity and work functions, and indicators of organizational progress. Further, these diversity perspectives had implications for workgroup functioning.

The three perspectives—integration and learning, access and legitimacy, and discrimination and fairness—can be effective motivators for increasing statistical presence, but only the first two *frame* that presence as substantively meaningful to the organization, albeit in different ways. The "access and legitimacy" regards inclusion as a means of penetrating specific markets or communities, while the "integration and learning" framework views diversity as a source of broad, substantive organizational enrichment, specifically through the often contentious but productive activity of soliciting and reconciling competing interests and viewpoints.

Implications for a hypothetical police or court organization are not difficult to imagine. In an organization where the "access and legitimacy" perspective prevails, hiring Asian police or prosecutors may be envisioned as a means of increasing effectiveness and perceived legitimacy in Asian community contexts, and the value of ties to Asian associational life will be similarly framed. Yet Asian operatives will likely resent this constrained organizational purpose and influence, and their positions may be devalued in the organization, leading to conflicts surrounding segregated group functions. By contrast, in an "integration and learning" environment, Asian police or court actors are more likely to be envisioned as general contributors to the organization, so too associational ties, and valued alongside other racial and ethnic group collectives as sources of enrichment in core workgroup functions. While this more robust perspective invites more active contention, in the form of productive disagreements, the "integration and learning" frame is ultimately found to be associated with enhanced organizational innovation, productivity, and satisfaction (Ely and Thomas 2001: 261).

The ideal of deliberative racial justice envisions an *actual* participatory process premised upon "integration and learning," resulting in what we call racially democratic social control. Yet realities of racial endogeneity present challenges as translating policy into practice is concerned and to empirical research that might evaluate the status and impact of deliberative racial justice. Contexts surely vary in terms of how well diverse constituencies are enabled to participate in decision-making, over time and across space. The extent of shared dominion over crime control processes (i.e., processes of defining, interpreting, and enforcing criminal law) is difficult to impose or observe from without, contributing to a noted overreliance on distributive proxies (e.g., "percent black") of these more nuanced deliberative ideals in research and policy.

Several studies reliant on such measures cast doubt on the impact of "diversity among legal authorities" (see Ward 2006 for a review), but more recent work employing nuanced assessments of representation challenges this conclusion (see, e.g., Lyons et al. 2013; Sharp 2014; Ward et al. 2009). What is clear is that we have not lived in a world where participatory parity in crime control is sufficiently widespread to evaluate its symbolic or substantive impact. Mixed and unimpressive findings to date seem more likely to reflect qualitative variation in this absence of participatory parity—and limits of theoretical and empirical engagement with deliberative inclusion within specific contexts—rather than evidence of the actual irrelevance of racially democratic crime control.

Conclusion

In Ferguson, Missouri, where Michael Brown, an 18-year-old African American was shot multiple times by white police officer Darren Wilson in 2014, demonstrators quickly highlighted the police force's history of targeting young black American men for aggressive policing and the exploitative practices of municipal courts (Apuzzo and Ferdandez 2014). Challengers noted that the city of Ferguson was 67 percent African American, but 94 percent of the police force was white, as were the mayor and five of the six city council members. After a lengthy and unusual grand jury process, Wilson was not indicted for Brown's death. An ongoing expose of widespread racist cultural and institutional practices of Ferguson officials, bolstered by the noted Justice Department report finding conditions that harken to debt peonage, along with the pressures of emergent social movement frames and resources, seems to make certain some formal reconfiguration of participatory parity in that region and a relative increase in deliberative racial justice.

Events in Ferguson recall those in Anaheim, California, two years before, when the police shooting of Manuel Diaz, a 25-year-old Latino man, was followed by protests and demonstrations that highlighted that city's increased Latino population and its experience of police violence. Though over 50 percent of Anaheim's residents were Latino, its mayor and city council, chosen in at-large elections, were white. Among the demands of activists was a move to council districts and the appointment of a Spanish-speaking Latino police chief, presumably advancing Latino recognition, representation, and participatory parity (Whiting 2015). These are not foregone conclusions.

The apparent pursuit and promise of participatory parity is kept alive in these moments of crisis, especially when there are faint signs of changing power relations. Marilyn Mosby, the prosecutor for Baltimore City and a young black woman, presented such a moment when she rose in stark contrast to her middle-aged white male counterpart in Ferguson, announcing indictments of six police officers for the death of Freddie Gray, a black man who died in police custody. Her announcement not only presented a different legal outcome, provisional as it was, but seemed to convey a different representative process and relationship, evident in her own outrage and apparent identification with the aggrieved. Would there have been the same outcome if narrative traces of national (esp. black American) outrage were not so intense in that moment and in the deliberations of that particular city administration, led as it is by a black mayor and majority black city council? We cannot answer that question empirically, but the anecdotal distinctions are no less striking and relevant to our discussion.

While these moments undoubtedly generate important civic dialogue, policy changes, and shifts in formal representation, they are never certain to sustain the change in political culture envisaged by democratic social control. For the government of a multi-racial and ethnic polity to be representative in an expansive and meaningful way requires more than the removal of *de jure* barriers to participation and more than mere statistical diversity in the ranks of formal authorities. It requires active inclusion that recognizes *de facto* barriers and creates pathways to overcome them, not simply in the ranks of authorities, but within the civil polity broadly—where ideas about social control circulate and become fashioned into priorities and rendered as norms, policies, and practices.

As we have noted, this ultimately calls on the citizenry to remain engaged in democratic deliberations and to create and sustain democratic institutions that translate group interests into collective decisions and actions. This ongoing representative engagement of a diverse citizenry—what Young calls "deep democracy"—is crucial to social justice. As Young (2000) explains,

> We deepen democracy when we encourage the flourishing of associations that people form according to whatever interests, opinions, and perspectives they find important. Strong, autonomous, and plural activities of civic associations offer individuals and social groups maximum opportunity in their own diversity to be represented in public life. (153)

What are the present and future prospects of such a robust system of racially democratic control? Focusing on the US context, but confident that this is true elsewhere, we acknowledge that this society is far from achieving a deeply democratic system of criminal social control, and governance more generally. The mix of continued exclusion, often illusory progress, and discouraging cultural and institutional obstacles makes this unlikely to change dramatically in the foreseeable future. Yet, continued contestation over substantive representation and the relative rather than absolute ideal of deeply democratic control provide considerable space for optimism and progress.

Bibliography

Cases cited

Dred Scott v. Sanford, 60 U.S. 393 (1857).
Pennsylvania v. Local Union 542, Int'l Union of Operating Eng'rs, 388 F. Supp. 155 (D. Pa. 1974).
Plessy v. Ferguson, 163 U.S. 537 (1896).

Works cited

Alexander, M. (2010) *The New Jim Crow: Mass Incarceration in the Age of Colorblindness*. New York, NY: The New Press.

Anderson, D. and Killingray, D. (1992) *Policing and Decolonization: Nationalism, Politics, and the Police, 1917–1965,* Manchester: Manchester University Press.

Apuzzo M. and Fernandez, M. (2014) 'Justice Dept. inquiry to focus on practices of police in Ferguson', *New York Times.* 3 September.

Appiah, K.A. (1989) 'The conservation of race', *Black American Literature Forum,* 23(1) Spring: 37–60.

Ashkenas, J. and Park, H. (2015) 'The race gap in America's police', *New York Times,* April 8, 2015. Online: http://www.nytimes.com/interactive/2014/09/03/us/the-race-gap-in-americas-police-departments.html (accessed August 10, 2015).

Associated Press. (2014, August 13) 'Immigration judge sues over recusal from cases'.

Austin, L. and Shehabi, S. (2015) 'The United States Department of Justice turns the clock back sixty years to reinstate "separate but equal"', *The Huffington Post,* June 6. Online: http://www.huffingtonpost.com/leila-golestaneh-austin/the-united-states-departm_b_7537896.html (accessed August 1, 2015).

Berrey, E. (2015) *The Enigma of Diversity: The Language of Race and the Limits of Racial Justice*, Chicago, IL: The University of Chicago Press.

Bies, K.J., Deporto, I.M., Long, D.G., McKoy, M.S., Mukamal, D.A. and Alan, D. (2015) 'Stuck in the '70s: the demographics of California prosecutors', A report of the Stanford Criminal Justice Center. Standford, CA:University Law School.

Bolton, K. and Feagin, J. (2004) *Black in Blue: African-American Police Officers and Racism*, New York, NY: Routledge.

Bonilla-Silva, E. (2006) *Racism without Racists: Color-blind Racism and the Persistence of Racial Inequality in the United States*, Lanham, MD: Rowman & Littlefield Publishers.

Brogden, M. and Shearing, C.D. (2005) *Policing for a new South Africa*, New York, NY: Routledge.

Brown, M.K., Carnoy, M., Currie, E., Duster, T., Oppenheimer, D.B., Schultz, M.M. and Wellman, D. (2005) *Whitewashing Race: The Myth of a Color-Blind Society*, Berkeley, CA: University of California Press.

Carbado, D., Fisk, C. and Gulati, M. (2008) 'After inclusion', *Annual Review of Law and Social Science*, 4: 83–102.

Cashmore, E. (2001) 'The experiences of ethnic minority police officers in Britain: under-recruitment and racial profiling in a performance culture', *Ethnic and Racial Studies*, 24(4): 642–59.

Chapman, A. (1912) 'Red Police: The faithful service of the Red Men who maintain the peace on the reservations, often at risk of life and dishonor among their own people', *Harper's Weekly*, 56: 13–16.

Chow, J. (1991) 'Sticks and stones will break my bones, but will racist humor: a look around the world at whether police officers have a free speech right to engage in racist humor', *Loy. LA Int'l & Comp. LJ*, 14: 851.

Crenshaw, K. (1989) 'Demarginalizing the intersection of race and sex: a black feminist critique of antidiscrimination doctrine, feminist theory and antiracist politics', *U. Chi. Legal F.*, 139.

Crenshaw, K. (1991) 'Mapping the margins: intersectionality, identity politics, and violence against women of color', *Stanford Law Review*, 1241–99, 1244.

Darder, A. and Torres, R.D. (2004) *After Race: Racism after Multiculturalism*, New York, NY: NYU Press.

Dayan, C. (2011) *The Law Is a White Dog: How Legal Rituals Make and Unmake Persons,* Princeton, NJ: Princeton University Press.

Delaney, M. (1852) *The Condition, Elevation, Emigration, and Destiny of the Colored People of the United States*. Baltimore, MD: Humanity Books.

Dulaney, W.M. (1996) *Black Police in America*, Bloomington, IN: Indiana University Press.

Ely, R.J. and Thomas, D.A. (2001) 'Cultural diversity at work: the effects of diversity perspectives on work group processes and outcomes', *Administrative Science Quarterly,* 46(2): 229–73.

Esquivel, P. (2013) 'Anaheim's changes not enough for Latino community', *Los Angeles Times,* July 28. Online: http://articles.latimes.com/2013/jul/28/local/la-me-anaheim-unrest-20130729 (accessed August 5, 2015).

Fandos, N. (2015) 'A study documents the paucity of black elected prosecutors: zero in most states', *New York Times,* July 7, 2015. Online: http://www.nytimes.com/2015/07/07/us/a-study-documents-the-paucity-of-black-elected-prosecutors-zero-in-most-states.html?_r=0 (accessed August 10, 2015).

Foner, E. (1998) *The Story of American Freedom,* New York, NY: Norton.

Fraser, N. (2005) 'Reframing justice in a globalizing world', *New Left Review,* 36.

Goldberg, D.T. (1993) *Racist Culture: Philosophy and the Politics of Meaning,* Malden: Blackwell.

Hall, S. (1997) 'The work of representation', in S. Hall (ed.) *Representation: Cultural Representations and Signifying Practices*, London: Sage.

Harris, C.I. (2000) 'Equal treatment and the reproduction of inequality', *Fordham L. Rev.*, 69: 1753, 1765.

Heyman, J. (2002) 'US immigration officers of Mexican ancestry as Mexican Americans, citizens, and immigration police', *Current Anthropology*, 43(3): 479–507.

Johnson, D. and Lichtblau, E. 'Critical study minus criticism of Justice Dept.', *New York Times,* October 31, 2003. Online: http://www.nytimes.com/2003/10/31/national/31JUST.html?hp (accessed February 25, 2015).

Lauter, D. and Pearce, M. (2015) 'After a year of high-profile killings by police, Americans' views on race have shifted', *Los Angeles Times,* August 5, 2015. Online: http://www.latimes.com/nation/la-na-race-poll-20150805-story.html#page=1 (accessed August 10, 2015).

Lawton, B. (2007) 'Levels of nonlethal force: an examination of individual, situational, and contextual factors', *Journal of Research in Crime and Delinquency,* 44(2): 163–84.

Lichtblau, E. (2003) 'Inquiry is sought about deletions in report on Justice Department', *New York Times,* November 4, 2003 Online: http://www.nytimes.com/2003/11/04/us/inquiry-is-sought-about-deletions-in-report-on-justice-department.html (accessed August 10, 2015).

Litwack, L.F. (1998) *Trouble in Mind: Black Southerners in the Age of Jim Crow,* New York, NY: Vintage Books.

Lovelace R. (2014) 'Immigration judge sues Justice Department for anti-Iranian discrimination', *National Review,* August 22, 2014. Online: http://m.nationalreview.com/article/386098/immigration-judge-sues-justice-department-anti-iranian-discrimination-ryan-lovelace (accessed January 25, 2015).

Lyons, C.J., Vélez, M.B. and Santoro, W.A. (2013) 'Neighborhood immigration, violence, and city-level immigrant political opportunities', *American Sociological Review*, 0003122413491964.

McCluskey, J.D. and Terrill, W. (2005) 'Departmental and citizen complaints as predictors of police coercion', *Policing: An International Journal of Police Strategies and Management*, 28: 513–29.

McElvain, J.P. and Kposowa, A.J. (2004) 'Police officer characteristics and internal affairs investigations for use of force allegations', *Journal of Criminal Justice*, 32: 265–79.

Menjívar, C. and Abrego, L. (2012) 'Legal violence: immigration law and the lives of Central American immigrants', *American Journal of Sociology*, 117(5): 1380–1421.

Miles, R. (1989) *Racism,* London: Routledge.

Miller, L.L. (2010) 'The invisible black victim: how American federalism perpetuates racial inequality in criminal justice', *Law & Society Review*, 44(3–4): 805–42.

Mills, C.W. (1997) *The Racial Contract*, Ithaca, NY: Cornell University Press.

Montagu, A. (1974) *Man's Most Dangerous Myth,* Oxford: Oxford University Press.

Muhammad, K.G. (2011) *The Condemnation of Blackness: Race, Crime, and the Making of Modern Urban America*, Cambridge, MA: Harvard University Press.

Norton, M.I. and Sommers, S.R. (2011) 'Whites see racism as a zero-sum game that they are now losing', *Perspectives on Psychological Science*, 6(3): 215–18.

Obasogie, O. (2013) *Blinded by Sight: Seeing Race through the Eyes of the Blind,* Stanford, CA: Stanford University Press.

Oliphant, J. and Savage, D.G. (19 July 2009) 'Diversity a touchy topic at Sotomayor hearings', *Los Angeles Times*.

Rawls, J. (2001) Justice as Fairness: A Restatement. Cambridge, MA: Harvard University Press.

Rosaldo, R. (1994) 'Cultural citizenship and educational democracy', *Cultural Anthropology*, 9(3): 402–11.

Rowe, M. (2012) *Policing, Race and Racism*, London: Routledge.

Salamon, L.M., Sokolowski, S.W. and List, R. (2003) *Global Civil Society*. Baltimore, MD: Johns Hopkins Center for Civil Society Studies.

Seligson, S. (2015) 'The NAACP is not done', *Bostonia*, summer (2).

Sharp, E.B. (2014) 'Minority representation and order maintenance policing: toward a contingent view', *Social Science Quarterly*, 95(4): 1155–71.

Smith, J.C. (1993) *Emancipation: The Making of the Black Lawyer, 1844–1944*, Philadelphia, PA: University of Pennsylvania Press.

Sotomayor, S. (2002) 'A Latina judge's voice', *Berkeley La Raza Law Journal*, 13 (Spring): 87–94.

Travis, J., Western, B. and National Research Council (US) Committee on Law and Justice. (2014) *The Growth of Incarceration in the United States: Exploring Causes and Consequences*, Washington, DC: The National Academies Press.

US Department of Justice. (2003) 'Justice Department initiates new diversity program', Press Release (03–070), February 5. Washington, DC: US Department of Justice.

Ward, G. (2006) 'Race and the justice workforce: a system perspective', in R. Peterson, L. Krivo and J. Hagan (eds.) *The Many Colors of Crime: Inequalities of Race, Ethnicity, and Crime in America*, New York, NY: NYU Press.
Ward, G., Farrell, A. and Rousseau, D. (2009) 'Does racial balance in workforce representation yield equal justice? Race relations of sentencing in federal court organizations', *Law & Society Review*, 43(4): 757–806.
Ward, G.K. (2012) *The Black Child-Savers: Racial Democracy and Juvenile Justice*, Chicago, IL: The University of Chicago Press.
Whiting, D. (6 August 2015) '"We've come a long way since 2012": Anaheim's first Latino chief helps rebuild trust after riots', *The Orange County Register.*
Wilkins, D.B. (1998) 'Identities and roles: race, recognition, and professional responsibility', *Md. L. Rev.*, 57: 1502.
Young, I.M. (1989) 'Polity and group difference: a critique of the ideal of universal citizenship', *Ethics*, 250–74.
Young, I.M. (2000) *Inclusion and Democracy*, Oxford, New York, NY: Oxford University Press.
Zilberg, E. (2004) 'Fools banished from the kingdom: remapping geographies of gang violence between the Americas (Los Angeles and San Salvador)', *American Quarterly*, 56(3): 759–79.

19

Fetishizing the will in juvenile justice policy and practice

Alexandra Cox

Our preoccupation with young people's capacities to successfully develop, grow up, and to change is age-old. When a young person is accused of a crime, those concerns become more acute and the questions more perplexing: Do young people grow out of crime? Do they need assistance in doing so? If so, what form should that assistance take? We know more clearly than ever before that the vast majority of young people age out of crime, even those charged with serious offenses (Mulvey 2011; Mulvey et al. 2004). Thus, do interventions matter? If so, *how* do they matter with respect to a young person's role as a citizen-in-waiting? Juvenile justice programs demand that young people work on their capacities to be compliant with the law and thus exercise self-control and control over their will. Juvenile justice interventions raise critical ethical questions because they are aimed at shaping young people's roles as compliant citizens in the liberal state.

It is arguable that these questions about the relationships among paternalism, justice, and liberty are particularly salient in the study of juvenile justice systems in the United States today. Since the country's first juvenile courts were founded at the turn of the twentieth century, they have sought to distinguish their role—ostensibly one aimed at "rehabilitation"—from that of the adult justice system—"punishment" (Tanenhaus 2002; Schlossman 1977). Today, many states are shifting toward what they describe as a more "rehabilitative" approach to juvenile punishment in response to what has been presented by advocates for reforming the system as the overreaching, punitive, and zero tolerance mentality of the 1990s-era forms of punishment aimed at teenagers. The rhetoric of reformers quite consistently focuses on the need for softer, more caring forms of "treatment" over ostensibly harsher forms of "punishment." This rhetorical strategy is not a new one: there have been a number of previous eras of reform in which advocates have sought to distinguish an older, more punitive system against the newer, more rehabilitative system they seek to build (Bernard and Kurlychek 2010). The approaches endorsed by system reformers today have included the expansion of treatment programming within facilities, particularly cognitive behavioral therapies and so-called "trauma-based" modalities National Research (Council 2012; National Juvenile Justice Network 2012). The new approaches are distinct in that they rely heavily on the idea that the practices are evidence-based, rational responses to previous regimes that have failed children. The positive outcomes found in these so-called "evidence-based practices" are those which result in lower recidivism rates than comparable programs. As so-called "evidence-based" treatment programming has expanded in these juvenile facilities, it has arguably become more critical to assess the ethics of these programs, particularly in the ways that they impact on young people's abilities to participate as social agents and citizens in a liberal democratic order. The reason these ethical questions are particularly relevant is that the state's reliance on and appeal to "evidence" sometimes prevents scrutiny of the underlying motivations and morality of such practices. The focus on the singular outcome of a reduction in recidivism (often over a short period of time) also obscures the significance of softer dimensions of "success" in individuals' lives, such as their ability to build a "good life" where avoidance of arrest and prosecution is not central to their existence and instead they are full participants in the social world, engaged in pro-social relationships, housed, and productive in their labor (Ward and Brown 2004). In practice, policy-makers' invocation of the term "evidence-based" builds the legitimacy of their choices to employ rehabilitative practices that are immune from the critiques of those who might deem them "soft" on crime.

As scholars have long suggested, juvenile justice interventions have long been understood to be repressive—particularly in their effectiveness of maintaining class positions and hierarchies—rather than liberating (Platt 1969/1977; Schlossman 1977). Thus, as we see a new form of reform more focused on treatment and less focused on harsh discipline, do these newer programs do a better job at facilitating young people's future role as social agents and citizens?

As social agents, individuals require adequate conditions under which they can develop, grow, and act in the world in a way that is functional for their well-being and that of those they are connected to (see also Farrall, Bottoms, and Shapland 2010). The conditions under which they can arguably develop and grow into their potential as social agents are those that nourish the dimensions of human agency most related to the "capacity for autonomous social action" (Calhoun 2002): the habits and routines—or dispositions—that undergird the human's position in a social world (Bourdieu and Wacquant 1992) and the space for reactive, unconscious desires to be understood and developed in relationship to one's understanding of choice and action (Elliott 2002; Hitlin and Elder 2007).

This research

These questions about paternalism and governance in the juvenile justice system were explored through two qualitative research studies inside New York's juvenile justice system, conducted over a period of three years, from 2008 until 2011. The first study explored young people's capacities to exercise agency and ultimately to get out and stay out of the juvenile justice system in the context of rehabilitative programming that was explicitly aimed at facilitating "change" in them (see, e.g., Cox 2011). Staff members within these institutions are trained to implement programs that seek to stimulate young people's acceptance of responsibility for their actions, their acceptance of the rules of the institution, and by extension, a form of self-regulation. The second study examined staff members themselves, analyzing some of the ways that they engaged with and resisted these tools aimed at young people's self-change (Cox 2013).

The programs in New York's juvenile facilities are putatively aimed at stimulating young people's capacities to lead lives that are compliant with the law upon their departure from the facility. The facilities employ a medley of programming that focuses on stimulating individual change; they range from cognitive behavioral approaches to those with crudely behaviorist orientations.

This chapter explores the ways that these programs uphold a notion of the will—and in fact *fetishize* that idea of the will—in ways that damage and can destroy young people's agential capacities. I use the term "fetishize" here to suggest that the idea of the will that is possessed by program administrators in juvenile facilities is in fact one that is both impossible and irrational for young people to control. I also argue that power over the will is fetishized by program administrators as the source of change in young people who have committed wrongdoing, when in fact this is a false or misleading site of preoccupation.

Many contemporary policy-makers and advocates focus on the damages of juvenile incarceration on young people's bodily integrity—the harms of physical and sexual abuse, for example, or the dangers of regimes focused entirely on punishment and deprivation (Bernstein 2014). While it is important not to disregard these critiques, it may be useful to explore some of the "persuasive" forms of discipline (Schlossman 1977) aimed at facilitating change in young people's capacities for self-control, rather than the more explicitly and overtly physical forms of punishment.

Many contemporary programs in juvenile facilities seek to change the individual through a combination of incentives and earned privileges. In his recent study of the role of behavioral change regimes in men's prisons in England, Ben Crewe (2009) has found that behavioral change programs in prisons exhibit a form of what he calls "neopaternalism," in which people in prison are induced to improve themselves in ways that are "soft" in their influence, as opposed to the "hard" and authoritarian prison regimes of the past, where the forms of control were overt in their physical demands on inmates, their unilateral forms of power and control, and their clear and rigid forms of spatial separation and control. This form of "soft" power also arguably exists in contemporary juvenile facility life, but in a more embedded form: The behavioral change expectations are woven into the fabric of daily life of the facilities and affect young people from morning until night. From the making of their beds to the way they hold their bodies, they are monitored and assessed by staff members who use those assessments to determine a young person's progress in a way that is described in facility life as "the program."

The program of change

In juvenile facilities across the United States, programming is structured around a model of behavioral advancement; young people progress through "stages" of change that map onto ideas about the stages of moral development that were proposed by developmental psychologists (Piaget 1955; Kohlberg 1976).[1] Many facilities employ a token economy to try to incentivize such advancement; in New York State, young people receive privileges associated with their progress through the behavioral stage system. Their place in that system is symbolized by the color of their shoelaces, with white being the lowest stage and green the highest.

The ideal typical resident in New York's juvenile facilities is constructed through the program design and literature as an individual with a fully pliable and programmable will. The young person's exercise of will is arguably the primary aim of the behavioral intervention. A model resident—and one who obtains the privileges and advantages associated with such a status, including an opportunity for early release—is one who can successfully demonstrate control over his or her will.

There are four core ways in juvenile facilities in which young people can demonstrate this ability to control their will: through their bodies, through their embrace of a philosophy of self-change and self-help, through deference to staff rules, and through the acceptance of responsibility for both the actions that led them to the facility and the responsibility of maintaining order—both physical and social—within the institution.

Ironically, although those in charge of the institutions described the institutions as treatment-oriented, little in the way of treatment was observed within the institutions on a daily basis. It is theorized that this in part occurred *as a result of* the extensive reforms aimed at introducing new treatment modalities. Facing confusion about what treatment and behavioral change modalities they were expected to use and which ones they were expected to abandon, and noting that many of the new tools resembled older ones, a number of staff members simply gave up on employing treatment strategies, and instead relied upon the enforcement of rules and the expectation that they might facilitate change. Staff would occasionally engage in group treatment with young people and employ cognitive behavioral change curricula, but they more fully relied upon behavioral expectations rather than interventions to guide change within young people. In this sense, then, it is arguable that staff in the institutions was not in fact concerned with change as much as focused on institutional order and management. It is also arguable that juvenile justice systems have long been concerned with the idea that young people's engagement in juvenile delinquency represents a failure of personal control (Reiss 1951). One of the most direct avenues to a form of control that staff members found they could exercise over young people was through the route of rules and regulations, as opposed to treatment for change.

Bodily change

Throughout institutional life, young people's bodily functions, habits, and expressions were monitored and policed by staff in ways that were connected to the regulation of the will. Self-control over one's physical actions thus came to be equated with personal control. Policing of the body was almost exclusively focused on directing young people to regularly keep themselves clean and, at least outwardly, self-possessed. Staff often focused on what was described as "hygiene," directing young people to shower, braid their hair, and keep themselves regularly clean, often in infantilizing ways for the overwhelmingly late adolescent population who was ostensibly capable of self-grooming and dressing. The staff often demanded that young people's uniforms be tucked in and that their pants be pulled up. In classrooms, they made young people sit up straight in their chairs or walk straight in lines as they moved throughout the facility. Although there were no facility rules that enumerated these forms of bodily control, they were the unwritten priorities of staff within the facility. In over four years of observational research, I noted many instances of staff members urging young people to demonstrate that they were in *control* of their bodily functions and their bodies in ways consistent with and demonstrable of an expression of willful self-control.

You come here alone, you leave here alone

The expression "you come here alone, you leave here alone" was used by a number of staff members in institutions, often in an effort to discourage young people from engaging in conflict or from seeking the approval of their peers. The expression reflected staff members' attempts to engender notions of "personal responsibility" among the young people.[2] It grows out of the personal responsibility discourses that these young people came of age in—many of them were born in the early 1990s, and their parents were forced to participate in onerous welfare to work programs as a result of Clinton-era welfare reform programs, enacted in 1996, that explicitly relied upon discourses of personal responsibility (c.f., Fraser 1993). The welfare reforms of the 1990s increased the number of sanctions that individuals faced if they failed to meet the requirements imposed by state welfare administrations that mandated individual movement toward jobs and education, sometimes at the cost of the lives of children and families. Some states chose to impose a federal law that required that those with felony drug convictions would lose access to food stamps; other states imposed a federal rule banning access to public housing for those with a drug conviction. The welfare rolls decreased sharply after welfare reform, but not necessarily to the advantage of poor people (Soss, Fording, and Schram 2011).

The program of behavioral change in the facilities was often explicitly linked to ideas of personal responsibility by staff members. For some staff members, the notion of personal responsibility was seen as perhaps the *most* integral part of the change process. One staff member refused to accept my offer to donate the book *Race, Crime and the Law*, by Randall Kennedy, because he said that the title of this book might convey the young people that they could blame racism instead of taking personal responsibility for their actions (he had never read the book). While speaking to a group of young men at a juvenile facility, a judge echoed this sentiment when he said "you have the keys to your jail cell in your control."[3] Staff would routinely implore young people to avoid engaging systemic or structural critiques of the juvenile justice system and their routes into it.

These notions that "getting out" of treatment are connected to an individual's focus entirely on themselves is one that also has increasing purchase in contemporary prisons, which have highly individualized forms of punishment and treatment (Crewe 2009). In the facilities, staff members often suppressed young people's assertions of racial identity and racism in favor of what they said was a more liberal-minded assertion of `colorblindness' and individualism (Bonilla-Silva, 2003). Fused with their critique of youth claims of structural disadvantage, the focus on the individual melded well with staff members' promotion of the notion of hard work on oneself as a "way out" of the juvenile justice system and thus their endorsement of the "American Dream." In many senses the staff members were themselves living what they felt that "Dream" was—they possessed a secure, unionized, and well-paid state job, and many of them had made it out of the impoverished urban core into a secure rural, middle-class existence.[4] Thus, there is a sense in which they were projecting their own notions of success onto the young people under their care.

The notion of "freedom coming from within" can be found in some prisoner narratives and literatures (see, e.g., McCall 1994) and is one that is arguably a source of ontological security—or a sense of continuity and order in the events of one's life (Giddens 1991)—and grounding for some people who are incarcerated and a source of relief from some of the feelings of loss of control that imprisonment causes. A number of the young people felt that time in custody was their sole responsibility and that it was entirely "on them" to do that time. However, their expressions of doing their time on their own may be distinct from this notion of freedom from within in that it was actually about managing and surviving the behavioral change program they were expected to complete. A number of young people spoke about the notion of change coming from within while simultaneously acknowledging their struggles with managing the behavioral change program and their fears about surviving beyond it.

Young people would reflect these notions of individualized progress in their descriptions of their experiences in the facilities. One young woman spoke about how each young resident's program was her "responsibility" and that this could only be accomplished successfully alone. A young man said that while he was in the residential facility "I've been in control 100 per cent of the time," and that "every decision I made was on my own." Another young man similarly spoke about his realization that the only way he could do his time in residential custody was to "do me," and that it was best to ignore other people in that process:

> ... all you gotta do is ignore. If you can ignore somebody, if you can ignore negativity, you will be the best person that you can ever be. You can be the best.

Many staff members encouraged young people to do their time "alone"—through contemplation, introspection, and self-control—rather than with the assistance of others. Staff relied upon familiar narratives of self-reliance and willful self-change that some have argued are a key component of our contemporary mood economy (Silva 2013). Yet it seemed that the staff members' inducements to the young people to "do me" were more like attempts to get those young people to avoid conflict with others in the period of their incarceration, and thus seemed to serve staff interests and institutional prerogatives rather than the developmental needs of young people. In fact, "doing me" might actually work *against* a young person's interest in the sense that they were asked to be introspective and independent in a context where interdependency and relationships might better serve their broader needs in growing, developing, and building character.

These narratives of responsibility were supported by the philosophy of the cognitive behavioral change treatment programs that were in use in the juvenile facilities. These "evidence-based" programs are undergirded by a philosophy of personal responsibility and control; in their deep focus on the psychological nature of self-control, and deliberate shift away from socio-structural explanations for offending, these programs work to support an emphasis on the responsible self. In some program curricula, for example, a young person's decision to speak about their previous experience with abuse or violence may be an indicator of their inability to take full responsibility for their actions.

Other scholars examining the lives of young working class people in the context of contemporary life have identified the ways that young people embrace a self-change narrative in the face of structural disadvantage and social insecurity (Silva 2013; Furlong and Cartmel 2007). Structural changes in recent years have severely limited opportunities in the labor market for young adults (Rampell 2009; Sum et al. 2008). We live in a changing social order, where transitions to adulthood have become less fixed, lengthening young people's periods of dependency upon their parents and guardians and slowing their transition to full citizenship (Furlong and Cartmel 2007). In the face of this insecurity and uncertainty, young people—especially working class and poor young people—have increasingly embraced self-help and self-change narratives (Silva 2013). The narratives are, in a sense, a means of exerting control over a future that seems increasingly out of their control. These experiences of economic uncertainty were arguably magnified by the stigma of the criminal conviction and the collateral consequences of incarceration, perhaps leading to many young residents ironically embracing the idea that their happiness and well-being lay in their own hands and that their change process belonged to themselves. The staff in the facilities actively rewarded young people for embracing these ideas about selfhood and often discouraged them from relying upon their peers and others for support in such change.

Peer contagion and relational ethics

Consistent with the notion that "peer contagion" was the cause of delinquency, staff often appealed to the idea that young people's engagement with their peers was dangerous and toxic—that peers are only sources of tension or conflict, or temptation, not of progress. These ideas are as old as the inception of America's juvenile justice system (Schlossman 1977). Young people were not allowed to speak to each other at meals and during movements throughout the facility, and they were discouraged from talking to each other during their down time in their rooms. They were not allowed to remain in contact with each other or staff members once they left the facilities. While there has been a great deal of research literature devoted to the negative effects of peer relationships on adolescents' capacities to offend, the knowledge about which is in part leveraged by institutional authorities to discourage peer interaction, we increasingly know and understand that adolescent friendships can be an important facilitator of healthy development and wellbeing (Way 2011).

This opens up a puzzle: Can juvenile justice interventions recognize the role of healthy relationships in the development of character? Juvenile justice institutions typically conceptualize adequate behavioral change on the part of young people through their emphasis on young people's individual self-change; this is rooted in the notion that individual change facilitates a change in character. Yet, what we are increasingly learning in the literature on adolescent development and also in that about desistance from offending is that stopping offending happens *with others*—in fact, one's relationship to others is critical to an individual's ability to change (Weaver 2012; McNeill 2009). It is arguable that the staff members' focus on young people's individual-level change, barring them from peer interaction, fails to appreciate the importance of an approach to treating young people that is concerned with and engaged with the potential of relationships to develop and sustain an individuals' ethical engagement in the world; this has been termed *care ethics* by some. Care ethics seek to "structur[e] relationships in ways that enhance mutuality and well-being" (Lawson 2007: 3). They acknowledge the critical importance *and existence* of interdependency in a world that increasingly imagines the liberal subject as an autonomous, willful individual (Lawson 2007: 3). Care ethicists argue that interdependence, mutuality, and care are actually critical to the establishment of a political economy rooted in justice, dignity, fairness, and trust (Lawson 2007: 3).

It was arguable that the juvenile facilities and their staff had a paradoxical relationship to such "care." Juvenile justice institutions often distinguish themselves from adult institutions in their differential focus on treatment and "care." Yet, as many scholars have argued, care and control are often two sides of the same coin (Sharland 2006; Phoenix 2009). The ban on relationship-building among teenagers in the facilities—ostensibly articulated as a form of "care" or treatment—served facility management purposes as opposed to preventing peer contagion. The notion of peer contagion finds its roots in long-standing sociological ideas that young people tend to commit crime in groups and that they learn crime in interaction with others; the idea is that if delinquent peers are grouped together in institutions like juvenile facilities, they may develop and learn antisocial behavior from each other. Researchers have found compelling evidence that peer group interventions, including those in juvenile facilities, aimed at reducing delinquent behavior actually amplify that behavior (Bayer, Hjalmarsson, and Pozen 2009; Dishion, McCord, and Poulin 1999; Dishion and Tipsord 2011; Mennis and Harris 2011). However, some researchers have found that young people can also exert positive, protective peer influences on each other and that not all interactions are negative ones (Lee and Thompson 2009).

This culture of individualism gave rise to some considerable ironies. The staff themselves knew that they were not only far outnumbered by youth residents in the facility, but that if they never allowed these young people down time on the unit to play cards, watch television, and talk to each other—to build relationships—that they would not be able to effectively run the facility. The staff members did not allow young people to engage in this kind of down time for purely instrumental reasons; this was in part a tacit recognition of young people's need for an "escape" from the indignities of facility life, including behavioral change programming. They found this "escape" through care and concern for each other. The staff members' decision to allow these relationships to proceed was arguably an acceptance of the dignity of the residents amidst facility rules and demands for order. The staff could also enjoy their own down time in these moments; I often observed them reading books, snacking, catching up on paperwork, playing cards with the young people, and even sleeping.[5] While discussions about "structure" and "control" were very much part of the public transcript in the institutions, it was these moments of unstructured down time that arguably enabled the young people and staff to thrive.

The moments in which staff members prevented young people from speaking to each other—during movements, meals, and classes—were those times when they were perhaps able to exert the least amount of control over the young people. These were delicate, tightrope-like moments—those in which the young people were expected to obediently follow the directives of staff about movement and bodily control, but also ones in which they were most interested in resisting the terms of their domination because the prohibition on speaking seemed most illogical to them. These moments were also an effort to get young people to express willful control over their engagement with others at times that were beneficial to the institutional staff, not necessarily to the young people themselves. In other words, the irony of willful self-change narratives in juvenile facilities was that they supported and sustained facility order as opposed to actually facilitating change. It is the moments in which willful self-change was *not* encouraged that its fictional underpinnings were revealed. The units were quiet, calm, and free of violence when young people and staff were able to rest and be introspective and be engaged and relational and involved in voluntary, self-motivated interactions but not be bored. While the experience of boredom is typical for many teenagers, it could be quite dangerous in the facilities: it led to higher rates of violence and the greater use of physical restraints by staff against young people.

Deference

Upon entering a facility, residents were given a manual in which they learned about the behavioral stage expectations and rules they needed to follow. The basic rules required deference to staff authority, compliance with rules and procedures, "work[ing] out problems" through treatment programs, exercising "self-respect" and respect for others, honesty, cleanliness, and being quiet (New York State Office of Children and Family Services 2008). The facility staff convened "treatment team" meetings, at which a young person's progress in treatment would be monitored. At each treatment team meeting, staff filled out forms that identified the extent to which each resident was making progress in meeting his or her behavioral goals and expectations. Deference to staff members formed a core part of the expectations outlined in the forms. These included items demanding that young people follow the rules of the facility and exhibit respect toward staff. If a young person successfully exhibited such deference, he or she was rewarded within the treatment team process.

A resident's compliance with treatment in juvenile facilities is considered analogous to the normative processes of development and maturation, in which one moves from dependence on others to independence. The principles behind this behavioral change model stem from the idea that, through these treatment interventions, young people will be prepared to make more rational choices—they will be more *willful* in their actions. The young person's evolution toward these choices is expected to closely follow models of moral development developed by the psychologist Jean Piaget (Morash 1981). This process is considerably more bounded than the parallel experience of maturation in a non-coercive context. The first stage (Orientation, described as a *"Reluctant Learner"* stage in a staff training manual) teaches residents that they "will be watched very closely by staff," who will tell them what to do, and that if they stay on track, "it will also improve the way you control yourself." In the next stage (Adjustment, described as an *"Enthusiastic Learner"*), a resident is expected to work without direction, demonstrate improvements in programs, and to show "other evidence that you are accepting your placement and understand why you have been placed here." In the third stage (Transition, a "*Cautious Performer*"), residents are expected to take more initiative in their deference to the rules of the program, using the "skills" that they have obtained in the facility (such as "anger control" and "problem solving") and show that "you are able to say that you feel sorry for your crimes and take responsibility for your negative behaviors, without blaming others." In the highest-level stage (Honors, a "*Competent and Committed Performer*"), residents should be encouraging their peers to "be positive and to make good choices" by showing "improved self-esteem by cooperating with staff and program expectations." Residents are given what is called a "Resident Behavior Assessment" at their treatment team meeting, on which their stage progression is based. They are also sometimes given "Behavior Improvement Plans."[6]

These forms of assessment comprise what Banks (2008) describes as "scripted" notions of change. The programs are largely aimed at encouraging residents to follow the rules. According to one "Resident Progress Report" issued to him, a young resident named David engaged in multiple incidents and rule violations, which are the markers of resistance to change in the institutional setting, at least in terms of his ability to be released and to receive a higher-level stage. Yet, he complied with or exceeded all of the expectations listed in the report, except for the expectation to "describe acceptable methods for controlling impulsive behavior and use them with staff direction." His initial delinquency offense, like that of many others, is less important in this context than his continuing misbehaviors, which play a role in defining his identity as someone who needs to learn the significance of compliance with norms (Banks 2008).

David arrived at the residential center after a long period of time in the "community," doing an alternative-to-incarceration program. He lived with foster parents, who had adopted him after his mother abandoned him as a child, choosing to maintain her drug addiction. While he was in residential care, David started receiving letters from his incarcerated father for the first time in his life, learning that his father was going to be released within months and wanted to see him. During my visit with David at the residential facility, he showed me the letters he had received from his father, which were posted up on the wall of his room. David's abilities to make choices and solve problems, however, were not evaluated with his family history and circumstances in mind, even though they may have played a role in shaping his behavior in the facility and arguably in his demonstration of self-control and personal control.

Was the behavioral stage model actually a treatment tool, or was it in fact a tool for social control within the institutions? In other words, did the stage process and the rule-making that accompanied it, actually facilitate behavioral change? There was little evidence to suggest it did. Instead, I observed that the expectation that young people exhibit deference to staff members more often than not discouraged or inhibited reflection on, and expression of, their personal histories and emotions in ways arguably detrimental to their character development.

Jacob's story[7]

Like a number of other young residents around him, Jacob was able to articulate his investment in the process of "willful self-change."[8] He worked hard in the facility on what he felt was his self-improvement: He got a coveted job in the facility's kitchen; he earned his way into a college course; and he was on the highest behavioral change level. He spoke about how he wanted to become a police officer after he left the facility. On the day he left the facility, he felt his life had been transformed as a result of his own hard work in the facility; he was ready to be successful because he had changed while he was inside. Yet, when he arrived at home, he had to confront his structural disadvantage and the collateral consequences of his incarceration. He faced serious difficulties in re-enrolling in school, finding a secure and sustaining job, navigating the foster care system in which he remained, and building pro-social relationships and emotional stability after receiving no support or interventions while he was inside that would equip him with the skills to do so.

Jacob, an ideal and successful juvenile facility citizen, found himself struggling after his release. The programming and interventions in the juvenile facilities weren't concerned with Jacob's past; in fact, as a number of criminologists have sought to argue, psychotherapeutic programs based in insight development are seen as too costly and ineffective to implement and have been abandoned in favor of Moral Reconation Therapy, Aggression Replacement Training, and Thinking Errors curricula, all of which were in place at Hooper. As far as the system was concerned, Jacob's ability to develop the impulse control skills necessary to prevent him from exploding in anger in his low-wage job that he got after he left the facility was one of many similar aims—these programs conceive of desistance in a rather static way, as the ultimate state of self-control. Jacob, like other young people in the facility, was discouraged from forming bonds with his peers and prohibited from staying in touch with the facility staff he had connected to and anyone else who might be connected to the facility while he was on parole. So, his "success" in the facility—his ability to follow the rules—was intended to signal his ability to stay crime free on the outside.

Throughout his young life, Jacob was abandoned by his biological parents and by the systems and safety nets (including the child welfare and mental health systems) that were intended to protect him against such abandonment. And he suffered: Shortly before he was incarcerated for his case, his mental health had deteriorated, and he was in a crisis. Yet, as many putatively competent and intelligent young people do, he was able to mask this crisis in the context of a criminal case that necessitated self-protective behavior, both at the jail where he was initially sent and then at the boys' facility, Hooper, where he was sentenced. His mental health and child welfare records didn't follow him to Hooper and when offered medication, he refused; this would have meant he appeared weak to his fellow residents. He found "the program" of behavioral change at Hooper relatively easy to manage because he was a fairly compliant young man; he had to be, as someone who had grown up with few attachments to his biological parents, he aimed to please whatever adult figures with whom he could form even a minimal bond.

But when a crisis struck, Jacob's past quickly haunted his present. He had no friends beyond those who were selling guns and drugs; he was manic and paranoid and had received no consistent mental health care in confinement, and he had no understanding about how to leverage resources in the community on his own behalf after he lost his foster parent very suddenly. His life spiraled out of control, and he is now incarcerated with only a handful of people who remain in contact with him. Jacob had developed limited abilities to engage in what has been termed as "ethical self-correction" (Jacobs 2014). After his foster parent died, Jacob was robbed. Despairing and panicking, Jacob felt that the only possible solution to this perceived injury was to injure someone else.

In part, these actions emerge quite logically from an institution that fetishized willful self-change. From the ages of 14 to 17, Jacob was in an institution that taught young people that the only power to change was under their own control. If they engaged in conflict with others, the philosophy of the institution was that they should be separated until they "cooled off," as opposed to learning how to mediate conflict through ethical engagement with one another. They were taught that they should follow the rules of all adults but not learn how to set rules themselves or cultivate an understanding about moral engagement with others; that they should change their behavior but not their values. In other words, they were taught to simply perform their responsibility for their actions as opposed to developing insight into why they engaged in those actions. There weren't any facility-based curricula or interventions aimed at facilitating young people's understandings of difficulty and disappointment and how those difficulties and disappointments were not only inevitable, but might also lead them to gain greater insights into the antecedents of their harmful actions (Craib 1994). They were only taught the very individualized form of "anger management," as opposed to empathy, care, and concern.

Jacob's story illustrates some key questions about agency and the will. Interventions in the juvenile court context have, even as they take on different shapes and forms over the history of this country's juvenile justice system, specifically been centered around the idea that young people are citizens-in-waiting. They are unformed, underdeveloped, and so on, and it is in part the role of the intervention to help to shape that character (c.f. also Kennelly 2011). Young people who offend are in a sense bearing a multiple burden through the intervention. Not only are they being "corrected" for their criminal behaviors, but they are also expected to learn adult-imposed "responsibilities," which, it is assumed, will help them to grow up and learn how to abide by the rules—and moral standards—of the adult world. As Jacqueline Kennelly puts it, they "must be carefully guided toward suitable degrees of self-regulation" (2011).

The interventions in the juvenile justice context are arguably ones which are really deeply concerned with character *development*. Yet, they operate with a paradoxical construction of young people—malleable, yet also, ultimately, capable of a great deal of resistance to being shaped and governed. Thus, the solution used by juvenile justice administrators is to create programs of change that are highly simplistic in their vision of what constitutes "agency." In the latest iteration of the juvenile justice system, the interventions are deeply informed moral development theories, which inform the behavioral "stage" system used in the facilities I studied, yet in a crude and often coarse way. What I observed was that their translation was one that ultimately resulted less in moral "development" than in a kind of adaptive conformity. Without the ability to develop one's moral responsibilities in a context that provided thicker opportunities for questioning, relational insight building, and so on, the facilities simply enforced passive compliance with rules, rather than active engagement with them.

Many of the young people in the juvenile facility are in a sense deeply alienated from their sense of agency, despite the fetishizing of the will that occurs in the facilities. This alienation, I think, is actually *enhanced* by three discrete processes: the literal alienation and isolation that comes along with incapacitation; the existentially demanding and potentially troubling form of alienation that occurs when one must devote his or her entire time in confinement to compliance with "the program"; and the deep forms of despair and isolation that accompany the copious amounts of "down time" and thus boredom they experience—which explains why the average amount of sleep the young people get each day sometimes exceeds 12 hours.

Juvenile facility practices raise key questions about the governability and regulation of young people accused of crimes. Within the context of the juvenile prison, those young people who are rewarded the most are seen to be those who are the most "governable." Yet what appears to be wrong here are the terms by which governability is set. I argue that the forms of regulation themselves have a very crude vision for what constitutes the redeemable subject of reform; this is ultimately a young person who is, in a sense, a "bad" citizen—one who is passive, deferential, lethargic, apathetic, and under-informed. Those who are seen to be ungovernable find themselves in the adult criminal justice system.

Conclusion

The juvenile facility programs fetishize the expression of the will in order to regulate and control young people as opposed to facilitating their development and the development of their character. I found in my research that the programs actually acted to *inhibit* young people's capacities to make decisions for themselves both within the facility and beyond it. If performed perfectly, program participation served program ends rather than benefiting the young people; the form of agency that they were taught to exercise sometimes facilitated order within the prison and young people's short-term adherence to the law (at least for a few months after they left the facility), but the young people rarely accrued any real benefits in the form of agency they were taught to enact. In this sense, it was not "agency" per se, it was a form of enforced self-regulation. The facilities' programs squelched young people's development as relational, insight-driven beings, capable of coping with despair and difficulty as well as the legitimate barriers they faced as individuals with the stigma of a criminal record or experience in a juvenile prison, as well as their near-constant exposure to criminalization via stop and frisk and other policing tactics. This has serious consequences for the development of character and the capacity to care for others.

Notes

1 See Abrams and Anderson (2013), Inderbitzen (2007), Fader (2013), Nurse (2010), and Reich (2010) for contemporary accounts of residential juvenile facilities in states around the country.
2 The notion of "personal responsibility" is said to be consistent with the "ethos of individual autonomy" associated with philosophies of advanced liberalism, and it relates to inducements to self-government (Rose 2000: 329).
3 This judge would often speak of his own story as an individual raised in a working class community in New York City and making it out to the middle class through hard work and thrift.
4 See Watkins-Hayes (2009) for her analysis of bootstrapping language employed by black and Latino welfare bureaucrats.
5 These activities by staff may not have been allowed, but they often became a way of coping with time, particularly when staff were given mandated overtime shifts, which required them to work for 16 hours straight.
6 Those residents who have been designated as sex offenders must admit responsibility for their actions as a prerequisite for release from the Sex Offender Treatment Program.
7 Some identifying details about Jacob's relationships and this incident have been changed in order to protect his confidentiality.
8 I use pseudonyms throughout this chapter for the names of young people and the facilities they were in.

Bibliography

Abrams, L. and Anderson-Nathe, B. (2013) *Compassionate Confinement: A Year in the Life of Unit C,* New Brunswick, NJ: Rutgers University Press.

Banks, C. (2008) *Alaska Native Juveniles in Detention: A Qualitative Study of Treatment and Resistance.* Lewiston, NY: The Edwin Mellen Press, 2008.

Bayer, P., Hjalmarsson, R. and Pozen, D. (2009) 'Building criminal capital behind bars: peer effects in juvenile corrections', *The Quarterly Journal of Economics,* 124(1): 105–47. doi:10.1162/qjec.2009.124.1.105.

Bernard, T. and Kurlychek, M. (2010) *The Cycle of Juvenile Justice,* 2nd edn., New York, NY: Oxford University Press.

Bernstein, N. (2014) *Burning Down the House: The End of Juvenile Prison,* New York, NY: New Press.

Bonilla-Silva, E. (2003) *Racism without Racists: Colorblind Racism and the Persistence of Racial Inequality in the United States,* Lanham, MD: Rowman and Littlefield.

Bourdieu, P. and Wacquant, L. (1992) *An Invitation to Reflexive Sociology,* Cambridge: Polity Press.

Calhoun, C. (2002) *Dictionary of the Social Sciences,* Oxford, NY: Oxford University Press.

Cox, A. (2011) 'Doing the programme or doing me? The pains of youth imprisonment', *Punishment & Society,* 13(5): 592–610.

Cox, A. (2013) *Juvenile Facility Staff Responses to Organizational Change,* New Paltz, NY: SUNY New Paltz.

Craib, I. (1994) *The Importance of Disappointment,* New York, NY: Routledge.

Crewe, B. (2009) *The Prisoner Society: Power, Adaptation, and Social Life in an English Prison,* Oxford: Oxford University Press.

Dishion, T.J., McCord, J. and Poulin, F. (1999) 'When interventions harm: peer groups and problem behavior', *American Psychologist,* 54(9): 755–64.

Dishion, T.J. and Tipsord, J.M. (2011) 'Peer contagion in child and adolescent social and emotional development', *Annual Review of Psychology,* 62(1): 189–214. doi:10.1146/annurev.psych.093008.100412.

Elliott, A. (2002) *Psychoanlaytic Theory: An Introduction,* Durham, NC: Duke University Press.

Fader, J. (2013) *Falling Back: Incarceration and Transitions to Adulthood among Urban Youth,* New Brunswick, NJ: Rutgers University Press.

Farrall, S., Bottoms, A.E. and Shapland, J. (2010) 'Social structures and desistance from crime', *European Journal of Criminology,* 7(6): 546–70.

Fraser, N. (1993) 'Clintonism, welfare, and the antisocial wage: the emergence of a neoliberal political imaginary', in A. Callari, S. Cullenberg and C. Biewener (eds.) *Marxism in the Postmodern Age,* New York, NY: The Guilford Press.

Furlong, A. and Cartmel, F. (2007) *Young People and Social Change: New Perspectives,* Berkshire: Open University Press.

Giddens, A. (1991) *Modernity and Self-Identity: Self and Society in the Late Modern Age,* Stanford, CA: Stanford University Press.

Hitlin, S. and Elder, G.H., Jr. (2007) 'Time, self, and the curiously abstract concept of agency', *American Sociological Association,* 25(2): 170–91.

Inderbitzen, M. (2007) 'Inside a maximum security training school', *Punishment and Society,* 9(3): 235–251.

Jacobs, J. (2014) 'Character, punishment, and the liberal order', John Jay College of Criminal Justice, Institute for Criminal Justice Ethics.

Kennelly, J. (2011) 'Policing young people as citizens-in-waiting', *British Journal of Criminology,* 51(2): 336–54.

Kohlberg, L. (1976) 'Moral stages and moralization: The cognitive developmental approach', in T. Lichona (ed.) *Moral Development and Behavior: Theory, Research, and Social Issues,* New York, NY: Holt, Rinehart and Winston.

Lawson, V. (2007) 'Geographies of care and responsibility', *Annals of the Association of American Geographers,* 97(1): 1–11.

Lee, B.R. and Thompson, R. (2009). 'Examining externalizing behavior trajectories of youth in group homes: is there evidence for peer contagion?', *Journal of Abnormal Child Psychology,* 37(1): 31–44. doi:10.1007/s10802-008-9254-4.

McCall, N. (1994) *Makes Me Wanna Holler: A Young Black Man in America,* New York, NY: Vintage Books.

McNeill, F. (2009) *Towards Effective Practice in Offender Supervision.* Glasgow: Scottish Center for Crime and Justice Research.

Mennis, J. and Harris, P. (2011) 'Contagion and repeat offending among urban juvenile delinquents', *Journal of Adolescence,* 34: 951–63.

Morash, M.A. (1981) 'Cognitive developmental theory', *Criminology,* 19(3): 360–71.

Mulvey, E.P. (2011) *Highlights from Pathways to Desistance: A Longitudinal Study of Serious Adolescent Offenders,* retrieved from Washington, DC: US Department of Justice. Available at: https://www.ncjrs.gov/pdffiles1/ojjdp/230971.pdf. (Accessed 28 March 2016).

Mulvey, E.P., Steinberg, L., Fagan, J., Cauffman, E., Piquero, A.R., Chassin, L., ... and Losoya, S.H. (2004) 'Theory and research on desistance from antisocial activity among serious adolescent offenders', *Youth Violence and Juvenile Justice,* 2(3): 213–36. doi:10.1177/1541204004265864.

National Juvenile Justice Network. (2012) *Advances in Juvenile Justice Reform,* Washington, DC: National Juvenile Justice Network.

National Research Council. (2012) *Reforming Juvenile Justice: A Developmental Approach,* Washington, DC: National Academies Approach.

New York State Office of Children and Family Services. (2008) *Resident Manual: Secure Facilities,* Rensselaer, NY: New York State Office of Children and Family Services.

Nurse, A. (2010) *Locked Up, Locked Out: Young Men in the Juvenile Justice System,* Nashville, TN: Vanderbilt University Press.

Phoenix, J. (2009) 'Beyond risk assessment: the return of repressive welfarism?', in F. Mcneill and M. Barry (eds.) *Youth Offending and Youth Justice,* London: Jessica Kingsley Publishers.

Piaget, J. (1955) *The Construction of Reality in the Child,* New York, NY: Basic Books.

Platt, A. (1969/1977) *The Child Savers: The Invention of Delinquency,* Chicago, IL: The University of Chicago Press.

Rampell, C. (2009) 'Teenage jobless rate reaches record high', *The New York Times.*

Reich, A. (2010) *Hidden Truth: Young Men Navigating Lives In and Out of Juvenile Prison,* Berkeley, CA: University of California Press.

Reiss, A. (1951) 'Delinquency as the failure of personal and social controls', *American Sociological Review,* 16(2): 196–207.

Rose, N. (2000) "Government and Control." *British Journal of Criminology* 40 (2000): 321–39.

Schlossman, S. (1977) *Love and the American Delinquent: The Theory and Practice of "Progressive" Juvenile Justice, 1825–1920,* Chicago, IL: The University of Chicago Press.

Sharland, E. (2006) 'Young people, risk taking and risk making: some thoughts for social work', *British Journal of Social Work,* 36(2): 247–65.

Silva, J. (2013) *Coming Up Short: Working-Class Adulthood in an Age of Uncertainty,* New York, NY: Oxford University Press.

Soss, J., Fording, R. and Schram, S. (2011) *Disciplining the Poor: Neoliberal Paternalism and the Persistent Power of Race,* Chicago, IL: The University of Chicago Press.

Sum, A., McLaughlin, D., Khatiwada, I. and Palma, S. (2008) *The Continued Collapse of the Nation's Teen Job Market and the Dismal Outlook for the 2008 Summer Labor Market for Teens: Does Anybody Care?* Boston, MA: Center for Labor Market Studies, Northeastern University.

Tanenhaus, D. (2002) 'The evolution of juvenile courts in the early twentieth century: beyond the myth of immaculate construction', in M. Rosenheim, F. Zimring, D. Tanenhaus and B. Dohrn (eds.) *A Century of Juvenile Justice,* Chicago, IL: The University of Chicago Press.

Ward, T. and Brown, M. (2004) 'The good lives model and conceptual issues in offender rehabilitation', *Psychology, Crime & Law,* 10(3): 243–57.

Watkins-Hayes, C. (2009) 'Race-ing the bootstrap climb: black and Latino bureaucrats in post-reform welfare offices', *Social Problems,* 56(2): 285–310.

Way, N. (2011) *Deep Secrets: Boys' Friendships and the Crisis of Connection,* Cambridge, MA: Harvard University Press.

Weaver, B. (2012) 'The relational context of desistance: some implications and opportunities for social policy', *Social Policy and Administration,* 46(4): 395–412.

20

The moral justification for the police use of lethal force

Seumas Miller[1]

In this entry I examine the moral justification or, better, justifications (plural) for police use of lethal force.[2] Presumably police officers, along with the rest of us, are morally justified in using lethal force in self-defence or in defence of the lives of others. But do police officers have a moral justification for the use of lethal force that the rest of us do not have? Of particular interest here is the claim that police officers have an *institutional* and moral right and duty to use lethal force in circumstances in which ordinary citizens do not have any such moral right or duty. Certainly, police officers have an institutional moral right and duty to uphold the law. So do police officers have an *institutional* moral right and duty to use *lethal* force to uphold the law, above and beyond their moral right and duty to use lethal force in self-defence or defence of others? Here there is a contrast between an institutional right or duty and a natural or pre-institutional one. Arguably, the right to self-defence (and to defend the lives of others) is a natural, as opposed to an institutional, right.

Killing in order to defend one's own life or the life of another is typically morally justified on the grounds that each of us has a right to life.[3] Moreover, speaking generally,[4] we are entitled to defend that right to life by killing an attacker under three conditions and if we do so in compliance with the three principles of imminence, necessity, and proportionality. Firstly, there is the condition that the attacker is deliberately trying to kill someone – either oneself or another person – and will succeed if we do not intervene immediately. Moreover, in accordance with the principle of imminence the deadly threat needs to be imminent. We are not entitled to shoot dead an attacker whom we know is threatening us with a replica of a gun or (speaking generally) pre-emptively kill someone who is planning to kill us in the distant future. Nor are we entitled to kill an attacker who is only engaged in a minor assault (principle of proportionality).

The second condition is that we have no way of preserving our own or the other person's life other than by killing the attacker (principle of necessity). For example, we are not able to flee to safety. I note that the principle of necessity may operate in a different manner in cases of collective violence, such as wars fought by the military forces of nation-states. Thus in the context of an ambush of an enemy force in a theatre of war it may not be necessary for a military combatant to kill a particular enemy combatant in order to protect his own life (i.e., in self-defence) or to protect the life of a fellow combatant. For perhaps the enemy force being ambushed is entirely unaware of the presence of the ambushing force; therefore, the latter is in a position to avoid armed conflict. Nevertheless, it may be a *military necessity* in the sense that killing the enemy combatant (and his fellow enemy combatants) contributes to degrading the enemy force, and degrading this force is in turn necessary if the war is to be won.

The third condition in the one requiring that our attacker does not have a morally justifiable reason for trying to kill us. This is straightforward in many cases, e.g., an armed robber who tries to kill a defender in order to get his money. Other cases are less so. For example, since the death penalty is controversial then it is controversial whether a legally appointed executioner has a good and decisive moral justification for carrying out the death penalty in the case of a serial killer. If the executioner does have such a justification, then presumably the serial killer is not morally justified in trying to kill the executioner in self-defence, supposing the opportunity arose.[5] If not, then perhaps the serial killer is morally justified in trying to kill the executioner in self-defence.

1 Police use of lethal force in defence of the rights of others: An institutional (moral) duty

To reiterate, police officers evidently have a *natural* moral right to use lethal force in self-defence and a *natural* moral obligation to use lethal force in defence of the lives of others. In these respects, they are no different from ordinary citizens. But evidently police officers also have an *institutionally based* moral *duty* to use lethal force to protect innocent lives under certain circumstances. Moreover, this institutional duty is arguably different from the natural obligation from which it is presumably, at least in part, derived. One indicator of this is that police, but not ordinary citizens, can be held legally liable if they fail to take the opportunity to shoot dead an armed and dangerous criminal who then goes on to (say) take the lives of innocent citizens.

What of ordinary citizens? As noted, they have a natural moral obligation to use lethal force to protect others, at least in cases where the threat to life is immediate and certain, and there is no non-lethal alternative. However, this natural moral obligation comes with some important qualifications.

The qualifications are threefold. Firstly, the obligation of ordinary citizens to use lethal force to protect others is evidently a *general natural* moral obligation and not a *special institutionally based* moral duty, as is the case with the police.[6] Secondly, in the context of a well-ordered, contemporary, liberal democratic nation-state this moral obligation of ordinary citizens is only triggered in the absence of police; in the first instance, it is the moral and institutional duty of police to protect threatened lives. Thirdly, not having been trained, and not having accepted a special institutional responsibility to protect the lives of others, ordinary citizens ought not to be expected to go to the same lengths or to take the same risks as police officers are obliged to. Police officers, but not ordinary citizens, have a moral duty to put themselves in harm's way to protect the lives of others. In summary, the moral obligation of ordinary citizens to kill to protect others is less stringent than the special institutionally based moral duty of police officers to do so.

In addition to the justification for using lethal force to protect the right to life (whether in self-defence or in defence of the lives of others) there is the question of a wider justification in terms of the protection of rights other than the right to life. Evidently, the use of lethal force can be justified to protect moral rights other than the right to life. However, in speaking of using lethal force in defence of rights, one should not include *all* moral rights, or at least *all violations* of all moral rights. For example, property rights are arguably moral rights, but for a police officer to shoot someone dead to prevent him stealing a handbag would be morally unacceptable. So the question becomes: Are there any moral rights, apart from the right to life, the protection of which would justify police use of deadly force? Candidates for such rights might include a right not to be severely physically or psychologically damaged. Perhaps rape, serious child molestation and grievous bodily harm are actions the prevention of which might justify use of deadly force. Maybe police, in particular, are justified in shooting a fleeing serial rapist if that is the only way to ensure his arrest. Henceforth I will use the terms 'self-defence' and 'other-defence' to include the list of rights that in most liberal democracies would be taken *prima facie* to justify the use of lethal force in their defence, albeit I have not fully specified this list.

Arguably, there are other moral rights, including some property rights, the violation of which under certain circumstances might justify the use of lethal force. Consider, for example, the policy of shooting on sight cattle rustlers in the old American Wild West, in circumstances under which the property crime of cattle rustling threatened ranchers' livelihoods? Perhaps the moral justification in such cases is *indirect*; it is *ultimately* to be understood in terms of the right to preserve one's life (or the right to a minimal standard of living or some such[7]) against culpable aggressors including, in some extreme circumstances, pre-emptively.

The lethal response of police officers to various forms of collective violence provide a different kind of case. What of police shooting rioters or those engaged in communal violence? Here we need to distinguish the question of the *types* of crime that might justify the use of lethal force, from the question of the *extent* of crime that might justify it. So there might be a general breakdown of law and order in some part of an otherwise well-ordered and law-abiding polity. This breakdown might consist in large-scale, serious violations of moral rights.

Arguably, the moral justifications for police use of force in general (as opposed to lethal force in particular) in public order policing, e.g., riots, communal violence, comprise considerations of self-defence, other-defence and in order to uphold the law (of which more in the next section). If so, then the moral justifications for the police use of force in public order policing are essentially the same as in policing practice more generally.

Public order policing strategies[8] tend to be divided into two broad groups, (a) pre-emptive or pro-active policing and (b) reactive policing. For example, pro-active public order policing is typically utilized in pre-organized election rallies and involves planned public order policing arrangements. By contrast, in reactive public order policing police have little or no notice of impending events, and police frequently confront collective violence. Accordingly, the use of force by the police is, correspondingly, both far more likely and easier to justify. However, even in reactive policing of collective violence situations, coercive force needs to be used judiciously and in tandem with non-violent strategies.

In some instances of reactive policing of collective violence, the violence is primarily directed at the police themselves, e.g., recent demonstrations in the US against police shootings of blacks. In other instances the violence is primarily directed at another group within the community, e.g., religious violence in India. An important factor in the policing of collective violence is the attitude of the community being policed to the police. Are the police seen as an occupying force or as an impartial enforcer of the law and protector of the community from criminal elements? Race riots in Ferguson, Missouri, in 2014 in the aftermath of the shooting dead of an unarmed black youth, Michael Brown, by a police officer indicated that the police in many US jurisdictions are not necessarily viewed by black communities as impartial enforcers of the law.[9]

Notwithstanding that members of a crowd are engaged in individual or collective violence, the police response ought to be driven by the requirements to uphold the law/preserve the peace and protect the moral rights (including property rights) of the citizenry. Hence, the aim of the police is to disperse violent crowds and do so with the minimum use of force and in a discriminating manner. Here the use of tear gas can be effective. Although tear gas is not discriminating it is also not particularly injurious. Additional more discriminating methods are available to target specific individuals, such as ringleaders or those engaged in violent acts, such as missile throwers. These methods include firing non-lethal rounds which, nevertheless, incapacitate, e.g., plastic bullets.[10] In this context, the apparent militarization of US law enforcement agencies in terms of their deployment of armoured vehicles, machine guns, and other military hardware is cause for concern.[11]

There are some instances of collective violence in which police use of lethal force may be required. For example, in Ahmedabad, Gujarat, in 2002 hundreds, if not thousands, of Muslims were killed by Hindus and incited to do so by Hindu leaders; moreover, hundreds of Hindus were killed by Muslims.[12] In these circumstances, police use of lethal force is justified both in terms of their own self-defence and in order to defend the lives of those being attacked. In such contexts the distinction between the police and the military use of force comes under some pressure. For example, effective use of lethal force by police in such circumstances might rely on a military style authority relationship between police leaders and subordinate police officers; the latter firing their weapons when instructed to do so by their superiors rather than on the basis of their own individual judgments.[13] On the other hand, the principle of military necessity (mentioned above) is not in play; so even in these extreme cases of collective violence the justification for police use of lethal force does not collapse into the justification for the use of lethal force in military combat. In such cases the police, unlike the military, are not seeking or, at least, ought not to be seeking to degrade an enemy force but rather to preserve lives.

Some instances of serous and ongoing collective violence undermine the legitimate political and, more broadly, legal order and, as such, constitute a threat to national internal security. Perhaps the riots in Thailand in 2014 directed at the democratically elected government of the day are an instance of this. At any rate, to unjustifiably undermine the legitimate legal order in this manner is – among other things – to indirectly violate the legal and political rights (institutionally based moral rights) of the citizenry. Arguably, if the extent of collective violence is undermining the legitimate legal order and all available non-lethal methods have failed, then the (minimally necessary) use of lethal force by police might be justified. It is at this point that the institutional roles of the police and the military meet. Nevertheless, even in these kinds of situations, arguably, the distinction between the police and the military role can be, and should be, maintained. The demarcation in question can be maintained by an institutional demarcation between granting emergency powers to police and imposing martial law. In effect, the latter, but not the former, takes operational authority away from the police and gives it to the military.

The various above-described collective violence scenarios involving a general breakdown in public order justify police use of force, including, potentially, lethal force, on a scale that would otherwise not be justified. Moreover, the typical response to such scenarios would be one in which there was a declaration of a state of emergency in a specified geographical area for a limited period of time and the granting of special powers of enforcement to police by the government of the day but only in that area for that period. Moreover, strict accountability measures would need to be introduced to ensure police did not abuse their new powers. However, the point to be stressed here is that the special powers in question (including, potentially, the use of lethal force) are ones granted only to police, i.e., not to the citizenry in general. Accordingly, these special legal powers (institutional rights and duties) should not be assimilated to natural moral rights and obligations to use lethal force, albeit they may in large part be derivable from them.

The upshot of our discussion in this section is as follows. As is the case with ordinary citizens, police officers have a natural moral right to self-defence. Moreover, both ordinary citizens and police have a moral obligation to use lethal force in other-defence. However, the justification for the police use of lethal force in other-defence while grounded in large part in the natural right to use lethal force in other-defence is, nevertheless, different in some important respects. Importantly, police officers, but not ordinary citizens, have an (institutionally based) moral duty to put themselves in harm's way to protect the lives of others. Moreover, police officers have a moral duty to defend the legitimate legal (including political) order including, if necessary, by the use of lethal force. But this duty is presumably not a *natural* obligation since it pertains to an *institutional* arrangement.

Thus far we have explicitly discussed the self-defence and other-defence moral justifications for police use of lethal force. Arguably, these moral justifications simply involve an extension of pre-existing natural (moral) rights or obligations, e.g., the natural moral right to defend one's own life against a culpable attacker. However, we have also introduced a third putative moral justification for police use of lethal force: defence of the legitimate legal order. Evidently, this latter moral justification does not simply involve an extension of a pre-existing natural moral right. Rather it is seems to involve an institutional moral duty, namely, police use of lethal force to enforce the law. Moreover, conceptually at least, we can separate police use of lethal force in self-defence and in defence of others, on the one hand, from police use of lethal force to enforce the law. At any rate, let us now turn explicitly to this third (putative) moral justification for police use of lethal force.

2 Police use of lethal force to enforce the law

Thus far we have considered police use of lethal force to enforce the law in situations involving collective violence and, in particular, situations in which the established (morally legitimate) legal order is under threat. But what of the small-scale, police-offender encounters that are more characteristic of policing in well-ordered liberal democratic states? After all, it might be argued that by focusing on these collective violence scenarios we are invoking highly unusual, if not fanciful, emergencies and, thereby, argumentatively 'stacking the deck'.

The collective violence scenarios in question (scenarios that might justify police use of lethal force) are, of course, highly unusual in *well-ordered* liberal democratic states; but, as we saw above, they take place all too often in disorderly ones, such as parts of India. Moreover, even if these scenarios are highly unusual emergencies, nevertheless, apparently some of them – some of those involving a threat to the legal and political order – demonstrate that there is a third kind of moral justification for police use of lethal force. At any rate, let me now turn to a consideration of small-scale, police offender encounters with a view to determining whether some of these might provide further reason to believe that enforcing the law is a third acceptable moral justification for police use of lethal force.[14]

As already discussed, police use of lethal force, while morally justified in self-defence and in other-defence, it is not in general morally justified in relation to less serious offences, such as property crimes, e.g., police are not morally justified in shooting dead an unarmed pickpocket. This is the case even if the only way to prevent escape is by shooting the offender dead.

Nevertheless, there is apparently a type of case, thus far neglected, in which police officers are morally and legally entitled – and perhaps morally and legally obliged – to use lethal force in order to uphold the law. Consider the case of Burglar who has successfully burgled a large number of homes containing expensive items, (e.g., jewellery, large amounts of cash) and gotten away with millions of dollars of other people's money. His modus operandi is to steal from empty homes; he does not use the threat of violence to get his loot. Nevertheless, Burglar knows the police are investigating his crimes, so he arms himself and is prepared to shoot in order to avoid capture, though if left alone with his money, he will not shoot anyone.

This scenario involves a property crime and to this extent evidently does not warrant a lethal response on the part of the police. On the other hand, it also involves a *repeat* offender who is armed and prepared to use lethal force to avoid capture, albeit not otherwise.

The police need to consider their options when they realise Burglar is armed and prepared to use lethal force to avoid arrest. Perhaps they can arrest Burglar at a later time, and do so when he is not armed. Or perhaps they can contain Burglar (e.g., by means of strategic positioning of armed police officers) and successfully negotiate with him. However, neither of these options might be available. Suppose, for example, Burglar is always armed in order to avoid arrest. Suppose also that the chances of the initial confrontation between Burglar and the police involving more than one or two police officers is extremely small; they don't know where Burglar lives and cannot predict which of numerous homes will be next on his list. In short, containment and negotiation is not an available option.

It might be argued that the police officer who comes upon Burglar should allow Burglar to go scot-free. The police officer should do so on the grounds that by doing so his or her own life and that of Burglar will not be put at risk; and ensuring that no life is lost is more important than protecting property[15] and seeing to it that justice is done by imprisoning Burglar for his crimes.

Now consider a related scenario, Wife-killer. Wife-killer has a gun and, having just killed his adulterous wife in their home, refuses to give himself up to the police officer who is present. Instead Wife-killer threatens to shoot the officer dead, if he tries to arrest him, though if allowed to escape he will not harm anyone. Wife-killer hated his adulterous wife but is otherwise not dangerous, let us assume. Moreover, Wife-killer is about to leave the country, never to be found.

It might be argued that the police officer should allow Wife-killer to go scot-free. The police officer should do so on the grounds that by doing so his or her own life and that of Wife-killer will not be put at risk; and ensuring that no additional life is lost is more important than ensuring justice is done by imprisoning Wife-killer for his crime of murder.

The arguments in favour of the police officers allowing Burglar and Wife-killer (respectively) to escape are not in my view compelling, but let us up the ante. Let us assume that in a certain police jurisdiction large numbers of offenders arm themselves and threaten to kill police officers who try to arrest them for their offences. The offences in question are serious property crimes (as in Burglar) and one-off serious crimes of murder, grievous bodily harm, and rape (as in Wife-killer). Moreover, the armed offenders in question will kill or, at least, try to kill the police officers, if the latter try to arrest them, but not if these officers simply allow the offenders to escape.

One possible police response to this (let us assume) widespread law enforcement problem is to comply with the wishes of these offenders by allowing them to escape. However, such a police practice would surely be a gross dereliction of their institutional and moral duty; it would essentially consist of a failure to enforce the law on any occasion in which an offender was prepared to use lethal force to resist arrest (in circumstances in which allowing the offender to escape did not pose a risk to the lives or limbs of police officers or third parties). In the circumstances in question such a practice would render police officers impotent in relation to a very wide range of serious crimes; as such, it is arguably not a sustainable law enforcement practice. Evidently, police officers need to retain as a last resort the use of lethal force to enforce the law, even in small-scale, police-offender confrontations in which their resort to lethal force is not necessary to prevent loss of life or limb (either their own or that of offenders or ordinary citizens).

So far so good. But it might now be argued that although the police are morally and, presumably, legally obliged to use lethal force against offenders prepared to use lethal force to avoid arrest (assuming it is necessary to do so on pain of allowing the offenders to escape), the moral justification for such use of lethal force by the police is self-defence rather than, as has been suggested, to enforce the law.

Before proceeding to engage directly with this argument there are a couple of preliminary matters to be dealt with. Firstly, it is important not to conflate the type of scenario in question with a related type that is irrelevant to the argument. In these irrelevant scenarios the armed offenders will try to kill the police officers whose job it is to arrest them, *even if* these officers are prepared to allow the offenders to escape. In short, in this second type of scenario the officer's life is at risk, irrespective of whether he or she proceeds to try and effect an arrest of the offender. A moral justification for police use of lethal force in this second type of scenario may well be self-defence; but this type of scenario is *not* in question here. In the scenarios in question here the police officer has the option of allowing the offender to escape without putting his own life (or that of the offender or, for that matter, any third party) at risk.

More generally, it is important not to conflate the type of case of interest to us here with that of fleeing *dangerous* offenders. Unlike the offenders of interest to us, dangerous offenders in this sense are a threat to the life and limb of police officers and ordinary citizens, even if they are allowed to escape. So dangerous offenders are a *standing* threat to life and limb; the threat to life and limb that they pose cannot be removed by leaving them alone. Hence it is legally and, presumably, morally permissible to use lethal force against such dangerous offenders if they are trying to escape arrest; if they are so-called 'fleeing felons'.

In the US the fleeing felon rule under which lethal force could be used against a fleeing person suspected of a felony was curtailed by the US Supreme Court in 1985.[16] Roughly speaking, under this ruling lethal force is legally justified only if it is necessary to prevent the escape of someone who is reasonably believed to pose a significant threat to the life or limb of the pursuing police officer or to others. Consider the recent case mentioned above of the unarmed black youth Michael Brown. After stealing from a shop in Ferguson, Brown fled from police, was shot at by a police officer (and hit in the hand), and was finally shot dead by the police officer. Perhaps this use of lethal force was lawful prior to 1985, but *prima facie* it was unlawful thereafter, given Brown was unarmed. On the other hand, there remains the issue as to whether or not the police officer might be held to have had a reasonable belief that Brown constituted a threat since, arguably, he was moving towards the officer rather than surrendering when he was shot.[17] In the recent case of Walter Scott shot dead by a police officer in North Charleston, South Carolina, there could not have been any such reasonable belief. Scott was an unarmed black person stopped by the officer. The officer shot Scott in the back multiple times as he fled, and the incident was caught on video. The officer was charged with murder.

A second preliminary point is that the argument under consideration here (that the law enforcement justification for police use of lethal force collapses into the self-defence justification) should not be confused with a related argument involving the other-defence justification. According to the latter argument, in the scenarios in question the police, even if they are not engaged in killing in self-defence are, nevertheless, necessarily killing in defence of others. As we saw above, this may well be true of *dangerous* fleeing offenders (e.g., serial killers) or offenders who will try to kill would-be arresting police officers, even if the latter would allow them to escape. However, as scenarios Burglar and Wife-killer (again) illustrate, neither the lives of police officers nor those of ordinary citizens need be at risk. So with respect to the scenarios in question the other-defence justification is not relevant.

Let us now directly engage with the actual argument at issue; the argument that these putative cases of police use of lethal force to enforce the law in cases such as Burglar and Wife-killer are simply cases of police using lethal force in self-defence. To reiterate: the type of case of in question is that of fleeing offenders who only use lethal force, or threaten to use lethal force, to avoid arrest.

What if in these cases the police do their duty and choose *not* to allow such offenders to escape? So the police proceed to try to arrest these offenders, but in doing so they no longer have the option of using non-lethal means; so the police use lethal force. I have suggested that the police are now using lethal force to enforce the law. The alternative suggestion is that the police are using lethal force in self-defence. But at the point at which the police decide to enforce the law in the knowledge that the offender will use lethal force to resist arrest, the police are not engaged in an act of self-defence. After all, at this point the police have another option, if they are primarily interested in preserving their only life and/or that of the offender: get back into their patrol cars and return to the police station. Accordingly, at this point the self-defence justification is not available to the police officer. It is not available since it is not necessary for the police officer to use lethal force to protect his life (or that of his fellow officers or other third party); the option of flight is available to the officer(s). However, it is necessary for the police officer to use lethal force if the officer is to enforce the law. Therefore, in these scenarios the moral justification for the police officer using lethal force is that it is necessary to do so if the law is to be enforced.

Against this it might be argued as follows. It is agreed on all hands that the police officer in question is doing his legal and moral duty in trying to arrest the offender and that the offender ought not to resist arrest. However, so the argument goes, if the offender does resist arrest by (say) shooting at the officer then the officer's action of killing the offender is self-defence. For at *that* point – the point at which the offender tries to kill the officer – the offender would have killed the officer if the officer had not killed the offender first.

This response is flawed insofar as the possibility of flight remains available to the police officer. Naturally, at *some* point in *some* scenarios the possibility of flight might not be available, e.g., the officer and the offender are exchanging fire and the officer is unable to flee for some reason but is, nevertheless, blocking the offender's exit path. At this point in these scenarios it may well be that the officer is not aiming at arresting the offender but is simply trying to preserve his own life. However, this does not vitiate the claim made above that prior to such a point being reached the police officers may well be using lethal force to enforce the law and not in self-defence, given that the option of flight remains available to the officer. Moreover, the option of flight or of allowing the offender to escape may well remain even after the officer and/or the offender have fired their weapons. Consider the following Australian policing real-life scenario: the killing of Ian Turner by police constable Wayne Sherwell.[18]

Officer Sherwell stopped a car driven by Turner for speeding near St. Arnaud in country Victoria. Turner had no ID, and in the course of conversation aroused Sherwell's suspicions. Turner said he would look for ID in his bag, but instead pulled a sawn-off .22 on Sherwell. He then took Sherwell's police revolver. Sherwell grabbed Turner's hand and a struggle ensued. During the struggle, Turner called on Sherwell to give up and simply let him go free. Sherwell disarmed Turner and, now in possession of both weapons, ordered Turner to lie on the ground and allow himself to be handcuffed. He refused to do so, calling on Sherwell to let him go. When Sherwell refused his request and tried to radio for assistance, Turner blocked his way, calling on Sherwell to shoot him. Sherwell fired his gun in the air. Turner ran to his car while Sherwell called on his radio for assistance. Turner ran back to his car and produced a sawn-off shotgun which he pointed at Sherwell. Sherwell fired a couple of shots. Both men hid behind their respective cars. Further shots were fired by Sherwell. Turner did not fire any shots at any time. When other officers arrived at the scene, they found one of Sherwell's shots had killed Turner. Turner, it later emerged, was an armed robber.

Evidently throughout the whole episode, Turner had no desire to kill Sherwell, but rather acted in order to escape from Sherwell. Thus, initially Turner used the threat of lethal force pre-emptively in order to escape arrest, and subsequently he grabbed his shotgun because Sherwell was holding him prisoner and using the threat of lethal force to do so. So Turner essentially threatened, but never in fact used, lethal force in order to avoid arrest.

For his part, Sherwell, while prepared to *threaten* to use lethal force to prevent Turner's escape, only in fact seemed prepared to use lethal force in self-defence. In other words, if Turner had simply got into his car and driven off, Sherwell would quite possibly not have shot him. Moreover, if Turner had known that Sherwell would not have shot him other than in self-defence, Turner would not have pulled a gun on Sherwell in the first place, but would simply have driven off.

The Sherwell-Turner scenario illustrates an offender who is prepared to kill (or, at least, threaten to kill) to avoid arrest and also the distinction between killing in self-defence and killing to enforce the law.

A further point is that the Sherwell-Turner scenario contrasts sharply with various episodes in policing in which police sought to artificially create a situation in which they could use lethal force against offenders, notwithstanding that it was unnecessary to do so, and yet allege with some credibility that they acted in self-defence. Consider, in this connection, the following type of scenario involving the Special Investigation Section of the Los Angeles Police Department, who targeted armed robbers during the period 1965 to 1992: 'The most controversial of the home-baked rules is the SIS practice of standing by and watching its surveillance subjects victimise innocent citizens, then confronting offenders as they leave the scene of their crime.'[19] Here the SIS provided known offenders with the opportunity to commit very serious crimes by failing to arrest them for the less serious crimes they had already committed. The SIS did so in order to enable the offenders to commit the more serious crimes and thereby either receive longer prison sentences or be shot by the police while attempting to flee the crime scene or resisting arrest.[20]

Conclusion

In this entry I have distinguished three moral justifications for police use of lethal force, namely, self-defence, other-defence, and law enforcement. Moreover, I have provided arguments to the conclusion that the latter moral justification (law enforcement) does not collapse into one or other of the first two (self-defence or other-defence). I have offered two general kinds of scenarios by way of evidence for this conclusion. First, there are some instances of collective violence that threaten the established legal and political order. Arguably, police are entitled, indeed obliged, to use lethal force in order to protect the morally legitimate, legal, and political order, supposing non-lethal methods are to no avail and the use of lethal force is likely to be effective. Second, there are small-scale, police-offender encounters in which the offenders use, or threaten to use, lethal force simply in order to escape arrest and in which it is necessary for police to use lethal force to enforce the law on pain of the serious crimes in question becoming a widespread phenomenon.

Notes

1 Seumas Miller is a professorial research fellow at the Centre for Applied Philosophy and Public Ethics at Charles Sturt University (Canberra) and the 3TU Centre for Ethics and Technology at Delft University of Technology (The Hague).

2 See Jeffry Reiman 'The social contract and the police use of deadly force', in Fredrick Elliston and Michael Feldberg (eds.) *Moral Issues in Police Work,* Totowa, NJ: Rowman and Allanheld, 1985; Jerome Skolnick and James Fyfe *Above the Law: Police and the Excessive Use of Force*, New York, NY: The Free Press, 1993; John Kleinig *Ethics of Policing*, Cambridge: Cambridge University Press, 1996, Chapter 6; Edwin Delattre *Character and Cops*, 4th Edition, Washington, DC: AEI Press, 2002, Chapter 13; Seumas Miller and John Blackler *Ethical Issues in Policing*, Aldershot: Ashgate, 2005, Chapter 3; (eds.) Simon

Bronitt, Miriam Gani and Saskia Hufnagel, *Shooting to Kill: Socio-legal Perspectives on the Use of Lethal Force,* Oxford: Hart Publishing, 2012.

3 There is, of course, a voluminous literature on this topic but see: G. P. Fletcher 'Right to Life', Monist. vol. 63 (1980); P. Montague 'Self-defense and choosing between lives', *Philosophical Studies*, vol. 40 (1981); C. C. Ryan 'Self-defense, pacifism and the possibility of killing', *Ethics*, vol. 93 (1983); J. J. Thomson 'Self-defense', *Philosophy and Public Affairs*, vol. 20 (1991); Seumas Miller 'Killing in self-defence', *Public Affairs Quarterly,* vol.7 no. 4 1993: 325–40; Sue Uniacke *Permissible Killing: the Self-Defence Justification of Homicide,* Cambridge: Cambridge University Press, 1994; Jeff McMahan 'The basis of moral liability to defensive filling', *Philosophical Issues,* 15 2005: 386–405.

4 There are, of course, exceptions such as a standing and unavoidable lethal threat that might justify a pre-emptive strike.

5 But see J. Teichman, 'Self-defence', in her *Pacifism and the Unjust War,* Oxford: Blackwell, 1986.

6 Although, arguably, there are some analogous special natural duties, e.g., of a parent to protect his or her child.

7 See Henry Shue *Basic Rights*, 2nd edition, Princeton, NJ: Princeton University Press, 1996.

8 P. A. J. Waddington *The Strong Arm of the Law* Oxford: Clarendon Press, 1991.

9 'Ferguson Police: A Stark Illustration of Newly Militarised US Law Enforcement', *The Guardian* 15th August 2014 www.theguardian.com/world/2014/aug/14/ferguson-police-military-restraints-violence.

10 Plastic bullets can be lethal, e.g., if fired at very close range. However, they are, at least in principle, non-lethal weapons and, in any case, should not be used to disperse non-violent crowds or against members of violent crowds not actually engaged in violent acts.

11 Ibid.

12 R. Zakaria, *Communal Rage in Secular India*, Mumbai: Popular Prakasham, 2002, pp. 20–24. See also Seumas Miller, Sankar Sen, Prakash Mishra and John Blackler *Ethical Issues in Policing in India*, Hyderabad: National Police Academy, 2008.

13 In fact in India there is a sharp institutional division between ordinary police and the armed police used to quell community violence; the latter are a separate paramilitary force.

14 The basic argument in this section is taken from Miller and Blackler op. cit. Chapter 3.

15 I am assuming the theft of the items in question will not lead to the death or near death of the property owners, e.g., by depriving them of the means to buy food.

16 See Daryl Close and N. Meier (eds.) *Morality in Criminal Justice*, Boston, MA: Wadsworth Publishing Company, 1995, Chapter 7 "Tennessee v. Garner" pp. 366–79.

17 'What Happened in Ferguson?' *New York Times*, August 10 2015.

18 John Silvester, Andrew Rule and Own Davies, *The Silent War: Behind the Police Killings that Shook Australia*, Melbourne: Floradale Production and Sly Ink, 1995, pp. 125–30. This description is from Miller and Blackler op. cit.

19 Jerome Skolnick and James Fyfe, op. cit., p. 146.

20 The police might argue that in some of these situations they would be unable to convict these offenders of any serious crimes, due to the difficulties of, for example, proving a conspiracy to commit an armed robbery, or even to prove attempted armed robbery. Accordingly – the argument might run – they had to choose between increasing the risk to life and limb (their chosen option), or allowing armed robbers to either get off scot-free (when they failed to be convicted of (say) conspiracy to conduct an armed robbery) or simply be convicted of minor offences, such as (say) car theft.

Bibliography

Bronitt, S., Gani, M. and Hufnagel, S. (eds.) (2012) *Shooting to Kill: Socio-legal Perspectives on the Use of Lethal Force,* Oxford: Hart Publishing.

Close, D. and Meier, N. (eds.) (1995) *Morality in Criminal Justice,* Boston, MA: Wadsworth Publishing Company.

Delattre, E. (2002) *Character and Cops*, 4th edn, Washington DC: AEI Press.

Fletcher, G.P. (1980) 'Right to life', *Monist,* 63: 135–55.

Guardian, The. (2014) 'Ferguson Police: A Stark Illustration of Newly Militarised US Law Enforcement' 15 August. Available at: www.theguardian.com/world/2014/aug/14/ferguson-police-military-restraints-violence.

Kleinig, J. (1996) *Ethics of Policing,* Cambridge: Cambridge University Press.

McMahan, J. (2005) 'The basis of moral liability to defensive killing', *Philosophical Issues,* 15: 386–405.

Miller, S. (1993) 'Killing in self-defence', *Public Affairs Quarterly,* 7(4): 325–40.

Miller, S. and Blackler, J. (2005) *Ethical Issues in Policing,* Aldershot: Ashgate.
Miller, S., Sen, S., Mishra, P. and Blackler, J. (2008) *Ethical Issues in Policing in India,* Hyderabad: National Police Academy.
Montague, P. (1981) 'Self-defense and choosing between lives', *Philosophical Studies,* 40: 207–19.
New York Times. (2015) 'What Happened in Ferguson?' 10 August.
Reiman, J. (1985) 'The social contract and the police use of deadly force', in F. Elliston and M. Feldberg (eds.) *Moral Issues in Police Work,* Totowa, NJ: Rowman and Allanheld.
Ryan, C.C. (1983) 'Self-defense, pacifism and the possibility of killing', *Ethics,* 93: 508–24.
Shue, H. (1996) *Basic Rights,* 2nd edn, Princeton, NJ: Princeton University Press.
Silvester, J., Rule, A. and Davies, O. (1995) *The Silent War: Behind the Police Killings that Shook Australia,* Melbourne: Floradale Production and Sly Ink.
Skolnick, J. and Fyfe, J. (1993) *Above the Law: Police and the Excessive Use of Force,* New York, NY: The Free Press.
Teichman, J. (1986) *Pacifism and the Unjust War,* Oxford: Blackwell.
Thomson, J.J. (1991) 'Self-defense', *Philosophy and Public Affairs,* 20: 283–310.
Uniacke, S. (1994) *Permissible Killing: The Self-Defence Justification of Homicide,* Cambridge: Cambridge University Press.
Waddington, P.A.J. (1991) *The Strong Arm of the Law,* Oxford: Clarendon Press.
Zakaria, R. (2002) *Communal Rage in Secular India,* Mumbai: Popular Prakasham.

21

Ethical perspectives on interrogation

An analysis of contemporary techniques

Maria Hartwig, Timothy J. Luke, and Michael Skerker

Introduction

Interrogation is a central component in criminal justice settings as well as military, intelligence, and national security contexts. In the last decades, the practice of interrogation has received widespread attention, in particular from psychologists, criminal justice scholars, and sociologists. There is now a substantial body of empirical research on the nature and effects of interrogation techniques commonly used in practice (Kassin et al. 2010). Moreover, the last few decades have seen a wave of research aiming to improve the practice of interrogation through the development and empirical evaluation of interrogation methods derived from psychological science (Vrij and Granhag 2012).

However, there has been less sustained academic effort to examine the ethical elements of interrogation, despite the fact that such elements are prominent in the public discussion about interrogation. For example, the use of psychologically and physically coercive interrogation techniques that aim at breaking resistance and eliciting compliance has received substantial attention in the media, in particular the so-called enhanced interrogation techniques employed under the Bush regime (e.g., Hersh 2004). The recent release of the Senate report detailing the CIA's use of these techniques reignited the public debate about ethics in the context of interrogation.

In this chapter, we attempt to provide an overview of some of the key ethical elements involved in the practice of interrogation. By doing so, we hope to add to the hitherto scarce body of academic work on the ethics of interrogation. Our discussion will focus primarily on interrogation in criminal justice settings, but some of the techniques reviewed will be of relevance for interrogation in military and intelligence settings. Although we will briefly discuss torture, we will primarily focus on interrogation techniques that are psychological rather that physical in nature. More specifically, we will outline what we call three eras or schools of interrogation research, policy, and practice. These three schools will be described in some detail, and the empirical literature on their underpinnings and effectiveness will be described. Subsequently, we will provide an ethical analysis of each of these schools. However, we will begin this chapter by providing our definition of interrogation, followed by an outline of some of the most central ethical issues involved in interrogation.

Interrogation and related key terms

In this chapter, we use the term *interrogation* to refer to the questioning of a person who may possess information desired by investigators. Since disclosure of this information may be against the self-interest of the person who holds the information, it is possible that the subject of questioning will be uncooperative and/or deceptive. As such, interrogators may use a variety of social influence techniques to obtain the targeted information. We have adopted the term *suspect* to refer to the person being questioned in an interrogation. Some legal jurisdictions distinguish between interviews and interrogations. In some jurisdictions, "interrogations" trigger particular regulations (e.g., video recording) or legal rights that "interviews" do not. Here, we are interested in the morality of the substantive behavior of the investigator, rather than the nuances of the law that are in place to protect citizens' legal rights and facilitate effective and efficient investigations. That is, because we are interested in moral rather than legal issues, we do not draw a distinction between interviews and interrogations.

Rights and autonomy

Since the Enlightenment, deontological moral theories focusing on rights have gained currency around the world and especially in Western countries, undergirding domestic and international canons of law and international treaties such as the UN Declaration of Human Rights. Rights theory speaks directly to the liberties people find fundamental, particularly in liberal democracies.

Rights and autonomy are intertwined. Autonomy is the capacity to reach decisions about how one wants to behave and live. Autonomous people are able to control their desires, order their priorities, and act in an intentional manner consistent with their self-chosen actions. As permissions to think, speak, and act, rights also entail the legitimate power to resist unjust interference with rights expression and with autonomy. Operating on the assumption that all people are morally equal, one person's rights exercise must be self-limited in deference to other people's rights exercise. Failure to freely choose to defer to others' rights effectively proves that one is unable to responsibly enjoy one's autonomy. This failure entails ceding the otherwise legitimate expectation that others will defer to one's rights. Others may restrain one's rights-violating behavior with enough force to halt the active or imminent rights violation, provided in most circumstances, that the response is proportional to the threat. In this view, an armed assailant may be liable to be a target of defensive force (i.e., temporary forfeiture of a right not to be harmed). This means that it may be permissible to use force against him in self-defense—though it would be morally impermissible to attack him for some other reason (e.g., his race) or to continue to harm him once he has halted his attack.

Going forward, it will be important to bear in mind the distinction between a rights infringement and a rights violation. An infringement is a material curtailment of the normal exercise of a right. An unjustified infringement is a rights violation, an illegitimate assault against a person's autonomy. However, infringements are not inherently morally wrong. As we have just seen, though, some infringements, like self-defensive violence, are justified and therefore not rights violations.

Moral problems in interrogation

Regardless of the techniques employed, interrogation poses several moral hazards. Many of the moral problems raised by specific techniques are variations of these broader issues. Before discussing specific techniques, we will discuss some broad moral difficulties present in virtually all interrogations.

Autonomy and the imbalance of power

Interrogations involve an imbalance of power. The investigators possess more power and resources than the suspect. Frequently, they have the legal authority to detain the suspect and isolate him or her from family, friends, and social support. In military contexts, interrogators may possess even greater authority over the suspect. One military interrogator, quoted in Sherman (2010), articulates this point clearly: "I interrogate for eight hours a day and can then leave the cell and talk to my friends or call my family. These detainees can't. They are totally under my control. They are at my mercy" (121). In law enforcement contexts, the imbalance of power may not be as stark as it is in military contexts, but police interrogators are still empowered to deprive suspects of much of the freedom they might otherwise enjoy in normal life.

Interrogation inherently threatens the autonomy of the suspect. As we will discuss in further detail below, different interrogation techniques infringe upon autonomy to different extents, but detaining and questioning a person necessarily reduce that person's ability to act and even think freely. Interrogation entails behaviors that are, under normal circumstances, morally unacceptable. In our everyday social lives, we are not typically permitted to keep people in custody; deceive and emotionally manipulate them; and ask extremely personal questions about their relationships and actions.

Secrecy and privacy

Bok argues that privacy and secrecy are essential components of autonomy. Privacy is a precondition for autonomy in the sense that one will not have any personal plans or thoughts of one's own without a private "mental space" to consider ideas and formulate plans. Constant demands to reveal one's thoughts deprive one of this mental space and expose one to unfair critiques based on one's partially formulated ideas. Hence, "[t]o have no capacity for secrecy is to be out of control over how others see one; it leaves one open to coercion" (1983: 19).

Concerns about secrecy and privacy can be raised with respect to both interrogators and suspects. Interrogation infringes on suspects' right to privacy, and it provides ample opportunities for interrogators to abuse their own right to keep secrets in order to deceive the suspect. Infringements on privacy are not the same thing as illegitimate violations of privacy; infringements are material curtailments of normal rights exercise but may be permissible, as in cases of justified self-defense, discussed above. It remains to be addressed, for example, if guilty suspects have a moral right to privacy concerning their transgressions.

Epistemic limitations

The problem of *epistemic limitations* is closely related to the issue of overriding autonomy and the imbalance of power entailed in interrogation. Even if under certain circumstances it is defensible to override people's autonomy, there still exists a problem pervasive in the context of interrogation: We are limited in our knowledge of whether the subject of interrogation has, in fact, done anything to warrant infringements on his or her autonomy. As stated earlier, interrogations are inherently threatening to the autonomy of the suspect. Because we frequently cannot know whether the suspect has, in fact, committed any wrongdoing that could justify curtailments of autonomy, interrogation is highly morally risky.

Interrogations are, in part, aimed at establishing whether the suspect has committed a transgression that justifies limiting that person's autonomy by convicting and imprisoning him. However, the process of interrogating someone in order to ascertain his or her legal status may involve infringing on the suspect's autonomy. Even the most benign interrogations involve disrupting the normal progress of the suspect's life and possibly temporary detention. Thus, interrogation is fraught with opportunities to misuse power and infringe on the rights of those who have done nothing wrong.

Skerker (2010) argues that though innocent people have a right to privacy and a reasonable expectation that others will not generally interfere with their autonomy, they also have an expectation that the state will attempt to detect and prevent crime. In this view, innocent people are not wronged by being questioned when there is reasonable cause to do so. Indeed, Skerker (2010) argues that it is in principle irrational for people to object to investigators' questioning (again, when they are acting with a reasonable cause) since investigators are engaged in an enterprise vital to securing a relatively crime-free environment necessary for the enjoyment of everyone's rights.

Torture and physical coercion

There are at least two consequentialist objections to torture. First, the costs of torture outweigh the benefits. There is no empirical evidence that physical coercion is an effective means of obtaining accurate information (Biderman 1960; Skerker 2010). If little or no useful information is obtained from the act, torture produces ample harm (for the suspect) without sufficient value gained to justify the cost. A practice that regularly produces more harm than good is indefensible on consequentialist grounds. The second, more distal, objection is that the widespread use of torture damages the reputation—and therefore the effectiveness—of organizations or states that use it. This second objection does not assume that torture is necessarily ineffective as a means of obtaining information; it only assumes that any proximal utility gained from torture is outweighed by the damage to organizations' reputations.

The primary deontological objection to torture is that it destroys an individual's autonomy. An individual's moral status (e.g., culpability for a moral transgression) may make it permissible to reduce the extent to which that person may act freely (see the discussion of rights above), such as when an unjust attacker is fought or restrained. A permissible degree of defensive violence is limited to what is necessary to halt the attacker's unjust attack. Yet a shackled suspect is not posing any physical threat. Therefore, physical violence against him is unjust. Further, torture is worse than simple assault because of the intent of the torturer and the effect on the victim. The purpose of torture is not to temporarily diminish, but to completely erode autonomy—to induce a state wherein the victim is as compliant as a trained animal. Eroding the distinctive qualities that make one human constitutes a clear moral violation.

Three schools of interrogation and their moral implications

A nuanced discussion about the ethics of interrogation entails a consideration of ethical principles as well an understanding of the practical reality of interrogation. Below, we will provide an overview of the main findings stemming from empirical research on interrogation techniques. More specifically, we will discuss three broad schools of techniques. These methods are highlighted because they either dominate Western interrogation practice or have been proposed and examined by scholars. A proper ethical analysis of these techniques is not only of value from a scholarly perspective; it may also be relevant from a policy and practice perspective.

School 1: Confession-oriented techniques

Although there is little systematic data on interrogation practice in the nineteenth century and first part of the twentieth century, it is clear that interrogation in this era at least occasionally involved so-called "third-degree" techniques. These techniques involved a range of coercive methods including physical assault, deprivation of food and sleep, and explicit threats of violence (Leo 2004; Wickersham Commission Report 1931). The purpose of these methods was to extract confessions from suspects. By the 1960s, the use of such methods had declined significantly in the United States, and they were replaced with methods that were almost entirely psychological in nature (Leo 1996a). However, the ultimate goal of these techniques remained the same: to generate confessions.

There are numerous police interrogation manuals available to advise law enforcement on how to conduct interrogations with the purpose of eliciting confessions (Gordon and Fleisher 2006; Holmes 2003; Walkley 1987; Walters 2003). The most widely used and influential of these is the so-called Reid manual (*Criminal Interrogations and Confessions*), which was originally developed in the 1940s and revised repeatedly thereafter (Inbau et al. 2013). The technique is practiced widely in the United States and Canada (Kassin et al. 2010), and other confession-oriented techniques share much in common with it.

The Reid technique of interrogation consists of nine steps aimed at eliciting confessions. These steps entail confronting the suspect with a direct accusation of guilt, followed by the development of one or more *themes*, which are face-saving excuses for the crime intended to make it easier for a suspect to confess. Reducing the moral seriousness of the crime in this way is known as *minimization*. Denials and objections by the suspect are prevented or deflected until the suspect accepts the theme offered by the interrogator. If the suspect resists, the interrogator will often emphasize the futility and potentially severe consequences of denial. Emphasizing the gravity of the situation in this way is known as *maximization*. When the suspect's resistance is depleted, the interrogator then elicits an admission of guilt, followed by a written confession to the crime (see Kassin et al. 2010). Observational studies show that these three tactics are common in American interrogations (e.g., Leo 1996b). As we will discuss in further detail below, the Reid technique has been criticized widely in the research community, on the basis of a substantial body of research showing that the technique is linked to false confessions (Gudjonsson 2003).

A variety of theoretical perspectives derived from psychology explain why minimization and maximization techniques are effective in eliciting both true and false confessions (Kassin and Gudjonsson 2004). Of particular relevance for the present context, social psychologists have long argued that confession-oriented interrogation techniques are powerful social influence and persuasion tools (Zimbardo 1967), designed to change a suspect's attitude from the view that denying is rational to the view that confessing is the best option. Furthermore, a decision-making model suggests that (implied) threats of punishment and promises of leniency, which form the core of the minimization/maximization approach, are effective in that they manipulate the perceived costs and benefits with denying and confessing (Hilgendorf and Irving 1981). These techniques thus seek to maximize the anxiety associated with denial and minimize the perceived loss associated with confessing. Simply put, these interrogation techniques are designed to create the illusion that confessing is the suspect's most rational option. Interrogation techniques may create a psychological illusion where the suspect may believe that confessing will provide the opportunity to leave the police station and avoid further confinement. That is, while minimization techniques may not explicitly promise leniency, their psychological effect is such that people expect leniency through a process called pragmatic implication (Kassin and McNall 1991). For example, if an interrogator suggests that a crime was accidental rather than intentional, the suspect may believe that the consequences of admission are not severe and may hence offer such an admission either as a short-term decision to terminate the stress of interrogation, to terminate confinement, or because of a belief that the admission will not carry any penalties (or all three).

As mentioned before, the Reid technique also uses interrogation themes that encourage confession. These may involve offering face-saving excuses for the commission of the crime (e.g., that the crime was based on a misunderstanding, that it was the fault of the victim, or that it was an isolated event) or justifications for confession (e.g., suggesting that the suspect will feel better if he or she admits to the crime). A suspect may thus (wrongly) determine that agreeing to having committed a crime characterized by the interrogator as morally excusable does not amount to a criminal confession.

Confession-oriented techniques and deception

Minimization and maximization techniques, as well as the use of themes, are clearly manipulative. Arguably, the entire Reid technique rests on a form of deception (Leo 1996a). That is, interrogators are taught to deliberately misrepresent the situation—for example, by presenting themselves as being on the suspect's side and framing the interrogation as the suspect's way out of trouble. The Reid technique also involves blatant forms of deception, particularly in the form of so-called false evidence ploys, through which the interrogation exaggerates or completely invents evidence. Such false evidence ploys are implicated in the majority of known false confession cases (Kassin et al. 2010). There are several mechanisms behind the effect of false evidence ploys. First, it is well known that a suspect's perception of the strength of the evidence against him or her predicts whether he or she will confess (Gudjonsson 2003). That is, the stronger the suspect believes the evidence to be, the more likely he or she is to confess. False evidence ploys thus manipulate suspects' view of the situation they are facing, which in turn influences their decision to confess or deny the accusations against them. Moreover, false evidence ploys can contribute to the formation of false memories. The malleability of memory in response to misinformation is a well-established and fundamental principle of cognitive psychology (Loftus 2005). Thus, false evidence ploys can lead to what is known as *internalized false confessions*, which occur when innocent but malleable suspects not only capitulate behaviorally (by confessing), but also come to believe that they have actually committed the crime (Kassin and Wrightsman 1985). Again, the occurrence of such an internalized false confession is demonstrated both by archival analyses of proven false confessions and by laboratory research (Gudjonsson 2003; Kassin and Kiechel 1996).

Confession-oriented techniques and false confessions

Confession-oriented techniques have received harsh criticism from a variety of directions on the basis of the concern that they may produce false confessions (Kassin et al. 2010). That false confessions occur with some regularity is beyond dispute. Although the exact frequency with which false confessions occur is not known, false confessions and admissions are frequently present in post-conviction DNA exonerations (Drizin and Leo 2004; Kassin 1997; Lassiter 2004; Leo and Ofshe 1998; Scheck, Neufeld and Dwyer 2000). At the time this chapter was written, the Innocence Project's database of DNA exonerations indicates that 27 percent (88 of 325) of exonerees in their sample were convicted at least partially on the basis of false confessions or admissions (innocenceproject.org). Because this sample fails to include data on confessions that were proven to be false before trial, those in which no DNA evidence is available, and minor crimes unlikely to receive post-conviction scrutiny, it is likely that the data from post-conviction DNA exonerations represent the mere tip of an iceberg. The findings from post-conviction DNA cases are supported by a substantial body of research on false confessions using a variety of methodologies, including field studies, case studies, self-report studies, and laboratory research (Gudjonsson 2003). Importantly, because laboratory research allows for causal inferences, it is possible to conclude that confession-oriented techniques are not merely associated with false confessions, but that they are actually a causative factor (Kassin et al. 2010).

Ethical considerations of confession-oriented techniques

The (implicit) argument of exceptionalism

In his landmark interrogation manual *Lie Detection and Criminal Interrogation*, Inbau (1942) defends the practice of deception and manipulation in law enforcement interrogations:

> In dealing with most criminal offenders, it is impractical or futile merely to give them a pencil and paper and trust that their conscience will impell [sic] them to confess. … Something more is required [to obtain a confession], and at times the interrogator must deal with a criminal offender in a somewhat lower moral plane than that in which ethical, law-abiding citizens are expected to conduct their everyday lives. (118)

This passage, in a brief section on the ethics of interrogation, remains largely unchanged in the subsequent editions of the manual (Inbau 1942, 1948; Inbau and Reid 1953), and similar statements appear in its successor *Criminal Interrogation and Confessions* (Inbau and Reid 1962, 1967; Inbau, Reid, and Buckley 1983; Inbau, Reid, Buckley, and Jayne 2001, 2013).

As the argument is portrayed in the above quotation from Inbau (1942), there appears to be a pragmatic concern that it would not be possible to elicit confessions from guilty suspects without the use of trickery and psychological manipulation. The community, therefore, would be less safe if we disallowed interrogators to deceive and manipulate suspects. Thus, necessity is used to justify the use of such methods that would, under most circumstances, be morally impermissible. However, these concerns assume that trickery is, in fact, the only way to accomplish this objective. As we will review below in our discussion of information-gathering techniques, there are empirical reasons to suspect that this assumption is unfounded.

In her analysis of the moral and psychological hazards faced by members of the armed forces, Sherman (2010) has referred to interrogation as "the moral shadowland." "[D]eception and betrayal, manipulation and exploitation, tools morally questionable in ordinary transactions," she describes, "[are] standard tools of [the interrogator's] specialized trade" (115). Sherman's (2010) discussion of interrogation deals exclusively with military intelligence contexts, so its implications do not necessarily extend to law enforcement or other contexts. However, it is clear that she acknowledges that deceit and manipulation are permissible in particular contexts, although they are often impermissible in everyday life.

Inbau and Sherman appear to suggest a moral divide between ordinary life and interrogation (or interrogation in specific contexts). Yet, even if it were the case that practical necessity demanded the use of trickery, deceit, and other rights infringements, necessity in itself might not render them permissible. Many moral systems condemn the pursuit of just ends using unjust means. This issue is extensively discussed in the philosophical literature on the morality of war (see Walzer 1977, especially sections on sieges and "supreme emergencies"; see also McMahan 2009, 2006). Making a community safer by interrogating and prosecuting criminals is likely a just goal, but it may still be impermissible to pursue that goal with techniques that unjustly infringe on suspects' rights. Whether confession-oriented techniques are unjust infringements of suspects' rights is a question we will turn to now.

Autonomy and consent

Confession-oriented techniques raise a number of moral concerns. Interrogators using these techniques intentionally create stress for a suspect, so much so that a guilty suspect will sometimes go against his material self-interest and confess in order to alleviate the stress. Further, interrogators deceive suspects by presenting the crime as more or less serious than it actually is, by pretending to sympathize with suspects, and by presenting "face-saving" interpretations of the event the interrogator probably does not believe. Finally, confession-oriented techniques appear to run the risk of generating false confessions, which frequently, in turn, lead to unjust convictions.

Behavior that is otherwise immoral can sometimes be permissible if the affected party consents to the behavior, such as when a patient explicitly consents to her dentist causing her physical discomfort in the course of a root canal. Barring explicit consent, it is even possible to justify adversarial actions by government officials if the action is *worthy* of citizens' consent. All people want to be protected from crime and so should consent to certain types of police activity meant to keep them safe. Given a range of possible police techniques, we can see that in the abstract, the most reliable, effective, proportionate, and efficient tactics would be more consent-worthy than techniques scoring lower on these metrics. Further, since police tactics might infringe on people's rights (questioning, arrest, searches, violence, interrogation, etc.), we can assume that the most rights-respecting among efficacious tactics would be worthy of consent versus efficacious techniques that are relatively more rights infringing. Do confession-based techniques meet this consent-worthy standard?

Deceptive techniques

Suspects obviously cannot explicitly consent to being deceived in interrogation. It is impossible for suspects, innocent or guilty, to knowingly consent to being subjected to deceptive techniques; by definition, they do not know they are being deceived. Are deceptive techniques worthy of consent in the sense that a citizen should consent to police using deceptive techniques because they are the most efficient, effective, proportionate, reliable, and rights respecting means of creating a relatively crime-free environment?

More broadly, are there *any* cases in which people would (or should) consent to being deceived? We believe so. A benign example illustrates this point: Some years ago at an academic conference, the second author of this chapter (Luke) conspired with several others to deceive the first author (Hartwig) into entering a hotel room in which a surprise party for her had been arranged. Doing this required someone luring her to the room under false pretenses. This deceit limited her ability to make choices in accord with available information. Her autonomy was, as such, (mildly) curtailed. Nevertheless, Luke maintains that this deception was morally permissible. Why? At the time, Luke considered whether Hartwig would have consented to the act if she were informed about it in advance and concluded that she likely would have. Actual consent for a surprise party is obviously impossible to obtain. Instead of obtaining real consent, Luke appealed to hypothetical consent and decided the deception was morally permissible.

Although this example is somewhat frivolous, it demonstrates that people can hypothetically consent to being deceived, especially when the deceit results in benefits for them. If deceptive interrogation techniques produce clear societal benefits (i.e., assisting in the prosecution of criminals), they might be worthy of consent. Is it the case that people should consent to the deception involved in confession-oriented techniques? There is ample reason to believe they should not.

The empirical research reviewed above suggests there are substantial risks (e.g., the production of false confessions and subsequent wrongful convictions) involved in the use of confession-based techniques. Considering the damage the techniques can cause to innocent suspects, it is difficult to imagine that people would (hypothetically) consent to the deception on which confession-based techniques depend. Additionally, there are empirical reasons to believe that these hazards are unnecessary. We review relevant research in our discussion of information-gathering techniques below. The existence of efficacious and reliable alternatives is important since it is conceivable that people would consent to even a risky technique with frequent good outcomes if no alternatives existed.

Confession-oriented techniques raise another ethical concern worth noting briefly. The development of themes that minimize the moral seriousness of the crime is a core component of the Reid technique and other confession-oriented techniques (Buckley and Jayne 1999; Senese 2008). Interrogation themes are intended to make it psychologically easier for suspects to confess.[1] There is no assumption that the theme accurately reflects what actually occurred, and it is not likely that the interrogator, in fact, believes the theme. However, the Reid technique advises interrogators to prevent the suspect from objecting to the theme or denying involvement (Inbau et al. 2014). To the extent that an interrogator is effective at overcoming objections to the theme, this tactic effectively prevents the suspect from telling the truth, which seems morally problematic. Also, this could make wrongful conviction more likely by preventing people from providing accounts that may help clear them of suspicion.

Broader effects of confession-based techniques

Two final concerns are worth noting, viz., the potential effect of confession-based techniques on the interrogator and on the wider community. The practice of confession-oriented techniques may have negative effects on those who practice them. There are some moral views that advocate complete bans on lying since lying violates the natural purpose of speech (see Bok 1978). For those thinkers willing to countenance lying and deception toward people who lack the right to the truth, there is still concern expressed over the effect of repeated lying on the liar's character. Repeated actions lead to habits. We can imagine how interrogators could be accustomed to lying, deception, and manipulation and become increasingly cavalier about manipulating people in their private life. Even if they are able to compartmentalize their professional skill-set from ordinary life, they might still feel a personal sense of alienation and self-disgust at their ability to manipulate people. While it is difficult to quantify this risk, we have found another reason for preferring less manipulative and deceptive interrogation techniques if efficacious alternatives are available.

Second, a regime of confession-oriented techniques, especially those involving deception of suspects, may diminish society's trust in the police. If the community becomes aware that the police routinely lie to suspects, people may be less inclined to cooperate with the police when they otherwise would have. It is an interesting question to consider whether community relations with police are further coarsened if even guilty suspects' interactions with police are regularly marked by deceit and manipulation. It is difficult to assess whether there would be a reduction in crime if police always dealt with suspects in a completely honest manner. Perhaps careful studies could be done on this question comparing otherwise similar communities in countries where police mostly use the confession-oriented techniques (e.g., the US and Canada) and countries where information-gathering techniques are practiced (e.g., the UK and Norway). Again, it is difficult to quantify the risk of confession-based techniques, but it is yet another potential reason to discourage the use of these techniques.

School 2: Information-gathering techniques

Over the last decades, there has been substantial reform of interrogation practice in England and Wales. Subsequently, several countries have implemented similar reforms (e.g., Norway, New

Zealand and Australia; see Oxburgh, Walsh, and Milne 2011). The reform in England and Wales was initiated by a series of highly publicized cases of wrongful convictions, including the Guildford Four, the Birmingham Six, and the Maguire Seven (Gudjonsson 2003; Huff, Rattner, and Sagarin 1996; Victory 2002). These cases led to outcries for legislation regulating the interrogation of suspects, which resulted in a fundamental shift in law, policy, and practice (Baldwin 1993; Milne and Bull 1999; Sear and Williamson 1999; Williamson 1993). In terms of legal change, the introduction of *the Police and Criminal Evidence Act* (PACE) in 1984 imposed restrictions on the treatment and questioning of suspects in police custody and introduced mandatory tape recordings of all interrogations. In terms of police training and practice, a new model of police interrogation was introduced, which entailed a different ethos as well as a different set of interrogation tactics (Bull 1999). This new model is referred to as *information-gathering interrogation*, or *investigative interviewing* (Bull 2014; Bull and Milne 2004; Williamson 1993).[2]

Basic principles of information-gathering interrogation

The information-gathering model is based on a profoundly different view of the purpose of interrogation. While interrogation prior to PACE was heavily confession-oriented (Gudjonsson 2003; Irving 1980), the information-gathering approach instead emphasizes, as the label indicates, a focus on yielding as much information as possible. Expressed differently, the goal of information-gathering interrogation is to establish the truth about what has happened. In this view, suspect interrogations have a similar aim as interviews with victims and witness: to aid investigators in generating an accurate and complete picture of what has occurred.

Another difference between confession-oriented techniques and information-gathering techniques lies in the extent to which the principles are derived from psychological theory and research. Information-gathering techniques are grounded in theories about human communication, conversation management, and the psychology of memory (Clarke, Milne and Bull 2011). Furthermore, there has been extensive effort to empirically evaluate the effectiveness of the basic principles that information-gathering techniques are based on Milne and Bull (2001). This sharply contrasts with confession-oriented techniques, elements of which are derived from lay psychological notions (Masip, Barba and Herrero 2012) and are either contradicted by scientific research (Vrij, Mann, and Fisher 2006), unsupported (Gudjonsson 2003), or buttressed by pseudo-evidence (Horvath, Jayne, and Buckley 1994).

The practice of information-gathering interrogation

The principles of information-gathering interrogation were articulated in the framework *PEACE*, an acronym that stands for Planning and preparation (occurring prior to the interrogation), Engaging and explaining the process, gaining an Account, Closure, and Evaluation (occurring after the interrogation; Milne, Shaw, and Bull 2007). The planning/preparation as well as evaluation phases are designed to engender a more thoughtful and systematic approach to the interrogation, in addition to a consideration of how the information (potentially) generated during the interrogation might fit into the larger picture of the investigation. The engage/explain and closure phases are designed to promote rapport and trust and to create a sense of transparency. The account phase is aimed at developing a statement from the suspect. In simple terms, this is accomplished through an emphasis on the use of open- rather than closed-ended questions, and avoidance of leading or misleading questions. Subsequent to the initial introduction of PEACE in 1992, there have been revisions and additions to the model, which now consists of a five-tiered approach built on research and developments in the criminal justice system (Griffiths and Milne 2006).

Observational and quasi-experimental research in the UK has examined the characteristics of police interrogations pre- and post-PACE, as well as the effectiveness of training in the PEACE model. As noted earlier, research prior to the implementation of PACE established that confrontational and coercive techniques were common, despite the fact that there was no systematic training in confession-oriented approaches (Irving 1980; see also Softley 1980). For example, interrogators often emphasized the futility of denial and attempted to influence suspects' perceptions of the consequences of confessing. In contrast, post-PACE research suggests that there was a significant reduction in coercive interrogation techniques (Baldwin 1992, 1993; Moston and Engelberg 1993; Moston and Stephenson 1993; Pearse and Gudjonsson 1996). Importantly, and perhaps counter-intuitively, there is no convincing evidence that confession rates dropped after the introduction of PACE (Gudjonsson 2003; Irving and McKenzie 1989; Softley 1980).

Research directly measuring the effect of PEACE training is relatively scarce, and the picture is mixed. In an early evaluation, interrogation skills were found to improve after training in the model (McGurk, Carr, and McGurk 1993). A more recent study corroborated the finding that PEACE training had positive effects, but some skills appeared to deteriorate over time (Griffiths and Milne 2006). A third study found a higher degree of skill among interrogators who had received PEACE training. The latter finding was qualified by the observation that the performance of trained interrogators still showed deficits. A fourth study found no substantial differences between interrogations conducted by PEACE trained officers compared to those conducted by untrained officers (Clarke, Milne and Bull 2011).

A shift in ethics

Information-gathering techniques were developed partly on the basis on pragmatic considerations. As described earlier, there was concern that confession-oriented techniques were so powerful that they might compel innocent people to confess. In broader terms, there have been concerns about the reliability of information gained through the use of these techniques (Gudjonsson 2003).

Importantly for this chapter, information-gathering interrogation is based on a different ethical view of interrogation. In contrast to confession-oriented techniques, information-gathering interrogation strongly emphasizes treating the suspect with fairness and dignity and involves acknowledging, explaining, and honoring suspects' legal rights. Information-gathering interrogation also includes an emphasis on honesty and transparency. This means that deception in general, and false evidence ploys in particular, are not permitted. Moreover, statements generated through the use of such techniques are usually inadmissible in court in the countries that have implemented reform in interrogation practice (Memon, Vrij, and Bull 2003).

These reforms remove most of the rights-infringing concerns raised above with respect to confession-based techniques. There is still a degree of psychological pressure associated with being in police custody, but this degree of pressure would be present in any kind of police interrogation. Concerns about the interrogator's character are also minimized with these techniques since the interrogator is not engaging in deception or manipulation. Another advantage of utilizing information-gathering techniques may be their effect on the larger society. In line with theories of procedural justice, employing fair and transparent procedures might lead citizens to be more compliant and cooperative with authorities in general (Tyler 2006).

As described above, research shows that information-gathering techniques are not associated with a drop in confession rates (Gudjonsson 2003) and that the information generated by these techniques tends to be more reliable than that produced by confession-oriented techniques. Therefore, the argument that confession-based techniques are necessary to gain judicially useful confession evidence seems to be based on a false premise. Given their greater reliability and greater respect for suspects, we believe that information-gathering techniques are superior to confession-oriented techniques.

School 3: Strategic interviewing techniques

For around a decade, researchers have developed a number of interrogation techniques that emphasize strategic considerations (Granhag and Hartwig 2008; Levine, Shaw, and Shulman 2010; Vrij and Granhag 2012). While these interrogation techniques share some of the goals of information-gathering interrogation (e.g., an emphasis on the search for reliable information), they deviate from pure information-gathering techniques in that they view interrogations of suspects as a different form of enterprise than the interviewing of witnesses and victims. This should not be taken to mean a reversal in ethos to coercive methods, but rather that the recent techniques emphasize that interrogation entails the use of strategies employed by both interrogators and suspects. In this sense, these interrogation methods go beyond information-gathering and incorporate a set of more in-depth considerations about the strategic mindsets held by both the interrogator and the suspect. Strategic interrogation techniques are typically based on principles derived from cognitive and/or social psychology. However, they differ in their primary objectives. It is possible to make a distinction between techniques that attempt to elicit cues to deception based on strategic questioning and those designed to induce information disclosure. Below, we will provide an overview of some techniques under the umbrella of strategic interrogation methods, followed by a discussion of ethical considerations that these techniques raise.

The cognitive load techniques

The *cognitive load technique* is based on the well-established finding that cues to deception are scarce (DePaulo et al. 2003), and that judging deception based on simply observing a person's behavior while providing a true or false statement generates mediocre hit rates, at best (Bond and DePaulo 2006, 2008; Hartwig and Bond 2011). The cognitive load technique is further based on the notion that lying is more cognitively demanding than telling the truth (Vrij 2008). More specifically, people who wish to establish whether a person is lying or telling the truth (henceforth referred to as lie-catchers) can exploit this difference by imposing further cognitive load on the person being interviewed (Vrij et al. 2006, 2008; Vrij et al. 2012). The reasoning is that such load will be more difficult to manage for liars compared to truth tellers, since the former are already taxed by the process of generating a false account. Cognitive load has been induced by having suspects provide their account in reverse chronological order, by asking them to maintain eye contact, or by employing dual task paradigm, all of which are mentally taxing (Vrij and Granhag 2012). Indeed, this reasoning is supported by research showing that cues to deception become more pronounced when suspects are questioned under cognitive load. Also, accuracy in judging deception is improved by the use of the technique (Vrij et al. 2008).

The Strategic Use of Evidence technique

The *Strategic Use of Evidence (SUE) technique*, like the cognitive load technique, is based on the notion that accuracy in judgments of credibility may be improved by actively eliciting cues to deception, rather than passively observing behavior. In particular, the SUE technique revolves around acknowledging that truth telling (i.e., innocent) and deceptive (guilty) suspects may employ different strategies to convince; these are called *counter-interrogation strategies*; Granhag and Hartwig in press). Specifically, suspects differ in information management strategies—guilty suspects need to conceal information, while innocent suspects typically do not. Liars' concealment may entail their involvement in a crime or other knowledge that they wish to keep the interrogator ignorant about (Hartwig, Granhag, and Strömwall 2007). Empirical work on liars' counter-interrogation strategies shows that they use verbal strategies either of *avoidance* (i.e., not mentioning visiting a particular place when asked an open-ended question) or *escape/denial* (i.e., denying visiting a particular place when asked directly about it). Truth tellers instead tend to use forthcoming strategies whereby they volunteer even potentially incriminating information (Kassin 2005; Strömwall, Hartwig, and Granhag 2006).

As the name indicates, the SUE technique attempts to make differences in liars' and truth tellers' approaches salient by using the available evidence strategically. A simple illustration of this might be helpful. In the first study on the SUE technique, liars had taken a wallet from a briefcase left in a store, while truth tellers simply moved the briefcase in order to look for an object (Hartwig et al. 2005). The interrogator possessed evidence that suspects had been at the scene of the crime, as well as suspects' fingerprints on the briefcase. Note that this evidence was true for both liars and truth tellers. When this information was strategically withheld during the interrogation, and the suspect was asked a series of systematic questions about their whereabouts and actions (see Hartwig et al. 2011), liars' stories tended to be inconsistent with the evidence (e.g., they tended to avoid mentioning being at the scene of the crime, and they often denied having seen or handled the briefcase). In contrast, in a control condition where the SUE technique was not used, it was not possible to distinguish between the statements given by liars and truth tellers.

Since the SUE technique was introduced a decade ago, it has been developed substantially. There have been refinements in the theoretical reasoning about the technique as well as in the specific tactics incorporated under the SUE umbrella (for a comprehensive review, see Hartwig, Granhag, and Luke 2014). The applications of the technique have also been expanded to include methods to elicit information (Granhag and Hartwig in press). At this point, two studies (one in Sweden, and one in the United States) have shown that training in the SUE technique leads to more systematic use of the evidence, clearer differences in the statements from liars and truth tellers, and higher accuracy rates in judging credibility (Hartwig et al. 2006; Luke et al. 2015).

The unanticipated questions technique

Similar to the SUE technique, the *unanticipated questions technique* is based on a consideration of liars' and truth tellers' strategies. The fundamental assumption is that liars plan their accounts (Hartwig et al. 2007; Strömwall et al. 2006). Such planning makes sense as it makes lies more difficult to detect (DePaulo et al. 2003). From the interrogator's point of view then, asking questions that liars have *not* anticipated is probably more strategic, since liars might face more difficulties answering such questions. Truth tellers should find anticipated and unanticipated questions roughly equally difficult to answer.

In one study on the unanticipated questions technique, pairs of truth tellers went to lunch together (Vrij et al. 2010). Liars committed a mock crime and were instructed to deny the crime and instead claim that they went to lunch together. The interrogation consisted of a mix of anticipated (e.g., "What did you do while in the restaurant?," "What did you talk about during lunch?") and unanticipated ("In relation to the front door, where did you sit?" and "In what order did you talk about the topics mentioned earlier?"). As predicted, lies were more detectable when the questions were unanticipated compared to when they were anticipated, as measured by the overlap in the statements given by the members of each pair.

The approach to pose unanticipated questions can also be used in interviews with single suspects (Lancaster et al. 2013). Moreover, there is evidence that an unanticipated format of questioning—being asked to draw the scene rather than describe it verbally—produces similar effects (Vrij et al. 2012). The general pattern is that liars provide fewer details in response to unanticipated prompts.

The Scharff technique

The Scharff technique is conceptually related to the SUE technique, in the sense that it involves an understanding of the suspect's point of view and in particular his or her counter-interrogation strategies. The goal of the technique is to elicit information, primarily in intelligence settings. It is based on accounts of the legendary German intelligence officer Hanns Joachim Scharff, who was active during World War II (Toliver 1997). Inspired by descriptions of Scharff's highly sophisticated interrogation strategies, Granhag and colleagues developed a series of principles that have recently been tested in laboratory settings (Granhag, Montecinos, and Oleszkiewicz 2013; Scharff 1950).

The counter-interrogation strategies identified by Scharff and articulated by Granhag et al. are threefold: a) refraining from providing information if possible, b) arriving at an understanding of what information the interrogator is seeking, and c) not denying information that the interrogator already knows, as this would be pointless. Based on these counter-interrogation strategies, Scharff outlined his own strategies, which can be summarized as follows. First, he attempted to create a friendly environment. Second, he did not press suspects for information and instead told detailed stories that provided the opportunity for the suspect to add information or correct errors. Third and relatedly, he used the "I-already-know-it-all" illusion, which was designed to convey the sense that the interrogator was very well informed.[3] Fourth, he employed a tactic referred to as "confirmation/disconfirmation." Through this tactic, interrogators present a number of claims that they know are correct, but occasionally introduce claims that they are uncertain of. The suspect may confirm or disconfirm this information, without understanding that he or she revealed new information to the interrogator. This tactic might thus produce disclosure while at the same time keeping the information objectives of the interrogation opaque (May, Granhag and Oleszkiewicz 2014).

The relationship between suspects' counter-interrogation strategies and the Scharff tactics is intricate, but it is possible to summarize some of the principal mechanisms in the following fashion: The Scharff tactics employ an understanding of the suspect's mindset as well as one's own information to induce the suspect to disclose new information. If these tactics are executed in a successful fashion, the information can be obtained while the suspect is unaware that he or she has provided new information and ignorant or uncertain about what the interrogator sought to find out. Indeed, laboratory tests of the Scharff techniques provide support for the basic premises: In the first test of the technique, suspects interrogated with the Scharff technique indeed incorrectly believed that they had revealed less information than participants interrogated with the Direct Approach derived from the Army Field Manual. They also found the information objectives of the Scharff interrogation more difficult to read. Two other studies found support for the prediction that the Scharff approach generates more information compared to a control interview (May et al. 2014; Oleszkiewicz et al. 2014).

Embodied cognition and priming techniques

A line of recent research has examined whether it is possible to employ principles of unconscious influence to promote information disclosure in interrogations. While the underlying reasoning here is somewhat different from the methods that exploit suspects' (presumably) deliberate counter-interrogation strategies, the priming techniques share features with the techniques we have just reviewed. For example, the reasoning is derived from psychological theories, and the interrogator employs this reasoning in a strategic fashion order to achieve certain goals within an interview.

This program of research is anchored in theories of implicit and embodied cognition. Implicit cognition theories posit that a large portion of cognitive processes operate outside conscious awareness (Bargh 1997). Moreover, memories and associations from previous experiences can be primed (i.e., activated), which may unconsciously influence cognition and behavior. Embodied cognition is a form of implicit cognition that states that mental processes are grounded in physical experience and that there is a bidirectional relationship between psychological and physical states (Lakoff and Johnson 1980). In this view, metaphors used in common parlance are not mere linguistic devices, but instead convey a deep relationship between the two types of states. For example, a classic study showed that participants who held a warm cup of coffee formed a "warmer" impression of another person than those who held a cold drink (Williams and Bargh 2008). In another study, participants who were led to think of social exclusion reported experiencing the room as colder than those in a control condition (e.g., Zhong and Leonardelli 2008).

These principles apply in the domain of interrogation: It is possible to predict that priming may have advantageous cognitive and behavioral effects. If the goal of the interrogation is to generate information, as is often the case in intelligence-gathering settings, it may be useful to activate the concept of openness as this concept is closely linked with disclosure. A series of recent studies has tested this possibility. In one study, subjects either were or were not primed with the concept of an open and trusting relationship. Subsequently, they were exposed to details about a mock terrorism plot, followed by an interrogation that sought information about the plot (Dawson, Hartwig, Leps, and Brimbal 2015). As hypothesized, subjects who had been primed with the concept of an open and trusting relationship provided more information about the plot than those in the control condition. A related study using a similar procedure primed openness through a semantic prime: In the experimental condition, subjects were interrogated with a script that included words related to openness (e.g., forthcomingness, transparency, trust), while the control condition excluded such words (Dawson, Hartwig, Luke, and Denisenkov 2015). Here, too, it was found that subjects in the experimental condition provided more details than those in the control condition.

Recent research also examined the extent to which disclosure can be activated through activation of the metaphor of openness. More specifically, subjects who had information about a mock terrorism event were either interrogated in an "open" room (i.e., more spacious one with windows), or in a prototypical interrogation room. As in the previous studies, subjects in the "open" condition were more prone to disclose information than those interrogated in the standard interrogation room (Dawson, Hartwig, and Denisenkov 2015).

Ethical considerations of strategic interrogation techniques

The unexpected question technique is the least concerning of the four canvassed above since there is no reasonable expectation on the part of a suspect that an interrogator ask a specific list of questions or ask them in a particular order. Assuming police interrogation as such is justified, the practice gives the prerogative to the interrogator to ask the questions he thinks most conducive to learning about the crime in question. The confusion and stress a guilty suspect might feel upon being asked unanticipated questions could be avoided if the suspect was truthful from the start. It is important to empirically verify that innocent suspects can indeed reliably narrate true events backwards, draw pictures of places they visited, and so on.

We can categorize priming as manipulation under the broadest definition of the term. The interrogator is acting strategically, attempting to trigger certain states of mind on the part of the interviewee in order to lead him to an outcome the interrogator desires. The Scharff-style interrogator also engages in a degree of manipulation. He affects a friendly demeanor and attempts to control the suspect's understanding of the interrogator's knowledge of the alleged crime. Manipulation may be considered morally controversial since the manipulator takes advantage of an asymmetry of knowledge, control, perspective, or authority to shape the target's perception of the relevant situation. Manipulation reduces the target's autonomy, leading him to choose the action the manipulator wants him to choose, an action the target perhaps would not otherwise choose.

Assuming a context of a just state, a guilty suspect does not appear to be wronged by the low level of manipulation and deception present in the priming and Scharff techniques. This follows, if we can agree he has ceded his otherwise legitimate expectation to be treated with the same respect as an innocent person. The guilty suspect has wronged an innocent person by committing a crime. Now, his recalcitrance in the interrogation booth delays the process of justice. He has no standing to object to mild strategic behavior on the part of police to bring about a just conclusion to the case. His understandable desire to avoid punishment is not a moral concern (others have to respect) given that he has voluntarily placed himself in jeopardy by wronging another.

That said, the police are usually not in a position to know that a suspect is guilty. So we have to consider if police may engage in priming or the Scharffian illusion of extensive knowledge, even when targets may be innocent. In order to address this question, one approach is to consider whether a person could consent to such police behavior if one was wrongly suspected of a crime. On this line of thinking, one could not logically consent to actions that undercut the rights that crime prevention is meant to protect. For example, torture fails this test of consent-worthiness, because no one would rationally choose to live in even a crime-free state if one risked being falsely accused and tortured by police. Above, we argued that confession-based techniques may fail this test as well.

Regarding priming, being invited to answer questions in a comfortably appointed room does not seem to pass this threshold of a significant rights violation. Assuming the style of questioning is closer to the information-gathering approach than to the confrontational and potentially demeaning confession-based approach, presumably, it would be less stressful to sit in a room resembling a therapist's office than in a typically Spartan interrogation booth. Additionally, the relatively mild psychological manipulation entailed in priming, in itself, is unlikely to result in any harm to an innocent suspect.

Having a friendly conversation with an interrogator using the Scharff technique might prove somewhat concerning to a suspect since it will become obvious to him that the authorities have been investigating him for some time. Yet this concern would occur in any type of interrogation. The positive aspect of the Scharff technique as far as an innocent person is concerned is that the interrogator lays more of his cards on the table, perhaps providing more occasions for an innocent person to correct the errors that led to him being falsely implicated in a crime. Similarly, the Scharff technique might be preferable to styles of interrogation where the interrogator reveals fewer details because the suspect can gain a picture of the interrogator's concerns faster, thus forestalling the stress that might come from wondering why he was arrested when the interrogator is more withholding.

Again, what is distinctive about the priming and Scharff techniques is their tendency to elicit a greater amount of information from suspects than would have been obtained with other techniques. It is important to confront concerns related specifically to this dynamic. Being more forthcoming about, say, one's whereabouts or activities at the time a crime was committed in a relaxed environment might lead a suspect to reveal private but non-criminal details he would have concealed in a more adversarial setting. Similarly, it is possible that an innocent suspect in a more "open" mental state would decline to request a lawyer he would have demanded in a more adversarial setting, and then go on to reveal information that nonetheless makes police more suspicious of him. This may be relatively unlikely, but it is possible.

If priming openness poses a strange kind of peril in the interrogation booth, it must be remembered that the more typical interrogation room also presents problems on this score. The anxiety produced by a Spartan interrogation room—certainly heightened by confrontational techniques—might lead to nervousness the police could wrongly interpret as indications of guilt (cf. Kassin, Goldstein, and Savitsky 2003). Anxiety might also lead an innocent suspect to share intimate but non-criminal secrets with police he would have preferred to conceal. It is difficult to weigh these risks, but if priming and Scharff techniques are highly reliable and efficacious, it seems reasonable for innocent people to consent to these risks in exchange for an interrogation regime that frequently produces true confessions from guilty suspects.

Let us turn to the Strategic Use of Evidence. Using this technique, the interrogator might deliberately conceal his or her knowledge from the suspect. Guilty suspects likely do not have cause to complain that an interrogator is acting strategically with them for the reasons already discussed. Frustration a guilty suspect may feel when the interrogator reveals the withheld evidence could have been avoided had the suspect been truthful from the start. Neither innocent nor guilty suspects necessarily have a right to know what information investigators hold. Suspects do not have a right to compromise investigations, which could occur if evidence is revealed to either innocent or guilty suspects. Thus, the SUE technique's withholding of information does not appear to unjustly violate suspects' rights.

It should be further noted with respect to innocent suspects that interrogators and innocent suspects may never have a confrontation where the former's deception is revealed, because the innocent suspect simply confirms all the evidence in the detective's possession. Second, the suspect should understand that the interrogator may have more information than he is sharing since he is performing an investigation, not just having a chat with the suspect. The interview or interrogation likely starts with some preamble along the lines of "we've asked you down here/arrested you because we have reason to believe that you have information regarding. ..." So an interrogator who reveals evidence he did not mention at the start is not necessarily doing something the suspect should not have reasonably expected.

Broader effects of strategic interrogation techniques

Concerning effects on the interrogator's character, these techniques may raise slightly more questions than the information-gathering techniques, but they are clearly less troubling than the confession-based techniques. The manipulation present with the priming techniques is more oblique since the interrogator sets the scene in the interrogation booth rather than directly manipulates the suspect. Thus, the negative effects on an interrogator's character are likely less significant than they would be with direct manipulation.

The Strategic Use of Evidence technique and Unanticipated Questions technique both seem to involve minimal amounts of manipulation. The interrogator engages in a more or less rational game[4]—like chess—wherein one compares the facts one has at one's disposal with those the suspect is presenting and engages in gambits to expose the suspect's lies. It is conceivable that the discrete, factual, non-emotional nature of this process makes it separable from the interrogator's private life—something one can "leave at the office."

Using the Scharff technique, the interrogator actively produces an illusion about the extent of his or her knowledge and conceals his or her objectives. Scharff's (1950) own writing about his methods seems to indicate that the production of this illusion, much like with the SUE technique and unanticipated questioning, is rationally calculated and game-like. Although the technique involves imposing strategic considerations onto an ostensibly friendly interaction, given the ubiquity of self-presentation in human communication (see Schlenker 2012), the Scharff technique may not involve much more social strategizing than people are prone to do in their everyday lives. Scharff himself appeared to suffer no ill psychological effects from the use of his technique, and, in fact, after the war, he had numerous amiable interactions with former

POWs he had interrogated (Toliver 1997). Although this evidence is merely anecdotal, it is suggestive that Scharff's techniques are injurious neither to the interrogator nor to the person being questioned.

Concluding remarks

Overall, we have seen that the information-gathering and strategic interrogation techniques pose fewer moral concerns than the confession-based techniques. If the scientific literature continues to show support for the former schools of techniques in both laboratory and field settings, we believe that it would be preferable for the justice system to move toward implementation of these more modern schools of interrogation.

One might reasonably ask, however, whether there may exist circumstances under which it would be justifiable to use confession-oriented approaches. That is, are there situations in which the stakes are sufficiently high that the moral restrictions on interrogation techniques are loosened. As this argument goes, situations Walzer (1977) might call "supreme emergency" demand actions that would ordinarily be impermissible.

Earlier, we briefly discussed a version of this argument we described as "exceptionalism." There, we pointed out that the argument that confession-oriented approaches are necessary in order to prosecute dangerous criminals is a case of begging the question: It assumes that confession-oriented approaches are effective. From what we have seen, it appears that although such techniques are effective at eliciting confessions, they run a high risk of inducing innocent people to confession, and moreover, the rights-infringements they entail are more extensive than techniques that are just as effective, if not more effective, and carry a lower risk to innocent people. If the necessity of prosecuting criminals compels action, it would be difficult to justify the use of such unwieldy tools, especially when better ones exist.

Stepping away from reality, one might imagine a plausible alternate universe in which confession-oriented approaches were more effective than the alternatives. Such a world would pose a dilemma in which the respect for autonomy competed against the just cause of averting harm for innocent people (i.e., by allowing dangerous criminals to elude prosecution). To prohibit the use of confession-oriented techniques in this alternate reality runs the risk of negligently allowing the community to be less safe than it could be. However, we believe that, in such a world, our foregoing moral reasoning would still apply: The deception and manipulation entailed in confession-oriented techniques still pose serious risks of violating the rights of both the innocent and the guilty.

The problem might, thus, be intractable: In such a world, there may be no option that satisfies all of our moral concerns. Nagel (1979) has discussed the idea of such a "moral blind alley" in which "a previously innocent person [is faced] with a choice between morally abominable courses of action [and is left with] no way to escape with his [sic] honor" (74). At least in the domain of interrogation, the practical reality is that we need not make such grim compromises. Those techniques that are most effective are also those that are respectful of autonomy. This is a fact for which we should be grateful.

Notes

1 There is no direct empirical evidence that interrogation themes, in fact, function as intended.
2 As part of this change, the term 'interrogation' was largely abandoned in favor of the term 'interview'. Here, we have retained the term 'interrogation' throughout the discussion, which should not be taken to indicate disagreement with the terminology of investigative interviewing.

3 It must be emphasized that this illusion is created in a very different fashion, and has different goals, than the false evidence ploys described earlier. For a more detailed of the 'I-already-know-it-all' illusion, see Oleszkiewicz, Granhag & Montecinos (2014).

4 We use the term 'game' to indicate an interaction with strategic considerations. The use of this term should not be taken to suggest the interaction is of trivial consequence.

Bibliography

Baldwin, J. (1992) 'Videotaping of police interviews with suspects: An evaluation', *Police Research Series*, Paper No 1. London: Home Office.

Baldwin, J. (1993) 'Police interview techniques: Establishing truth or proof?', *The British Journal of Criminology*, 33: 325–52.

Bargh, J.A. (1997) 'The automaticity of everyday life', in R.S. Wyer, Jr. (ed.) *The Automaticity of Everyday Life: Advances in Social Cognition*, Mahwah, NJ: Erlbaum, pp. 1–61.

Bok, S. (1978) *Lying*, New York, NY: Vintage.

Bok, S. (1983) *Secrets: On the Ethics of Concealment and Revelation*, New York, NY: Vintage Books.

Bond, C.F., Jr. and DePaulo, B.M. (2006) 'Accuracy of deception judgments', *Personality & Social Psychology Review*, 10: 214–34.

Bond, C.F., Jr. and DePaulo, B.M. (2008) 'Individual differences in judging deception: accuracy and bias', *Psychological Bulletin*, 134: 477–92.

Buckley, J. and Jayne, B. (1999) *The Investigator Anthology*, Chicago, IL: John E. Reid and Associates.

Bull, R. (1999) 'Police investigative interviewing', in A. Memon and R. Bull (eds.) *Handbook of the Psychology of Interviewing*, Chichester: Wiley, pp. 279–92.

Bull, R. (2014) *Investigative Interviewing*, New York, NY: Springer Science.

Bull, R. and Milne, B. (2004) 'Attempts to improve the police interviewing of suspects', in G.D. Lassiter (ed.) *Interrogations, Confessions, and Entrapment*, New York, NY: Kluwer, pp. 181–96.

Clarke, C., Milne, R. and Bull, R. (2011) 'Interviewing suspects of crime: the impact of peace training, supervision and the presence of a legal advisor', *Journal of Investigative Psychology and Offender Profiling*, 8: 149–62.

Dawson, E., Hartwig, M. and Denisenkov, P. (2015) *Interviewing to Elicit Information: The Effect of Spatial and Openness Primes on Disclosure*, Manuscript in preparation.

Dawson, E., Hartwig, M., Leps, C. and Brimbal, L. (2015) *Interviewing to Elicit Information: Using Priming to Promote Disclosure*, Under review.

Dawson, E., Hartwig, M., Luke, T.J. and Denisenkov, P. (2015) *From Theory to Application: Testing a Method of Priming to Influence Disclosure in Human Intelligence Interviews*, Manuscript in preparation.

DePaulo, B.M., Lindsay, J.J., Malone, B.E., Muhlenbruck, L., Charlton, K. and Cooper, H. (2003) 'Cues to deception', *Psychological Bulletin*, 129: 74–118.

Drizin, S.A. and Leo, R.A. (2004) 'The problem of false confessions in the post-DNA world', *North Carolina Law Review*, 82: 891–1007.

Firstman, R. and Salpeter, J. (2008) *A Criminal Injustice: A True Crime, a False Confession, and the Fight to Free Marty Tankleff*, New York, NY: Ballantine Books.

Gordon, N.J. and Fleisher, W.L. (2006) *Effective Interviewing and Interrogation Techniques*, 2nd edn, San Diego, CA: Academic Press.

Granhag, P.A. and Hartwig, M. (2008) 'A new theoretical perspective on deception detection: on the psychology of instrumental mind reading', *Psychology, Crime & Law*, 14: 189–200.

Granhag, P.A. and Hartwig, M. (in press) 'The strategic use of evidence (SUE) technique: a conceptual overview', in P.A. Granhag, A. Vrij and B. Vershuere (eds.), *Deception Detection: Current Challenges and New Directions*, Chichester: Wiley.

Granhag, P.A., Montecinos, S.C. and Oleszkiewicz, S. (2013) 'Eliciting intelligence from sources: the first scientific test of the Scharff technique', *Legal and Criminological Psychology*, 20: 96–113.

Griffiths, A. and Milne, B. (2006) 'Will it all end in tiers? Police interviews with suspects in Britain', in T. Williamson (ed.) *Investigative Interviewing: Rights, Research, Regulation*, Devon, United Kingdom: Willan Publishing, pp. 167–89.

Gudjonsson, G.H. (2003) *The Psychology of Interrogations and Confessions: A Handbook*, Chichester: Wiley.

Hartwig, M. and Bond, C.F., Jr. (2011) 'Why do lie-catchers fail? A lens model meta-analysis of human lie judgments', *Psychological Bulletin*, 137: 643–59.

Hartwig, M., Granhag, P.A. and Luke, T.J. (2014) 'Strategic use of evidence during investigative interviews: the state of the science', in D.C. Raskin, C.R. Honts and J.C. Kircher (eds.) *Credibility Assessment: Scientific Research and Applications* Academic Press, 1–36, Amsterdam: Elsevier.

Hartwig, M., Granhag, P.A. and Strömwall, L.A. (2007) 'Guilty and innocent suspects' strategies during police interrogations', *Psychology, Crime & Law,* 13: 213–27.

Hartwig, M., Granhag, P.A., Strömwall, L. A. and Kronkvist, O. (2006) 'Strategic use of evidence during police interviews: when training to detect deception works', *Law and Human Behavior,* 30: 603–19.

Hartwig, M., Granhag, P.A., Strömwall, L.A. and Vrij, A. (2005) 'Detecting deception via strategic disclosure of evidence', *Law and Human Behavior,* 29: 469–84. doi:10.1007/s10979-005-5521-x.

Hartwig, M., Granhag, P.A., Strömwall, L.A., Wolf, A., Vrij, A. and Roos af Hjelmsäter, E. (2011) 'Detecting deception in suspects: verbal cues as a function of interview strategy', *Psychology, Crime, & Law,* 17: 643–56.

Hartwig, M., Granhag, P.A. and Vrij, A. (2005) 'Police interrogation from a social psychology perspective', *Policing & Society,* 15: 379–99.

Hersh, S. (2004) 'Torture at Abu Ghraib', *The New Yorker,* May.

Hilgendorf, E.L. and Irving, M. (1981) 'A decision-making model of confessions', in M. Lloyd-Bostock (ed.) *Psychology in Legal Contexts: Applications and Limitations,* London: MacMillan, pp. 67–84.

Holmberg, U. and Christianson, S.-Å. (2002) 'Murderers' and sexual offenders' experiences of police interviews and their inclination to admit or deny crimes', *Behavioral Sciences and the Law,* 20: 31–45.

Holmes, W. (2003) *Criminal Interrogation: A Modern Format for Interrogating Criminal Suspects Based on the Intellectual Approach,* Springfield, IL: Thomas.

Horvath, F., Jayne, B. and Buckley, J. (1994) 'Differentiation of truthful and deceptive criminal suspects in behavior analysis interviews', *Journal of Forensic Sciences,* 39: 793–807.

Huff, C.R., Rattner, A. and Sagarin, E. (1996) *Convicted But Innocent: Wrongful Conviction and Public Policy,* Thousand Oaks: Sage.

Inbau, F.E. (1942). *Lie Detection and Criminal Interrogation,* 1st edn, Baltimore, MD: Williams and Wilkins.

Inbau, F.E. (1948) *Lie Detection and Criminal Interrogation,* 2nd edn, Baltimore, MD: Williams and Wilkins.

Inbau, F.E. and Reid, J.E. (1953) *Lie Detection and Criminal interrogation,* 3rd edn, Baltimore, MD: Williams and Wilkins.

Inbau, F.E. and Reid, J.E. (1962) *Criminal Interrogation and Confessions,* 1st edn, Baltimore, MD: Williams and Wilkins.

Inbau, F.E. and Reid, J.E. (1967) *Criminal Interrogation and Confessions,* 2nd edn, Baltimore, MD: Williams and Wilkins.

Inbau, F.E., Reid, J.E. and Buckley, J.P. (1983) *Criminal Interrogation and Confessions,* 3rd edn, Baltimore, MD: Williams and Wilkins.

Inbau, F.E., Reid, J.E., Buckley, J.P. and Jayne, B.C. (2001) *Criminal Interrogation and Confessions,* 4th edn, Sudbury, MA: Jones and Bartlett.

Inbau, F.E., Reid, J.E., Buckley, J.P. and Jayne, B.C. (2013) *Criminal Interrogation and Confessions,* 5th edn, Sudbury, MA: Jones and Bartlett.

Irving, B. (1980) 'Police interrogation: a case study of current practice', *Research Studies No. 2,* London: HMSO.

Irving, B. and McKenzie, I.K. (1989) *Police Interrogation: The Effects of the Police and Criminal Evidence Act,* London: Police Foundation of Great Britain.

Kassin, S.M. (1997) 'The psychology of confession evidence', *American Psychologist,* 52: 221–33.

Kassin, S.M. (2005) 'On the psychology of confessions: does innocence put innocent at risk?', *American Psychologist,* 60: 215–28.

Kassin, S.M., Drizin, S.A., Grisso, T., Gudjonsson, G.H., Leo, R.A. and Redlich, A.D. (2010) 'Police-induced confessions: risk factors and recommendations', *Law and Human Behavior,* 34: 3–38. doi:10.1007/s10979-009-9188-6.

Kassin, S.M., Goldstein, C.C. and Savitsky, K. (2003) 'Behavioral confirmation in the interrogation room: on the dangers of presuming guilt', *Law and Human Behavior,* 27: 187–203.

Kassin, S.M. and Gudjonsson, G.H. (2004) 'The psychology of confessions: a review of the literature and issues', *Psychological Science in the Public Interest,* 5: 33–67. doi:10.1111/j.1529-1006.2004.00016.x.

Kassin, S.M. and Kiechel, K.L. (1996) 'The social psychology of false confessions: compliance, internalization, and confabulation', *Psychological Science,* 7: 125–28.

Kassin, S.M. and McNall, K. (1991) 'Police interrogations and confessions: communicating promises and threats by pragmatic implication', *Law and Human Behavior,* 15: 233–51.

Kassin, S.M. and Wrightsman, L.S. (1985) 'Confession evidence', in S.M. Kassin and L. Wrightsman (eds.) *The Psychology of Evidence and Trial Procedure,* Beverly Hills, CA: Sage, pp. 67–94.

Lakoff, G. and Johnson, M. (1980) *Metaphors We Live By*, Chicago, IL: University of Chicago Press.

Lancaster, G.J., Vrij, A., Hope, L. and Waller, B. (2013) 'Sorting the liars from the truth tellers: the benefits of asking unanticipated questions on lie detection', *Applied Cognitive Psychology,* 27: 107–14.

Landau, M.J., Meier, B.P. and Keefer, L.A. (2010) 'A metaphor-enriched social cognition', *Psychological Bulletin,* 136: 1045–67.

Lassiter, G.D. (ed.) (2004) *Interrogations, Confessions, and Entrapment,* New York, NY: Kluwer Academic.

Leo, R.A. (1996a) 'Miranda's revenge: police interrogation as a confidence game', *Law and Society Review,* 30: 259–88.

Leo, R.A. (1996b) 'Inside the interrogation room', *Journal of Criminal Law and Criminology,* 86: 266–303.

Leo, R.A. (2004) 'The third degree and the origins of psychological police interrogation in the United States', In G.D. Lassiter (ed.) *Interrogations, Confessions, and Entrapment,* New York, NY: Kluwer Academic pp. 37–84.

Leo, R.A. and Ofshe, R.J. (1998) 'The consequences of false confessions: deprivations of liberty and miscarriages of justice in the age of psychological interrogation', *Journal of Criminal Law and Criminology,* 88: 429–96.

Levine, T.R., Shaw, A. and Shulman, H.C. (2010) 'Increasing deception detection accuracy with strategic questioning', *Human Communication Research,* 36: 216–31.

Loftus, E.F. (2005) 'Planting misinformation in the human mind: a 30-year investigation of the malleability of memory', *Learning & Memory,* 12: 361–66.

Luke, T.J., Hartwig, M., Joseph, E., Brimbal, L., Chan, G., Dawson, E., Jordan, S., Granhag, P.A. and Donovan, P. (2015) *Training in the Strategic Use of Evidence: Improving Deception Detection Accuracy of American Law Enforcement Officers.* Under review.

Masip, J., Barba, A. and Herrero, C. (2012) 'Behaviour Analysis Interview and common sense: a study with novice and experienced officers', *Psychiatry, Psychology And Law*, 19: 21–34.

May, L., Granhag, P.A. and Oleszkiewicz, S. (2014) 'Eliciting intelligence using the Scharff-technique: closing in on the confirmation/disconfirmation tactic', *Journal of Investigative Psychology and Offender Profiling,* 11: 136–50.

McGurk, B.J., Carr, M.J. and McGurk, D. (1993) 'Investigative interviewing courses for police officers: An evaluation' (Police Research Series Paper, No. 4), London: Home Office.

McMahan, J. (2006) 'On the moral equality of combatants', *Journal of Political Philosophy*, 14: 377–93.

McMahan, J. (2009) *Killing in War,* Oxford: Oxford University Press.

Memon, A., Vrij, A. and Bull, R. (2003) *Psychology and Law: Truthfulness, Accuracy and Credibility,* 2nd edn, Chichester: Wiley.

Milne, R. and Bull, R. (1999) *Investigative Interviewing: Psychology and Practice*, London: Wiley.

Milne, R., Shaw, G. and Bull, R. (2007) 'Investigative interviewing: the role of research', in D. Carson, R. Milne, F. Pakes, K. Shalev and A. Shawyer (eds.) *Applying Psychology to Criminal Justice,* Chichester: Wiley, pp. 65–80.

Moston, S. and Engelberg, T. (1993) 'Police questioning techniques in tape recorded interviews with criminal suspects', *Policing and Society,* 3: 223–37.

Moston, S. and Stephenson, G. M. (1993) 'The changing face of police interrogation', *Journal of Community and Applied Social Psychology,* 3: 101–15.

Nagel, T. (1979) 'War and massacre', in T. Nagel (ed.) *Mortal Questions,* Cambridge: Cambridge University Press, pp. 53–74.

Oleszkiewicz, S., Granhag, P.A. and Montecinos, S.C. (2014) 'The Scharff-technique: eliciting information from human sources', *Law and Human Behavior,* 38: 478–89.

Oxburgh, G.E., Walsh, D. and Milne, B. (2011) 'The importance of applied research in investigative interviewing: a real-life perspective', *Journal of Investigative Psychology and Offender Profiling,* 8: 105–109.

Pearse, J. and Gudjonsson, G.H. (1996) 'Police interviewing techniques at two south London police stations', *Psychology, Crime and Law,* 3: 63–74.

People v Thomas, 22 N.Y.3d 629. (2014).

Scharff, H.J. (1950) 'Without torture', *Argosy,* 39: 87–91.

Scheck, B., Neufeld, P. and Dwyer, J. (2000) *Actual Innocence*, Garden City, NY: Doubleday.

Schlenker, B.R. (2012) 'Self-presentation', in M.R. Leary and J. Tangney (eds.) *Handbook of Self and Identity,* 2nd edn, New York, NY: Guilford Press, pp. 542–70.

Sear, L. and Williamson, T. (1999) 'British and American interrogation strategies', in D. Canter and L. Alison (eds.) *Interviewing and Deception,* Darmouth: Ashgate, pp. 67–81.

Sherman, N. (2010) *The Untold War: Inside the Hearts, Minds, and Souls of Our Soldiers,* New York, NY: W. W. Norton & Company.
Senese, L. (2008) *Anatomy of Interrogation Themes*, Chicago, IL: John E. Reid and Associates.
Skerker, M. (2010). *An Ethics of Interrogation*, Chicago, IL: University of Chicago Press.
Softley, P. (1980) *Police Interrogation: An Observational Study in Four Police Stations. Home Office Research Study No. 61*, London: HMSO.
Strömwall, L.A., Hartwig, M. and Granhag, P.A. (2006) 'To act truthfully: Nonverbal behaviour and strategies during a police interrogation', *Psychology, Crime & Law,* 12: 207–19.
Toliver, R. (1997) *The Interrogator*, Atglen: PA: Schiffer Publishing.
Tyler, T.R. (2006) *Why People Obey the Law*, Princeton, NJ: Princeton University Press.
Victory, P. (2002) *Justice and Truth: The Guildford Four and the Maguire Seven,* London: Sinclair-Stevenson.
Vrij, A. (2008) *Detecting Lies and Deceit: Pitfalls and Opportunities,* 2nd edn, New York, NY: John Wiley & Sons.
Vrij, A., Fisher, R.P., Mann, S. and Leal, S. (2006) 'Detecting deception by manipulating cognitive load', *Trends in Cognitive Sciences,* 10: 141–42. doi:10.1016/j.tics.2006.02.003.
Vrij, A., Fisher, R.P., Mann, S. and Leal, S. (2008) 'A cognitive load approach to lie detection', *Journal of Investigative Psychology & Offender Profiling,* 5: 39–43. doi:10.1002/jip.82.
Vrij, A. and Granhag, P.A. (2012) 'Eliciting cues to deception and truth: what matters are the questions asked', *Journal of Applied Research in Memory & Cognition,* 1: 110–17.
Vrij, A., Leal, S., Granhag, P.A., Mann, S., Fisher, R.P., Hillman, J. and Sperry, K. (2009) 'Outsmarting the liars: The benefit of asking unanticipated questions', *Law and Human Behavior*, 33: 159–66. doi:10.1007/s10979-008-9143-y.
Vrij, A., Leal, S., Mann, S. and Fisher, R.P. (2012) 'Imposing cognitive load to elicit cues to deceit: inducing the reverse order technique naturally', *Psychology, Crime & Law,* 18: 579–94. doi:10.1080/1068316X.2010.515987.
Vrij, A., Mann, S. and Fisher, R.P. (2006) 'An empirical test of the Behaviour Analysis Interview', *Law and Human Behavior*, 30: 329–45.
Vrij, A., Mann, S., Leal, S. and Fisher, R.P. (2012) 'Is anyone there? Drawings as a tool to detect deceit in occupation interviews', *Psychology, Crime & Law*, 18: 377–88.
Vrij, A., Mann, S., Leal, S. and Granhag, P. (2010) 'Getting into the minds of pairs of liars and truth tellers: an examination of their strategies', *Open Criminology Journal*, 3: 17–22.
Walkley, J. (1987) *Police Interrogation: Handbook for Investigators*, London: Police Review Publication.
Walters, S. (2003) *Principles of Kinesic Interview and Interrogation,* 2nd edn, Boca Raton, FL: CRC Press.
Walzer, M. (1977) *Just and Unjust Wars*, New York, NY: Basic Books.
Wickersham Commission Report. National Commission on Law Observance and Law Enforcement. (1931) *Report on Lawlessness in Law Enforcement*, Washington, DC: US Government Printing Office.
Williams, L.E. and Bargh, J.A. (2008) 'Experiencing physical warmth promotes interpersonal warmth', *Science*, 322: 606–607.
Williamson, T.M. (1993) 'From interrogation to investigative interviewing: Strategic trends in police questioning', *Journal of Community and Applied Social Psychology,* 3: 89–99.
Zimbardo, P.G. (1967) 'The psychology of police confessions', *Psychology Today,* 1: 17–20, 25–27.
Zhong, C.B. and Leonardelli, G.F. (2008) 'Cold and lonely: Does social exclusion literally feel cold?', *Psychological Science*, 19: 838–42.

22

The moral ecology of policing

A mind science approach to race and policing in the United States

Phillip Atiba Goff and Rachel Godsil

Introduction

A casual observer of recent events in US policing would be hard pressed to conclude that race plays anything other than a central role in encounters with law enforcement. The shooting deaths of Michael Brown Jr., Walter Scott, and Tamir Rice each shocked the nation's conscience. Eric Garner's deaths at the hands of NYPD officers and Freddy Gray's death in a Baltimore Police Department van have all made it seem outlandish to imagine that these are isolated cases or that the same treatment befalls most white citizens encountering police. And, in part because both lay and scholarly understandings about how race operates are so limited, this often leads to the conclusion that policing in the US is rife with racial bigotry (Gambino and Laughlin 2015). However, even if racial prejudice is appreciably elevated in police (as compared to the general population), all of the best science on the nature of racial discrimination suggests that prejudice alone is insufficient to explain observed racial disparities (Goff 2013). In other words, racial bigotry is not sufficient to explain racial discrimination.

How then, are we to understand what appear to be widespread racial disparities in police outcomes—especially when the encounters caught on camera seem to reveal such visceral reactions to young Black men? Drawing on decades of research in the mind sciences, we employ the scientific consensus that situations often matter more than character in order to understand the moral ecology of police decision-making as influenced by race. That is, by understanding the contexts of policing, this chapter attempts to reveal the mechanisms by which racial disparities come into being. The present chapter sketches the moral ecology of law enforcement at three levels: 1) the line officer, 2) the first line supervisor, and 3) the executive. This is accomplished by examining the ways in which the mind sciences can be translated into the chronic contexts that influence decision-makers at each of these three levels, focusing on mid-sized to large urban police departments.[1]

Our goal is to provide an outline of the social forces that influence each of these decision-makers with an eye towards how they over-determine the outcome of street-level bureaucratic encounters between communities and law enforcement. We divide the chapter into four sections:

First, we briefly detail two of the major advances in mind science approaches to the understanding of racial disparities, namely implicit bias and self-threats (also understood as fast and slow traps).

Second, we broadly outline some of the features of municipal policing that create localized "police culture." Here we also highlight the reasons why it is important to understand all levels of a police organization with respect to how they influence the street level bureaucracies that communities and police navigate. In other words, we formally stress the need to bring even policy-level analyses back to the level of the daily distribution and consumption of law enforcement services by the communities police are sworn to protect.

Third, we translate those advances to three common levels of police bureaucracy (i.e., line officers, supervisors, and executives). At each level of decision-making we will provide both a brief overview of social forces and an accounting for how the contexts of individuals in these positions influence their susceptibility to psychological processes that tend to produce disparate outcomes. Specifically, we outline the primary audiences of each bureaucratic level—providing the network of social forces that influence each level—as well as the decisions traditionally made at each level. Within each decision, we review the mind science literature relevant to how these kinds of decisions are vulnerable to the influence of implicit bias and self-threats.

Finally, we conclude with some summary thoughts on the state of the evidence base regarding racial equity in policing and some modest policy and research recommendations for the field.

Our intent is to provide a guided tour of the ways that the mind sciences might be used to understand race and policing in the United States. By foregrounding the set of contexts negotiated by officers in each of the most important bureaucratic levels within the organization, we also hope to provide an ecological roadmap for future research and policy interventions.

When prejudice is not enough

High profile incidents of Black men and boys killed by law enforcement, and the protests that follow, bring into the public discourse the toxic dynamics that too often exist between law enforcement and non-White communities. Nearly every level of government, most broadcast and digital media, and many American households are now deeply engaged with questions about police culture and how it intersects with America's most vulnerable communities in the wake of unprecedented attention to police involved deaths of unarmed Black men, as well as increasing attention to more minor daily conflicts. To understand that intersection, however, one must first understand the chronic contexts that police officers, administrators, and executives routinely negotiate.

For those who position themselves as reformers, the problem is often cast as one of police racism (Goff 2013; Tyler and Huo 2002; Swarts 2015). As with the rest of the population at large, some police officers do continue to hold blatantly racist views. For instance, in March of 2015, four Florida police officers were fired after sending "a trailer-style video amongst themselves containing a Ku Klux Klan hood, attacks against minorities, derogatory images of President Obama and racist comments about Hispanics and homosexuals" (Campbell 2015). But such individuals are highly unlikely to be the norm within police departments (note that these officers were fired when their views became known). Most police officers, like the rest of the population, are loathe to think of themselves as "racist" (Tyler and Huo 2002), a group that is nearly as reviled as child sexual predators in the general public (Crandall, Eshleman, and O'Brien 2002). However, it has long been apparent that this gentling of overtly hostile racial attitudes has not brought with it a resolution to conflicts between non-white communities and law enforcement, as it has failed to do so in many segments of American public life (Goff 2013; Richardson and Goff 2015). So, if racial inequality has remained persistent in the wake of declining racial prejudice, what new language might one use to make sense of that persistent inequality? Innovations in the mind sciences provide two promising courses of explanation.

Over four decades of research in the mind sciences reveal that many of our conscious thoughts, behaviors, and judgments are affected by automatic mental processes (Godsil et al. 2014; Richardson and Goff 2012). Similarly, a growing body of research demonstrates how seemingly unrelated self-directed processes fundamentally shape interpersonal and intergroup behaviors (Fein and Spencer 1997; Goff, Steele, and Davies 2008; Richeson and Shelton 2003; Vorauer and Kumhyr 2001; Vorauer, Main, and O'Connell 1998). In the present chapter, we explore the ways in which these mind science innovations might help provide a rubric for making sense of the moral ecology of policing in the context of race relations in the United States.

The limitations of conscious attitudes in predicting behavior

While relatively few people in the US today believe consciously—i.e., explicitly—that all black and Latino people are poor, intellectually dim, and prone to criminality, the scientific consensus is that racial stereotypes continue to affect behaviors (Godsil et al. 2014). Racial stereotypes also affect what Goff (2013) contends are identity traps, social psychological phenomena that intersect in human behavior. This explains the apparent paradox between the low occurrence of explicit thoughts of non-whites as deficit and discriminatory behaviors toward the group. Identity traps can be divided into fast and slow identity traps: A fast trap is an automatic or uncontrolled response such as an implicit bias and conversely, a slow trap is self-directed, ruminative, and conscious. A self-threat—something a person sees as a threat to a belief he holds about himself—is an example of a slow trap (Hochbein 2014).

Implicit racial bias and its consequences

Implicit social cognition refers to the process by which the human brain orders the vast amount of stimuli we encounter through the use of categories ("schemas") and automatic associations between concepts that share related characteristics (Tajfel and Forgas 1981; Anderson 1983). Schemas are comprised of traits and attitudes—evaluative valences (Eagly and Chaiken 1993)—and they are constructed for people as well as objects. While critical to social functioning, social categories translate into "stereotypes"—generalizations about particular identity categories—and are often far from neutral. Of particular concern to policing in the United States, of course, are those stereotypes associating blacks, and to some degree Latinos, with violence, criminality, and poverty (Bobo 2001; Eberhardt et al. 2004; Trawalter et al. 2008). Implicit racial biases thus refer generally to automatic stereotypes and attitudes that result from repeated exposures to the cultural stereotypes of different racial groups that pervade society (Richardson and Goff 2012).

Implicit bias is a result of the automatic, unconscious association of negative attributes with different groups. But at an explicit or implicit level, bias can also manifest as a result of comparatively positive preferences for one group over another. Social scientists refer to this phenomenon as "in-group" bias or preference (Brewer 1999; Tropp and Molina 2012). In-group bias is more likely to be explicit than is animus, but it can often be implicit as well. It is most prevalent when in-group members perceive a threat to resources that benefit the in-group (Riek et al. 2006) or norms that legitimize the status quo (Tropp and Molina 2012; Sidanius et al. 1996).

In-group bias can include the failure to attribute a full range of emotions to out-group members (Leyens et al. 2001). "Primary" emotions such as pleasure, fear, and rage are understood to be experienced by both human and non-human animals, while "secondary" emotions such as mourning, admiration, resentment, and hope are believed be experienced exclusively by humans (Levin et al. 2003; Demoulin et al. 2004; Gaunt, Leyens, and Demoulin 2002; Leyens et al. 2001; Leyens et al. 2003; Vaes et al. 2003; Vaes, Paladino, and Leyens 2004, 2006). Goff and colleagues

(Goff, Eberhardt, Williams, and Jackson 2008) state that because these secondary emotions are an important part of what makes us "human," denial of secondary emotions to out-group members constitutes a form of dehumanization. Other researchers describe this phenomenon as "infrahumanization" and note that it includes ascribing greater intelligence (Crocker, Major and Steele 1998) and language competency (Giles and Coupland 1991) to in-groups (Cuddy et al. 2007).

Related research has documented distinct neural reactions to the level of empathy in-groups show to the pain of out-groups using fMRI studies measuring the level of activity in the amygdala (an area of the brain that mediates pain). In a 2009 study, researchers showed participants video clips of faces contorted to reflect the experience of pain (Xu et al. 2009). When participants viewed pictures of in-group members experiencing pain, the fMRI documented high activity levels in the relevant brain region, but the activity level dropped when in-group members viewed clips of out-group members experiencing pain (Xu et al. 2009). A similar study used transcranial magnetic stimulation (TMS) to measure corticospinal activity levels in participants who were shown short video clips of a needle entering into the hand of either a white or black target (Avenanti et al. 2010). As with the 2009 fMRI study, researchers here found that region-specific brain activity levels are higher when a white participant views the clip of a white target experiencing pain than when a white participant sees a clip of a black target experiencing pain. Neither implicit bias nor the neural reaction to the pain of particular out-groups is inherent or universal. Both are mediated through the relative status and perceived worth of different racial groups (Trawalter, Hoffman and Waytz 2012). The combination of implicit negative associations with black people particularly and in-group preferences among whites appears to result from our country's hardened racial categories and pervasive racialized associations.

Implicit racial bias and in-group preference are integral to workplace hierarchies and dynamics. They have been shown to cause individuals to interpret identical facial expressions as more hostile on black faces than on white faces (Hugenberg and Bodenhausen 2003) and identically ambiguous behaviors as more aggressive when engaged in by blacks than by whites (Duncan 1976; Richardson and Goff 2015). Field studies demonstrate that black and Latino job applicants are significantly less likely to receive callbacks than are equally qualified white applicants (Pager et al. 2009), and studies mimicking job interviews (Word et al. 1974) found that whites showed more positive non-verbal behaviors toward other whites than toward black candidates, such as sitting closer to them; at the same time, whites spent 25 percent less time with black candidates and had higher rates of speech errors with them than with white candidates (Word et al. 1974).

Because they operate automatically and outside of awareness, implicit racial biases are difficult to fight consciously. Researchers have amassed powerful evidence that those with negative implicit racial attitudes, or those who automatically stereotype, display behaviors consistent with those attitudes (McConnell and Leibold 2001). Experiments related to law enforcement include studies of participants directed to "shoot" video images of people with a gun as quickly and accurately as possible. When "civilians" are tested, those with higher implicit bias levels shoot black targets holding guns faster and more accurately than white targets holding guns (Payne, Shimizu, and Jacoby 2005; Payne, Lambert, and Jacoby 2002; Correll et al. 2002; Correll et al. 2006). Police officers' training appears to prevent their implicit biases from affecting accuracy, but they do correlate with speed—like civilians, police officers are quicker to shoot black targets holding guns than white targets (Correll et al. 2007). Additionally, Correll and colleagues have found that police officers who worked in high crime areas with large percentages of blacks and Latinos were more likely to exhibit shooter bias (Correll, Hudson and Guillermo 2014).

Also salient to policing are studies of the effect of "priming" on visual attention as well as decision making (Eberhardt et al. 2004; Graham and Lowery 2004). Eberhardt, Goff, Purdie, and

Davies (2004) demonstrated that after having been subliminally primed with images of weapons, police officers were more likely to look at black faces than white faces and also to remember them as having more stereotypically African American features, resulting in the potential for false identification. Graham and Lowery found that subliminally priming police officers with words associated with blacks—"Harlem" or "dreadlocks"—led the officers to recommend harsher sentencing decisions (Graham and Lowery 2004).

Importantly, however, the research literature on implicit bias, vast and growing as it is, should not be used as an epistemic substitute for explicit bias. That is, while implicit biases do reside within the functioning of an individual's mind, they are best understood not as properties of an individual character—as we often consider explicit bigotry. Rather, since most estimates suggest that many Americans hold implicit anti-black racial biases (FAQs Project Implicit 2015), it is often less crucial to determine who does and who does not hold implicit biases, and more crucial to understand the situations that make us more vulnerable to our implicit biases that influence our behaviors.

What the science reliably reveals is that a wide array of factors including (ironically) the presumptions of objectivity (Uhlmann and Cohen 2007); elevated emotional states—particularly those linked to social categories such as resentment, disdain, or disgust (Dasgupta 2009); time pressure (Greenwald, McGhee, and Schwartz 1998; Kang et al. 2012); cognitive depletion (e.g., being tired, mentally exhausted, or distracted) (Ito et al. 2015; Mendoza, Gollwitzer, and Amodio 2011; Monteith et al. 2009); and threats to one's self-concept (Rudman, Dohn and Fairchilde 2007; Fein and Spencer 1997) all make us more likely to rely on the "mental shortcuts" of implicit biases in guiding our behavior. Again, these factors are particularly pernicious because they elicit biases that function outside of our awareness, making them difficult to detect for even the most self-critical person and harder still to exercise conscious forms of correction. As we shall see, the contexts in which officers work are rife with conditions that can trigger biases (e.g., multiple demands on one's time, the need for decisive and split-second decision making, and negative feedback from communities) (Glaser 2014; Goff 2013; Goff, Epstein, and Reddy 2013; Goff, Epstein, Mentovich and Reddy 2013). Consequently, when understanding how implicit biases may influence law enforcement behaviors, it is important to emphasize these chronic contexts rather than the character of individual officers or of police as a group.

Self-threats in intergroup contexts: The dangers of "it's not you, it's me"

In addition to the research on implicit biases, an emerging consensus among discrimination researchers reveals that threats to one's self-concept play an under-appreciated role in the production of racial inequality (Goff, Steele, and Davies 2008). For instance, the concern that many whites have, that they may be presumed to be racially biased, predicts cognitive depletion (Richeson and Shelton 2003); anxiety (Apfelbaum et al. 2008; Voraeur, Main, and O'Connell 1998); the activation of negative in-group stereotypes (Goff, Steele, and Davies 2008); and the avoidance of the topic of race—and the people who might raise the topic in the first place (Apfelbaum Norton and Sommers 2012; Apfelbaum et al. 2008; Goff, Steele, and Davies 2008; Word et al. 1974; Butz and Plant 2011; Dovidio et al. 2006; Plant and Butz 2006; Plant and Devine 2003; Tropp 2003).

Concerns with appearing prejudiced are far from the only identity-related concerns that influence intergroup interactions. For instance, researchers have found that men become more aggressive when their masculinity is threatened as a way to reassert their masculine identity (Willer et al. 2013; Bosson and Vandello 2011). In a recent study, college students who were told that their answers to a survey indicated feminine traits claimed higher levels of support for war, as well as homophobic attitudes, than those who were told that their answers were consistent with masculine traits (Willer et al. 2013). In a study in which men were required to engage in a behavior associated with femininity—braiding hair rather than rope, they overwhelmingly chose to punch a bag rather than do a puzzle. When both hair and rope-braiders punched the bag, the hair-braiders consistently punched harder than the rope-braiders (Bosson and Vandello 2011). Given that black men are stereotyped as hyper-masculine (Goff, Thomas, and Jackson 2008) and that confronting racial prejudice facilitates threats to black men's masculine self-concepts (Goff, Di Leone, and Kahn 2012), it is not difficult to imagine how non-compliant black men might disproportionately provoke threats to officers' masculine self-concept as well.

Taken together, these literatures offer examples of how threats to self-concept—independent of explicit or implicit prejudice—can influence intergroup interactions. Importantly, the solution to reducing intergroup disparities provoked by self-threat is not to "de-threaten" individuals. Rather, a productive endeavor would be to engage in self-enhancement on an individual level in order to have a sense of self that cannot be threatened. Moreover, it is also an efficient solution to protect individuals from contexts that tend to threaten self-concepts. In other words, the solution does not reduce to the character of officers (or civilians), but rather to structuring interactions differently through policies, procedures, and practices.

The set of factors identified above that tend to exacerbate implicit bias such as cognitive depletion (Devine 1989), time-pressured decision-making (Greenwald, McGhee, and Schwartz 1998), threats to self-concept (Fein and Spencer 1997), elevated emotional states, and low motivation to resist bias (Kang et al. 2012) are typical of the conditions that line officers encounter regularly. Self-threats tend to be exacerbated by strong identification with the domain, the high stakes of the event (Steele and Aronson 1995), and the large numbers of out-group members (Inzlicht and Ben-Zeev 2000). Again, all of these would appear to apply to both officers and the residents they encounter, making police interactions nearly the perfect provocations for the set of factors most likely to produce racially disparate outcomes even in the absence of explicit racial bias.

How, then, should we think about understanding the science of implicit bias and self-threats in the context of policing? What is the appropriate level of analysis? In the next section, we argue that understanding three broad levels of bureaucracy is informative for structuring an understanding of the moral ecology of policing. At each level, we outline the primary audiences, vulnerable decision-making points, and the mind science relevant to those vulnerabilities with an emphasis on the so-called "street-level" bureaucracy navigated by line officers and residents.

The many cultures of US police departments

Given both scholarly and popular tendencies to individualize racial disparities in treatment (Goff 2013; Plaut 2010), an obvious translation of the mind science of bias into the policing world would begin and end with a "psychologizing" of police officers. Because line officers are the face of both law enforcement and (often) the State, this tendency is both epistemologically seductive and dangerous. It is seductive because it relies on a widely held assumption about the role of internal states in producing racial disparities (Goff 2013) and dangerous because this tacit explanation for racism is conceptually myopic and belied by the facts. Goff (2013) previously referred to the difficulty we have understanding persistent racial inequality in the absence of explicit racial bigotry as the Attitude-Inequality Mismatch (AIM) problem. The crux of the AIM problem is that the conceptual framework for understanding racial inequality has often been reduced to racial animus. Consequently, in the absence of explicit bigotry (or amidst its steep decline), both lay and scientific explanations of inequality are robbed of their dominant mechanism. In the context of policing, there is both the danger that locating the mechanism for racially disparate treatment principally inside line officers distracts from powerful situational factors and the multiple layers of roles within major urban police departments. Each bureaucratic layer within a department has its own audience and organizational functions, each with its unique vulnerabilities to implicit bias and self-threats.

Consequently, in the present chapter, we have chosen to draw a rough map that delineates the levels of police responsibility in a mid-size to large police department, the kind responsible for public safety in the majority of urban areas in the United States. Within each bureaucratic level, we outline the primary audiences of those roles as well as the kinds of decisions most likely to be influenced by implicit bias and self-threats at each level. However, at each level of organizational analysis, it is crucial to understand the ways in which the context of that role filters down to the street-level officer. The street-level bureaucracy is the primary point of contact between communities and the men and women sworn to defend them. And, as previous scholars have noted, it is essential to understand the cultural context of these line officers to understand what factors shape a community's experience with its public safety force. The themes of this previous literature are three-fold. First, police departments have multiple "micro-cultures" that make up the character of the agency. Therefore, understanding those micro-cultures is crucial to understanding the logistic mechanisms by which any organizational tendency comes to be observed by residents. Second, culture/chronic context is a fundamental lever in shaping the behavior of line officers. And third, police/community relations are fundamentally defined at the level of street bureaucratic exchanges.

For instance, the literature addressing the social ecology of police misconduct includes an array of hypotheses for the link between race and coercive policing (for a review, see Kane 2002). Among these are the "minority group threat hypothesis" (Jackson 1989) that contends that increases in the percentage of minorities triggers a threat response by the dominant group and a resultant increased deployment of police, coercive policing strategies, and undermined legitimacy of police in minority communities (Jackson 1989). In support of this theory, Jacobs and O'Brien (1998) found that increased racial composition was linked to police use of deadly force across metropolitan areas in the United States. Campbell et al. (1998) found that, even controlling for crime, police dog deployments across Los Angeles Police Department divisions were 4.61 times more likely in divisions that were at least 50 percent black and twice as likely in divisions that were 50 percent Latino compared with primarily white divisions.

Klinger's (1997) formative article setting forth an "ecology of patrol" model does not focus on police violence but rather police lenience. He argues that officers deployed in high-crime areas develop a norm of greater leniency in policing than peers in low-crime communities because of a general sense that the residents of such a community are themselves likely to be "deviant." Klinger's argument is based upon two primary suppositions: the first, that police officers have a high degree of autonomy from the work rules of their superiors, and second, that group norms emerge among officers who work in particular precincts that are linked to the levels of perceived crime and "deviance" within the areas in which they work. Klinger's "ecology of patrol" model rests on the idea that officers in particular precincts develop a sense of what constitutes "normal" based upon the level of criminality that occurs in public and the general sense of disorder they encounter. The conditions that trigger a perception of disorder as described by Klinger are essentially the conditions that often accompany poverty—overcrowding and disrepair of residential and commercial properties and even the express perception that residents are impoverished. Klinger contends that the police understand their role as regulating "deviance" to protect the conventional citizenry—and accordingly, if the residents of a particular area are generally presumed deviant, they are undeserving of protection themselves. Two other factors are salient to Klinger's model: police cynicism and police workload. In high-crime precincts, he posits, police officers are apt to become cynical about the efficacy of the criminal justice system as they see those they've arrested out on bail or otherwise free from legal consequence and in addition, are likely to have significantly higher workloads than those in low-crime districts. Klinger's thesis supports the "broken windows" theory of policing—his contention is essentially that allowing low levels of crimes to continue, particular districts will either become or stay "high crime." However, the underpinnings of his argument are also consistent with police misconduct to the extent that officers in particular precincts—those that are poor—are more likely to see residents as undeserving and distinct from the "conventional" citizenry to whom they owe fealty to protect.

Herbert (1998) similarly identified different cultures arising from the contexts of particular precincts but relied upon a different theoretical framework. He postulated that six normative orders—law, bureaucratic control, adventure/machismo, safety, competence, and morality—provide both guidelines and justifications for the style of policing engaged in by officers. He also explored the effects of internal structure—such as assignment and rank. Herbert's analysis differed from Klinger's in his emphasis on the role of leadership in establishing a particular culture—using the LAPD as an example of an "ass-kicking" department following a mandate of aggressive policing stemming from a series of police chiefs (notably Daryl Gates). Herbert and Klinger both note the role of workload as salient—but with different identified outcomes. Klinger described higher workload from "high-crime" precincts resulting in more lenient policing, while Herbert contended that lower officer ratios could trigger a stronger police response to particular incidents to make the police presence more palpable despite the small numbers. Herbert concludes with a set of observations about necessary steps to reform departments in which the interplay of normative orders have led to policing styles that undermine community police relations. He suggests, for example, that competence be redefined from aggressive pursuits of large numbers of felony arrests to engaging with the community to address their issues of concern.

Kane in 2002 extended this literature by examining longitudinally whether variations in social ecological conditions in NYC precincts and divisions predicted patterns of police misconduct from 1975 to 1996. He found:

> in New York City from 1975 to1996, communities characterized by structural disadvantage and increases in Latino populations may have experienced processes that both attenuated informal social control mechanisms while providing a source of conflict necessary to encourage police misconduct. Moreover, because population mobility has been linked to the disruption of neighborhood bonds and networks (Bursik and Grasmick 1993; Bursik and Webb 1982; Kasarda and Janowitz 1974; Sampson and Groves 1989), communities characterized by high residential turnover may have further experienced a decreased capacity to engage in informal social control.
>
> (Kane 2002)

This literature provides a valuable foundation for examining the role of social organization and levels of police misconduct/ethical reasoning in policing. They emphasize the local level at which cultures form, the foundational role culture plays in police behavior, and the primary status of patrol officer contact in police/community relations. However, the literature has yet to incorporate evolving insights in the relationship between social psychological processes and the structure of police decision-making at different levels within police organizations.

In order to integrate these literatures, we divide police organizations into three bureaucratic levels and articulate the primary audiences and crucial decision points each bureaucratic level must negotiate and how these render each level uniquely vulnerable to the influences of implicit bias and self-threats. Again, the goal is to provide a kind of practical and scientific roadmap to considering racial justice within a framework of police moral ecology.

Three bureaucratic ecologies of race in American policing

One can roughly divide police responsibilities into three categories: officers, supervisors, and executives. Officers have the most direct contact with residents. They are evaluated and disciplined by supervisors, who are in turn instructed by the policies of executives. This results in a three-tiered hierarchy in which officers are the lowest status and executives are the highest. Though the vast majority of US Police Departments are numerically small and, consequently, lack this level of bureaucratic complexity (Interim Report of the President's Task Force on 21st Century Policing 2015), it is useful to divide departments into these bureaucratic layers for three reasons. First, the audiences, responsibilities, and vulnerabilities we articulate below are present in all departments, regardless of bureaucratic complexity. Second, the distinctions among line officers, supervisors, and executives provide a generally natural split into the administrative responsibilities of most bureaucratic police organizations. Third, the focus of contemporary police reforms has disproportionately involved sizeable urban metropolitan areas, where a majority of blacks reside—outside of the South. Additionally, a higher proportion of blacks live inside the largest principal cities in 15 out of the 20 largest metro areas, compared to whites, Hispanics, and other race populations (US Census Bureau 2010). Still, it is worthwhile to be mindful of the fact that the bureaucratic units we outline are only rough guideposts and are not intended to suggest a standardized system of roles and responsibilities that generalize to all police departments.

In this section we review each of the three bureaucratic units in terms of their primary audiences and responsibilities where implicit bias and/or self-threats might influence decision-making. We outline the primary audience at each level to provide a context of the interests to which each level is structurally held accountable and outline the responsibilities for much the same in order to trace the possible ecological vulnerabilities to racially disparate behavior.

Line officers

As others have covered exhaustively elsewhere (Crank and Crank 2014), line officers are often motivated by the pressures of peer social culture. In other words, the principal audience for officers is often other officers. Previous literature has argued, intuitively, that this peer referencing stems from an occupational need to rely on other officers for fundamental physical safety (Farkas and Manning 1997) and that all paramilitary organizations tend to produce these kinds of peer-referent cultures of accountability (Chappell and Lanza-Kaduce 2010; Conti and Doreian 2014; Getty, Worrall, and Morris 2014). For the purposes of understanding the moral ecology of officer's contexts, this means that the culture created by departmental patterns and practices becomes the most important lever for influencing police reform. That institutional culture trumps other factors relevant to reform is not a new insight (Chappell and Lanza-Kaduce 2010; Conti and Doreian 2014; Getty, Worrall and Morris 2014). However, the fact that supervisory reviews and civilian responses to line officers are often listed as far less influential is important for understanding both how officers view their own accountability and, consequently, how they may interpret their own moral standing.

In the context of this audience, there are three major responsibilities wherein officers may find themselves vulnerable to the influences of implicit bias and self-threats. Namely: 1) decisions

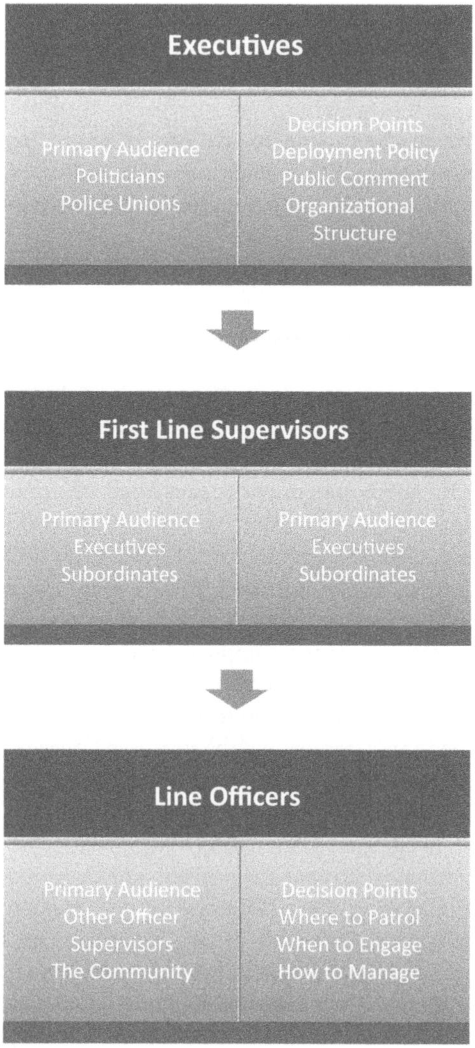

Figure 22.1 Three bureaucratic units in mid-size to large law enforcement agencies.

about where to patrol; 2) decisions about when to contact a resident; and 3) decisions about how to engage a resident once a decision to make contact has been made.

While decisions about deployment are often made by line supervisors or executives and can be further curtailed by budgetary constraints that (in extreme cases) can leave departments, like Detroit's, functionally unable to provide more than reactive policing (Skolnick and Bayley 1988; Scott 1998), officers in major cities frequently find themselves with significant latitude regarding where they patrol and what they are looking to identify (Brown, Novak, and Frank 2000). However, both implicit biases and self-threats can influence decisions about where one searches for criminal behavior. On a basic level, being aware that non-whites in general—and a majority non-white neighborhood in particular—are stereotyped as high in criminal activity is enough to justify disproportionate police scrutiny from some line officers. Even those who may not consciously subscribe to those stereotypes may find themselves affected by them in deciding where to patrol and what to seek. Research shows that simply being aware of these stereotypes can shape decisions (Devine 1989). For example, as we describe above, words and images that are linked to criminality, such as weapons, tend to cause a visual tuning to black people and to result in the recollection of more stereotypically African American features (Eberhardt et al. 2004 on visual tuning). To the extent that officers are making decisions about where they are most likely to encounter criminal activity, these automatic stereotypical associations will all too often come into play.

Similarly, the decision to stop an individual is often made based on a cascading array of observations that research demonstrates have almost undoubtedly been informed by the stereotypical associations of criminality and blackness (Richardson and Goff 2012). As Richardson and Goff explained, if a line officer observes two men—one obviously black, the other racially ambiguous—running from a convenience store after a robbery, the officer is likely both to pay more attention to the unambiguously black suspect (Eberhardt et al. 2004) and to recall the black suspect as the person of greatest interest—whether or not he was the culprit (Richardson and Goff 2012). The risk that the infusion of implicit associations informing other crucial moments in the criminal justice system is present as well. For example, Eberhardt and Goff (2004) found in a study of police officers identifying suspects from a line array that, while officers generally picked the right suspect, to the degree that they "got it wrong" and misidentified the suspect, they tended to pick out more racially stereotypical black suspects.

Recent research demonstrates that these implicit biases may be compounded by concerns among non-whites that they will be seen and treated as criminals. Najdowski (2012) hypothesized that stereotypes about black criminality may trigger stereotype threat in African Americans, who, concerned about confirming the stereotype, engage in self-regulatory efforts (e.g., vigilance to threat-related cues, active monitoring efforts) when interacting with the police. This self-threat has the risk of having the tragically ironic consequence that African Americans may be more likely than whites to behave in ways that police commonly perceive as indicative of deception, increasing the likelihood that innocent African Americans will be misclassified as guilty by police (Najdowski 2012). Najdowski, Bottoms, and Goff (in press) conducted experimental research of this hypothesis, finding black men, though not black women, reported feeling concerned that police officers might judge them unfairly and stereotype them as criminals. In a study of anticipated behavior in the face of a police encounter, they found that African American men were significantly more likely than white men to think they would feel anxious, anticipate they would monitor the situation and their behavior for risk of being stereotyped, and, ironically, behave in ways that police have been shown to perceive as deceptive or suspicious (e.g., Akehurst et al. 1996). This form of stereotype threat, then, produces behaviors that are "objectively" treated as suspicious by officers (Najdowski 2012).

The slippage between noticing, "suspicion," and making decisions about appropriate treatment has been identified in the literature. Stereotype threat during interracial interactions has been found to be broadly depleting (Richeson and Shelton 2013) and to cause both general performance decrements and specifically more harsh punishments among decision-makers (Danzinger, Levav, and Avnaim-Pesso 2011; Goff, Steele, and Davies 2008; Steele and Aronson 1995; Stone 2002; Stone, Lynch, Sjomeling, and Darley 1999). In a recent study, Okonofua and Eberhardt (2015) found that teachers engaged in harsh and biased decisions toward Black children as compared to White children when the children were described as engaging in misconduct a second time though they were treated similarly for the first offense. In a context where officers often know the repeat offenders in the neighborhoods they navigate, the likelihood that officers will 1) choose disproportionately non-White neighborhoods to patrol; 2) disproportionately contact non-Whites in those neighborhoods; and 3) treat non-Whites disproportionately poorly is compounded by the above range of factors.

First line supervisors

The primary audiences for first line supervisors are executives, who evaluate supervisors, and line officers, whose trust it is necessary to maintain in order to be effective (Shockley-Zalabak, Ellis, and Winograd 2000; Tyler and Degoey 1996). The culture of line officers casts a long shadow over the institutional incentives of many levels within the bureaucracy. That said, there is emerging evidence that first line supervisors play a critical role in attenuating the worst instincts of line officers and promoting the best values of the organization. For instance, researchers have found that high quality supervision, or even sufficient numbers of supervisors can reduce the number of justifiable homicides (Brown 1988; Martin 1994; Matulia 1982). The effects of these dual audiences can easily create conditions under which implicit bias and self-threat can leak into behavior.

Evaluations comprise a key component of supervisors' role in the ecology of policing. In light of their evaluation responsibilities, they face three decision points: 1) aggregate evaluations, 2) individual evaluations, and 3) informal evaluations. By aggregate evaluations, we mean accounting for the performance of a district, precinct, or division. This accounting often takes the form of responsibility for crime statistics or departmental areas of emphasis, usually at COMPSTAT-like meetings (Glaser 2015; Henry 2002; Walsh 2001; Weisburd, Mastrofski, Greenspan, and Willis 2004). For those unfamiliar with COMPSTAT and/or its progeny, it is a performance management system based on problem solving that police departments use to reduce crime and achieve other department goals. COMPSTAT is based on four primary tenets: 1. timely and accurate information/intelligence gathering and sharing; 2. rapid deployment of resources; 3. effective tactics; and 4. relentless follow-up (Bureau of Justice Assistance, 2013). Supervisors are held accountable for crime statistics in their command. Regular command-level meetings allow relative increases or decreases in the performance of the rate of officers they manage, and are given crime to be targeted for praise or additional enforcement resources. While COMPSTAT meetings are often not attended by first line supervisors (who usually hold a rank of sergeant), these first line supervisors are often enlisted to compile the numbers and report them to lieutenants, captains, commanders, majors, and/or division chiefs. Consequently, at each level of supervisory middle management, the COMPSTAT system helps to organize professional activity, encouragement, or negative feedback in keeping with that performance.

In certain large urban police departments, the accounting mechanisms become the primary "audience" meaning that supervisors are motivated to manage crime numbers above all other law enforcement outcomes. Because positive police interactions are difficult to measure, this can mean that "getting good numbers" sometimes can trump positive policing. This phenomena is not unique to policing, (Melnyk, Stewart, and Swink 2004; Nel 2011; Steers 1975), however, contrary to other contexts, the numbers reflect arrests—a negative—rather than sales or some other metric that incentivizes positive behavior. Here, the critical metric is wholly detached from positive police behavior.

Importantly, while the seeming objectivity of COMPSTAT and other evidence-based approaches to crime reduction have been heralded by some as a way to militate against racial biases (MacDonald 2003, 2010), the reality can be quite different. That is, rather than providing an explicitly race-neutral tool for engaging criminal elements within a community, COMPSTAT relies on the "symptoms" of crime in order to deploy resources. These numbers necessarily come from community calls for service and police actions—input systems that cannot be treated as if they are free of biases despite the cold, evidence-based ethos of COMPSTAT. In addition to rarely including incentives for positive police behavior toward residents, other aspects of evidence-based policing can trigger biased behavior by supervisors.

For instance, the fact that supervisors must rely on officers to "keep their numbers down" can have the ironic effect of causing supervisors to leverage biased practices in order to increase arrest numbers and drive down categories of crime. Large numbers of low-level drug arrests of people in non-White communities, for example, can fulfill the obligation to show aggressive policing and have had the much-documented effect of criminalizing behavior that in the suburbs is essentially ignored (Beckett 2008; Alexander 2012; Edwards, Bunting, and Garcia 2013; Haroscopos 2005; Corsaro, Hunt, Hipple, and McGarrell 2012).

Similar vulnerability to implicit biases exists when providing feedback to line officers about deployment and patrol patterns. A significant body of research shows that people perceive places as less safe and more apt to contain criminal activity simply because Black people are seen in the space (Bonam 2010). This application of stereotypes of danger and criminality applies to neighborhoods and thus is likely to affect deployment decisions even without empirical support for levels of criminality. In a study that showed white subjects videos of neighborhoods, simply seeing Black (as opposed to White) residents in a neighborhood elicited significantly more negative evaluations of neighborhood conditions—even though the neighborhoods were identical in all respects other than race (Krysan, Couper, Farley, and Forman 2009). Bonam also found that this tendency goes beyond residential neighborhoods to any spaces—business, outdoor leisure, religious, entertainment—as associated with Black or White and in a second study, those spaces considered Black were rated as dangerous or poor (Bonam 2010). To the extent that a larger police presence is linked to a more significant likelihood of higher level of arrests, often for minor activity, a vicious feedback loop emerges. Spaces that are racialized as Black are presumed to contain more criminality, line officer visual attention is tuned to Black people, resulting in higher surveillance and, likely, arrest levels of Black people—and a numerical metric that then supports the stereotypes.

In addition to aggregate evaluations, line supervisors also conduct the individual evaluations of line officers—the routine performance evaluations of line officers that are common in urban police departments. Here supervisory implicit racial bias and self-threat can have a different set of consequences. Performance evaluations are relevant to the racial dynamics of policing more generally in two distinct ways: first, the likelihood that implicit racial bias and self-threat will bleed into supervisors' evaluations of Black and Latino police officers creating a racially skewed internal culture; and second, the metrics that are in use to evaluate line officers even when not applied disparately are likely to slant against police officer behavior that is consistent with justice.

White men remain the norm both as line officers and supervisors, which often has the effect of creating identity salience for female officers and non-White male officers in the eyes of supervisors and colleagues. Supervisors' implicit bias can seep into performance evaluations, particularly when criteria for performance evaluation are subjective (Kang et al. 2012). The standard identity salience that stems from being one of the few in any workplace is likely to be exacerbated in the policing context by the role that race plays in identifying suspects by race and the association of race and criminality. As Crosby, Monin, and Richardson (2008) have identified, people have a tendency to visually attune to members of particular identity groups when potentially offensive remarks are made about that group. In other words, the cross-racial navigation challenges that often accompany "minority" status in the workplace, which are taxing and cognitively depleting, include regular social referencing and negative associations made about one's identity group which then pile on to the depletion (Richeson and Shelton 2003; Richeson, Trawalter, and Shelton 2005; Richeson and Shelton 2007). In addition, the evaluative role for supervisors may well be fraught by their own self-threat if they are concerned that constructive negative feedback will be interpreted as "racist" (Godsil et al. 2014; Cohen, Steele, and Ross 1999).

In the policing contexts, gender and racial workplace dynamics are exacerbated by the volatile nature of the work. Racialized misconduct by other officers, for example, places officers in a position of having to choose between maintaining silence in alliance to their identity as police officers or acting as whistleblowers. And while no one likes whistleblowers generally, women and non-white whistleblowers seem to face particularly harsh derogation (Good, Moss-Racusin, and Sanchez 2012; Rasinski and Czopp 2010), making it exceptionally challenging to observe racial disparities (as an officer is sure to do) and feel supported in addressing them within the organization (as many may wish to do). Taken together, this can create an environment in which non-white officers are paradoxically hypervisible in ways that provoke performance depleting self-threats and invisible in contexts where they need supervisorial support.

As in most workplaces, supervisors perform "informal evaluations" as well as formal performance reviews. These refer to the myriad ways that supervisors subtly affirm and censure behavior daily. These evaluations suffer from the same racialized risks described above, but in addition, because they are constant, generally automatic rather than deliberative, and subtle, may be at even greater risk of perpetuating racialized hierarchies.

While supervisors tend to be less cognitively depleted and under time pressure than line officers, their decision points have the cloak of more objectivity, making it, in some ways, more difficult for them to sense their own complicity in any resulting disparities. The consequences of these processes can be both that police cultures may tend not to encourage non-traditional officers (e.g., blacks, Latinos, women, etc.) and tend not to track/incentivize positive police behaviors. In other words, the chronic contexts of police supervisors are far from ideally situated to promote a just workplace or just police outcomes.

Executives

It is said that being a chief in a large urban setting is like sitting on a three-legged stool. Chiefs must have the support of at least two legs if they are to remain upright. Lose support of two at the same time, and a chief topples. The three legs are: 1) the political class, 2) the police union, and 3) the public. These three audiences vary in importance depending on the chief, but each is always fundamental to the ecology of moral decision-making for each chief (Geller 1985; Rainguet and Dodge 2001).

In their capacity overseeing departments as a whole, chiefs face three critical decision points: 1) deployment, 2) public comment, and 3) organizational priorities. In each category, the decisions tend to be far more deliberative and well informed than decisions at lower levels can be. However, each also often requires chiefs to explain—or justify—the behaviors of the department. This may trigger self-threats with regard to self-efficacy and/or fears of being perceived as racist. But, perhaps more importantly, since most chiefs are former officers and supervisors, it is likely that the areas of bias that have seeped in to the lower-tier bureaucracies will be embedded in thought processes and unexamined by reflective distance. Consequently, deployment patterns, public statements, and organizational priorities can miss the science of bias and the ways it has rendered line officers vulnerable. Importantly, this may also lead to communities feeling that chiefs are not able to speak about the reality of their officers' behavior. Ironically, the converse is also true. If communities feel that a chief can speak with fidelity to his experience, the difficulty detecting implicit bias and self-threats can make officers—and consequently, unions—feel that a chief has betrayed them. We have recently seen classic examples of this in New York, St. Louis County, and Baltimore (Parascandola 2015; Graham 2015; Swain 2014).

In addition to the above problems posed by dent of a chief police executive's potential worldview, there are also chronic situations surrounding police chief executive decision points that are also likely to leave them vulnerable to implicit biases and self-threats. For instance, no chief can keep her job long if her response to a pattern of resident calls for services is that "we are not responding to that community's calls because they are probably racist." That is, deployment of police services is not—and cannot be—immune to the biases of the communities they serve. Consequently, cultural conflict in neighborhoods experiencing demographic transition is often compounded by police deployments that are (necessarily) responsive to community biases. This can be compounded, again, by political pressure to remedy these conflicts if elected officials feel their constituent supporters require a public stance.

In the context of public statements, self-threats can plague a chief. In the past year, we have seen several high-profile racially charged incidents and several police chiefs make statements that have rankled the public, police unions, and elected officials. Some were influenced no doubt by the fact that the undercurrent of these incidents has been that police character is at issue—that police chiefs and officers are racist. The stereotype of police racism and the resultant concern with appearing racist is a common theme in police research (Goff 2013; Tyler and Huo 2002). And a significant psychological literature demonstrates that such concerns lead to interpersonal discomfort (Richeson and Shelton 2003), interpersonal distancing (Goff, Steele, and Davies 2008), and out-group antipathy (Vorauer, Main, and O'Connell 1998). Similar experiences can also lead to increased verbal disfluencies and non-verbal behaviors that tend to provoke the perception of guilt, untrustworthiness, or racial hostility (Richeson and Shelton 2003; Najdowski, Bottoms, and Goff 2015; Word, Zanna, and Cooper 1974).

Finally, when imagining a set of organizational priorities for police departments, chiefs frequently encounter the specter of past conflicts with non-white communities. For both internally promoted chiefs and chiefs who were hired from outside the organization, this is often a point of both emphasis and vulnerability. The vulnerability often comes for two reasons: first, because in the culture of most police departments, individuals who are arrested are not seen as part of the community that must be placated—a view that many community members share (Gunnison and Helfgott 2011; Hirschfield and Piquero 2010; Leverentz 2011; Ross 2000), and it is often threatening to one's self-concept to take responsibility for others' past or current moral failings (Aronson 1999). Both situational threats leave police executives vulnerable to a "gut resistance" to prioritizing deep organizational change necessary to address previous wrongs (Mentel 2012). This structural tendency can thus lead to an organizational "blindspot" and the need for deeper racial reconciliation, a point recently recognized by a US Department of Justice Initiative: The National Initiative for Building Trust and Justice (Department of Justice Office of Public Affairs 2014) that relies, in part, on reconciliation processes to promote community/police collaboration.

Conclusion

The multiple decision points at which implicit bias and self-threat can manifest reveal how an organization can be set up to appear racially neutral while leaving itself vulnerable to human psychological frailties. A department that is responsive to community concerns may still fall short of providing effective service that is free of racially biased behavior. In the above sections, we have reviewed a few of the ways that this is most likely to happen at three bureaucratic levels of police administration.

At the line officer level, decisions about where, when, and how to engage communities are each susceptible to implicit biases and self-threats. Moreover, the chronic contexts of line officers—the need to work long shifts, multi-task, navigate abuse language directed toward them, and make quick decisions about life and liberty—are perfectly designed to render officers even more vulnerable to the biases that are so well rehearsed by our minds.

Police supervisors are positioned to be less vulnerable to time constraints but likely more so to the vagaries of ostensibly objective numbers and the ways in which they organize both the outcomes of line officers and the supervisors themselves. Armed with metrics that track crime and violence, but not positive engagement and behaviors that enhance the public's cooperation with police, supervisors are often set up poorly to evaluate their staff fairly or sufficiently encourage equitable behavior.

Finally, police executives are situated among three constituencies: politicos, unions, and the public. Each presents a unique set of decision-making challenges. But the decision points chronically encountered by police executives are also fraught with opportunities for implicit biases and self-threats to interfere with chiefs' genuine desire to promote a fair workplace and a just police force.

Taken together, we hope that the organizational roadmap presented in this chapter can help those working to enhance racial justice within policing to understand the different ways in which the mind sciences can be leveraged in the pursuit of that goal at each level of police bureaucracy. Additionally, this chapter can be used as a roadmap for advocates and researchers who seek to broaden the exceptionally thin evidence base around police justice (Goff 2013; Goff and Kahn 2012; Goff et al. 2010), communicate all the way down the hierarchy, and provide opportunities to leverage existing audiences to provide support for reforms in these areas. For without a map of the ways police departments make decisions, how can we understand the moral ecology that leads to the decisions they make?

Note

1 While the vast majority of police departments in the United States have 25 or fewer officers (Interim Report of the President's Task Force on 21st Century Policing, 2015) the majority of unrest and protest about racial disparities in policing have taken place in or near major urban metropolitan areas. Consequently, we focus on these more thoroughly bureaucratized departments in order to provide context for the departments that provide public safety to the majority of traditionally vulnerable non-white communities. The analysis provided, however, can be extended to smaller departments by understanding that levels of bureaucracy articulated in this chapter may be collapsed.

Bibliography

Akehurst, L., Köhnken, G., Vrij, A. and Bull, R. (1996) 'Lay persons' and police officers' beliefs regarding deceptive behaviour', *Applied Cognitive Psychology*, 10(6): 461–71.

Alexander, M. (2012) *The New Jim Crow: Mass Incarceration in the Age of Colorblindness*. New York, NY: The New Press.

Anderson, J.R. (1983) 'A spreading activation theory of memory', *Journal of Verbal Learning and Verbal Behavior*, 22(3): 261–95. doi:10.1016/S0022-5371(83)90201-3.

Apfelbaum, E.P., Norton, M.I. and Sommers, S.R. (2012) 'Racial color blindness emergence, practice, and implications', *Directions in Psychological Science*, 21(3): 205–209.

Apfelbaum, E.P., Pauker, K., Ambady, N., Sommers, S.R. and Norton, M.I. (2008) 'Learning (not) to talk about race: when older children underperform in social categorization', *Developmental Psychology*, 44(5): 1513–18.

Apfelbaum, E.P., Pauker, K., Sommers, S.R. and Ambady, N. (2010) 'In blind pursuit of racial equality?', *Psychological Science*, 21(11): 1587–92.

Apfelbaum, E P. and Sommers, S.R. (2009) 'Liberating effects of losing executive control when regulatory strategies turn maladaptive', *Psychological Science*, 20(2): 139–43.

Aronson, E. (1999) 'Dissonance, hypocrisy, and the self-concept', In Aronson, E. (Ed.), *Readings about the Social Animal*, New York, NY: MacMillan pp. 219–236.

Avenanti, A., Sirigu, A. and Aglioti, S.M. (2010) 'Racial bias reduces empathic sensorimotor resonance with other-race pain', *Current Biology*, 20(11): 1018–22.
Beckett, K. (2008) 'Race and drug law enforcement in Seattle', Report prepared for the ACLU Drug Law Reform Project and the Defender Association. Retrieved on July 10, 2015, from https://www.aclu.org/files/assets/race20and20drug20law20enforcement20in20seattle_20081.pdf.
Bobo, L. (2001) 'Racial attitudes and relations at the close of the twentieth century', *America Becoming: Racial Trends and Their Consequences*, 1: 264–301.
Bonam, C.M., Eberhardt, J. L., Markus, H., & Ross, L. (2010) 'Devaluing black space: Black locations as targets of housing and environmental discrimination', (dDoctoral dissertation). Retrieved from Stanford Digital Repository. (gz102cb9731).
Bosson, J.K. and Vandello, J.A. (2011) 'Precarious manhood and its links to action and aggression', *Current Directions in Psychological Science*, 20(2): 82–86.
Brewer, M.B. (1999) 'The psychology of prejudice: ingroup love or outgroup hate?', *Journal of Social Issues*, 55: 429–44.
Brown, M.K. (1988) *Working the Street: Police Discretion and the Dilemmas of Reform*, New York, NY: Russell Sage Foundation.
Brown, R., Novak, K. and Frank, J. (2000) 'Identifying variation in police behavior between juveniles and adults', *Journal of Criminal Justice*, 27: 200–208.
Bureau of Justice Assistance & Police Executive Research Forum. (2013) 'Compstat: its origins, evolution, and future in law enforcement agencies', retrieved on July 10, 2015, from http://www.policeforum.org/assets/docs/Free_Online_Documents/Compstat/compstat%20%20its%20origins%20evolution%20and%20future%20in%20law%20enforcement%20agencies%202013.pdf.
Bursik, Jr. R.J. and Grasmick, H.G. (1993) 'Economic deprivation and neighborhood crime rates, 1960–1980', *Law & Soc'y Rev.*, 27: 263.
Bursik, Jr. R.J. and Webb, J. (1982) 'Community change and patterns of delinquency', *American Journal of Sociology*, 24–42.
Butz, D.A. and Plant, E.A. (2009) 'Prejudice control and interracial relations: the role of motivation to respond without prejudice', *Journal of Personality*, 77(5): 1311–42.
Butz, D.A. and Plant, E.A. (2011) 'Approaching versus avoiding intergroup contact: the role of expectancies and motivation', in *Moving Beyond Prejudice Reduction: Pathways to Positive Intergroup Relations,* American Psychological Association. pp. 81–98
Campbell, A., Berk, R.A. and Fyfe, J.J. (1998) 'Deployment of violence: The Los Angeles Police Department's use of dogs', *Evaluation Review*, 22(4): 535–61.
Carney, R.N. and Levin, J.R. (2003) 'Promoting higher-order learning benefits by building lower-order mnemonic connections', *Applied Cognitive Psychology*, 17(5): 563–75.
Chappell, A.T. and Lanza-Kaduce, L. (2010) 'Police academy socialization: understanding the lessons learned in a paramilitary-bureaucratic organization', *Journal of Contemporary Ethnography*, 39(2): 187–214.
Cohen, G.L., Steele, C.M. and Ross, L.D. (1999) 'The mentor's dilemma: providing critical feedback across the racial divide', *Personality and Social Psychology Bulletin*, 25(10): 1302–18.
Conti, N. and Doreian, P. (2014) 'From here on out, we're all blue: interaction order, social infrastructure, and race in police socialization', *Police Quarterly*, 17(4): 414–47.
Correll, J., Hudson, S.M., Guillermo, S. and Ma, D.S. (2014) 'The police officer's dilemma: a decade of research on racial bias in the decision to shoot', *Social and Personality Psychology Compass*, 8(5): 201–13.
Correll, J., Park, B., Judd, C.M. and Wittenbrink, B. (2002) 'The police officer's dilemma: using ethnicity to disambiguate potentially threatening individuals', *Journal of Personality and Social Psychology*, 83(6): 1314.
Correll, J., Park, B., Judd, C.M., Wittenbrink, B., Sadler, M.S. and Keesee, T. (2007) 'Across the thin blue line: police officers and racial bias in the decision to shoot', *Journal of Personality and Social Psychology*, 92(6): 1006.
Correll, J., Urland, G.R. and Ito, T.A. (2006) 'Event-related potentials and the decision to shoot: The role of threat perception and cognitive control', *Journal of Experimental Social Psychology*, 42(1): 120–28.
Corsaro, N., Hunt, E.D., Hipple, N.K. and McGarrell, E.F. (2012) 'The impact of drug market pulling levers policing on neighborhood violence', *Criminology & Public Policy*, 11(2): 167–99.
Cortes, B.P., Demoulin, S., Rodriguez, R.T., Rodriguez, A.P. and Leyens, J.P. (2005) 'Infrahumanization or familiarity? Attribution of uniquely human emotions to the self, the ingroup, and the outgroup', *Personality and Social Psychology Bulletin*, 31(2): 243–53.
Crank, J. and Crank, J.P. (2014) *Understanding Police Culture*, New York, NY: Routledge.

Crandall, C.S., Eshleman, A. and O'Brien, L. (2002) 'Social norms and the expression and suppression of prejudice: The struggle for internalization', *Journal of Personality and Social Psychology*, 82(3): 359–78. http://dx.doi.org/10.1037/0022-3514.82.3.359.

Crocker J., Major B., Steele C. (1998) Social stigma. In Gilbert D., Fiske S.T., Lindzey G. (Eds.), *The handbook of social psychology*, New York, NY: McGraw-Hill pp. 504–53.

Crosby, J.R., Monin, B. and Richardson, D. (2008) 'Where do we look during potentially offensive behavior?', *Psychological Science*, 19(3): 226–228.

Cuddy, A.J., Fiske, S.T. and Glick, P. (2007) 'The BIAS map: behaviors from intergroup affect and stereotypes', *Journal of Personality and Social Psychology*, 92(4): 631.

Danziger, S., Levav, J. and Avnaim-Pesso, L. (2011) 'Extraneous factors in judicial decisions', *Proceedings of the National Academy of Sciences*, 108(17): 6889–92.

Dasgupta, N. (2009) Mechanisms underlying the malleability of implicit prejudice and stereotypes. In Nelson, T.D. (Ed.), *Handbook of Prejudice, Stereotyping, and Discrimination*, New York, NY: Psychology Press p. 267–84.

Departmentof Justice, Office of Public Affairs. (2014, September 18) 'Justice department announces national effort to build trust between law enforcement and the communities they serve' [Press release]. Retrieved from https://www.justice.gov/opa/pr/justice-department-announces-national-effort-build-trust-between-law-enforcement-and

Demoulin, S., Leyens, J.P., Paladino, M.P., Rodriguez-Torres, R., Rodriguez-Perez, A. and Dovidio, J. (2004) 'Dimensions of "uniquely" and "non-uniquely" human emotions', *Cognition and Emotion*, 18(1): 71–96.

Devine, P.G. (1989) 'Stereotypes and prejudice: their automatic and controlled components', *Journal of Personality and Social Psychology*, 56(1): 5.

Devine, P.G., Plant, E.A., Amodio, D.M., Harmon-Jones, E. and Vance, S.L. (2002) 'The regulation of explicit and implicit race bias: the role of motivations to respond without prejudice', *Journal of Personality and Social Psychology*, 82(5): 835.

Dovidio, J.F., Piliavin, J.A., Schroeder, D.A. and Penner, L. (2006) *The Social Psychology of Prosocial Behavior*, Mahwah, NJ: Lawrence Erlbaum Associates Publishers.

Duncan, B.L. (1976) 'Differential social perception and attribution of intergroup violence: testing the lower limits of stereotyping of blacks', *Journal of Personality and Social Psychology*, 34(4): 590.

Eagly, A.H. and Chaiken, S. (1993) *The Psychology of Attitudes*, San Diego, CA: Harcourt Brace Jovanovich College Publishers.

Eberhardt, J.L., Davies, P.G., Purdie-Vaughns, V.J. and Johnson, S.L. (2006) 'Looking deathworthy perceived stereotypicality of black defendants predicts capital-sentencing outcomes', *Psychological Science*, 17(5): 383–86.

Eberhardt, J.L., Goff, P.A., Purdie-Vaughns, V.J. and Davies, P.G. (2004) 'Seeing black: race, crime, and visual processing', *Journal of Personality and Social Psychology*, 87(6): 876.

Edwards, E., Bunting, W. and Garcia, L. (2013) *The War on Marijuana in Black and White*, New York, NY: American Civil Liberties Union.

Farkas, M.A. and Manning, P.K. (1997) 'The occupational culture of corrections and police officers', *Journal of Crime and Justice*, 20(2): 51–68.

FAQs Project Implicit. (2015, July 10). Retrieved from https://implicit.harvard.edu/implicit/demo/background/faqs.html#faq22.

Fein, S. and Spencer, S.J. (1997) 'Prejudice as self-image maintenance: affirming the self through derogating others', *Journal of Personality and Social Psychology*, 73(1): 31.

Gambino, L. and Laughlin, O. (2015, February 15) 'Three years after Trayvon Martin, a new civil rights movement grows in strength', *The Guardian*. Retrieved from http://www.theguardian.com/us-news/2015/feb/27/trayvon-martin-new-civil-rights-movement-grows-strength.

Gaunt, R., Leyens, J. and Demoulin, S. (2002) 'Intergroup relations and the attribution of emotions: control over memory for secondary emotions associated with the ingroup and the outgroup', *Journal of Experimental Social Psychology*, 38(5): 508–14.

Geller, W.A. (ed.) (1985) *Police Leadership in America: Crisis and Opportunity*, New York, NY: American Bar Foundation.

Getty, R.M., Worrall, J.L. and Morris, R.G. (2014) 'How far from the tree does the apple fall? Field training officers, their trainees, and allegations of misconduct', *Crime & Delinquency*, 0011128714545829.

Giles, H., Coupland, J. and Coupland, N. (1991) *Contexts of Accommodation: Developments in Applied Sociolinguistics*, Cambridge: Cambridge University Press.

Glaser, J. (2014) *Suspect Race: Causes and Consequences of Racial Profiling*, New York, NY: Oxford University Press.

Godsil, R.D. and Freeman, J.S. (2015) 'Race, ethnicity, and place identity: implicit bias and competing belief systems', *Hawaii L. Rev.*, 37: 313–535.

Godsil, R.D., Tropp, L.R., Goff, P.A., & Powell, J.A. (2014, November) *The Science of Equality, Vol. 1: Addressing Implicit Bias, Racial Anxiety, and Stereotype Threat in Education and Healthcare.* New York, NY: Retrieved from: http://perception.org/app/uploads/2014/11/Science-of-Equality-111214_web.pdf

Goff, P.A. (2013) 'A measure of justice: what policing racial bias research reveals', In F.C. Harris and R.C. Lieberman (eds.) *Beyond Discrimination: Racial inequality in a Postracist Era*, New York, NY: Russell Sage Press, pp. 157–85.

Goff, P.A., Di Leone, B.A.L. and Kahn, K.B. (2012) 'Racism leads to pushups: how racial discrimination threatens subordinate men's masculinity', *Journal of Experimental Social Psychology*, 5: 1111–16.

Goff, P.A., Eberhardt, J.L., Williams, M.J. and Jackson, M.C. (2008) 'Not yet human: implicit knowledge, historical dehumanization, and contemporary consequences', *Journal of Personality and Social Psychology*, 94(2): 292.

Goff, P.A., Epstein, L.M., Mentovich, A. and Reddy, K.S. (2013) 'Illegitimacy is dangerous: how authorities experience and react to illegitimacy', *Psychology*, 4(3A): 340–44.

Goff, P.A., Epstein, L.M. and Reddy, K.S. (2013) 'Crossing the line of legitimacy: the impact of cross-deputization policy on crime-reporting', *Psychology, Public Policy, and Law*, 19(2): 250–58.

Goff, P.A., Jackson, M.C., Di Leone, B.A.L., Culotta, C.M. and DiTomasso, N.A. (2014) 'The essence of innocence: consequences of dehumanizing black children', *Journal of Personality and Social Psychology*, 106(4): 52.

Goff, P.A. and Kahn, K.B. (2012) 'Racial bias in policing: why we know less than we should', *Social Issues and Policy Review*, 6: 175–207.

Goff, P.A., Steele, C.M. and Davies, P.G. (2008) 'The space between us: stereotype threat and distance in interracial contexts', *Journal of Personality and Social Psychology*, 94: 91–107.

Goff, P.A., Thomas, M.A. and Jackson, M.C. (2008) '"Ain't I a woman?": towards an intersectional approach to person perception and group-based harms', *Sex Roles*, 59: 392–403. [Part of the special issue of Sex Roles honored with the Association for Women in Psychology Distinguished Publication Award, 2009].

Goff, P.A., Tyler, T.R., Sidanius, J., Dovidio, J. F., Deaux, K., Sommers, S.R., Keesee, T.L., Baldwin, M., Biernat, M., Beletsky, L., Brooke, J., Eberhardt, J.L., Epstein, L.M., Smiedt, M.G., Glaser, J., Goff, E.L., Hagan, J., Harris, D., Jackson, M.C., Jones-Brown, D., Kahn, K.B., Kliengklom, T.J., Land, K., Moon, S.H., Motto, M., Najdowski, C., Plaut, V., Sesko, A., Smith, P., Sturm, S., Thomas, E. and Zatz, M. (2010) 'The contract for policing justice', A report published by the Consortium for Police Leadership in Equity at the Salt Lake City Police Department.

Good, J.J., Moss-Racusin, C.A. and Sanchez, D.T. (2012) 'When do we confront? Perceptions of costs and benefits predict confronting discrimination on behalf of the self and others', *Psychology of Women Quarterly*, 36(2): 210–26.

Graham D.A. (2015, July 8) 'Baltimore's Mayor fires her police commissioner', *The Atlantic.*, Retrieved on 9 July 2015, from http://www.theatlantic.com/politics/archive/2015/07/the-defenestration-of-anthony-batts/398042/.

Graham, S. and Lowery, B.S. (2004) 'Priming unconscious racial stereotypes about adolescent offenders', *Law and Human Behavior*, 28(5): 483.

Greenwald, A.G., McGhee, D.E. and Schwartz, J.L. (1998) 'Measuring individual differences in implicit cognition: the implicit association test', *Journal of Personality and Social Psychology*, 74(6): 1464.

Gunnison, E. and Helfgott, J.B. (2011) 'Factors that hinder offender reentry success: a view from community corrections officers', *International Journal of Offender Therapy and Comparative Criminology*, 55(2): 287–304.

Harocopos, A. and Hough, A. (2005) *Drug Dealing in Open-Air Markets.* U.S. Department of Justice Office of Community Oriented Policing Services. Retrieved from: http://ric-zai-inc.com/Publications/cops-p067-pub.pdf

Hirschfield, P.J. and Piquero, A.R. (2010) 'Normalization and legitimation: modeling stigmatizing attitudes toward ex-offenders', *Criminology*, 48(1): 27–55.

Hugenberg, K. and Bodenhausen, G.V. (2003) 'Facing prejudice implicit prejudice and the perception of facial threat', *Psychological Science*, 14(6): 640–43.

Hochbein, K. (2014, November 11) 'A new language for racial inequality', retrieved from http://www1.lehigh.edu/news/new-language-racial-inequality#sthash.RtbitlGj.dpuf.

Henry, V.E. (2002) *The COMPSTAT Paradigm: Management Accountability in Policing, Business, and the Public Sector*, Flushing, NY: Looseleaf Law Publications.

Herbert, S. (1998) 'Police subculture reconsidered', *Criminology*, 36(2): 343–70.

Inzlicht, M. and Ben-Zeev, T. (2000) 'A threatening intellectual environment: why females are susceptible to experiencing problem-solving deficits in the presence of males', *Psychological Science*, 11(5): 365–71.

Ito, T., Friedman, N., Bartholow, B., Correll, J., Loersch, C., Altamirano, L. and Miyake, A. (2015) 'Toward a comprehensive understanding of executive cognitive function in implicit racial bias', *Journal of Personality and Social Psychology*, 108(2): 187–218.

Kane, R.J. (2002) 'The social ecology of police misconduct', *Criminology*, 40: 867.

Kang, J., Bennett, M.W., Carbado, D.W., Casey, P., Dasgupta, N., Faigman, D.L., ... and Mnookin, J. (2012) 'Implicit bias in the courtroom', *UCLA Law Review*, 59(5).

Kasarda, J.D. and Janowitz, M. (1974) 'Community attachment in mass society', *American Sociological Review*, 328–39.

Klinger, D.A. (1997) 'Negotiating order in patrol work: an ecological theory of police response to deviance', *Criminology*, 35: 277–306.

Krysan, M., Couper, M.P., Farley, R. and Forman, T. (2009) 'Does race matter in neighborhood preferences? Results from a video experiment', *AJS; American Journal of Sociology*, 115(2): 527.

Leyens, J.P., Cortes, B., Demoulin, S., Dovidio, J.F., Fiske, S.T., Gaunt, R., ... and Vaes, J. (2003) 'Emotional prejudice, essentialism, and nationalism: the 2002 Tajfel lecture', *European Journal of Social Psychology*, 33(6): 703–17.

Leyens, J.P., Rodriguez-Perez, A., Rodriguez-Torres, R., Gaunt, R., Paladino, M.P., Vaes, J. and Demoulin, S. (2001) 'Psychological essentialism and the differential attribution of uniquely human emotions to ingroups and outgroups', *European Journal of Social Psychology*, 31(4): 395–411.

Jackson, P.I. (1989) *Minority Group Threat, Crime, and Policing: Social Context and Social Control*, New York, NY: Praeger Publishers.

Jacobs, D. and O'Brien, R. (1998) 'The determinants of deadly force: a structural analysis of police violence', *American Journal of Sociology*, 103: 837–62.

Leverentz, A. (2011) 'Neighborhood context of attitudes toward crime and reentry', *Punishment & Society*, 13(1): 64–92.

MacDonald, H. (2003) *Are Cops Racist: How the War Against the Police Harms Black Americans*. Chicago, IL: Ivan R. Dee.

MacDonald, H. (2010, January 4) 'A crime theory demolished', *Wall Street Journal*. Retrieved on 7 July 2015 from http://www.wsj.com/articles/SB10001424052748703580904574638024055735590.

Martin, S.E. (1994) '"Outsider within" the station house: the impact of race and gender on black women police', *Social Problems-New York*, 41: 383.

Matulia, K.J. (1982) 'A balance of forces: executive summary' (Vol. 74, No. 5), US Department of Justice, National Institute of Justice.

McConnell, A.R. and Leibold, J.M. (2001) 'Relations among the Implicit Association Test, discriminatory behavior, and explicit measures of racial attitudes', *Journal of Experimental Social Psychology*, 37(5): 435–42.

Melnyk, S.A., Stewart, D.M. and Swink, M. (2004) 'Metrics and performance measurement in operations management: dealing with the metrics maze', *Journal of Operations Management*, 22(3): 209–18.

Mendoza, S.A., Gollwitzer, P.M. and Amodio, D.M. (2010) 'Reducing the expression of implicit stereotypes: reflexive control through implementation intentions', *Personality and Social Psychology Bulletin*, 36(4): 512–23.

Mentel, Z. and the US Department of Justice Office of Community Oriented Policing Services. (2012) 'Racial reconciliation, truth-telling, and police legitimacy', retrieved from http://trustandjustice.org/resources/guide/racial-reconciliation-truth-telling.

Monteith, M.J., Lybarger, J.E. and Woodcock, A. (2009) 'Schooling the cognitive monster: the role of motivation in the regulation and control of prejudice', *Social and Personality Psychology Compass*, 3(3): 211–26.

Najdowski, C.J. (2012) 'Stereotype threat in police encounters: why African Americans are at risk of being targeted as suspects', Doctoral dissertation, University of Texas at El Paso.

Najdowski, C.J., Bottoms, B.L. and Goff, P.A. (2015) 'Stereotype threat and racial differences in citizens' experiences of police encounters'. *Law and Human Behavior*, 39(5): 463–77.

Nel, P.S. (2011) *Human Resources Management*, Oxford: Oxford University Press.

Nosek, B.A., Smyth, F.L., Hansen, J.J., Devos, T., Lindner, N.M., Ranganath, K.A., ... and Banaji, M.R. (2007) 'Pervasiveness and correlates of implicit attitudes and stereotypes', *European Review of Social Psychology*, 18(1): 36–88.

Okonofua, J.A. and Eberhardt, J.L. (2015) 'Two strikes race and the disciplining of young students', *Psychological Science*, 26(5): 617–24.

Paladino, M.P., Vaes, J., Demoulin, S. and Leyens, J.P. (2004) 'Emotional infra-humanization in intergroup relations: the role of national identification in the attribution of primary and secondary emotions to Italians and Germans', *Cahiers De Psychologie Cognitive/Current Psychology of Cognition*, 22(4–5): 519–36.

Pager, D., Western, B. and Bonikowski, B. (2009) 'Discrimination in a low-wage labor market a field experiment', *American Sociological Review*, 74(5): 777–99.

Parascandola, R., Moore, T., Fermino, J. and Siemaszko, C. (2015, 8 January) 'Bratton, NYPD union bosses fail to resolve differences with City Hall during meeting without Bill de Blasio,' *New York City News*, retrieved on 9 July 2015, from http://www.nydailynews.com/new-york/bratton-nypd-union-bosses-meet-work-slowdown-article-1.2069051.

Payne, B.K., Lambert, A.J. and Jacoby, L.L. (2002) 'Best laid plans: effects of goals on accessibility bias and cognitive control in race-based misperceptions of weapons', *Journal of Experimental Social Psychology*, 38(4): 384–96.

Payne, B.K., Shimizu, Y. and Jacoby, L.L. (2005). 'Mental control and visual illusions: toward explaining race-biased weapon misidentifications', *Journal of Experimental Social Psychology*, 41(1): 36–47.

Plant, E.A. and Butz, D.A. (2006) 'The causes and consequences of an avoidance-focus for interracial interactions', *Personality and Social Psychology Bulletin*, 32(6): 833–46.

Plant, E.A. and Devine, P.G. (2003) 'The antecedents and implications of interracial anxiety', *Personality and Social Psychology Bulletin*, 29(6): 790–801.

Plaut, V.C. (2010) 'Diversity science: why and how difference makes a difference', *Psychological Inquiry*, 21(2): 77–99.

President's Task Force on 21st Century Policing. (2015) *Interim Report of the President's Task Force on 21st Century Policing*, Washington, DC: Office of Community Oriented Policing Services.

Rainguet, F.W. and Dodge, M. (2001) 'The problems of police chiefs: an examination of the issues in tenure and turnover', *Police Quarterly*, 4(3): 268–88.

Rasinski, H.M. and Czopp, A.M. (2010) 'The effect of target status on witnesses' reactions to confrontations of bias', *Basic and Applied Social Psychology*, 32(1): 8–16.

Richardson, L.S. and Goff, P.A. (2012) 'Self-defense and the suspicion heuristic', *Iowa Law Review*, 98: 293–336.

Richardson, L.S. and Goff, P.A. (2015) 'Interrogating racial violence', *Ohio State Journal of Criminal Law*, 12: 114–52.

Richeson, J.A. and Shelton, J.N. (2003) 'When prejudice does not pay: effects of interracial contact on executive function', *Psychological Science*, 14(3): 287–90.

Richeson, J.A. and Shelton, J.N. (2007) 'Negotiating interracial interactions costs, consequences, and possibilities', *Current Directions in Psychological Science*, 16(6): 316–20.

Richeson, J.A., Trawalter, S. and Shelton, J.N. (2005) 'African Americans' implicit racial attitudes and the depletion of executive function after interracial interactions', *Social Cognition*, 23(4): 336–52.

Riek, B.M., Mania, E.W. and Gaertner, S.L. (2006) 'Intergroup threat and outgroup attitudes: a meta-analytic review', *Personality and Social Psychology Review*, 10(4): 336–53.

Ross, D.L. (2000) 'Emerging trends in police failure to train liability', *Policing: An International Journal of Police Strategies and Management*, 23(2): 169–93.

Rudman, L.A., Dohn, M.C. and Fairchild, K. (2007) 'Implicit self-esteem compensation: automatic threat defense', *Journal of Personality and Social Psychology*, 93(5): 798.

Sampson, R.J. and Groves, W.B. (1989) 'Community structure and crime: Testing social-disorganization theory', *American Journal of Sociology*, 774–802.

Scott, J. (1998) '"Performance culture": the return of reactive policing', *Policing and Society: An International Journal*, 8(3): 269–88.

Shockley-Zalabak, P., Ellis, K. and Winograd, G. (2000) 'Organizational trust: What it means, why it matters', *Organization Development Journal*, 18(4): 35.

Sidanius, J., Levin, S. and Pratto, F. (1996) 'Consensual social dominance orientation and its correlates within the hierarchical structure of American society', *International Journal of Intercultural Relations*, 20(3): 385–408.

Skolnick, J. and Bayley, D. (1988) 'Theme and variation in community policing', *Crime and Justice*, 10: 1–37.

Steele, C.M. and Aronson, J. (1995) 'Stereotype threat and the intellectual test performance of African Americans', *Journal of Personality and Social Psychology*, 69(5): 797–811.

Steers, R.M. (1975) 'Problems in the measurement of organizational effectiveness', *Administrative Science Quarterly*, 546–58.

Swain, J. (2014, November 17) 'St. Louis police chief says only criminals were teargassed at Ferguson protests', *The Guardian* retrieved on July 8, 2015 from http://www.theguardian.com/us-news/2014/nov/17/st-louis-police-chief-denies-teargas-rubber-bullets-ferguson.

Swarts, P. (2015, January 13) 'Police need better training and community relations, presidential task force is told', *The Washington Times*, retrieved from http://www.washingtontimes.com/news/2015/jan/13/police-brutality-solutions-are-training-community-/?page=all.

Tajfel, H. and Forgas, J.P. (1981) 'Social categorisation: cognitions, values and groups', in J.P. Forgas (ed.) *Social Cognition*, New York, NY: Academic Press.

Trawalter S., Hoffman, K.M. and Waytz, A. (2012) 'Racial bias in perceptions of others' pain', *PLoS ONE*, 7(11): e48546. doi:10.1371/journal.pone.0048546.

Trawalter, S., Todd, A.R., Baird, A.A. and Richeson, J.A. (2008) 'Attending to threat: race-based patterns of selective attention', *Journal of Experimental Social Psychology*, 44(5): 1322–27.

Tropp, L.R. (2003) 'The psychological impact of prejudice: implications for intergroup contact', *Group Processes & Intergroup Relations*, 6(2): 131–49.

Tropp, L.R. and Molina, L. (2012) 'Intergroup processes: from prejudice to positive relations between groups', in In Deaux, K. & Snyder, M. (Eds.), *Oxford Handbook of Personality and Social Psychology*. Oxford: Oxford University Press. pp. 545–70.

Tyler, T.R. and Degoey, P. (1996) Trust in organizational authorities: The influence of motive attributions on willingness to accept decisions. In Kramer, R.M., & Tyler, T.R. (Eds.) *Trust in Organizations: Frontiers of Theory and Research*. New York, NY: SAGE Publications pp. 331–56.

Tyler, T.R. and Huo, Y.J. (2002) Trust in organizations. *Trust in Organizations: Frontiers of Theory and Research*. New York, NY: SAGE Publications pp. 16–38.

U.S. Census Bureau. (2010) 'The Black population: 2010', retrieved July 10, 2015, from https://www.census.gov/prod/cen2010/briefs/c2010br-06.pdf.

Uhlmann, E.L. and Cohen, G.L. (2007) '"I think it, therefore it's true": effects of self-perceived objectivity on hiring discrimination', *Organizational Behavior and Human Decision Processes*, 104(2): 207–23.

Vaes, J., Paladino, M.P., Castelli, L., Leyens, J.P. and Giovanazzi, A. (2003) 'On the behavioral consequences of infrahumanization: the implicit role of uniquely human emotions in intergroup relations', *Journal of Personality and Social Psychology*, 85(6): 1016.

Vaes, J., Paladino, M.P. and Leyens, J.P. (2006) 'Priming uniquely human emotions and the in-group (but not the out-group) activates humanity concepts', *European Journal of Social Psychology*, 36(2): 169–81.

Vorauer, J.D. and Kumhyr, S.M. (2001) 'Is this about you or me? Self-versus other-directed judgments and feelings in response to intergroup interaction', *Personality and Social Psychology Bulletin*, 27(6): 706–19. doi: 10.1177/0146167201276006.

Vorauer, J.D., Main, K.J. and O'Connell, G.B. (1998) 'How do individuals expect to be viewed by members of lower status groups? Content and implications of meta-stereotypes', *Journal of Personality and Social Psychology*, 75(4): 917–37. http://dx.doi.org/10.1037/0022-3514.75.4.917.

Walsh, W. (2001) 'Compstat: an analysis of an emerging police paradigm'. *Policing: An International Journal of Police Strategies and Management*, 24(3): 347–63.

Weisburd, D., Mastrofski, S.D., Greenspan, R. and Willis, J.J. (2004) *The Growth of Compstat in American Policing*, Washington, DC: Police Foundation.

Willer, R., Rogalin, C.L., Conlon, B. and Wojnowicz, M.T. (2013) 'Overdoing gender: a test of the masculine overcompensation thesis', *American Journal of Sociology*, 118(4): 980–1022.

Word, C.O., Zanna, M.P. and Cooper, J. (1974) 'The nonverbal mediation of self-fulfilling prophecies in interracial interaction', *Journal of Experimental Social Psychology*, 10(2): 109–20.

Xu, X., Zuo, X., Wang, X. and Han, S. (2009) 'Do you feel my pain? Racial group membership modulates empathic neural responses', *The Journal of Neuroscience*, 29(26): 8525–29.

Ziegert, J.C. and Hanges, P.J. (2005) 'Employment discrimination: the role of implicit attitudes, motivation, and a climate for racial bias', *Journal of Applied Psychology*, 90(3): 553.

23

Hunting gruffalo with a blunderbuss

On the ethics of constructing and responding to English youth gangs

Jon Shute

In this chapter I outline a critique of recent English youth gang policy, focusing on how the issue has been formulated and also on the ethical role of the criminologist as evaluator and policy commentator. The discussion highlights methodological and evidential gaps at the heart of policy and argues for the more active, engaged role of the criminologist. There should be a more direct connection between the methodology of studying the phenomena and practices aimed at addressing the issues.

This chapter's title derives, in part, from a pair of short policy essays (Shute, Aldridge, and Medina 2012; Shute and Medina 2014) written as a critical response to a major piece of English and Welsh youth crime policy entitled *Ending Gang and Youth Violence: A Cross-Government Report* (HM Government 2011). Published in the political aftermath of serious urban rioting in major English cities, the report set out a youth-focused violence reduction strategy combining better co-ordination of existing policy levers with a small number of new proposals focused on suppression. Much of the initial report was problematic and, among other things, we criticised its partial and misleading construction of the gang 'problem', together with a complex and confusing mesh of poorly-described initiatives that did not seem amenable to evaluation. It seemed that a policy 'blunderbuss' – an indiscriminate, scattergun set of proposals – was being aimed at an imagined and convenient folk devil (the 'gang member') summoned into existence in a process analogous to that described in the feted children's story *The Gruffalo* (Donaldson 1999). In the context of the time, this seemed particularly problematic given that rapid analysis of the riots (*Guardian*/LSE 2011) explicitly dismissed youth gangs as a causal factor and revealed an unusually wide age range of participants. We continue to feel that the shortcomings of the 2011 report and subsequent annual reports (HM Government 2012, 2013, 2015) say something important about the nature and limitations of late modern policy-making in an era of financial austerity.

In this chapter, I rehearse and amplify a number of our arguments, choosing to stress their normative-ethical dimension. Reflecting on the relationship between academic research and policy construction is especially important, and I advance a normative position of 'duty to expose and reduce harm' that I argue *should* motivate criminological policy engagement despite the numerous obstacles that exist to 'research utilisation'. I then apply this logic to *Ending Gang and Youth*

Violence (hereafter, *EGYV*) as a case study that illustrates the potential harm consequent on rapid, partial, poorly described and unevaluated policy, arguing that this is as likely to obscure effective practice as it is to promote ineffectiveness and counter-productivity. I also suggest that the broader UK political context – at the time of writing, an unstable coalition government making major budgetary cuts with uneven impact across populations – makes this form of policy-making increasingly likely, and introduces into it core characteristics (complexity, misdirection, invisibility) that render the role of the engaged criminologist more important than ever. To the extent that many Western governments find themselves in a similar financial-policy predicament at the time of writing, I hope to draw more general lessons regarding criminal justice policy in political context from what may at first seem a parochial and time-limited example.

Policy, research and the 'public' role of the criminologist: Towards a normative emphasis on harm reduction

Since Burawoy's (2005) address to the American Sociological Association on the nature of and need for a 'public sociology', there has been a healthy discussion about the proper role of the criminologist in taking their methods and findings beyond the academy in ways that inform policy, practice and more general public discourse on crime. There is a rewarding literature in this area (see, for example, Chancer and McLaughlin 2007; Loader and Sparks 2010; Uggen and Inderbitzen 2010) that I will not review here but selectively allude to in relation to the process of policy-making. I tend to agree with Tonry (2010) that 'public' and 'policy' criminology is something academics have always tried to do, albeit not always very well. But I go further by stating that criminologists have an essential and positive *duty* to engage critically with law and order policy for the following reasons:

First, crime presupposes intentional and socially-mediated *harm*, not only from the perspectives of the legislator and the enforcers of the criminal law, but also, perhaps, for many people much of the time in relation to a 'core' set of personal and property offences (van Kesteren et al. 2013). Naturally, criminal prohibition is not co-terminous with harm more broadly/thoughtfully conceived (Hillyard et al. 2004; Pemberton 2007 on definitions), and it is the nature of the harm (physical, psychological, economic, cultural), the conditions of its imposition (intention or indifference), its relevant source (cultural, structural, organisational, individual) and target (victim, offender, bystander) that animates the rich, dynamic and contested field of criminological theory and practice, with one's precise location within that field constituting to a great extent, the professional self-identify of the criminologist. What I want to emphasise here – echoing Uggen and Inderbitzen (2010: 726–27) – is that what attracts students to the discipline and keeps academics engaged in their subject matter is this principal Durkheimian interest in harm and its explication and the fact that the interaction of one's political convictions with methodological and theoretical preferences determines precisely *how* this is viewed does not detract from this essential normative fact. Many of us do what we do, in other words, because we recognise harm and are committed to seeking politically supportable strategies for reducing it.

Second, criminologists are essentially interested not only in harm but in its *reduction*, that is, that something actively be done to recognise and limit harm. Even when that 'something' appears to be the imposition of further harms – for example, criminal justice penalties applied to the offender – proponents tend to do so for future-oriented reasons of utility, requalification, or restoration, all of which are thought to be ways of reducing harm. Even purely retributive rationales for punishment can be argued in their essential 'rightness' to leave non-offending bystanders 'feeling better' that societal harm has not been tolerated. Again, one's conception of the nature of harm is fundamental, but it can be argued that much of the 'core business' of criminology, whether it is recognised as 'public' or not, is concerned with exposing hidden harms (for example, domestic violence, corporate and state crime), defining down or reframing supposed harms (for example, the decriminalisation and better regulation of drugs), arguing the best strategy for harm reduction (developmental, situational, criminal justice), or the proper focus and scope of intervention (from systemic macro-economic reform to the micro-economic decision-making of individuals). While globalisation has necessitated a growing 'transnational' sensibility and a recognition of the role of a variety of social actors in governance (Shearing and Wood 2003), that most criminologists still look to the nation-state as the prime co-ordinating or monopolising executive agent to formulate, fund, and enact harm-reduction strategies. Even those interested in 'state crime', seldom propose anarchy or the absence of the state, merely that it does not abuse its power and is held accountable for any abuses. In other words, then, if we do what we do to expose, explicate, and reduce harm, we also look to government as a prime means of achieving the latter.

Third and finally, it follows from the above that criminologists should take an essential interest in examples of government *policy* – the use of public money to address ideologically inflected issues of socio-political interest – that directly and indirectly aim to reduce the harms associated with crime (Loader and Walker 2007). Whether they are formally contracted to evaluate that policy or not, it seems to behove the criminologist to apply their training to comment on the overall premise and rationale of the programme, its theory of change, likelihood of success in its own and in other terms, its practical implementation and summary change claims. Even if one, as a critical criminologist, does not support the government of the day or elements of the overall political order it represents, the normative focus of the discipline should still ensure an essential duty to engage with policy, if only to point out a fundamental misguidedness. This normative stance can be taken one step further if one concedes that *not* to do so – to fail to engage in the assessment of harm reduction – risks a form of complicity in harm *promotion*. This can happen if a policy contains elements that are known to be counterproductive (for example, the various costs of increased use of prison, of stop-and-search, or of drug sanctions, outweighing the benefits), but also from lack of transparency and accountability, for example, where unevidenced claims of success are made due to lack of good evaluation data. Poor or no evaluation can be harmful in that it risks rejecting successful but obscured harm reduction as well as accepting the ineffective and the counterproductive. This is also harmful in that it is a culpable waste of public funds; the taxpayer ideally expects some form of palpable 'return' for their salary sacrifice and expects that governments will not use this to make a situation actively worse.

In short, I agree again with Uggen and Inderbitzen (2010: 743) that criminologists should be 'acting to challenge false statements, question shoddy evidence, and debunk harmful myths and scare tactics' but also constructively to engage in taking their skills and knowledge beyond the academy and to positively shape policy and public discourse in the direction of harm reduction. Many, or even most of the criminological community would say that this is precisely what they do most of their time, whether it be in the classroom or in their funded research and its dissemination. What I have tried to stress in this section, however, is the normative dimension of this activity: that we do what we do to expose and explicate and reduce harm; that we look to government policy as a prime means of achieving harm reduction; and we therefore have a responsibility – a duty – to critically engage with that policy in order to assess its worth and to avoid complicity in harm promotion.

The contours of UK[1] youth gang research and policy 1997–2011

I now turn to the application of the above principles to an analysis of a specific piece of criminal justice policy: *Ending Gang and Youth Violence*. I attempt this most directly in the next section;

however, it is first necessary to contextualise *EGYV* in light of recent formative developments in politics, policy, and scholarship. This is important, not only because it is precisely this detail that is excluded from the main report, but also because it makes clear just how 'new' recognition of youth gangs is in the English and Welsh context, and therefore how remarkable it is that it should become an important trope in contemporary crime and justice policy.

The author (Shute 2013) has previously characterised the short history of constructing and responding to youth gangs in the UK in terms of C. Ronald Huff's (1990) stage model of denial, over-reaction, and mis-identification. Here I reframe elements of that analysis to fit with my overall concern with harm, and do so in a time frame that begins in the late 1990s with the first British official usage of the term 'gang', and ends with the publication of *EGYV*.

Exposing and explicating the harm of youth gangs

Youth gangs have been studied in the US for the best part of a century (Thrasher 1927), and while some academics (for example, Davies 1998) have argued that the phenomenon has, in fact, a venerable history in Britain, a sociological preference for sub-cultural explanations of youth group formations successfully impeded recognition of the applicability of an extensive American literature until the turn of the twenty-first century (see, e.g., Campbell and Muncer 1989). Perhaps conscious of a new police-led willingness to acknowledge gangs (see below), the picture began to change when, independently, academics in Wales and Scotland (Bennett and Holloway 2004; Smith and Bradshaw 2005) began to apply self-report survey methods to establish the prevalence of gang membership using varied samples and definitions. A scientific impetus here was to establish common definitions with American survey research in order to aid cross-national comparisons. This direction of development was also apparent in the establishment and influence of the US/European 'Eurogang' international research network (see Klein 2001) whose central concern with developing common methodologies led sympathetic researchers in Manchester to test them in a major government-backed survey (Sharp et al. 2006) and a research council funded ethnographic study (Aldridge et al. 2008). At the same time, researchers at the University of Bedfordshire conducted a detailed mixed-methods study with a strong single-community focus (Waltham Forest, London; Pitts 2008), and critical work on definitions and nomenclature was being conducted (see Hallsworth and Young 2004) that usefully distinguished among youth gangs, organised criminal gangs, and non-delinquent peer groups.

While much could be said about this lively and productive literature, I focus here on two key points of material relevance for an argument as it relates to *EGYV*. First, all empirical studies confirmed that gangs can be said to exist in the UK and validated the basic American (now international) literature in that *time in the gang is associated with a substantially increased risk of harm* relative to time out of the gang and association with other youth group formations. As an example, Sharp and colleagues (2006) employed a modified 'Eurogang' definition[2] in a representative English survey of around 4,000 10- to 19-year-olds and found: an overall prevalence of 6 per cent; roughly equal participation of females, who tend to leave the gang earlier; variable age composition, with a peak age of involvement of 14 to 15; variable group size, high turnover rates and loose structure; variable ethnic composition reflecting broader neighbourhood demographics; and broader family and community conditions of multiple social exclusion. Nearly two thirds (63 per cent) of the sample had committed an index criminal offence over the preceding year as opposed to 26 per cent of non-gang youth; and gang members were two to four times more likely to be categorised as serious or frequent offenders, to have carried a knife or a gun, to have taken illegal drugs, and committed offences under the influence of alcohol. Youth gang members in England are also more likely to experience physical and gendered sexual violence (e.g., Pitts 2008).

The second point to stress is that there exists *considerable and ongoing disagreement* among British (and international) gang researchers, for example, regarding definitions, methods, and emphases of study, the importance of territory and group structural features, the centrality of violence to identity and reputation, and the processes and meaning of gang entry and exit (see e.g., Pitts 2012). An example might be to contrast the work of Aldridge and colleagues (2008) in an anonymised northern English urban setting – 'Research City' – with Pitts's (2008) work in Waltham Forest, a metropolitan borough of London. While similarities probably outweigh differences, Aldridge and colleagues found that becoming involved in a gang entailed a subtle qualitative shift in existing peer and family relations and that the groups had loose structure, limited vertical integration, and a generally short active period; Pitts, by contrast, stresses the 'grooming' of 'reluctant' socially marginalised youth who are recruited into a highly organised, differentiated, and territorialised system linked to 'glocal' drug markets.

Policy and practice attempts to acknowledge and reduce harm

If, before the index period under consideration, few UK police forces were willing to admit to the existence of 'US-style' gangs (see Sanders 1994, cited in Bennett and Holloway 2004), the operational picture changed very quickly in the late 1990s. Greater Manchester Police led the way, with Stelfox (1998) reporting the problem of firearms being used by 'gangs' (undefined) in 16 UK police force areas; and Shropshire and McFarquar (2002) briefing the same force about the potential of multi-agency gang strategies to tackle escalating gun crime in the city. It is difficult to locate precisely how and why the police's ontological shift[3] of acceptance of the existence of gangs occurred, but it seems the construction focused on very serious drug-related crime committed by older youths and young adults in primarily 'black' communities. Absent data, one can only speculate, but an important reason in the context of escalating firearm incidents may have been the increased relevance, perceived importance, and success of 'Operation Ceasefire' (also known as the Boston Gun Project: Braga et al. 2001), an American police co-ordinated multi-agency deterrence and suppression strategy aimed at reducing gang-related gun crime. While high-level youth crime policy was more concerned at this time with low-level anti-social behaviour (the Antisocial Behaviour Order or 'ASBO'), police forces benefitting from greater public spending instigated five 'Ceasefire-like' gun and gang suppression operations in London, Manchester, and other UK cities between 1999 and 2004 (H.C. Hansard, 15 November 2004). By the late 2000s, political priorities had shifted in light of high profile media treatment of a series of urban youth stabbings and shootings, and a racialised, conflated discourse of gangs, guns, and knife crime was being endorsed at the highest level in speeches by the then Prime Minister Tony Blair (Wintour and Dodd 2007). In the last three years of the Labour administration under Gordon Brown, a seemingly unstoppable law enforcement-led multiagency approach to suppression was strengthened in gang-specific Home Office initiatives (the *Tackling Gangs Action Plan*) and key policy documents (*Tackling Gangs: A Practical Guide for Local Authorities, CRDPs and other Local Partners*, Home Office 2008; *Saving Lives, Reducing Harm, Protecting the Public, An Action Plan for Tackling Violence*, HM Government 2008).

Academic and related commentary on the official harm reduction policy

What will be clear from the above is that during this period, British academic gang research and operational police work often seemed to be describing very different phenomena. There was perhaps some limited common agreement as to the species of harms done to and by 'gangs' and 'gang members', but survey work in particular suggested youth, low prevalence, high turnover, and elevated but often relatively petty offending, in contrast to police constructions which focused on 'heavy-end' drugs and firearms offences committed by older black and mixed-race figures involved in organised crime. This split in understanding also seemed to encourage a split in academic and related commentary. On the one hand, some academics shifted focus from the harm committed by gangs to the *harms attendant on constructing and policing gangs.* For example, Hallsworth and Young (2008) criticised a generally partial, inexact, media- and ideologically-driven set of operational working definitions; Ralphs et al. (2009) pointed to the stigmatic and false labels applied to those identified by police 'intelligence' as gang-affiliated; and Bullock and Tilley (2008) found concrete evidence of both problems in a south Manchester explicitly 'Ceasefire' inspired policing initiative.

On the other hand, the greater compatibility of Pitts's Waltham Forest gang work with police understanding of serious and organised drug and weapon-enabled offending seemed to lead that construction to 'win out' in influencing policy, and it began to be featured heavily in the campaigning policy work of the centre-right think tank – the *Centre for Social Justice* – set up by the former leader of the Conservative Party, Iain Duncan Smith. Its 2009 report *Dying to Belong: An In-Depth Review of Street Gangs in Britain* supported a mixed portfolio of enforcement, intervention, and prevention, and was associated with further work on family-focused initiatives (Allen and Duncan Smith 2008). Pearce and Pitts (2011) also conducted work at this time on female sexual victimisation in gangs for the Office of the Children's Commissioner.

In sum then, the period 1997 to 2011 was an extraordinary period of activity where, in effect, gangs were given an absolute ontological status[4] previously denied in the UK, and from this standing start became the object of enquiry, rhetoric, and action to finally appear at the forefront of high-profile policy and practice on youth violence. It is fair to say that all who accepted the existence of gangs in this period also accepted that they were deserving of attention because, as both a dependent and independent variable, they are associated with a diverse range of harms. It is equally fair to say that the sometimes fundamental disagreements of researchers, policy-makers, and practitioners as to the nature and source of those harms produced a contested and ideologically charged field. Academic evidence was clearly being used by police to apprehend and reduce harm in law and order terms; however, further evidence was also accumulating of the dangers of doing so.

Ending gang and youth violence 2011 to 2015: A case study and critique

I now turn to the policy documents themselves as a case study of how harm is constructed, argued, and evidenced in a particular political context. In the first section, I summarise something of the nature and content of the original (2011) policy report *Ending Gang and Youth Violence* (*EGYV*) and amplify our initial reactions to it (Shute et al. 2012). I then analyse the truth claims made in subsequent (2012, 2013a, 2013b, 2015) progress documents. Finally, I add a coda in terms of observations regarding 2014–15 parliamentary review of the policy via the Home Office Affairs Select Committee, to which I contributed evidence. My overall argument is that the policy strikes an ambivalent tone that is strongly reminiscent of David Garland's (1996, 2000) 'adaptations' to the understood limits of the sovereign state, but that the nature of the weak and austerity-compromised coalition government that created it also meant little new money and lent a somewhat desperate sense of 'restate and recycle' activity to the project. I claim that while the policy was not entirely un-evidenced in conception, it was extremely partial in what it took to be relevant evidence, and, most culpably, did not concern itself with generating action that was capable of being adequately described or evaluated. Robust *new* evidence cannot, therefore, be produced. I contend that *EGYV*, in sum, exemplified only unreasoned activity over achievement and actively risked a range of quite profound harms that may be felt well beyond the coalition's time in office. In so doing, I attempt to bring to bear all the observations on evidence and ethical duty to prevent harm that I have rehearsed above.

Ending gang and youth violence: A cross-departmental report (HM government 2011)

EGYV was published on November 1st 2011. Two points might be made for the non-British reader by way of context. First, the report was the first major piece of youth crime policy announced by the Coalition government – a combination of the centre-right Conservative Party and centrist Liberal Democrat Party – that emerged from the first hung (no overall majority) parliament in post-war Britain. After over a decade of economic deregulation and credit-driven growth under Tony Blair's Labour party, the UK suffered a major recession and increase in sovereign debt as a result of the 2008 global 'credit crash'. The Coalition government was more inclined to austerity than its predecessor, and as result of the May 2010 election, the new Coalition's agreed agenda focused strongly on punitive public spending cuts in order to quickly reduce national debt.

A second contextual point relates to events immediately prior to the publication of *EGYV*. In the wake of a mishandled community protest at the police shooting to death of a young black man, Mark Duggan, rioting began in the north London borough of Tottenham on the evening of 6 August 2011, spread to a number of other boroughs and English cities, ending in Greater Manchester on 9 August. Analysis indicated over 4,000 arrests and 3,000 court appearances; an argued role in five deaths; and an estimated £1 billion cross-sector 'bill' in insurance, compensation, criminal justice, and lost revenue costs (Riots Communities and Victim Panel 2011). Quickly-produced criminal justice (Ministry of Justice 2011, 2012) and research data (Morell et al. 2011; *Guardian*/LSE 2011; Lightowlers and Shute 2012; Lightowlers and Quirk 2015) indicated, *inter alia,* strong crime-deprivation links at both the area and individual level, a high prevalence of prior adverse criminal justice experiences (including proactive 'stop and search' policing), and strong evidence of punitive sentencing.

The report itself – a co-product of the Home Office and Department for Work and Pensions – was framed clearly in terms of a response to the riots, which were referred to by the departmental heads in the Ministerial Foreword (*EGYV*: pages 3–4[5]). In the two months between the riots and publication, the government convened three events consisting of representatives of local authorities, voluntary sector organisations working with gangs, and police. It also consulted with the *Centre for Social Justice* on the outcome of a similar event, held a 'young persons' roundtable, and convened an 'International Forum of Experts on Gangs' to inform its deliberations. The policy product was an intended programme of activity that combined targeted co-ordination of existing measures across government with new gang-focused measures: 'We need to combine action to tackle the causes of gang and youth violence with tough enforcement to crack down on those that commit crime'; '… intensive police action is needed to stop the violence and bring perpetrators to justice, but we must match this robust enforcement response with a robust offer of support to exit gang life, and an equally intensive prevention strategy' (3–4). Five areas of activity were stressed (Executive Summary: 7–9). First, '*Providing Support* to local areas to tackle their youth violence problem', involving the establishment of an *EGYV* Team and network of advisers to provide practical advice to gang affected communities; £10 million to improve the targeting of services in 30 such areas; and £1.2 million to improve services for young victims of sexual violence. Second, the report emphasised the need for better gang and violence *Prevention* via support for an existing early childhood intervention for socially deprived teenage mothers (Family Nurse Partnerships) and new advisory materials for parents and schools. Third, *Pathways Out* for established gang members were to be offered via emphasis on intensive tertiary intervention (Multisystemic Therapy), education and rehousing programmes, and diversion into support at the point of arrest or injury (hospital accident and emergency). Fourth, greater *Punishment and Enforcement* was intended via extended gang-injunctions, new mandatory sentences for knife-related and repeat serious violence, consultations on police curfew powers and new firearms offences, and a restated commitment to deport gang members who were not UK citizens. Finally, an emphasis was placed on *Partnership Working,* including guidelines on inter-agency data sharing and the co-location of relevant public services.

On the face of it, these measures seemed to offer a rapidly-formulated yet consultative and rational set of actions representing a *tour de force* of 'evidence-based', 'joined-up' government. I did not and do not doubt the sense, goodwill, or ability of many of those involved and agree that many individual points and policies appear to be *prima facie* valid and reasonable. I also want to stress that we do not doubt the existence of youth gangs *as we understand them* nor of the existence and effects of serious youth violence on individuals and communities. In our early policy commentary (Shute et al. 2012) what we regarded as objectionable was the studied manipulation of a real sense of crisis emanating from the riots to focus on a largely unrelated and diffuse set of policy scapegoats constructed around an intensely selective and partial view of 'the evidence'. If the construction of the problem was problematic, so was a planned response that was so complex that it defied description, could not lend itself to a clear theory of change that linked inputs to outputs, and contained no clear plans for evaluation. We felt that the plans had real potential to be wasteful and even counterproductive and therefore took a critically normative stance in the spirit of harm reduction. I will now discuss these points in detail.

We can describe two major sets of flaws in the *construction of the problem*: a fallacious sense of crisis and the selective use of evidence. Regarding the first of these, crisis is apparent in the language used in the Ministerial Foreword, in the clear linkage to the objectively ruinous costs of rioting and in the interesting narrative use of harrowing fictional 'life-stories' of ideal-typical gang members ('Boy X'; 'Girl Y') which personalise the abstract and mix pathos with a sense of unfolding but preventable societal cost. This sense of crisis was no doubt felt by many observers in the wake of the riots, but to what extent could it be substantiated as a problem of youth violence in general or gang violence in particular? A Home Office Statistical Bulletin released one month before the riots (Chaplin et al. 2011) revealed that nationally, police recorded incidents of violence had fallen by six per cent relative to the previous year, after falls of between four and eight per cent for each of the preceding four years. Firearms offences were down by 13 per cent on the preceding year and 37 per cent down on 2005/6; and knife offences down 10 per cent relative to the preceding two years. The same publication revealed violent crime as recorded by the British Crime Survey to be up six per cent relative to 2009/10 against an overall fall of 47 per cent since its peak in 1995. Youth Justice statistics for the same period (Ministry of Justice 2012) revealed an overall drop of 33 per cent in proven offences involving violence against the person between 2007/8 and 2010/11. Naturally, these are national trends that mask local variation, but it is striking given the title of the report that none of the above statistics were cited and none at the local level. Regarding the August 2011 riots (*Guardian*/LSE 2011: 21–23), swiftly organised qualitative interviewing revealed youth gang hostilities to be absent or explicitly dismissed in 270 participant accounts, and early Home Office analysis of the backgrounds of arrestees revealed that only 26 per cent were aged 10 to 17 years, slightly less than the 28 per cent found to be 25 years or older (Home Office 2011). I think the basic point is made: that the riots, disturbing and damaging as they were, were in no credible straightforward sense 'gang' or 'youth' phenomena and that isolated high-profile and tragic cases of death aside, they occurred against a backdrop of long-term decreases in violence and youth violence.

Regarding the selective use of evidence in *EGYV*, a number of points can be made. First, the same Home Office document just described noted (18–19 and table A15) that 13 per cent of riot arrestees could be described as 'gang-affiliated' by police definition only to admit in a compensation sentence and footnote that there existed no standard operational definition of 'gang' or 'gang-affiliated', meaning 'estimates will not be directly comparable between forces and should be treated as indicative'. This is the first mention of the broader and fundamental ontological problem we noted in our contextual section above. *EGYV* contains a definition of 'gang' inspired by the Secretary of State for Work and Pensions' own think-tank, the *Centre for Social Justice*, but there is no indication of the extent to which this was or could possibly be applied to police operational practices. In fact, British police generally rely on 'gang intelligence' gathered from 'practice wisdom', and from surveillance, self-report, police informers, and partner agencies; it is inherently speculative and not easily amenable to the small range of social science operationalisations available (see Association of Chief Police Officers 2007; Pitts 2008; Ralphs et al. 2009). This being the case, the validity of *EGYV's* reliance on police 'gang' statistics to make its case risks severely misleading the reader and reifies the concept without reference to the more nuanced and critical literature.

The emphasis on police operational constructions of the 'gang' is also seen in that of the 34 non-governmental attendees at a consultative 'international forum of gang experts', 24 (70 per cent) were current or former senior police officers. The contested plurality of British gang research was represented at that meeting (and, as far as we are aware in the whole consultative process) by a single British gang researcher – John Pitts – and no reference was drawn in *EGYV* to at least two pieces of academic research that might have challenged the understanding of the gang 'problem' no doubt voiced there. The first is the Sharp and colleagues' (2006) analysis of Home Office generated data that found a low overall prevalence of gang membership (6 per cent) as defined by a clear set of criteria, and where 37 per cent of the sample had committed no offence in the preceding year, 66 per cent had not committed a serious offence, 87 per cent had not carried a knife, and 99 per cent had not carried a gun. While still higher in prevalence than non-gang members, this set of findings tends to downplay the strong conflation of guns, gangs, knives, and serious offending portrayed in *EGYV*. A second set of findings relates to Bullock and Tilley's (2002; 2008) evaluation of an early example of a Manchester-based multi-agency gang-reduction programme mixing welfarist and enforcement aims. The project began with a formal intention to repeat the kind of police-led co-ordinated suppression and deterrence model of Boston's 'Operation Ceasefire', but disagreements among agencies as to the definition of 'gang' together with concerns about imparting stigma by applying the term led to programme 'drift' and an unsustainably large number of 'eligible' young people being identified. The authors concluded that absent a potentially unattainable consensus on assessment of 'gang' and hence (risk of) gang membership, policy should focus on behaviour and not social identity or risk counterproductive 'net-widening' and widespread labelling.

In addition to flaws in the basic construction of the policy problem, I also draw attention here to problems with describing and understanding the *prescribed plan of action*. The most striking feature of *EGYV* is the sheer number of public and voluntary sector initiatives adduced as being relevant, effective, or promising: I counted over 60 in an 84 page document in addition to four Bills spanning the activities of at least four government departments. This was deliberate, no doubt, in order to emphasise the degree of thought, consultation, and co-ordination necessary in a multi-agency, multi-sectoral response and to showcase the quality of existing resources.

Identifying, distinguishing, and even naming such a large number of potentially relevant initiatives is also problematic, however. First, it is clear that only a small number of these initiatives were substantively 'new' in that a service that did not previously exist was created, or existing services were given additional monies; in fact only those initiatives described under the *Providing Support* priority area clearly involved extra money. The amount explicitly committed – a total of £11.2 million – was not inconsiderable in absolute terms, but set against total UK public spending in 2010–11 of £697 billion, including £20 billion for the Home Office and Ministry of Justice combined (Rogers 2013), this represented a very modest commitment. Like many initiatives in the report, the two flagship childhood/young adult interventions named in the *Prevention* and *Pathways Out* – respectively, Family Nurse Partnerships and Multisystemic Therapy – were 'existing commitments' of the government. However, while both are high quality evidence-based programmes with a strong North American evidence base suggesting effectiveness in reducing behavioural problems, they were recommended before UK effectiveness data from full randomised controlled trials was available and have never been offered explicitly to gang members nor evaluated for their impact on gang membership (Shute 2008, 2013). No plans were announced to gather such data, so although promising, it is difficult to see how it would be possible to evidence impact on the youth gang 'problem'. A third set of issues relates again to the selective use of evidence: *EGYV*-like local policy failures such as those described by Bullock and Tilley (2008) above are entirely omitted; and there was uncritical acceptance of the success of programmes that were not evaluated to high standards due to lack of resources for that purpose. One example is the Strathclyde Police's Community Initiative to Reduce Violence (CIRV), a co-ordinated suppression, enforcement, and exit programme. Success claims at the time of the publication of *EGYV* were built on a non-independent evaluation involving simple descriptive comparison of pre-post violence among a group of police-defined 'gang members' who engaged with the programme versus those who did not (Violence Reduction Unit 2011). Violence was also reduced in the comparison group[6], meaning success could not confidently be attributed to the programme.

It could be argued that the only really concrete, achievable, and clear set of intentions expressed in *EGYV* related to *Punishment and Enforcement* and *Partnership Working*: the latter due to its technocratic nature; the former due to the inherent legislative advantage possessed by a government in power. Both sets of measures, however, tended towards greater surveillance, greater 'intelligence-gathering' and greater punishment and were not therefore 'harm free'.

One final point to be made about the 2011 report and its action points relates to *plans for evaluation*. A further problem associated with citing so many potentially relevant initiatives is that their independent, additive and interactive effects as they operate in varied local contexts are extremely hard to evaluate with confidence (Shute et al. 2012). The only evaluation plans referred to in *EGYV* (60–61) relate to potential criminal justice and injury-related (hospital-derived) outcomes and 'common-sense' progress indicators at the individual, family, and community levels. While sensible, no hint of any research design is given, nor the recruitment of an independent evaluation team to oversee the process.

Overall then, *EGYV* emerged in a somewhat unique constellation of micro- and macro-level political contexts where chronic public anxieties over the economy were acutely overlain with intense debate in the wake of urban rioting on a wide range of policy questions regarding social harm: concentrated social exclusion, youth crime, police-community relations and legal inequality. While the focus on harm seems proper, and the policy response expressed in *EGYV* seems focused on harm-reduction, I have tried to argue here that rather like an impressionist painting, the report seems to make much more sense at a distance than close-up. When the detail is inspected closely in context with other publicly available research data, it seems that the sense of crisis it invokes could not be justified, that the construction of gangs and youth violence was largely police-led and made only by selectively ignoring evidence that inconveniently challenged it, and that, truly, a metaphorical 'blunderbuss' of mostly pre-existing policy was being advocated without any clear theory of change or plans for evaluation. I objected to this approach (Shute et al. 2012) as both youth gang and policy evaluation researcher, and address the moral consequences of this predicament in the conclusion below. I first analyse follow-up documents to the main report.

Ending gang and youth violence: Follow-up documents (HM government 2012, 2013; Home Office 2013)

As might be expected *Ending Gang and Youth Violence: One Year On* (2012) was to a great extent a 'work in progress' report that detailed activity in key areas, for example 'Partnership working and information sharing' which involved the *EGYV* Team conducting 'peer reviews' of relevant service provision in most of the 29 priority areas. Other areas of activity included advising a separate set of initiatives on the sexual exploitation of girls in gangs and raising awareness of violence as a public health issue. Progress was in relation to *Punishment and Enforcement* (reframed as 'the Criminal Justice response') included the extension of gang injunctions to children aged 14 to17 years and the introduction of mandatory minimum sentences for weapon-carrying in a school. No further detail on evaluation was given.

Two further documents were released in December 2013: one by HM Government, *Ending Gang and Youth Violence: Annual Report 2013* and a Home Office evidence review, *Ending Gang and Youth Violence: Review 2012–13*. Both the tone and content of the annual report were similar to the previous year's document and evidenced a significant amount of further activity in the redrawn/labelled priority areas. Notably strong success claims were made by the Home Secretary regarding overall effectiveness: 'The initiative is working, the crimes that the programme aims to tackle are diminishing … the programme has led to more effective leadership and a greater sense of strategic direction. That has helped those on the frontline increase the effectiveness of their work. And that has contributed to the drop in youth violence' (6).

I invite the reader to assess this claim in the light of our (Shute and Medina 2014) critical response to the accompanying evidence review which had an explicit evaluation focus. The findings therein consisted principally of: an 'in-house' (Home Office) self-report online survey to community contacts in the 33[7] pilot areas, an analysis of the 'peer review' process whereby *EGYV* Team members assessed local service provision, and an analysis of police-recorded violence in programme areas over the previous two years and in comparison to non-programme areas. A positive picture was drawn: pilot areas strongly appreciated the peer review process and more general assistance and strategic focus provided by *EGYV*, and general reductions in violence and weapon-use were evident in pilot areas.

In fairness to the authors of the report, the limitations of the methods employed are explicitly discussed and conclusions do not, in general, go beyond them. It is, however, worth enumerating them in order to further illustrate problems associated with the lack of attention to evaluation in the 2011 report.

A first point to make is that no independent evaluation was conducted, so the funders were also evaluators of their own policy using information gained directly from fundees with a strong stake in current and future funding. In the context of significant and ongoing budgetary cuts for local authorities (see below), it is not hard to see how, despite professionalism, objectivity, and goodwill, a more positive picture of *EGYV* might have emerged than would have been the case had information been gathered by external researchers. Second, the two longitudinal surveys of community contacts and three attempts at telephone interview were not compulsory. In fact, only 10 out of 29 (34 per cent) initially funded pilot areas completed both surveys, and 13 out of 29 (45 per cent) provided an interview. Six trial areas 'did not contribute to the research in any way'. It is unsurprising that busy practitioners do not always respond with enthusiasm to evaluation; however, it is surprising that participation was not made compulsory as a condition of funding. As admitted in the *Review* document, such a low return can only further limit/bias findings. Finally, underlining a point made earlier, selected police-recorded crimes of violence declined in project areas relative to the first year of programme implementation; however, this continued a trend seen in the year before that implementation, and, as we have seen from national data, a much longer reduction over the past five to 20 years. No individual-level data on gang membership, violence, or gang-related violence was measured in any area.

The authors of the review (6–7) describe the considerable challenges of evaluating what is in effect a complex community initiative (Connell and Kubisch 1998) with great inter-site variation in context and practice. As in our 2014 article, I agree but argue that this is the nature of national policy shaped by and devolved to the local level, and *had more time and effort been expended embedding evaluation plans in the initial 2011 report*, a much more simple, targeted, and theory-infused set of initiatives could have been implemented and directly evaluated using established longitudinal quasi-experimental comparisons of individuals in matched areas. In other words, the problems of evaluating *EGYV* could and should have been avoided, and severely limit the learning that can be taken from this complex and contested venture.

Home Affairs Select Committee on gangs and youth crime (2014–15)

No annual report was published in 2014; however, a prominent parliamentary committee – the Home Affairs Select Committee (HASC[8]) – set up a review of *EGYV* in March of that year. The Committee system of the UK parliament selects issues of concern and/or importance by government department, subjects them to inquiry by collecting oral and written evidence, and produces a report to which government is obliged to respond within two months of publication. It has no formal powers but is a form of retrospective accountability where prominent political figures are often publicly subject to difficult and direct questions. HASC sessions are minuted and all submitted evidence made publicly available.

Here, I add some brief observations attendant on my participation in and analysis of that process. In collaboration with fellow gang researchers, the authors collectively submitted written evidence as the 'Manchester Gang Research Network', which made constructively critical comments along the lines discussed here and that drew on the findings of major empirical gang projects (Medina et al. 2013; Smithson et al. 2013). Of 33 documents detailing written and oral evidence we formed the only independent academic contribution raising fundamental issues of definition, lack of evidence, and possible counter-productivity. Of the remaining 32 documents, 12 (37.5 per cent) were from voluntary sector organisations involved with *EGYV*, eight (25 per cent) from individual police officers or representatives of police gang initiatives (for example, Operation Trident in London), two from *EGYV*-engaged Local Authorities (London Boroughs of Hackney and Lambeth), two from individual practitioners, and the remainder (n=8; 25 per cent) from representatives of major posts and institutions (for example, the Minister for Crime Prevention, the Children's Commissioner, Youth Justice Board, the London Mayor's Office). Given the investment of virtually all of these actors in *EGYV* itself (not least, the Home Office and *Centre for Social Justice*), it is perhaps unsurprising that the 'evidence' is broadly supportive of the programme. However, no further empirical evidence was adduced, and we, the author, found ourselves to be an academic minority of one.

In late February 2015, the HASC final report *Gangs and Youth Crime: Thirteenth Report of Session 2014–15* was published. It is, to my mind, something of a 'curate's egg', that is, not all bad. The first headline recommendation of the report stated: 'The Home Office has spent over £10 million on its Ending Gang and Youth Violence programme, but has failed to effectively evaluate the project. The Home Office must undertake high-quality comparative evaluation in order to assess what works best in combating gang and youth crime and in identifying areas for improvement' (3), later adding 'This will be vital in ensuring the ten new priority areas receive the full benefit of the programme' (8). This exceeded our expectations and, to our surprise, even invoked our contribution (7–8). However, the recommendation also sat alongside others, for example, the increased use of primary school educational prevention and mentoring programmes, which, while intuitively appealing, have a somewhat equivocal evidence base (Esbensen et al. 2012; Medina et al. 2012). As ever, quite what 'effective evaluation' means in social scientific terms will be of fundamental importance to any successor policy.

Coda: Ending gang and youth violence: Annual report 2014–15

Two weeks *after* the HASC report (mid-March 2015), and immediately prior to submission of this chapter, the delayed 2014 annual report was published by HM Government. In structure and content, the document was broadly comparable to previous annual reports, and I here draw attention only to a subtle but possibly significant change in language, tone, and emphasis. Published two months before the UK General Election, and in the likelihood that the conservative-dominated Coalition would not retain overall power, there was an understandably valedictory but reflective end-of-policy-cycle feel to the document. What was also notable was the absence of grandiose effectiveness claims and a re-framing of success in 'softer', more processual terms: supporting and enabling local areas and services; better understanding gang dynamics, and its relation to organised criminal networks; strengthening regulation; and providing 'improved communications with partners such as the police' (6–7, 9). Whether these change were related to the criticisms voiced in the HASC report is unknown.

Conclusions: The tricky moral business of policy engagement

I return at last to a discussion of the normative-ethical issues at the heart of my observations. I make three sets of points in relation to the nature and limitations of policy engagement with *Ending Gang and Youth Violence*.

Late modern law-and-order policy making in times of austerity

David Garland (1996, 2000) suggested that, faced with chronically high crime levels as a normal social fact, the UK, like other Western countries was learning to come to terms with the end of the 'sovereignty myth' – that government could guarantee internal security for its population. Though there are no doubt other interpretations of *EGYV* in terms of risk, securitisation, and 'governing through crime', we see the applicability of Garland's analysis 15 years on. True, crime in England and Wales has fallen considerably since 1995, however, it is still high by historical standards and in comparison with many Western jurisdictions. *EGYV*, for me, displays both adaptive and denial-based reactions to high crime as normal social fact. Elements of the programme are *adaptive* in that they draw on a rational, if heavily selective, evidence-base intended to 'cool' (Loader and Sparks 2010) a heated post-riot situation, and in doing so, invoke the 'criminologies of the self' that treat gang-members as rational calculators able to perceive and react to the sets of deterrents and incentives behind 'Operation Ceasefire' and related programmes. There is also very extensive evidence in *EGYV* of 'responsibilisation': suggesting that effectively addressing the issues should involve a drawing-in of a range of voluntary sector actors, NGOs and non-law-and-order agents[9] to 'network' the response, rather than the State accepting primary responsibility for its own policy failings. At the same time, elements of the language and invocation of crisis displayed in the reports, together with its suppression-focused content more than hint at Garland's 'hysterical *denial*' of this situation and attempt to reaffirm the State's 'tough'[10] role as final arbiter of justice and security.

I would, however, modify this analysis to suggest that law-and-order policy post-2008 is very clearly shaped by the context of public spending austerity and unstable Coalition government. I have argued that, despite the consultation, policy detail, celebration of initiatives, and so forth, *EGYV* displays more *activity* than it does *achievement*; its main business is to advise, assess, monitor, co-ordinate and 'govern at a distance', not because it is a preferred way of exercising power but because *there is no money or political will to do otherwise.* What is wholly absent from the reports is the financial reality of average year-on-year cuts to Home Office and Ministry of Justice departmental budgets of 5.6 per cent and 8.1 per cent respectively between 2010–11 and 2015–16 (Keynes and Tetlow 2014) and a 37 per cent estimated real-terms reduction in Local Authority budgets over the same period (National Audit Office 2014). Regarding the 'prevention' focus of *EGYV*, it is also the case that spending on early education, childcare, and child-centred community services fell by 25 per cent between 2009–10 and 2012–13 (Lupton 2015). In this context, £10 million of extra *EGYV* money spread over two years and 30 local sites is put firmly into perspective.

From an ethical point of view, the main and primary issue facing policy-makers at the time of writing[11] is how credibly to claim an avowed interest in harm reduction when the services employed to do so are being disinvested in to such an extent. It is this essential but undeclared/invisible normative point that frames all others, and that lurks behind every fine word and sentiment of *EGYV*. Granted, resources are scarce, perhaps more scarce than is often the case. That, however, makes it especially important that they should not be misused or wasted in needless ways.

The centrality of high quality research to effective harm reduction

Much of what I have argued proceeds from a strong normative position: that policy aimed at harm reduction, if it is to have any chance of success in anything other than symbolic terms, must be evidence-based from its inception, must specify the context and theory of change that links inputs to outcomes, and build-in robust evaluation that is capable of comprehending its effects. This has not happened in *EGYV*. This means that an extremely effective initiative or combination of initiatives, supremely well-suited to the needs of a proportion of local youths but with the potential to be generalised, may be overlooked because it cannot be evidenced. It also means that a poorly founded, ineffective programme that does little but create activity and consume time and public money, may be overlooked because it cannot be evidenced. It also means that a poorly founded, counterproductive programme that actively increases social harm 'iatrogenically' may be overlooked because it cannot be evidenced. It is likely that all three of these scenarios have occurred under the auspices of *EGYV*.

This emphasis on theory-led evaluation will no doubt be interpreted by some as an unrealistic, technocratic exercise in nit-picking that valorises the role of the (generally unglamorous) academic researcher. Perhaps. All I will say to this is to point out the extraordinary but obscured irony that a report nominally created as a response to the August 2011 riots should so favour US-style gang suppression projects when the initial 'spark' of those riots was the shooting to death of an unarmed black man by officers from such a project. I might also point out the high ethnic disparities in stop-and-search in the UK (Hurrell 2013), the impact on perceived legitimacy and police co-operation of poor experiences of procedural justice (Hough et al. 2010), and the net-widening and labelling fears attendant on vague gang definitions (Bullock and Tilley 2008). To *not* test for unintended effects such as these – among others – is not only immoral but highly inefficient in terms of heavily curtailed public funds. Theory-led, well evaluated policy is the only ethical response. Political imperatives – genuine ones that are not merely political– involve substantial ethical elements, both in regard to how the issues in question are formulated and in regard to how they are studied and addressed. Those projects are unavoidably ethical, whether or not there is explicit recognition of the fact.

The limits of a public criminology

I began this chapter by arguing that criminologists interested in harm reduction had an ethical duty to engage with policy aimed at doing precisely that; to not do so in one's field of expertise risked complicity in harm production. What my experience of commenting on the foregoing case study confirms is Tonry's (2010) conclusions that public criminology can influence policy and debate but that this is a noisily multivocal and contested process governed by timing, choice of subject, divergent understandings of 'evidence', and the fit of one's research findings to developing official narratives that discount nuance and inconclusiveness. As he states, it also requires stamina and energy that few researchers possess. There are real and profound obstacles to the potential of a public criminology then at particular times and in particular contexts; however, I maintain that it is right to continue to do so, particularly in times of financial austerity when social harms escalate and the rational use of public funds is at a particular premium. Becker's (1967) fundamentally moral-ethical question of 'whose side are we on?' has never been so relevant.

Notes

1 I use the term 'UK' here in order to incorporate relevant findings from academic and policy analysis in Scotland. The nature of devolved governance, however, means that *EGYV* applies only to policy and practice in England and Wales, which is my prime focus.

2 'A durable street-oriented youth group whose involvement in illegal activity is part of their group identity'. This definition has been found to have cross-national validity (see, e.g., Decker and Weerman 2005).

3 That is, a novel and unprecedented acknowledgement that gangs 'exist' as a concept and empirical entity that are thereby amenable to policy action.

4 see footnote 4.

5 Home Secretary Teresa May: 'One thing the riots in August did was to bring home to the entire country just how serious a problem gang and youth violence has now become'; Secretary of State for Work & Pensions Iain Duncan Smith: 'In the immediate aftermath of August's disorder the Prime Minister rightly called for a report into Britain's street gangs'.

6 A later quasi-experimental evaluation (Donnelly et al. 2014) confirmed non-significantly greater reductions in the intervention versus comparison group, with reductions seen in both groups at two-year follow-up. Significant reductions relative to comparison were seen for weapons carrying. None of these results were available at the time *EGYV* was published.

7 A further four sites had been added to the initial 29.

8 See http://www.parliament.uk/business/committees/committees-a-z/commons-select/home-affairs-committee/inquiries/parliament-2010/gangs-and-youth-crime/.

9 As stated in the Ministerial Foreword of the original 2011 report, 'Stopping such violence is not a task for the police alone. Teachers, doctors and youth workers all have a vital role to play. ...'(4); 'health visitors, GPs, teachers, A&E departments, local youth workers and Jobcentre Plus staff – need to be involved ...'(8).

10 This term is used 13 times in *EGYV* (2011).
11 It should also be noted that in the run up to the UK General Election of 7th May 2015, both main political parties are committed to further public spending cuts over the lifetime of the next parliament.

Bibliography

Association of Chief Police Officers (2007) *Gun Crime and Gangs: A Response to the Home Secretary,* London: ACPO.

Allen, G. and Duncan Smith, I. (2008) *Early Intervention: Good Parents, Great Kids, Better Citizen,* London: Centre for Social Justice.

Aldridge, J. and Medina, J. (2008) *Youth Gangs in an English City: Social Exclusion, Drugs and Violence: Full Research Report ESRC End of Award Report.* RES-000-23-0615, Swindon: ESRC.

Becker, H.S. (1967) 'Whose side are we on?', *Social Problems*, 239–47.

Bennett, T. and Holloway, K. (2004) 'Gang membership, drugs and crime in the UK', *British Journal of Criminology*, 44(3): 305–23.

Braga, A.A., Kennedy, D.M., Waring, E.J. and Piehl, A.M. (2001) 'Problem-oriented policing, deterrence, and youth violence: An evaluation of Boston's Operation Ceasefire', *Journal of Research in Crime and Delinquency*, 38(3): 195–225.

Bullock, K. and Tilley, N. (2002) 'Gangs, shootings and violent incidents in Manchester: developing a crime reduction strategy', *Criminology and Criminal Justice*, 4(2): 255–76.

Bullock, K. and Tilley, N. (2008) 'Understanding and tackling gang violence'. *Crime Prevention & Community Safety*, 10(1): 36–47.

Burawoy, M. (2005) 'For public sociology', *American Sociological Review*, 70(1): 4–28.

Campbell, A. and Muncer, S. (1989) 'Them and us: a comparison of the cultural context of American gangs and British subcultures', *Deviant Behavior*, 10(3): 271–88.

Centre for Social Justice. (2009) *Dying to Belong: An In-depth Review of Street Gangs in Britain* London: CSJ.

Chancer, L. and McLaughlin, E. (2007) 'Public criminologies', *Theoretical Criminology*, 11(2): 155–73.

Chaplin, R., Flatley, J. and Smith, K. (eds.) (2011) *Crime in England and Wales 2010/11. Findings from the British Crime Survey and police recorded crime,* 2nd edn, London: Home Office.

Connell, J.P. and Kubisch, A.C. (1998) 'Applying a theory of change approach to the evaluation of comprehensive community initiatives: progress, prospects, and problems', *New Approaches to Evaluating Community Initiatives*, 2: 15–44.

Davies, A. (1998) 'Youth gangs, masculinity and violence in late Victorian Manchester and Salford', *Journal of Social History*, 349–69.

Decker, S.H. and Weerman, F. M. (eds.) (2005) *European Street Gangs and Troublesome Youth Groups,* Walnut Creek, CA: AltaMira Press.

Dondalson, J. (1999) *The Gruffalo,* London: MacMillan Books.

Esbensen F., Osgood, D.W., Peterson, D., Taylor, T. and Carson, D.C. (2012) 'Short and long-term outcome results from a multi-site evaluation of the G.R.E.A.T. programme', *Criminology and Public Policy*, 12(3): 375–411.

Garland, D. (1996) 'The limits of the sovereign state strategies of crime control in contemporary society', *British Journal of Criminology*, 36(4): 445–71.

Garland, D. (2000) 'The culture of high crime societies', *British Journal of Criminology*, 40(3): 347–75.

Guardian, The and London School of Economics. (2011) *Reading the Riots: Investigating England's Summer of Disorder – full report.* http://www.guardian.co.uk/uk/interactive/2011/dec/14/reading-the-riots-investigating-england-s-summer-of-disorder-full-report, accessed 15 February 2015.

Hallsworth, S. and Young, T. (2004) 'Getting real about gangs', *Criminal Justice Matters*, 55(1): 12–13.

Hallsworth, S. and Young, T. (2008) 'Gang talk and gang talkers: a critique', *Crime, Media, Culture*, 4(2): 175–95.

Hansard, H. C. vol. 425 col. 1108W (15 November 2004).

Hillyard, P. (2004) *Beyond Criminology: Taking Harm Seriously,* London: Pluto Press.

HM Government. (2011) *Ending Gang and Youth Violence: A Cross Governmental Report Including Further Evidence and Good Practice Case Studies,* London: The Stationery Office.

HM Government. (2013) *Ending Gang and Youth Violence: Annual Report 2012–13,* London: The Stationery Office.

HM Government. (2015) *Ending Gang and Youth Violence: Annual Report 2014–15,* London: The Stationery Office.

Home Affairs Select Committee. (2015) *Gangs and Youth Crime: Thirteenth Report of Session 2014–15,* London: The Stationery Office.

Home Office (2011). *An Overview of Recorded Crime and Arrests Resulting from Disorder Events in August 2011,* London: Home Office.

Home Office. (2013) *Ending Gang and Youth Violence: Review 2012–13,* London: Home Office.

Hough, M., Jackson, J., Bradford, B., Myhill, A. and Quinton, P. (2010) 'Procedural justice, trust and institutional legitimacy', *Policing,* 4(3): 203–10.

Huff, C.R. (1990) 'Denial, overreaction, and misidentification: a postscript on public policy', *Gangs in America*, 310–17.

Hurell, K. (2013) *Race Disproportionality in Stops and Searches, 2011–12. Equality and Human Rights Commission Briefing Paper 7,* London: EHRC.

Keynes S. and Tetlow G. (2014) *Survey of Public Spending in the UK. IFS Briefing Note BN43,* London: IFS.

Klein, M. (1971) *Street Gangs and Street Workers,* Englewood Cliffs, NJ: Prentice Hall.

Klein, M., Kerner, H.J., Maxson, C. and Weitekamp, E. (eds.) (2001) *The Eurogang Paradox: Street Gangs and Youth Groups in the US and Europe,* Dordrecht: Kluwer Academic.

Lightowlers, C.A. and Shute, J. (2012) 'Rioting and area deprivation in Greater Manchester', *Radical Statistics*, 106: 22–29.

Lightowlers, C.M. and Quirk, H. (2015) 'The 2011 English "riots": prosecutorial zeal and judicial abandon'. *British Journal of Criminology,* 55(1): 65–85.

Loader, I. and Sparks, R. (2010) 'What is to be done with public criminology?', *Criminology & Public Policy*, 9(4): 771–81.

Loader, I. and Walker, N. (2007) *Civilizing Security,* Cambridge: Cambridge University Press.

Lupton, R. (2015) 'The coalition's social policy record: policy, spending and outcomes 2010–2015', *Social Policy in a Cold Climate, Research Report 4.* Available at http://sticerd.lse.ac.uk/dps/case/spcc/RR04.pdf.

Medina, J., Cebulla, A., Ross, A., Shute, J. and Aldridge, J. (2013). *Children and Young People in Gangs: a Longitudinal Analysis*, London: Nuffield Foundation.

Medina, J., Ralphs, R. and Aldridge, J. (2012) 'Mentoring siblings of gang members: a template for reaching families of gang members?', *Children & Society*, 26: 14–24.

Ministry of Justice. (2011) *Statistical Bulletin on the Public Disorder of 6th to 9th August 2011 – October Update,* London: Ministry of Justice.

Ministry of Justice. (2011) *Statistics on Race and the Criminal Justice System 2010,* London: Ministry of Justice.

Ministry of Justice (2012) *Youth Justice Statistics 2010–11,* London: Ministry of Justice.

Morrell, G., Scott, S., McNeish, D. and Webster, S. (2011) 'The August riots in England', in *Understanding the Involvement of Young People,* London: National Centre for Social Research.

National Audit Office. (2014) *The Impact of Funding Reductions on Local Authorities,* London: NAO.

Pantazis, C., Tombs, S. and Gordon, D. (eds.) (2004) *Beyond Criminology: Taking Harm Seriously,* London: Pluto Press.

Pearce, J.J. and Pitts, J. (2011) *Youth Gangs, Sexual Violence and Sexual Exploitation: A Scoping Exercise for the Office of the Children's Commissioner for England,* Luton: University of Bedfordshire.

Pemberton, S. (2007) 'Social harm future (s): exploring the potential of the social harm approach', *Crime, Law and Social Change*, 48(1–2): 27–41.

Pitts, J. (2008) *Reluctant Gangsters: The Changing Face of Youth Crime,* Cullompton: Willan.

Pitts, J. (2012) 'Reluctant criminologists: criminology, ideology and the violent youth gang', *Youth and Policy*, 109: 27–45.

Ralphs, R., Medina, J. and Aldridge, J. (2009) 'Who needs enemies with friends like these? The importance of place for young people living in known gang areas', *Journal of Youth Studies*, 12(5): 483–500.

Riots Communities and Victims Panels. (2011) *Five Days in August: An Interim Report on the 2011 English Riots,* London: Riots Panel.

Rogers, S. (2013) 'UK public spending since 1963', published on 18 March 2013 with Simon Rogers as the author, and the URL being http://www.theguardian.com/news/datablog/2010/apr/25/uk-public-spending-1963. Accessed 18 February 2015.

Sharp, C., Aldridge, J. and Medina, J. (2006) *Delinquent Youth Groups and Offending Behaviour: Findings from the 2004 Offending, Crime and Justice Survey* (Vol. 14, No. 06), London: Home Office.

Shearing, C. and Wood, J. (2003) 'Nodal governance, democracy and the new denizens', *Journal of Law and Society*, 30(3): 400–19.

Shropshire, S. and McFarquhar, M. (2002) *Developing Multi-Agency Strategies to Address the Street Gang Culture and Reduce Gun Violence among Young People,* Manchester: Steve Shopshire and Michael Mac Farquhar Consultancy Group.

Shute, J. (2008) 'Parenting and youth gangs: risk, resilience and effective support', unpublished report prepared for Manchester City Council's Children's Services Division, Manchester: Centre for Criminology and Criminal Justice.

Shute, J. (2013) 'Family support as a gang reduction measure', *Children & Society*, 27(1): 48–59.

Shute, J., Aldridge, J. and Medina, J. (2012). 'Loading the policy blunderbuss', *Criminal Justice Matters*, 87(1): 40–41.

Shute, J. and Medina, J. (2014) 'Hunting gruffalo: "gangs", unreason and the big bad coalition', *Criminal Justice Matters*, 96(1): 26–27.

Smith, D.J. and Bradshaw, P. (2005) *Gang Membership and Teenage Offending*. Edinburgh: University of Edinburgh, Centre for Law and Society.

Smithson, H., Ralphs, R. and Williams, P. (2013) 'Used and abused: the problematic usage of gang terminology in the United Kingdom and its implications for ethnic minority youth', *British Journal of Criminology*, 53(1): 113–28.

Stelfox P. (1998) 'Policing lower levels of organised crime in England and Wales', *The Howard Journal,* 37(4): 393–406.

Thrasher, F.M. (1927) *The Gang: A Study of 1,313 Gangs in Chicago*, Chicago, IL: University of Chicago Press.

Tonry, M. (2010) '"Public criminology" and evidence-based policy', *Criminology & Public Policy*, 9(4): 783–97.

Uggen, C. and Inderbitzin, M. (2010) 'Public criminologies', *Criminology & Public Policy*, 9(4): 725–49.

van Kesteren, J., van Dijk, J. and Mayhew, P. (2013) 'The international crime victims surveys: a retrospective', *International Review of Victimology*, 0269758013511742.

Violence Reduction Unit. (2011) *The Violence Must Stop: Glasgow's Community Initiative to Reduce Violence: 2nd Year Report,* Glasgow: Strathclyde Police.

Williams, D.J., Currie, D., Linden, W. and Donnelly, P.D. (2014) 'Addressing gang-related violence in Glasgow: a preliminary pragmatic quasi-experimental evaluation of the Community Initiative to Reduce Violence (CIRV)', *Aggression and Violent Behavior*, 19(6): 686–91.

Wintour P. and Dodd V. (2007) 'Blair blames spate of murders on black culture', *The Guardian, 12 April.*

Index

For Product Safety Concerns and Information please contact our EU
representative GPSR@taylorandfrancis.com
Taylor & Francis Verlag GmbH, Kaufingerstraße 24, 80331 München, Germany

www.ingramcontent.com/pod-product-compliance
Ingram Content Group UK Ltd.
Pitfield, Milton Keynes, MK11 3LW, UK
UKHW051322190926
475701UK00011B/1055

9780367581589